MEMBERSHIP AND MORALS

MEMBERSHIP AND MORALS

THE PERSONAL USES OF PLURALISM IN AMERICA

Nancy L. Rosenblum

PRINCETON UNIVERSITY PRESS   PRINCETON, NEW JERSEY

Library of Congress Cataloging-in-Publication Data

Rosenblum, Nancy L.
Membership and morals : the personal uses of pluralism in America /
Nancy L. Rosenblum
p.   cm.
Includes bibliographical references and index.
ISBN 0-691-01689-5 (cl : alk. paper)
1. Pluralism (Social sciences)—United States. 2. Associations, institutions,
etc.—United States. 3. Civil society—United States. 4. Political participation—United States. 5. Democracy—United States. 6. United States—Social
conditions—1980–.   I. Title.
HN59.2.R67 1998
306′.0973—dc21 97-27937   CIP

This book has been composed in Times Roman

Princeton University Press books are printed
on acid-free paper and meet the guidelines
for permanence and durability of the Committee
on Production Guidelines for Book Longevity
of the Council on Library Resources

http://pup.princeton.edu

Printed in the United States of America

10 9 8 7 6 5 4 3 2 1

Contents

Acknowledgments

I AM GRATEFUL to Brown University for granting me a sabbatical leave and to the Harvard University Law School for a Liberal Arts Fellowship in 1992, which gave me the opportunity to become immersed in the law of groups.

I have benefited from the opportunity to present my work at a number of conferences and colloquia, where I received helpful comments from Amy Gutmann, George Kateb, and their colleagues at the Center for the Study of Human Values, Princeton University; Stephen Macedo and colleagues at the Maxwell School of Citizenship and Public Affairs, Syracuse University; Bernard Yack, Marion Smiley, and their colleagues at the University of Wisconsin; Stephen Elkin for the opportunity to present "The Democracy of Everyday Life" to a distinguished group organized by the Committee on the Political Economy of the Good Society; and fellow members of the faculty study group on civil society organized by Dietrich Rueschemeyer at the Watson Institute for International Studies, Brown University.

Friends and colleagues read portions of the manuscript, offering cautions and corrections, and encouragement even when they disagreed; I am in their debt: Daniel Bell, Jean Cohen, Harry Hirsch, Wendy Kaminer, Sanford Levinson, Jane Mansbridge, Susan Okin, Yael Tamir, John Tomasi, Sherry Turkle, and Cheryl Welch.

Lucas Swaine and Joel Oestreich hunted down a seemingly endless stream of research material, and gracefully endured the role of sounding board, for which I am grateful. I want to thank Ann Wald, Editor-in-Chief at Princeton University Press, for the enthusiasm she has shown for this project from the start, for her acute suggestions for cuts and changes, and for shepherding the manuscript smoothly through production. I also want to thank Maria E. den-Boer for editing my prose lightly and scrutinizing my documentation severely, saving me from many errors.

Above all, I am indebted to my husband, Richard Rosenblum, who has never joined a group and poses a daily reminder of the virtue and happiness of romantic individualism.

MEMBERSHIP AND MORALS

Introduction ———————————————————

Associations and the Moral Anxieties of Liberalism

THIS BOOK is about voluntary associations in the United States and the uses we make of freedom of association. Voluntary associations are a boasted characteristic of American social life. They are an essential element of democratic representation. And Americans' propensity to join groups is famous.

Associations have always been a staple of American political thought, but in recent years interest in the subject has heightened. National and state governments have flirted with privatization, assigning secondary associations a greater part in providing for public welfare and social well-being. Debates about multiculturalism and differential group rights have made us ask whether restricted-membership groups are desirable or legally permissible. And moral and political theorists have made voluntary associations central to their explorations of civic virtue and community. Apocalyptic warnings about arrant, atomistic individualism contribute to the present enthusiasm for associational life. Doubtless, people's own strong affiliations (or their longing for affiliations they feel they lack) do as well. My own fascination with voluntary associations, however, is fed by a contrary sensibility—resistance to the attractions of membership, appreciation of individualism and tolerance (dispositional, not moral) for at least an iota of detachment, if not anomie.

Liberal democratic thought has traditionally concentrated on the *political* functions of groups. Associations appear chiefly as a means of checking government, as elements of interest group pluralism, as inhibitors of unrestrained majoritarianism, and as training grounds for participation and leadership. But the instrumental political purposes of groups is not the whole story. There is also the intrinsic value of association. Though the U.S. Supreme Court has identified this exclusively with "intimate associations," I want to acknowledge at the outset that associations of all kinds have intrinsic satisfaction and value for members. The meaning and value of associations is not coextensive with the stability or well-being of liberal democracy, with justice, or with cultivating civic virtue. It is as extensive as human flourishing, self-development, and self-affirmation. Above all, freedom of association is "integral to a free human life," which is why George Kateb is exactly right in saying that "the seriousness of the association is not inevitably proportional to the value of the experience accommodated by it."[1]

My subject is narrower than the value of association, however. It is the effects of associational life on the moral disposition of members personally and individually, and the often indirect and unintended consequences for liberal democracy. Membership in voluntary associations is formative, sometimes powerfully so, and the currents of associational rise and decline have added drama if the moral tides of American liberal democracy can be said to shift with them. This explains the distress with which social scientists document the apparent falling off of membership in beneficial groups. It also explains the alarm that accompanies what some see as the "relentless tribalization" or balkanization of American life, and the proliferation of associations whose norms and purposes are antiliberal or undemocratic.[2]

In the political science lexicon, pluralism indicates multiple centers of power, but I am interested in the broad gamut of associations, whether or not these groups have a political voice. I discuss the way the day-to-day activities of voluntary associations promote or inhibit characteristically liberal democratic virtues—tolerance, say, or fairness. In fact, liberal democracy rests on a wide range of virtues and practices that are not directly promoted by public institutions and official public culture. Some, like habits of cooperation, are not specific to political life at all; they are requisites of social order generally. We depend on many developmental contexts to form aspects of character, including associations that are incongruent with liberal democratic principles and practices. They are hopeless as sources of civic virtue. They may be outright averse to liberal democracy ideologically and in their own practices. But their homely moral lessons are vital, and they often reach individuals who are otherwise unconnected.

Appreciation for the moral importance of voluntary associations does not lead by itself to a particular position on freedom of association and its limits. It does not guide political theorists or policy-makers in settling how much autonomy associations should enjoy in choosing their members and exercising authority over them. It does not dictate when government should intervene to uphold or overturn decisions by the group's leaders, resolve internal disputes, enforce adherence to due process, or impose the principle of nondiscrimination on restricted-membership groups.

If our concern is to encourage liberalizing and democratizing practices or to inhibit illiberal and antidemocratic ones, we might want to use government incentives or regulations to shape groups.[3] We will set limits on the power incongruent associations have over their members, or criminalize them altogether, denying in these cases the freedom to associate. Moral concerns might even inspire the demand that secondary associations be congruent with public norms and institutions "all the way down," so that the membership and internal organization of associations should be a matter of public policy, legally enforced. Yet appreciation of the formative importance of group life can inspire the opposite conclusion: that demands for congruence are psychologically naive and politically misguided.

We may argue that associational pluralism is an inevitable result of liberty, and that both practical and principled justifications for liberty, freedom of association in particular, are overriding. Or that the requisite moral dispositions are principally fashioned in associations that are *not* congruent with liberal democratic principles of justice. Precisely to the extent that associations impress their distinctive characters on members, they excite a kind of ecological concern to preserve them as endangered forms of cultural life.

Finally, we may take the chary view I do in this book, that associations indifferent or patently adverse to liberal public culture can serve personal development and can be beneficially exploited; at a minimum they are not fatal to and may even serve political legitimacy and stability, though that is not part of their purpose.

Where and how American government regulates the internal life and authority of these groups, and what limits on freedom of association are necessary and justifiable is part of my subject. The answer varies by context, of course. Voluntary associations range from Rotary clubs and Jaycees to paramilitary groups. And, as my subtitle indicates, the actual uses members make of associational life personally and politically go well beyond anything a group's formal objectives might suggest. The motives for forming groups are wonderfully diverse, as are the bases on which we see ourselves as members. Werner Sollors explains: "the Americans' unsystematic desire to identify with intermediary groups . . . may be based on real or imagined descent, on old or newly adopted religions, on geographic area of origin, socialization or residence, on external categorization, on voluntary association, or on defiance. In all these cases, symbolic boundaries are constructed in a perplexing variety of continuously shifting forms."[4]

My intention is not to fix the social or legal boundaries of the right of association, but to examine the uses we make of this freedom and how we understand what we do. This book is an inquiry into the way Americans employ familiar moral and political principles, appeal to established expectations, and invoke ideology and legal categories to justify freedom of association or limits on this freedom.

Moving Targets

The term "associations" refers to groups, of course, but also to the stream of ideas and experiences that buffet our thinking about them. My discussion is guided by the far-flung resonances voluntary associations evoke in the context of American political thought and institutions. There is a logic to this discussion, provided by the psychological logic of our political ideas. For example, I explore the conjunction of ideas that make up the strange dance of secret societies, exclusionary groups, and democratic equality in America. Or the connection between corporatism and localism, which explains why we see homeowners' associations alternately as experiments in neighborhood self-government and as hostile to democratic community. Or the nexus linking republicanism, conspiracism, and paramilitarism.

This book is not an intellectual history of our thinking about voluntary associations, though I could not have written it without the resources provided by fine historical studies. I do not uncover a single submerged ideological stream or retrieve a neglected tradition of American political thought. Still, my attempt to illuminate associations has the drama of discovery if we find exciting the chaotic compounding of groups and layered accounts of their place in liberal democracy. One of the tasks of political theory is to make sense of how we think about these matters and to show why our thinking is complicated, conflicted, even irrational.

Two things make my design by association appropriate to the subject. One is the hybrid character of associations themselves. Gross references to "voluntary" associations (with its choice of opposites—involuntary, ascriptive, or governmental) and general terms like "secondary" and "intermediate" associations obscure the mixed makeup of most groups. Classification driven by political advocacy does too, as when libertarians portray every membership as voluntary and strong democrats portray every association as a school of civic virtue. There are always alternative understandings of an association's nature and purpose, and competing classifications. My aim is to bring these myriad associations to mind. Is a residential homeowners' association a corporation or a local community? Can homeowners contract into a private government that has greater discretion to control their conduct and use of property than would be permitted local government? Should voting rights be distributed to member-owners on the basis of ownership share or one person, one vote? The facts about homeowners' associations do not settle these questions. Neither does political ideology; at least, each characterization points to real social goods and relationships (and costs).

Legal categorization discounts many-sidedness and settles the parameters of the right of association in practice. The U.S. Constitution does not provide for a general right of association; Mill's prescription of "freedom to unite, for any purpose not involving harm to others" is not law.[5] U.S. courts do not recognize association as a fundamental right under the due process clause. Instead, the right is ancillary to enumerated First Amendment liberties. Courts have adopted a categorical approach by which some associations are protected by the religion and speech clauses, and a narrow view of the potential rationales for constitutionally guaranteed associational autonomy. The result is concerted judicial efforts to type groups as religious or expressive (or intimate) on the one hand, and to show why particular groups fall outside these protected categories on the other.

This categorization proceeds by selecting out characteristics of a group relevant in the law; it demands a willful disregard for a group's actual mixed purposes and uses. Judges settle on certain features of an association as salient when they decide that the Jaycees are a commercial organization rather than a political group, for example, or that the workers in a religious cult are employees, not volunteers in a religious mission.

Judges' reflections on prototypical cases are set out in legal precedents, available for ongoing inquiry by us as well as by courts. In thinking about freedom of association for particular groups, we can make use of this material. We can consider competing accounts of the salient features of an association, and draw alternative analogies between a given group and a business corporation, or church, or local government.

In practice, associations constantly confront us with their mixed nature and purposes. These emerge with force when an association's formal objectives conflict with their members' expectations or outsiders' judgments. Thus, Minnesota classified the Jaycees as a public accommodation regulable under the state's human rights law, but the young men who joined saw it as a restricted social membership group, and compelled association with women was anathema. The janitor in a Mormon-owned gymnasium saw it as a workplace subject to federal prohibitions against discrimination in employment, but the church saw the gym as an extension of religious community that the law should accommodate. We can try to fix the category, as we see the Supreme Court doing in *Roberts v. Jaycees* and *Corporation of Presiding Bishop of the Church of Jesus Christ of Latter-Day Saints v. Amos*. Or we can take the opposite tack, as I do, highlighting the several aspects groups present and the way these reflect divergent elements of American thought.

Not surprisingly, the hybrid character of associations affects the expectations we have of any group and bring to the experience of membership. For any individual in any association, membership normally has multiple and shifting associations. This is another reason for my title.

While I was writing this book I edited a volume of Henry David Thoreau's political writings. Thoreau is famous for his radically individualist stance: "minding one's own business" and "washing one's hands of it" were favorite prescriptions. He was uncomfortably unable to name all of the societies he had never joined but that nonetheless claimed his loyalty and imposed their obligations, and he repeatedly disavowed affiliation. I found that my study of Thoreau had surprising resonance for this project, for one thing because he raises not only the question of consent to membership but also the difficulty of disassociation.

Thoreau was also acutely sensitive to the hybrid character of association. Although he assumed the pose of detachment, he did not disclaim identification as an American citizen, and in a striking passage toward the end of *Civil*

Disobedience he records his shifting perspective on that singular association, confessing that his experience of citizenship and sense of its worth was not of a piece:

> Seen from a lower point of view, the constitution, with all its faults, is very good; the law and the courts very respectable; even this State and this American government are, in many respects, very admirable and rare things, to be thankful for. . . . Seen from a point of view a little higher, they are what I have described them; seen from a higher still, and the highest, who shall say what they are, or that they are worth looking at or thinking of at all?[6]

Not even the evil of slavery and high ground of abolitionism permanently eclipse other perspectives. Thoreau's judgment of the value of political membership to him, and the feelings accompanying his identification as citizen, shift from appreciation of real benefits, to declaring war with the state, to disavowing the obligations of citizenship in favor of quietist retreat, and back again.

We are not all Thoreau; his exquisite sensibility is rare. Some people experience membership in a group as fixed and normally immutable, and for them the meaning and value of belonging appear singular and clear. Still, Thoreau reminds us that voluntary associations are personally and politically evocative and changing, and that the vicissitudes of personal life affect what we take from membership.

The significance of association depends on the experiences individuals bring to it, including the unique obstacles we each face in cultivating and exhibiting particular competencies or dispositions. So I caution against the unwarranted assumption that the effects of an association on members can be predicted on the basis of a group's formal purpose or system of internal governance. The moral valence of group life is indeterminate.

The Indeterminate Valence of Associational Life: #1

Together, the hybrid character of associations, the categories we use to think about them, and the unpredictable dynamic of membership make it difficult to assess the moral significance of freedom of association, even in particular cases. A few examples suffice to give a taste of the wild plurality of associational life and add concreteness to my introduction of the theme of individualism and the moral uses of pluralism.

Roughly 75 million Americans belong to small religious fellowship groups and secular recovery and support groups. Does membership fuel narcissism or cooperation?[7] These small groups seem to reinforce self-involvement, since members talk mainly about their own lives, the proposed solution to problems is self-transformation rather than collective action, and "the measure of any

political or social event, as well as any relationship, is how it makes us feel."
"Caring" is defined strangely and minimally as hearing one another out non-
judgmentally.[8] In any case, these small groups are too fluid to create sustained
responsibilities. Members shop the crowded marketplace of support groups,
electing the elements of identity they want to exhibit as joiners. On the other
hand, small groups provide the experience of reciprocity: even if members
mainly take turns speaking about themselves, they do take turns, and they are
expected to take a turn at encouraging others. If only in a miniscule way, they
create the expectation that our indignation at arbitrariness and unfairness will
not be met with indifference or hostility. They may cultivate the iota of trust
necessary for democratic citizens to speak out about ordinary injustice.

Residential homeowners' associations now number about 150,000 and constitute an increasing share of the housing market throughout the country. Association members vote for boards of directors and for rules and restrictions that
govern the use of their property, and they are allotted votes in proportion to the
number or size of their units. Does this transform neighbors into shareholders
preoccupied with efficient management and property values, creating an arid
"corporate culture at home"? Or are housing associations part of the long
American tradition of elective community? They are not antiworldly utopias,
of course, but like communal experiments these associations provide members
with the experience of common ownership, rule-making, and self-governance.
Or are both views insufficiently sensitive to the political character of homeowners' associations? Should we want them to conform to the model of local
government and constitutionalize them by extending votes to all residents, for
example, and restricting the associations' ability to regulate residents' conduct
and use of their property?

Citizen militias are one of many types of paramilitary association. A Montana Militiaman is described as "alive with conspiracies. They whirr in his
mind and welter in his heart, and they fill him so full of outrage and nervousness that he cannot ever stay still."[9] Are the seventeen states that outlaw paramilitary groups right? Or should we take comfort from the fact that this conspiracist is securely ensconced in a remote Northwest compound? Minutemen
leader Robert DePugh advised that it is better to have "kooks and nuts" inside
the organization than outside on their own: "Out," he told an interviewer,
"they're liable to do most anything at any time without anybody knowing it
except them. If they decide they want to go out and blow somebody up, okay,
they go out and blow somebody up. But if they're part of a group . . . well, then
there's a good chance someone in the organization will know about it and
they're going to take steps to bring this person under control."[10]

We could multiply evocative associations indefinitely, and in the following
chapters I add religious groups and quasi-social, quasi-civic, quasi-business
groups like the Jaycees. Most of us have established expectations of the beneficial formative effects of religious and civic association. We are generally con-

fident, to the contrary, that the moral consequences of membership in hate groups and secret societies, to say nothing of their paramilitary offshoots, are far from benign. Precisely because of these expectations, the unanticipated moral uses of membership, for good and ill, emerge sharply.

The moral valence of membership in other associations is more puzzling even from the start. Consider the distinctive culture of retirement communities of the elderly, for example, or the myriad voluntary associations based on members' publicly acknowledged identity as addicts, co-dependents, and victims—psychological identities that for increasing numbers of Americans eclipse every other affiliation.

I am tempted to call the array of voluntary associations in the United States "our multiculturalism." The internal norms and authority of corporations, fellowship groups, and paramilitary groups are as salient for social diversity and conflict in American public life as ethnic differences, though they are notably absent from the literature on "diversity," with its focus on ascriptive attachments. Except that these associations are voluntary, and forming, joining, and leaving are as much a part of their moral use as belonging.

The Permanent Cycle of Liberal Anxiety

These points on the terrain of American associations suffice to conjure up the difficulties that plague what has emerged as a leading proposition in political theory and public policy: that the relation between civil society (that is, our associational life) and liberal democracy is, or must be, reciprocally supportive; that liberal democratic character and commitment must find their origin and vital complement in an array of independent groups. Associations are potential schools of virtue. At the same time, associational pluralism is inescapable so long as there is personal freedom, and many groups are incongruent with liberal democratic norms and institutions. No wonder the moral anxiety of liberalism is irrepressible, and efforts to allay these anxieties are a permanent feature of liberal political thought.

Beginning with the thought that the genius of liberal democracy is that it can function in the absence of *civic* virtue. If virtue is always exceptional, "auxiliary precautions" are necessary. Nothing is further from preoccupation with the cultivation of specifically liberal and democratic dispositions than assigning the defense of liberal democracy to "a policy of supplying by opposite and rival interests, the defect of better motives." Kant's assurance that a constitution can be designed for a race of intelligent devils is the perfect expression of this thesis: "A good constitution is not to be expected from morality," Kant wrote in *Perpetual Peace*, "but, conversely, a good moral condition of a people is to be expected only under a good constitution."[11] A well-ordered representative system can arrange selfish inclinations so that one moderates the ruinous effects of another, contriving to modulate conflicts of interest and make the outcomes of clashes tolerably fair.

These ideas are Montesquieu's, of course, and Madison's, and Robert Dahl's on polyarchy. In them, constitutionalism joins with social pluralism. And the good citizen and good person cease to overlap. Montesquieu thought the English model citizens in their support of excellent institutions, including their willingness to bear the burden of taxes; their politics and national character were admirable. But he also thought the English personally were exemplars of eccentricity and vice, who cared nothing for others.[12] Mill chose this quotation from Tocqueville for his review of *Democracy in America*: In the United States the general and permanent working of the government is beneficial, although the governors are often unskillful and sometimes despicable, frequently inferior, both in point of capacity and of morality. . . . the hidden tendency of democratic institutions makes us instruments of the general good in spite of our vices and stupidity.[13] For many liberals, "this was misanthropy's finest hour."[14]

Apart from hopeful expectations for the effects of institutional design, liberals have been tempted to allay moral anxiety by leaving open the question whether there is a single liberal democratic character type, even ideally. Many moral dispositions can arguably sustain representative government and civil liberties if people are only occasionally politically self-defensive and express their sense of injustice when it is aroused.[15] Anxiety makes us cautious about demanding too much and advises us to "more carefully distinguish . . . between what is and is not required for liberal public order."[16] In ideal theory, too, the moral requirements for a just liberal democracy may not be very severe. John Rawls reassures us that the capacity for moral personality "is not all that stringent," and concedes that the morality of principle may be necessary only for "a substantial majority of politically active" members.[17]

So we may deny the necessity for everyone to be liberal, or for anyone to be a good liberal democrat all the time or in every sphere of life. Only some people have to exhibit the self-discipline involved in respecting rights, say, or the capacity to deliberate in the face of moral disagreement, and it is an open question how many must and how often they are required to call on that capacity, and in what contexts. Certainly when it comes to pluralist politics, commitment to democratic procedures can be pragmatic. Compromise emerges in practice because group interests are normally self-limiting. Shared procedural norms moderate but are not intended to overcome substantial conflict between values and loyalties.[18]

We also appreciate that historically American liberalism has successfully tolerated and in some cases hospitably accommodated bizarre elective communities, religious and secular, quietist and not-so-quietist, whose members see themselves as internal exiles. It has withstood secret societies and snobbish, exclusive ones, defiant counterculture groups, and racial and religious separatists. Liberal democracy in America seems to be compatible with a great deal of incorrigible apathy, withdrawal, indifference, and deviance. It survives political incompetence and egregious lapses in public judgment, to say nothing of a citizenry that enthusiastically exercises "the right to live unexamined as well as examined lives."[19] All this is consonant with the popular attitude that unless we run for political office we do not think of ourselves as publicly accountable for our conduct, much less our characters, so long as it remains within the law.

These considerations may temporarily abate the moral anxiety of liberalism. At the same time, the impetus is always there to back off from this relaxed stance. Even those who applaud "contingency" and self-made identity as the heart of democratic life acknowledge that "there may be some lethal—or at least quite dangerous—contradiction or tension between what the political system requires and what it as it were helplessly and ineluctably engenders. It is as if a system of chastened authority could endure only if the people did not take its basic moral teaching too seriously."[20] It is an empirical question how widespread deviations from any specified set of liberal democratic dispositions can become before political functioning or stability is upset, much less a sense of political community. It is hard to discern which evidence of demoralization is critical—crime, for example, or failure to cross some threshold of political participation, or incivility and public shows of disrespect toward other citizens?

Nothing is more common than insistence on the public consequences of even our private vices. We are familiar with admonitions that failure to support one or another public policy is evidence not of political disagreement but of moral lapse, as in the charge that "consistently unbalanced budgets . . . are signs of a citizenry unwilling to moderate its desires or to discharge its duties."[21] There is little in liberal democracy to invite complacency. We rarely lose sight for very long of the particular need for virtue where "authority is to be controlled by public opinion, not public opinion by authority."[22] We recognize that the proliferation of moral types goes on against the background of liberal institutions and public purposes that presuppose citizens reasonably disposed to value and protect them.

So historians of political thought draw our attention back to neglected discussions of moral education in liberal democratic philosophy.[23] And contemporary political theorists affirm the thought that liberal democracy is a distinctive political culture whose promised secular goods and principles are authoritative ideals, and that liberal democracy depends on producing men and women who identify with this public culture and exhibit its characteristic excellences.[24]

Liberal democratic virtues do not pretend to encompass the sum of human fulfillment, "the good life," or the whole of moral identity. Nonetheless, the catalogue of requisite dispositions is more extensive than philosophers' preoccupation with justice suggests. These virtues are wide-ranging: modest law-abidingness, willingness to work to support oneself, and the self-control necessary to refrain from exhibitions of hatred and violence, to more demanding tolerance or fairness. Some accounts require the disposition to provide collective goods and to accept sometimes painful policies. Others require the capacity for political deliberation in accord with "public reason." And if not rigorous republican virtue, at least a miniscule concern for the common good. (The specific habits demanded by political pluralism—bargaining, negotiation, and compromise—unaccountably take a back seat when they are mentioned at all.)

Moreover, these excellences *are* stringent. The perfectly mundane requirements of due process presuppose considerable self-restraint. Resisting self-preference and demonstrating normal regard for the rights of others is difficult, as is overcoming solidarity with our friends and kin, if only because sociability and sympathy "make us want to go along, be liked, follow orders, and win approval."[25] It is hard to accept obligations to strangers, especially if they are unlike ourselves and have different backgrounds and standards of public and private conduct. Looking beyond justice, blunting the inclinations of interest and passion takes more than a miniscule amount of self-control. Controlling impulsivity is learned; there is nothing simple about avoiding cruelty, humiliation, or even bad manners.

We realize how much we count on the exhibition of moral dispositions in everyday life, and that we are normally immune to the full force of Camus' warning: "We all carry within us our places of exile, our crimes and our ravages, but our task is not to unleash them on the world; it is to fight them in ourselves and others."[26] When restraint breaks down, whether on the part of public officials or ordinary men and women, our latent assumptions about the moral requirements of democracy in everyday life come into focus.

Still, it is a long way from appreciation of liberal democratic dispositions to the view that the chief purpose of liberal democracy is to reproduce citizens, and that public policy should cultivate and motivate us to exhibit specific virtues. Even if we can identify a morally laudable liberal democratic self (or a plurality of selves, keeping in mind Thoreauvian individualism and Lockean self-direction, to name just two), and even if we do not insist that the self is heroically self-made and radically revisable, we may be reluctant to say that the imperative to produce a certain character or range of characters should govern the organization of social or political life. Or that laws should require us to embrace liberal democratic principles or exhibit moral dispositions in every aspect of our own lives. Nothing provokes anxiety like the proposition that in American democracy "statecraft is soulcraft."[27] Anxiety encourages us to fall back on the self-restrained liberal nostrum that "one can argue for a particular conception of self and politics without being obliged to entertain an explanation of how people come to be like that."[28]

For the heart of liberal democracy has been to guard against the tutelary or manipulative intent of authorities, particularly political authorities, who want to mold minds, call up moral sentiments, or exact displays of virtue and enthusiasm. Governments are perfectly capable and often inclined to change our motives, call on our affections, influence our deepest inclinations, and demand internal assent. Nothing is more common than the political exploitation of personal longings, including the not uncommon desire for self-improvement. We tolerate many attempts to whip up passions and direct enthusiasm: businesses exciting their sales forces, preachers seeking donations from congregations, politicians eliciting solidarity from their volunteers, football players stirring up crowds, among others; "scenarios for inspiring intense involvement are permanent aspects of the human comedy."[29] But in the hands of officials, these are familiar excuses for tyranny. They are inseparable from the impulse to shape people's characters, lives, and self-understanding. Modern despotism differs from ancient, Benjamin Constant advised, because it "pursues the vanquished into the interior of their existence, it maims them spiritually in order to force them to conform."[30]

Contemporary liberal democrats may share Constant's wariness of compulsory moral and political inspiration. This goes a long way toward explaining the assertion that "if anything is clear, it is that the only opportunity, the only hope we can possibly have for self-improvement, is under conditions of freedom and the strict enforcement of legal rules."[31] It explains the resilience of the view that character formation should not be forced or even promoted by political authority. And the resigned conclusion that if the absence of public pedagogy makes us worse, more corrupt and selfish, it also avoids the worst.

The obvious avenue of retreat from rigorous public moral education is to leave the cultivation of moral dispositions largely to the family and private life. Or to look to the formative effects of voluntary associations, and to leave associations alone. But this path has obstacles of its own, and in any case is not unambiguously inviting. We have come the full anxious circle. Insulated from government, people form associations to meet all sorts of emotional and ideological needs, amplify selfish interests, and give vent to exclusionary impulses that the "mischiefs of faction" don't begin to cover. And liberal democracy is committed to providing protection against private tyranny and tutelage. We look to laws to oversee not only the political power of groups but also the power private groups exercise over their members. For Hobhouse, "the function of Liberalism may be rather to protect the individual against the power of the association than to protect the right of association against the restriction of the law."[32]

The nervousness attached to leaving public and private virtue to associations is understandable, too, given inescapable moral and cultural pluralism. Alasdair MacIntyre has made us aware of the historical overlay of moral tradition on dissimilar tradition. And there is America's unique multiculturalism, both the usual ethnic and religious varieties and the profound incongruity among voluntary associations that is my subject. We differ dramatically in our assessments of what counts as a virtue or vice, much less their rank order.

Every virtue has its detractors. And vices have positive functions. Montesquieu thought that vanity was a spur to commerce and consumption. Tocqueville lauded the hypocritical "courtier spirit" of politicians who privately deplore the want of enlightened wisdom, but talk incessantly in public of the natural judgment of public opinion. Mistrust is constructive if it makes us suspicious of the powerful, who are always prepared to take unfair advantage of weakness. Democratic politics with its promise of egalitarianism is inseparable from mistrust, intrigue, and mutual accusation: every secret society is designed to counter a sinister elite or conspiracy against the people, real or imagined. No wonder it is hard to tell when suspicion of authority is a "democratic distemper" or sheer irrationality and when it is virtuous independence and sane self-protection.[33]

All the famously difficult puzzles associated with ceaselessly shifting boundaries between public and private spheres recur here. All the fears of the effects of unrestrained government regulation of freedom of association on the one hand, and experience of the cruelty and damage done by unrestrained private interest and private relationships on the other are stirred up when we propose that liberal democracy must be concerned with the sort of people we are and therefore with the formative associations where we become, or fail to become, good citizens: The cycle of anxiety and tentative resolution is continuously generated from within liberal democratic thought. It is sheer parochialism to see it as simply a rejoinder to communitarian challenges.

The Indeterminate Valence of Associational Life: #2

There is no systematic answer to whether we can depend on the associations of civil society to cultivate the moral dispositions liberal democracy requires, or whether to use public incentives and the force of law to create and enhance liberalizing, democratizing groups. Associational pluralism and the vicissitudes of personal experience militate against a coherent answer. Recall the groups I used to introduce the range of associational life: small support groups, homeowners' associations, and paramilitary groups. I chose them because of their currency, and because jeremiads about the decline of association membership in the United States give them short shrift. They also serve as introduction because excellent studies document their variable effects.

The hundreds of thousands of fellowship and support groups may not inspire members to take on onerous obligations of mutual care or create close communities, as some wish. But there is evidence of their indirect democratic effects. These groups encourage members to overcome humility and passivity, which are not democratic virtues. And they accustom members to treating one another identically and with easy spontaneity, which is a pretty good definition of the democracy of everyday life.

White racist groups present a hard case. The "scared, stranded" youths who join have typically dropped out of school years before graduation and have no prospects of work. Their lives are devoid of attachments. They are not driven by hate to join groups that mirror their beliefs; they are simply available, and sheer lack goes some way toward explaining why membership may be easy for them. In *The Racist Mind*, Raphael Ezekiel reports that members "derive a degree of self-confidence and dignity from the suggestion that they are engaged in a heroic struggle for the sake of a larger entity, the reborn family of Whites." "The white supremacist movement—for a while, at least—is a lifeline for these kids."[34]

The fact that membership fulfills the "need" for a sense of belonging somewhere is no argument for the moral uses of these groups, certainly not if the association fails to provide some potentially constructive compensatory experience or to help contain aggression and avoid the worst. (Ezekiel discovers that hate groups do both for some of their members.) An association may fatally inhibit members from looking outside the group to other affiliations. Or membership may be inconsequential; joiners may have no more resources for good or ill when they exit than when they entered. For those without the prospect of other connections, leaving is a matter of aimless drift rather than competing social pulls.

I recognize the tenuous evidentiary status of case studies of associations, and do not claim my examples are typical. It should be clear that I have no interest in reporting trends. Simply, accounts of members' experiences, especially when they include their own words, make the moral uses of pluralism vivid. This material is meant to be illustrative; in fact, I use examples chiefly to make the neglected or counterintuitive point.

These examples introduce a family of ideas I intend to pursue. No single formative context is determinative of moral disposition. One experience of association can compensate for the deprivations and degradations of another. And except for cruel and violent settings, almost any association has potential for being either constructive or destructive of moral dispositions in an individual case. It follows that if some associations inhibit democratic virtues, not all illiberal settings do. Even those may not be debilitating for all members and may perform vital moralizing and socializing functions for some. Vices may be amenable to containment if not correction. We should not hastily conclude that incongruities between associational and public life are beyond the pale on the grounds of moral effects on members alone.

There is nothing to recommend hate groups. The example simply anticipates what I see as the key to reciprocity between liberal democracy and voluntary associations in the United States: whether and how experiences of association come together in the lives of individuals. The governing idea I advance in this book is that by itself, the simple *existence* of a dense array of associations—whether congruent with the public norms of liberal democracy or incongruent, alien, and adverse—may contribute little to the moral uses of pluralism. To be sure, there are aesthetic and sometimes political reasons to value pluralism per se. But it does not suffice for moral development that the social stock of values and practices carried by associations is abundant if the lives of men and women are terminally fixed and situated, if they are unable to exploit freedom of association. The possibility of shifting involvements among associations—the *experience of pluralism* by men and women personally and individually—is what counts.

Individuals draw on membership for personal psychological, moral, and political goods, sometimes intentionally as when we seek and find the pleasures of sociability or political influence or a community of faith, but often serendipitously. Members may join a group in pursuit of one of these goods and find another. They leave for similar reasons. That is why I emphasize the dynamic of association, pointing out that forming, joining, schism, and disassociation are as much a part of freedom of association as the solidity of identification and belonging.

Since personal vicissitudes make moral and political education variable and unpredictable, a general theory of the moral uses of pluralism may be impossible. But the emergence of liberal democratic dispositions and containment of illiberal ones is not a matter of serendipity. Given pluralism and our ideas about voluntary associations, we can say something meaningful about the parameters of freedom of association in a liberal democracy. We can also identify government responsibility for the background conditions that make the moral uses of pluralism possible.

Situating This Study

Readers familiar with contemporary moral and political philosophy know that one of its dominant themes is justifying institutions and the exercise of authority in a pluralist setting where moral disagreement is inescapable. It is reasonable to wonder how I locate my discussion of the moral uses of pluralism in relation to a just political order.

If I subscribed to a fully theorized account of liberal democracy like that of John Rawls, I would have to focus on how ideal theory should deal with "unreasonable pluralism" and the theoretical status of groups that do not share a commitment to public principles of justice. I would owe an explanation for beginning with voluntary associations as we understand them and trying to arrive at an account of freedom of association, rather than beginning with strictures derived from commitment to principles like "reasonable pluralism" or "reciprocity" and applying them to groups. I would have to show that my discussion is at least consistent with a prior theoretical commitment to inclusiveness, or fair democratic outcomes, or self-respect.

However, in this book I do not adopt a political ideal of justice or moral justification as a guide to thinking about the sort of character that liberal democracy requires. Indeed, I am reluctant to advance even the modest claim that what I call "the moral uses of pluralism" offers the best possibility for developing specific liberal democratic virtues—deliberative capacities, say—under conditions as they exist. As will become clear, I have come to think that generous freedom of association for groups and shifting involvements by individuals offer the best chance of correcting and containing the vices that subvert the general moral climate of democracy in everyday life. I also think that many character types are compatible with and lend support to democracy in America, not least because the moral dispositions on which it depends and which it normally cultivates are not limited to justice or any other civic virtue. There *are* moral dispositions peculiarly important to liberal democracy, I believe, the disposition to fairness and tolerance among them, just as there are political competencies uniquely important for liberal democratic citizens. But it should be plain that the moral concerns animating my work extend beyond liberal democratic virtues strictly understood to moral dispositions more generally: cooperation and trust, generosity and civility, and so on.

In short, my study and the main concerns of contemporary democratic political philosophy run along roughly parallel tracks. I do not engage concerns of justice or justification directly. Though implicit in my account is the thought that insofar as political philosophers take their bearings from a process of "reflective equilibrium," they should have recourse to a sophisticated understanding of the plurality of groups and the moral psychology of membership.

I am convinced that it is not enough simply to argue for a catalogue of liberal democratic virtues, whether that catalogue is tied to a comprehensive moral account of liberalism, to political liberalism, or to historical experience. What political theory owes in addition is a moral psychology of how dispositions are developed in actual social contexts. And a dose of realism in thinking about the bearing these processes of development have on the relation between voluntary associations and government.

This book is a brief for going beyond ethics. The thought that social and "value" pluralism is not only a fact of modern life but also a condition for developing moral capacities has a solid place in both moral and political philosophy. Contemporary moral philosophers observe that tolerance has no more meaning in the absence of moral difference and disagreement than does courage in the absence of fear. John Rawls offers the related suggestion that the virtues of truthfulness and sincerity gain importance under conditions of pluralism and social change, where there is doubt and loss of faith in long-established values and authorities. For philosophers who take autonomy to be the defining human trait and the ground of liberal justice, critical reflection and capacity for choice make sense only where authoritative norms face competition from alternative values, social expectations, cultural options: "If having an autonomous life is an ultimate value, then having a sufficient range of acceptable options is an intrinsic value."[35] In each case, the moral uses of pluralism must allow for at least the possibility of the *experience* of pluralism.

Having said this, however, value pluralism, "moral complexity," "difference," and so on, typically make their appearance in political philosophy as they do in ethics, divorced from institutional settings. In J. S. Mill's marketplace, ideas and values are free-floating. Contemporary philosophers refer to norms and practices abroad in society or to the diffuse "cultures" of a multicultural order rather than to the concrete associations in which they are learned, and still less to the dynamic by which they are learned.[36]

The principal business is to take up where ethics leaves off—with the question of how and where moral dispositions are formed. Political theory is plainly indebted to moral philosophy for inspiration on the subject of moral character, but not for instruction in where or how character is shaped, still less for guidance in addressing the political question of how much congruence among the contexts of development, public and private, is necessary and justifiable in a liberal democracy, and whether it should be legally enforced. With this task in mind, I thread my way through the associations that guide our thinking and our experience of voluntary association.

Thematic Outline

In part 1, I assess the point to which liberal democratic theory in this country has come. Chapter 1, "Civil Society," sets the subject in political context and American notions of civil society in comparative perspective. It canvasses competing diagnoses of associational life and the difficulty we have getting the dangers right. Its main purpose is to provide a typology of current approaches to the moral uses of pluralism.

Chapter 2, "The Morality of Association," argues that the dynamics of membership are as significant as a group's formal structure and purposes in understanding its moral effects. I explore how the dynamic operates. I argue, too, that the standard assumption that dispositions shaped through membership, good and bad, spill over into other spheres is simplistic. The formative effect of membership may be compensatory rather than complementary. It may counterbalance bad habits and inclinations, or substitute for missing virtues. Associations may provide the materials for the reparation of deficits—chastening egotism, or integrating otherwise disconnected individuals into some company, or assisting in loosening the hold of gripping attachments. Or associations may check and contain irreparable vices. Of course, given the variable uses of association by members personally and individually, any given group may do all these things. I also explain why I focus on adulthood rather than on childhood.

Part 2, "Voluntary Associations," is organized thematically, and it may be helpful to signal some of the questions that order the discussion. In keeping with my interest in the variety of ideological associations that attach to our thinking about religious groups, say, or homeowners' associations, specific types of voluntary association and legal cases dominate each chapter. But the themes and examples introduced here reappear throughout with what I hope is cumulative force in bringing home the moral uses of pluralism.

One question is when government intervention in the lives of associations undermines key activities, inhibits self-definition, chills expression, or threatens viability. We know, for instance, that activities central to religious doctrine, faith, and ecclesiastical authority are presumed to be protected from government by the First Amendment. What activities are peripheral to religion and thus regulable? Exercises of faith that are not required by doctrine—singing in the church choir, for example? Does advertisement in the Yellow Pages by a church-affiliated school make it a "commercial enterprise" subject to federal regulation, or is this an exercise of the evangelical duty to reach out to the community to attract converts, part of its proselytizing mission?

Similarly, when are the membership practices of an expressive association constitutionally protected from government control? Can the state mandate membership policies, for example? Is requiring a voluntary association to admit unwanted members—women or racial minorities—impermissible interference with its "voice" by definition? Or is it permissible so long as it does not alter the group's political expression; that is, does freedom of association depend on a logical nexus between membership and message?

The question of association integrity reappears when we turn to corporations. Are corporate purposes expansive and discretionary so that a business board of directors can spend shareholder assets on political activities? Can local governments use their authority under home rule to pass zoning ordinances that exclude the poor? Or are municipal corporations and businesses "artificial beings," legal entities limited to the purposes for which they were chartered by the state?

Perhaps the most disruptive interference with groups is compelled association. Open primary election laws permit independents and voters registered with other parties to participate in the opposition primary. What could justify limits on the freedom of political associations to determine who qualifies as a Democrat or Republican for the purpose of selecting party candidates? Closed shops require unions to represent all workers and compel workers to contribute financially to a union as a condition of employment. Does that mean employees must contribute to union activities unrelated to collective bargaining? To the union's political voice?

In this country, the chief rationale for constitutionally compelling associations to admit unwanted members is democratic equality. When are the advantages of membership in a voluntary association so material and significant for citizens' public standing that the group is brought under the antidiscrimination provisions of public accommodation law? And what about compelling association for the purpose of preventing dignity harms or securing self-respect?

Impediments in the path of would-be joiners receive more attention than obstacles to breaking away from membership, and democratic theorists typically give little thought to public responsibility for facilitating disassociation. It is true that "you can join the Labour Party without slaughtering a sheep . . . and you can leave it without incurring the death penalty for apostasy."[37] Still, when a church discriminates on the basis of religion in its employment practices, it has power to force employees to choose between faith and their jobs. "Totalistic" groups, whether an ultra-Orthodox Jewish yeshiva or a paramilitary commune, immerse members in the organization, and liberals committed to protecting citizens against private as well as public despotism and exploitation will be tempted to intervene. Should they? What securities must members have qua citizens—rights of which they are aware, or material supports—to insure that leaving is possible?

Finally, I pursue two themes in a "contrarian" spirit, with the intention of offering correctives to what I see as simplistic orientations toward associational life. My emphasis on the conditions for *forming* groups is contrarian, given the emphasis of communitarians and advocates of cultural group rights on protecting and preserving groups. Not only does the communitarian orientation overlook the salience of schism, separation, and the ceaseless multiplication of groups. Also, exclusive preoccupation with group preservation over formation is misguided from the standpoint of the moral uses of pluralism. Understandably, the hope is to explain and stall what many see as the decline of American associational life (a trend that I would characterize rather as a change in the predominant types of associations). But that is no reason for confusing the instability and attrition of associations with demoralization. Genuine anomie is the critical, intractable problem. For people segregated from the arenas where we are normally recruited into associations, and who are without resources for creating associations of their own, the moral uses of pluralism are impossible. If so, the formation of associations is at least as important as their preservation; indeed, the two may be in tension.

Another theme focuses on containing vices; it is a contrarian antidote to the attention usually trained on cultivating and diffusing virtue. We are increasingly knowledgeable about antiliberal, antidemocratic strains of American political thought—racism, nativism, anti-Semitism to name a few—and their carrier groups. These ideological traditions are not unique to the United States, though they have such a secure place here that they cannot be said to be violations of America's "true" democratic values. Other ideologies antithetical to liberal democracy are what Harold Bloom called, in the context of religions like Mormonism and Christian Science, "American originals." They arise in response to the frustrations or unintended consequences of American democracy, and fuel our secret societies, militias, and grim variations on our traditions of localism, separatism, and privatism. There is also the permanent dynamic of social affiliation and exclusion, driven by snobbery or self-celebration, which marks voluntary association here and elsewhere. None of these associations are schools of civic virtue, even potentially. But they may serve the purpose of containment. They can provide safety valves. Associations can circumscribe exhibitions of hate and hostile outbreaks of envy. Loathsome groups can be lifelines.

I do not propose that these themes coalesce around a single principle of freedom of association. There is no "law of groups." Once again, my task is to follow the threads of association, underscoring the elements of American thought that make these problems so difficult for us. And to propose "the personal uses of pluralism" as a guide to the relation between our liberal democracy and our associational life.

Part One

PLURALISM AND LIBERAL EXPECTANCY

1

Civil Society: Getting the Dangers Right

Hegel's Moment

The moment we begin to conjure up associations—Jaycees or the Michigan militia, homeowners' associations or the Mormon Church—we see difficulties with what has emerged as a driving force in public policy and a leading proposition in both social science and political theory: the idea that the relation between civil society and liberal democracy must be reciprocally supportive. Liberalism's origin in the context of religious wars is a reminder of the historical promise of reciprocity: limited government and a policy of toleration would protect the associational life of religious groups, and for their part, an array of independent churches and sects would insure the civil, secular character of government. Extended to voluntary associations of every kind, this idea has become a staple of liberal democratic thought.

The classic formulation focuses on the *political* role of groups as both complementary and countervailing forces to government. Like a wide dispersion of private property, a multiplicity of associations with resources of leadership and organization checks government and insures the possibility of political resistance. Some groups in America are self-appointed political guardians. Secret societies and patriot groups aggressively assume this role; alertness to danger and readiness for resistance are their raison d'être. The checking value of associations capable of mobilizing against arbitrary or oppressive government is attributed to groups whether or not they are formed for political purposes, though, or intended as centers of power and opposition. Apart from overt political activity, their independence offers protection for members and for the overall system of freedom. The defensive political function of the associations of civil society as counterweights to the state is a liberal democratic orthodoxy.

There is also the Madisonian conviction that the interplay of groups advancing and defending interests and opinions prevents consolidation of a permanent tyrannical majority. And the fact that competition for members normally breaks up the power of groups and moderates inclinations to extremism. Associations facilitate democratic representation, setting the agendas for political conflict and cooperation. They are the means of collective action generally, and the chief resource for those whose interests are disregarded and who lack influence of other kinds.

These considerations support a general thesis in favor of pluralism. But they are of little help in identifying the associations that at any moment are salient for political self-defense or participation. That is a contextual, contingent question, and specific perceptions of danger give specific groups first place.

Alongside the political function of voluntary associations in the history of liberal thought is the significance of associational life for personal liberty. For liberals of many stripes, freedom of association should be understood as a fundamental right. Escape from hereditary and ascriptive attachments (or their willing reaffirmation), the formation of new affiliations for every conceivable purpose, and shifting involvements among groups are essential aspects of liberty. Associations serve private, even idiosyncratic values that may have little to do with public life. They are a condition of self-perfection; Wilhelm von Humboldt insisted that the highest and most harmonious development of our powers requires a privileged sphere where circles of friends cultivate "beautiful individuality" and regard one another as works of art to be created and loved. The whole justification for liberalism was that limited government preserved this sphere.[1] "Ways of life," "value pluralism," the "pluralist collage" that Clifford Geertz says provide "the possibility of quite literally, and quite thoroughly, changing our minds" are the materials of self-creation. They are embodied, confronted, exploited, and altered in actual associations.[2]

The orthodox preoccupation with associations as buffers against government and avenues to political participation, and with freedom of association as an aspect of personal liberty, has been eclipsed. Today, the dominant perspective is moral: civil society is seen as a school of virtue where men and women develop the dispositions essential to liberal democracy.

The term "civil society" has a definite place in the history of political thought, and its current use in American discourse is a legacy from Hegel, the philosopher for whom "the creation of civil society [is] the achievement of the modern world."[3] I am not proposing that Hegel's philosophy figures centrally in the intellectual history of American political thought on the subject. Only that his writing produces a shock of recognition today, and that the moral intensity driving retrieval of the idea of civil society echoes Hegel's, sometimes self-consciously. Despite the gulf separating nineteenth-century German corporations from the complexity and fluidity of contemporary civil society, *The Philosophy of Right* identifies the ethical project of integrating individuals into the life of public community. The career of the Hegelian concept stands in plain contrast to the Lockean emphasis on civil society as bulwark against despotism. It contrasts with the class-centered, property-centered Marxian view in which "bourgeois society" and "bad privacy" are anathema and noneconomic groups insignificant.[4]

Hegel taught that civil society must be seen against the historical background of the rise of individualism. Civil society goes the final step toward alienation from premodern groups and particularist privileges: it "tears the individual from his family ties, estranges the members of the family from one another, and recognizes them as self-subsistent persons." Individuals receive in civil society their identity as persons bearing rights. In an age of romanticism Hegel's extravagant picture of atomistic individualism was hardly unique. But he was exceptional in pointing the way to political reconciliation. For at the same time that it disconnects individuals from traditionalist moorings, civil society is the "tremendous power" that draws individuals into itself, provides them with a "second family," and reorients them: "the sanctity of marriage and the dignity of Corporation membership are the two fixed points round which the unorganized atoms of civil society revolve." Where others see only arbitrariness and contests among disconnected individuals, Hegel comprehends "the world of ethical appearance." "Individuals can attain their ends only in so far as they ... make themselves links in this chain of social connexions."[5]

Civil society is a system of needs: "the livelihood, happiness, and legal status of one man is interwoven with the livelihood, happiness, and rights of all. . . . Only in this connected system are they actualized and secured."[6] It is where individuals find satisfaction in cooperation at work: "for it is not enough that the citizen is allowed to pursue a trade or calling, it must also be a source of gain to him; it is not enough that men are permitted to use their powers, they must also find an opportunity of applying them to purpose."[7] Hegel brings to his sober analysis a keen recognition of romantic expressivism and plenitude. He describes the ceaseless multiplication of day-to-day demands for personal satisfaction, the unleashing of personality as "measureless excess" and "a riot of self-seeking." It leads to an explosion of "contrivances and organizations": "the whole sphere of civil society is the territory of mediation where there is free play for every idiosyncrasy, every talent, every accident of birth and fortune, and where waves of every passion gush forth, regulated only by reason glinting through them."[8]

There is not only a discernible system but also a "liberating discipline" in all this, however. "Vain subjectivity" is tempered by the constraints of contract and civil law and by activity in accord with public laws and the administration of justice. "Personal arbitrariness ... is broken against such authorized bodies," Hegel wrote.[9] Civil society is at once an economic system of acknowledged mutual welfare, an arena for free expression, and a public juridical culture that imposes its discipline.

The principal "ethical entity" that provides members "with work of a public character over and above their private business ... which the modern state does not always provide" is the corporation, meaning the circles of civil life: economic organizations, religious bodies, learned societies, and so on.[10] Members have espirit de corps, that is, "the disposition to make oneself a member of one of the moments of civil society by one's own act, through one's energy, industry, and skill, to maintain oneself in this position, and to fend for oneself only through this process ... while in this way gaining recognition both in one's own eyes and in the eyes of others." The propensity of members of associations to cooperate, contract, and recognize rights is a genuinely ethical disposition. For the education that goes on in corporations experienced as "a second family" is no mere external imposition. Nor is it just a necessary means to the comforts of private life.[11] Without membership "an individual is without rank or dignity, his isolation reduces his business to mere self-seeking, and his livelihood and satisfaction become insecure."

Corporations have diverse *Sittlichkeits*; the social identity of their members, modes of life, characteristic virtues and practices, and political representation. There is only one "universal class" in Hegel's system, "dispassionate, upright and polite," whose collective ethos is public service.[12] But each corporation in pluralist civil society provides members with self-respect and is integrative.

> Through working with others, his particularity is mediated; he ceases to be a mere unit and eventually becomes so socially conscious, as a result of the educative force of the institutions of civil society, that he wills his own ends only in willing universal ends and so has passed beyond civil society into the state. . . . The history of civil society is the history of the education of . . . private judgement until the particular is brought back to the universal.[13]

The Philosophy of Right also illuminates the limitations of civil society, in particular, the "most disturbing" problem of poverty. Poverty disconnects people from associations, with "a consequent loss of the sense of right and wrong, of honesty and the self-respect which makes a man insist on maintaining himself by his own work and effort." That is what makes the poor a "rabble." Poverty is marked by "dissoluteness, misery, and physical and ethical corruption." Lacking self-respect, yet armed with the publicly justified demand for subjective satisfaction and rights, the poor may incline to criminality and social destruction.[14]

The limits to Hegel's interest for us are also illuminating. He had nothing to say about the tenaciousness of ascriptive affiliations, or the re-creation of new particularist communities. Hegel worried that corporations might ossify "into a miserable system of castes."[15] But he did not anticipate the persistent strength of religious or ethnic communities (much less myriad other self-styled identity groups) that do not share the norms of public juridical culture. His teleology made them historically, if not practically, inert in any case.[16]

For Hegel, the great Idealist, recognition of ethical life is conceptual, a matter of understanding the rational necessity of civil society and the modern state. Wholeness and belonging are apprehended through thought, specifically, through the transformative recognition that comes from grasping the system set out in *The Philosophy of Right*. For Hegel, the *idea* of the state is where the mind finds itself at home.

This reading is meant to drive home a single point. Associations brake arrant willfulness and selfishness. They provide "the discipline of culture." At the same time, civil society holds out the "right to satisfaction," loosening hereditary and ascriptive affiliations so that individuals are able to see themselves at liberty to seek self-realization. Both detachment and voluntary association are permanent dynamics of civil society. That is why—outside of a teleological philosophy in which civil society and the modern state rise together (outside Hegel's moment, that is)—at any moment reciprocal moral support between civil society and public life may be hard to discern, much less manage in practice.

In contemporary American political thought, the perception is that both government institutions and civil society are failing to serve their disciplining, integrative functions. And it is not surprising that demoralization appears to proceed from opposite directions: atomistic individualism and narrow communalism, too much and too little voluntarism and privatism, an absence and a surfeit of authoritative public norms and regulations. So nothing is more important than getting the dangers right.

Getting the Dangers Right

The idea that liberal democracy depends on the conscious reproduction of citizens is nothing new, but in contemporary political thought the ante has been raised. Expectations for moral development go beyond tempering self-interest and enlarging parochial views: Tocqueville's and J. S. Mill's concern. At the same time, few convictions are as widespread as the belief that the cultivation of even minimal civic capacities and commitment to liberal democratic values and institutions is inadequate.

Jeremiahs marshal empirical evidence of the falling off of American public life. The catalogue is familiar: Analyses of declining voter turnout, along with a sorry decline of expectation from the standard of the "reasonable voter" to the "rational voter" to the minimally "reasoning voter."[17] Surveys documenting political mistrust (once thought to keep citizens alert to abuses of power, but now wayward) and "pervasive contempt" for major institutions. Data on crime rates and litigation explosions. Even clinical depression, inspiring Robert Lane to call the United States a "joyless polity."[18]

Citizenship is not autonomous, the argument goes, and official "seedbeds of civic virtue" such as public schools and local governments cannot do the work of liberal democratic character formation alone. The reproduction of citizens must go on in the networks of civil society. Once the preserve of conservatives, the imperative "to recapture the density of associational life and relearn the activities and understandings that go with it" is echoed across the political spectrum.[19] Associations are supposed to integrate members into liberal democratic public culture. Either directly, by cultivating specific democratic competencies. Or indirectly, by instilling general moral virtues in members and building up the "social capital" without which collective action is inconceivable. Civil society must compensate for what is seen as either the natural limitations or perverse failings of political institutions.

As soon as we proceed beyond simple, hopeful invocations of civil society, however, we are caught up in grim observations that associational life, too, is faltering. Surveys of membership in voluntary associations report declines, particularly in church-related groups, labor unions, the PTA, and fraternal organizations. Since "members of associations are much more likely than nonmembers to participate in politics, to spend time with neighbors, to express social trust," the result is an erosion of "social connectedness" and trust, a fraying of the "fabric of community life."[20]

Of course, the problem will appear less intractable if we challenge this vision of associational life as fragile, fatally vulnerable to disintegrative economic and cultural forces and overweening government. (In fact, it seems to be an American tradition to view with alarm the future of voluntary organizations.[21]) Or if we can plausibly argue that new forms of association take the place of declining membership in traditional groups.

Another strategy for mustering a sanguine outlook is to disregard the actual incongruous array of associations and keep references to civil society very general, even vacuous—for example, "the space of uncoerced human association"; "concrete and authentic solidarities"; the "sphere of autonomous institutions, protected by the rule of law, within which individuals and communities possessing divergent values and beliefs may coexist in peace."[22] The complaint that civil society has "much resonance and little content" is well taken.[23] Alternatively, terms can be exquisitely refined and civil society identified with specific associations judged supportive of liberal democracy. Democratically organized public interest groups and civic-minded volunteer groups open to all comers are on every list. Other associations are excluded by definition; business corporations, for example, or any association engaged in market-oriented production and consumption, perhaps on the assumption that even if decentralized ownership is a precondition of civil society it is not part of its moral significance.[24]

There is widespread agreement that voluntary associations play a key part in personal moral development, then, and that they are endangered. The thought that "increasingly, associational life in the 'advanced' capitalist and social democratic countries seems at risk" is a commonplace, rarely unchallenged.[25] However, there is striking disagreement on the diagnosis of the breakdown of reciprocity between civil society and government when it comes to reproducing liberal democratic citizens.

One current designates America a mass society and warns that the "megastructures" of American government are hallmarks of totalitarianism. Government undermines healthy pluralism directly by official regulation, subsidy, and control, or by gobbling up social functions and displacing secondary institutions in its ever-expanding roles as speaker, educator, employer, and player in the market. Government institutions are overbearing and inhospitable to "concrete particularities." They displace or erode the independent life of groups and subcommunities.

As a historical, causal account this is certainly wrong. Social historians have shown that voluntary associations in America multiplied and flourished in tandem with the growth of government activism at every level, and were supported rather than choked off by government policies. But this has not undermined the perception that overall, strong government has weakened basic values and social attachments. Nor has it erased the perception of widespread anomie.

Beginning in the 1970s, Peter Berger and Richard Neuhaus, early authorities for this diagnosis, identified a critical need for mediating groups capable of "giving private life a measure of stability" and "transferring meaning and value to the megastructures of public order."[26] It is necessary to connect people who are aliented from (or more likely never knew) the associations in which moral dispositions and social attachments are developed. When Berger and Neuhaus proposed the axiom that "psychologically and sociologically . . . *any identity* is better than none," the danger of anomie evidently loomed larger than anything that could be feared from the tendencies of strong affiliation with antiliberal, antidemocratic groups. The axiom is repeated today: "the basic fact of liberal sociology," William Galston argues, is that "the greatest threat to children in modern liberal society is not that they will believe in something too deeply, but that they will believe in nothing very deeply at all. Even to achieve the kind of free self-reflection that many liberals prize, it is better to begin by believing something."[27]

Joan Didion gave this picture of disintegration haunting expression in her essay on the radical disconnection of children in Haight-Ashbury in the 1970s:

> The center was not holding. It was a country of bankruptcy notices and public-auction announcements and commonplace reports of casual killings and misplaced children and abandoned homes and vandals who misspelled even the four-letter words they scrawled. . . . Adolescents drifted from city to torn city, sloughing off both the past and the future as snakes shed their skins, children who were never taught and would never now learn the games that had held the society together.[28]

The picture is sadly accurate for several generations of street children adrift in cities and towns since Didion wrote *Slouching towards Bethlehem*.

Small wonder traditionalism and particularism are lauded. "Balkanization," "parochialization," even "retribalization" are not wholly critical terms for those fixed on the atomizing government behemoth.[29] From this perspective the appropriate remedy is not obvious, though. Downsizing, limiting, and privatizing federal and state government activity may not be a sufficient condition of reinvigorated civil society. Indeed, since a zero-sum view of state versus voluntary activity is erroneous, displacing government would be fatal to general well-being.[30]

Besides, separate, sometimes incompatible reasons for celebrating connections are run together by those who share the diagnosis of atomistic individualism and mass society. Is the chief aim to revive associations capable of countering cold loneliness, providing the psychological goods of solidarity and affective attachment?[31] Or is it to buttress cultural practices on the assumption that "individual freedom and well-being depend on unimpeded membership in a respected and prosperous cultural group"?[32] Or are mediating groups prized for their capacity to cultivate dispositions that support liberal democratic political life specifically? Michael Walzer has voiced this concern: conflicts among dissociated individuals may be "too dispersed and trivial to threaten the stability of social life, but they are also too dispersed and trivial to energize social life," and he would "look for ways of limiting protestantism, separatism, and privatization."[33]

This is a partial account of the obstacle to reciprocity between liberal democracy and civil society, at best. A second and opposite diagnosis focuses on the dangers of wildly proliferating group life, which is seen as the consequence of a generally weak and permissive public culture. Liberal democracy has laudable moral as well as political ideals and institutional arrangements, on this view, but fails by being self-effacing. Committed to freedom of association, liberal democracy becomes home for every imaginable formal and informal group—authoritarian, elitist, bureaucratic and hierarchic, "feudalistic," sexist, racist, blindly traditionalist, and paramilitary, committed to detachment, Nietzschean nihilism, or bohemianism, to say nothing of overt disobedience. Fortuitously insulated from the conflicts of ethnically or linguistically defined nationalities that dissolve citizenship, still, the United States is awash in identity groups. Liberal democracy harbors private despotisms—domestic and communal. It is positively inviting to "counterculture" enclaves (mostly white and middle-class) of New Age believers, eccentric religious sects, walled residential communities dedicated to re-creation, racial separatists, and paramilitary camps. Not surprisingly, they find one another grating if not loathsome: San Francisco's gay Castro district and Jerry Falwell's Liberty Baptist Church community "haunt each others' dreams."[34]

The danger is not atomism and a "missing middle," then, but the undisciplined multiplication of associations that amplify self-interest, encourage arrant interest group politics, and exaggerate cultural egocentrism. Civil society is rife with associations dedicated to the exhibition of presumably exemplary differences. These groups claim us as their own, attribute obligations to us, and insist that we should feel as if we belong—labeling us traitors and self-haters (or "in denial") if we do not. Liberalism gives scope to fierce group loyalties that look on characteristic liberal democratic practices as unwanted, oppressive assimilation. Joan Didion gives this expression, too, in *Miami*:

> In the continuing opera still called, even by Cubans who have now lived the largest part of their lives in this country, *el exilio*, the exile, meetings at private houses in Miami Beach are seen to have consequences. . . . Revolutions and counter-revolutions are framed in the private sector . . . This particular political style, indigenous to the Caribbean and to Central America, has now been naturalized in the United States.[35]

"La lutta" is no one's version of democratic politics.

The prescription that flows from this diagnosis is not "connection" but disassociation: loosening the hold of gripping affiliations so that members have the psychological latitude to look beyond the group and identify themselves as citizens. What is needed is a stronger assertion of liberal democratic values in both public and private life.

This picture of a segmented society of societies is as partial as the characterization of the United States as a mass society. Whether the greater danger is social groups in a culture war with liberal democratic norms and institutions, or overweening government that threatens the independence and distinctive characters of associations can only be settled retrospectively, by political history. But as a practical matter, the enormous diversity of associational life in this country means that invariably these processes go on simultaneously, which is why accounts of danger diverge dramatically, depending on the element in view.

A dose of sociological and psychological realism suggests that things are more complex than either allows. Anomie and aggressive self-interest coexist, along with solidaristic groups that inhibit their members from looking outside. So civil society's formative purposes properly include chastening egotism and crass self-interest, integrating disconnected individuals into formative associations, and loosening the exclusive hold of gripping communities. Both greater government regulation and greater solicitude for associational life may be useful, and neither is a substitute for the other.

The answer to the question of what political and legal relations hold, or should hold, between voluntary associations and government depends on getting the dangers right. A comparative perspective may be helpful.

Getting Things in (Comparative) Perspective

"Civil society" is a reigning slogan and aspiration globally, particularly in Central and Eastern Europe. It is salutary to expose our sense of danger to the comparative politics of civil society, especially since the peculiar tides of intellectual influence have American theorists drawing on the postcommunist literature for inspiration. As if the turn to civil society in a period of political crisis and state collapse corresponds to the recurrent ups and downs of associational life here. As if the struggle in democratizing countries to link associations to representative institutions and to constitutionalism has lessons for the United States, where the problem if anything is a falling off of political commitment, self-dramatized as de-democratization.

"Civil society" entered the contemporary political lexicon of Eastern Europe as an oppositional idea. Where the political imperative was liberation from party dictatorships that controlled the economy, politics, and ideology and where overt opposition was ineffective and suicidal, resistance to centralized authority had to be chiefly intellectual and cultural. Civil society referred to an underground "parallel polis" of groups attending peacefully to ostensibly nonpolitical affairs. It signaled hope for an iota of negative liberty: "Let me be, leave me alone, don't try to tell me how to live."[36] Poland's Solidarity epitomized another facet of civil society, as seedbed of human rights and dissident movements actively opposed to Party authority. Since the fall of communist regimes, civil society has exhibited yet another face; trade unions, professional organizations, churches, and political parties are prized as decentralized loci of independent economic and social activity. They are the material for social restructuring. "The social self-organization of society" is supposed to move into every space state power has abandoned.[37] In contrast to the implacable authority of a centralized communist regime, civil society signifies "a living society in which public life and activities originating 'from below' are possible."[38]

One thing is clear: the idea of conflicting political groups advancing particular interests and opinions is not anathema. After all, the whole idea is to recover from the stifling myth of collective harmony and to move out into the fresh air of adversary politics. Associations are recognized engines of collective action; they enable the advancement of interests; they play a part in securing democratic legitimacy and, hopefully, stability. Bargaining, negotiation, party alliances, and the rest of the apparatus of interest group politics do not have the appearance of an amoral pursuit of "naked preferences" they do for American thinkers distressed by the perceived excesses of political pluralism here, or attracted to some more demanding deliberative democratic ideal.

That is a luxury. In postcommunist countries the challenge is precisely to see beyond civil society as oppositional and as an imagined utopia of self-organized groups, and to conceive of practical, reciprocal relations between associations and government. Accounts of the possibilities for this relation are as contested as theories of the transition to democracy.[39] How to channel freedom of association into representative institutions? How to constitutionally secure the legal independence of associations capable of counterbalancing government?[40] And, on the other side, how to insure that government is strong enough to perform its own vital countervailing and ordering functions? And to generate sufficient commitment to compete with centrifugal loyalties. As intractable and destabilizing as disagreements on these matters are, they pale when the alternative to civil society and constitutional government as a replacement for communist authority is communalism based on nationalist cultural identities.

From the standpoint of postcommunism, the United States has a well-developed civil society with a plurality of independent social, economic, and political groups and without ideological or institutional monopolies. Declarations that associational life is "at risk" must seem histrionic. There is no danger of wholesale rejection of freedom of association, and no challenge to the stability and legitimacy of liberal democratic arrangements. From a comparative perspective, we enjoy a deep historical reservoir of reciprocity between voluntary associations and democratic institutions: "in the United States, at least, private associations have . . . contributed to order and stability through a pattern of relationships with government to a degree which is seldom acknowledged."[41]

Consider, for example, that when it comes to addressing social needs such as caring for the elderly or educating children, all sorts of semipublic/semiprivate organizations—churches and neighborhood groups, ethnic associations and civic charities, commercial and for-profit organizations—share these responsibilties with local, state, and federal governments. It is incorrect to call this self-help or voluntarism; since the 1960s, almost all of the groups delivering social services, from Catholic Charities to the Boys Clubs, have been publicly subsidized, often on the order of 70 percent or more of their funding.[42] Goals are set or endorsed by public policy, and the rationale for delivery by a profusion of associations has a good deal to do with moral and political education as well as efficiency. Lester Salamon calls this "third party government."[43] The "welfare state" is a misnomer, not only because it falls short of securing welfare but also because it is not coextensive with the state.

Salamon's phrase is also more apt than privatization, since calls for government self-restraint and devolution of activities to voluntary associations have settled limits, too. Reinvigorated associations are seldom intended to undermine government's capacity to undertake energetic action, mobilize resources, and address collective problems.[44] Despite the "myth of pure virtue" that attaches to voluntary associations, and despite disputes over policy and political jockeying over how to divide and characterize these functions, cooperation is the accepted norm.[45] So much so that it is profitless to settle whether voluntary associations fill in for government failure in the United States or government is a derivative response to market and voluntary failure.[46]

Moreover, as viewed from outside the American debate, our internal disagreements about the health of civil society and the dangers threatening the reproduction of liberal democratic depositions take place within fairly well-defined political parameters. The settled points are clear. On the side of official incursions on freedom of association, government criminalizes few groups.

Laws do not require the internal life of *every* association to conform to public norms and practices; they do not prohibit racial, religious, or gender discrimination, enforce due process, or impose a democratic structure of authority on every group. We do not favor congregational churches over hierarchic ones, or mandate worker control over other forms of management. We do not foster democratic family life by outlawing not just polygamy as "patriarchal" but also unequal and gendered divisions of domestic labor. In short, liberal democracy in the United States does not command strict congruence everywhere and "all the way down."

But neither do associations have unlimited authority to discriminate and exclude unwanted members, govern their own affairs, or define their public obligations for themselves—not even families or religious groups. The conditions that led Mill to speak of the subjection of women in private life have been largely overturned by law. Government accommodates particular religious or cultural groups by granting exemptions from general obligations, but rarely, and separatist self-rule and "internal exile" fall outside this parameter.[47]

There is broad agreement about the parameters of association demands and incursions on government, too. Liberal democracy must be representative, and is expected to mirror ever-changing pluralism. Associations significantly determine the course of public policy. But that is consistent with a messy array of formal and informal mechanisms that fall short of the guaranteed integration of groups into government characteristic of corporatism. It precludes the constitutionally mandated representation of national minorities.

Within these parameters, we raise and address our moral concerns about the formative influence of associational life. What does contemporary liberal democratic theory have to say about the kind and degree of congruence between the internal life and organization of associations and the public norms of liberal democracy? Is congruence considered necessary, or incongruity considered tolerable, not to say welcome? Should government intervene, regulate, or protect these groups? It will help us traverse the terrain of actual groups, the complex American ideology of freedom of association, and the laws governing association life in part 2, to have a typology of approaches at hand. (The usual advisory about mixed types and merely illustrative cases applies.)

The Logic of Congruence

The neatest conceptual approach to the moral uses of pluralism thinks it imperative that the internal life and organization of associations mirror liberal democratic principles and practices.[48] A standard social science thesis views congruence between public institutions and private associations as a key to political stability; recast by political theorists, congruence appears as the key to moral education.

The logic of congruence demands more than assurance that associations are free of force, fraud, and the most egregious private despotisms. "Only a democratic state can create a democratic civil society," Michael Walzer wrote; "only a democratic civil society can sustain a democratic state."[49] Civic habits are developed through practice, the argument goes, and the requisite moral and political dispositions are cultivated only by regular, repeated interactions.

So proponents look for ways to bring the experience of liberal democracy home to us. Political associations are the obvious starting point. Neighborhood political groups, popular referenda, innovative schemes for refashioning political forums reminiscent of Robert Dahl's "minipopulus" are one way to heighten civic engagement. There are always hopeful new venues. Residential housing associations seemed to offer a fresh chance at localism, at neighborhood community and democratic control. Electronic democracy is a technologically utopian attempt not only to bring home one or another form of democratic politics (plebiscitary on some accounts, deliberative electronic town meetings on others) but also to rationalize public discourse by sanitizing it of campaign advertising, political sloganeering, and other presumably distorting influences.

Of course, even congruent political groups can fail to serve the demanding purpose. Democratically organized political interest groups and "new social movements" may serve the classic function of political representation, and they may cultivate a sense of political efficacy in their active members. Yet they may fail to serve as important reference points for the moral dispositions of members or to foster deep commitment to democratic values or to the political community as a whole. Jürgen Habermas directed this caution at Claus Offe's enthusiastic claim that "relations of association" would "ready citizens to engage in 'responsible behavior.'" What insures that the pluralization will provide new sources of public identity, Habermas asked, instead of "impotence in the face of an impenetrable systemic complexity"?[50]

In any case, political institutions pale as potential schools of virtue beside the array of associations available to "mediate and order the distance between the people and the government."[51] John Dewey's vision of democracy as a way of life that permeates society indicates the potential dimensions of the logic of congruence: "all the agencies and influences that shape disposition . . . every place in which men habitually meet—shop, club, factory, saloon, church, political caucus—is perforce a school house even though not so labelled."[52] We recognize the congruence thesis from Harry Eckstein's work on authoritarian family patterns and Carole Pateman's on participatory workplaces. In *Making Democracy Work* Robert Putnam draws a causal connection between horizontal networks of interaction and civic engagement on the one hand, and between vertical patron–client relations and political dysfunction on the other.

As these examples suggest, congruence generally refers to patterns of authority, but not necessarily. If the vital moral disposition is fairness and a propensity to defend one's rights and those of others, the defining characteristic of congruence will be associations whose practices emphasize rights and due process. Alternatively, if the disposition to care for others is seen as the critical democratic trait, congruence means associations modeled on empathic family relations, replicating relationships of heightened mutual vulnerability and responsibility.

Workplace democracy illustrates the congruence approach nicely. In Carole Pateman's classic *Participation and Democratic Theory*, the decisive reason for workplace democracy is the psychological effect authority structure has on the sense of political efficacy. This dictates a stringent standard for democratization. After all, it is possible to have participation without democratic authority; small doses of low-level participation in the immediate work process may enhance confidence, and studies confirm that even modest egalitarian distributions of authority result in greater self-respect. But Pateman insists that only genuine worker control, where the whole body of employees makes management decisions, can generate the requisite sense of political efficacy.[53]

There are other arguments for reorganizing workplace authority that fall outside the logic of congruence: increasing productivity, insuring material benefits like health insurance, controlling the distribution of jobs, or using democratic decision-making to equalize wealth. We also know that accounts of the workplace as the crucial formative environment do not always see authority structure as critical. Self-respect is rightly said to be essential to liberal democratic citizenship, and on a view that can be traced to Adam Smith and Karl Marx, routinized, repetitive work is dehumanizing and damages self-respect, regardless of who makes decisions.[54] Similarly, the exhibition of excellences through work may be essential to democratic individualism, but it, too, has nothing to do with workplace control.[55] As Michael Sandel's reading of American political thought suggests, if we doubt that a nation of "hirelings" can cultivate the independence and judgment necessary to genuine self-government, we will be chiefly concerned about the economic independence of producers.[56]

Every variation on the congruence theme rests on the assumption that dispositions and practices shaped in one association spill over to other contexts. This is a vulnerable point. (I leave aside for now the assumption that reiteration is desirable.) For the logic of congruence does not come automatically equipped with a social or psychological dynamic to explain why dispositions cultivated in one association can be expected to be stable and transmitted to other spheres.

In fact, Pateman was skeptical that a sense of political efficacy cultivated in voluntary associations translates to political institutions, and she challenged Almond and Verba's classic study of civic culture, which said that the principal factor in a sense of political efficacy was a "cumulative pattern of participatory opportunities."[57] She fastened onto the workplace as the singular context for democratic education because it was the most 'political' arena in which ordinary individuals interact.[58] But Pateman does not offer a plausible dynamic to explain the presumptive transmission of a sense of political efficacy from industrial democracy to political arenas either.[59] Although workplace participation and political participation may be complementary, they could just as reasonably be seen as substitutes for one another. Or as entirely independent of one another so that men and women interpret the work situation as requiring different qualities from them than citizenship. Of course, if workplace democracy did inspire political participation, there is little indication what considerations would guide worker-citizens' judgment or enhance the quality of their decisions. When it comes to industrial matters that affect the wider political community such as investment policy, pollution, or the size of the workforce, for example, do workers identify themselves as citizens concerned for the common good? Or as workers concerned with their own or their enterprise's particular good, which is, after all, in potential conflict with workers in other sectors or firms, the unemployed, shareholders, or some broader public—local, state, or national?

It is not always clear whether the proposition that congruent associations alone serve the purpose of cultivating democratic dispositions is a matter of principle—part of a normative theory of ideal democracy. Or whether it is an empirical claim about the actual moral effects of institutional design. Social scientists have had more success demonstrating the moral (typically ill-) effects of *incongruence* between associational life and liberal democracy in particular instances than the logic of congruence. If we cannot show conclusively where or how "participation begets participation," there are a host of good reasons, moral but also practical and organizational, why an absence of participatory experience can make collective action harder.[60]

In his work on patterns of authority Harry Eckstein traces what he calls "civic inclusion and its discontents" to the authoritarian culture of the poor, beginning with the family. The absence of decision-making processes in family life along with persistent experience of peremptoriness and unpredictability explain why the poor often exclude themselves from participation in politics, the workplace, and educational institutions that are formally open and egalitarian.[61] The consequence of this particular incongruence for democratic citizenship, Eckstein proposes, is submissive acceptance of ruling elites and mass behavior. But the study does not demonstrate the congruence thesis: that democratically organized families produce participatory citizens enthusiastic about taking advantage of their inclusion.

Even if we accept the logic of congruence, with its assumption that moral dispositions spill over from a formative association to other spheres and ultimately to exercises of citizenship in public life, the political question remains. Should congruence between the norms and practices of public institutions and the internal life of voluntary associations be enforced by law?

Many areas of social life have been constitutionalized, of course. Race and gender antidiscrimination law is generally applicable. Due process is the rule if not effective practice in most organizations, and courts enforce the regulations of even private clubs against objecting members. Restricted-membership groups can be legally coerced to admit unwanted members, and government can compel association as the Supreme Court did in *Roberts v. Jaycees*, deciding that the Jaycees could not successfully invoke the First Amendment right of association to assign women second-class membership.

The rationales for constitutionalizing certain groups have little to do with the moral uses of pluralism, however, at least not directly. And there are legal and ideological constraints on publicly enforced congruence. In general, "we do not expect the same religious tolerance of the United Presbyterian Church . . . nor the same political tolerance of the Sixth Ward Republican Club, as we do of the state."[62]

It is not hard to see why the question of legally enforced liberalization or democratization is seldom addressed, or is addressed piecemeal even by advocates of the logic of congruence. Concern for personal liberty and freedom of association is understandably aroused. And the direction of causality is in dispute: who is responsible for initiating the beneficial cycle of mirroring and reciprocal support, government or voluntary associations? Nevertheless, advocates of congruence typically go further in mandating intervention than current law permits. "Constitutive groups," the argument goes, must themselves be constituted and shaped by the "gentle interventions" of government if they are "to be of use to our political order," and "a crucial task of educational statecraft is to foster a healthy structure and mix of group life."[63]

Every element of society is a candidate for congruence. If "a society that is committed to equal respect for all of its members, and to justice in social distributions of benefits and responsibilities, can neither neglect the family nor accept family structures that violate these norms," Susan Okin argues, then gender inequality must be erased through shared parenting and a fair division of paid and unpaid domestic labor.[64]

If business corporations represent narrow interests and are generally undemocratic, their political participation and speech rights should be sharply curtailed. Or they should be reformed through worker control, shareholder democracy, or public interest representation on corporate boards.[65]

The logic of congruence does not permit religious or cultural communities to deny children democratic education, strictly defined. It narrows the zone of permissible religious accommodation and restricts exemptions from general obligations. Where deliberation is considered an essential democratic competence, congruence prescribes constraining religious groups from participating in politics unless they frame their arguments in terms of secular rationales or in accord with the norms of "public reasonableness."[66] (The demand for self-restraint from religiously *motivated* purposes and reasons is even more severe.)

The thought that "civil society and the state . . . must become the condition of each other's democratization" can translate into demands for powerful central coordination by government.[67] Given the potentially imperialist logic of congruence, it is not surprising that proponents are more comfortable mandating government support for associations that mirror public values than active intervention to correct deviations in their internal life and governance. Walzer looks for "the creative forces in our society that might benefit, as the labor movement once benefited, from political authorization."[68] The idea behind "associative democracy" is to make civic consciousness "an explicit goal of institutional design." Using a variety of incentives and creating new channels for representation, government can "harness group contributions to democratic order."[69]

The logic of congruence sees associations as critical formative contexts for shaping liberal democratic dispositions, then, but like corporatist institutions, they are in danger of becoming 'artifacts" of public policy. The oppositional spirit of voluntary association disappears.[70] Liberal democracy is less a mirror of civil society than tutor and creator.

Mediating Associations

A mediating approach to civil society, in contrast, orients us *away* from civic and politically inspired associations and toward the social networks believed to inculcate civility, sociability, responsibility, and cooperation that hold any society together. The concern is not for specifically, liberal democratic dispositions, but for a whole range of moral dispositions, presumably supportive of political order. Individuals learn to cooperate in shared purposes in social groups, John Rawls wrote, describing "the morality of association."[71] Currently, the reigning formulation is that civil society generates "social capital," defined in moral as well as institutional terms as "features of social organization such as networks, norms, and social trust that facilitate coordination and cooperation for mutual benefit."[72]

The mediating vision "endows small moral worlds with an ultimate significance in creating, sustaining, and improving the nation."[73] It reflects familiar assumptions about American social life, in particular, that voluntary associations rather than general institutional authorities, social classes, or tradition, are the agents of moral education and social control, with the emphasis on "social" over control. The "deep structure" of "linkages among person, community, and larger society" is "congregational" on this account, not in the sense of democratic but based on interpersonal relations on a relatively small scale, on moral self-regulation rather than public education from above.[74]

This is a more capacious approach to the moral uses of association than the logic of congruence, clearly. The business of instilling habits of responsibility, reciprocity, cooperation, or trust is compatible with a variety of political orientations and substantive values. Associations are not expected to cultivate specifically democratic political competencies in members, either, at least not by design. (Though the process of association helps define interests and goals, so that association per se is often a step toward transforming inchoate beliefs and wants into a political agenda.) And countless social unions can serve, whether or not they are structurally or ideologically liberal and democratic.

In studying the United States, Robert Putnam seems to place less emphasis on congruent horizontal groups specifically, invoking instead the "density of associational life" in general.[75] In fact, special merit may attach to nonliberal, undemocratic sources of virtue. Francis Fukuyama argues that the roots of social capital are in *incongruent* associations: "democracy and capitalism work best when they are leavened with cultural traditions that arise from nonliberal sources."[76] No group is immune from recruitment to the cause. Public funds and foundation grants have been used to subsidize street gangs, for example, with the thought that they might turn from crime and self-destruction and substitute for the "natural" social organizations allegedly missing from urban ghettos.[77]

This picture of the mediating approach to civil society is sharpened if it is juxtaposed to the theoretical tradition of British pluralism, which flourished in the first decades of this century. For J. N. Figgis, the state was simply a "community of communities" or "society of societies," a political framework and guarantor of peace among vital self-organized associations, including universities, trade unions, and churches, which arranged social life and were responsible for moral development.[78] These associations are primary and autonomous, a "natural fact, the expression of the social union." It is a mistake to represent them as outgrowths of contingent contractual agreements, Figgis argued, or as legal creations of parliamentary or popular sovereignty, corporate creatures of "the great Leviathan."[79] The contemporary mediating approach to civil society shares the British pluralist view of social groups as the "native soil" of moral and political life. They arise spontaneously, define their own goals, and are accountable only to themselves. Whether formative groups are voluntary or ascriptive, they do not owe their existence or moral purposes to government initiative or direction, or to the general impress of liberal democratic public life.

But having said this, those who put their faith in mediating associations today have a more fluid and contingent view of groups, as stands to reason in the United States, where there are few foundings far enough in the past to encourage the claim of natural origin or unity typical of British pluralism.

Alcoholics Anonymous, for example, could not have been invented by a government policy-maker. Mediating associations are more likely to be AA or an independent church formed by a charismatic preacher than a historic establishment. Informal groups have standing along with permanent institutions.

Nor can American advocates concede autonomy and priority to associations as the British pluralists did, or concede that associations are properly the chief claimants on our allegiance. Liberal democracy is more than a framework prized for its hospitality to pluralism. It embodies political ideals that associational life ideally supports, if only indirectly. Public values have independent justification and force. Associations and political institutions need not form a seamless web, but contemporary proponents of civil society would hesitate before affirming Figgis's fond observation that associations "limit and develop your life, make you do, or refrain from doing, what otherwise you would not, and in so far prevent you being a free and untrammelled citizen of the state."[80]

For "mediating" is meant to convey the idea that social networks do more than inculcate cooperation and a sense of shared responsibility in their members; cooperation begets cooperation. It is reiterated. And the resultant moral dispositions and "social capital" they generate are supposed to redound to political society as a whole.[81] But unintentionally, so to speak, and without government direction.

So it is significant that, like the logic of congruence, mediating approaches fail to offer a social or psychological dynamic capable of explaining whether and how trust, say, or cooperation, is transferred from sphere to sphere, including democratic arenas. Virtues are not contagious, though it goes without saying that certain generalized moral dispositions—against violence or malfeasance, for example—are necessary to the functioning of *any* institution. Virtues supportive of liberal democracy, or at least consistent with it, are at issue, not the bare requirements of "civilization." Without a plausible dynamic, the idea of mediating institutions rests on little more than an optimistic "liberal expectancy."

Tocqueville's *Democracy in America*, not the political theory of British pluralism, is considered the authoritative statement. He characterized voluntary associations as "partial publics" where individualism is chastened, and intoned: "feelings and ideas are renewed, the heart enlarged, and the understanding developed only by the reciprocal action of men upon one another."[82] In fact, Tocqueville's account is more severe than these often cited passages suggest.

Americans have perfected "the art of pursuing in common the objects of common desires and have applied this new technique to the greatest number of purposes," he thought.[83] They had to. Alone, individuals "can do hardly anything for themselves, and none of them is in a position to force his fellows to help him. They would all therefore find themselves helpless if they did not learn to help each other voluntarily."[84] Associations take the place of "the powerful private persons whom equality of conditions has eliminated," and cooperation gives citizens confidence and pride (hence Tocqueville's description of them as "aristocratic"). The alternative to cooperation was a fall into barbarism, or state despotism. That is why the counterpart of voluntary associations impressed Tocqueville just as much: corporations were a practical invention to make up for the scarcity of capital and accumulated wealth and enabled large-scale undertakings and projects of improvement.

Moral anxiety caused Tocqueville himself to sentimentalize certain institutions, notably religion and the family, but not voluntary associations. He never doubted that "individual interest will more than ever become the chief if not the only motive behind all actions." The real question was "how each man will interpret his individual interest," and what makes the pursuit of self-interest in America notably "orderly, temperate, moderate, careful, and self-controlled." "Self-interest rightly understood," or "refined and intelligent selfishness," follows from the understanding that increasing the prosperity of our district, the right to direct its affairs, the hope of pressing through plans for improvements that enrich us and so on depend on cooperation. It was eminently practical. Tocqueville gives prime place to associations formed for political cooperation, principally in local arenas, "in the centre of the ordinary relations of life." Local political institutions do most of the work of chastening individual passions, in part for practical reasons now obsolete, in part because he thought that desire for public esteem, thirst for the exercise of influence, and taste for authority and popularity "change their character when they find a vent so near the domestic hearth."[85]

Whether Tocqueville is properly appreciated for his cold-eyed reflections or sentimentalized, it is fair to say that his importance for contemporary American political thought is mainly inspirational. *Democracy in America* offers no guidance on the question of government's relation to mediating associations.

The principal prescription at present is public endorsement and aid. Modest proposals to increase tax credits for charitable contributions aim not only at reducing direct government spending but also at fostering group life.[86] "Left Tocquevillians" recommend public funding for specific categories of beneficial associations—educational and charitable groups, both religious and secular—so long as support is distributed in a way that cannot be construed as a special privilege.[87] Multiculturalists favor policies to foster the prosperity of cultural groups: state-funded education in their own language, public support for cultural institutions, guaranteed media air time, and so on.[88] In more ambitious "welfarist" proposals, government is justified in using tax exemptions and rebates, matching grants and vouchers to support virtually any voluntary association, whatever its character. Indeed, government should monitor the results of freedom of association with a view to insuring a novel kind of social equality. It should act as a "guiding hand" by helping "socially disadvantaged groups" form associations so that they can deliver the goods of associational life to their members.[89]

However, other theorists of civil society would stringently curtail government's authority to confer benefits on associations and prescribe leaving them to themselves. John Gray argues that the chief result of government solicitude and support for associations is a tendency to grabbiness and "state-subsidized ghettos." Given machinery for private litigation and legal restraints on government from taking on and crowding out social roles and responsibilities, civil society will flourish. There seems to be no acceptable middle ground between minimal government and corporatist behemoth, on Gray's or any view so repulsed by the jockeying of interest groups. Fearful of the twin evils of aggressive state "capture" and passive clientelism, there is apparently little to regret if associations turn away from political engagement altogether. Indeed, for Gray civil society has priority over liberal democracy, which is instrumental at best; "liberal" authoritarianism will do.[90]

Libertarian philosophers insist even more strongly on unregulated and unsupported freedom of association for all groups, whether or not they value or practice freedom. The principal criterion for lawful association is the possibility of exit. A society is free only if "individuals can dissociate themselves from options they cannot abide," though it may be costly and entry into other groups may be difficult.[91] At the extreme, liberalism is compatible with what amounts to internal secession by self-governing groups (though it is unlikely libertarians have the white racist Northwest Imperative or enclaves of Posse Comitatus in mind). In any case, libertarians are more interested in justifying near-total freedom of association than in support for government, which must create the legal framework for association and presumably insure the right to exit groups. Government remains a cipher.

We have located the outer limit of mediating approaches to associational life: where liberalism is justified because it provides the most ample and secure framework for associations to form and flourish but without equivalent concern for whether and how associations support liberal democratic character and public life. Reciprocity between civil society and liberal democracy has disappeared. Libertarian or not, mediating approaches to civil society are typically more solicitous of the conditions for associational life than of the conditions that lead them and their members to support government. Where there is freedom of association, groups will arise spontaneously—that is, owing to the entrepreneurial talents of organizers or schism within existing groups. But what reason is there to think that minimal commitment to liberal democratic virtues or political life is also spontaneous, especially if support for liberal democracy imposes some cost on an association's own purposes and internal culture? In fact, what reason is there to think that associations cultivate benign dispositions in their members at all? Proposals for public support provide at least a pragmatic reason why associations might have a commitment to liberal government sufficiently strong to weigh in against each group's loyalty to its own, though this rationale is seldom made explicit. For the most part, the mediating approach to civil society rests, again, on an airy "liberal expectancy."

Individualism and the Moral Uses of Pluralism

This is the point to which we have come. The *congruence* approach to civil
society gives undue priority to political competence and participation over
other moral uses of pluralism, and suffers from the hubris of thinking that
government can fill social voids and generate liberalizing, democratizing
groups by incentive or fiat. Democratic political culture threatens to colonize
personal and social life. The *mediating* approach indulges romantic enthusiasm for spontaneous associations and for the undifferentiated "moralizing"
effect of membership without an equivalent concern for attachment to the legal
and political institutions that sustain associations in the first place. Freedom of
association threatens to balkanize public life.

I do not intend to depreciate the theoretical sophistication and good political
sense in both approaches. In separate ways, congruent groups and mediating
associations chasten egotism, provide attachments, widen outlooks, and enlarge sentiments and some may generate distinctly liberal virtues such as tolerance; both may be useful and neither is a substitute for the other. But as guides
to the moral uses of pluralism they are inadequate. Both ignore the lesson of
"Hegel's moment." Association membership is a distinctive "moment" in social and personal life. It cannot be dissolved into citizenship on the one hand
or genuinely private life on the other.

Neither the logic of congruence nor a mediating approach to civil society
attends to the principal consideration: that, by itself, the *existence* of a dense
array of associations—whether congruent or not—may fail to contribute to the
moral uses of pluralism. It is the *experience of pluralism* by men and women
personally and individually that counts. We must be able to exploit, willfully
and inadvertently, the moral possibilities of membership in diverse associations. So the crucial considerations are the extent to which individuals' lives
are bound up with a single group, whether membership in a particular association inhibits or encourages other affiliations, what experiences of association
life are vivid and accessible, and the possibility of shifting involvements.

I have charged congruence and mediating approaches to civil society with
failing to explain not only how moral dispositions are cultivated in groups but
also whether and how these virtues (or vices) are transmitted to other spheres.
Why should we think that transitivity is desirable in any case? It remains for
me to say something more about the dynamic of associational life. In the following chapter I review what we know about "the morality of association" and
the dynamics of personal moral development, and why these ideas are useful
for thinking about freedom of association.

2

The Morality of Association

Three Ounces of Psychological Realism

The approaches to civil society surveyed in chapter 1 share a set of failings stemming from a common, misplaced focus. They attend predominantly to social structure, to the density and formal character of groups in civil society, and are disturbingly inattentive to the *dynamics* of membership. This orientation skews perceptions of associational life. Without regard for the dynamics of membership, the insights of moral psychology are unavailable to us. Without a modicum of insight into the regularities and vicissitudes of personal moral development, understanding of the moral uses of pluralism is stunted.

For one thing, standard approaches assume that a group's formative effects on members can be predicted on the basis of its express purpose or formal organization, which is why the usual listing of groups by social science category (commercial/political, say, or "secondary"/"mediating") is made trivial by its abstraction. Listing by title—the Mormon Church or Knights of Columbus—is just as unhelpful. It may indicate the "sort" of person who is a member and the general structure of authority, but says little about the group's moralizing, socializing power, if any, for those who join.

From the point of view of formative effects on individual members, the valence of associational life is often indeterminate. Why? The sources of anti-liberalism, and undemocratic temper vary among individuals, so it really should not be surprising that what works as an effective school of virtue will vary too, depending on whether the obstacle in each instance is arrant self-interest, some gripping and exclusive affiliation, or anomie. Members bring predispositions, constitutions, prior histories, and ideological expectations to groups, and they attribute meaning to association and have moral and emotional responses to belonging that are far from generalizable. The variable, personal uses of association are confirmed by personal experience and by an ounce of psychological realism. Social structure and phenomenology do not work independently, and neither should be considered alone.

In the second place, the temptation to concentrate single-mindedly on whether and how civil society cultivates and diffuses virtues, justice or tolerance, say, is irresistible if we disregard the dynamics of associational life. Political theorists and policy-makers set their sights on bettering our dispositions. Some look to civil society for nothing less than human flourishing and self-fulfillment. We should always be open to improvement, but a reforming temper is liable to be blind to the irrepressibility of our vices. And to what it indicates about the moral uses of membership in voluntary associations.

We would do well to absorb sociology's reminder that deviance is as much a part of social life as the reproduction of norms, and to consider whether and how associations temper illiberal vices and circumscribe mistrust. Surely it is important that groups provide relatively benign outlets for ineradicable viciousness, intolerance, or narrow self-interest, and that antidemocratic dispositions are contained even if they cannot be corrected.

This is perfectly consistent with the political objectives of a good deal of liberal political thought, which has never been exclusively idealist, much less perfectionist. Liberal democracy frequently takes its bearings from the conditions that threaten to give partiality and cruelty, ordinary and extraordinary vices, and potentially global irrationalities like conspiracism free rein. It is soundly rooted in guarding against the worst.

Finally, there is the tendency to adopt a simplistic "transmission belt" model of civil society, which says that the beneficial formative effects of association spill over from one sphere to another. As if we can infer enduring traits from behavior in a particular setting. As if moral dispositions shaped in one context, public or private, are transferable to dissimilar ones. The "transmission belt" model is simplistic as a general dynamic. It is one thing to say that within face-to-face rotating credit associations "social networks allow trust to become transitive and spread: I trust you, because I trust her and she assures me that she trusts you," and quite another thing to show that habits of trust cultivated in one social sphere are exhibited in incongruent groups in separate spheres.[1]

The propensity to assume a "transmission belt" or spillover doubtless reflects the optimistic thought that if we get one set of formative associations "right," whether by promoting congruence or the proliferation of key mediating groups, the beneficial effects are multiplied. (Logically, of course, ill effects multiply too.) It borrows power from the related thought that dispositions like justice spread contagiously.

Part of the problem with this governing assumption is that transmission is unexplained. Even if psychologists are correct that empathic mothering is the principal source of the adult capacity for strong attachments and responsibility for others, for example, the steps indicating how these translate from intimate relations to wider ones remain to be taken. (Particularly so, absent an account of the mechanisms of reinforcement.) The same is true of trust and fairness, cooperation and a sense of political efficacy. Empirical studies suggest that in very specific areas cumulative patterns of experience do hold sway; longitudinal analyses of political behavior reveal continuity, in particular, the strong impact of previous political participation on current rates of voting.[2] But we have reason to question whether, to continue this example, participation is transferrable from democratically organized voluntary associations to political institutions.

Of course, "some degree of trust must be assumed to operate" in most arenas, "since institutional arrangements alone could not entirely stem the force of fraud."[3] But the fact that at a high level of abstraction a generalized morality is discernible in ordinary social dealings says little about the mechanism at work, or its limits.

Another part of the problem with the "transmission belt" is that it is not the only dynamic at work. Thankfully, since there is no reason to suppose that reiteration is desirable. It is just as important that one experience of associational life offsets others. The lessons of one affiliation may provide countervailing force to the formative effects of another area of social life. Or they may compensate for the deficits and deprivations suffered outside; membership is a sort of reparation. Or association may provide a unique outlet for some set of dispositions unacceptable in other arenas. After all, it is simply not the case that labor in an authoritarian workplace produces incorrigibly submissive characters, or that observant Roman Catholics are ritualistic, Orthodox Jews legalistic, and followers of charismatic ministers enthusiastic in every domain.

We have overwhelming evidence that individuals exercise capacities for discrimination and moral adaptation all the time, even among seemingly close situations. This includes a refined capacity to *resist* spillover. Indeed, part of the "discipline of culture" is to discriminate among associations. At the extreme, the inability, say, to assign or withhold trust or mistrust appropriately approaches paranoia or pathological fusion. National surveys asking whether Americans believe that "people in general can be trusted" are doubly bleak: disheartening and unenlightening

We differentiate among contexts all the time. For example, we attribute different meanings to subjection to authority depending not only on the formal rules of a particular association and our role within it but also on subjective states and the residues of powerful experiences in other spheres that may "leak" from one to another, sometimes unconsciously. We are alarmed when our expectations for authority, which normally vary from setting to setting, do not respect social boundaries.

Thus, women may experience their position in a business or professional relationship as one of habitual deference to male authority or as vulnerable to sexual domination.[4] This "sense" is a complex mix: part conscious experience, accessible to introspection; part a way of behaving, observable to others; part unconscious inner state.[5] It may be an accurate reflection of the situation, but it may also be projection, or irrational fear, or exaggeration. In any case, the result is dissonance.

The point is, although boundaries are rarely perfectly clear, we have a normal desire and capacity to discriminate among social contexts. And the *expe-*

rience of pluralism enhances the ability to differentiate among spheres and to adjust our conduct and call up alternate dispositions. So even if we are subject to (or inflict) prejudice, arbitrariness, or deference in one domain, we may be able to exhibit an iota of tolerance in public arenas or fairness in hiring. If spillover and reiteration were the only or principal dynamic, the confinement of attitudes, behavior, and moral dispositions would be inconceivable.

These three ounces of realism come together, and I put these cautions to work in part 2. The vicissitudes of personal development affect the moral significance of membership and whether the dynamic of associational life is principally one of reinforcement, compensation, or reparation. The valence of associational life is as much a matter of how experiences come together in the lives of individuals as the formal structure and ideology of groups.

The experience of association has regularity as well as variability and indeterminacy, however. The principal constant is that associations cultivate members' capacity for cooperation. That is the core of "the morality of association," and John Rawls' account of moral development in *A Theory of Justice* is a good focal point. It gives the "morality of association" central place; incorporates moral psychology; sets moral development squarely in the context of actual associations; and assumes a pluralist array of groups.

Rawls also assigns the morality of association a distinctive role in the moral development of liberal democratic citizens: he casts the morality of association as a stage on the way to comprehending and acting on principles of justice. We can appreciate the significance of the morality of association without adopting either his theory of justice or his "liberal expectancy." For the dispositions cultivated in associations are *not* characteristically liberal or democratic. We can, however, discern that the moral uses of voluntary associations *do* serve a constructive and distinctly political function: as compensation for the characteristic failings of American liberal democracy.

The Morality of Association

"The morality of association" arises, as its name suggests, from membership in groups. There, individuals learn the social roles and rules impressed on them by the approval and disapproval of other members and by the group's authority. How does this happen? As Rawls explains it, members come to appreciate that the group's system of cooperation requires a variety of actions and points of view, and they learn to take on the perspectives of others. Ties of friendly feeling and trust are generated as they see that others intend to do their share. As individuals become attached to these arrangements and develop mutual confidence, they are motivated to comply with the obligations of membership and to live up to the ideals of their station. Qua members, they learn to habitually overcome the vices that impede cooperation—partiality, deceit, and graspingness, to name a few.

Notice what is *not* at the center of this process. No innate internal mechanism or drive is inexorably at work inclining us to cooperate. "Socialization," "internalization" of authoritative norms, or some notion of a self "embedded" in community or "penetrated" by it have no part. These processes have passive implications, and suggest external forces operating on us to instill roles and rules. Rawls adds that moral development has nothing to do with acquiring "missing motives" to do right. His observation about justice applies as well to the morality of association: "a person's sense of justice is not a compulsive psychological mechanism cleverly installed by those in authority in order to insure his unswerving compliance with rules designed to advance their interests."[6]

The dynamic of the morality of association is rooted in affective ties. Its essence is reciprocity: "Now this tendency is a deep psychological fact. Without it our nature would be very different and social cooperation fragile if not impossible."[7] A number of influential social theories and psychological laws trace conformity to moral standards to regular interactions and affective attachments. The difference is, they do not give the disposition to willingly cooperate central place.

Rawls sets the morality of association in the framework of a theory of justice. He says plainly that his end point—a just, liberal society—provides a way to distinguish moral stages, proceeding from the simpler to the more complex. The morality of "authority," "association," and "principle" he adopts correspond to Lawrence Kohlberg's stages of moral development (a modification, in turn, of Jean Piaget's cognitive theory of moral judgment). The roles and rules of association life are intermediate steps on the way to the higher-stage "morality of principle," in Rawls' case, principles of justice. "We eventually come to hold a conception of right on reasonable grounds that we can set out independently for ourselves."[8]

From the standpoint of development, a plurality of associations presenting an array of ideals and demands on individuals, some more complex and comprehensive than others, is crucial. So is access to associations by individuals. The idea is that as we assume a succession of more demanding roles in more complex schemes of rights and duties, we enlarge our experience of cooperation and our moral horizons, and our capacity for commitment to liberal principles of justice increases. We are prepared for the way in which the just system as a whole generates moral support:

> the recognition that we and those for whom we care are the beneficiaries of an established and enduring just institution tends to engender in us the corresponding sense of justice. We develop a desire to apply and to act upon the principles of justice

once we realize how social arrangements answering to them have promoted our good and that of those with whom we are affiliated. In due course we come to appreciate the ideal of just human cooperation.[9]

"In due course" suffices. There is a continuum suggested here, between the origin and expression of moral dispositions in associations and the inclination to public justice. Instead of division between our moral orientation qua members and qua citizens, there is psychological continuity. Indeed, from the highest stage, morality of principle, Rawls looks back at associations: "persons understand their sense of justice as an extension of their natural attachments, and as a way of caring about the collective good."[10]

Rawls' principles of justice are famously demanding as applied to the basic structure of society, where the burdens and benefits of social cooperation are distributed. But once inside a reasonably just order, he seems to make modest claims on individuals. Capacities for justice differ as do other natural assets, but the basic capacity for moral personality is "not at all stringent."[11] Men and women can be assumed to have the moral powers that enable them to take part in social cooperation.

In fact, it seems that progress to the morality of principle may not be necessary to support just institutions, at least not for everyone.[12] It is enough that moral sentiments are fixed at the stage of social cooperation, and follow from specific bonds and from the desire to do our share. Some people, perhaps most of us most of the time, comply with the public requirements of justice from ties of fellow-feeling and concern for the approbation of the wider society, and not out of attachment to highest-order principles. In "Overlapping Consensus" Rawls allows that an allegiance to public institutions may be based on the desire to conform to what is expected and normally due. He steps back, it seems, from saying that the morality of association is a stage that must be traversed and left behind before justice is possible.

This would help explain Rawls' open-ended definition of association as a system of cooperation in the service of some end, and why his list of associations includes the family and political society. Political society, too, is a system of cooperation.[13] Regular experience of reciprocity in public life increases trust and confidence in "the social union of social unions," and generates the disposition to conform to civic roles and rules.

Other philosophers sympathetic to the project of a theory of justice also concede that "few individuals will come to embrace the core commitments of liberal society through a process of rational inquiry." Typically, the alternative to reflective commitment to principles of justice is rhetorical pedagogy: a moralizing history and pantheon of heroes that confer legitimacy on political institutions.[14] Or, commitments are said to arise from "identification" with the political community and feelings of belonging: we are affiliated and therefore morally obligated, not vice versa.[15] For Rawls, attachment to public institutions and social arrangements comes about as a continuation of the dynamic operating in voluntary associations. (This account corresponds to the adviso that a person's level of reflective moral judgment does not determine the place that morality occupies in his or her life.)

We now have a compelling account of how the disposition to cooperation is cultivated in associations. The thought that citizens also experience liberal democracy as a whole as an association is less compelling. Its force derives from the well-ordered society of Rawls' ideal theory, and it is built into justice from the start.

If we step outside this ideal framework, why should we expect that a plurality of associations with freely articulated social roles and rules prepare members for either a reflective commitment to principles of justice or *any* liberal democratic disposition? We know that apart from habitual cooperation, the moral content of associational life is given by the "ideals of one's station" in a particular group, where members cooperate to achieve whatever it is that motivated them to join. Rawls could not be clearer: "the appropriate notion of fair terms of cooperation depends on the nature of the cooperative activity itself: on its background social context, the aims and aspirations of the participants, how they regard themselves and one another as persons, and so on."[16] Why would we think the disparate moral content of dispositions, generated as they are by membership in all sorts of incommensurate, incongruent groups, supports or complements liberal political society?

Perhaps it suffices that groups are beneficial to members and generate a sense of fellow-feeling and self-worth? Or instill habits of cooperation? If so, it is hard to see why the morality of association is peculiarly important for liberal democracy; virtually every form of social and political life depends on cooperation, after all. To be consistent with sociological and psychological realism, the "liberal expectancy" attached to the morality of association needs explaining.

The Question of Congruence

Rawls portrays his overall philosophical project as completing and extending "the movement of thought that began three centuries ago with the gradual acceptance of the principle of [religious] toleration," and invites us to generalize from liberty of conscience. A well-ordered society "will presumably contain countless social unions of many different kinds." From the perspective of liberal justice "we are not to try to rank them in value," and "government has no authority to render associations either legitimate or illegitimate any more than it has this authority with regard to art and science." Liberalism dictates that "particular associations may be freely organized as their members wish, and they may have their own internal life and discipline subject to the restriction that their members have a real choice of whether to continue their affiliation."[17]

There are limits. Freedom of association is subject to the necessity of preserving public order, Rawls argues, and there is the usual problem of where to draw the boundaries of basic liberties when they conflict (where to "set the wall" between church and state, for example). If "bitter dissension" threatens constitutional order, Rawls allows that it may be necessary to forbid paramilitary groups to arm, for example, and I return to this in chapter 8. Still, he counts even this interference with associational life an injustice, and "all that can be done is to limit these injustices in the least unjust way."[18] Provocations that lead to restrictions on the freedom of association are rare. We are meant to take government nonintervention seriously.

In any case, the question here is not what basic liberty permits or political stability requires, but what conditions make the morality of association as it plays itself out in social life compatible with, much less directly supportive of liberal democracy?

One possibility is that associational life is part of the "basic structure" of a well-ordered society, whose organization and norms must conform to principles of justice because their effects on defining men's rights and duties and influencing their life-prospects "are so profound and present from the start."[19] Of course, what counts as so "profound and present" as to justify public regulation is a key question not only for a theory of justice but also for freedom of association in practice, and I discuss the constitutionalization of associations in the United States in part 2.

Where do associations stand in Rawls' scheme? The answer is complicated by the fact that as regards even indisputably basic institutions, application of the liberal principles of justice is somewhat fluid.

Rawls does not prescribe a single form of family, for example, though certain life-chances may be fixed there. Certainly the family is the scene of early moral development, the stage he calls "the morality of authority."[20] It is one thing to recognize that many family arrangements can excite self-worth in children and obedience to justifiable demands. But having suggested that persons who have developed a sense of justice and self-esteem "are more likely to care for their children with manifest intention," Rawls does not go on to discuss what social and psychological resources men and women need or can depend on in their role as parental authorities. As feminist critics point out, he does not extend the principles of justice to the family.[21]

Some associations, it seems, must be "semicongruent" with the basic structure. Political parties should be publicly funded and independent of private economic interests if they are to play their part in a liberal constitutional scheme. Rawls says nothing about the organization of parties, though— whether they must be democratically structured, for example, and whether the principle of one person, one vote applies, and so on.[22]

Finally, Rawls affirms "there is no reason to suppose ahead of time that the principles satisfactory for the basic structure hold for all cases."[23] Most associations fall outside the domain of principles of justice; their arrangements and practices are contingent on their particular ends, and apart from cooperation, the content of the virtues they generate is supplied by members' respective status or role.

Rawls speaks in this connection of learning the "virtues of a good student and classmate, and the ideals of a good sport and companion." These suggest cooperation among peers, if not democratic practices or strict equality. But we know that the role of good worker is not always characterized by cooperation among equals, certainly not good priest or Orthodox Jew. So it would be wrong to conclude that the morality of association is frustrated by hierarchic or authoritarian structures, as long as they inspire attachment and cooperation.

Michael Sandel has pointed out the ambiguity in Rawls' moral vocabulary: "a 'community' cannot always be translated without loss to an 'association,' nor an 'attachment' to a 'relationship,' nor 'sharing' to 'reciprocating,' nor 'participation' to 'co-operation.'" Nonetheless, it is reasonably clear that "co-operation" here does not designate a particular authority structure or internal culture but any system in which various roles contribute to a common task, where there is mutual benefit, and where a desire to live up to the association's standards follows from an appreciation of these things. "Different persons with similar or complementary capacities *may co-operate so to speak* in realizing their common or matching nature."[24] Except for serfdom and slavery Rawls does not identify arrangements that must be prohibited as a condition for the morality of association.

We can conclude that associations do not fail in serving their formative moral purposes by being incongruent with the public norms of liberal democracy, or by being insufficiently complex and comprehensive to move members in the direction of appreciation for principles of justice. Rather, they fail to serve moral development if they cannot create the conditions for effective rules and roles and settled expectations. That is, if they cannot generate in members the disposition to live up to their ideals and to cooperate in their purposes. That said, the morality of association provides a pluralist background culture, much of it incongruent with liberal democracy. What remains of liberal expectancy?

Liberal Expectancy and the Strains of Commitment

Rawls insists that in a reasonably well-ordered society incongruence between the roles and rules of associational life and the requirements of public justice rarely causes tension or erupts into public dissension. If associations threaten the stability of constitutional order, they may be regulated or prohibited outright. But these are treated as exceptions.

The orthodox reason for being sanguine is that more than any other known or conceivable regime, liberal democracy is capacious. It minimizes the strains of commitment.[25] "Political liberalism" offers theoretical grounds: liberalism is expounded without reference to any wider background of beliefs and is supported by an "overlapping consensus." In addition, and less contentiously, it does not require associations to conform to the basic structure of the overall system of social cooperation.[26] Rawls' formulation is that "a conception of political justice must contain within itself sufficient space, as it were, for ways of life that can gain devoted support." As a result, "the values of community are not only essential but realizable, first in the various associations that carry on their life within the framework of the basic structure, and second in those associations that extend across the boundaries of political societies, such as churches and scientific societies."[27]

In practice, too, American government is accommodating. Even without assuming an impossibly neutral stance or disappearing, in effect, by disavowing strong liberal principles it has been able to generate broad cooperation. Government employs strategies for lessening the strains of commitment, including exemption from public obligations and "internal exile." (It goes without saying that this presumes political stability. The priority of liberal principles and institutions is asserted more vigorously where liberals are a minority.)

Liberal expectancy depends only in part on the capaciousness of liberalism, though. It also rests on assumptions about our affiliations. Rawls is well aware that citizens "may regard it as simply unthinkable to view themselves apart from certain religious, philosophical, and moral convictions, or from certain enduring attachments and loyalties." Because the comprehensive doctrines of most people are not "fully comprehensive," that is, do not cover "all recognized values and virtues within one rather precisely articulated system," however, they provide scope for allegiance to liberal practices.[28] Moral incoherence is not necessarily brought out, much less provocative of conflict between associational life and public norms.

Conflict arises mainly if men and women encounter public intolerance and discrimination when they express their incongruent views and values or engage in alien and distasteful practices. Or if groups bring to democratic politics the core demand of "identity politics": that "what is just for the group ought to be defined by it alone. What is due to people—what in hot politics, their 'rights' are—is for them to say."[29] For the most part, however, "many if not most citizens come to affirm their common political conception without seeing any particular connection, one way or the other, between it and their other views."[30] Because we can generally subscribe to separate conceptions in the public world and social and personal affairs, the "strains of commitment" are not severe.

This falls short of the distinct claim that "within different contexts we can assume diverse points of view toward our person without contradiction so long as these points of view cohere together when circumstances require."[31] This recalls us to the priority of justice in Rawls' theory, and seems to make his liberal expectancy more stringent. For the thought is that either associations themselves change in directions indicated by liberal justice, or do not inhibit their members from doing so "when circumstances require."

We have neither a theory of motivation nor a normative account of justifiable measures that would achieve this transition.[32] Which is where "liberal expectancy" comes in. I use the phrase because it is evocative, suggesting a process that is presumably undirected—a moral sea change that may be felt and observed but is largely unexplained, or even empirically demonstrated. It is reminiscent of the historical transformation we call "secularization," as much mysterious global label as measurable social process.

The idea behind liberal expectancy is that the principles and practices of liberal democratic institutions are diffused, and their advantages are plainly felt and publicly acknowledged. So an appreciation of justice becomes an element in people's motivations. And associational life is altered to the extent that members also take on liberal democracy as a moral commitment. The particular roles and rules of cooperation within groups increasingly conform to liberal democratic norms.[33] Rawls concedes that some groups will suffer a decline in authority and cohesion as a result of liberalizing forces; their survival may be threatened. Simply, "there is no social world without loss—that is, no social world that does not exclude some ways of life that realize in special ways certain fundamental values."[34]

Not all liberal theorists are preoccupied with justice, but virtually all who look to civil society to cultivate distinctively liberal democratic virtues exhibit this liberal expectancy. Something like the "protestantizing" of American religion is said to operate in associational life overall. Or, the effect of the "informal gravitational influence" of public values is said to be discernible.[35] Liberal ideals "cannot help but shape people's lives broadly and deeply and relentlessly over time"; they do not "'stay on the surface,' and their consequences cannot be confined to a particular sphere of our lives."[36] Associations cannot be effectively sheltered from contrary experiences. Their permeability to other groups and to the public culture of liberal democracy is a real obstacle to representing themselves to their members as total, William Galston explains, just as "the basic features of liberal society make it virtually impossible for parents to seal their children off from the knowledge of other ways of life." Members of groups with incongruent moral and political cultures are faced with opportunities and temptations to "drift out of their native cultural group into another."[37]

Liberal expectancy extends to associations overall, then, including gripping identity groups. George Kateb describes the transformation of ascriptive groups into voluntary associations:

> the aspiration to democratic individuality in a society slowly and imperfectly re-makes the nature of group attachment. The tendency in fact has been towards less immersion, less self-loss, more ambivalence, and moments or years of secession from cultural group attachments. In becoming limited and truly voluntary, group attachments have changed, for many people, from a fate or an inheritance into something flimsier but more charming and humane.[38]

Even strong advocates of cultural group rights, dedicated to protecting incongruent cultural communities from outside influences that threaten their viability, insist at the same time that substantial autonomy does not inhibit liberalization: "Liberals inside the culture would seek to promote liberal principles through reason or example, and liberals outside would lend their support to any efforts the community makes to liberalize their cultures," Will Kymlicka writes reassuringly.[39]

Apparently resisting this optimistic liberal expectancy, Joseph Raz speculates that existence in a liberal society often makes minority cultural groups *more* repressive than they would be in relative isolation: "the insecurity of existence . . . tends to encourage conservative elements. . . . It also tends to increase pressure on members of the group to turn inward . . . as the only guarantee against defection."[40] At least some highly "traditional" ways of life survive and thrive, and Galston suggests that the lush profusion of Orthodox and Hasidic Jewish groups in Brooklyn might be seen "as beneficiaries of a sociological backlash."[41] But Raz, too, ends up positing a "transforming effect": absent coercion, interaction with other groups is "bound to have its impact" and produce liberalizing change, including tolerance.[42]

If liberal expectancy seems to sit uneasily beside jeremiads about the falling off of moral dispositions that support liberal democracy with which I began, the two are not necessarily inconsistent. For one thing, historical perspectives and the urgency with which we regard liberalization of associations differ and affect the temper of discussion. For another, a single, undifferentiated process of "liberalization" is implausible. It is possible to concede the gradual liberalization of traditional ethnic or religious groups, for example, yet worry about the incongruence of what I have called "our multiculturalism"—the array of orientations associated with everything from retirement communities of the elderly, to the culture of self-help groups, to secret societies, to hate groups. Finally, of course, whether we incline to liberal expectancy or jeremiads depends to some extent on what we think liberal democracy requires in the way of moral dispositions, and on what we expect from voluntary associations as schools of virtue.

Liberal Expectancy and the Moral Uses of Pluralism

If the standard is whether associations in liberal democracy cultivate the disposition to cooperate in members, then the morality of association is almost certainly effective. This is the normal dynamic of associational life, whatever a group's purpose; engagement and the experience of reciprocity produce cooperation, though in other respects the dispositions called up by membership in associations are diverse. Unquestionably, this is a vital element of personal development, but it has no special affinity to liberal democracy. Cooperation is a universal requisite of social order, and it hardly bears mentioning that it carries no normative implication. Cooperation enables the worst as well as the best social actions—"force and fraud are most efficiently pursued by teams."[43] Liberal democracy has a unique relation to this process only insofar as it guarantees freedom of association.

If the expectation is that associational life produces distinctively liberal democratic virtues, however, it will be regularly disappointed. Clearly so if liberal virtue is identified with justice; the ideologies and internal lives of few voluntary associations conform to public principles of justice. The same holds for other liberal dispositions as well: tolerance, say, or adherence to due process. Liberal expectancy makes sense only if we are willing to intervene in the organization and purposes of voluntary associations to enforce congruence "all the way down," with all the ensuing strains.

The problem is obscured somewhat by expanding the list of civic virtues to include everything from "broad sympathies" to "self-control" to "an appreciation of inherited social ideals."[44] Of course, many admirable human traits are exhibited in American social life and most are compatible with the requirements of liberal democracy. In an effort to show that liberalism is not hostile to these dispositions the impulse is to class them as elements of liberal democratic character. Moreover, as the number multiplies, so do the groups that can be described as beneficent schools of virtue. This expansive field of virtues has less to do with support for characteristically liberal democratic institutions and practices, however, than with modern social life and human flourishing generally. The "strains of commitment" are not lessened in any case; they are merely diffused.

As "the morality of association" indicates, the chief and constant contribution of associations to moral development is cultivating the disposition to cooperate. On my view, that is what we can reasonably expect as a regular matter. So long as we admit pluralism and are committed to freedom of association, we cannot expect that groups will encourage their members to grasp or exhibit specifically liberal democratic virtues. Voluntary associations fail, then, only if they cannot engage members in cooperation. I want to add one thing to this minimalist position: associations also fail to serve the moral uses of pluralism if they inhibit members from looking outside the group to other attachments and experiences of social cooperation. That is, if they are total and conform to what Lewis Coser called "greedy institutions."[45] If their hold on members is such that they make shifting involvements and the cultivation of specifically liberal democratic dispositions in other spheres inconceivable.

Thus, members of organized religious or cultural communities, isolated racial enclaves, secret societies, and extremist political associations may have little psychological latitude to look beyond the group. Association inhibits other affiliations in the wider society. Members look outside, when they do, solely for self-protective reasons, to anticipate and resist interference, to heighten their sense of distinctiveness, or to claim their share, fair or not, of resources. Though not necessarily; self-enclosed associations that neither replicate nor reinforce liberal democracy may have the unplanned, unanticipated effect of preparing their members for reentering the wider society.

Whatever their affiliations, men and women must be able to see themselves also as citizens of liberal democracy with publicly recognized rights and obligations. Given American pluralism, the "strain of commitment" is always a possibility. It can be circumscribed, however. Particularly if the burden of enabling shifting involvements does not fall on associations and require alterations in their character, but on government. After all, the grip associations have on their members is exacerbated by weak and ineffective public institutions. It is the responsibility of liberal democracy to insure the background conditions that make exit possible, and the conditions that facilitate the ceaseless formation of new associations. Certainly, citizens' public standing must be unaffected by changes in or lack of affiliation.

This should inform arguments for disconnecting health care benefits and pensions, say, from specific residence and employment. It argues for requiring even self-contained communities—whether newly invented religious cults like the Alamo Foundation or traditionalist groups like the Amish—to pay minimum wages and contribute to social security taxes so that economic dependency does not make leaving inconceivable. Homeowners in residential housing associations resist what they call "double taxation," but municipalities should require them to pay community property taxes as well as the association's internal assessments.

The morality of association does not support an optimistic liberal expectancy when it comes to cultivating specifically liberal democratic dispositions. (Though some associations will continue to fulfill our loftiest hopes as schools of virtue.) In particular, the moral consequences of associational life rarely relate directly to justice, the predominant concern of most liberal democratic theorists today; they often cut against strong claims of justice. Still, it is perfectly clear that liberal democracy benefits from moral dispositions that have only an indirect bearing on justice and that associations help cultivate.

Moreover, the morality of association *does* bear a distinctive relation to liberal democracy. Americans make certain characteristic moral uses of membership in voluntary associations: membership provides defense against the rash of snubs, painful exclusions, restrictions, and inequalities that are a part of social life in our pluralist society. Wherever there is pluralism and freedom of association, expectations for democratic equality will be frustrated, and association membership will provide a buffer and a compensation.

Compensating for the Limitations of Democracy in America

Two steps carry us from the thought that associations provide experience in cooperation to their compensatory uses. The first step leads from cooperation to self-respect. Recall the dynamic at work in the morality of association. Individuals are motivated to live up to the ideal of their station as a result of ties of friendly feeling and trust. Reciprocity is key, and members must do their share. Since associations have diverse ends and embrace different things as contributions, individuals must find arenas suitably adjusted to their abilities and wants, where their specific capacities and talents are appreciated. They must have some place where their notions of the good life are affirmed, Rawls argues, and where they reduce the likelihood of failure and get support against the sense of self-doubt.[46]

It is not just a question of moral development being consistent with a variety of formative contexts, but actually requiring them. (The point is reinforced if we consider the "Aristotelian principle" as a "deep psychological fact" accounting for why we prefer complex activities to duller, simpler ones. Perfectionism, too, requires associational pluralism.) Membership is a source of self-respect, which Rawls sees as the psychological precondition for pursuing a plan of life "with zest" and for acting justly toward others.

The step from cooperation to self-respect goes by way of active participation in associational life. This is worth emphasizing because it contradicts the view that self-worth derives from racial or cultural "identity"—"identification," really, not putative identity. More specifically, self-respect is said to be enhanced by identification with the accomplishments or social advancement of others we claim as our own, often but not always as a matter of descent. Sympathetically describing the "imagined sense of togetherness" that is nationalism, Yael Tamir suggests that

> in every field of human activity—music, theatre, literature, sports, the army, or the economy—every action performed within a national context counts both as a contribution to that particular field and as a contribution to the national endeavor. . . .

Willingly or unwillingly [the poet, athlete, or painter is] also contributing to the advancement of their nation.[47]

Any "identity group" can substitute for nation in this formulation.

Whatever its merits in community-building, identification is a dubious route to individual self-respect. The "complacent confusion" of one who "introjects" the group and feels enlarged damages moral personality, George Kateb advises. So does the indirect and dishonest self-love that is pride in the group's achievements.[48] K. Anthony Appiah cites Bertrand Russell's "the virtues of theft over honest toil" in this connection.[49]

Awareness of one's status as a member of a group will naturally color both our attempts to contribute and our judgment of what counts as a contribution.[50] The point is, whether associations are voluntary or ascriptive, the morality of association depends on *personal* contributions, not psychological identification. Self-respect is inseparable from actual participation in an association's ends, and affirmation of the worth of an individual to a particular group will depend on internal assessments of his or her usefulness. Unless roles and rules are unusually simple or transparent, the effects of belonging to a particular association on a person's self-respect may be almost impossible to assess much less predict from outside or by objective means. Members' expectations are also frequently disappointed. Which is why, again, individuals must be able to find some place where they "reduce the likelihood of failure and get support against the sense of self-doubt."

The connection between self-respect and concrete contributions to associational life also distinguishes the moral uses of membership from citizenship. Contributions to this or that association have nothing to do with the worth to liberal democracy of its citizens, or should not. Nor do specifically civic contributions. As Rawls puts it, "their worth in a just and well-ordered society is always equal."[51] In practice, things are not equal, both because individuals and groups are unjustifiably debased and because one of Americans' considered judgments seems to be that a fairly circumscribed set of contributions to society are a moral prerequisite for "first-class citizenship." Awareness of self-worth developed in smaller associations is not always confirmed in the wider liberal society.[52] Nonetheless, liberal democracy in the United States promises equal public standing and creates institutional guarantees, which are often effective.

Even if equal public standing is secure, however, there are limits to its significance for personal self-respect. *First-class citizenship is not enough.* Americans are, after all, members of "two interlocking public orders": democratic public culture, where citizens have or should have equal public standing, and the realm of pluralist groups and associations, where inequality and social exclusion are everyday occurrences.[53] We are reminded of Tocqueville's description of how, in the absence of European hierarchy and social status,

Americans form "small private circles . . . little private societies held together by similar conditions, habits, and mores. . . . Each freely recognizes every other citizen as equal, but he only accepts a very small number as his friends or guests."[54] The self-respect that comes from membership is incommensurate with the public respect distributed, presumably equally, by the public institutions of liberal democracy. Neither is a substitute for the other.

The second step follows, and takes us from associations as settings of cooperation, appreciation, and self-respect to associations as compensation for disappointed social and political expectations. Membership is no compensation for second-class citizenship, but it *is* a defense against other inequalities, and does offset failure and defeat in other realms. Rawls points to associations as correctives for the adverse effects of economic inequality on self-worth. Despite equal citizenship, social status is often tied to a hierarchy of income and wealth. Associations act as a brake on competition, rivalry, and hostile outbreaks of social envy, which turn on income shares. The plurality of associations, he explains, "tends to reduce the visibility, or at least the painful visibility, of variations in men's prospects." The idea is that the various associations in society "tend to divide it into noncomparing groups."[55] This dynamic is exactly right. But Rawls' hope for "noncomparing" associations is his one striking lapse in sociological common sense.

Except for differential economic prospects, Rawls seems to ignore relative status, rivalry, and enmity *among* groups. Cooperation in a group requires members to overcome graspiness and unfairness, dishonesty and deceit, prejudice and bias that tempt them to self-preference over reciprocity.[56] But this check is internal to groups, and says nothing about the disposition members of one association exhibit vis-à-vis others or the wider society. Nothing is more common than restricted-membership groups that excite snobbery and exclusiveness, enforce strict rules of inclusion and exclusion, and cultivate a sense of superiority along every imaginable dimension. The "pleasures of animosity" should not be discounted.[57]

In short, associations mirror, reinforce, and actively create social inequalities. At the same time they offer the best antidote to the vicious effects of pluralism. The compensatory dynamic of associational life does not stop with material distributions and their social offshoots, not if everyone has appropriate occasions for inclusion and exclusion. The principal thing is the possibility for individuals to have associations in which they feel at home, even if that also means feeling superior.

From this standpoint, it is easy to see why expansive freedom of association—"the full and diverse internal life of the many communities of interests equal liberty allows"—is desirable.[58] And why not only varied associations but open ones facilitate the moral uses of pluralism. A society of terminally closed and bounded groups limits the chances of finding one whose internal life matches (or cultivates) our capacities and ideals. What is wanted is the most extensive pluralism combined with chances to exploit it, where men and women can enter and exit groups freely, where new associations are spontaneously formed and where shifting involvements is commonplace.

On the other hand, if we are to experience some degree of cooperation and control over common tasks in a setting that is "our own" and where our ends are confirmed, then gatekeeping is a principal part of association. Members themselves or the group's leaders must be able to determine the association's character, which includes enforcing restrictive criteria for entry and acting on particular notions of desert. The free and open marketplace of groups has the obvious advantage of expanding opportunities for finding personally complementary contexts, but there is little reason to suppose that every association must be open to all comers. Or that public policy should aim at mandating inclusiveness and eliminating rejection, dismissiveness, secretiveness, even discrimination despite the pain these cause those who are excluded. Nothing in the compensatory moral uses of association suggests that it operates only in *voluntary* associations, either. The morally important aspects of associational life do not turn on free choice but on generating attachment, cooperation, and a sense of being appreciated. The principal thing is that alternative associations are available for the alien or unwanted. And that associations do not keep their members captive or permanently cut off; that members have a real choice of discontinuing affiliation.[59]

Freedom of association and shifting involvements increase the possibility of finding a fitting context for self-respect. But we should not assume that individual joiners (or exiters) aim self-reflectively at this or any other moral result. The moral uses of association do not rest on our being "strong evaluators." We know from experience that our reasons for affiliation range from serendipity—circumstantial appeal and opportunity, such as recruitment by a friend or colleague at work—to sober intent with particular goals in mind. Our motives may be unconscious, or we may be guided by dim visions of our "possible selves," both aspirational and dreaded possibilities, fears of what we have been or might become. These are only tenuously connected to sociologically sophisticated views of the options available, which is why there is frequently a disjuncture between our notions of possible selves and our sense of possibility.[60] Changes in ascriptive affiliation correspond to a similar range from reflective to unintentional. Both self-distancing and disavowal of one's ethnic or cultural background and fervently adopting a lapsed, newly discovered, or invented identity may be choices; we may decide to be included. Or they may be choices only in the weak sense that they are uncoerced. Or they may come about gradually, without foresight, and have meaning only in retrospect.

Opportunities for the moral use of associations—for self-defense and self-respect, compensation and reparation, are manifestly diffuse and cannot be legislated. They are best secured by expansive freedom of association. Even if we count self-respect as a "primary good," unlike wealth and income and opportunities for public office, principles of justice cannot govern its distribution.

Just institutions can insure the element of self-respect that is derived from democratic public standing, but that is not the whole of self-respect. Indeed, it may not always have priority.

One assumption is implicit in everything said so far about civil society and the morality of association: moral change is commonplace in adults. Every thesis about the moral uses of pluralism rests on the fact that moral development continues beyond childhood. I want to consider briefly whether this focus on adult experience is defensible.

Beyond Childhood

The point that development is ongoing is built into developmental theory of every kind: cognitive and psychoanalytic approaches, theories focused on moral reasoning or moral sense, self-theory, and comprehensive theories of "identity." We need not settle on a particular account of an internally regulated course of development, specification of stages, or teleological end point— "maturity," or in Rawls' case, the "morality of principle," to grasp the simple point. It is brought home in the idea of a life cycle, whose essential outlines have been popularized. Every person passes through a series of stages, each with its specific developmental task, its particular conflicts and successful resolutions. For Erik Erikson, to take the best-known example, the components of the stages of childhood are basic trust, autonomous will, and initiative.

Erikson's work was notable for moving beyond "childhood and society" to study the critical juncture of adolescence and young adulthood, and in *Seasons of a Man's Life* David Levinson extended life-cycle analysis into adulthood.[61] Phases that used to be subsumed under the single idea of (genital) maturity are now marked by distinctive developments—the capacity for intimacy, generativity, and integrity:

> Identity formation neither begins nor ends with adolescence; it is a lifelong development . . . that involves the synthesis and resynthesis of constitutional givens, idiosyncratic libidinal needs, favored capacities, significant identifications, effective defenses, successful sublimations, and consistent roles.[62]

Even psychoanalytic theory has begun to move away from the orthodoxy that oedipal crises or infant object-relations are determinative, or even uniquely salient:

> There is remarkably little reliable evidence regarding the general effects of early experience upon later development or even regarding the question whether early experiences have a special and irreversible determinative role in personality formation.[63]

Moral psychology, too, has moved beyond the thought that development is fixed early, and away from an emphasis on continuity over change.

Popular belief has it that aging decreases change. This goes unchallenged because there has been little systematic research on relative stability versus growth after early childhood, and moral change in adults is virtually unstudied. Nonetheless, aspects of moral development are marked by evident discontinuity. Studies of the inverse correlation between age and crime indicate as much. So does the seldom-noted erasure of difference between men's sphere of activity and women's as we grow old. Accounts of extraordinary altruism indicate a capacity for moral change so dramatic that the term "development" is inapt.[64]

This should come as no surprise given American popular culture, where the possibility of personal improvement and being "born again" is commonplace, where groups and literature advertising moral transformation are big business, and where there is a long history antedating the current "recovery movement" of religious and secular associations aimed at the beneficial conversion of adults. It should come as no surprise where the current generation of people in their sixties and seventies and older are not only the most privileged generation of elderly people in history, the most mobile, independent, and powerful (with a feared political lobby) but also a cultural avant-garde. The elderly as a group has evolved unique institutions and customs, "its own distinctive attitudes toward death and toward marriage, its own style of 'interpersonal relationships,' its own argot, its own leisure activities, and its own rituals."[65] Whole cities of elderly exist by choice, where for weeks you can see no one under sixty, communities as unique as counterculture communes in the 1960s and 1970s or New-Age enclaves today.

Despite the need for a balanced concern about moral development across the life cycle, the propensity to fix on early developmental moments as decisive holds sway. Indeed, theorists armed with an ideal of democratic citizenship are sometimes guilty of what has been called the "radical instrumentalization of childhood."[66] It is a preparation for citizenship. In the same way, Marxist theorists made the "extraordinary error of believing" that "people were born when they first enter capitalist employment" and begin to engage in political and industrial action.[67]

Two assumptions prevail, both eminently contestable and neither well grounded in social science. One is that what is learned earliest is "basic" or most important, so if moral development in childhood is inhibited or misguided the result is incorrigible. The other is that children's moral development goes on largely in the family, and secondarily in schools. Other contexts are discounted. The family is singularly important for moral and social life, of course; and there are good reasons as well as easy political and sentimental ones for preoccupation with family breakdown and for casting it as the foundation of civic renewal. Still, nothing is more important for both political theory and public policy than soberly identifying what elements of moral education *are* crucial to childhood, which of these can take place *only* in the family (or school), what moral capacities are developed outside these settings, and what early deficits are reparable.

We know that the sense of "basic trust" and capacity for attachment is established young. There is considerable controversy over whether the mother-child bond specifically is the foundation of trust and subsequent moral development, or whether, as seems clear, other attachments can serve. In any case, to receive the moral benefits of authoritative relations children must be "productively engaged," usually but not always with a parent.[68] For there is a strong connection among attachment, moral sensibility, and the translation of moral emotions into the substance of rules, values, and standards. According to William Damon in *The Moral Child*, parental authority and the rules of conduct they maintain are crucial: "the child's respect for this authority is the single most important moral legacy that comes out of the child's relation with the parents." In families, we first learn to keep promises, resist temptations, reciprocate affections, take others' feelings into account. Some moral dispositions, like reciprocity, emerge from sociability and love with little direction. More deliberate parental effort is required to cultivate others, such as self-control. So social scientists like James Q. Wilson rightly attend to "the moral sense" initially cultivated, or not, in early childhood.

What we get *exclusively* from early relationships, then, is love and the capacity to form intimate attachments. If these relations are cold, erratic, or discordant, children are at moral risk. Emotional security does not lead to good character or good citizenship. But radical insecurity interferes with the formation of every social connection in which moral awareness is sharpened and translated into responsibility. It increases the chance that we will react to others with avoidance, fear, anger, hostility. A recent study indicates that an individual's propensity to trust others is rooted less in whether he or she has had positive experiences in civic associations, though that is a factor. Rather, it is mainly rooted in whether the individual sees himself or herself as personally trustworthy.[69] This is contingent on adult circumstances and experiences, of course, but trust and trustworthiness are learned first as a child at home.

It is clear, though, that children's moral development goes on outside families as well. There are many reasons for wanting just families, as Susan Okin prescribes, but cultivating fairness in children is not chief among them. Sharing and reciprocity among peers are principally the work of natural empathy, the fun of play, pragmatic concerns about the consequences of falling from the good graces of other children, and sheer imitation. "The day-to-day construction of fairness standards in social life must be done by children in collaboration with one another."[70] To take another, counterintuitive example, we learn that *ethnic identity* is often stimulated by school projects (and other official, institutional pressures) as much as by families![71]

We have more reason to resist exclusive preoccupation with childhood in light of the literature on political morality, which fails to convincingly establish either a connection or lack of connection to adult political orientations.[72] The effects of schools on broadly defined political attitudes, on thinking about politics, and on emergent political competence and civic virtue are inconclusive.[73] The best evidence pertains to racial attitudes: schooling in cooperative, racially mixed settings has been shown to produce tolerance, though no research has been done to confirm the long-term effects of democratic education on racial attitudes.

Paucity of evidence for continuity between childhood and adulthood does not mean that efforts to reproduce liberal democratic citizens are irrelevant or misguided. Adult political orientations—apathy, say, or illiberalism—do not disconfirm the importance of early cultivation of democratic capacities. They simply suggest that later experiences may undermine or fail to reinforce early moral development, positive democratic attitudes, and a sense of political efficacy. A sober developmental view is one reason not to treat the school as a "metaphor for society" rather than a distinctive institution (or set of institutions).[74]

Children are both vulnerable and resilient, and society has redundant opportunities to fail them and to compensate for these failings. This, of course, intensifies the moral responsibility of particular adults and social arrangements:

> Human childhood is long, so that parents and schools may have time to accept the child's personality in trust and to help it to be disciplined and human in the best sense known to us. This long childhood exposes the child to grave anxieties and to a lasting sense of insecurity which, if unduly and senselessly intensified, persists in the adult . . . and contributes specifically to the tension of personal, political, and even international life.[75]

Erikson's point about time and redundant opportunities holds for the life cycle overall. The personal uses of authority is just one aspect of the moral uses we make of associations but it gives a taste of what is at issue.

J. S. Mill drew a simple distinction between the moral needs of children and adults, arguing that paternalism enables children to attain the maturity of their faculties. We know the matter is more complex. The moral effects of different types of authority differ from child to child, which is why we try to find the right match of teacher or school. We also know that deep needs (and good reasons) for authority continue into adulthood. Diverse experiences of authority serve self-development in many ways, providing contexts for working through crises of personal identity or averting conditions in which we are liable to "get stuck." The effects of different types of authority are variable, which is why we seek out a physician–patient relation that is paternalistic or collaborative, to say nothing of the implicit choice we make about our tolerance for emotional or material dependence (or for mutuality) when we choose a partner, husband, or wife. Writings on mentor relations describe how authority can facilitate the transition to full responsibility. Individuals require different situations for creativity; some people work productively within a closely managed, hierarchical organization and others under conditions of cooperation or even isolation. Less apparent is the fact that the same person may need all of these at some time. At different points in their lives, and depending on personal as well as social circumstances, people feel more secure, confident, and self-respecting in one sort of authority relation than another.[76]

So it bears mentioning that it is not always weakness, infirmity, or moral cravenness to choose to be subject to authority, even in situations where independence is expected of us or considered ideal. And while the contingencies of personal history and social situation should not govern us, still, as Rawls points out, moral sentiments very often will cease to be regarded as neurotic compulsions if we understand the essential features of the psychology of moral development.[77]

The Vicissitudes of Personal Development

"Development" implies an orderly, sequential move from earlier to later stages, but the course is not seamless or irreversible. Nor is dramatic resolution of conflict and crisis guaranteed. Every developmental theory allows for developmental lags; even Piaget, who posits a wholly internal dynamic of cognitive development, speaks of "horizontal decolage," and psychoanalytic theory gives regression and developmental "arrests" central place. Closely related to the fact that development is ongoing, then, is the dynamic of deficit and reparation. We know that internal conflicts are overcome, reparations made, vices contained. In thinking about associations, it is well to recall these vicissitudes as well as regularities. Men and women have personal and social histories, not just a life cycle.

The notion of reparation of injury or compensation for lack is familiar mostly from accounts of clinical therapy. For Freud, interpretive insight brings conflicts to the surface and transforms "extraordinary misery" into ordinary unhappiness; trauma and conflict cannot be erased but their hold on us can be loosened. An alternative view sees therapy as a corrective interpersonal experience in a safe environment; lapses are made up and deficits repaired.

Parallels between therapy and moral and social reform are often noted. Harmless outlets for aggression, sports for hostile adolescents, say, correspond to the first account of correction. Remedial action to repair poor self-esteem, such as supplying idealizable adults who take an interest in particular youths (Big Brother/Sister programs are singularly successful), corresponds to the second.[78] Obviously, a single social program may produce both dynamics. Which (if any) is effective depends on a particular person's receptivity. Robert Kegan has described the fit and misfit between two patients and their therapeutic programs. One program, geared to encouraging cooperation, mutuality, and joint decision-making, was fortuitously attuned to the patient's developmental need for an increased sense of competence and personal control. The other program, requiring group discussion of mental life, was an "unlucky match" for a patient unprepared to participate in an intense interpersonal community; the therapy was "an unwitting form of cruelty."

Instead of seeing therapy as a model for social organization, Kegan proposes that clinical therapy should take its cues from the successful workings of ordinary associations, which see people through periods of crisis and evolution. "Rather than make psychotherapy the touchstone for all considerations of help, look first to the meaning and makeup of unselfconscious 'therapy' as these occur again and again in nature."[79] Kegan's work is a cautionary tale for clinicians, not political theorists, and I do not take a therapeutic view of associations. I mention this research because it confirms the value of attending to moral development beyond childhood, and reminds us that associations take members as they are; they are not formative "from scratch."

Consider Saul Levine's sensitive account of the thousands of adolescents who abruptly leave home to join a communal group—fundamentalist, mystic, political, and therapeutic. In *Radical Departures*, he explains when and why the experience of membership in communities marked by uncritical acceptance and suffusion of self-righteousness is beneficial, and under what conditions it sets off a worsening spiral into personal chaos.[80] These groups are abhorrent to outsiders, who invariably characterize them as cults and regard them as the very opposite of a haven, much less a medium for moral development. But Levine concludes that membership normally has benign or salutary effects, and that virtually all joiners leave within two years.

In short, the alterations associations stimulate in individuals are indeterminate and often unintended. If I am right, the key to reciprocity between civil society and liberal citizenship is exploiting *incongruence* by making the *experience of pluralism* available to men and women personally and individually. This way of thinking is a bit reminiscent of the Rolling Stones lyric, "you can't always get what you want, but if you try sometimes you just might find, you'll get what you need."[81] Chance is unpredictable, but the word is not merely a label for our ignorance.[82] The moral uses of pluralism is not a matter of serendipity.

I do not mean to overemphasize the vicissitudes of personal development as either a description of the moral uses of pluralism or a rationale for freedom of association. The indeterminate moral effect of groups also turns on the fact that associations are complex, often real hybrids. The psychological logic of American political thought also insures that the uses of association will be complex. No wonder their consequences for members vary. Or that the law of groups has such difficulty setting boundaries. Or that our ideas about freedom of association buffet us about.

Part Two ————————————————————————

VOLUNTARY ASSOCIATIONS

3

Religious Associations: Constitutional Incongruence

Religion as Voluntary Association

The U.S. Constitution does not name freedom of association as a distinct right, and constitutional interpretation has not extended it beyond churches, political advocacy groups, and intimate associations like the family, as I will show. Even there, personal freedom *of* association does not mean unfettered freedom *for* associations in their internal lives, certainly not their external affairs. "Ardent believers in the richness and diversity of a pluralist society, where a variety of voluntary private associations and groups operate simultaneously to maximize opportunities for self-realization and minimize the strength of centralized power, will find little comfort in the doctrine of freedom of association as developed by the U.S. Supreme Court," Laurence Tribe advised.[1] But this has not inhibited the ceaseless proliferation of voluntary associations, their connection in the public mind with personal liberty, and the presumption that membership in associations often shapes us in powerful ways.

For historical reasons and in response to claims arising under the religion clauses of the First Amendment, American political thought has explored association freedom most closely in connection with religion. I begin with religious associations for this reason, and because despite their exceptional constitutional status these groups are viewed as the quintessential voluntary association. Inherited religious status, like other inherited privileges and liabilities, is considered undemocratic.[2] The traditional view of religious membership as ascriptive or by descent cannot be sustained in any case, when so many people arrive at religious beliefs independent of churches, and actively join (and leave, and join other) religious groups rather than stay with their childhood faith. Nothing could underscore the voluntarism of religious associations more than the open and aggressive competition for believers that characterizes religion in the United States.[3]

The free exercise clause helps insure that religious association is voluntary by restraining government from prohibiting adherence to one or another religion or requiring adherence to any. Neither affiliation nor nonaffiliation affects our standing as citizens, not if we are true to Thomas Jefferson's insistence that "our civil rights have no dependence on our religious opinions, any more than our opinions in physics and geometry." The religious test provision of the

Maryland constitution that required state officials to declare their belief in the existence of God was finally overturned in 1961 as a patent denial of political rights to nonbelievers. And in 1978, the Supreme Court overturned a provision of the Tennessee constitution disqualifying clergy from legislative office, explaining: "the American experience provides no persuasive support for the fear that clergymen in public office will be less careful of anti-establishment interests or less faithful to their oaths of civil office than their unordained counterparts."[4]

I begin with religious associations, too, because they are universally viewed as depositories of moral values and scenes of moral education. We may doubt the formative effects of a political interest group or homeowners' association, but the connection between secular ethics and religion is undisputed. Religious belief has a moral imprimatur, and membership in religious associations is presumed to shape public as well as private virtue (presumably positively!), which is why political theorists are often preoccupied with restoring what they see as the "delicate balance" between juridical liberalism and its religious preconditions.[5] The proposition that "the moral structure of religious community should be treated as an island of autonomy" is intended to protect associations from government policies that undermine their authority over their members, not to recommend isolation, precisely so religious groups can effectively cultivate moral dispositions and advance the public welfare.[6]

American Political Culture: Religion and Morality

The relation between religion and morality can be stated at the highest level of generality: "a spirit of religiousness in general" is a "necessity of the soul" that yearns for perfection, Humboldt wrote.[7] Typically, moral claims for religion in American political life are similarly lofty and divorced from the institutional features of faith. They are not always tied to specifically liberal democratic virtues, but they are focused on public conduct. Jeremiahs lament what they contend is Americans' fall from faith because they celebrate the link between religion and middle-class values, personal and national improvement. (Hence the increasingly common practice of chaplains performing ministering and counseling services in private-sector industry, hospitals, and so on.)[8] People disciplined by the moral persuasion of religious beliefs may require less legal compulsion, one argument goes, because these commitments motivate them to be law-abiding or economically independent. Or, religion "helps to overcome the aggressive individualism that so threatens civil order."[9] A "taste for the infinite," Tocqueville wrote, can "purify, control, and restrain the excessive and exclusive taste for well-being."[10] Religion is seen as a "beneficial and stabilizing influence in community life." Or if not stabilizing, inspiring. "Great Awakenings" and evangelical "revitalizations" are the most studied instances of recurrent claims that religion advances the moral welfare of the American political community.

Confidence in harmony between secular public purposes and spiritual missions finds literal confirmation in partnerships between government and religious agencies. The Supreme Court's reminder that "it long has been established . . . that the State may send a cleric, indeed even a clerical order, to perform a wholly secular task" is an understatement for those who think that joint ventures are not just permissible but vital wherever social problems have moral dimensions. From this standpoint, government partnerships are not just a matter of supporting valuable activities—well-run hospitals, adoption agencies, or soup kitchens—regardless of the sponsor; to the contrary, the religious character of the sponsor is what counts. *Bowen v. Kendrick* upheld the constitutionality of federal support for religious organizations counseling teenagers about sexuality under the Adolescent Family Life Act, also called "The Chastity Act." By actively soliciting the involvement of religious organizations, the act incorporated the Senate's judgment of "the limitation of government in dealing with a problem that has complex moral and social dimensions." "It seems quite sensible," Chief Justice Rehnquist reflected, "for Congress to recognize that religious organizations can influence values."[11]

Familiar theses in American cultural history go beyond cooperation and propose the democratization of religion in America and the religiosity of American democracy. The first points to the voluntarism of religious membership. And to the dominance of dissenting Protestantism with its antihierarchicalism and antiestablishment stance, its populist clergy, and its corrosion of elite ecclesiastical traditions. (All are said to affect other faiths, notably Roman Catholics and Jews in the United States.) The democratization of religion also refers to competition for believers.[12]

For its part, the religiosity of American democracy refers to the manifest vitality of religion in the United States (95 percent of the population profess belief in God or some universal spirit and 68 percent belong to a church or synagogue) and the extraordinarily high percentage (88 percent) who confidently affirm that God loves them.[13] Beyond that, it points to the commingling of American political identity, patriotism, and religion captured in Conor Cruise O'Brien's characterization of America as "Godland" and institutionalized in the pledge of allegiance. Or better still in the President's National Prayer breakfast, invoking God's blessing on the military budget. We find it in Justice Douglas's unabashed assertion in *Zorach v. Clauson* that "we are a religious people whose institutions presuppose a Supreme Being." It is demonstrated every time a court or legislature opens its session with prayer (the Supreme Court's begins: "God save the United States and this Honorable

Court"), and in innumerable other invocations of the direct link between government officials and heaven.[14]

Given what Harold Bloom has called our "religiously mad culture," it is not surprising that avowed unbelievers rarely run for public office. Or that there is a virtual taboo against overt atheism and demonstrated hostility toward religion, a socially enforced restraint accorded no other group; from business corporations to "Queer America," associations are targets of ridicule and disbelief.[15] Surveys conducted in the 1980s show that while nearly 70 percent of Americans agree that freedom to worship applies to all religious groups regardless of their views, only 26 percent thought that freedom of atheists to make fun of God and religion should be legally protected.[16]

This is not to concede that religious associations are "seedbeds of civic virtue." Or even that they are benign. Religious principles can be abhorrent, leaders advocates of hate, and believers homicidal. There is abundant evidence, historical and contemporary: nativism, violent anti-Catholic mobs, pervasive anti-Semitism, persecution of Mormons, harassment of non-Western sects. The policy of religion-matching in adoption was advocated by Catholic immigrants attempting to stop the removal of Catholic children from their families and farming them out for adoption in a bigoted crusade to "Save the Children for Protestantism."

American ideologies of inequality are almost always steeped in religion, and hate groups make these ideologies the cement of association life. Armed paramilitary groups, convinced that the federal government is "zionist occupied," combine anti-Semitism and white racism with Christian fundamentalist theology, a subject to which I return in chapter 7 on secret societies and private armies.

Accusations of disloyalty are regularly leveled at religious groups with ties to countries of the world in conflict. The revival of the long-dormant law of sedition in the case against Sheik Omar Abdul Rahman for preaching "jihad" is a recent instance.[17]

Religion continues to earn its reputation for arrogance and pious cruelty and as instigator of civil strife: Christian groups targeting health practitioners who perform abortions for harassment and murder, or fanatical Jewish Zionists.[18] To say nothing of the religious associations that encourage their members to remain ignorant, limit their opportunities, and exploit their labor.

Nonetheless, Americans typically agree on the moral advantages of a God-fearing people even when they disagree about government support for religion and about the role of religious associations in politics. And academic studies tend to point up affinities between religion and the moral requirements of liberal democratic public life rather than incongruence, if only because "in a society where a lot of people share the same general religious beliefs, their cultural biases will alone work to shape public life."[19]

From Symbolic Endorsement to Autonomy
for Religious Associations

As this suggests, the symbolic and practical commingling of religion and official public culture may diminish some citizens' sense of belonging. Government endorsement of religion, Justice O'Connor observed, "sends a message to nonadherents that they are outsiders, not full members of the political community, and an accompanying message to adherents that they are insiders, favored members of the political community."[20] Catholic resistance to using the Protestant Bible in common schools was not mollified by the sort of "nonsectarian" readings of selective passages Horace Mann prescribed, and the result was a parochial school system. Attempts to publicly invoke Christian unity, and now "our Judeo-Christian heritage," may be an improvement over the millennialism of "redeemer nation," but they are far from inclusive. The counterpart of parochial schools today is the explosion of Muslim academies.[21]

Symbolic issues of government identification with religion take center stage, and there is no better example than the series of cases challenging government displays of Christmas trees, Santas, creches, and menorahs that has turned "creche law" into a legal specialty.

It is not only fastidious atheists who oppose even government "acknowledgment" of religion much less endorsement and assistance. Roger Williams' fear of the corruption of religion by democratic politics is far from obsolete. The "three plastic animals rule" in Christmas display cases seems to confirm that religious symbols must be disrespectfully cheapened to be widely acceptable. (The Supreme Court ruled that one creche display violated the establishment clause precisely because "nothing in the creche's setting detracts from that [patently Christian] message"; there was no talking wishing well to serve as an alternative "center of attention."[22]) It would not surprise Roger Williams to find the Court reassuring challengers to prayer in state legislatures that through rote repetition "ceremonial deism" has lost any significant religious content, and that opening sessions of courts and legislatures with prayer serves "in the only way reasonably possible in our culture, the legitimate secular purposes of solemnizing public occasions, expressing confidence in the future, and encouraging the recognition of what is worthy of appreciation in society."[23] To believers of every stripe, this is absurd: prayer is worship, not simply speech, and "praying means to take hold of a word, the end, so to speak, of a line that leads to God."[24]

For some believers, however, removing creches from public squares and erecting purely secular displays creates the appearance of state hostility toward religion or favors secular celebrants of the Christmas holiday over religious observers.[25] From this standpoint, official public culture should mirror the fact that society as a whole is infused with religions, and government should actively promote "a regime of religious pluralism." Michael McConnell argues:

> I make no claim that religious positions should be privileged because they are religious, but only that secular positions should not be privileged because they are secular. . . . Ours is not a Christian republic, but it is not a secular republic, either. It is a free and pluralistic republic, in which religious voices from a variety of traditions . . . have an equal right to speak and to strive for their visions of justice.[26]

(The counterpart is the multiculturalist argument that liberal democracy should not pretend to neutrality but "recognize the equal standing of all the stable and viable cultural communities existing in that society. . . . None of them should be allowed to see the state as its own, or to think that the others enjoy their standing on sufferance."[27]) Anything less is the real impermissible establishment, because it promotes a sort of "Universal-Unitarianism" or "civil religion" or, more extravagantly, establishes not just a secular but an atheistic state.[28]

It is reasonable to think that the simultaneous endorsement of Judaism and Christianity, or any number of religions—which will always fall short of *all* faiths—is as constitutionally impermissible as the endorsement of Christianity alone. Particularly if the issue turns, as Justice O'Connor proposes, on how the message of government endorsement is received. One count identified 1,400 distinct religious groups in the United States today, "only" 800 of them with Christian roots.[29] (To say nothing of members of mainstream churches who also attest to their belief in astrology and reincarnation.) Muslims outnumber Episcopalians, peculiarly American faiths are invented and flourish, non-Western religions are modified, and charismatic groups spring up irrepressibly all the time. Rajneesh Meditation Centers, the Society for Krishna Consciousness, and Jews for Jesus can appear positively "mainstream" beside satanic cults and benign devotees of angels, or groups organized around psychotic leaders.

Novelist Don DeLillo describes the arranged marriage of 6,500 couples by Reverend Moon in Yankee Stadium. A father watches his daughter's wedding through binoculars from the grandstand:

> Here they come, marching into American sunlight. They are grouped in twos, eternal boy–girl, stepping out of the runway beyond the fence in left-center field. . . . There is a strangeness down there he never thought he'd see in a ballpark. . . . The brides and grooms exchange rings and vows and many people are taking pictures . . . whole families snapping anxiously . . . trying to neutralize the event, drain it of eeriness and power. Master chants the ritual in Korean. . . . When the Old God leaves the world, what happens to all the unexpended faith? . . . He keeps the glasses trained, feeling a slight desperation now, a need to find her and remind himself of who she is.

Healthy, intelligent, twenty-one, serious-sided, possessed of a selfness . . . grids of pinpoint singularities they will never drill out of her. Or so he hopes and prays, wondering about the power of their own massed prayer.[30]

It is not hard to see that believers might also object to government appropriating their holidays and religious symbols to advance its patriotic message of tolerance and pluralism. Not all religious groups favor religious diversity and tolerance, after all. They are hostile to one another, refuse to participate in ecumenical services, and do not want to be implicated in secular celebrations of pluralism.[31]

Debates about government's symbolic association with religion is part of the story. Another part, as we have seen, is the presumed affinity between religiosity and characteristic liberal democratic values, which justifies encouragement for religious groups' participation and influence in political arenas— lobbying, electioneering, alliance-building, and direct policy initiatives—as well as access to public goods. Together, these are the most visible and contentious aspects of the relation between government and religion. But they do not exhaust the subject.

Self-government for religious associations stands out from these familiar puzzles and commands our attention because the internal life of religious associations, particularly its congruence with public norms or resistance to them, is the heart of the moral uses of pluralism. Religious associations habituate members to forms of authority, to altruism or reciprocity among members and between members and outsiders (or not), to race and gender segregation or integration and equality, to expectations of due process or clerical discretion with its danger of arbitrariness and oppression. Religious associations encourage or discourage dispositions of tolerance, fairness, or nondiscrimination in their members through tenets of faith, but also through practices such as admitting and excluding members, educating children, managing internal affairs, and relating to outsiders in the course of hiring or proseletyzing.

Religious associations claim "a spirit of freedom . . . an independence from secular control or manipulation—in short, power to decide for themselves, free from state interference, matters of church government as well as those of faith and doctrine."[32] The structure of religious authority, ownership and control of church property, decisions to appoint, fire, and defrock clergy and officers, to admit and discipline members, and to designate what aspects of the group's activity are properly religious rather than secular are often protected by judicial deference to the religious "polity."

Although freedom for religious associations owes in large part to the reluctance of liberal government to define, interpret, and enforce forms of worship or tenets of faith, we will see that the freedom accorded religious associations extends to affairs only tangentially connected to belief, or unconnected altogether. The question is, "power to decide for themselves" in what areas?

Advocates have proposed a categorical right to self-determination by religious associations, on grounds that "religious groups are a locus for certain of the constitutive, foundational activities by which Americans define and determine who and what they are, both individually and communally."[33] But absolute protection for religious association is not necessary, practicable, or justifiable. What legal restrictions are actually imposed on the internal life and organization of religious associations? What deviation from public norms of due process and nondiscrimination is permitted? And what can we learn from the reasons given?

Out of ignorance or for ideological reasons, liberalism is often charged with seeing religious experience as a "wholly private matter" for the solitary individual. If the political history of toleration and accommodation of religious associations does not correct this silliness, then insight into freedom for religious self-government should.

Association Autonomy and Due Process of Law

The most common religious case law involves internal disputes about who controls church property. These little-known conflicts are dramatic as well as significant because they revolve around who is the rightful religious authority. So whether courts become involved in deciding these disputes, and if so what standards they apply, is crucial. The imposition of external standards such as insistence that clerics adhere to due process is arguably the most important form of government interference with association freedom, with consequences for the moral experience of associational life.

Historically, courts used ecclesiastical law to settle controversies over authority and property, employing the "departure from doctrine" test. Formalized in "Lord Eldon's Rule," the idea was that church assets were held as an "implied trust" in favor of the fundamental doctrines of the religious body. In the event of internal conflict, property was awarded to the faction that adhered to the original doctrine of the church, thus requiring courts to interpret which claimant was faithful to church tenets. (In early American history, the alternative was to interpret the act of incorporation as placing control of church affairs in the hands of the majority of the congregation. This is a radical example of a public policy of congruence—legally enforced democracy. It was anathema to hierarchical churches, and short-lived.[34]) The "departure from doctrine" test had problems, among them doubt about courts' competence to interpret the body of constitutional and canon law that "tasks the ablest minds to become familiar with." So, beginning in 1871 with *Watson v. Jones*, the Supreme Court reduced its reliance on "implied trust," first at common law, then in 1952 as a matter of constitutional free exercise. After *Everson v. Board of Education* it applied First Amendment rulings about "the forbidden process of interpreting and weighing church doctrine" to the states.[35] The pithy rule goes: "the law knows no heresy."

That leaves civil courts to resolve church property disputes by constructing deeds, contracts, or trusts in terms of neutral principles of civil law. Judges can look to documents to determine whether the intent of a local church was to give authority over its property up to the hierarchical organization, for example. In this respect, religious associations are treated like other private organizations. The same approach holds for other areas of church affairs. If religious associations codify their wage and hiring practices and arrange to make employment agreements enforceable in secular courts, for example, states can adjudicate disputes. Thus, priests employed as law professors at Catholic University in Washington, D.C., could only challenge the university's policy of paying ordained faculty less than lay faculty if the university had formally agreed to eliminate the disparity. Without a contract, the court would not apply external standards to judge the disparity illegal; the dispute had to be resolved within the church.[36]

The neutral principles approach has limited applicability because not all religious associations are incorporated or have formal charters and bylaws. It is not just theology that may be convoluted and "idiosyncratic beyond belief." New, rapidly changing, and unorthodox religious groups may be independent and unincorporated. They may not have constitutions, or documentation of the terms of their affiliation with national denominations, or contracts with officers and employees. Requiring them to adhere to quasi-juridical standards of printed texts and codified regulations "might inhibit their formation by forcing the organizers to confront issues that otherwise might never arise."[37]

An alternative approach to cases involving internal disputes over property and authority is for courts to defer to the religious association's own decision-making processes and to the rulings of its highest authority:[38] "whenever the question of discipline, or of faith, or ecclesiastical rule, custom, or law have been decided by the highest of these church judicatories to which the matter has been carried, the legal tribunals must accept such decisions as final."[39] *Serbian Eastern Orthodox Diocese of America and Canada v. Milivojevich*, decided in 1976 after thirteen years of litigation, is a window onto the limits of government intervention and its significance for the moral uses of pluralism.

The conflict revolved around the authority of the Serbian Eastern Orthodox Holy Synod and Assembly of Bishops to defrock an American bishop and control church property in the United States. Like many precedents in this line, the controversy was as much political as theological, which is why judicial nonintervention is justified in part by the reasonable fear of *political* favoritism toward one or another church faction.[40] In this instance, afraid that the hierarchy in Belgrade would fall under communist control, the American church attempted to remove governance of the diocese and its assets from the Mother Church. This precipitated the American bishop's defrocking, and the American church's charge in court that his removal was arbitrary and in violation of the church's constitution and penal codes.

The Supreme Court refused to interfere with the Holy Synod's ruling: all the decisions of the Assembly of Bishops "in regard to faith, officiation, church order and internal organization of the church, are valid and final." Indeed, the Court refused even to inquire whether the relevant church governing body had power under ecclesiastical law to decide the dispute: "to permit civil courts to probe deeply enough into the allocation of power within a hierarchical church so as to decide . . . religious law governing church polity would violate the First Amendment in much the same manner as civil determination of religious doctrine." Finally, it prohibited courts from inquiring whether church authority had acted arbitrarily, in contravention of its *own* laws; this would "inherently entail inquiry into the procedures that canon or ecclesiastical law supposedly requires the church judicatory to follow. . . . But this is exactly the inquiry that the First Amendment prohibits."[41]

Justice Rehnquist forcefully objected to the decision. If courts rubber-stamp ecclesiastical decisions when such deference is not accorded similar acts of secular voluntary associations, he cautioned, it would create serious problems under the establishment clause. Rehnquist's chief concern, however, was the rights of believers. Consent to membership in a religious polity does not extend to clerical action in violation of its constitution, and government nonintervention subjects individual members to "domination by oppressive religious authorities." "If the civil courts are to be bound by any sheet of parchment bearing the ecclesiastical seal," he warned, "they can easily be converted into handmaidens of arbitrary lawlessness." Invoking a Hobbesian state of nature, Rehnquist anticipated that unless courts decide disputes, conflicts over church property and authority will be resolved "by brute force."[42]

Religious associations' own procedures need not mirror judicial norms of due process exactly, on this view. And *Serbian Diocese* was not a matter of forcibly imposing alien external rules or of a government inspectorate making sure the church's own constitution is enforced. Simply, where religious procedures exist, and where members lodge a civil complaint against church authorities for failing to adhere to them, courts should consider the merits of the case and uphold these rules.

In a 1978 keynote address at the University of Miami Law School Rehnquist seemed to soften his position a bit, acknowledging the "special weight" that should be given churches and other "communities of memory and mutual aid." He conceded that occasional deference by courts is justified "in situations where adversary litigation of the propriety of internal decisions would have more disadvantageous consequences in terms of diminishing the usefulness of the institution than would the ultimate resolution by the court of the claim of individual right."[43] What sort of balancing is this? What "usefulness" commends flexibility?

We can understand why *members* might exercise self-restraint and decline to challenge religious authorities, even under the trying political circumstances that provoked the American bishop's challenge. It is perfectly reasonable to think that clergy and lay members might believe serious violations of the church constitution had occurred and still choose not to challenge the decision, pursue internal appeals, or look to courts to enforce ecclesiastical order. Deference to the decision of the highest authority cannot be presumed to be blind obedience. It may be a demonstration of the priority of faith and of commitment to the community. Restraint may reflect the conviction that other values outweigh due process: harmony, forgiveness, or the preservation of the "community of memory or mutual aid." The "usefulness of the institution" is for believers to decide.

But why should Justice Rehnquist retreat from his insistence that once parties to the conflict appeal to courts, judges should take the matter up and insure internal due process? Why recommend *judicial* self-restraint? His original position had clarity and considerable force. Liberal democracy's interest in settling internal religious disputes in a manner reasonably consistent with the due process norms of public order is neither trivial nor ill-defined. Faithfulness to established rules and practices is the heart of legalism. It is our protection against the chief evil in the liberal worldview—vulnerability to arbitrary authority. And from the point of view of forming character, due process in associations generates habitual expectations of procedural safeguards. It may cultivate or reinforce a propensity to fairness on the part of individual members. Or encourage a disinclination to consent to unchecked exercises of private power. Moreover, when it comes to inquiring whether religious authority acted arbitrarily in violation of its own rules, the liberal interest in due process is likely to be effectively furthered by judicial intervention.[44]

Not every government interest in regulating religious associations is as substantial as this. Cost-savings and administrative efficiency ought to be insufficient reasons to interfere with religious authority, for example. (In the same vein, the Supreme Court's decision in *Sherbert v. Verner* to extend unemployment benefits to sabbatarians should not have depended on the fact that the administrative costs would be insignificant because the government apparatus for reviewing cases and granting individual exemptions was already in place.[45])

Nonetheless the *Serbian Diocese* majority decided "it is the essence of religious faith that ecclesiastical decisions are reached and are to be accepted as matters of faith whether or not rational or measurable by objective criteria. Constitutional concepts of due process, involving secular notions of 'fundamental fairness' or impermissible objectives, are therefore hardly relevant."[46] What can be said for supporting association autonomy over protecting members against arbitrary authority, and over promoting the regularities of due process?

Judicial Deference, Freedom of Association, and the Proliferation of Groups

Government nonintervention rests on the assumption that membership in a religious association is voluntary and based on faith. We will see that consent to membership does not immunize secular associations from publicly enforced rules of "fundamental fairness." Voluntarism and religious faith together are key.

And in this context, voluntarism is a modest assumption. It has nothing to do with a theology of volitionalism. Nor does it imply that obedience to a religious law or tribunal is experienced as a "choice" by believers themselves rather than as an imperative. From a perspective internal to some beliefs, the First Amendment free exercise clause protects unyielding, unchosen obligation, not consent. (It is perfectly clear that the Orthodox Jew does not "select" the day of the week on which to refrain from labor; the choice is God's.)[47] Voluntarism certainly does not mean that subjection to religious authority is the result of rational deliberation.[48] How people arrive at their beliefs is a matter of indifference. Simply, whether or not ecclesiastical authority's conformity to established internal procedures is decisive for obedience and ongoing membership must be decided by believers themselves.

Members are bound to contemplate religious authority and practices in light of their experience in other spheres, of course, including civil and political life. Their expectations of secular due process may spill over into their understanding of religious membership. Or the two may be kept distinct.[49] There is no authority to dictate which set of values individuals apply in assessing associational life; that is left to individual judgment. Moreover, the permeability of religious associations does nothing to dilute their claim to autonomy. Religious groups are inevitably altered (indeed, formed in the first place) in response to external events, from shifts in political and legal culture to the raw ambition of leaders. A baseline presumption of a religious state of nature is wildly ahistorical, a version of pastorale. So the case for deference to association self-government is not strengthened by dramatizing its purity and vulnerability to "outside" influences. While it is perfectly true that religious groups "establish a *nomos* of their own," the "church in the world" is an inescapable fact.

This contributes to the fact that membership is often internally divided over whether religious authorities have been faithful to established rules or have acted arbitrarily. Over whether or not procedural correctness and faithfulness to the church constitution are essential to the group's "nomos." And finally over whether arbitrariness is decisive for their continued faith and consent. Judicial nonintervention recognizes the deep conflicts that cleave religious groups, and the "crises from which we cannot be spared."

When the *Serbian Diocese* majority decided "it would be a vain consent and would lead to the total subversion of such religious bodies, if any one aggrieved by one of their decisions could appeal to the secular courts and have them reversed," the intention was not to endorse the Holy Synod's decision.[50] (Nor, or in other instances, decisions reached by the congregational majority.) Nothing suggests that *members* ought to defer to religious authority rather than pursue internal appeals, resist, or threaten separation or schism.

And judicial nonintervention does not condemn dissidents to discipline and punishment. If aggrieved clergy and lay members fail to persuade church officials that deviation from the association's rules or "fundamental fairness" is intolerable (or if they are denied an opportunity to persuade or appeal), if their faith in authority is shaken, they can leave. Judicial deference may override some members' due process claims, but it is not a state-created obstacle to their religious freedom. It does not deliver them into the hands of tyrants or exile them into a moral vacuum—not in a society alive with religious groups and liberty to form new ones. The assumption of voluntarism that underlies liberal self-restraint is made effective by a background of fluid pluralism, where other religious homes are open to splitters and the formation of new associations is a real possibility.

In practice, government nonintervention can have either a conservative or progressive thrust. Internal revision might be effectively thwarted if members knew they could obstruct change by appealing to the civil courts. Or, dissidents might be able to enhance their power and prestige by having a judicial platform to air grievances or win a favorable verdict. The only certainty is that nonintervention amounts to an acknowledgment that the decisions of religious authorities may not reflect the views of all the faithful, and that religious associations must keep their faithful or lose disaffected members all on their own. The famous passage from *Zorach v. Clauson*—that in competition among religious associations "we sponsor an attitude on the part of government that . . . lets each flourish according to the zeal of its adherents and the appeal of its dogma"—holds for factions in intrareligious disputes as well.[51]

In effect, government deference to the highest religious authority also gives notice that ferment and adversarial relations and the rise and decline of religious associations are as normal a part of "living faith" as the evolution of theology. Decriminalization of blasphemy and freedom to vilify faith are other areas where law requires established religious groups "to suffer offense so that new religious groups can be born."[52]

Historians confirm this point. The history of religious associations in the United States is a story not of pluralism simply, but of instability. There is ceaseless splitting and schism. There is the fantastic invention of "American originals," Mormons and Jehovah's Witnesses. There is the array of religious associations continuously imported by immigrants, "new religion" variants on non-Western faiths, and New Age spiritual movements. Since "cult" is a pejo-

rative, one scholar suggests calling these groups "first-generation religions"—
Christian Science, Jehovah's Witnesses, Mormonism, and Seventh-Day Ad-
ventism were once cults and are now among the fastest-growing groups in the
country.[53]

From early on legal doctrine contributed to letting spiritual freedom go its
way by prohibiting colonial governments from forcing local churches to take
a congregational form.[54] Nonintervention has encouraged denominationalism,
less rigorous standards of admission to membership, and competition for believers. One case study describes the two decades after 1920 when new sects
began twenty-six different churches in Gastonia, North Carolina—highly atomistic units, each initiated by an individual minister setting out to organize a
group of his or her own.[55] The recent decline of denominationalism and "restructuring" of American religion, characterized by the mushrooming of small
groups, is well documented.[56] As Richard Posner and Michael McConnell
have accurately but gracelessly observed: judicial nonintervention produces
"product differentiation" in religion.[57]

Government deference and solicitude for association autonomy might
evoke contemporary communitarianism, except for the *spirit* in which the factions of a religious association are left to themselves. The *Serbian Diocese*
decision points up internal conflict, voluntarism, and institutional change. The
communitarian concern is protecting the integrity of established religious
groups, shielding them from outrage and externally imposed change, so that
they can continue to provide "the options that give life meaning" undisturbed.[58] The communitarian paradigm is of religious community and tradition
as "given," authoritatively imposed. (Communitarians would see it as a loss,
for example, that fund-raisers for the United Jewish Appeal are now hesitant
about soliciting contributions from Jewish donors by saying, "This is the tax
you owe.")[59] The implication is that the community's way of life is right for its
members, and that switchers are morally unserious, their commitments tenuous. The Court's voluntarist emphasis would strike communitarians as an invitation to the unfettered choice they abhor.

A more instructive comparison is to the British pluralist tradition of Maitland, Figgis, and Laski, whose core idea is that an association "is no fiction, no
symbol, no piece of the State's machinery, no collective name for individuals,
but a living organism and a real person, with a body and members and a will
of its own."[60] Nothing is gained by reviewing here the metaphysical controversy inflamed by the notion of legal personality. (Morris Cohen's wry litany
of "communal ghosts" is justly famous: "Groups are not begot through the
union of father and mother, they do not suck their mother's milk, do not play
children's games, do not spend weary hours in school, do not work for wages,
strike for shorter hours, and do not suffer the trials and joys of anxious parent-
hood.")[61] The political impetus behind the pluralist theory of association "personality" is plain enough. It was directed against the view that corporations are

state-created, legal entities bound by their founding statements of corporate purpose and subject to unlimited parliamentary regulation. Among other things, pluralism was an attack on the "departure from doctrine" test, which allowed government to interpret religious tenets and identify the rightful authority.

It is unlikely that British pluralists would have been any more satisfied than contemporary communitarians with the *Serbian Diocese* Court's voluntarist justification for nonintervention, though. As Figgis put it, the state is a "community of communities" that must share sovereignty with all the self-governing sources of law within it—a formulation designed to *increase* the authority and hold of associations over their members.[62] The point of calling religious associations sovereign is that we should recognize them as independent societies, and be willing to commit people to their care.[63]

In any case, the "sovereignty" of groups cannot have much resonance in the United States, where patently voluntary religious associations, often based on a charismatic individual and a few followers, crop up all the time. Where the First Amendment is interposed between government and religious groups. And where balancing freedom for religious association against state interests is a regular feature of legislation and judicial decisions.

Exemption and Accommodation

It is rare to find legislation that interferes with worship directly or discriminates among religions on its face today. Instead, religious free exercise and self-government are burdened as a consequence of government enacting general laws for valid secular purposes—imposing regulations, meting out benefits like unemployment insurance, and acting in its ever-expanding capacities as proprietor, employer, educator, and patron. For advocates of freedom for religious groups, the constitutional agenda is to carve out "a zone of permissible accommodation."[64] Without it, "where government advanced, religion must retreat."[65]

As a result, statutory accommodation of religious associations and constitutional claims for mandatory exemptions mark every area of the law, from zoning, taxes, and licensing requirements to legislation that directly implicates liberal practices and dispositions—antidiscrimination law, employment law, and the protections of due process.[66] At the same time religious associations proliferate and become ubiquitous in all the activities of social life, so do the ways liberal democracy impinges on them. No wonder claims of exemption and accommodation multiply.

Given the connection between religious self-government and faith and consent, we might expect to find a bright line separating solicitude for associations in matters of authority over doctrine, worship, and church government from authority over nonreligious activities and dealings with nonmembers. Spurred by an appreciation of the plurality of religious groups and theological notions of religion, the Supreme Court's *definition* of religion is capacious: "It is no business of courts to say that what is a religious practice or activity for one group is not religion under the protection of the First Amendment."[67] But that still requires courts to discriminate between religious and nonreligious activities. As ministries expand beyond charities, schools, and hospitals to businesses, family counseling centers, broadcasting networks, and legal aid clinics, and as church–state partnerships multiply, so do efforts at categorization. All have proved difficult to determine, some say unworkable, in part because ascertaining whether the group's activities are close to the heart of religion implicates the very questions of faith and authority that government is supposed to avoid.[68]

A host of distinctions have been tried: conduct required by doctrine or individual conscience from exercises of religion that are not required—singing in the church choir, for example; denominational schools, hospitals, or charities that are an integral part of a church's religious mission and "infused with religious purpose" from "affiliated institutions" that are not "pervasively sectarian" (and are therefore eligible to receive federal and state grants, contracts, and reimbursements for social welfare services); church-owned businesses run in "intrinsically religious ways" from those formed for a "purely business purpose."

The difficulty increases when the question turns on "divining the good faith and legitimacy of religious grounds asserted as a defence" against having to conform to the law.[69] As Christian theologians witnessed and Hegel philosophized, the paralyzing question of a pure heart can never be resolved, even for oneself. Consider the New Testament Baptist Church, which claimed a free exercise exemption from federal antidiscrimination law to permit them to exclude black children from the church school. The circuit court judges in *Brown v. Dade Christian Schools* had to determine whether or not the school's segregation was based on a "sincerely held religious belief that socialization would lead to [the sin of] racial intermarriage." Pointing to testimony by church officials that the basis for forbidding commingling of whites and blacks was a "policy directive" by the school board, it characterized this discriminatory exclusion as "a recent policy developed in response to the growing issue of segregation and integration" in the public schools, and ruled it constitutionally impermissible.

No area of exemption is more important for my purposes than antidiscrimination law in hiring. It underscores the hybrid nature of associations, in this case religious groups as employers. It affects nonmembers directly. And the workplace is a key arena for cultivating specifically liberal virtues. Title VII of the 1964 Civil Rights Act permits religious associations to discriminate on the basis of religion in the area of employment, and the act has been interpreted to allow race and gender discrimination in matters of "purely ecclesiastical cognizance" too, such as the selection of ministers (including commissioned officers in the Salvation Army). Thus, a church successfully defended discharging its homosexual organist in a suit brought under a local gay rights ordinance, on grounds of belief that homosexuality is a sin.[70] A civil court declined to hear the case of a deposed minister who claimed he was fired because of his wife's race: "who will preach from the pulpit of a church and who will occupy the parsonage" is a purely ecclesiastical question.[71]

On the other hand, the "nonreligious activity" designation has been applied to hiring and EEOC regulations enforced. Courts found Seventh-Day Adventists guilty of sex discrimination against an employee with editorial and secretarial responsibilities in a nonprofit publishing house, for example, and racial discrimination against a white receptionist-typist discharged for having a "casual relationship" with an African American.

We can understand both the impetus to enforce congruence with public norms of nondiscrimination and the difficulty of judging when activities are sufficiently "religious" to warrant a free exercise exemption. But what is the thinking behind exempting religious associations from public obligations when their activities are admittedly not central to doctrine or authority? Why would Congress and courts refuse even to require religious associations to prove the case for exemption?

Corporation of Presiding Bishop of the Church of Jesus Christ of Latter-Day Saints v. Amos is the Supreme Court's most expansive inquiry into accommodation in this sensitive area.[72] A janitor who had worked for sixteen years at a nonprofit Mormon-run gymnasium open to the public was fired for not complying with the eligibility test for attendance at Mormon temples (the standards involved church attendance, tithing, and abstinence from coffee, tea, alcohol, and tobacco). The district court found the Deseret Gymnasium indistinguishable from any other health club operated for profit, and the janitor's job similar to jobs in those facilities. It thus failed to find a sufficiently close connection between the work the employee performed and tenets of faith to say that government regulation would burden religion. Nothing in the church's operation of the gym was "even tangentially related to any conceivable religious belief or ritual of the Mormon church or church administration."[73] An exemption from Title VII this broad is impermissible. The Supreme Court overturned the district court's decision in 1987 and granted the gym an exemption from antidiscrimination law, but not because it had uncovered a close connection between exclusionary hiring and Mormon faith. Why then?

The majority determined that the legislative intent was not to advance religion but to avoid interference in the group's religious mission. More important here, that courts must avoid independently assessing whether an activity is central to religion. And religious associations should not be forced to predict which of their activities a court would consider regulable and which it would judge close to the heart of religion, and exempt. Echoing a consideration at the heart of free speech doctrine, Justice White wrote that fear of potential liability could "chill" associational life. Justice Brennan concurred:

> ideally, religious organizations should be able to discriminate only with respect to religious activities, [but] while a church may regard the conduct of certain functions as integral to its mission, a court may disagree. A religious organization therefore would have an incentive to characterize as religious only those activities about which there likely would be no dispute. . . . As a result, the community's process of self-definition would be shaped in part by the prospects of litigation.[74]

The "conditionals" peppering Brennan's formulation suggest that *any* risk of having to demonstrate the religious nature of an activity would affect the group's ongoing "self-definition" and is too risky. The idea is to ward off the unanticipated influence not of government regulation per se but of government inquiry into religious belief as well as the need to justify an exemption from regulation—that is, effects stemming from the *fear* of public justification and litigation. The argument assumes that religious communities are fragile. The Court does not portray exemption as a condition for religious flourishing; it sees enforcement of antidiscrimination law as a threat to the association's viability.

This goes beyond the danger government intervention would pose to religious autonomy by settling internal disputes over who is the rightful church authority and controls church property, addressed in *Serbian Diocese*. It also constrains government more than the rule against "entanglement" in a religious association's daily business, which was an element in the decision in *Walz v. Tax Commission* to include religious associations in the broad category of tax-exempt institutions.

For constitutional separationists keenly sensitive to establishment, tax exemption amounts to state subsidy of religion and a de facto financial exaction from unbelievers; it is perfectly clear that money saved from taxes can be used by churches for religious purposes. Nevertheless, the religious exemption was upheld in *Walz* against an establishment clause challenge in part on grounds that *it* is the true separation. The broad class of exempted secular and religious groups avoids any appearance of selectivity or favoritism. Tax-exempt status *restricts* fiscal relations between church and state, since taxation requires government evaluation of church property, tax liens and foreclosures, and accompanying legal and recording procedures.[75] Similarly, when the NLRB was denied jurisdiction over unionization of lay teachers in parochial schools in 1979 the issue was not the Catholic Church's doctrinal objection to unions. Rather, *NLRB v. Catholic Bishops of Chicago* turned on the fact that official resolution of charges of unfair labor practices or official findings related to bargaining would require intrusive investigation, since "nearly everything that goes on in the schools affects teachers and is therefore arguably 'a condition of employment.' "[76]

The proviso against government "entanglement" in associational life has nothing to do with the direct effects of particular regulations, then. It gives independent weight to official activities connected to regulation—investigation, monitoring, auditing of routine administrative affairs, and so on.[77] It does not require concrete evidence that oversight procedures actually burden free exercise or subvert self-government, either. No substantive inquiry goes on. (As the dissent in *NLRB* notes, the claim that jurisdiction over lay teachers would implicate the religion clauses by undercutting the bishop's authority "is mere assertion.")[78] Rather, exemption from state and federal legislation is granted with an eye to the unpredictable, cumulative effect of government interest in the internal management of church affairs.

This is the mirror image of arguments made by opponents of government accommodation of religion, who fear the unpredictable, cumulative effect of religious exemptions on the administration of public business. References to slippery slopes and ungovernability are common. Justice Scalia warns that religious exemptions from general laws "would be courting anarchy" and could initiate "a system in which each conscience is a law unto itself." Indeed, "consistent subordination of secular norms to religious ones would threaten the social cohesion produced by generally applicable law."[79]

Amos takes this logic a step farther. After all, enforcement of antidiscrimination employment law to protect the janitor is more removed from day-to-day association affairs than taxation or resolution of labor disputes. The avowed danger is chilling the church's "self-definition." What is the significance of liberal self-restraint?

The Costs of Liberal Self-Restraint

Hiring only faithful Mormons may not reflect religious intolerance or a generally discriminatory attitude toward outsiders, and we do not know whether the operators of the gym were disinclined to respect the religious liberty and other rights of non-Mormons in other settings. (Practices like strenuous proseletyzing and even conversion of the dead are not coercive, though they have been called disrespectful.) From this narrow perspective on shaping moral dispositions, the decision in *Amos* is indeterminate. But a religious association with liberty to define for itself what falls within the scope of activity that is *conceivably* part of its self-definition has consequences for the moral uses of pluralism, particularly when it comes to cultivating specifically liberal virtues.

For one thing, church autonomy comes at the expense of the janitor's free exercise rights. By lifting the requirement of nondiscrimination in hiring, the

Court gave the Mormon Church power to force the janitor to choose between qualifying for a "temple recommend" or losing his job. The potential for coercion is plain. There is no sharper deviation from liberalism than coercing belief by conditioning vital secular benefits on declarations of faith. The gym is not a government agency, of course, and this is not a case of "unconstitutional conditions." Although it was *government* that lifted the general regulatory burden from the religious organization, Justice O'Connor concurred in the outcome, satisfied that an objective observer would not perceive the statutory exemption as conveying a message of government endorsement of religious discrimination. Still, the Deseret Gymnasium employee's liberty (which includes the right *not* to believe) was clearly burdened by the church's exemption from federal law, as was the religious liberty of other non-Mormon, potential employees. So there is a question whether discrimination in employment by religious associations is a tolerable incongruence, particularly without a showing that hiring touches on church government in matters of administration or faith.

Some shifting of burdens is inevitable wherever there is religious liberty. Exempting religious associations from taxation adds to the burden on nonbelievers, though these costs are diffuse and impersonal. The *Amos* Court acknowledged that its decision gave the church economic leverage in the secular realm, where Mormon Church activities are firmly and successfully planted. What weight did this have, if any, in Congress's legislation or the judges' ruling?

We saw in *Serbian Diocese* that deference to decisions by religious authorities is justified because members are free to leave and to join or form some other association, or none—though they may have to give up access to church property when they split. When a religious association's life is felt to be "unfair" according to its own internal rules or members' expectations, the result is internal dissent, separation, and the success of rival institutions. Religious associations evidently see employment in these voluntarist terms, and take the view that government may not intervene to protect workers against "merely" arbitrary or unfair treatment: "the remedy for that is to resign or renegotiate the terms of employment."[80]

Were assumptions of economic opportunity parallel to assumptions of religious opportunity implicitly at work in *Amos*? The justices may have assumed that alternative employment existed for the fired janitor and other potential employees, though they did not inquire into the facts. Or they may have assumed that workers are able and should be willing to move from the local community to earn their living elsewhere. Or that the janitor could always fall back on public welfare; perhaps the assumption was that government would compensate for the consequences of religious freedom to discriminate.

It is an empirical question when hiring on the basis of religious belief measurably redistributes employment opportunities from the population generally to the faithful of particular groups, and becomes a significant constraint on the free exercise of nonmembers. At some point, a religious association, especially if it is a dominant establishment and economic force in a region, may wield power over members and nonmembers that is practically inescapable.[81] A notion of "sacred space" that swallows up the domain of employment where public principles of justice are supposed to reign can be imperial. This is a valid consideration in any balance between the free exercise claims of the janitor and the Mormon Church, and between religious claims for exemption from federal law and the public interest in nondiscrimination. The Court's assumption that the group was fragile was explicit (its self-definition easily "chilled"), presumably more tenuous than the janitor's religious liberty since association autonomy is allowed to override it. In fact, neither the background condition of economic opportunity nor the extent of the church's economic leverage appears to have figured in congressional or judicial reasoning.

Conflict between employees' free exercise rights and the rights of religious associations (and their members) are not the only concern, however. The consequences of liberal self-restraint are also specific to religious associations as workplaces. Discrimination has implications for liberal dispositions even if workers are indifferent to religion and willing to obey temple rules as a condition of employment. And even if Justice O'Connor is right to think that an "objective observer" would not view this exemption as government endorsement of discriminatory hiring.

From the point of view of shaping moral dispositions, workplaces play a crucial part. They are sites for cultivating skills, exhibiting excellences, and garnering self-respect. Beyond that, workplaces are quasi-public settings normally governed by at least some liberal democratic norms of cooperation, one of the few such settings to which most men and women are regularly exposed and expected to conform. When they abide by or assert state and federal antidiscrimination law, work relations can introduce them to at least minimal practices of impartiality. They can foster expectations that the disposition to avoid discrimination will be exhibited (and be subject to scrutiny) at least in the limited area of hiring, promotion, and firing. For individuals whose other affiliations may well be incongruent, workplaces provide the principal experience in the discipline of liberal democratic culture.

Not that work experiences compensate for or offset the moral effects of other, incongruent settings, so that character as a whole is liberalized. Simply, employment practices require us to differentiate among social contexts and the dispositions they countenance. They call up the capacity to adjust practices as we shift involvements. The *Amos* Court was keen to avoid the messy business of sorting out work that is by its nature religious from work that is not. It ruled against concrete, case-by-case judgments of claims for exemption from liberal democratic regulations. And it went along with Congress's decision not to require the Mormon Church to demonstrate that discrimination in hiring was a matter of faith or affected its religious life. Decisions analogous to these are inescapable for ordinary men and women, personally. As a daily matter we have to discriminate among social spheres and muster the moral habits appropriate to each. Quite apart from cultivating specific virtues, workplaces are where most people get experience in negotiating the complex moral demands of liberal democracy. That is one reason why *Amos* concedes too much.

Another is the way the Court assessed the dangers enforcing liberal democratic norms would pose to associational life: its elastic notion of "viability."

Viability and Voice

"Viability" is a recurrent consideration in deciding on exemptions and accommodation for secular as well as religious groups, so it merits attention. It helps to contrast *Amos* with *Wisconsin v. Yoder*, where the Court had the bottom of the presumptively slippery slope of government interference—the group's survival—in clear view. Also, in *Yoder* the threat to viability has concrete content: attrition through the loss of willing members and failure to attract new ones. Viability is a matter of the critical number of believers necessary for carrying on a particular way of life.

In this case, the Supreme Court granted the Old Order Amish an exemption from Wisconsin's requirement that children attend school until the age of sixteen. The community did not claim that its religious tenets forbid public school education or compelled strict separatism at adolescence. The argument was that their religious faith and way of life were interdependent, and that it could only maintain its exclusive hold over Amish youth by sheltering them from the worldly seductions they would encounter in high school. The Court upheld the exemption on grounds that the religious community's viability was at stake. Without accommodation, Chief Justice Burger concluded, the Amish could reasonably fear for the survival of their community, and would be "forced to migrate to some other and more tolerant region." He evoked the sort of sympathy we associate with the fate of oppressed outcasts and exiles: "what will become of these poor people?"[82]

Plainly, the community's way of life depends on commitment by future generations, but how many defections would threaten its viability? What sort of internal changes might some Amish tolerate in order to keep members? The preservation of the community as it exists in Lancaster, Pennsylvania, is identified with the preservation of their faith. The Amish order, recall, originated in separation from the Mennonites. Insistence that the church is an "organic entity not reducible to a mere aggregation of individuals" obscures these questions.[83] So does the test of viability.

Taken literally, the standard of viability is too stringent; it seems to allow government interference up to the crisis point that puts survival in doubt. As applied in *Amos*, on the other hand, the standard of viability is impossibly lax. The institutional survival of the Mormon Church was not at stake in the exemption from antidiscrimination law but rather the elusive risk of chilling the association's self-definition.

It is clear from *Amos* that solicitude for association autonomy acquires force from the presumption that groups are fragile. This is a doubtful generalization that flies in the face of evidence that "religious organizations have had the resources with which to respond to the challenges set before them. Rather than simply being eroded, as the secularizationists would have it, American religion has been able to play its cards with the advantage of a tremendously strong hand."[84] Vulnerability may make sense in the case of "internal exiles" like the Amish, with a history of communal separatism. But Mormon assimilation was accomplished some time ago (what could be more in step with popular culture than a gym?). Fragility is simply asserted in *Amos*, as if the condition for exemption is that a chill on "self-definition" is near-fatal: "these matters are so highly reactive when placed in contact with public authority that religious liberty requires any appreciable risk of involvement be avoided."[85] There are no parameters to "highly reactive," no standards of vulnerability or "appreciable risk." In *Amos*, self-definition/viability/survival are fused.

Without doubt, a religious association's ability to create Amish or Mormon believers depends on freedom to organize its own affairs. But "self-definition" gets its force from its abstraction from any particular aspect of self-government. It smacks of concern for some elusive group "identity" or "integrity" rather than the specifics of authority, discipline, doctrine, or management. Justice Brennan seemed to make even the possibility that the Mormon community's self-definition "might be shaped in part by the prospect of litigation" the equivalent of a coerced change of identity.

We can appreciate the sound core of Brennan's concern. He wants to avoid requiring either courts or associations to rigidly settle on the defining characteristics of the religion that warrant protection. But he swings to the other extreme, replacing essentialism with fluid "self-definition." Faced with a similar dilemma, advocates of cultural group rights in liberal democracies try to avoid specifying and protecting only presumptively essential characteristics of a culture. Will Kymlicka, for example, allows that a group's "character" is changeable, and would aim legal protections at externally coerced change in the group's "structure" (its institutional existence and capacity for self-government).[86] Whether or not these guidelines for weighing association claims for exemption from government mandates, accommodation, or positive assistance make sense, the attempt to unpack viability is vital and I return to this subject in chapter 9 on "the politics of recognition."[87]

We can sharpen the significance of liberal self-restraint by looking at the matter from another direction, and considering what it can mean for government to judge the centrality of an activity to faith, and to balance its significance for the group against the requirements of liberal democracy.

Recall *Brown v. Dade Christian Schools*, where in 1977 the circuit court decided the New Testament Baptist Church did not qualify for a First Amendment exemption from antidiscrimination law. Its policy of excluding black children from its school was designed to circumvent government-mandated school integration, the court ruled. Judge Arthur Goldberg diverged from the plurality in his concurrence. He viewed the school's segregation as a genuine expression of faith, but that did not lead to him to automatically grant the group an exemption from federal law. The court should have balanced the right of religious expression against the state interest in desegregation.

Performing this balance, Goldberg concluded that "the rights of African Americans to participate in our society on equal terms must have ascendancy over a religious practice that can be subordinated *without impairing* the religion's viability."[88] Equal protection does not outweigh free exercise and association, simply; Goldberg would have upheld the state interest because doing so would not endanger the church's survival.[89] His conclusion was based on the assessment that the belief in racial segregation was a minor tenet of faith.

Clearly, balancing is less painful if one side is weighted ("a more compelling governmental interest has perhaps never been enlisted in opposition to a free exercise claim") and the other side lightened from the start.[90] The church's viability is unlikely to appear at risk by being forced to contradict a minor tenet of faith. How did Goldberg decide it was minor, then?

He does not search the church's twenty-two-year history, or inquire into the centrality of the belief to members personally and individually. Simply, after conceding that according to church tenets, departure from the command to segregate would constitute disobedience to God, he refuses to concede that disobedience would endanger salvation! He invents his own theology, in short, and draws practical conclusions from it. Membership in the church, presumably motivated by faith, will not be affected by publicly enforced integration so long as salvation is not imperilled. The church will not lose its faithful. Its viability will be unimpaired.

Behind this remarkable, speculative conclusion is the argument that members of the church and school could go on believing and advocating segregation while being required to practice integration without impairing faith. In fact, belief is likely to be impaired if members cannot fully act on it within the circumscribed arena of church and affiliated school; that is the whole point of autonomy for religious communities. As Figgis pointed out in another context, only those who "seem almost unable to conceive what churchmen mean by claiming any freedom for religious bodies" would imagine otherwise.[91] It would surely matter to associational life and faith that black students do not subscribe to the religious tenets that support racial segregation. (If they did, why would they voluntarily enter a school that practices integration? *Their* membership is not compulsory; they are not condemned to hypocrisy or self-contradiction.)

Dade is a near-perfect illustration of the truth of the observation that "the power to change the membership of a bona fide private association is unavoidably the power to change its purpose, its programs, its ideology, and its collective voice."[92] Goldberg proposes a strange reversal of Locke's historical argument in his *Letter on Toleration*. Locke would require churches to teach civil toleration as a condition of their own liberty; Goldberg would require the all-white church school to give up its liberty to refuse fellowship to African Americans as a condition for preaching racial separation and intolerance.

It is impossible to predict based on the facts given whether forced integration of the church school would cause a falling off of membership and threaten its survival, but Goldberg's reasoning does not inspire confidence. He employs an analogy between competition for customers and believers: "much as merchants were freed by the Civil Rights Act of 1964 from any fear that white customers would react adversely to the acceptance of black business, parents and school leaders are freed . . . from any fear that children will interpret acceptance of blacks as an indication of church approval of the practice."[93] If every school is forced to carry the government's message of racial equality, the reasoning goes, no church has a competitive edge and the ability to attract and keep adherents is unaffected. This argument is dubious too, since some churches are likely to do a more plausible job than Dade Christian of convincing a court majority that their opposition to segregated schools is theological.

Goldberg did not take even the modicum of care Justice Burger had in *Yoder* to consider the conditions for socializing children into a community as a condition for its continued existence.[94] Clearly, the circuit court did not share the Burger Court's sympathy for the religious association before them; the Amish were economically self-supporting and law-abiding, and the sacrifices accepted by members were testimony to their sincerity. Also operating in the Amish case was marginality and the assumption of harmlessness in comparison to the powerful, armed Mormon population resisting antipolygamy law in *U.S. v. Reynolds*, or Baptist segregationists in *Dade*.

The problem with Goldberg's reasoning is not his insistence that autonomy for religious associations should be balanced against the demands of liberal democracy; that is proper and unavoidable. The problem is the dubious attempt to ascertain—really, to concoct on his own—the centrality of a matter of faith, to speculate about the developed and practical significance of being required to contravene it, and to make this conclusion key to the balance. A judgment that the compelling liberal principle of desegregation simply takes priority over religious expression, though wrong, would be preferable to bad faith weighing and blind stabs at prediction.

One key to a sounder balance is the specific nature of government intervention here: control over membership.[95] Compelled association *is* a threat to the viability of groups whose liberty is grounded in voluntary association and fellowship. Religious liberty means individuals are not forced to join or prevented from leaving groups; *Dade* introduces a third element—freedom from compelled association. The ruling compelling a church school to admit unwelcome members is the very definition of loss of self-government. And it disregards the basis for liberal deference to religious self-government set out in *Serbian Diocese*: that the advancement or decline of a church should come only from the voluntary support of its followers, determining for themselves the requirements of faith, not from the political support or inhibition of government.

Totalistic Religion, Voluntary Association, and Exit

The moral consequences of membership in associations that forcefully reject liberal democratic norms and practices take center stage when it comes to totalistic religious groups. "Totalistic" does not refer to the number and kind of religious directives issued but to "greedy institutions," from a Rajneeshee ashram to an ultra-Orthodox Jewish yeshiva, which immerse members in the organization and take up every moment of their lives. Totalistic groups are closed and set themselves apart, in the spirit of separatism or exhibition of exemplary differences. Often at their core is a keen sense of danger and the discipline this demands of members—obedience to jealous, unchallenged authority. Jerry Falwell's notion that "Christians, like slaves and soldiers, ask no questions" gives a "cultish" aspect to his congregation, and to others that would be horrified at the title.[96]

For in popular consciousness the cult label suggests malignant conduct—suicide, murder, prostitution, starvation, torture, and brainwashing. (For which there is rarely much evidence. When criminal charges are brought, it is usually for fraud or income tax evasion. Anxious families and professional "deprogrammers" are the ones engaged in indisputable kidnapping and coercion.) Jonestown is the bad memory of mass irrationality projected onto every totalistic group. Currently, indiscriminate fear focuses on "jihad," though its opposite, quietude, is also disturbingly alien.

Don DeLillo gives us the voice of the daughter married in the mass ceremony in Yankee Stadium:

"Cult." How they love to use it against us. Gives them the false term they need to define us as eerie-eyed children. And how they hate our willingness to work and struggle. They want to snatch us back to the land of lawns. That we are willing to live on the road, sleep on the floor, crowd into vans and drive all night, fund-raising, serving Master. That our true father is a foreigner and nonwhite. How they silently despise. They keep our rooms ready. . . . But we're a lifetime away, weeping through hours of fist-pounding prayer.[97]

Particularly when antiliberalism is not made palatable by a long history of self-chosen "internal exile" like the Amish, and when a group's strange mix of commercial activities and evangelical mission is aggressively in the world, the impetus to enforce congruence is strong. These gripping associations have unchecked opportunity to shape members, and liberals committed to protecting citizens against private as well as public despotism and exploitation will be tempted to intervene. Again, as Hobhouse cautioned: "the function of Liberalism may be rather to protect the individual against the power of the association than to protect the right of association against the restriction of the law."[98] Without publicly enforced limits, associations can terrorize people and engross resources.[99] Here, Justice Rehnquist's concern about "domination by oppressive religious authorities" seems more apt than in the *Serbian Diocese* case. These groups are a reminder that the obstacles to liberal virtue are not always ordinary vices but sometimes extraordinary ones: terrible impulses to mastery and control over vulnerable followers, or irresistible urges to self-effacing submission and discipleship.

At the same time, the attractions of totalistic religious groups bring to mind the desperate hunger some people feel for strong affiliation, which cannot be repressed. Too many people are lost and lonely, and feel unutterably useless and diminished, without opportunities. "The army of children waiting to be led" could be led by political forces much less benign than the weirdly original, spiritually potent "remnant churches" that gather in and organize the disassociated. The thought that *some* association to alleviate radical disconnection is the condition for combatting anomie and for exciting moral capacities at all may apply.

Tony and Susan Alamo Foundation v. Secretary of Labor is a window onto the twin question of protection for and protection from totalistic religious groups. The nonprofit religious Alamo Foundation derived its income by operating service stations, retail clothing and grocery outlets, hog farms, roofing and electrical construction companies, a recordkeeping company, a motel, and candy companies staffed by Foundation "associates." Entrepreneurial efforts of this sort are not unusual; leaders of religious organizations in the United States typically agree that "profit-making enterprise is a legitimate and necessary way of sustaining a nonprofit organization."[100] It is not only ministers of "megachurches" who learn from business, though the senior pastor of Willow Creek Community Church may be the only one with a Peter Drucker poster on his office wall.[101]

In the 1985 case involving the Alamo Foundation, the secretary of labor filed action under the Fair Labor Standards Act, charging the group with violating minimum wage and overtime provisions. The Supreme Court held that the Foundation business was a commercial enterprise whose substandard wages gave it unfair economic advantage over competitors, which the laws were designed to prevent. It also observed that wage and hour regulation was no more intrusive than conformity to fire inspection or building and zoning regulations; there were no grounds for religious exemption on the basis of "entanglement."

That did not end the matter, because the Court still had to determine whether the underpaid, overworked associates were "employees" within the meaning of the act or volunteers engaged in a religious mission and thus outside the reach of government. We have seen that religious associations may be exempt from economic and labor regulations, [whether or not they are explicitly required by church doctrine] particularly when activities come close to the heart of their religious missions. Foundation members represented themselves as volunteers "bringing good news to a pagan world" and objected to receiving wages. But applying the "economic reality" test, the Court found that they were entirely dependent on the Foundation for food, shelter, and clothing, and that they worked in expectation of these benefits, which were wages in another form.

Moreover, the Court ruled, receipt of federally mandated wages would not burden associates' free exercise since they could return them to the Foundation, "provided they did so voluntarily." This is a clue that the categorical question whether the Foundation is predominantly a commercial or religious enterprise, and the question whether enforcing wage laws is simply the neutral application of public principles of justice to an organization whose commercial activities are judged peripheral to its religious mission, obscure the chief concern. That is, the quintessential liberal matter of consent to authority, especially when it diverges radically from public norms.

Before their conversion and rehabilitation, Foundation associates were mostly drug addicts, criminals, and derelicts. Like the Unification Church, Alamo was widely thought to prey on the vulnerable and to take advantage of the intense need for connection and care, perhaps by engaging in infantilizing and guilt-inducing recruiting practices that made voluntarism doubtful. Former associates testified that they had been "fined" heavily for poor job performance and were prohibited from getting food from the cafeteria if they were absent from work due to illness or bad weather; members' standing seemed closer to indentured servitude than volunteerism. This gives an edge to Justice White's otherwise routine argument about unfair competition and the downward pressure on wages:

> That the associates themselves vehemently protest coverage under the Act makes this case unusual, but the purposes of the Act require that it be applied even to those who would decline its protections. If an exception to the Act were carved out for

employees willing to testify that they performed work "voluntarily," employers might be able to use superior bargaining power to coerce employees to . . . waive their protections.[102]

From the standpoint of the moral uses of pluralism, the conditions under which members enter a totalistic subcommunity—whether they are born into it or join under conditions that cause outsiders to doubt the reasonableness or sanity of consent—may be less important than whether they can leave. Strong advocates of autonomy for religious associations argue that "the state has no legitimate interest sufficient to warrant protection of church members from their church with respect to discrimination, economic exploitation, or a wide range of other evils that the state tries to prevent in the secular economy." Member-employees should have no official protection against unfair or irrational treatment, on this view, because they can leave.[103]

This ignores the real conditions of exit. *Amos* raised them indirectly by drawing attention to the question of alternative opportunities for employment; *Alamo* raises them directly in the form of a social safety net. It is one thing to decline to protect adult members from the consequences of their religious "choices" in matters of internal discipline or control of church property, as the Court did in *Serbian Diocese*. It is another to fail to insure access to general public protections and benefits. This is a more stringent public obligation than monitoring the conditions of consent to membership or intervening to alter the internal life of groups.

This question was raised in *Wisconsin v. Yoder* (though it was not decisive): whether exempting Amish children from mandatory school attendance to the age of sixteen would interfere with their ability to leave the separatist community and participate in the wider society. Chief Justice Burger called public education "the very apex of the function of the state," but argued that Wisconsin's interest in enforcing its school attendance requirement was not compelling because the community successfully instilled the virtues and competencies of democratic citizens in its members. In a rare authoritative statement of what these are, Burger pointed to economic self-sufficiency and law-abidingness. Basic schooling and the vocational skills and habits of industry acquired in the religious community guarantee that Amish children "are capable of fulfilling the social and political responsibilities of citizenship."[104]

It is bizarre to identify the antiworldly Amish, whose religion determines their entire mode of life, with Jefferson's "sturdy yeomen," but Burger's pragmatic point is plain. The community's survival can be allowed to take precedence because the restraint on future generations' opportunity and liberty is modest. True, the intention was to insulate children from alternatives in order to insure automatic adoption of the prescribed adult roles of Amish farmers and housewives. But Justice Douglas's prediction that the children would be "forever barred from entry into the new and amazing world of diversity that we have today," his concern that their whole lives would be "stunted and deformed" by a decision in favor of their parents' free exercise, is extravagant.

What about traits more distinctively liberal than ability to earn? Justice Douglas pointed out that the state's school attendance laws were designed to cultivate tolerance, broaden sensibilities, kindle imagination, and foster a spirit of free inquiry. The Amish repudiate all that. They want their children to acquire just enough basic skills to be able to deal with outsiders "when the need arose." "What is at issue," Amy Gutmann observes, "is not *whose* values, but *what* values ought to be imposed on children." Parents "have an obligation to allow their children to be exposed to the choices available in their extra-familial society."[105] This argument is compelling only if we accept a particular account of the constitutive moral elements of liberal democratic citizenship. Neither Burger's self-supporting earners nor Douglas's autonomous choosers are the only moral types compatible with liberalism. Even those inclined to support mandatory democratic education might doubt whether public high schools develop the capacities Justice Douglas describes, except ideally. Besides, this has little bearing on the question of whether the Amish are free to leave.

In this connection, the Supreme Court rejected another Amish claim of exemption from general laws, this time from the requirement that Amish employers pay their workers' social security taxes. The community cares for its own, the Amish argued, and members do not draw on the fund.[106] The Court's decision in *U.S. v. Lee* (1982) was correct, but not its reasoning. Justifying mandatory social security contributions in order to prevent administrative "anarchy" or out of concern for the viability of a "comprehensive national social security system" is hardly compelling. Needless to say, Amish farmers' marginal contributions were trivial. It does not make sense to worry about a wave of unprecedented religious exceptions to a broad-based tax either; the religious community is sufficiently singular. But mandatory contributions to social security are justified for the same reason conformity to wage and hour laws was in *Alamo*—because exempting the religious community from payment would provide it with extraordinary economic leverage over its members. It would contribute to the armament of private coercion, inhibit members' real and symbolic identification with citizenship, and create an obstacle to shifting involvements and the experience of pluralism.

In liberal democracy, individuals can opt out of exercising civil and political rights and can decline to draw public benefits. They can disavow that "worker" or "citizen" is part of their self-conception; "believer" may eclipse them. But government should not participate in the alienation of rights or foreclosure of entitlements by a religious association in the name of its member-employees. It should not give the religious polity's claim to totalism and separatism official imprimatur. Joseph Raz is right: "Given that even oppressive cultures can give people quite a lot, it follows that one should be particularly wary of organized campaigns of assimilation and discrimination." But it emphatically does not follow that "they provide many of their members with all that they can have."[107] Liberal democracy's imperative is to insure that it is *not* all they can have.

The decision to extend fair labor protection to workers in Alamo Foundation businesses reinforces voluntarism. It helps make exit conceivable. It removes at least one impediment to the moral uses of pluralism. When petitioners tried to suggest that the state interest was not compelling because minimum wages would have no appreciable effect on association—that is, members would simply return them to Foundation coffers—they missed the point. The object is not to liberalize the group's beliefs by instilling a sincere commitment to wage equity or members' financial independence. Much less to propose that economic justice is essential to relations within the group. The state interest is also misunderstood if it is seen as enforcing public principles of justice on an organization judged more commercial than religious. Or as minimizing public expense when Foundation employees are forced to seek state medical or welfare assistance.

Instead, like all rights and benefits, its impact is edifying as well as practical. Protection under the Fair Labor Standards Act is an affirmation of the inescapability of liberal democratic civic culture. It insists that citizens have rights, even if they choose not to exercise them in the context of religious community. Even if bearing rights is not currently part of their self-understanding or motivation. Addressed to members of a self-styled totalistic religious association, enforcement of wage and hour laws is both a public declaration and a material demonstration of their standing as citizens. It assists in assuring at least the possibility of shifting involvements, the avenue to membership in associations more likely to cultivate liberal democratic dispositions.

Unintended Moral Consequences

Plainly, religious associations do not all promulgate liberal democratic principles (though they may) or inculcate liberal democratic dispositions through their practices (though some do). The cases I have discussed should also help us see that the formative effect of any religious association is always variable. When church authority and discipline deviate from rules of "fundamental fairness," as American bishops charged in *Serbian Diocese*, the result may be to inhibit the cultivation of habits of due process, or to stifle them where they exist. Or it may lead to invigorated respect for constitutionalism in church government, and strengthen commitment to established procedures. And members' decision to defer to religious authority regardless of its faithfulness to procedures, and to refrain from appeals out of commitment to the association, is perfectly compatible with scrupulous conformity to the demands of due process in other spheres.

That said, it is easy enough to list the obstacles religious associations pose to liberal dispositions, both known and potential. The thought I would import from *Yoder*'s discussion of mandatory schooling to the grimmer facts of *Alamo* is that while associations may not cultivate every or any characteristically liberal virtue, and may habituate members to conduct that is normally anathema such as self-effacing submissiveness to "the Enlightened Master," they may nevertheless instill vital moral dispositions and social competencies. This is not to recommend enacting public policy expressly aimed at supporting these associations and their religious values. Only that freedom of association may not incur the costs we assume.[108]

Consider that the "face value" of an association and system of belief may be misleading. It may suggest troubling self-abjugation, asceticism, elimination of personal choice, and adoration, but in practice these may be only part of the dynamic of associational life. By relieving anomie and cultivating habits of work and rule-following, the Alamo Foundation may have compensated for experience members did not receive anywhere else, or needed to have reinforced by "starting over."

In her study of Liberty Baptist Church, Frances Fitzgerald observed that while the church was officially posed in opposition to "the world," "many of their prescriptions for life look very much like tactics for integrating people into society rather than like tactics for separating them from it."[109] The same point has been made about "cults," where members' financial contribution through work is routine and believers exercise organizational, administrative, and business skills much as they would outside. For nine out of ten joiners, the life cycle of membership in totalistic communities is under two years, and many continue in the line of work they began inside after they leave. "The values to which the group subscribes are only thinly veiled versions of middle-class ideals—all that hard work, sharing, caring, scrubbed floors, and good food," one scholar observes.[110]

Not that charismatic groups are the equivalent of junior achievement clubs; still, from the standpoint of the moral uses of pluralism their unintended effects bear noting. Most important, if rehabilitation, habits of industry, and ability to earn are not sufficient conditions for being able to leave a totalistic environment, they are enabling.

Indeed, incongruent associations can have the wholly unintended effect of contributing to specifically liberal democratic practices and dispositions. Several illustrations emerge from this discussion, beginning with the fact that religious associations can be hostile to consent and choice yet heighten perceptions of the voluntarism of membership. They can deprecate personal liberty yet provide a powerful experience of social experiment and elective affinity.

Joining a church is often viewed as starting over—the theology of being "born again" is just one manifestation of this common experience. Converts have it, of course, as do people enthusiastically embracing an ancestral faith from which they or their families have fallen off. So do those who, like Malcolm X, exhibit a conversion pattern away from assimilation and childhood faith.[111] Shifting affiliations in the United States is commonplace: a sound estimate is that one person in three has switched from the faith in which he or she was raised, and one person in five changes affiliation three times or more, a phenomenon described as religious "musical chairs."[112]

Joining may be motivated as much by the attractions of group social life or the association's moral culture as anything else. A good example of elective affinity is the salience of a religious group's reputation on issues of concern to women or gays and lesbians, both its doctrinal position and its outreach and hospitability in practice. Joining is also guided by tastes in popular culture— what one United Methodist minister, a "nationally known parish consultant," calls "the Americanization of the Christian church."[113] A typical suburban "mega-church" offers several styles of service: country music, traditional, and pop-style in its six-thousand seat stadium. "You're not intimidated by any ceremonies," one member reports. "We probably came here for a year before we knew it was Lutheran."[114]

Religious association is not solely about beliefs and worship, after all; it is expected to provide important services: marriages, baptisms, and funerals and a host of fellowship and support groups geared to self-improving activities of every kind.[115] The proliferation of these groups, which for many have become the heart of religious membership, are direct acknowledgment that religious associations must be relevant to an array of personal, even therapeutic needs, including "a good relationship" with God, friendship groups promising intimacy, exercise groups, and parents-without-partners.[116]

The point is, even orthodox religious associations and authoritarian sects may simultaneously embody some ideal of gripping constitutive community as the followers of Reverend Moon do, yet contribute indirectly to undermining inherited religious status, inviting experimentalism, and supporting institutional as well as personal transformation. Religious polities may advertise strong tutelary authority and unyielding imperatives for conduct and faith, but they, too, compete for believers, who join for purely personal reasons, including a desire for radical personal change.[117]

We should be skeptical of a group's self-description as orthodox or traditionalist, particularly where "traditionalism" is an avowed reaction against current social changes. Indeed, we should be wary about concluding that religious associations are *functionally* traditionalist even if their organizational structure is, and not take their claims to be opposed to individualism at face value. We should certainly be wary in drawing conclusions about the self-understanding of members from the self-description of groups.

Unintended liberal consequences also result from overt clashes between religious associations and public norms. Litigation by religious groups resisting government policy is an integral part of American history, which escalates in lockstep with increases in both the diversity of faiths and state action. When government can burden or prohibit religious exercise and autonomy in every area, from zoning to antidiscrimination law, and where government accommodation to associational life is largely discretionary, religious groups are bound to raise frequent challenges. Neither fear of establishment nor concern for oppressed minorities is outmoded, although Catholics are not hounded, Quakers jailed, or dissenters tithed.[118] Except for *Wisconsin v. Yoder* and *Sherbert v. Verner* (the case brought by the sabbatarian for unemployment benefits), most recent constitutional challenges have been denied. Every one was brought by a "marginal" religious group: Old Order Amish, Seventh-Day Adventists, Orthodox Jews, Muslims, Mormons, and the Native American churches. (I put "marginal" in quotes to indicate that a group falls outside traditionally dominant faiths and has tenuous standing in public sympathies, not that its adherents are few; Islam is the eighth largest denomination in the United States.)

Doubtless, some litigiousness is objectionable, but the disposition to check public power and to express a sense of injustice when it is aroused by appealing to the courts or taking direct political action should not be anathema in a liberal democracy. Self-defensive legal recourse is preferable to timidity, submission, and self-hatred. It should certainly be appreciated by those who complain that secular liberal society silences believers, and who represent religious souls as fragile victims.[119] The moral education of membership in a group that asserts rights should not be overlooked, particularly when it appears to be in tension with the group's own norms. Then, self-protective claims of rights and exemptions appear even more starkly as experience in liberal democracy, and in differentiating among spheres.

Barbara Grizzuti Harrison describes her education as a member of Jehovah's Witnesses, principal litigants for First Amendment rights:

> all Witnesses learned to equip themselves to deal with police and judges. At weekly "service meetings" during the war years, they received paralegal training. They had mock trials, some of them lasting for weeks. . . . They were coached in how to respond to arresting officers, and how to behave procedurally in order to establish the basis for appellate review of convictions."[120]

They had to. Jehovah's Witnesses refused to apply for conscientious objector status during World War II because they weren't conscientiously opposed to war—they would fight at Armageddon. Unlike Quakers, they would not perform alternative civilian service on grounds that the only true service is witnessing. They applied for ministerial exemptions instead, and four thousand male Witnesses spent the duration of the war in federal penitentiaries for draft violations. The development of public forum doctrine is the work of Jehovah's

Witnesses and Hare Krishnas. The Witnesses' flag salute cases are only the best known of 150 state supreme court cases and forty precedent-setting Supreme Court cases brought by the church.[121]

Today, followers of the Santeria faith, who mix Catholicism and African tribal religion, have emerged from underground to challenge local health ordinances that interfere with their animal sacrifices. They have a special spell for winning court cases, but followers are also schooled in their rights and legal avenues of resistance.

The doctrinal history of the First Amendment owes to religious claims framed not in terms of self-referential exemption but in terms of norms broad enough to apply to other groups. This is important: although religious associations may exploit constitutional freedom, thinking in terms of general rights and liberties from a general perspective is unavoidable.

This is not to say that membership in religious associations is generally liberalizing or democratizing, or that the principles advocated in court are brought home to associational life and pervade relations there. My point is simply that members are well situated to feel the effects of government strings on the growing array of benefits and entitlements, sometimes amounting to "unconstitutional conditions," and to observe when government takes a rigid administrative-efficiency stand against exemptions and accommodations. They are in a position to articulate structural concerns about the difficulty of collective action and the distribution of democratic power. Religious self-assertion provides at least some members with a modicum of experience with liberal democratic practices; it encourages resistance and the disposition to protest.

The question, "Does anyone believe that the annual outbreak of lawsuits over the symbols of the December holidays advances the cause of religious harmony or civic understanding?" was meant to be rhetorical and answered in the negative. In fact, the answer is "yes." At least public debate surrounding these cases advances civic understanding, at a minimum insight into theological and ideological differences on the question of religion in public life.

It is churlish to imply that legal challenges for and against religious accommodation (or establishment, as in the creche case) are the work of a few zealous groups and a lot of greedy attorneys. Chief Justice Burger did just that in *Lynch*: "apart from this litigation there is no evidence of political friction or divisiveness over the creche in the 40-year history of Pawtucket's Christmas celebration. . . . [A] litigant cannot, by the very act of commencing a lawsuit, create the appearance of divisiveness and then exploit it as evidence." Justice O'Connor has displayed a similar distemper: "there is little record of support for the proposition that New York City's admirable Title I program has ignited any controversy other than this litigation."[122] The implication is that First Amendment challenges are unwarranted disruptions of public harmony. In fact, these disputes generate ecumenicism, albeit on each side of the question.

Harmony is not a preferred liberal good, in any case; unlike civil peace, tolerance, and inclusive first-class citizenship, which *are* indisputable political
goods.

In short, the formative effects of association life are not of a piece. The
absence or rejection of some liberal practices is compatible with the presence
of others. Active rejection of liberal virtues within associations is compatible
with fostering other, positive moral dispositions. For liberals attempting to
assess the morality of association and the parameters of freedom for religious
associations, this is the crisis from which we cannot be spared.

Democratic Expectancy

One set of unintended consequences is the standard fare of political pluralism:
contests among religious groups and between them and government cultivate
dispositions and competencies required by democratic politics. The ability of
religious associations to win legislative accommodation depends on "their
skill at self-protection in the halls of Congress," for example, so that in practice
"religious groups in America seem forced to choose . . . between adopting the
techniques of secular special-interest groups or else having no influence what-
sover on American public life."[123]

The sanguine assumption is that the public culture of liberal democracy can
never "deviate too far from the 'overlapping consensus' among social subcultures, including religious subcultures," and that "participation by antagonistic
groups in a political and legal system that all regard as fair can bring mutual
respect; such mutual respect can be the first step toward mutual recognition,
understanding, and empathy."[124] Recall Joseph Raz's confidence in liberalism's "transforming effect," and his optimistic claim that members of all cultural groups "will have to acquire a common political language and conventions of conduct to be able to participate effectively in the competition for
resources."[125]

Thus, religious associations are drawn to make common cause with one
another and form pragmatic alliances across faiths for lobbying and litigation,
as many did for the Religious Freedom Restoration Act. Evangelical groups
join secular environmentalists in preserving the Endangered Species Act as
"the Noah's ark of our day." Buddhists petition for membership on local councils of Christians and Jews. Religious associations create parachurch organizations geared to political and social missions, form think-tanks, and train political organizers and fund-raisers—and they invent political techniques like
direct-mail campaigns and television evangelism that have become an integral
part of electoral and issue campaigning.[126] Interfaith and denominational divisions are supplemented by special purpose groups organized along moral and
cultural fault lines. The conservative Moral Majority included several million

Roman Catholics, Mormons, and Orthodox Jews as well as evangelizing fundamentalists; Jerry Falwell is quoted as saying, "if we ever opened a Moral Majority meeting with prayer, silent or otherwise, we would disintegrate."[127]

We know that some religious leaders do abandon "paranoid styles" and world-rejecting stances and become integrated into larger organizations. Sectarian colleges founded to oppose "the world" often change their goals and aim at public respectability, career advancement, worldly goods, and a share of power in society—institutionalized in sectarian schools of business and communications.[128] The white Pentecostal Fellowship of North America disbanded, in recognition that all members of the denomination were "brothers."[129]

But we also know that the demands of religious groups, symbolic and concrete, may be non-negotiable, compromise unabidable. Groups do not always regard the "system as fair" or want fairness for themselves, insisting that preferential treatment is warranted by the truth, value, or popularity of their faith. They may not engage in "strategic self-censorship" that keeps them from uttering the unspeakable, morally offending others. Their sense of crisis may be so extreme that the most radical action is called for to alert potential sympathizers to danger. Their thinking may be apocalyptic, their revelations live and of the moment, not safely in the past. Provocation, making themselves detested, may be a way of exciting internal solidarity.

Only willful blindness ignores the fact that spiritual revolutions need spiritual leaders, who can be expected to frame complex social and political questions in "unequivocal, moralistic terms."[130] Or, as we will see, in conspiracist terms. "It is one of the unappetizing paradoxes of American society that it is composed of individualists in search of charisma" and that "the most anti-eschatological political system in the modern world was devised for the most eschatologically inclined society in the modern world."[131] I have emphasized the ceaseless proliferation of religious groups; new ones crop up all the time.

Today, in addition, the rhetoric of even mainstream religious groups is often aggressively oppositional. It is conspiratorial, pointing to "judicial tyranny" and to a cabal of liberal secular humanists. In the antechamber of the Senate Majority Leader, the Catholic priest Richard John Neuhaus announced: "It is not hyperbole to say that we are at a point at which millions of conscientious American citizens are reflecting upon whether this is a legitimate regime." This heightened pitch is not reserved for specific issues such as abortion rights either. It is not just a matter of the illiberal or undemocratic substance of religious belief. Or of explicit appeals to religious "warrants and imperatives" rather than to generally accessible reasons. Or of the lack of self-discipline that enables persons of faith to speak differently about matters of law and policy in civil society and in political arenas than they do within their church.[132] Contributions to the illiberal tenor of public life are disturbing enough.

We cannot expect to infuse liberal democratic principles and protections into the self-understanding of religious groups, not even when it concerns self-presentation in official arenas. To imagine we can "neutralize their oppressive aspects" is abject optimism on the part of liberal democrats guilty of taking "their own philosophy, and its appeal, too much for granted."[133] The most that can be said is that the disposition to pursue legal challenges and electoral or interest group politics are benign alternatives to separatist withdrawal, overt hostility, and violence. But it can never overcome them altogether, as we are reminded by Christian Identity or the Nation of Islam, two of a long, sobering list of religious hate groups and conspiracists, sometimes armed (the subject of chapter 7).

Nonetheless, religious associations provide normally safe settings for expressing illiberal dispositions and living out antidemocratic impulses—submission to authority, self-effacement, avowed discrimination, and favoritism toward "one's own" in hiring or admission of members. Particularly if they are antiworldly, associations circumscribe these vices. In any case, they may give them relatively harmless expression. "Religion is only good for good people," the novelist Mary McCarthy pronounced in a skepticist's overstatement. She understated things too, since even if particular religious associations are not good for anyone, they may contain the worst.

Like religious groups, secular voluntary associations advance claims to autonomy, though obviously not on the same constitutional grounds. The issues discussed in this chapter arise again and again. All associations want self-direction, particularly control over governance and membership practices. They all want to be buffered from unwanted external change, especially change mandated by law. Periodically, the stability of associational life is unsettled by challenges brought by members or contesting authorities, who are divided as well over whether to welcome or ward off judicial intervention to resolve conflicts.

Secular associations present a similar set of challenges to liberal democracy. There will be calls for public regulation insofar as illiberal, antidemocratic practices deviate from public norms and undermine public interests. On the other hand, precisely to the extent that associations *are* incongruent, there will be advocates for leaving them alone as expressions of personal liberty, out of concern to protect endangered forms of social life, or, as I argue, with an eye to the moral uses of pluralism by men and women, personally and individually.

I turn next to residential homeowners' associations. Hybrid entities—part democratic community, part corporation—they bring into play a remarkable range of legal and ideological arguments for and against freedom for their associational life. "Constitutional incongruence" dictates freedom for religious associations in the United States, but no constitutional right of association applies to these neighborhood/property arrangements. One person, one vote does not apply to voting shares in elections for condominium directors, and the right to privacy does not apply to keeping pets. Instead, corporate law, the interpretation of covenants, and inventive analogies to local government provide frameworks for defending association independence on the one hand and enforcing congruence with liberal democratic norms on the other. Few associations are this interesting: homeowners' associations underscore our conflicted ideas about the moral dispositions required of neighbor-citizens, and the settings we believe instill or inhibit them.

4

Corporate Culture and Community at Home

Homeowners' Associations: Community/Corporate Hybrid

The shaping power of membership comes from the fact that groups control admission and realize common purposes they alone define. Joining represents commitment to the particulars of associational life, to internal rules and authority. When we want to indicate that the "morality of association" is especially intense, self-government especially far-reaching, and that the day-to-day proximity of members to one another is essential, we speak of "community." But the phrase is more often metaphor than fact. Occasionally, religious or political groups form separatist enclaves. Members of ethnic and cultural groups often gravitate to the same location, so that the political boundaries of a locality sometimes coincide with the residences of co-religionists—as they did in the much-publicized case involving the Satmar Hasidim, who incorporated as an independent village, Kiryas Joel, in New York. Normally, however, belonging to a local community comes with residency, and neighbors are little more than a loose aggregate of strangers.

But for a growing number of residential communities, membership is literal. When buyers purchase property in a residential community governed by a homeowners' association they become members as well as owners. They are subject to the association's restrictions and obligations, and can only disassociate by selling their homes. This peculiar hybrid association does not quite conform to any of our standard images of community. Yet it is not a typical voluntary association with discrete purposes separate from home and daily personal life.

As of 1994, an estimated 32 million people were members of 150,000 homeowners' associations, or residential community associations (RCAs).[1] That is approximately 15 percent of the population, with the figure predicted to rise to 25 percent by the year 2000. Every section of the country has condominiums, cooperatives, and homeowners' associations, ranging from under ten units to thousands. Eighty percent are "territorial" and resemble a residential area rather than a single high-rise building. In Los Angeles and San Diego counties, RCAs account for 70 percent of the new housing market; they make up more than 50 percent of new home sales in the fifty largest metropolitan areas; more than one million New Yorkers live in cooperative apartments.[2]

The form is not new, but what was once the preserve of the wealthy is widely available today, and many moderate-income developments are designed to meet the needs of first-time home buyers and the elderly. "Typically, RCAs are an integral part of retirement communities, recreational communities, large-scale suburban subdivisions (and many smaller ones as well), townhouse projects (including today's version of the starter house), and multiple-building, high-rise and mixed-use developments."[3] There are "amenity cooperatives" like Manhattan's Gramercy Park; specialty cooperatives like the Fenway Studios for artists in Boston; the "environmentally sound" co-housing development in Acton, Massachusetts, organized to reproduce small-town life (including curfews for children); and Sun City, the retirement community Frances Fitzgerald made famous in *Cities on the Hill.*

The significance of RCAs for my subject goes beyond their prevalence. It is often noted that "what makes RCAs unique . . . is that they are private organizations that strain the distinction that normally exists between public and private association."[4] In interesting and subtle ways, RCAs raise the question of congruence with liberal democratic practices and dispositions. As we have seen, once an association is identified as religious it is buffered by the First Amendment, and courts and legislatures, reluctant to specify which of the group's activities are really secular and subject to public directives, generally give them latitude. Freedom for the internal life and authority of private residential communities is more tenuous; they cannot claim First Amendment protection. Their freedom is also more vulnerable to how they are defined; they are messier hybrids. Since one or another governmental intervention or regulation (or immunity from the state) follows from how the group is classified, identifying RCAs as a property arrangement, corporation, voluntary association, or functional equivalent of local government is crucial. It determines whether government should intervene in these associations, and if so whether standards drawn from contract law, civil liability and tort law, corporate or constitutional law apply.

So an unusually broad cast of ideological elements come into play in defining RCAs, setting limits to their freedom, and assessing their moral consequences for members. They hold a mirror up to our complicated understanding of voluntary associations, corporate responsibility, and local community.

RCAs exhibit two different aspects of "community" as the term is used today, and inspire the hopes and criticisms that attach to each. By "community" political scientists typically mean local government, and in some respects RCAs are analogous to a municipality. They govern a territorially defined area; are involved in "zoning"; provide "public services" to residents and "tax" property to support them; and make and enforce "laws." Association boards of directors are elected, and RCAs have been represented as a new form of face-to-face local community: little democratic societies, potential schools of civic virtue.

This view of RCAs as functional equivalents of local government has a darker side. For they seem to replicate and reinforce the politics of privatism and self-interest. Charges that members lack civic spirit and have an attenuated sense of responsibility to the association community are confirmed when angry owners claim that the association violates their "rights" and resort to litigation. RCAs "take an American preference for private home ownership and, too often, turn it into an ideology of hostile privatism."[5] The grim accusation is that "in giving second place to personal relationships with neighbors and first place to economic interests, homeowners may be putting limits around the local fund of social trust."[6]

Homeowners' associations are said to lack public spirit vis-à-vis the wider local community as well. It is estimated that "in all probability, RCAs account for the most significant privatization of local government responsibilities in recent times." But what libertarians portray as exemplary "secession" from political control, critics decry as the "secession of the successful."[7] I will consider in what sense this is true. And whether "secession" is incongruent with our political ideology of local community. After all, law and public opinion authorize municipal officials to consider the property values and welfare of local residents only, to the exclusion of the interests of nonresidents and a broader public good. RCAs may disappoint hopes for an idealized democratic community of engaged and civic-minded citizens, yet be perfectly accurate reflections of "our localism."

RCAs have characteristics of community in a second sense, as "elective communities" designed to create a distinctive social environment. Members agree to common ownership and to regulations that reflect their values and preference for a certain way of life. So RCAs are *expected* to diverge from standard property and governance arrangements and from official public norms. The whole point is to create an exemplary private community. In America, self-improvement and reinvention are often the work not of individuals alone, as Thoreau would have it, but of groups. It is worth recalling that throughout U.S. history, states tolerated experimental communities in their midst and enforced the contractual arrangements on which their survival depended. Carol Weisbrod's legal history demonstrates that "the legislatures did not force the utopias to reimburse seceders; they did not refuse the [sexually nonconformist] communities permission to raise children . . . ; and they did not, even in the case of Oneida, move to close [them] down."[8] Freedom of contract was legitimizing and enabling, and state governments typically enforced the contractual arrangements on which their survival depended.

When an ex-Shaker demanded wages for his years of work in the community, arguing that the Shaker covenant (requiring celibacy as well as shared property) was "contrary to the genius and principles of free government, and therefore void," the court responded that "one of the blessings of a free government is, that under its mild influences, the citizens are at liberty to pursue that mode of life and species of employment best suited to their inclination and habits."[9] So state courts upheld the unconventional property and authority arrangements, divisions of labor and programs of education that marked classic nineteenth-century utopian communities, religious and secular, their heirs in the 1960s, and the New Age communes that continue to crop up today.

Few RCAs aim at social reform or spiritual purity or belong on any index of utopias—which is simply to say that developers are rarely visionary community-builders. (Though the ideas behind "new towns" like Reston, Virginia, *were* innovative. Retirement communities are an entirely unprecedented social form. And some housing developments are experiments in living designed by owner-founders.) Utopian or not, supporters of this face of RCAs want to preserve the possibility of creating distinctive private communities by minimizing state regulation. They insist on the enforceability of covenants and restrictions whether or not they conform to judicial standards of "reasonableness." As one commentator observes, liberals and communitarians should be prepared "to accommodate minor deviations from majoritarian norms as readily as we do more divergent subcultures."[10]

The negative view of this face of community has it that internal restrictions on conduct and the use of property are unwarranted violations of personal liberty. They undermine rather than enhance "the availability of neighborhoods conducive to human flourishing, where each individual's identity can be based on personal control of a unique place in a residential environment."[11] Far from being elective expressions of freedom, RCAs tend to be "custom-made" legal structures supplied by real estate developers.[12] Worse, "much of the suburban sprawl controlled by association-administered servitude regimes has become aesthetically undifferentiated and culturally desolate."[13] The corrective, on this view is to *increase* personal autonomy by *limiting* association autonomy—imposing stricter statutory and judicial constraints on their freedom to regulate the lives of members.

In addition to presenting two faces of community, hybrid RCAs are private corporations run by elected boards of directors, and in many respects RCA governance is closer to business management than government. True, they are not committed to profit maximization (though appreciation of property values is every owner's wish), and owners have longer-term economic stakes than investors in stock. Nonetheless, as owners they bear as much affinity to corporate shareholders as they to do members of a voluntary association or citizens of a municipality. Critics are appalled by the fact that residents "often behave like the stockholders in any large corporation, who neither know nor care about corporate affairs as long as their stock goes up. . . . This peripheral interest is especially disturbing when the corporate affairs in which people are disinterested are the workings of their own neighborhood."[14]

Corporate culture has created a distinctive and pervasive "morality of association" in the United States, and there is good reason to consider its relevant aspects. Little is gained by using "corporate" simply as invective. On reflection, "shareholder democracy" is a useful supplement to democratic theory for understanding members' experience of homeowners' associations. And debates about the social responsibility business corporations have to "stakeholders" can help us assess whether RCAs are democratically irresponsible, a form of "secession" from the wider political community.

So RCAs "flip" back and forth, exhibiting aspects of quasi-democratic local government, elective community, and corporate culture. Are RCAs democratizing or privatizing? Mainly infused with habits of business management or communitarianism? The several faces of associational life color members' experiences, and RCAs vividly demonstrate my proposition that the moral uses of pluralism turn not on the existence of diverse associations simply, but on the uses of association by men and women, personally and individually. The moral uses of this association are bound to be multiple and variable because RCAs are a veritable Rorschach test of associational life.

Private Property and Private Government

The proliferation of RCAs is a byproduct of a form of zoning that replaced lot-by-lot development with construction of large-scale, planned residential communities. Developers like this arrangement because clustering buildings on sites creates open spaces and room for swimming pools, playgrounds, community meeting places, and golf courses. These make the units desirable without making costs prohibitive. Moreover, developers can divest themselves of management responsibilities by turning the common property over to the association. Hence the view that "the entire phenomenon of homeowners' associations is based on private initiative, private money, private property, and private law concepts."[15]

The specific legal form that permits this development is a "servitude" on land that binds its use. The term is unfortunate because it lends rhetorical support to those who represent these arrangements as illiberal constraints on liberty, but the technical legal mechanism is less ominous than its name. Simply, potential investors value land more highly when incompatible uses of neighboring property are prohibited. "Obligations run with the land," that is, they restrict the use of surrounding property even in the face of ownership change. So durable "servitudes" replace a multitude of contracts among present owners. There is no limit on their life span either.

Along with servitude restrictions, RCA buyers acquire mandatory membership in the association that owns the common areas and imposes and enforces regulations on the use of property and on members' conduct. RCAs allow buyers to purchase an environment, not just a house. The legal structure of the community is contained in recorded "covenants, conditions, and restrictions" (CC&Rs). They establish a variant of the phenomenon Grant McConnell called "private government." They assign the association authority to levy regular assessments and to impose liens on property if members default. They lay out procedures for the election of an unpaid board of directors (typically with five to seven members) from among the owners, rules for quorums, proxy voting, and how often general meetings of the entire membership must be called. Most states impose a statutory requirement of a supermajority of all owners to alter the covenant or to approve new amendments, usually 67 percent, and a requirement of unanimous ratification to undo the servitude altogether. Finally, associations are legally required to allocate votes by ownership share.

Private government is brought home in the day-to-day lives of RCA residents through association rules and obligations, regular reminders that homeownership is also membership.

> Inherent in the . . . concept is the principle that to promote the health, happiness, and peace of mind of the majority of the unit owners since they are living in such close proximity and using facilities in common, each unit owner must give up a certain degree of freedom of choice which he [or she] might otherwise enjoy in separate, privately owned property.[16]

Architectural harmony and a distinctive physical environment are key elements, and restrictions aim at preserving physical congruence. There are regulations on altering building exteriors, parking vans or boats in driveways, clotheslines, exterior painting, the color and style of curtain liners or shades. RCAs may set limits on the use of yards, impose standards for landscaping, and require that garage doors be kept closed. Regulations also govern conduct in common areas: bans on liquor at the pool or shopping carts in the condominium lobby. RCAs may restrict the number of occupants in a unit, or pets (the bylaws of my mother's condominium permit dogs, but attempt to limit their size with a rule that they must be carried in elevators and hallways). Contrary to what we might expect, the chief source of internal conflict is not financial assessments, but rules regarding parking and pets!

Responses to association regulations vary dramatically. Some residents see them as a "small price to pay for protection from the potential misdeeds of one's neighbors." One owner observed: "Sure, they have some rules, like the one that regulates campers. But the community associations are here to protect our interests, not let the community deteriorate. That's not regulation; it's common sense. I don't know why anyone would look at it differently than I do, do you?" Another refers to his association board of directors as "little Hitlers," and an Urban Land Institute Report described residents as "unhappy, resentful, discouraged, and disillusioned about their associations . . . [and] what they think of as strait-jacket controls on their lives."[17]

The restrictiveness of regulations, the strictness with which they are enforced, and owners' tolerance for rule-following are all variable. Members are vulnerable to directors' discretion; there is ample opportunity for partiality and capriciousness. They are also vulnerable to intrusive communitarianism. Common ownership and the right of enforcement invite vigilantism, "condo commandos" on patrol for minor violations of rules.

The flip side of arbitrary and overzealous regulation, of course, is failure to enforce. Board members are typically untrained neophytes with no experience in governance. They are tentative and inept, or simply lax. It is not hard to see why they are often reluctant to exercise authority. They are neighbors who take hostile criticism (to say nothing of harassment and threats) personally; unlike government officials they are not well insulated from complaints. (Accounts of resident management of public housing also report that balancing efficient business and communal relations is prohibitively difficult.[18])

Association members have good reason to want to see rules complied with, though: predictability, stable property values, respect for communal norms. What critics characterize as "rigidly enforcing technical rules against people's use of their own homes" can be seen as protective legalism.

When news articles report overbearing directors and excitedly announce a "litigation explosion" in homeowners' associations, the unstated comparison is to ordinary homeownership, not to other sorts of residence. It is unclear that either RCA oversight or the level of conflict they produce is greater than for many tenants in private rental housing, mobile home parks, public housing, housing on military bases, or for private homes in historical districts.[19] Still, the subjective experience of restrictions on personal liberty in RCAs *is* distinctive. As hybrids they generate incompatible expectations for property and community, and inevitably create discrepancies between buyers' anticipations and actual experiences.

Bruce Ackerman has noted the gulf between the law's view of property as a bundle of rights with respect to a thing (none of which approximates absolute control or identifies a single person as owner) and the layperson's view of ownership as nearly absolute personal control.[20] Nowhere is this expectation more apparent than when it comes to *dominium* over one's home. Wherever possible homeowners use fences, hedges, yards, and gates to mark their boundaries. Polls show that Americans think of the single-family house as the most private form of housing, and owner control as an inviolable right.[21] At the extreme, "the isolated house came to represent the individual."[22]

In RCAs these expectations come up against the fact that private territorial rights are reduced. For in these associations "the institution of private property is . . . stood on its head: property rights, which tend to protect individuals from interference in the use of their property outside RCAs, facilitate such interference inside RCAs."[23] No wonder members may see the association as wielding unfair power over them. At the same time that property rights over one's home are contracted, collective property rights are expanded. Members purchase an environment, recall, so their definition of ownership and control extends to common areas and to the larger neighborhood, increasing occasions for conflict.

The stake RCA owners have in neighboring property is made graphic by the physical congruence of the community, and is formalized through common ownership. But a proprietary attitude toward surroundings is not unique to RCAs. In suburbia generally, a well-cared-for lawn has been described as "a kind of compulsory public housekeeping . . . a tax imposed by neighborhood consciousness." This is more than conformity to "bourgeois" taste. Many homeowners have put all their resources into buying a house, and its value depends on everybody else on the block. Neither inside RCAs nor outside do property values respect property lines. So RCA members complain to boards of directors about their neighbors just as homeowners complain to city officials.

> "We do take people to court, and that news gets around," says one local building inspector. "They say this is a city of laws, not people. You have to maintain some sort of balance in the neighborhood. . . . [T]he lady that complained . . . about the fellow with the seven cars in his yard, the lady next door to her has her house up for sale. And that motivated part of the complaint, although they've complained lots in the past."[24]

Insofar as RCA members see other owners as neighbors rather than business partners, they fall into familiar patterns. "Neighbor" is an intractably vague and undefined relation. Neighborhoods are idealized as sites of community warmth and shared values. In practice, dissension over the appearance and use of property and over day-to-day conduct is universal. *Anything* is sufficient cause: noise, dogs, fences, garbage, crab grass, parking, snubs and slights result in irritation, quarrels, verbal harassment, lawsuits, and violence. Every cause and occasion of conflict is compounded by expectations of privacy, and the fact that no strategy can eliminate the innumerable opportunities neighbors have for witting and unwitting invasion. They may impinge not only on our privacy but also on some people's guarded anonymity. Neighbors are implacably audible and visible, and may act or seem like treacherous informants.

We also know that the linchpin of neighbor relations everywhere is children. "Neighboring is not a lifelong activity, and it doesn't come naturally. Neighboring is almost wholly contingent on offspring in American society, and it frequently lasts only one long moment in the life cycle." As a measure of interaction, children take precedence over income, education, ethnicity, religion, and race.[25] Children are also the chief source of disagreement among neighbors. RCAs are subject to the 1988 amendments to the Fair Housing Act, which outlawed discrimination on the basis of age, with an exception for retirement communities. So they follow the usual pattern—a mix of residents at different stages of the life cycle increases conflict.

If RCAs seem to exacerbate these difficulties, it is because the association adds another layer to neighbor relations. Owners are conscious of their rights as members and join with the expectation that the use of neighboring property will conform to association rules. They also join with the expectation that effective mechanisms exist to enforce the rules and preserve harmony.

One critic of RCAs describes the plight of a new member whose neighbor created an eyesore by parking nonconforming vehicles in his yard. Instead of talking to the offender personally, the owner wanted the governing board to enforce the parking ban. His expectations were disappointed by a passive association board that refused to act. So he consulted a lawyer. "Consensual agreement between neighbors was not his goal," James Winokur comments. "By choosing instead to telegraph his complaint by lawyer, he was hoping to coerce removal."[26] Winokur's comment implies that the complaining owner's desire for "community" must have been hopelessly confused, or hypocritical. As if exercising membership rights chills community. As if the genuine communal impulse is to settle with one's neighbor personally (presumably amicably) or to withhold one's claim for the sake of amity.

Of course, members may refrain from exercising their rights in a spirit of generosity; indeed, RCAs generate innumerable, unrecordable occasions for self-restraint as well as informal ways of appreciating and rewarding it. Likely, exhibitions of generosity are reiterative. Occasions for this virtue and others are generated by associational life, but are not part of the morality of this association, which is predominantly legalistic. In fact, in this instance, the owner's action conformed to his status as RCA member, and may well have been guided by concern for communal relations, not just his own rights in the matter. Both keeping peace with his neighbor and holding the irresponsible board accountable are association goals.

In fact, Americans are generally reluctant to confront neighbors over transgressions. They prefer to complain anonymously to building inspectors, dog wardens, homeowner associations, and the police. They complain only if they do not have to identify themselves, because they do not want to generate lasting hostility or because they fear retaliation. We should recognize the democratic disposition that often underlies an appeal to third parties, too. We want to avoid taking on superior and censorious attitudes toward our neighbors, "and criticizing another's behavior certainly carries that connotation. Directly complaining can readily be seen as telling them what to do. When a personal show of superiority is culturally forbidden, substituting the impersonal, yet legitimate, authority of local government and homeowner boards makes much sense."[27]

Elective Community: Consent to Servitudes

When owners buy property in an RCA, they elect membership in a proprietary community and agree to its restrictions.[28] Economists argue that consent reflects consumer preferences, and that "covenants resolve a coordination problem."[29] Since municipal boundaries seldom coincide either with residents' differential demands for services or with their aversions to certain activities or land uses, homeowners' associations offer a set of services and amenities that better suit buyers' needs. Moreover, they apportion fees to benefits.[30] Economists also use market forces to explain the fairly standard array of RCA restrictions and obligations. Since developers have incentives to offer "the ideal mix of burdens and benefits," the argument goes, the proliferation of RCAs indicates that buyers want more in the way of mutual restrictions on conduct and use than the common law of nuisance or trespass provides.[31] They "expressly purchase quality control that is generally unavailable in the public sector. In return, RCA members subject themselves to control without the checks that must accompany the exercise of public power."[32]

Dissenters from this market analysis concede that ownership in an association is a matter of consent, not force or fraud, but deny that it indicates preference. For one thing, choice is undercut by the fact that many buyers are apparently unaware of the extent of their obligations. Even with explicit notice, they may not review documents written in complex legal language, or understand them if they do, which is why "many of the important intergovernmental issues regarding RCAs and citizenship are consumer protection issues."[33]

Beyond that, ideal market assumptions about options, mobility, and information do not hold. Regulatory oversight by state real estate agencies and federal secondary mortgage agencies make it easier for developers to conform to bureaucratic tastes and use standard forms than not, for example.[34] So, at best, RCAs accommodate some low common denominator of consumer choice, or "adaptive preferences."

Of course, limited options, the "bundling" problem that requires us to accept restrictions we do not want in order to get some we do, "ulysses contracts" in which we forgo short-run choice for a longer-run good characterize agreements of all kinds. For that matter, they characterize traditional homeownership. A recent study confirms that in the United States homeownership is an enduring personal goal and that prospective buyers are willing to compromise their ideal for smaller, affordable dwellings. They want to own a home per se more than they want to simply improve the quality or size of their housing.[35]

This shifts attention from the conditions of consent to RCAs to the broader question of why "there is *no* second most popular choice" to owning a single-family house, even among people over sixty-five, unmarried singles, families renting larger dwellings than one they could afford to own, and young non-apartment renters.[36] Over 85 percent of Americans surveyed give owning a home as the primary component of the good life—above an automobile, a happy marriage, an interesting or high-paying job, even above good health! They choose a home and neighborhood, within or outside RCAs, principally because it is affordable. For every group that can imagine the possibility of owning, renting is considered "temporary, transient, and socially undesirable."[37] Why?

There are disadvantages to renting. The private rental market may not have sufficiently high standards at reasonable prices. The public rental sector means-tests applicants; access is retricted to those with the lowest incomes and is stigmatized as a form of welfare. Tenancy is insecure. (Though these may be consequences rather than causes of the overwhelming preference for ownership.) Another impetus is the fact that suburbs have become the locus of jobs (67 percent of suburban employed are commuting to suburban workplaces), moves are made for employment reasons, and the suburban rental market may be so tight that all those who can are driven to own.

But homeownership in the United States is related to entrenched *public* values and policy, as well as private preferences. Federal tax policy and the financial institutions that make the benefits of owning readily accessible encourage buying. There is also a connection between homeownership and national social policy. The point of accrued equity (and potential appreciation of property value) is that as the mortgage is paid, owners can borrow against it for personal consumption, college tuition, retirement, and so on.[38] The worth of this asset to us is tied to the sort of goods and services we must privately pay for over the course of a lifetime. In a comparative country study Jim Kemeny found a correlation between high levels of homeownership and low government involvement in the provision of social services.[39]

Full information and a perfect market would not appease critics of RCAs, who see the home as a unique zone of enhanced liberty and individual flourishing, and consent to servitudes as "escape from freedom." From this standpoint, RCA membership is evidence of "pathology in the process of preference formation" and "nonautonomous preferences," and irrational choice should be grounds for legally restricting servitudes.[40] Buyers demonstrate "the narcotic effects of affluence upon the culture."[41] The argument turns on the harm individuals sustain by subjecting themselves to an authoritarian regime:

> The central importance of home to an individual's sense of self, and to the shaping of that individual's unique history and future by the expression of his or her own distinctive personality, requires that—presumptively—each resident should control the details of his or her own residential uses.

The proposed solution is for courts and state legislatures to limit association autonomy, and to overturn even standard RCA restrictions, from bans on pets to the duration of covenants.

As a measure of whether a restriction on the use of property is justifiable and legally enforceable "the central importance of home to an individual's sense of self" offers little guidance. "Sense of self" is hopelessly boundless. No restriction is trivial if the stake is personal identity. The requirement to install a wooden rather than metal swing set may be an irritation, but is it an inhibition of "distinctive personality"? That is precisely the charge:

> respect for, and promotion of individual identity requires protection for each resident's right, for example, to determine when he or she takes out the trash, to select the color of the family swing set, to fly the American (or other) flag from the balcony, to choose his or her own interior curtains and liners, and to decide how many sixteenths of an inch thick the plexiglass shall be on a balcony enclosure.[42]

We could logically infer from this extravagance that the distinctive personalities of renters everywhere are crippled. Even as a purely subjective matter, the expressivist view of homeownership is overstated. The American penchant for public signatures—bumper stickers, T-shirts with slogans, yard sculptures—has many outlets. None are universal. For some people, even property in one's home is a fungible investment.

At a minimum, the connection between ownership and identity is mediated by established expectations. Jeremy Bentham described the dynamic:

> Every part of my property may have, in my estimation, besides its intrinsic value, a value of affection.... Everything about it represents to my eye that part of myself which I have put into it—those cares, that industry, that economy which denied itself present pleasures to make provision for the future. Thus our property becomes a part of our being, and cannot be torn from us without rending us to the quick.[43]

Bentham's concern was the forcible alienation of property through revolutionary changes in property law, government expropriation, or voiding of contracts. He did not think in this connection of restrictions on use imposed through a formal agreement. To his mind, contract was a principal *source* of legitimate expectations.

Margaret Jane Radin has considered what forms of property are so bound up with personhood that they make "commodification" inappropriate. Unique and irreplaceable personal property qualifies, but what about the property arrangements of an RCA? Radin suggests that the distinctive forms and social environments of an elective community are expressive. RCA controls over the use and alienation of property should be seen as models of the positive connection that can exist between property and personality rather than as restrictions on individual liberty and flourishing. Her chief hesitancy in commending this form of property is concern for future generations. In some areas virtually all new housing is in RCAs, and since servitudes run in perpetuity, subsequent purchasers may be bound by the "dead hand" of original promissors. Present liberty of contract conflicts with future markets, at least potentially. Homeowners' associations are vehicles of personhood insofar as they do not "create monolithic exclusions that make it impossible for minorities and dissenters to form communities and live out their alternative visions," and "are such that those who live under servitudes can freely go elsewhere if they find them onerous."[44]

Disillusioned members have the same recourse as owners and residents of a municipality who find their local government, taxes, or neighbors unabidable—they can leave, keeping in mind that relocation is costly and people are not equally mobile.[45] Exit is not the only option. Elected boards of directors and amendments to CC&Rs give members a voice, though changes require a supermajority vote. Members also find "voice" through litigation. They challenge directors' interpretation of the original covenant and the enforceability of new restrictions in everything from expulsion to disapproval of architectural plans. They demand judicial intervention in associational life. Which is why, "it is through resolution of these disputes that the legal system reveals the value we ultimately place on autonomous associations."[46]

Unreasonable Rules and Judicial Intervention

In deciding whether an association rule is enforceable courts look beyond the fact of consent. Should judges defer to association regulations as interpreted and applied by boards of directors? Or should they actively interpret covenants and restrictions themselves in light of association purposes? Or should they apply an independent standard of "reasonableness" to association rules? Or some other external criterion?

Most jurisdictions use the standard "enforceable so long as they are reasonable." "Reasonableness" is a ubiquitous legal adjective. It is not self-defining (consider the singularly unhelpful decision: "If a rule is reasonable the association can adopt it; if not, it cannot"[47]). Although the rulings of state courts are far from uniform, overall the doctrine that has emerged from civil case law upholds RCA regulations that provide a reasonable means to further the collective "health, happiness, and enjoyment of life" of owners. Unreasonable regulations are "arbitrary or capricious," violate public policy, or bear no rational relationship to the purposes of the association as set out in enabling statutes and bylaws.[48]

A typical case involves an appeal from the judgment of an architectural review committee. Association regulations normally provide only very general guidelines for construction, such as "conformity to the harmony of external design and location in relation to surrounding structures and topography." Courts look at the reasonableness of the review committee's decision in light of the building patterns already established.[49]

In other cases the "reasonableness" standard may do the work of constitutional review, as in *Cashio v. Shoriak*, a 1986 Louisiana case involving limitations on speech. Owners appealed an association order enjoining them from erecting "We have a right to clean water" signs in their yards. The covenant contained a provision prohibiting signs of any kind, but made exceptions for small professional signs and advertisements for property for sale or rent. The court ruled that a literal interpretation of the "no signs" clause would lead to absurd results—to removing "season's greetings" signs, "beware of dog" signs, political candidate signs, and resident name signs.[50] The exceptions listed in the bylaws indicate that the purpose was not to preserve the beauty of the neighborhood from the litter of signs generally, they ruled, but to keep most *commercial* signs out of the subdivision.

Challenges to reasonableness review come from several directions. Some critics find it insufficiently protective of personal liberty and recommend a judicially enforced "antirestrictions policy." What standard should guide review of RCA regulations then? One proposal would allow latitude for restrictions in common areas but not when it comes to personal choices within the home—keeping pets or home offices, for example. Alternatively, restrictions would be permissible only if they were designed to prevent "harmful spillovers" arising from the use of property, such as noise or traffic.[51] The trouble is, neither view is determinate when it comes to judging the bulk of restrictions—on aesthetics, say, or uses of property most owners think impact on neighborhood ambience or property values, which is the principal reason for covenants in the first place.

Strong supporters of the elective character of RCAs have the opposite fear: that judicial review of the "reasonableness" of regulations provides an opening for the imposition of external standards of reasonableness, restricting the liberty of those who elect communal restrictions. The "no signs" ruling against the association board is a case in point. Indeed, judicial oversight seems to provide an opening for the imposition of criteria more stringent than reasonableness.[52] Defenders of association autonomy worry about "an apparent invitation to Lochnerian activism" (curiously, since *Lochner* does not invoke activism generally but judicial defense of existing property rights, which is precisely what they advocate here).[53]

This apprehension is excited more by theoretical debate than by actual rulings, however. The tendency is to defer to the rules promulgated by the association. Courts may be reluctant "to find that unit owners have ceded more power over the use of their property and their actions than is necessary to serve the ends for which the condominium exists."[54] But the language of CC&Rs grants associations broad rule-making power. And the pattern of state court decisions "tends to honor the suggested principle of greater private associational autonomy."[55] Thus, in *Hidden Harbour Estates v. Norman* a unit owner tried to enjoin enforcement of a regulation adopted by the board and ratified by a two to one vote of owners prohibiting liquor in or around the clubhouse. The Florida court upheld the new regulation, citing the association's authority to adopt rules governing the use of common areas: condominium unit owners "comprise a little democratic sub society of necessity more restrictive as it pertains to use of condominium property than may be existent outside."[56]

Courts are reluctant to apply *any* test, even reasonableness, to the original covenant. In *Hidden Harbour Estates v. Basso* (1981) the Florida court distinguished use restrictions set forth in the master deed from others:

> [The original] restrictions are clothed with a very strong presumption of validity which arises from the fact that each individual unit owner purchases his unit knowing of and accepting the restrictions imposed. . . . Although case law has applied the word "reasonable" to determine whether such restrictions are valid, this is not the appropriate test. . . . Indeed a use restriction in a *declaration of condominium* may have a certain degree of unreasonableness to it, and yet withstand attack in the courts. If it were otherwise, a unit owner could not rely on the restrictions found in the declaration . . . since such restrictions would be in a potential condition of continuous flux.[57]

A hypothetical example that crops up in the legal literature is an association formed by Orthodox Jews whose condominium covenant stipulates that males must wear yarmulkes in common areas on holy days. The consensus of commentators is that courts should enforce this covenant in deference to the unanimous wishes of the original members.[58]

Yet another line of criticism attacks the standard of reasonableness as judged by association purposes from a democratic perspective, as a limitation on self-government. On this view, RCA restrictions on personal liberty are justifiable if they result from open-ended and "conversation-inducing" deliberations. Process is key: whether rules are arrived at "deliberately and socially," as a result of "dialogic inquiry." "Reasonableness," in short, is deduced from the vision of "a society committed to the ideal of community"—specifically, democratic community as a deliberative forum. On this view, courts are assigned the role of monitoring and correcting for the tendency of RCAs to become "nomic bunkers" by enforcing an open-ended dialogic reasonableness rule.[59]

The reasonableness test courts actually apply to RCA restrictions shapes the internal life of these associations to a limited extent. But from the point of view of the actual *experience* of membership, the substance of reasonableness review may be less important than the point at which *any* test is applied. Is it used to judge whether a restriction serves a legitimate association purpose overall? Or is it used to judge whether the association should be permitted to enforce its restriction given the facts specific to an objecting homeowner? Thus, a prohibition against parking a truck, camper, trailer, or boat in carports may be reasonable given RCA purposes, but held unreasonable as applied to a new pickup truck with camper shell the owner uses for personal transportation. Or, a court may refuse to enforce a legitimate ban against satellite dishes in an instance where the dish is not visible to other residents or the public.

The answer can be crucial for the tenor of associational life and the dispositions it cultivates in members. It may affect whether associations encourage habits of meeting obligations, or encourage individual owners to seek personal exemptions. It contributes to whether association governance will incline to strict enforcement or to discretion. It is the contest over the merits of legalism brought home.

The argument was joined in 1994 in *Nahrstedt v. Lakeside Village Condo*. A pet owner claimed the prohibition against dogs and cats was "unreasonable" as applied to her because she kept her three noiseless cats, Ruffin, Muffin, and Fluffin, indoors. The majority agreed with the association's position: reasonableness must be determined by reference to the community as a whole, not case by case. Restrictions on pets are rationally related to the health, sanitation, and noise concerns of residents of a high-density condominium project.[60] In short, courts should uphold the board's decision "unless [the] owner could show that the burdens it imposed on affected property so substantially outweighed benefits that it should not have been enforced against *any owner*."[61]

Passions ran high in *Nahrstedt*. The dissent came close to accepting the majority's challenge, implying that all covenants restricting pets are unreasonable, and putting the full weight of popular culture in the balance. They invoked not only the universality of pets but also the American dream of owning a home of one's own:

> Taking into consideration the well established and long-standing historical and cultural relationship between human beings and their pets and the value they impart . . . enforcement of the restriction unduly burdens the use of land for those deprived of their companionship. [And,] with no demonstrated or discernible benefit, the majority arbitrarily sacrifice the dream to the tyranny of the "commonality."

The dissent's chief legal point, however, was that enforcing the "no pets" rule in *this* case is "patently arbitrary." "The balance of benefit and burden is disproportionate and unreasonable" where the benefits of pets can be had without nuisance to others, indeed without others even being aware of their presence.

The *Nahrstedt* dissenters were incensed at the "narrow, indeed chary, view of the law that eschews the human spirit in favor of arbitrary efficiency."[62] This opinion illustrates the view that upholding restrictions unless they are unreasonable for the community as a whole is unjustifiable if individual consideration, neighborly tolerance, flexible decision-making, and face-to-face communitarianism are valued. Can anything be said for judicial deference to association rules and support for limiting discretion in applying them against members?

The goal is not "arbitrary efficiency" but preserving the "social fabric" of the community.[63] Plainly, the particulars of a decision regarding three noiseless cats are not likely to threaten the association's viability. But the particulars of a decision regarding silent indoor cats *are* likely to produce a deluge of petitions for exceptions and costly and prolonged legal challenges.

More important, as a matter of institutional competence RCA boards are ill-equipped to weigh the burdens and benefits of enforcing restrictions against individual violators. Directors are uncompensated amateur managers. Wavering, hesitance to act, and inclinations to favoritism are endemic. Directors' decisions are always vulnerable to charges of partiality and unevenness, even when restrictions are universal and categorical. If boards must estimate the reasonableness of applying a legitimate rule in each case, occasions for challenging their judgment multiply. So do occasions for directors to indulge their reluctance to enforce compliance, which is certain to arouse unpleasantness. So judicial support for across-the-board enforcement also serves to strengthen directors' resolve, which can be critical for the stability of associational life. Each turnover in the membership of a board of directors brings in tentative new officers; it can take years to settle a problem, and conflict only increases when directors have "no backbone." Those who favor discretion and friendly exceptions are disinclined to appreciate the difficulties of RCA governance. Antilegalism is the view from outside. Trust and cooperation are facilitated, rather than stomped out, by regulations that secure expectations and reduce risk.

This is a compelling argument with regard to homeowners' associations, which are defined by a covenant that creates a distinctive environment. That is their whole purpose. Recall that religious associations do not always conform to formal legal norms and procedures in exercising authority over members or dealing with employees. And, for the most part, legislatures and courts do not intervene to enforce standards of "reasonableness" there, not even the association's own constitution. As *Serbian Diocese* showed, "it is the essence of religious faith that ecclesiastical decisions are reached and are to be accepted as matters of faith whether or not rational or measurable by objective criteria. . . . [S]ecular notions of 'fundamental fairness' or impermissible objectives, are therefore hardly relevant."[64] In contrast, environmental restrictions define RCAs, and owners consent to CC&Rs with the assurance that they may rely on them. Restrictions on the use of property and conduct in common areas (and sometimes at home) is the association's whole rationale. The elderly are promised that children will not move into neighboring units. Buyers who purchase architecturally uniform units have recourse when neighbors or association review committees violate established expectations. The preservation of property value is inseparable from stability, too; one court held a homeowners' association liable for failure to enforce its covenants.[65]

Covenants that run in perpetuity binding future owners, supermajority rules for amending CC&Rs, a deferential judicial rule of reasonableness in interpreting covenants are mechanisms designed to protect the integrity of these private communities. Stability is also underscored by the fiduciary responsibility of association directors. It provides a thread linking the elective and corporate faces of these associations.

Corporate Culture and Fiduciary Responsibility

Property owners in RCAs purchase not just a home but an environment, which requires ongoing management and business decisions: financing, asset and property management, assessment of fees, provision of services, insurance, employee relations, and so on.[66] The success of an association is said to depend on how well owners make the transition from the initial phase before the developer turns association government over to them, to electing a board that takes on the management role. (It is wryly reported that "upon turnover of the association to the unit owners, the first three things they do are raise the assessment, fire the manager, and sue the developer."[67]) The managerial face of the association is reinforced by owners' expectations of carefree living, which is why they may look on the RCA as an expanded set of services they have bought.

Their assumption that the elected board will run the association is confirmed by the legal status of directors as corporate officers, bound by duties to shareholders as defined by the Corporations Code. Because RCA directors are unit owners, we do not find the division of ownership and control that exists in business corporations, and association directors have more direct responsibility for management than the typical corporate board—which has been described as "merely the parsley on the fish."[68] But the fact that directors are unpaid owners does not eliminate opportunities for self-dealing, fraud, or negligence, or exonerate them from liability for breach of duty.

There are good reasons for applying corporate law to these associations, beginning with the business judgment rule, which says that a director must perform duties in good faith, in a manner he or she believes is in the best interests of the corporation, and with such care as an ordinarily prudent person in a like position would use under similar circumstances. The rule gives directors latitude in handling corporate affairs, in recognition of the fact that "the hindsight of the judicial process is an imperfect device for evaluating business decisions."[69] Courts avoid second-guessing corporate officers, then, but the standard is not empty. Since procedures are often evidence of good faith, the business judgment rule requires association boards to follow the procedures set out in their bylaws. If none are provided, they may require the equivalent of "sunshine" and open meeting laws, notice to members of meetings, and an opportunity to be heard.

A Florida court ruled that a "straw vote" was insufficient to amend an association covenant; it "would not be conducted with the same solemnity, deliberation and debate we would expect from a campaign to amend a declaration . . . in which the very property rights and obligations of the parties are formally spelled out." In some cases RCA boards have had to show that they took account of alternatives before coming to a management decision.[70] The business judgment rule also imposes an affirmative duty of care, so that directors may be liable for failure to act as well as mismanagement.[71]

The most important element of corporate responsibility from the standpoint of the morality of association is the "relentless and supreme" duty of undivided loyalty to owners.[72] The duty of loyalty prohibits self-dealing, but more to the point here, it prohibits weighing the interests of third parties over owners'. It governs the allocation of corporate resources: toward maximizing profits in the case of business corporations and toward preserving the value and stability of property in RCAs. In short, directors' duty of loyalty is to "shareholders" not "stakeholders."[73] RCA members have sued developers who allowed outsiders to use recreational facilities reserved for owners.[74]

Nothing prevents *consideration* of the interests of other constituencies. But there are virtually no guidelines for balancing public interests or charitable actions against costs to owners. I return shortly to the question of RCA responsibility vis-à-vis the wider community, and whether these associations amount to "secession." For now, my point is that the heart of the board's fiduciary duty is maintaining the value of owners' property in accord with association purposes. Because value in RCAs is closely tied to covenant enforcement, directors are accountable to owners for a duty of stability as well as fiscal responsibility.[75]

The fiduciary duties of RCA boards circumscribe the space for association self-government. So does the RCA's legal structure; association governance and voting schemes are designed for stability and enforcement, not for an "unexpected and unbargained-for right to promulgate *future* regulations and restrictions."[76] RCA directors are corporate officers, not political representatives of the owners who elect them. Democratic critics of RCAs see covenants as the weight of a dead hand on a potentially lively, self-governing community. They regret that "a culture of nonparticipation" is rooted in the very structure of these developments: "the chief obstacle to association democracy is the managerial mind-set."[77] They want to transform these associations from scenes of corporate management into arenas of democratic engagement.[78]

Even if lively democratization is desirable, more than one model is available. RCAs are hybrid associations. Should they be made congruent with the model of local government? Or should they follow the model of shareholder democracy? I will argue that neither would transform RCAs into schools of civic virtue because American law and political ideology regarding both corporations and local government are conflicted about democratic participation and responsibility. The interesting question, then, is not whether homeowners' associations are sufficiently congruent with democratic practices but what they reveal about these practices and about ourselves.

Which Congruence: Shareholder Democracy or Local Community?

In business corporations, directors are elected by shareholders, but the separation of ownership from corporate control lodges effective power in management. As a result, both managers and directors are imperfectly responsive to stockholders and the present version of "shareholder democracy" has been described as "nominal, tainted, coerced, or impoverished."[79] The proposed corrective is enhanced owner responsibility. Edward Johnson III, principal owner of Fidelity Mutual Fund, wrote a letter to investors warning against passive ownership in terms that echo democratic theorists' concerns about membership in RCAs:

> Owning stock and not being able to assert your ownership rights is like owning a piece of land over which you have little control. If you can't walk on it, garden it, put a fence around it, or build on it, it isn't worth much. If American corporations are owned by stockholders who can't assert their ownership rights eventually the ownership may not be worth much either. . . . They must read and vote proxies, understand the factors affecting the company's business, and make their views on important issues known to managers and directors . . . put pressure on directors to be more responsive to shareholder concerns about long-term strategies and the productive use of corporate assets. If directors are consistently unresponsive . . . they should be voted against.[80]

Johnson does not advocate activism by small stockholders, who are typically interested in short-run profitability rather than long-run operations.[81] Large institutional investors should supervise company affairs, and Johnson would require them to vote with the same "care, skill, prudence, and diligence" with which they trade. That is, to act like permanent owners—like homeowners in RCAs, who have incentives to monitor directors and to encourage them to take a long-term view.

Notice that directors remain accountable to *owners* in shareholder democracy, not to the wider public. Nothing suggests that reformed corporate government would incline to "corporate altruism," which is why those who want to see business decisions made for the benefit of constituencies besides shareholders propose other schemes, such as independent outside directors or "general public representatives" on corporate boards.[82] Arguments for greater par-

ticipation in homeowners' associations focus on the responsiveness of association governance to owners, too, not responsibility to the wider community.
And as in business corporations, voting rights in RCAs are required by law to
conform to economic share. These voting arrangements are our best indicator
of the association's hybrid character, and they help explain why it is difficult
to settle on a model of democratic participation and responsibility.

Distribution of votes by ownership stake and the practice of proxy voting
reflect the RCA's character as a corporation and owners' status as shareholders. It is clear from the legal requirement that both fees and benefits be appor-
tioned by ownership share, that RCAs are not redistributive. Unlike RCAs,
however, business corporations rarely use supermajority voting rules because
shareholders' interests are assumed to be the same. Since RCA members have
interests other than price, including life style and the overall character of the
community, amendments to association rules are more likely to upset a minority than ordinary business decisions. Supermajority voting rules are a practical
solution. Richard Epstein refers to association bylaws as a constitution.[83]

The reason for excluding nonowner residents (both tenants and adult family
members who are not sole owners) from voting is that while they have a stake
in association affairs (including an economic stake, given the cost of moving
if rents increase or services decline), they do not have a unity of interest with
owners. For example, tenants may not wish to see property values increase, if
the consequence is rising rents. If the proportion of tenants were large enough,
their preferences for restrictions on conduct and use could determine the com-
plexion of association life, to say nothing of owners' assessments. Of course,
owners' economic interests diverge too. Absentee owners are less interested in
quality-of-life improvements than resident owners and tenants, and they can
defeat measures for fee increases or amendments by proxy vote, or simply by
not voting at all. On any given issue, the lineup of interests may cut across the
class of shareholders and stakeholders. Nonetheless, the voting scheme mandated by state law assumes that intensity of interest in association affairs varies
with economic stake.[84]

In religious associations, and many secular voluntary associations as well,
authority can be distributed in every imaginable way: inheritance, hierarchy,
oligarchical arrangements, and decision-making by consensus to name a few.
Proponents who see RCAs as elective communities advocate changing the
statutory requirements on voting to allow for greater flexibility. They do not
suggest eliminating votes altogether, but would allow them to be allocated in
different ways. Robert Ellickson adopts Charles Tiebout's well-known thesis
that if there is competition among local governments and residents are mobile,
local expenditures on various kinds of services will be efficient. He applies this
thesis to RCAs, modifying it by counting governance itself as a consumer
good.[85] "Different voting systems accord different weight to the competing
interests of allocative efficiency, administrative efficiency, progressive redis-

tribution, and participation."[86] Some associations might permit tenants to vote on regulations but not on assessments, for example, or give all residents votes but weigh owners' more. Potential owners and tenants could go "shopping" for the association with the preferred voting system, increasing "consumer-voter" satisfaction and consensus within RCAs.

Variability is impermissible in local government elections today. Before the Supreme Court extended its Fourteenth Amendment equal protection ruling in *Reynolds v. Sims* to municipalities, states allocated votes in proportion to property tax assessments or land area, and in some cases on the basis of whether or not residents are directly affected by a governmental decision. But in a line of cases beginning with *Avery v. Midland County*, the Court held that only a compelling state interest could permit restrictions on grounds other than residence, age, and citizenship.[87] The justification for one resident, one vote in local government is that the distribution of interests and opinions is not property-bound; parents with children in public schools who see education as a budget priority do not distribute themselves along renter/owner lines, for example.

Even if local decisions *do* have differential economic effects, courts are less concerned about diluting the vote of those with more substantial interests by *inclusion* than about protecting the politically weak by prohibiting *exclusion*. There is no constitutional right to either local government or a municipal vote, but where a local franchise exists, the rule is one person, one vote.

At bottom (and in contrast to Tiebout), the right of residents to participate in decision-making, not their right of exit, is ground for local autonomy. Notice that justices are not concerned about the effects of local decisions on nonresidents who have no voice, however, which is why the residency standard may be more important than one person, one vote for local democracy, a point to which I return.

Democratic critics of RCAs want to eliminate incongruence between homeowners' associations and local government by enforcing the *Avery* decision there.[88] A constitutional strategy is unworkable, though. RCAs are not considered the functional equivalent of towns, and the Fourteenth Amendment does not apply. Besides, the main thrust of arguments for democratizing RCAs is not doctrinal. The principal goal is maximizing participation, which plays no part in judicial rulings extending the franchise.[89] In contrast to the case for greater shareholder democracy, the case for greater participation by RCA members has nothing to do with balancing long-term interests in value against short-term profitability. In contrast to Ellickson's proposal for variable voting schemes, the case for democratizing RCAs does not aim at consumer satisfaction. The argument for turning passive association members/shareholders into active citizens is moral: RCAs are potential schools of civic virtue.

Involvement in power changes individuals, the argument goes, "giving them a practical notion of the needs of social life and an interest in the welfare of their community."[90] Although political science has little to say about the effect of forms of tenure (tenancy versus ownership) or of voting schemes on political participation, the assumption at work here is that the franchise is a principal impetus to involvement, and that involvement is morally improving. "The practice of basing suffrage on home ownership instead of residence affects the internal political dynamics of RCAs in a way that diminishes their capacity to act as facilitators of civic virtue."[91]

Jane Mansbridge has commented on waning interest in the educative effects of participation, which she sees "ghettoized in the feminist and ecological movements, and faded even there."[92] Some democratic theorists have seized on RCAs as another potential scene of participation. It is not hard to see why. Their emergence coincided with a wave of enthusiasm for local participation in neighborhood organizations, block associations, federal model cities programs, and the "new town movement" (which was said to be "our best opportunity for experimentation" in "grass-roots democracy.")[93] Preoccupation with reviving local participation is a perfectly comprehensible response to the decline of political party machines, which had established neighborhood clubs and organized the local provision of goods in return for political support. Or to the increasing size of municipal government and consolidation of school districts. Or as part of a larger preoccupation with decentralization.

In each case, localism is thought to increase participation, and participation to create and reinforce democratic virtue. Michael Sandel reiterates the theme: "As the republican tradition taught, local attachments can serve self-government by engaging citizens in a common life beyond their private pursuits, by forming the habit of attending to public things."[94]

In this spirit, Gerald Frug has argued that by reducing the scale of decision-making we might meet "the need for the individual to gain control over those portions of his life now determined by others." He cast cities as "an alternative form of decentralized power in our society," as scenes of enhanced democratic participation and "public freedom." Invoking the free chartered cities of medieval Europe that combined the characteristics of economic, communal, and political associations, as well as early American towns Frug observes that: "both medieval and colonial towns were established by people who broke away from existing social restraints and who formed relatively closed societies with new social structures." Today, in contrast, cities have been reduced to state-created municipal corporations, administrative arms of state government. Frug wants to restore their legal and economic autonomy: cities should be given "the kind of power wielded by those entities that still exercise genuine decentralized power—private corporations."[95]

In short, democratic hopes for participatory RCAs are a spillover of enthusiasm for local self-government. Homeowners' associations are compact and votes count, a critical feature for those who see scale as the determinant of participation. Elected directors who serve without pay stimulate rotation in office. RCA business could be expected to engage members since it touches home. And in an optimistic leap from personal transformation to other-regardingness, participation can enhance commonality.[96] "The structure of the homeowners' association could unwittingly provide a mechanism for reversing the anti-community trends of the last century."[97]

Participatory hopes for RCAs have been disappointed. On average only 11 percent of members participate in association governance in some form, and in a significant number of associations too few people run for board of directors to fill the open seats. RCAs permit proxy voting in order to achieve a quorum, but one study shows that 30 percent of associations were unable to get a majority of owners to either vote or assign proxies in their previous election. (The turnout is no better in local government elections; in Mansbridge's study of a small Vermont town with an adult population of just 350, only one-third of voters attended town meetings.)[98] Fifty-three percent of RCA board members rated membership as apathetic, and 84 percent of residents responding to a survey in Florida thought that owner apathy is the biggest problem facing community associations.[99]

This should not be surprising. Inasmuch as membership is mandatory with ownership, RCAs are involuntary associations, a fact that should have dampened participatory expectations.[100] And contra Ellickson, there is no evidence that buyers anticipate or are motivated by opportunities for self-government. The assumption that participation in RCAs is gripping because matters touch home disregards the existence of competing centers of decision on issues like taxation and spending that affect the value of one's home and character of one's neighbors, schools, and so on. Besides, the sort of social problems and political conflicts that typically mobilize voters are absent.

A different picture emerges, however, if we focus less on RCA members as voters and more on volunteer boards of directors. With a typical board of five people and something on the order of 150,000 homeowners' associations, aproximately 625,000 people serve on governing boards. Many more if we take rotation into account. Barton and Silverman observe that at least initially directors often lack an understanding of RCAs as political communities. That is, they do not recognize disagreements as inevitable, owners as having both divergent interests and strong expectations about their rights, and continuous negotiation over property rights as a normal process in private government.[101] Once directors see the RCA as a political entity in these terms, and make efforts to garner support and participation from members, the association has fewer problems. RCAs provide education for directors in maintaining compliance and managing conflict, then.

They are also channels to involvement in local government. A 1990 survey found 70 percent of board members responding reported that they regularly monitored local government actions; 63 percent had personally attended at least one local meeting on behalf of the RCA during the preceding year; 78 percent said someone from their association had called or written to local officials on behalf of the association during the past year. RCA boards are incubators for political organizers. Directors know their neighborhoods, and local candidates turn to them to head get-out-the-vote efforts, and so on.[102] These democratizing effects are not universal, of course; directors may fail abjectly or suffer burnout, and owners often serve on boards for highly idiosyncratic reasons, not civic-mindedness. Though democratic education goes on nonetheless.

But democratic critics are concerned with general membership participation in association affairs, not leadership, and the restricted RCA franchise is just one incongruence they would change. The constitution-like status of CC&Rs, with their supermajority rules for amending covenants, also limit the scope of members' "voice," inspiring proposals to allow alteration by simple majoritarianism. The thought is that greater control is an incentive to participation. Thus, Winokur would overturn the indefinite life span of servitude regimes and legislate an automatic expiration of restrictions, in hopes of facilitating "consensual modification." He also proposes the creation of "enforcement pods" within large developments. Small areas (twelve units) of contiguous neighbors could unanimously change restrictions and create a neighborhood "character" distinct from the overall regime. (Winokur is vague about the degree of internal variation permissible; a "pod" might loosen restrictions on basketball hoops, for example, but not architectural style.) "While the promise of these smaller groupings cannot necessarily fulfill our most romanticized yearnings for community, we may regain something of what seems to have been lost in the modern age."[103]

Enthusiasm for face-to-face negotiations over association restrictions is misguided. It does not factor in the time and administrative costs of "associational federalism." Or consider that in a context combining "internal political debate with a culture that equates property ownership with sole rights to determine its use," the need to reach provisional majoritarian agreements about regulations would likely *multiply* occasions for conflict and increase dissatisfied minorities.[104] To say nothing of the fact that even socially homogeneous RCAs evolve their own snobberies and mysterious divisions. The painful politics of petty differences emerges in Fitzgerald's description of the "wrong side of the tracks" in one retirement community, with its insidious snubs and retaliations.[105]

If we concede that agreement is most likely on issues that relate directly to property values rather than infinitely negotiable matters of use and conduct, and that long-term strategies for value and security of expectation are best provided by stable covenants and the fiduciary duty of boards, then Winokur's plan seems not only burdensome but frivolous.

It is possible to turn this whole argument about RCA self-government on its head. That is, to see homeowners' associations as exemplary scenes of self-government in contrast to the degree of control citizens actually exercise over local government. Instead of seeing corporate RCAs as potential local communities and democratizing them, local neighborhoods should be seized on as a potential proprietary association and privatized.[106] Citizens should become shareholders. "The paradox is that a form of privatization is needed in order for city streets, at least, to fulfill the function of public property."[107] From this perspective, the vector of change should go in exactly the opposite direction.

Robert Nelson has made the populist case for the conversion of ordinary neighborhoods into homeowners' associations, with a view to enhancing self-government. Familiar forms of voluntarism in neighborhood groups and community development organizations, block watches and cleanup efforts, are typically short-lived. Instead, Nelson proposes that neighbors adopt covenants and request the transfer of ownership of streets, say, from the city to the new association, which would exercise property rights and collective control over common elements. In a limited form, this is nothing new. St. Louis has 427 private street associations that restrict access, control traffic, and pay for their own street maintenance.[108] Similar efforts have been tried in decaying neighborhoods in the Bronx, Baltimore, Tulsa, and Kansas City.[109]

In Nelson's scenario, residents could choose from a menu of controls along the lines of CC&Rs. Some neighborhoods could limit collective control to the exterior color of each house and the location of shrubbery. Private neighborhood associations could opt to provide their own services or continue to rely on the city. They could override local zoning laws and permit a commercial business such as a drug store or day-care center to operate. They could even sell "entry rights," with money accruing to the benefit of those immediately impacted by the new project.[110] Nelson expressly invites associations "to be subjective, emotional, arbitrary, value-laden, discriminating, and perhaps discriminatory." His hope is that privatization would set in motion a "virtuous cycle" of closer neighborhood relations and better property upkeep, "stronger personal values, longer-term stability, a firmer sense of belonging and community identity."[111]

Nelson's moral preoccupation and confidence in the participatory advantages of small-scale ownership is framed in terms of privatization. But it brings to mind republican theses about scale and the political economy of citizenship. Like other advocates of privatization, the scheme promises efficiency and consumer satisfaction. But Nelson is mainly interested in the economic arrangements that inspire self-government.

Neighborhood privatization faces profound obstacles. As a purely practical matter, the formation of an association would presumably require unanimous or near-unanimous consent. Legal permissibility is another question. In the case of ordinary zoning decisions, the Supreme Court has struck down neighbor-consent rules or processes that give abutters power to decide building setback lines. It has ruled that the procedures used in zoning must constitute "a classic demonstration of devotion to democracy." Zoning referenda have been allowed because they are seen as analogous to town meetings, but the Court has overturned "ambiguously founded neighborhood preference" decisions, which amount to delegation of governmental authority to "a narrow segment of the community, not to the people at large."[112]

I raise the issue of neighborhood privatization because it highlights the common thread linking the corporate and governmental faces of RCAs. Whether members are passive shareholders or active participants, the social and financial benefits of RCAs redound to them. The association is not internally redistributive, and cannot be, by law. Nor are RCAs oriented to responsibility toward the wider community. There is little reason to think that greater latitude for internal governance along the lines of either shareholder democracy or local government would increase member participation. There is less reason to think either model would shift the burden of responsibility. American law and ideology offer two frameworks for assessing RCA responsibility, corresponding to these faces of the association: corporate social responsibility and "our localism." Together, they put the "uncivic" character attributed to RCAs and demands for democratic congruence in perspective.

Corporate Responsibility

The United States is unusually preoccupied with corporate responsibility and with the thought that "profit maximization is increasingly at variance with the standards by which American society judges corporations' contribution to the public welfare."[113] Perhaps this is the result of the country's unusual reluctance to engage in structural reform of industrial capitalism (with its attendant political controversies) through national planning or decentralization. Instead, government uses fiscal and monetary policy, and regulation. This is supplemented by a popular and official chorus of moral exhortation urging corporations to be socially responsible.

Many corporations make voluntary contributions to public life. We know that corporate money has supplanted family money as the main funder of local social and cultural activities:

> Corporate chieftains became more important civic leaders than heirs to family fortunes, and corporate headquarters became a significant community asset. . . . Business associations in Atlanta, Seattle, and Philadelphia are moving from agreeing only to be against taxes to working across groups and sectors to create shared regional visions. . . . [These] recognize the importance of investment in public ameni-

ties such as ports, parks, and public schools. They are role models for cities such as
Boston or Pittsburgh that still have too many competing civic groups and little regional cooperation.[114]

But the corporate charitable deduction offers no more guidance about the right
level of giving or how to allocate resources among beneficiaries than do personal charitable deductions.[115]

Should RCAs direct their activities with more than property values and internal social life in mind? Or would that conflict with the legitimate purposes
of the association? The question applies to corporations generally. Increasingly, we look to business, including RCA developers, to do more than produce goods and services at the lowest possible cost.[116] But insofar as we have
settled standards for judging corporate "contributions to the public welfare,"
they find expression in state and federal law. Government regulations constrain the use of private property and control for an array of harms: air, water,
and noise pollution; consumer protection and unsafe products; workplace discrimination; health and safety hazards, to name a few. Corporate responsibility
toward employees, customers, suppliers, creditors, and various levels of government are set out in legislative and administrative decisions.

Public interest organizations use lawsuits, publicity campaigns, proxy-so-
licitation drives, and consumer boycotts to affect corporate conduct *indirectly*
by influencing public policy. David Vogel calls this the "politicalization of the
corporation."[117] As business entities, RCAs are subject to the gamut of rules
governing landlord–tenant relations, antidiscrimination policy, building
codes, employee relations, and so on.

There are good reasons *not* to look to corporations as trustees for the public
and to leave balancing of interests to political processes. Businesses are not
accepted as institutions for making public policy, after all. The justification for
shareholder election of corporate directors is precisely that they serve owners'
interests; it disappears if directors become in effect public employees or a
public conscience. So in an effort to have corporations move in the direction
of social responsibility, reformers propose structural changes like mandatory
"public interest representatives" on corporate boards. But what would guide
their decisions? Specific norms of corporate responsibility have proved intractable. Like the recommendation that Congress "establish a new norm, 'altruis-
tic capitalism' as the legal standard of review for corporate conduct," the norm
is empty.[118]

Candidates for corporate duty are usually framed in terms of avoiding harm.
For example, voluntary disclosure of public harms done, even when it is
against a corporation's long-run profits to publicize them. The principal formula for extending corporate accountability while avoiding impossibly diffuse
notions of responsibility for the public good is accountability to specific
"stakeholders": employees, consumers, (some add suppliers and dependent

businesses), and local communities in which corporations are situated. Here, too, it is unclear what level of sacrifice of shareholder interest social responsibility prescribes. What substantive responsibilities corporations have. Or even whether due process is owed those who are substantially affected by business decisions.[119] Proposals have been made to tie lower taxes and streamlined regulatory treatment to "good corporate citizens" that provide health and pension plans to workers, invest in training, and so on.[120]

Once corporate responsibility is defined, however, it is not left to corporate voluntarism. As of 1990, twenty states had passed statutes protecting local companies from pending takeovers that would adversely impact the local community. Pennsylvania's law (since rescinded) explicitly stated "that directors owed no special duty to *any* one corporate constituency, including shareholders"—in effect overruling the fiduciary duty of loyalty.[121] Antitakeover legislation reminds us that if tension exists between the selfish interests of corporate shareholders and the public interest of the local community, "our localism" is self-regarding too.[122]

Suburbs compete with cities and with one another for businesses and affluent residents—including RCA development—which add to the tax base with minimal fiscal impact. (The boroughs of New York City compete with one another to lure businesses or get them to expand there.)[123] From "home rule" to zoning, RCAs are embedded in a system of local autonomy without guidelines or enforceable obligations for responsibility to or for nonresidents or the wider region. The ideology of localism is clear: policy "ought to be controlled locally, with the interests of local residents as the exclusive desideratum of local decision makers."[124] Localism is systematically reaffirmed by public opinion and is judicially enforced. "The rise of fragmentary suburban localities," one expert on municipal law wrote, "calls into question basic assumptions about the 'public' nature of local political activity."[125]

My point is, it would be a mistake to see the uncivic aspects of RCAs as purely a function of their private corporate character. It is perfectly consistent with the association's communal aspects as well.

"Our Localism"

More Americans live in suburbs today than in either central cities or rural areas, and nearly half of urban Americans live in municipalities of fewer than fifty-thousand.[126] Central cities and incorporated suburbs have the same legal status and authority. As a formal matter they have only the powers delegated to them by state government, and "home rule" is potentially limited since few matters are "purely local." In practice, however, "local autonomy has taken on an air of permanence."[127] (The constitutional right to vote in local elections is based on a rejection of the argument that state legislative representation is a substitute for the local franchise.)[128]

States permit area residents to fix local boundaries and incorporate at will (the criterion of "community of interest" is simply deduced from the petition to incorporate). Indeed, municipalities have something of the character of voluntary associations like RCAs. There are 82,000 local governments in the United States. The multiplication of cities is the result of incorporation initiatives by residents or landowners brought for pragmatic, self-regarding, usually defensive, reasons. Local governments are "frequently created and defended . . . to insulate one set of local people or interests from the regulatory authority and population of another local government."[129] States enable municipalities to ward off annexation by other cities. They insure that they are free from any obligation to "take in" or consolidate poorer contiguous areas.[130] Once created, municipalities are protected against reorganization aimed at political or economic justice, for reasons of diversity or distribution. There is no analogue to periodic electoral redistricting.

In our effort to assess whether homeowners' associations are incongruent with the practices and dispositions of local democratic community, the relevant exercise of local government autonomy is exclusionary zoning. Zoning authority is a delegation from the state police power. It was designed to protect residents from interference with the enjoyment of their property, not to displace otherwise lawful land uses entirely. But it has become a protective device used by cities to establish and preserve the character of the area and to restrict new entrants.

The enabling acts and state constitutional provisions authorizing local zoning are broad. They provide for "comprehensive, flexible" plans enacted for the purpose of promoting the health, safety, morals, or general welfare of the community. And they are interpreted to give local governments tremendous discretion.[131] In *Eastlake v. Forest City Enterprises*, the Supreme Court surveyed the field:

> For most communities, zoning as long range planning based on generalized legislative facts . . . has proved to be a theoretician's dream, soon dissolved in a series of zoning map amendments, exceptions, and variances—reflecting, generally, decisions made on individual grounds . . . social and political changes, ecological necessity . . . economic facts . . . governmental needs, and, as important as any, market and consumer choice.[132]

Avoidance of economic harm to local residents is deemed a legitimate goal that includes "the maintenance of property values and the tax base, and the conservation of public services."[133] "Density" factors justify exclusion of multifamily dwellings, mobile homes, and subsidized housing. Courts have accepted an anticipated decrease in property values resulting from an influx of "apartment-type people" as a legitimate rationale for restrictions.[134] In *Village of Arlington Heights v. Metropolitan Housing Development Corporation* the Supreme Court upheld the authority of a white middle-class suburb to exclude low-income housing for the explicit purpose of protecting "property values and the integrity of the Village's zoning plan."[135] One comprehensive study of municipal law concluded: "the preservation of local wealth differences provides the motive for exclusionary actions; local zoning power provides the means."[136] In effect, zoning boards are accountable solely to local electorates.

The impetus to exclusion is mainly but not solely fiscal. Zoning is intended to give people a degree of control over "the look of the place" and who their neighbors will be. Religious missions are not immune. Neighbors have used zoning codes to force a Methodist church to end a program for assisting aliens seeking amnesty and to stop a Presbyterian minister from running a soup kitchen. "One need only attend a few public hearings on controversial zoning changes in suburban areas to realize that the people consider their right to pass judgment on their future neighbors as sacred."[137] The desire to "maintain the status quo within the community" defined in terms of "life style" or "character" receives judicial support.

In *Village of Belle Terre v. Boraas*, the Supreme Court upheld a small town's ordinance that restricted land use to family dwellings and required that members of a household be related by blood, adoption, or marriage (and excluded households of more than two unrelated persons) as a reasonable attempt to achieve an environment "addressed to family needs." Justice Douglas famously supported zoning designed to produce "a quiet place where yards are wide, people few, and motor vehicles restricted. . . . The police power is not confined to elimination of filth, stench, and unhealthy places. It is ample to lay out zones where family values, youth values, and the blessings of quiet seclusion and clean air make the area a sanctuary for people."[138] We can see why Robert Nelson called zoning a de facto collective property right, and the small community a private club.[139]

The extent to which cities are able to exploit their legal autonomy is another matter. "The republican tradition taught that to be free is to share in governing a political community that controls its own fate," Michael Sandel reminds us.[140] So local autonomy depends not on its formal authority but on its actual revenues and fiscal strains.[141] Fiscal autonomy gives reality to localism, as it does to federalism (and to freedom of association).

The property tax is the dominant *local* source of local revenue, and there is little relation between a city's wealth and its financial needs. Demands on local government and the ability to attract resources are both the result of forces largely beyond local control—history, migration patterns, federal and state welfare mandates, the mobility of labor and capital, that is, "the decisions of private taxpaying individuals and revenue- and employment-generating businesses to move to, remain in, expand in or depart from the geographical con-

fines of the city."[142] Historically, imagination and policy have made a difference, of course, and will continue to give the lie to determinism. Atlanta is a
case in point, welcoming carpetbaggers after the Civil War and reaching out to
national businesses as a self-declared progressive hub after World War II.[143]
Only a few cities are capable of taking care of "their own" in practice, however, typically because some location advantage makes them so desirable they
can control rents or impose burdensome taxes without economic penalty.

So economic development takes precedence over distribution, and cities are
reluctant to become attractive places for poor people to live. The realistic fear
is a "race to the bottom." Paul Peterson describes a liberal Massachusetts town
that offered "apartments for poor families, group homes for recovering drug
and alcohol abusers, halfway homes, counseling centers, and other programs
for the poor." The growing number of clients provoked complaints from town
leaders and taxpayers: "We can't afford this anymore."[144] No wonder Herbert
Gans advises that if they are to avoid irreconcilable conflict, municipalities can
tolerate only moderate heterogeneity: "since local institutions, including government, have little power to affect—and to ameliorate—the basic causes of
such conflict, they [are] unable to handle it constructively."[145]

These themes come together in the New Jersey supreme court decisions
collected under the title *Mount Laurel*, the principal challenge to the exercise
of zoning authority solely for the welfare of a particular community.[146] The
town of Mount Laurel was not antigrowth; its zoning scheme was explicitly
devised to oppose development that would detract from its average wealth. In
1975, a unanimous New Jersey court reasoned that since zoning is a delegation
of state police power, any scheme having an impact beyond the borders of the
local community must promote the general welfare of the "affected region"
rather than impair it. Significantly, the court did not resort to defining the
interests of nonresidents as basic liberties. Nor did it say that local zoning
authority and the desire to exclude residents were illegitimate. Only that this
desire had to be balanced against the "countervailing interests" of nonres-
sidents. In this case, the failure to make "realistically possible a variety and
choice of housing" sufficed to violate state constitutional due process and
equal protection.[147]

Mount Laurel and other communities would have to do their "fair share" to
meet the region's low- and moderate-income housing needs. The ruling required cities to develop "affirmative housing strategies based on private
sources of housing production and subsidies."[148] The prescriptions set by the
court, and modified by the New Jersey legislature's subsequent Fair Housing
Act of 1985, were modest, though, and the effects have been attenuated.[149] The
decision has not served as a precedent. There has been little change in judicial
deference to localities, even in states that have taken a regional view. As the
California supreme court put it, "suburban residents . . . may assert a vital
interest in limiting immigration to their community." After over a dozen years

of litigation, Mount Laurel's mayor continues to insist, "We'd just like to see our town develop in a nice way. We should have the right to run our town."[150] This remains the prevailing view.

The *Mount Laurel* court took the unusual step of declaring that "the state controls the use of land, *all* of the land," and that zoning had become "a form of public utility regulation." This was a dramatic departure not only from local autonomy in these matters but also from the standard representation of local governments as organic growths from some authentic prepolitical community. (We recognize this as a reprise of the debate about whether corporations are "natural" or state-created entities.) As one commentator points out, the tendency of courts is to romanticize local communities. Instead of seeing zoning or public education as state responsibilities provisionally delegated to local government as the New Jersey court did in *Mount Laurel*, local functions are seen as original and inalienable, sometimes as extensions of the family.[151]

It is not unusual to find social theorists casting neighborhoods as natural and familial, and arguing that "no realistic social alternatives" exist for the sort of "tribal" structure of community that is vital to civic renewal.[152] Popular political discourse especially has it that neighborhoods, viewed more as informal networks than as a structure of legal and political institutions, should be infused with community warmth. Their value is their moral homogeneity and capacity to support and transmit family values. Romanticism is latent in Laurence Tribe's sympathy for deference to local zoning schemes like the one upheld in *Belle Terre*: "The embedding of a choice within a close human relationship or network of relationships should always be regarded as significantly increasing the burden of justification for those who would make the choice illegal or visit it with some deprivation." Tribe regards communities seeking to preserve or restore what they see as traditional forms "as hardly less courageous, and even experimental, than the commune or the group attempting to share some other less widely understood pattern of life."[153]

Romanticization of local community has an argumentative thrust; it legitimates autonomy.[154] Critics point out that the phrase "character of a community" is code for expensive homes. In fact, it is code for self-government and for democratically condoned exclusion. Political responsibility for land use lies with municipalities. When they can afford to preserve their character through zoning, and when RCAs provide an additional strategy, they do. Cities could require mixed use. They could require RCA developers to build mixed associations. But political will and the ideology of localism incline to exclusion: "at the present time, population heterogeneity as advocated by planners is not workable. Neither home purchasers nor tenants seem to want it, and the housing market is not organized to provide it."[155] Nelson remarks that the trade-off between neighborhood identity on the one hand and erosion of a broader sense of metropolitan and national community on the other may already have been made.[156]

So "our localism" should put in perspective the charge that RCAs represent the privatization of cities without public deliberation. RCAs generally *reflect* the social character of the municipality. It is not surprising that a 1990 survey of RCA directors showed them rating relations with local government 16 percent excellent, 46 percent good, 15 percent fair, 4 percent poor.[157] To the extent they are more affluent than the locality overall, the effect of RCAs on a community can be mildly redistributive.[158]

If the democratic ideal of localism is homogeneity and small size, economic development and the life-style interests of home and family, then RCAs *are* congruent with democratic values and practices. Indeed, they come closer to fulfilling the ideal today than local communities, including suburbs. For the image of suburbia as "white, middle-class, family-oriented, and socially homogeneous" with "low-density, nonindustrial, and primarily residential" land use is outdated. They are increasingly heterogeneous, with high- and low-density development, industry, and jobs; 43 percent of all rental housing is in suburban metropolitan areas. The population is diverse: 50 percent of the Hispanic population lives in suburbs; 42 percent of Asians. The population is no longer solely middle-class or family-oriented either; suburbs have a growing proportion of young single adults, unrelated individuals, elderly, and the poor.[159] It does not follow from these facts that residents *want* local communities to diversify—only that they want to close the door to change behind them. RCAs go some way toward satisfying that wish. They are perfectly comprehensible responses to challenges to "our localism."

If local community is to be infused with appreciation for heterogeneity and social justice to go along with the changing social facts; if it is to be closely identified with interests besides residence and family—work, say, or unconventional life styles; if zoning is to be exercised on behalf of a wider polity, large changes in political culture and structure must take place. Localism "relies on a kind of invisible hand to bring the political system into moral equilibrium: the well-being of all affected citizens is best served by letting each jurisdiction look after only its own."[160] The alternative moral standards political philosophers propose for democratic decision-making—reciprocity, say, or due consideration for all those affected by local decisions—are rarely more sober, though. They have neither history nor ideology on their side. The standard of reciprocity cannot take us very far in defining the obligations local residents have to meet the housing needs of outsiders. On their own terms, they are not always persuasive in justifying why, in the absence of national health insurance, Arizonans should pay for the heart transplants of Californians.[161] Not so long as we have a system of democratic representation and accountability—with residency requirements for voting and "home rule"—designed to insure "our localism."

Exhortations of reciprocity are no substitute for structural change. Either local government authority must be limited, or its capacity to address distributional issues must be increased. Realistically, the focus should be on federal policy: "The enormous increments in federal dollars that came to the cities during the 1960s and early 1970s were rooted in a belief in cooperative federalism," Paul Peterson reminds us. "Public officials were committed to the principle that all governments working together could ameliorate the country's social ills."[162]

Indeed, if regional, state-centered, and federal programs were to offset the distribution of local resources, homeowners' associations would have an even stronger moral claim to be justified sites of voluntary localism, elective communities. The charge of "secession" would lose some of its edge.

The Illiberal Politics of Privatism: Segregation and Secession

Neither local communities nor RCAs are homogeneous. Within as well as among them there is diversity of age, occupation, ethnic or religious background, and stability/mobility. But for critics the key differentiation is economic, and RCAs seem to epitomize Robert Reich's "secession of the successful."[163] There is nothing new about economic segregation; it used to be the defining characteristic of suburbia. Moreover, "successful" is relative; RCAs cater to owners at every price range. Escape from poverty, which is really at issue, is nothing new, either: middle-class households—whether they are black, Mexican, Italian, Jewish, or Polish—always try to escape the poor. The push of crime and the pull of homeownership and suburban services explain these moves, and for most groups residential integration is a by-product of socioeconomic achievement, not a goal. They put up with integration to gain access to opportunities and resources.[164]

African Americans are the exception; their level of segregation does not decline as their socioeconomic status rises. In 1980, 71 percent of northern whites lived in suburbs; the figure for blacks was 23 percent. (Figures for homeownership overall are proportionately better; in 1990, 69.1 percent of white households owned their homes compared to 43.4 percent of black households.)[165] Suburbanization of African Americans has lagged far behind other groups of the same socioeconomic level, and "even within surburbs, levels of racial segregation remained exceptionally high."[166] The most striking thing about population shifts to suburbs is the maintenance of the color line and the "myopia" commentators Massey and Denton describe in *American Apartheid*:

> No group in the history of the United States has ever experienced the sustained high level of residential segregation that has been imposed on blacks in large American cities for the past fifty years. . . . The effect of segregation on black well-being is

structural, not individual. Residential segregation lies beyond the ability of any individual to change.[167]

Most discussions of residential segregation focus on the "hypersegregation" of the urban ghetto, where blacks are concentrated within a small area, centralized in an urban core, and isolated. Ghetto residents are unlikely to come in contact with whites within their own neighborhood or adjacent neighborhoods, and have little direct experience with other Americans. These are the conditions for what the authors choose to call the culture of segregation rather than the culture of poverty. The one-third of all African Americans who live under conditions of intense segregation "are unambiguously among the nation's most spatially isolated and geographically secluded people."[168]

Surveys show white support for fair housing in the abstract; 88 percent think black people have a right to live wherever they can afford to, which is why racial prejudice per se is an insufficient explanation of continued segregation. Support declines steeply, however, as the number of hypothetical black neighbors rises from one to more.[169] In practice, whites avoid settling in areas where there are or threaten to be a significant number of African Americans. Harassment and targeted violence make blacks reluctant to move into mainly white neighborhoods, too. And integrated areas resulting from happenstance or planning are notoriously unstable. Few remain integrated for long; "integration maintenance" policies in public housing, for example, face legal obstacles.[170]

As a result, holding education and occupational status constant, blacks are able to buy fewer goods distributed through housing markets with their income than other groups.[171] "Poor blacks live under unrivaled concentrations of poverty, and affluent blacks live in neighborhoods that are far less advantageous than those experienced by the middle-class of other groups."[172] And after decades of official desegregation and economic gains, the response to black middle-class neighborhoods is less likely to inspire the reaction Auburn Avenue in Atlanta did in the 1950s: "It was, for newcomers, like the first sight of Israel for a Jew, the first breathtaking sense of *majority*."[173]

There is no evidence suggesting that RCAs are more racially segregated than localities generally. If they bring to mind white "secession" it is because historically, neighborhood associations like Chicago's Hyde Park Improvement and Protective Club were created to prevent black entry. They implemented the restrictive covenants outlawed in *Shelley v. Kraemer*. But RCAs are regulable as businesses under state and federal antidiscrimination law. Despite being nonprofit, their overall function is to protect and enhance economic value, and they perform the customary business functions of the landlord in a landlord–tenant relationship.[174] Their control over membership by means of exclusion is restricted by the federal 1968 Fair Housing Act banning discrimination in the advertising, sale, and rental of housing, and injunctions against "blockbusting."[175] On the other hand, they have not changed the facts.

Across another dimension RCAs are a key site of segregation. Age restrictions in proprietary communities survived constitutional challenge when *White Egret Condominium, Inc. v. Franklin* ruled that "providing appropriate facilities for the differing housing needs and desires of the varying age groups" is a lawful purpose.[176] But state statutes rapidly filled in to prevent the exclusion of children from housing; RCAs are businesses within the meaning of California's Unruh Civil Rights Act, for example, which protects all persons from arbitrary discrimination in "accommodations, advantages, facilities, privileges or services." Housing for the elderly is an exception, with the result that the most segregated homeowners' associations are age-segregated ones, where in the normal course of a week residents rarely see anyone under age sixty. (Though within retirement communities, several generations now live side by side—the elderly and their "old, old" parents!). In many respects these associations are as culturally innovative as the communal experiments of counterculture types in the 1960s. They have evolved unique institutions and customs, distinctive attitudes toward death and marriage, styles of interpersonal relationships, and rituals.[177]

In fact, the charge of segregation is leveled at RCAs without much thought to a standard of social homogeneity or economic success. At root, it reflects hostility toward privatism or, more histrionically, "secession." Descriptions of RCAs point to barrier gates and cul-de-sacs, mazelike layouts, security monitors and alarms to underscore the charge that they comprise a "sinister subculture." According to one account, RCAs have a "communalistic, even cult-like isolationist nature" and signal "a reversion to feudalism." They are said to be infused with the "eerie detachment" of a commune.[178]

Some communities really do seem strange to outsiders; consider the first time the mayor of San Francisco made an appearance at a drag ball, or Jerry Falwell calling New York Baghdad.[179] But it is hard to reconcile "cultlike" with the reality of residential homeowners' associations. The truth about RCA detachment is mundane: private streets can be closed to through traffic, speed bumps installed, parking prohibited, and nonresidents denied use of association facilities.

And it is well to recall that an affluent proprietary community is no prerequisite for a guarded, enclave-like atmosphere. In 1995, the village of Rosemont, Illinois, near O'Hare airport erected a fence around its residential neighborhood and safety checkpoints at its entrances where video cameras record the license plates of entering cars.[180]

Something of the same spirit, minus the technology, inspires neighborhood watch policing schemes. Their effectiveness in preventing crime is doubtful, but they are powerful expressions of concern for safety and of the values of family, local community, and property. Confidence that people are looking out their windows and reporting suspicious activity creates an image of cohesion. This can be represented as spirited communitarianism or as polarizing "segregation"—"property owners against the propertyless; employed against unemployed; family, home, and community against the individual outsider."[181] If RCAs are "cultlike," neighborhood watches qualify as sinister surveillance networks. They are actually more dangerous; for them as for private police, there are few parameters of justifiable deterrence, accountability, or the use of force. These efforts, like RCA security measures, are best seen as simply the "determined preference" people exhibit again and again for a controlled environment.

In some cases, though rarely, RCAs are closed to uninvited public access. Advocates for constitutionalizing RCAs want courts to treat them as public property, and would apply Justice Black's ruling in *Marsh v. Alabama* that a "company town" was the functional equivalent of local government, and that violation of First and Fourteenth Amendment rights amount to unconstitutional state action.[182] Chicasaw, Alabama, the private town at issue in *Marsh*, had all the attributes of an ordinary town: residential buildings, streets, a system of sewers and disposal plant; a business block; a U.S. post office; and a deputy of the Mobile County sheriff, paid by the company, serving as the town policeman. RCAs may bear a closer functional resemblance to municipalities than do the private governments of businesses or churches, but they remain special-purpose associations. No court has accepted the argument that RCAs are company towns à la *Marsh*.

Nonetheless, there are judicially imposed limits on exclusion. Courts have ruled that homeowners' associations are not required to admit "religious evangelists, political campaigners, assorted sales-people, signature solicitors, or any other uninvited persons of the like."[183] Homeowners outside RCAs have an undisputed right to discriminate in excluding unwanted visitors, and courts treat RCAs as private property. But in a key case, *Laguna Publishing Co. v. Golden Rain Foundation* (1982), the California court of appeals recognized that "the gated and walled community is a new phenomenon on the social scene," and saw the need to determine when insistence on private property rights by a homeowners' association was "needless and exaggerated."[184]

The case was brought by a publishing company that had been prohibited by the association board from distributing its free circulars. The court struck down the exclusion as an unconstitutional deprivation of the rights of speech and press under the state constitution because the directors had permitted a rival publication to deliver its unsolicited paper to residents. Walled or not, exclusion cannot be at the discretion of the board of directors, or discriminatory.

Defendant owner, in the exercise of its private property rights, could choose to exclude all giveaway newspapers from the community. However . . . it impermissibly discriminated against plaintiff, when, acting with the implicit sanction of the state's police power behind it, and without authority from the residents of the community, it excluded plaintiff from the community.[185]

Justice Frankfurter's concurrence in *Marsh* sheds light on decisions permitting RCAs to exclude unauthorized visitors. Frankfurter shifted the focus away from whether a private community has the requisite attributes and functions of a town. Instead, he considered the extent to which private property is open for use by the public in general. From this perspective, RCAs can exclude unwanted visitors because their "community aspects" are restricted to members.[186] And since RCAs are located within a wider local community with public spaces to which RCA owners have access, there are effective alternatives for communicating with them.

Of course, physical boundaries are emblematic of exclusion and privatism. But it is fair to say that the chief concern is less RCA detachment than precisely the opposite—their potential for activism and political influence. "Secession's" other face is confrontational, a challenge to civic virtue.

"NIMBY"

We saw that the idea behind democratizing RCAs is to encourage members' participation in associational life. Advocates of congruence imagine RCAs as schools of citizenship. Yet there is little enthusiasm for association participation in local or state politics. Indeed, the animating concern is that these associations are the incarnation of selfish actors in interest group politics, whose orientation is "NIMBY."

In practice, the issues RCAs raise are the mundane staples of local politics: traffic patterns top the list, followed by stop signs, police protection, development issues, water and sewer, and trash. Their political activity is usually prompted by something "bad" happening.[187] There is nothing unusual or sinister about defending aesthetics or property values by appearing at zoning meetings or "packing" a school board meeting to oppose plans to build a new high school on contiguous land rather than in a location with fewer homes. This is no different than other organized neighborhood groups or disorganized residents agitating on their own. It is self-interested but not particularly base or selfish.

The animus expressed toward political activity by homeowners' associations is unaccountable, then, unless we recognize it as aversion to interest-based politics tout court. The classic democratic rationale for voluntary associations—as agents for identifying, expressing, and representing interests, and expanding the political agenda—has become anathema. The implication is that a system of political pluralism cannot produce justice, and that RCAs are forces opposed to the public good. They are the "them" of "special interests," made worse by their status as corporations. When interests are aggregated, they come out on top.

Do RCAs have some unfair advantage in local political arenas? Though political influence is notoriously difficult to estimate, unequal political resources, including the capacity for organization, is a legitimate democratic concern (to which I return in chapters 6 and 7). Unlike neighborhood groups, which depend on the chancey emergence of leaders, RCAs have built-in organization with their committees and boards of directors. RCAs are not megacorporations with resources to exert political influence, but some can afford to hire lawyers or planners.[188] Nonetheless, a comparative study from the mid-1970s showed that homeowners' associations are no better at local involvement and neighborhood ties than developments lacking an association.[189]

Barton and Silverman's 1986 study found that boards of directors avoid taking political positions, often because they are sensitive to the diverse views of members, and that they do not see keeping members informed much less agitating to act collectively as one of their functions. Other studies report that RCAs are *less* politicized and do less to facilitate participation than voluntary neighborhood civic associations.[190]

Association directors are not political representatives. A legal constraint designed to protect stockholders in business corporations from coerced political association applies in this context. *First National Bank of Boston v. Bellotti* raised the question of whether allowing corporations to engage in political speech threatens the First Amendment rights of shareholders. The same question arises in connection with stockholder suits against management that "wastes" assets by expenditures unrelated to corporate purposes, including promoting a political agenda.

RCA members are particularly vulnerable to compelled political association. They are not passive investors, and are thus more directly identified with association speech than stockholders in commercial businesses. They cannot easily sell their interests and disassociate. They cannot simply resign in disagreement, as they could membership in a political organization. The political priorities of members may not correspond with the decisions by directors to act in the name of the association even with regard to issues with a direct nexus to association business and property value. Unit owners in a New York City case successfully sued their condominium association for spending association funds to fight the developer of a nearby parcel of land, on grounds that the board action violated the bylaws about what constitutes a common expense.

Democratic attacks on RCAs simply echo the range of criticisms leveled at the politics of interest and corporate influence generally. They do not take us very far in understanding why these associations in particular are called "secessionist." The issue of "double taxation" does. It also helps us identify the appropriate limits on association freedom.

In a literal sense RCA owners are taxed twice on the value of common assets: they pay property taxes on their units (which are assessed to reflect the existence of common areas and amenities) and they pay their share of taxes on these common areas. But in most contexts, "double taxation" refers to something else: the fact that owners pay both local property taxes and fees to the association for services like snow removal or trash collection that the municipality provides other residents. And unlike municipal taxes, association dues are not deductible from federal income taxes. The claim "double taxation" amounts to a demand for local tax exemptions or rebates.

"Double taxation" sees the issue of taxes and services through the lens of "privatization," a term that confuses more than it clarifies. In the United States, it normally means assigning governmental tasks to private entities by contracting out for trash collection, say, or administrative services. It is more often a practical response to fiscal stress than ideology, and has been described as local shedding "almost by default."[191] RCAs are not recipients of public funds through grants, contracts, or payments to individuals who purchase their services.[192] They provide services only to their own members. They are not privatization in any strict sense.

But "double taxation" does assert that association assessments *should* be treated as taxes for privatized public services.[193] Houston and Kansas City provide rebates to RCAs, and New Jersey law requires cities to either provide residents with snow removal, street lighting, recycling, and trash collection or reimburse developments for the cost of providing their own services.[194] These examples aside, local rebates are rare, and they may reflect nothing more than the state's fiscal desire for RCA development rather than the justice of the claims underlying "double taxation."

For "double taxation" is a plausible characterization of the burden on RCA members only if property taxes are thought of as user charges for a discrete array of services, and if rebates can be pro-rated. Economists and political scientists are frankly uncertain about the second point. It is said that RCAs are "the most significant privatization of local government responsibilities in recent times as measured by the amount of expenditure relief given to the public sector for capital investment and operations."[195] But this is sheer assertion. The U.S. Advisory Commission on Intergovernmental Relations reports that public finance statistics do not include estimates of the extent to which RCAs are subsidizing the public services provided to non-RCA residents. (Or for that matter the increased costs attributable to RCAs that the locality must bear, for which it may demand exactions up front.) It is likely that RCAs derive some benefit from clean-up services to the city overall, as the city does from the security private police provide to a neighborhood. It is also unclear whether conceding the "double tax" claim would require cities to either raise local taxes or reduce services to other areas, though the question becomes increasingly salient as a significant portion of the population in a local area or state acquires RCA membership.

Calculable or not, "double taxation" is a misnomer because the analogy between association assessments and local taxes fails. RCAs provide services exclusively to their members, and are required by law to match association benefits to assessments. Directors are precluded from redistributing association goods, even internally. So owners expect to recapture their assessments directly as well as indirectly in the increased value of their units. By contrast, local taxes are levied on the basis of property value. And there is only a loose fit between a given taxpayer's burden and what he or she can expect to receive in services. Local citizen is not coterminous with taxpayer and consumer.

The analogy breaks down decisively if we consider that Montgomery County, Maryland, allows cash payments to RCAs for street maintenance, provided they allow general access to the street. This is the principal reason why "double taxation" is misleading. RCA residents have full use of public facilities; local residents do not have access to exclusive RCA services and facilities. They are amenities owners purchase for themselves.

The closest analogue to RCA assessment is the business improvement district, a special-purpose government authority that taxes neighborhood property owners for enhanced services. The democratic fear is that "instead of looking for public solutions to public problems, these districts encourage people to find private, exclusive solutions."[196] "Parts" of cash-strapped cities can be working effectively, but only parts, depending on their tax base: "In effect, advocates identify the CID [community interest development] interest with the community interest because, from their perspective, the CID is the community. Having attended to the property they own, CID residents would be deemed to have satisfied their duties to the community at large, and would be free to take advantage of its benefits without further obligation."[197] The same charge is brought against RCAs. To the extent separatism accurately reflects members' attitudes toward local government and taxes, the tag "secession" fits, even if it is hyperbolic.

Still, we should recognize that in the current political context, "double taxation" is better understood as part of a general trend toward fiscal populism than elite secession. Resistance to taxes is fueled by distrust in government and personal economic insecurity more than a shift in preference away from public services.[198] In this atmosphere, tax increases to support public programs are frequently designed as special-purpose taxes and raised from specific groups of potential "users":

a $10 increase in marriage-license fees in Colorado to pay for child-abuse prevention programs. Higher real-estate taxes for downtown property owners in an eighty-block area of Philadelphia to pay for enhanced security and special street-cleaning services. A dollar a year added to automobile insurance premiums in Michigan to pay for auto-theft prevention programs. Taxes on beer in several states to pay for anti-drunk-driving and alcohol rehabilitation programs . . . [S]pecial purpose taxes are the suburban ideal—not just private government but private taxes.[199]

Government officials are partly responsible for anticivic education insofar as they represent assessments to pay for public programs as fee for service. And insofar as they continue to use special assessments to get around popular limitations on property taxes—a strategy that encourages people to think in terms of fees and to avoid discussions of public responsibility and distribution. There is too little objection to the idea of "double taxation," only the practical, fiscal concerns of municipal officials.

Here, as in the case of religious associations, the moral uses of pluralism depend on a background of strong liberal democratic institutions, and on assertions of public values. Solicitude for voluntary associations justifies local government's hospitality to RCA development and deferential interpretation of RCA covenants by courts. But it is no argument for relieving members of public responsibility. Discussion of "double taxation" should be in terms of public policy and political education, not private benefits. States should prohibit local rebates uniformly, so that municipalities cannot compete for RCA development by acceding to the claim that members are "double taxed" and offering rebates. This confounds membership with citizenship, muddling an already complex mix of identifications. And it assigns membership priority, without justification.

Corporate Culture at Home

We acknowledge that habits drawn from public life infuse private relations all the time—when families vote about where to go on vacation, for example. Similarly, corporate culture at home is not just the invention of economists professionally disposed to think about family life and personal property in terms of assets and management. In everyday life in RCAs, joint ownership, concern for efficient management, economic obligations and restrictions shape residents' expectations for conduct, relations among neighbors, and their sense of home.

Many enthusiasts of "the density of association life" depreciate RCAs, claiming that they produce or reinforce antiliberal or undemocratic dispositions. By now the litany of charges is familiar. These associations encourage overriding preoccupation with protecting private property values. Strict enforcement of association rules rewards rigidity and inhibits face-to-face community. They steer members away from participation to management and the goal of maximizing amenities and minimizing expenses. Covenants constrain change and inhibit flexible self-government. The sternest critic despairs of the moral effect of RCAs' corporate character on members' understanding of personal liberty. McKenzie argues that when parents explain to their children that they must abide by prohibitions against changing their drapery liners or modifying their house's colors, they are delivering an illiberal lesson: "It is conceivable that children raised in CID housing may be undergoing a form of differential political socialization," he warns. "We have a generation in this country that doesn't know you *should be able* to paint your house any color you want."[200]

Strange "should." In fact, each fear about the consequences of RCA membership can be plausibly deflected or reversed. Responsibility defined as meeting economic obligations and conforming to the rules of voluntary association is nothing to despise. Compliance with restrictions preserves communal norms, checks arbitrariness and caprice, and channels personal conflict. By imposing another level of rules and authority close to home, RCAs alert members to the omnipresence of "private government"; is this de-politicizing? If RCAs make the economic stakes of homeownership vivid, and if joint ownership of common areas underscores the shared fate of neighborhoods (or highlights linkages among value, services, taxation, and local policy), is this anti-civic or sober political education? As for democratic practices proper, RCAs plainly cultivate leadership. Alongside their fiduciary duties as corporate board, directors willy-nilly rally members to meetings, direct decision-making, engage in negotiations, sustain an organization, and look outward to local and state government.

I am not suggesting that RCAs are schools of democratic virtue, only that here as elsewhere the moral uses of associational life by members are indeterminate. The effects of membership are dictated in part by the habits and expectations homeowners bring to the association. For some members managerial and ownership concerns are predominant and corporate culture looms large. But to the homeowner who is also a professional business manager, say, that aspect of the hybrid association may not be salient. We cannot predict whether she will relate to the business-like aspects of the association or not—whether the "hook" of membership is complementarity or compensation.

For some members, of course, the associational aspects of RCAs are personally inconsequential. RCA units are homes, first of all, and normally corporate and communal life can be ignored. Moreover, to the extent that members *are* immersed in the community, this is likely to entail social life rather than internal governance. Whether or not homeowners' associations are retirement communities, their internal life is attractive insofar as it mimics retirement. Buyers are attracted to RCA amenities. The lure of involvement is "life style": resident-run clubs, sports, and holiday get-togethers detached from jobs and divisive politics, from "pressure."[201] This is perfectly consistent with membership in activist groups outside the association, of course.

The assumption that the association has a powerful privatizing effect overall is unsubstantiated.

Similarly, there is no reason to think that the legalism of corporate culture and elective community overwhelms neighborliness. More than likely RCAs instill in members a vivid sense of their rights, and at the same time give rise to innumerable situations where members decide to refrain from exercising them. Individually, they make moral trade-offs all the time, between legalism or managerialism and generosity toward their neighbors, say. And their self-restraint and generosity are demonstrable virtues (not to be confused with abject passivity) only against the background of association rights and obligations. My daughter exhibits commendable neighborliness when she does not complain either to her abutter or to her condominium board when this neighbor plants a shade tree on her section of yard. She puts amiability ahead of procedural justice. She does not exhibit *civic* virtue here, however, nor any of the distinctive dispositions required by the morality of a homeowners' association.

So the moral valence of membership is variable. For any individual, residence may increase appreciation for community, for conformity to regulations, and for opportunity to take part in amending them. Or they may see themselves principally as shareholder-investors in common property with a stake in good management, enforcement, and a "maintenance-free life style."[202] Or residence can provoke a reaction, contrarian insistence on the rights of private ownership and unfettered personal liberty. Given the overlapping, shifting aspects of membership, at one time or another homeowners are likely to find different faces of the association and different norms salient. We can fairly assume that qua owner-member-citizens, individuals vote for directors, approve or disapprove association amendments, relate to one another and to the local political community with alternating interests and expectations in mind. It is likely that at one time or another they will find themselves on different sides: for and against liberty claims and owners' "rights" against the association, opposed to and supportive of strict enforcement.

The only certainty is that each face of associational life is experienced at a pitch. Consider the homeowner who refused to pay his assessment because he claimed that association gardeners using illegal pesticides had killed his two goldfish. After drawn-out legal wrangling he had to pay the assessment plus association attorney fees and court costs for a bill of over $58,000.[203] Arguments for and against the owner of the noiseless cats—arguments identified as legalist, corporatist, or libertarian, are levied with all the force of personal temperament and conviction brought home.

RCAs alert us to the fact that the moral experiences an association provides its members are not predictable on the basis of its formal purpose and authority structure. The internal life of groups is rarely singular; homeowners' associations provide opportunity for rule-following, collective self-government, and proprietary self-concern. RCAs also alert us to the disjuncture between popu-

lar moral concerns with insuring "the day-to-day virtues involved in neighborliness, self-restraint, and childrearing" on the one hand, and academic preoccupation with distinctive, often stringent, domocratic virtues on the other. They
offer an important insight: if we focus inflexibly on the structure of schools of
democracy, or on inculcating some specific democratic competence, we are
liable to be blinded to other powerful elements of moral and political education
that go on "at home" in the everyday life of these associations.[204] This discussion looks ahead to restricted-membership groups like the Jaycees and Rotary
Clubs. They are the classic voluntary associations, without the special characteristics of religious groups or corporations. So we might imagine that their
freedom of association is uncomplicated, and that the general encomium to
voluntary association applies: "The health of society will usually be promoted
if the groups within it which serve the industrial, mental, and spiritual needs of
citizens are genuinely alive. Like individuals, they will usually do the most for
the community if they are free to determine their own lives for the present and
the future."[205]

But here too the question whether we should prescribe legally enforced congruence with liberal democratic norms or protect association autonomy is
surprisingly complex. In part because categorization is key to association freedom, and groups like the Jaycees are perplexing hybrids. Freedom for association self-government, including the critical matter of control over admission of
members, has depended on whether the association is cast as a commercial
venture, a restricted-membership social group, or a political association. In the
next chapter, I focus on whether and when voluntary associations can claim
protection under the First Amendment against the most intrusive intervention:
the legal requirement that associations admit unwanted members.

5

Compelled Association:
Democratic Equality and Self-Respect

Compelled Association

When we think of voluntary associations, we think first of groups like the Jaycees—quasi-social, quasi-civic, quasi-business organizations that enlist local citizens and carry on a range of activities in the local community. And when jeremiahs bemoan a falling off of membership, they have groups like the Jaycees in mind.[1] "Liberal expectancy," meaning confidence in the progressive liberalization of the internal lives of groups and in the beneficial moral impact of membership, attaches unhesitatingly to these quasi-civic associations. Certainly, more spontaneously than it does to flourishing new phenomena such as homeowners' associations or fellowship and support groups. So the onus for cultivating the moral dispositions of liberal democratic citizens continues to fall heavily on the Jaycees and their myriad counterparts. With it comes the demand for congruence, especially for nondiscriminatory policies of admission. The paradoxical result is that the classic voluntary association is denied the core right of freedom of association—the ability to set restrictive membership criteria and to admit only wanted members.

Involuntary association is inescapable in daily life; as Justice Douglas remarked, "one who of necessity rides busses and streetcars does not have the freedom that John Muir and Walt Whitman extolled."[2] Legally compelled association is the rule in public institutions like schools and the military. In contrast, compulsion to join one or any religious association, or for these groups to admit unwanted members to fellowship, is plainly outside government authority. When it comes to voluntary associations, we regularly form, join, and disassociate ourselves from groups that are selective. We expect restrictions on who can join. In the spirit of civic inclusion Benjamin Franklin formed the first volunteer fire department, but he also founded the American Philosophical Society and a secret club of artisans. (I return to secret societies in chapter 7.)

With difficulty, we can imagine open organizations with which anyone can affiliate, but they have the look and feel of public accommodations rather than voluntary associations. Their common intentions and shared terms of sociability are necessarily attenuated. If associations cannot limit eligibility and control admission, their particular projects and expressive aspects will be inhibited, diluted, or subverted. As we know, sometimes the whole point of association is exhibition of some exemplary difference, whether the motivation is snobbery, celebration of a distinctive social identity without any pretense of superiority, or defensive self-protection. Restricted membership is a prerequisite of a fraternal society, the Jaycees pointed out.[3] Voluntary associations are bounded entities. The moral uses of pluralism require exclusion.

No wonder Herbert Wechsler's proposition that the right of freedom of association necessarily entails the freedom not to associate has immediate appeal. No wonder "there can be no clearer example of an intrusion into the internal structure or affairs of an association than a regulation that forces the group to accept members it does not desire."[4] Justice O'Connor put it simply: "the power to change the membership of a bona fide private association is unavoidably the power to change its purpose, its programs, its ideology, and its collective voice."[5]

"Open primary" laws are a vivid example of the threat compelled association poses to a group's ideology, practical effectiveness, and esprit. These state laws allowed not just independents but voters registered with another party to participate in the opposition primary, and mandated that the results should bind state delegates at the National Convention. It is clear why this violated political party rules and precipitated constitutional objections. At worst, Democrats or Republicans may vote with the express purpose of helping nominate the most beatable candidate. At a minimum, crossover voters have different voting patterns than party members, and the opportunity of declared party members to participate in the selection of delegates to the party convention is diluted. In a divided opinion in *Democratic Party v. Wisconsin*, the Supreme Court struck down open primary laws as a violation of freedom of association.[6]

The best-known instance of compelled association is the union shop. Labor history describes the turbulent shift in government policy from treating "combination" as criminal conspiracy, to upholding the right to join a labor association and opposing yellow-dog contracts, to government-mandated union representation and association. Because unions enjoy federally sponsored power to affect nonmembers through collective bargaining with regard to seniority, salary classification, grievances, and deciding whether to strike or to fight plant closings, laws compel them to represent all employees. At the same time, the public policy of eliminating free riders requires all employees to support the designated bargaining unit. Workers cannot join rival unions, or deal directly with employers, or disassociate at will. There is no protected conscientious objection to agency shops, and no violation of First Amendment free speech rights in compelling workers to contribute financially to a union as a condition of employment.[7]

This is made palatable by depreciating its significance for members personally. No worker has to espouse the cause of unionism or attend meetings, the thinking goes; the only obligation is payment of "periodic dues, initiation fees, and assessments." This is not a case of ignoring "the shibboleth that the law cannot compel the spirit of brotherhood," since the whole point is that no such spirit is necessary.[8] The personal obligations and effects of association are assumed to be nominal, even though membership ideally signifies much more than dues in return for contractual benefits—an intrinsically valuable set of relationships, an element of political identity, and more.

The union shop reminds us that in some instances men and women may view membership in a particular association as a practical necessity. Voluntary association can be *experienced* as compulsory if the benefits they afford seem crucial to reluctantly pragmatic or cynical joiners. We encountered an instance in *Amos*, where a janitor was fired from his job at a Mormon-run gym for failing to conform to the church's tenets of faith. Regional economic dominance can make religious observance a virtual condition of employment. Affiliation is not always as nominal as dues-paying, either; Jaycees must actively participate in the association's civic work and social life to reap the benefits of belonging.

The calculated advantage of joining is one thing. The legal requirement that groups open their membership to categories of people whom they wish to exclude is another. There is no question that associations can *advocate* discrimination and exclusion, or any other antiliberal, antidemocratic belief or practice. The Jaycees have a right to say that their organization should serve only the interests of young men, but what about the practice of discriminatory membership? When is official interference in the membership policies of secular *voluntary* associations justifiable?

It is worth noting briefly at the outset that compelled association is just one way government affects membership in voluntary associations. Government may directly punish the act of membership or prevent individuals from forming associations. Consider the history of legislation outlawing politically subversive groups ranging from criminal syndicalists, anarchists, and the Communist Party to paramilitary groups today.

Government may try to withhold benefits or privileges from members of certain associations. The principal evidence in determining an individual's qualifications for public employment on loyalty grounds was "guilt by association."[9]

Government has compelled disclosure of membership rolls in groups seeking anonymity, in what was really an effort by Alabama to drive the NAACP from the state. The Court first enunciated the constitutional doctrine known as the "right of association" in *NAACP v. Alabama* in 1958.[10]

Finally, as part of the attempt to protect individuals from the power of "private governments," courts insist on due process when associations discipline or expel members—the sort of intervention the Supreme Court ruled a violation of First Amendment freedom of religion in *Serbian Diocese*. A complaint by an Eagle Scout expelled from the Boy Scouts for being homosexual was upheld for wrongful denial of the right to fair procedure.[11]

But until *Roberts v. Jaycees*, states had not interfered with voluntary associations by mandating eligibility requirements for membership and compelling association.

The bylaws of the Jaycees national organization allowed women to participate in most activities as "associates" but denied them full membership. Local chapters in St. Paul and Minneapolis voted to admit women as regular members, and when the national organization threatened to revoke their charters, they challenged the organization's bylaws under Minnesota's Human Rights Act. *Roberts v. Jaycees*, decided in 1984, is the Supreme Court's most extensive discussion of the application of antidiscrimination law to voluntary associations.

It is not hard to see why "few cases in this Court's history have so deeply involved the shape and character of the private sector."[12] The *Roberts* decision goes to the heart of the Jaycees' self-definition as a group dedicated to the advancement of young men. Regular membership was restricted to men with like interests and backgrounds between the ages of eighteen and thirty-five. It was not a cross-section of young men either: 30 percent were upper management and another 20 percent middle management, though far less than half the population from which Minneapolis members were drawn fits that profile. The Jaycees' "voice" was altered once it was forced to admit young women as regular members. Moreover, the decision had implications for many other associations that restricted admission on the basis of either broad classifications such as race, gender, and ethnicity or subjective factors such as congeniality or social status.

Above all, the *Roberts* decision disturbed what had been a fairly stable equilibrium. Plainly, voluntary association could be a cynical strategy for circumventing civil rights laws: "an unbounded freedom to dis-associate would cripple the guarantees of equality contained in the constitution and our civil rights statutes, since every ban on discrimination would be checkmated by an assertion of individual autonomy phrased as a claim of associational freedom."[13] Legislation had created a sort of balance. On one side was a sphere of publicly available goods and services in which antidiscrimination law operated—the field of education, employment, housing, and "public accommodations." On the other side was a sphere of private, that is, social activity that legislatures and courts had not sought to enter. *Roberts* upset the prevailing understanding that "while classification on the basis of involuntary group affiliations is subject to attack in the name of equality, voluntary associations are protected in the name of liberty."[14] It represented an escalation of demands for congruence, and a further step in the constitutionalization of social life.

Like other redrawings of the perpetually shifting public/private boundary, this one was spurred by good intentions and invoked widely accepted principles of democratic equality. Designating the Jaycees a "public accommodation" so unsettled the public/private classification, however, that it effectively shifted the focus from marking out a privileged sphere of freedom of association. The protected private sphere was shrunk to encompass mainly "intimate" associations. The focus became the specific liberal democratic interests that justify compelling association.

In an early case involving the Benevolent and Protective Order of Elks, a district court had ruled that a black applicant's "interest in joining the private club of his choice surely does not constitute a basic right of citizenship."[15] This decision frames the issue correctly, I will argue. Government-mandated membership policies are justified when exclusion from an association denotes second class citizenship. But the *Roberts* majority does not stop here. Every item in the expansive catalogue of harms of exclusion makes an appearance in Justice Brennan's opinion: second-class citizenship but also, stigma, degradation, unequal status, injury to personal dignity and self-respect. In the Court's decision, and in moral and political theory more broadly, the harms of exclusion gain force from the aggregation and implicit conflation of independent evils.

Thus, in a representative statement, Kenneth Karst writes, "The most heart-rending deprivation of all is the inequality of status that excludes people from full membership in the community, degrading them by labeling them as outsiders, denying them their very selves."[16] "Inequality of status" indicates someone is assigned to an inferior caste; he or she is less than a full member of political society, a second-class citizen. "Outsider" ascribes subjective feelings to all parties; it indicates that recognized signs of "belonging" are willfully withheld, and that the person marked as alien feels alienated. (This criterion is problematic if we recall that casting oneself as an outsider is a familiar self-dramatizing and often self-aggrandizing mode in the United States. We conjure up a unified American society—"Christian" or "Judeo-Christian," "male," "white," "secular-humanist," or "middle-class"—in order to heighten our own group's distinctiveness and defiant marginality.) As for "denying them their very selves," the thought is indecipherable, or plainly wrong. But it *is* evocative of the gamut of notions associated with "identity" and the set of injuries to identity that includes harm to personal dignity and self-respect, and "misrecognition."

In order to assess compelled association from the standpoint of the moral uses of pluralism, it is necessary to disaggregate the evils liberal democracy purports to counter and the protections it promises. This entails taking a closer look at the *experience* of exclusion.

To anticipate: from the point of view of the moral uses of pluralism, our reasons for *insuring* freedom of association turn the argument for compelling association on its head. Membership in voluntary associations in which we are wanted and willing members is a key source of self-respect. Because associations often owe their origin to a dynamic of affiliation and exclusion, resentment and self-affirmation, the moral uses of pluralism are consistent with and may require incongruent groups. Indeed, groups functioning as "safety valves" for discrimination may help confine exclusion there. The history of voluntary association in the United States underscores the psychological logic of freedom of association.

The Legal Background: Nondiscrimination in Places of Public Accommodation and Compelling State Interests

The policy of enforcing congruence between the internal lives of voluntary associations and liberal democratic norms is a distinctive step in a family of statutory moves prohibiting private discriminatory actions. It began with repeal of laws *requiring* racial segregation. This was followed, a decade before enactment of the federal Civil Rights Act of 1875, by state laws prohibiting discrimination in "places of public accommodation." In his dissent in the 1883 Civil Rights Cases, Justice Harlan adopted the course states had marked out. He would have expanded the domain of legal rights to insure certain forms of "social intercourse," while maintaining the idea that "no legal right of a citizen is violated by the refusal of others to maintain merely social relations with him."[17] The majority famously and tragically disagreed, invalidating federal Reconstruction legislation on the grounds that the Civil War amendments were directed only at government actors, not private parties.

In response to this decision, more states adopted Human Rights Acts like the one applied to the Jaycees in *Roberts*. The legislative high point came with the 1964 federal Civil Rights Act, which denied associational freedom to discriminate in housing, employment, education, and access to basic goods and services, facilities of commerce and common carriers—in short, "places of public accommodation," though they are privately owned. Since then, federal and state governments have progressively broadened both the facilities and the groups covered. State constitutions have been amended to include public accommodation provisions prohibiting gender discrimination, as Minnesota did in 1973. Some local ordinances go further; New York City's Human Rights Law, for example, covers the physically or mentally handicapped and individuals discriminated against because of actual or perceived sexual orientation. (Though none embrace the broad principle that categorical exclusion should be prohibited when it is based on characteristics over which people have no choice.)

The precise terms of state public accommodation laws vary. They apply first of all to businesses, and since classifying a voluntary association as a business is an opening to state regulation, this construction is controversial. To take one example, in a 1983 case the Boy Scout Council was designated a business under California law because it received income from franchising copyrighted emblems and uniforms and from publishing and selling books. Some states construe "places of public accommodation" to mean an establishment with a definite geographical location. The Alaska Jaycees escaped the charge of unlawful sex discrimination in 1983 because the organization had no physical place of operation in the state. In *NOW v. Little League Baseball*, by contrast, the league was held to be a "place of public accommodation" because a fixed site was not necessary under New Jersey law.[18]

The 1964 federal Civil Rights Act did not apply to private clubs or other establishments not open to the public, however. Until *Roberts v. Jaycees*, either antidiscrimination laws contained specific exceptions for private associations, or "public accommodation" was interpreted narrowly. When the question of regulating membership of private associations was raised, these exceptions were upheld. Justice Douglas's reasoning in *Moose Lodge* reflected the rule:

> The associational rights which our system honors permit all white, all black, all brown, and all yellow clubs to be formed. They also permit all Catholic, all Jewish, or all agnostic clubs to be established. Government may not tell a man or woman who his or her associates must be. The individual can be as selective as he desires.[19]

Besides, states had less interventionist means to counter exclusion than mandating eligibility requirements and compelling association. They could use liquor licensing authority to withhold privileges from private discriminatory clubs, or withdraw tax concessions such as deductions for charitable contributions or nonprofit tax-exempt status.[20] State officials could be instructed not to appear at any function of an offending association and not to do official business with it. It could be made unlawful for an employer to subsidize employees' membership, and so on. In comparison, compelled association is extraordinarily intrusive.

The issue came to a head with three Supreme Court decisions, *Roberts v. Jaycees* and two others for which it provided the framework of constitutional analysis.[21] The Minnesota supreme court categorized the Jaycees organization as a *business* in that it sells goods and extends privileges in exchange for annual membership dues. (Specifically, "leadership skills are 'goods' [and] business contacts and employment promotions are 'privileges' and 'advantages.'") It is a *public* business in that it solicits and recruits members based on unselective criteria. And it is a *facility* in that it continuously recruits and conducts activities at fixed sites within the state.[22]

Judging that Minnesota has a "compelling interest" to see that women become full members, the state attorney general employed the arguments used to justify public accommodation law generally. "Clearing the channels of commerce of the irrelevancy of sex" is a public purpose of the first magnitude. And "the deprivation of personal dignity that surely accompanies denials of equal access to public establishments" (which is felt as deeply by women as persons denied it on the basis of color) is a harm the state should act to prevent.[23] The Supreme Court upheld the decision without dissent.

Categorizing Hybrids: "A Relatively Easy Case"

Justice O'Connor's important concurrence in *Roberts* adhered to the logic of the Minnesota supreme court. She distinguished commercial from expressive associations, assigned commercial associations only minimal constitutional protection, and judged that despite the group's "not insubstantial" volume of protected advocacy of political causes, the Jaycees is a "relatively easy case." It promotes and practices "the art of solicitation and management." It exists to serve the general public as "customers," not a more limited group as "members." "A shopkeeper has no constitutional right to deal only with persons of one sex," she argues, and rules as if the Jaycees were no different.[24]

O'Connor acknowledges that many associations cannot be described as purely commercial or expressive. The difficulties with her reasoning run deeper than overlap at the margins, however, since a large set of exclusionary social and cultural groups do not fit either category. Moreover, O'Connor's typology is vulnerable to conflicting interpretations. On one view, an association's purposes or activities determine whether or not they are *predominantly* expressive or commercial. On another view, whatever its purposes and activities, once an association enters the marketplace of commerce *in any substantial degree* it forfeits protection, though it is unclear how much commercial activity gives the state warrant to intervene.[25] (It goes without saying that membership activities, not the commercial investments of nonprofit associations, are at issue; the Catholic fraternal order Knights of Columbus, for example, operates a major life insurance company with $1 billion in revenues.[26])

These complications go unexplored because O'Connor declares the Jaycees to be first and foremost an organization that promotes and practices "the art of solicitation and management." Amicus briefs for the Jaycees had anticipated this argument. The Conference of Private Organizations pointed out that the Jaycees does not sell seats like the Dale Carnegie organization:

> if the U.S. Jaycees is merely a commercial business, it hardly would have expended hundreds of thousands of dollars in litigation fees, in courts throughout the country, defending its purpose and right not to engage in the allegedly lucrative "sale" of memberships to women. . . . Personal and business development, if they come, come not as products bought by members but as by-products of activities in which members engage after they join the organization.[27]

These include social, civic, and ideological activities. The Jaycees' rhetoric of "maximizing" recruitment and "marketing" their "product" may "hoist [the group] with its own petard," but this does not make them a sham association created to elude the Minnesota public accommodation statute.[28]

Whether the acquisition of commercial skills is simply one of the benefits of membership or bought, O'Connor's point is that the goods acquired through membership are commercial. More than 80 percent of the national officers' time is dedicated to recruitment, she observes, and "recruitment and selling are commercial activities, even when conducted for training rather than profit."[29] The problem with this characterization is that leadership, management, solicitation, and marketing skills are not specific to business. In a pluralist society distinguished by shifting involvements and where competition for people's time, attention, commitment, and money is commonplace, clergy "sell" their churches and partisans their advocacy groups. The "arts" O'Connor mentions are generalizable; they are learned and applied in innumerable contexts.

This is evident if we think of women who begin work outside the home as volunteers in nonprofit organizations large or small, and go on to exploit this experience in the labor market or in politics.[30] Volunteering reminds us that the origin and complement of Jaycee "training" is not business but nineteenth-century humanitarian reform societies. These early voluntary associations developed techniques for recruiting, dues-collecting, fund-raising, enlisting community support, selling publications, petitioning, and lobbying. Reform societies, not businesses, are the models for quasi-social/quasi-enterprise organizations like the Jaycees, whose activities involve a "not insubstantial" amount of charitable community work and political advocacy.[31] (In the same vein, the Court's identification of the "business like attributes" of Rotary International—its complex structure, large staff and budget, extensive publishing activities—describes many kinds of organizations, not just businesses.)

For Justice O'Connor, categorization is key to association freedom. The Jaycees are vulnerable to state public accommodation law because they are a commercial association, rather than because, commercial or not, the state has an interest in opening their membership. Her categorical approach was a wholesale rejection of the majority's reasoning. For Justice Brennan saw the Jaycees as an expressive association but ruled that the group's First Amendment right of association lost in the balance against the state's compelling interest in antidiscrimination. I argue in the next chapter that the decision is underprotective of expressive associations because it fails to appreciate the genesis of political association. My concern here is the misguided nature of the Court's understanding of the public interest in compelling association.

"Clearing the Channels of Commerce" and Second-Class Citizenship

The majority's argument for legally enforced congruence turns largely on the claim that "valuable goods and privileges" come from membership. Minnesota's extension of public accommodation to cover voluntary associations, Brennan wrote, "reflects a recognition of the changing nature of the American economy and of the importance, both to the individual and to society, of removing the barriers to economic advancement and political and social integration that have historically plagued certain disadvantaged groups, including women."[32]

When the connection between "clearing the channels of commerce" and second-class citizenship is secure, the harm of exclusion is not subjective. It is a violation of actual rights or public norms of civic equality (or of a generally recognized failure to apply and enforce rights and norms consistently). The injury is "logically entailed by, rather than merely contingently caused by" the conduct.[33] It is not erased by the fact that the victim may not experience injury, though normally the pain is real enough. That is why Charles Black was appalled by the "artificial mist of puzzlement" surrounding the question of whether racial discrimination inheres in legally imposed segregation in the twentieth century:

> It is true that the specifically hurtful character of segregation, as a net matter in the life of each segregated individual, may be hard to establish . . . [but] that a practice, on massive historical evidence and in common sense, has the designed and generally apprehended effect of putting its victims at a disadvantage, is enough for law.[34]

Historically, certain barriers and exclusions have been inescapable marks of inferior public standing in the United States. In a political society with a public ideology of political equality, where no special virtue or contribution was necessary for suffrage and "the worst white scoundrel" was declared fit to vote, to be denied the vote was to be degraded. It "is to make us an exception, to brand us with the stigma of inferiority," Frederick Douglass wrote.[35] This becomes perfectly clear if we contrast the women's suffrage movement with the attitudes of teenagers who had no reason to feel demeaned when they could not vote until the age of twenty-one, and did not value the franchise when it was thrust on them by constitutional amendment in 1971.[36]

Second-class citizenship is also sanctioned by diluting a group's vote, through gerrymandering, for example: "it is a fixed point in a democratic culture that public institutions should not establish or reinforce the perception that some people's interests deserve less respect or concern than those of others simply in virtue of their membership in one rather than another social or ascriptive group."[37]

The same rationales used to deny political rights were employed to justify other civil disabilities: denial of property rights, exclusion from certain occupations, and, what is probably the closest parallel to "associate membership" in the Jaycees, unequal pay for equal work.

The message of second-class citizenship is also communicated when the exercise of a right is frustrated or conceded in a manner that is grudging, humiliating, or effectively punitive. It is today when receipt of means-tested public benefits is made personally difficult. When welfare departments hassle recipients or require exhaustive documentation, frequent trips, and reapplications. When procedures assume recipients need policing—home visits characterized as "warrantless searches" by welfare workers turned into sleuths. (And when "no such sums are spent policing the government subsidies granted to farmers, airlines, steamship companies, and junk mail dealers.") Justice Marshall could not understand "why a commercial warehouse deserves more protection than does this poor woman's home." The message of second-class citizenship is delivered when denial of due process is condoned.[38] In *Goldberg v. Kelley*, a 1970 case requiring pretermination hearing before AFDC payments could be cut off, Justice Brennan's decision linked "dignity and well-being" as the twin goals of welfare.[39] Brennan was right to insist that the changing nature of the American economy can create new indiciae of second-class citizenship.

So when the *Roberts* court characterized the Jaycees' membership policy as "invidious discrimination" and denial of full membership to women as a "stigma," it used the most forceful terms available to say that the exclusion from the benefits of membership constituted debasement of women's public standing. "Stigma" refers not just to any prejudicial mark but to a badge of civic inferiority. It is a trigger for protective treatment. The Jaycees' response was blunt: "The fact that a few appellants do not like the . . . policy does not convert a benign exclusion into an invidious discrimination."[40] Feminist commentators concede that "not all females resent all forms of separatism and American society remains deeply divided over which forms are invidious."[41]

What makes exclusion from the "valuable goods and privileges" of Jaycee membership a legally cognizable barrier to "economic advancement and political and social integration that have historically plagued certain disadvantaged groups"? In terms of second-class citizenship, it is not clear that "economic advancement" is on a par with political inclusion. Or that all "opportunity interests" are on a par. Few writers would insist as Kenneth Karst has that full inclusion in public life for minority groups comes "only when the great preponderance of their members have visibly advanced into the middle class."[42] Discussion focused mainly on when exclusion from certain goods that are considered means to economic advancement amounts to debased public standing.

The Jaycees objected that there is simply no test of a voluntary association's "influence" in the business community. But a factual inquiry is possible. Evidence is available: personal testimony of members regarding the personal contacts that lead to jobs, records of business deductions of membership fees, and so on.[43] In *New York State Club Association* Justice Scalia upheld the exemption for benevolent orders by noting the absence of a showing that lodges "significantly contribute to the problem the City Council was addressing." A less restrained district court had scoffed at the thought of a compelling state interest in prohibiting the Elks from discriminating, describing the group as "ludicrous, harmless, innocent, anachronistic, defensive, evanescent, inconsequential."[44]

Judge Arnold's decision in favor of the Jaycees in the court of appeals had proposed that Minnesota's interest was not compelling because the record failed to show that membership was the *only* practicable way for a woman to advance in business or professional life.[45] But it is a misunderstanding of the purpose of public accommodation provisions to say that no compelling state interest exists unless the association is the sine qua non of economic advancement for women. That could never be demonstrated in any case; "as a practical matter it is probably impossible to identify from among the myriad of events in an individual's life a solitary decision or action which guarantees an advance in one's career."[46] Public interest in nondiscrimination does not require a showing that insuring access to a particular set of goods is the most helpful measure government could take, either. Even strong proponents of compelled association would agree that membership is less significant than vigorous enforcement of the Equal Credit Opportunity Act, for example, or affirmative action programs, which have proved their effectiveness. The decisive question is not whether Jaycee membership is an avenue to advancement but whether other parallel channels, adequately effective, are closed to women.

If so, exclusion may well be an inescapable stigma, debased public standing. But is it really of compelling importance that men and women have equal access to *every* association offering specific opportunities and advantages? Is the supposition that other channels of commerce are open "based upon the moribund theory of 'separate but equal'"? Or does a proliferation of associations, all-male, all-female, and gender-integrated, affect the challenge?[47] The appeals court thought the existence of alternative associations was legally significant:

> We know that membership in the Jaycees has been of some help to the complaining individuals in their corporate careers, but we do not know whether similar organizational experience in other clubs or associations, open either to both sexes or to women only, has been or could be of similar or greater help to these or other women.[48]

Of course, for strong egalitarians, whether or not a multiplicity of associations of varying degrees of openness exists, separatist institutions are intolerable because they sustain disadvantages. The Jaycees "perpetuate male hierarchies, not male sanctuaries," Deborah Rhode argues, and proposes a rule that would integrate all-male associations while leaving all-female associations alone. Legal differentiation is defensible, she writes in what has become a familiar argument, because "separatism imposed by empowered groups carries different symbolic and practical significance than separatism chosen by subordinate groups."[49] It is not clear how much this argument turns on the practical significance of membership versus symbolism. Or whether differential treatment is justifiable so long as women's social/civic/commercial associations are not on a social par with men's, or whether a more relaxed standard applies—the absence of alternative associations for women.

On all these points, the circumstances of the case are illuminating. *Roberts* involved an internal dispute over eligibility. In a 1981 national referendum Jaycees had voted 67 percent to 33 percent not to change the membership status of women. The St. Paul and Minneapolis chapters violated the organization's bylaws by deciding to admit women as full members, and when the national organization threatened to revoke their charters the Minnesota chapters brought action under the state Human Rights Act. The complaint was brought by members themselves. This is not surprising; associations engaged in a range of commercial and civic activities are highly permeable. The moral and social forces that led to legislation prohibiting gender discrimination in the mid-1970s were "out there," and local activists a decade later were not immune to them.

It is unlikely that a decision in favor of the national organization would have eliminated these integrated groups. The rebel local chapters would have separated permanently from the parent organization and gone their independent ways. Indeed, given the moral climate and organizational impetus of women's push for equality, integrated Jaycees and similar groups would very likely have been invigorated. In large cities, unreconstructed male Jaycees might have been marginalized in their own clubs. (The conditions of pluralism also vary; forming new or splinter groups is obviously more difficult in a small community of 25,000 than in St. Paul.) "It is almost a rule of associations," Grant McConnell advises, "that they have greater animosity for rivals than for opponents."[50]

Of course, it is also unlikely that compelled association eliminates restrictive groups, since discriminatory commercial and social relations go on defiantly "underground" all the time. (And I will leave aside the feminist question of whether the forced admission of women reduced pluralism by encouraging "assimilation.") Richard Epstein's argument in *Forbidden Grounds* for lifting antidiscrimination regulations applies much more convincingly to voluntary associations than it does to employment. Given widespread legal and political attacks on affirmative action and support for color-blind and gender-blind policies, he points out, permitting "private" discrimination may be the best strategy for integration. At least, it would guarantee that voluntary affirmative action could carry on undeterred.

In short, the alternatives facing would-be female Jaycees were not exclusion and segregation on the one hand and compelled association on the other. There was also voluntary association, separation and schism, and competition among groups. The parallel to the issues raised by *Serbian Diocese* in chapter 3 is plain. Faced with contested religious authority and doctrine, courts neither uphold religious orthodoxy nor side with dissenters. This creates an environment hospitable to the formation of new associations, and the result has been fluid denominationalism and a rash of independent religious groups.

Religious association is the original and model, but splintering and splitting mark humanitarian, labor, political, patriotic, ethnic, and cultural societies, and groups like the Jaycees. Eligibility for membership is high on any list of causes of splits. The Jaycees' institutional history illustrates the observation that "nothing has been more characteristic of voluntary bodies than the proneness of dissidents to exercise what has been termed 'the God-given right of every American to resign, tell why, and raise hell.'"[51]

Justice Brennan was right to reason that restricting freedom of association is warranted if it signifies and practically supports second-class citizenship. To the extent that he firmly tethers dignity harms to public standing, and connects both to exclusion from the specific goods meted out in places of public accommodation, his moral logic is sound. That certain exclusions have become inescapable marks of inferior public standing is a historical reality, and so are discriminatory barriers to public goods and opportunities. Preserving this connection serves as a reminder that second-class citizenship is not a historic relic. And it keeps the argument from expanding to cover every unjustified subordination and exclusion.

That said, Brennan's decision to classify the Jaycees as a public accommodation is not compelling. The group was not a general source of publicly available goods; participation was not widespread across all sectors of the community, or broadly representative. The Jaycees were not the exclusive purveyors of career advantages; other associations were open to women. Indeed, legally compelled association may have retarded the multiplication of groups capable of providing more people with a wider range of opportunities for commercial and professional advancement. These are arguable matters of judgment, however. There is no bright line indicating when exclusion from the option of membership makes equal public standing so difficult that association should be legally compelled. In specific instances the advantages of membership in a voluntary association might be so material and the obstacles to opportunities for economic advancement without membership so insuperable and so significant for "political and social integration" that it makes sense to include the association under public accommodation law. Certain associations have the character of civic groups. Professional societies like the integrated bar, for example. This is necessarily a case-by-case determination.

The only sure result of compelled association is that with *Roberts*, male Jaycees joined the company of those who see themselves as victims of powerful, hostile social forces and of public indifference to their freedom of association. The Rotary amicus brief anticipated this when it invoked constitutional protection for the Jaycees as an embattled, politically unpopular group: "At the present time, male-only organizations such as the Jaycees and Rotary are encountering governmental and social hostility akin to that directed at the NAACP in the 1960s."[52] (NOW was an amicus on the winning side.)

The critical problem with Brennan's decision is that he does not scrupulously preserve the promised tie to second-class citizenship. Perhaps because the Jaycees' importance as an avenue to public standing and to salient public goods was ambiguous, this rationale for interfering with its freedom seemed to need reinforcement. As I said earlier, in *Roberts* and in the arguments made by advocates of congruence generally, the public accommodation rationale rarely stands alone. It is swallowed up by the claim that second-class membership implies second-class citizenship tout court. The judgment that subordination in the Jaycees is a substantial barrier to economic advancement recedes. In its place Brennan invokes an unsupported parallel between subordination of women in the Jaycees on the one hand and in society at large and as citizens on the other.

Once the justification for compelled association is loosed from its tether to public accommodation law and the aim of "clearing the channels of commerce," there is nothing to stop it from expanding to cover every arbitrary and unjustified subordination and exclusion. A brake is needed, for the perfectly good reason that commitment to equal citizenship is "*not* identical to the general right of all citizens not to be arbitrarily discriminated against."[53] And because the conflation of exclusion from membership or second-class membership with debased public standing is an unfortunate invitation to set aside sociological and psychological realism.

Second-Class Membership = Second-Class Citizenship?

The national Jaycees' organization admitted women as "associate members" but they could not hold office, vote for officers or on organization policy, or receive achievement awards (though they participated in the programs on which awards were based). The state's "overpowering interest," Justice Brennan explains, stems from the fact that this membership policy is "invidious discrimination" and denial of full membership to women is a "stigma":

> this Court has frequently noted that discrimination based on archaic and overbroad assumptions about the relative needs and capacities of the sexes forces individuals to labor under stereotypical notions that often bear no relationship to their actual abilities. It thereby both deprives persons of their individual dignity and denies society the benefits of wide participation in political, economic, and cultural life.[54]

When *is* exclusion a mark of second-class citizenship? "To be a second-class citizen is to suffer derogation and the loss of respectable standing," Judith Shklar explains. The *Roberts* Court declares subordinate status *within* the association an independent harm to public standing. Supporters of the decision adopt Brennan's reasoning: "We might not be sure about the role gender ought to play in the 'good' society," Deborah Rhode observed, "but we can share a sense of the role gender ought not to play"—accepting that subordinate association membership entails a subordinate role in the good society overall, that it is stigmatizing.[55]

Full membership and public standing are seen as interdependent in the present on the assumption that social habits and moral dispositions cultivated and expressed in voluntary associations are carried over willy-nilly to public life. As one advocate of an expansive public "antidiscrimination project" puts it, "stigmatized social status and the concomitant withholding of respect are in a sense the central evil the [antidiscrimination] project seeks to remedy, since it is the source of the poison that contaminates, and renders unfair the outcomes of, public and private decision making."[56]

The position has the appeal of simplicity and holism. Second-class membership, the argument goes, is inseparable from debased public standing because their sources are the same. So are their consequences for victims: affront, outrage, "misrecognition," and self-loathing. And because "systems of stigmatizing meaning reproduce themselves systematically."[57] Congruence is necessary (and should be legally enforced) because moral dispositions are of a piece in their origins and effects, and spill over from sphere to sphere:

> Men who are uncomfortable associating with women in such social settings are unlikely to become less so if discomfort remains a valid justification for exclusivity. And such discomfort is not readily confined. Those who have trouble treating women as equals at clubhouse lunches will not readily escape such difficulties in corporate suites or smoke-filled rooms.[58]

Perhaps. But discrimination condoned in one sphere is not necessarily condoned, or exhibited, in all or any others. For one thing, individuals' attitudes toward others on the basis of race or sex serve different psychological functions for them in different domains. Moral psychology is more nuanced. For another, there are various reasons for discrimination, not just one reason that applies uniformly in all situations. "Myopic" prejudice may be amenable to correction by experience. If irrational prejudice were at work, compelled association might encourage male Jaycees to acknowledge women's contributions to their association, spilling over into appreciation of gender equality generally. *Roberts* assumes myopic prejudice, and in a related case involving Rotary clubs the Court adopted an overtly paternalistic line, announcing that the exclusion of women was not in the group's own interest. The club's mission—providing humanitarian service, encouraging high ethical standards in all vocations, and helping build world peace—would be improved by opening membership to women, Justice Powell prescribed, and would permit the Rotary to "obtain a more representative cross-section of community leaders with a broadened capacity for service."[59]

Paternalism was misplaced. It is doubtful that male Rotarians or Jaycees as a group were myopic, or that their membership practices were based on a stereotypical belief that women could not recruit new members or organize charity drives. After all, women "associates" contributed to the group's effectiveness. (Though for individual members, the affective content of exclusion as an expression of inferiority may have been at work.) The national Jaycees' resistance to Minnesota's law was not meant to defend a generalization about whether or not women could perform adequately as members, but to preserve the group as an association of young men. Withholding full membership from women illustrates "principled discrimination," which is cold-eyed and persists in the face of measurable costs, such as maximizing recruitment.

Moreover, principled discrimination is normally not a permanent disposition, unconsciously carried over from one sphere to another.[60] In the Jaycees, hierarchical membership is related to the association's avowed goal: the self-development and advancement of male management-types under the age of thirty-five (which is why they humorlessly object to the expression "old boys' network"). Under these circumstances, compelled association does not correct irrational prejudice but alters the association's deliberate, self-chosen purpose.

Powell's paternalism must have been galling. *Roberts* was decided in 1984, on the verge of the wave of "identity politics" that propelled a new vocabulary for group affiliation into everyday use. Constitutional strategy required the Jaycees to employ First Amendment arguments, including an emphasis on their political activities. But as we will see in subsequent chapters, the notion that membership itself is expressive was abroad. And the "politics of recognition," as the Jaycees could attest, demands acknowledging not just collective identity (in this case, young men with similar interests and social status) but also that the group's own view of its needs and interests should be determinative. If nothing else, with its untempered assertions about privilege and stigma, the *Roberts* decision reveals a failure of imaginative sympathy for the meaning exclusion might have for male Jaycees. The parallel is not exact, but here is General Bunting, superintendent of Virginia Military Institute, an all-male school facing a legal challenge by women (a case in which compelled association *was* justified):

> Wistful, plaintive; adjectives like that. It's like the Adagio section of Mahler's Fifth Symphony, Death in Venice, and there is a wistful quality that comes from the fact that those who go here really love it and adore it. They realize that once it's gone it can never be recovered. . . . This is a singular place; it's quiet; it has nothing to do with the screaming excesses of right-wing caricatures.[61]

Those who see a seamless web of public and private life and a unity of moral disposition deny that people have the capacity or inclination to discriminate discriminatingly. Beyond that, they argue that when government fails to interfere with an association's freedom and to eliminate "second-class membership," it "morally legitimizes and potentially encourages a practice both courts and legislatures have decried as one of the most significant evils in modern society."[62] On this view, government has an obligation to engage in civic education: to affirm the equal worth of excluded individuals, redress dignity harms broadly understood, and enforce acceptable democratic behavior in arenas except for the most intimate. Thus, Andrew Koppelman concludes: "The fact that the needed recognition can only be provided by the community creates a prima facie obligation on the part of the community to provide it." The state must use coercion to transform citizens' consciousness, recognizing the potential of antidiscrimination law "to function as an overt instrument of cultural transformation," to change patterns of cultural expression and even unconscious thinking.[63]

Government has many avenues for promoting approved conduct and messages, of course, in its authoritative capacity as educator and as employer, owner, grantor, and patron. But this case for the obligation to transform consciousness and practice goes far beyond seizing occasions for official proclamations. It goes beyond what ought to be the day-to-day demonstration of liberal democratic practices in public institutions. And beyond prohibiting "state action" that insinuates government in discriminatory private conduct.[64] Advocates of congruence are stern didacts. They would use the law to "press club members into service to send society a message of inclusion and equality." They disregard the liberal fundamental "that private individuals may not be used as the involuntary instruments of a state lesson."[65]

Plaintiffs in the *Tiger Inn* case, for example, acknowledged that the purpose of requiring Princeton University's all-male eating clubs to admit women was to send a message of equality to club members and society at large. "College years are very formative years, and students should not be taught the lesson that discrimination is acceptable and legitimate."[66] The same didactic intent informs arguments for the mandatory gender integration of Greek letter societies: "Integration may help teach young men and women to view one another as complete human beings rather than merely as potential sexual partners. Living together on a daily basis should encourage members of both genders to accept one another as social and intellectual equals."[67]

The argument proves too much. It is insensitive to the range of personal needs, and sexual and moral maturity of students. And it does not tell us when the "formative" years are over. Clearly, the justification for compelled association has shifted from avoiding presumptive harm to the public standing of those excluded to the moral education of discriminating members.

It is true that "the modern liberal state is best understood as energized by a distinctive ensemble of public purposes that guide liberal public policy, shape liberal justice, require the practice of liberal virtue, and rest on a liberal public culture."[68] And as a general matter we expect "circular reinforcement of politics, personal dispositions and behavior, and constitutional law."[69] But as a general matter, government is not thought to "morally legitimize and potentially encourage" a group's practices when it leaves the control of membership to members. Freedom of association is no stamp of public approval of the internal life of an association in a liberal democracy. If it were, the fundamental principle of toleration would be meaningless.

Public Standing and Self-Respect

Those who think that discrimination is one thing, that it cannot be contained and will spill over from sphere to sphere, see victimization as uniform across spheres as well. Stigmatizing reduces the victim "from a whole and usual person to a tainted discounted one," Erving Goffman observes, going on to describe stigma as "spoiled identity."[70] The idea is that those discriminated against and excluded internalize images of inferiority and incapacity, resulting in self-hatred.

This psychological logic was used effectively by Kenneth Clark and the NAACP in their argument in *Brown v. Board of Education*, which challenged government-mandated racial discrimination in public schools. The Court found officially inflicted harm to students, which Chief Justice Warren described as "a feeling of inferiority as to their status in the community that may affect their hearts and minds in a way unlikely ever to be undone."[71] Although this dynamic is widely invoked, there is reason to doubt whether what holds for black children's motivation to learn in officially segregated schools (and in an overtly racist public environment) is generalizable.

The assumption that second-class citizenship inexorably injures self-respect—a commonplace in philosophical discussions of democratic equality today, is even more troubling than the automatic identification of second-class membership with second-class citizenship. It is not just that self-respect is too subjective a state of mind to be the ground for public policy ("the consequences of discrimination both real and imagined, depend on an individual's temperament and past experience"—or the thickness of our skin).[72] Beyond that, the two are independent.

This may seem to claim too much. I could say, more modestly, that public standing is a necessary but not sufficient condition for dignity and self-respect, but I want to advance the stronger claim.

For one thing because the admonition that second-class citizenship is intolerable is not enhanced by heaping on the presumption of injury to self-worth. Its "elemental wrongness" is unchanged, whether or not victims suffer. The obligation of democratic government (and of citizens personally and individually) to insure equal public standing and refrain from public shows of disrespect is not diminished by the fact that self-respect may be invulnerable to these assaults.

More important here, the unproved overstatement that self-respect is mediated by public standing has serious consequences. It would be foolish to deny that second-class citizenship, accompanied as it normally is by public expressions of hate and denigration, can cause self-loathing. Or to prescribe stoic detachment, promising that debasement and humiliation only disrupt the equilibrium of those willing to be harmed. Nonetheless, there are good reasons not to overstate the capacity of law and public institutions to instill or to secure self-respect. And as I will explain, there are good reasons to acknowledge that exclusion and "invidious discrimination" are not inherently harmful to it. These goods are not as unambiguously related as political theory would have it.

Self-respect is rightly characterized as a "primary good," vital to well-being. It is a condition for any purposive action beyond the most narrowly instrumental: "The importance of self-respect is that it provides a secure sense of our own value, a firm conviction that our determinate conception of the good is worth carrying out. Without self-respect nothing may seem worth doing, and if some things have value for us, we lack the will to pursue them."[73] We know little about the conditions that instill self-respect, though, apart from the genuine need for attachment and basic trust in early childhood (a deficit at this stage is said to be irreparable.) We know even less about how self-respect is damaged or reversed; in particular, what conditions exacerbate or mitigate the effects of the public stigma of second-class citizenship.

But because liberal theorists fear that self-respect is vulnerable to unequal public standing, and because ardent civic-minded theorists positively insist it *should* be so, there is a strong impetus to adopt as a democratic tenet the tie between self-respect and first-class citizenship. With it comes the impetus to urge a uniform spirit of civic equality throughout public and private life, so that not only political institutions and public accommodations but also voluntary social groups function as mini-liberal democracies that cultivate and sustain self-respect. (It is another step to the "politics of recognition," whereby individuals identified with certain groups cannot be civic or social equals unless their "specific experience, culture, and social contributions are publicly affirmed.")[74] Again, the consequence of insisting that public standing is a necessary condition of self-respect is to assume a positive public obligation to insure self-respect, which is neither possible nor desirable.

Above all, this well-meaning view is carelessly cruel. By tying self-respect to public standing, defending oneself against discrimination becomes a moral imperative. This is not to deny that recognizing oneself as a person with rights and public standing is a defining characteristic of liberal democratic citizenship. So is appreciation of the moral obligations others have to perform in a way that respects these, and a keen sense of injustice when they do not. It is simply to distinguish having and exercising rights claims from self-respect.

For the frequent implication is that those who fail to resist unjust treatment lack moral backbone or psychological core. They are "damaged." Hannah Arendt feared that the school desegregation decisions required heroism of the black children forced into social stituations where they were not wanted. Ralph Ellison contradicted her, insisting that these children are required to master the inner tensions created by their racial situation, and must be inured to struggle.[75] The exchange reminds us that antidiscrimination law is not self-enforcing. Enforcement is dispersed, laid on men and women personally and individually. In this respect the *Roberts* case, which was an intraorganizational dispute brought by local chapters against the national organization, is misleading. It entailed little personal risk to complaining members.

Normally, effecting rights to equal treatment in housing, employment, education, and so on requires the personally consuming commitment of individual victims to righting the wrong through formal institutional proceedings, or in court. It means overcoming concrete obstacles: the costs of counsel, technicalities of evidence and burdens of proof, knowledge of what sorts of complaints are cognizable (after all, many forms of prejudicial treatment are permissible). Complainants must be prepared to verify their subjective experience of wrong in the form of records and evidence. They must call publicly for legal protection, and dedicate themselves to showing they deserve it.[76]

The inclination to see prejudice rooted in individual personality (the offender is "immature" or "just plain ignorant") rather than systematic discrimination, and viewing resignation as strength of character are unhelpful from the point of view of public education and political progress. We know that confrontations in the aggregate and over time can stem expressions of prejudice. The many political reasons to organize and motivate people to defend their rights are reinforced by the fact that activism itself is vitalizing and contributes to self-respect. But this is entirely different from the thought that passivity or alternative strategies of self-defense is an indication that second-class citizens are not self-respecting. In what appears to be a demonstration of empathy with victims, and in what is certainly a move to enhance the importance of equal citizenship by saying it is a necessary condition of self-respect, advocates come close to confirming that people treated as second-class citizens are degraded. Little good can come from suggesting that second-class citizens must publicly demonstrate that they are not lacking in self-respect—that they do not see themselves as "spoiled."

On reflection, we realize that discrimination occurs unostentatiously in the course of ordinary interpersonal relations, and self-assertion in accord with public procedures threatens to disrupt day-to-day life. Accustomed to speaking of rights and rights-holders in the abstract, we may tend to forget or depreciate the need to make the mundane calculation that one's situation will actually be improved. Like all subjective harms, the effects of second-class citizenship will vary among individuals, who must make a personal decision whether or not to defend their rights. Understandably, if victims fear that formal complaint and legal intervention will worsen their condition, they will devise alternative strategies. These include angry confrontation, stoic endurance, and exit—taking another job or moving to other housing or joining another group.

Christopher Jencks describes gender differences in the way African American men and women deal with discrimination:

> When a black man thinks someone has shown him disrespect or treated him unfairly, he is likely to show his anger, perhaps because this is the only way he can maintain his self-respect. Women are less likely to feel that their self-respect requires them to challenge their boss. . . . They tell one another stories about how unfair their boss's behavior is, or why they deserved the promotion someone else got.[77]

The second strategy is more constructive from the point of view of keeping one's job, but the point is not that women are the disciplined calculators. Both not complaining and lashing out may be expressions of dignity. People can maintain a sense of pride "by withstanding pain, avoiding confrontations, or completing humble work."[78]

Also, self-respect may lie in resigning oneself to mistreatment for the sake of fulfilling other obligations such as supporting a family. One of the subjects interviewed by Kristin Bumiller for *The Civil Rights Society* is a case in point: Carmen "accepts inequality as a worker because of the scarcity of jobs. At home, however, a husband who does not assume equal responsibility for the family is unacceptable."[79] This example highlights one of the reasons why a person can recognize herself as having rights and as being treated unjustly yet refrain from making claims. Other moral dispositions are imperative, too. They may not outweigh justice and the "antidiscrimination project" in public life. But they may well have priority when it comes to self-respect.

All these considerations apply to the tendency to identify both public standing and self-respect with employment. Again, the two dignity harms are separable. Arguably, paid work is a necessary condition for publicly recognized first-class citizenship in the United States. Everyone knows that unemployment may be beyond our control, but it is still a fall from public standing, and the connection between long-term joblessness and second-class citizenship is even clearer. The distinction between deserving and undeserving poor is as strong as ever, with one recent change. The influx of women into the labor market and the expectation that women should be able to support themselves and their children if they cannot depend on husbands or relatives means that "welfare mothers" as well as able-bodied working-age men are viewed as shiftless if they do not try to find regular employment. Women who are dependent on husbands or relatives are not similarly stigmatized; dependence on the state is key.

We sometimes acknowledge that compulsory workfare policies have less to do with economics than with getting the unemployed to maintain acceptable standards of civic conduct.[80] That this is in tension with structural economic changes and "the logic of jobless growth," which requires fewer people to work less and large numbers to remain unintegrated into the workforce has only recently gained attention.[81] It has made few inroads into democratic political ideology, whether the requirement of work is based on the obligation of self-sufficiency or reciprocity, a cooperative scheme of mutual obligation.

If paid work is represented as a condition not only of public standing but also of self-respect, reasons multiply for why the unemployed must take work, why public policy should make them work, and why government must guarantee work (and job training). We have only to think of the number of television dramas and situation comedies set in workplaces to recognize that they function as Rawlsian social unions, and are important arenas for cultivating self-worth. But we are also liable to lose sight of the fact that when it comes to work, public standing and self-respect may conflict.

It seems that any work that earns a living suffices for public standing. Any paid job signifies that able-bodied adults have taken on the common obligations of citizenship, or at least that they are not idlers, burdens on taxpayers. Self-respect, however, may require useful or "decent" work, or work that calls on specific capacities and talents. Contingencies of age and environment affect whether or not particular work or conditions of employment is considered respectable. Some jobless will take any job they can get, some do not want a job at all, and some want only a "good job," as Christopher Jencks explains: "Minimum-wage jobs are acceptable to many teenagers, who have no family to support and just want pocket money. But no native-born American male can imagine supporting a family on $3.35 [now $4.25] an hour. If that is the only 'respectable' alternative, he will usually conclude that respectability is beyond his reach."[82]

Work may diminish self-respect if the job itself or treatment there is considered demeaning, or if it is manifestly "make-work." Conflict between work as an avenue to public standing and self-respect also arises if a low-paying, seasonal, and temporary job means leaving the collective help and obligations of family and social networks. These are lifelines that provide an economic fallback for those who cannot save to meet unanticipated changes of fortune. They are also sources of moral independence and self-esteem.[83]

The gap enlarges if we subscribe to Michael Sandel's more demanding, republican argument that the aim of political economy should be to cultivate the qualities of character necessary for self-government. Ideally, public standing attaches to work fitting Senator Robert Kennedy's description: "dignified employment at decent pay, the kind of employment that lets a man say to his community, to his family, to his country, and most important, to himself, 'I helped to build this country. I am a participant in its great public ventures.'"[84] But it takes either an exercise of personal moral imagination or regular exhortations from public bully-pulpits to make all work fit that description, and for us to think of ourselves as workers in these terms.

Throughout this discussion I have followed the usual course of identifying the official marks of first-class citizenship that are our chief indications of public standing and democratic respect. These are backed up with civil and political rights and, hopefully, effective mechanisms of enforcement. But I want to insert the thought, to which I will return, that in everyday life our principal signals of public standing occur in the interstices of institutions—on the street, in stores, in the course of innumerable casual encounters with strangers. In a liberal democracy we are expected to refrain from public displays of cruelty and humiliation, and from expressing our moral and social judgments at every turn. This is the severe self-discipline liberal democracy asks of us. It is a discipline because democracy in everyday life does not necessarily reflect our private sentiments about whether individuals or groups warrant respect, or whether we think they have grounds for respecting themselves. It indicates nothing about whether we would voluntarily associate with them. Conduct in everyday life is where the moral dispositions of liberal democratic citizens are exhibited full force, without institutional props. It is legally untouchable. But it is an unavoidable arena of public education where, personally and individually, we have regular occasion to speak up for ourselves or others, to acknowledge and correct small acts of discrimination and disrespect.

That said, it is a failure of moral imagination to think that public standing is the sole, chief, guaranteed, or necessary condition of *self-respect*. After all, the dynamic frequently works in reverse. Self-respect bolsters us against slights and prejudice, social exclusion, second-class membership, and even second-class citizenship.

Restricted Membership and Self-Respect

So it should not be surprising that my objections to identifying self-respect with public standing apply even more strongly to identifying it with first-class membership in voluntary associations. What is wrong with assuming that personal dignity is mediated by "recognition" of the sort that comes from admission to restricted groups?

For one thing, it assumes that the intention to stigmatize others by excluding them is successful. It aggrandizes discriminators, and diminishes their targets by assuming they lack resources to resist being "spoiled."

It is also too stringent. Under the guise of protecting people against injury to self-respect, compelled association may simply protect them from "the raw insult of being kept out." Those who unjustifiably exclude others from consideration as candidates for membership may be guilty of a moral wrong. Or, they exhibit the "ordinary vice" of snobbery. Very often, what is taken as an expression of superiority is unintended:

> As we join a multiplicity of groups that include some people, we also exclude most others. These little societies are by no means equal in social standing and neither are their individual members. Inevitably some outsiders will be rebuffed and hurt, and this would be the case even if there were no groups that make social exclusion their chief business. Given any degree of inequality and any kind of choice of intimacies and interests, there is bound to be snobbery in effect.[85]

The fine line between disrespect and insensitivity is added reason to restrict official policy to exclusions that are inescapably marks of second-class citizenship, and to acknowledge that "the sense of injustice is as often ignited by injuries that the official agencies of justice cannot touch."[86] Simply, lack of consideration as a result of prejudice and ill-will is not a public harm and is not officially corrigible.

This is not to deny the painfulness of "the raw insult of being left out." "Psychologically," Arendt observed, "the situation of being unwanted (a typically social predicament) is more difficult to bear than outright persecution (a political predicament)."[87] Our sense of who we are, where we belong, and what constitutes respectful treatment varies wildly, along with the thickness of our skins. We know, for example, that members of white ethnic groups have reasonably accurate perceptions of the stereotypes others have of their group. But they have a distorted view of the valence of these characteristics, and imagine that others have a more negative view of them than is the case.[88]

There is another reason not to identify self-respect with membership in voluntary associations. It leads to a tendency to ennoble would-be joiners by assuming that crusading to open up a restricted-membership group is morally laudable, a self-respecting resistance to stigmatization. The grim self-righteousness of opponents of Princeton's eating clubs is unmistakable. Those storming the gates of exclusive associations may be frankly disposed to shut the door behind them. We have all witnessed the depressing spectacle of people desperately trying to "belong" in some milieu they imagine is superior to others. Characters without personal pride, who abandon one group and push their way into another, have been staples of the novel from its inception. The unwholesome drama is perfectly commonplace within as well as among racial, religious, and ethnic groups. Here is Melissa Fay Greene's description of Atlanta Jews in the 1950s:

> the upper class, the social comers, shinny up toward the summit until they feel they are but a hair's breadth from civil equality and social acceptance . . . if only they can shake the masses, the majority of their own people. And then here come the masses—ill timed, unwashed, tubercular, needy, reeking of the ghetto, raucously

shouting in dialect, and eagerly imposing on the hospitality and pocketbooks of their vaunted brethren. . . . From the point of view of the German-Jewish Reform Jews, it was the presence of the Orthodox Eastern European multitudes that *placed* them at risk, jeopardized their exalted positions; in short, blew their cover.[89]

Self-righteousness, hypocrisy, social-climbing, and envy do not undermine the principled justifications (and good motives) for legally compelled association—when it is necessary to defend citizens' equal public standing. But they do explain the moral ambivalence we may feel about crusading crashers. One scholar observed, in the related context of banning hate speech, that the motivation of censors is "hatred of those with bigoted attitudes and a desire to exercise power over them. . . . [I]f they cannot [force the association to open its doors], then they feel the frustration of impotence vis-a-vis those whose views they hate."[90]

These are reasons not to be deferential toward every self-described action in support of victims. They also provide some insight into passionate resistance from groups that want to preserve their exclusive characters. Sheer, illiberal prejudice is not the only force at work.

When those excluded from voluntary associations exhibit self-respect and democratic pride, they deserve moral approval. In fact, this is less rare than political and legal theorists seem to think. There is nothing inherently lamentable about individuals thrown back on themselves to "dredge up the meaning and stability" they require, rather than find it in membership.[91] Ultimately, that is what we all must do. No matter how emotionally identified we are (or imagine we could be) with a particular group, associations do not "constitute" us. Nor for that matter does public standing as citizens, no matter how fulsome official rituals of recognition.

In any case, personal resources and moral courage are not all we have to draw on in response to exclusion. Individuals' membership in voluntary associations where they are welcome members buffer them from public shows of disrespect, cultivate a sense of self-worth, and reinforce inner resources. That is why those who are excluded from one set of voluntary associations often disagree about whether the best response is to campaign for legally compelled association or to form their own restrictive groups.

Organized "support" is a major industry today. Innumerable self-help groups, fellowship groups, and self-styled "identity groups" form around personal disabilities and social disadvantages, stigmas, real or imagined victimization, disappointment and rejection of all kinds. Long lists of meetings fill local newspapers and bulletin boards. COYOTE (Call Off Your Old Tired Ethics), to take one example, has as its primary goal providing an educational and support network "to raise the overall self-esteem of women and men in the sex industry" and end the stigma surrounding "sexwork."[92] These groups are advertised instances of what goes on indirectly all the time in associations. For those who are not proud individualists, associations of one's own are the democratic response to exclusion and rebuff.

The argument for freedom to choose members does not depend altogether on weaknesses in the case for compelled association, then. Good reasons exist to support freedom to exclude unwanted members, even if the policy is pejorative, or taken as such. Self-worth comes in part from belonging to "social unions" in which we are wanted and willing members. And these associations frequently owe their origin to the dynamic of snobbery and exclusion, association and self-affirmation.

The Democratic Uses of "Comparing Groups"

John Rawls is surely right that to be self-respecting more is needed than the recognition of public standing demonstrated in the distribution of fundamental rights and liberties. Individuals need some place where their values and opinions are affirmed, their contributions acknowledged, where the likelihood of failure is reduced and they find support against lurking self-doubt. As we saw in chapter 2, voluntary associations provide these contexts whether or not they are congruent with liberal democratic norms and practices. Rawls also proposes that membership in associations protects self-respect by mitigating the effects of inequalities of income and wealth, a necessary function even if inequalities are just, as they are in his ideal scheme. A plurality of associations "tends to reduce the visibility, or at least the painful visibility, of variations in men's prospects," he observes. Associations "tend to divide [society] into noncomparing groups," and act as a brake on competition, rivalry, and hostile outbreaks of social envy.[93] Freedom of association operates as the antidote to its own vices if everyone has occasions for inclusion and exclusion, opportunities for self-protection and for bolstering self-worth.

A sociological precursor to Rawls' thesis is the 1892 essay, "The Great American Safety-Valve," which characterized voluntary associations as relatively harmless outlets for "these ambitions for precedence which our national life generates, fosters, and stimulates, without adequate provision for their gratification."[94] This suggests that even if voluntary associations temper economic comparisons as Rawls proposes, they are fertile ground for exhibitions of earned or unmerited superiority, organized elitism, separatism, snobbery, and genuinely hateful, prejudicial exclusion. Associations are often formed to demonstrate some exemplary difference from "mainstream" society as a whole. (Thus, the life history of the odyssey from immigrant or first-generation American to assimilated citizen and member—Jaycee!—has its counterpart in the life history of the shallow assimilationist discovering his or her roots and claiming superiority over "plain" Americans, like Malcolm X.) Or, associations are formed to reaffirm commitment to the public values of democratic society, exhibiting members' exemplary civic-mindedness and civility. Earlier, I quoted Werner Sollors' description of the range of purposes:

> Americans' unsystematic desire to identify with intermediary groups . . . may be based on real or imagined descent, on old or newly adopted religions, on geographic area of origin, socialization or residence, on external categorization, on voluntary association, or on defiance. In all of these cases, symbolic boundaries are constructed in a perplexing variety of continuously shifting forms.[95]

Anyone observing children's cliques gets a taste of the sheer arbitrariness of selective association in action, its irrepressibility and potential cruelty. I do not mean to suggest that "tribalism" is primordial. On the contrary, the dynamic I describe is distinctively democratic, and habits are learned early. Despite recurrent populist fears of elitism and subversion, Americans are not opposed to exclusive, even secret organizations for themselves: "The plain citizen sometimes wearied of his plainness," and wanted rites as well as rights, ceremonials, grandiloquent titles, exotic regalia, and comradeship.[96] In the United States, selective groups will be seen as advancing some claim to preference, privilege, or desert regardless of the association's purpose or members' intentions. Restrictive groups will provoke accusations that they violate the public ethos of democratic equality. According to David Brion Davis, "the subversive group was essentially an inverted image of Jacksonian democracy and the cult of the common man."[97]

The history of voluntary associations here reflects the permanent dynamic of association and exclusion, and challenges in the name of democratic equality. The very first collective enterprises apart from churches in the colonial era were nonsectarian benevolent societies like the American Bible Society, which charged churches with elitism in their competition for prestige and funds.[98]

Preoccupation with "entails, nobility, hierarchy, and monopolies" emerged full force in the Jacksonian era.[99] Social critics added professionals to the seemingly endless list of "social classifications" and "combinations" that smacked of pride and privilege. Every one of these groups would "become our dukes, lords, marquises, and baronets" if undeterred.[100] The proposed democratic antidote was the "voluntary principle," meaning free competition and voluntary association.

A few observers at the time were skeptical of this solution. We have a brilliant guide to the permanent dynamic of affiliation and exclusion in Nathaniel Hawthorne. This master of moral psychology took the American promise of self-made identity unencumbered by inheritances and the "voluntary principle" seriously, and pointed out every lapse and hypocrisy (not just the enormous contradiction of slavery). He called America a "Custom House" because society had enough in the way of inheritance and unearned privilege to make the social ethos of open, democratic egalitarianism seem like a chimera. To Henry James, America was a "thinly composed society"; it had no class, no status, no established church, no monarchy, no aristocracy, no guilds and closed professions, no nobility of sword or robe, no high culture, no polite society. To Santayana, America was a social vacuum, a ghastly "vacancy."[101] Hawthorne knew better, and predicted that the purported cure for hereditary social hierarchy and traditional exclusion—competing voluntary associations—would be a vast generator of restrictiveness and resentment in turn.

Hawthorne was right. There are always fresh waves of association and exclusion. As some forms of descent are thrown off as undemocratic fetters, others are invented. Associations celebrating ancestry are an American commonplace: pedigreed associations of the Sons and Daughters of the American Revolution and the Society of Mayflower Descendents; commemorative associations of survivors of the Civil War and heritage organizations such as the Sons of Confederate Veterans. These inspired the formation of groups of Jewish War Veterans, among others. Nativist anti-Catholic societies like the Order of United Americans and Brotherhood of the Union arose in response to the Ancient Order of the Hibernians imported by Irish Catholics in 1836, followed by dozens of Jewish fraternal orders, including B'nai Brith in 1843.

Freedom of association and social mobility are vast engines of social cliques. They generate groups that labor to preserve their social restrictiveness and pretended distinction, and to claim deference from others. Above all, there is the American penchant for secret societies and the groups formed in reaction, to combat their "conspiracies"—the Masonic fraternity, for example, and the rabid associations, also secretive, organized to counter Masonic power. In short, every restrictive association spawns accusations that they are subversively antidemocratic, and inspires counterpart groups, mirror images of exclusiveness.

I belabor this point because it is rarely noted. Apart from political science discussions of political interest groups and grassroots community organizing, group formation is a relatively neglected aspect of pluralism. Where it is considered, the standard thesis sees the process of voluntary association in America as determinedly practical. It stresses cooperation in useful tasks and generation of social capital. In contrast to aristocratic orders, Tocqueville explained, the "independent and feeble" citizens of a democratic nation must "learn voluntarily to help one another."[102] "The churches, clubs, lodges, temperance and reading societies of natives and immigrants" during the heyday of joining in the mid-nineteenth century "encouraged social ties that made the formation of death benefit, accident, and unemployment pools possible."[103] The Jaycees put themselves in this company when they warn that compelled association would have a "chilling effect" on their civic and charitable activities.

This standard, sanguine view has had its acid detractors. Accusations of faction, real or imagined, have been leveled at every imaginable group, beginning with Washington's Farewell Address condemning "all combinations and associations, under whatever plausible character, with the real design to direct, control, counteract, or awe the regular deliberation and action of the constituted authorities."[104] Civic republicans follow Rousseau in devising schemes to eliminate "Hobbesian" self-preferring groups and the social hierarchies that get a foothold in private circles. There are innumerable "lapsarian theories of groups" as combinations of individuals corrupted by self-love. And romantic individualists see all joining as a pitiful lack of self-reliance.

The usefulness of groups escaped Thoreau entirely; the best neighborliness is "minding your own business," he thought, and the true reformer is "one perfect institution in himself."[105] "At the name of a society all my repulsions play," Emerson confessed: "Men club together on the principle: 'I have failed, and you have failed, but perhaps together we shall not fail.'"[106] In liberal democracy, romantic aloofness is as insufferable as exclusive groups, however. It too is perceived as aristocratic self-distancing, and generally despised. Nonetheless, romantic individualism points up the dark underside of gregariousness: dependence, craving for the good opinion of others, hypocrisy, self-righteousness, and the desire of those excluded to join together and inflict the same on others. These are not just incidental accompaniments of voluntary association but key to the motivation and purpose of association.

The dynamic of affiliation and exclusion is permanent, and the character of "safety valves" constantly changing, because in liberal democracy conceptions of social status are unstable. It is reported that "private social clubs with discriminatory membership policies are fast becoming extinct" (the average age of membership is sixty-two). The reasons doubtless have less to do with legal challenges than changing ideas about social precedence. Freemasons, Shriners, Elk, and Moose are endangered species when groups of middle-aged white men are eyed with suspicion, and when prospective members find secret handshakes and the Moose's cape and tah (hat spelled backwards) laughable.

The St. Andrews Society recently contemplated admitting women to their 237-year-old club dedicated to upholding Scottish traditions and Scottish charity. They debated whether the association could survive without women members, or whether St. Andrews did enough for women already by allowing them to attend the annual banquet (seated at segregated tables in the balcony) and the Tartan Ball (where they could sit at tables with men). It is fair to suppose that potential young joiners were not so much outraged by the group's discriminatory practices as put off because St. Andrews could not possibly satisfy contemporary notions of social status, and its affairs do not appear to be fun.

The contemporary "politics of recognition" to which I turn in chapter 9 bears a family resemblance to the dynamics of affiliation and exclusion. But at least among academic theorists of cultural groups, the terms of discussion are maddeningly benign: "identity," "recognition," the emergence of self-understanding from "dialogue" with "significant others." We have lost Hawthorne's cold eye on the snobbery and malice of associations, aggressive assertions of uniqueness and self-celebration—whether members have power and privileges or not. The motivational root of affiliation is supposed to be the "epistemological comforts of home," not access to jobs and positions, social status or sheer resentment.[107] It is considered disrespectful to suggest that people who have been subject to discrimination want the solace and revenge of compensatory, exclusive, and sometimes hostile associations of their own. The dynamic of exclusion is a virtual taboo, or is attributed entirely to vulnerability and the contingent need for self-protection. Deference seems to demand that we disregard the fact that self-presentation in terms that emphasize identity and values "has often provided the excuse—as well as the emotional fuel" for action aimed at getting a share, fair or not, of social and economic goods.[108]

Again, this dynamic is eminently democratic. To the extent that the public culture and institutions of liberal democracy are sufficiently strong that exclusion cannot translate into withholding legal rights and publicly available goods, it will find expression in voluntary associations. Indeed, as gains in first-class citizenship by previously marginal groups and real security for public standing increase, we can expect to see the number and intensity of these associations increase. The genuinely antiliberal, antidemocratic claim that "we" are the "real citizens" and others permanently second-class because their inferiority is a matter of inherited or unalterable attributes will never disappear, but voluntary associations can serve as "safety valves."

What Rawls' picture of "noncomparing groups" gets wrong, then, is that the morally useful world of multiple associations and multiple hierarchies is one of *comparing* groups. Without this dynamic, which operates more freely in a liberal democracy than anywhere else, there would be many fewer sources of the "primary good" of self-respect. And less containment of irrepressible exclusiveness.

Democracy and Disassociation

The critical problem for voluntary association, public standing, and self-respect today is less exclusion from restricted membership groups per se than isolation. Political science has a lot to say about who lacks *political* association and the specific ways in which participation is unrepresentative. In a comprehensive study, Sidney Verba, Henry Brady, and Kay Schlozman surveyed the principal reasons for nonparticipation: paucity of necessary resources, lack of political engagement, and isolation from networks of recruitment. Their research also shows a gap between political participation and much higher levels of religious activity, so there is little reason to think that people without political association are without associational ties of other kinds. (The disposition to join is not peculiarly middle-class, either; many poor are joiners.)[109]

Genuine anomie is evidenced less by political nonparticipation or by overall declining membership in traditional associations (others are burgeoning) than by the fact that for some people the whole range of associational life is out of reach. Ghettoization, chronic unemployment ("unemployment means having nothing to do—which means having nothing to do with the rest of us"),[110] and characterological impediments to sociability (aggressiveness or depression) foster anomie.

The elusive designation "underclass" ordinarily points to the economic bottom of American social life, to apparent indifference to widely accepted social and moral values, and to a propensity for conduct believed to reflect this indifference: chronic hostility, impulsiveness, long-term joblessness, and criminality.[111] "Underclass" can be used as a term of abuse, of course. I think its persistence also owes in part to the perception of anomie. Its very emptiness is significant. Viewed from outside, alternative ways of aggregating and disaggregating the "members" of this class are not readily at hand. There are few buffering, overlapping associations and mediating identifications to soften the contrast between "the very bottom" and everyone else.

In the case of individuals condemned to a "culture of segregation" or isolation, both public standing and self-respect may well depend on being drawn into voluntary associations. But these are the very people who lack both resources for organizing groups of their own and occasions for being recruited into existing ones. Individuals do not simply "join" associations; they are recruited into churches or the Jaycees by friends or co-workers, which is one reason association breeds more association. We know very little about how to get isolated individuals to become joiners, still less about how to keep them engaged.

A newspaper report on the decline of the Loyal Order of Moose Lodge in Roxbury, Massachusetts, described the lodge's plan to give up its capes and to attract young men by launching a drum and bugle corps. The difficulty seemed immense even to the hopeful Moose: "If they're already into drugs, it'll be hard to get them into the drum and bugle corps."[112] Accounts of recruitment by hate groups indicate that young men are not attracted to them because they reflect their own racist ideas and ambitions, but simply because they are solicited. They have nothing better to do and nowhere else to go. Given this scenario, it is no surprise that the life span of membership in racist groups is short and that members cycle away, often into persistent disassociation and personal chaos.

It is unlikely that the energy and flux of voluntary association can be directed from above; associations implanted from outside have a high failure rate.[113] Recognizing that indigenous local efforts are the most successful, government has sometimes sought to fill the associational void by exploiting virtually any group "on the ground" as a basis for potentially positive social engagement. One program cast street gangs as sources of social capital, if only they could be diverted from apprenticeship for crime and self-destruction. We can sympathize with Nathan Glazer, skeptical but stumped: "In the absence of the natural forms of informal social organization, what alternatives do we have?"[114]

The terrible, palpable self-exclusion of anomie may be intractable. At least, it may not be amenable to public policy directed at assisting association. The indirect effect of redistributive policies on anomie, as on so much else, is another question. If it is tractable, however, the process of association capable of generating stable membership and self-respect in anomic outsiders will likely replicate the dynamic of affiliation and exclusion, of "comparing groups."

The limits on association freedom formulated by the majority in *Roberts v. Jaycees* were justified by the state interests I have dissected critically here. The Court also gave its most expansive interpretation of the constitutional right of association in *Roberts*, tying freedom of association to the First Amendment right of expression. The compelling demands of antidiscrimination were permitted to outweigh the expressive association's liberty to restrict membership in this case. But the fact remains that expressive associations, particularly when they advance political messages, are singled out for special protection. What is the rationale for this constitutional right of association? What, if anything, limits government regulation of the membership practices of an expressive group and interference with its distinctive "voice"? Why does constitutional doctrine obscure one of the key moral uses of pluralism—the genesis of both expression by a voluntary association and of expressive associations themselves?

6

Membership and Voice

IN A classic article, "Freedom of Association and Freedom of Expression," Thomas Emerson argued that a single doctrinal right of association is too broad and remote from concrete issues to offer voluntary associations protection against state intrusion. The question of associational rights is better separated out into "associational aspects of freedom of religion, freedom of expression, the right to engage in an occupation or profession, and the like."[1] I have observed Emerson's caution throughout this book. Freedom of association is not one thing, and neither is its justification—the moral uses of pluralism guarantees as much, in life if not law.

The focus of this chapter is the expressive use of associations; specifically, the relation between membership and voice. I consider the way compelled association can change an association's voice, and even coerce expression. It is not hard to see that an association's "voice" is dependent on its membership and is vulnerable to changes in membership policy. Voice is created, preserved, or altered by changes in the character of the group. So official impediments to choosing one's associates and compelled association have an impact on the group's voice. I also take up official attempts to curtail association expression on the one hand (to curb "undue electoral influence," for example) and to enhance voices on the other.

My particular interest is groups that are not initially formed as expressive associations but nonetheless engage in a considerable amount of expressive activity, beginning with the Jaycees, moving on to unions and corporations, and ending with "association" with electoral campaigns and causes via political contributions.

Associations are only sometimes formed for purposes of advocacy and political influence. More often, their members come to engage in political expression as a result of the unanticipated internal dynamic of group life or some external impetus. They publicly advance opinions or support the political activities of other groups as an adjunct to their principal purposes. I take a latitudinous view of the way members of an association arrive at political expression, and of the genesis of expressive associations themselves. Political expression is one of the key uses of pluralism, and I hope to drive home the often unintended, unpredictable entry of associations into public discussion and democratic politics. It is the reason why democratic justifications for freedom of association are inseparable from the moral uses of pluralism overall.

Freedom of Association and the First Amendment

Freedom of association is not mentioned in the text of the U.S. Constitution. Constitutional history and commentary generally represent the right of association as ancillary to enumerated freedoms of press, speech, petition, or assembly—what Justice Douglas called the "bundle of rights" protected by the First Amendment.[2] It confers a right to join with others to pursue activities independently protected by the First Amendment; association is necessary to make these express guarantees "fully meaningful." Justice Harlan forged this link in the NAACP case that formally enunciated a "right of association": "Effective advocacy of both public and private points of view, particularly controversial ones, is undeniably enhanced by group association, as this Court has more than once recognized by remarking upon the close nexus between the freedoms of speech and assembly."[3]

There is no independent constitutional right of association under the First Amendment, then. Not all lawful ends pursued through association are constitutionally protected, only these preferred freedoms.[4] The case has been made for a constitutional right of association loosed from its tether to other, enumerated rights. But speaking for the *Roberts* majority, Justice Brennan calls the right of association "instrumental." Despite impressions to the contrary, association is protected not for its own sake but to promote specific constitutional interests.[5]

The purposes of "instrumental" freedom of association mirror the democratic purposes of freedom of expression generally: to offset official orthodoxy, to shield dissident expression from suppression by officials or a political majority (captured in the thought that "the absence of seditious libel is the true pragmatic test of freedom of speech"),[6] to preserve other liberties by checking government, and to enable political deliberation. Expression need not be political advocacy; "we have long understood as implicit in the right to engage in activities protected by the First Amendment a corresponding right to associate with others in pursuit of a wide variety of political, social, economic, educational, religious, and cultural ends," Justice Brennan wrote in *Roberts*.[7] We will see, however, that a voluntary association's control of its own membership policy is more likely to be protected when the association is formed for specific expressive purposes.

The Jaycees had claimed the constitutional right of an expressive association to maintain their exclusionary membership policies. The eighth circuit court's ruling in their favor had focused on the group's traditionally privileged political speech. Though not a political party or pressure group, Jaycee organizations advocated positions on controversial public issues. They supported public policies in favor of the effort to reduce the size of the Minnesota legislature, the draft, FBI efforts to eliminate "disloyalty," a balanced budget, and voluntary prayer in schools. Jaycee chapters publicly favored a bill to support the economic development of Alaska, a bill to save seals, and a bill to change the form of city government in El Dorado, Arkansas. The association also embarked on a nationwide program of support for President Reagan's economic policy, and in this connection the Rotary amicus brief notes the substantial difference in support of the president by men and women—the "gender gap."

Bolstering this catalogue of political activity, briefs likened the Jaycees to other protected associations. They were portrayed as "a major organized voice of young men in the United States just as N.O.W. serves as an effective voice on behalf of women." (NOW filed an amicus brief on the opposing side.) On this view, when the government deflects the Jaycees from its purpose by requiring it to admit young women and presumably to advance their interests, it is no different than dictating to the NAACP that it must also devote its energies to matters of particular interest to white people.

Justice Brennan agreed that the Jaycees were an expressive association, acknowledging that political advocacy is "a not insubstantial part" of their activities. Although the right of association is not absolute, this should have made it very difficult to override the group's First Amendment freedom. Why wasn't the group protected?[8] Freedom of association lost in the balance against the state's compelling interest in applying antidiscrimination law to the Jaycees in order to clear the channels of commerce, combat gender stereotyping, and protect excluded individuals from injuries to self-respect. In the previous chapter I discussed the strengths and weaknesses of these arguments for congruence between voluntary associations and public norms of nondiscrimination. Here, I look at the other side of the balance. Specifically, at how, even in the privileged area of expression, the significance of association autonomy is diminished.

A doctrinal argument weighed in against the Jaycees' freedom of expressive association. The ACLU's amicus brief to the Supreme Court in *Roberts* employed familiar developments from the areas of speech and religion. Legislation not aimed at speech or religion, which is designed to serve other legitimate government purposes and has only an incidental effect on speech or religious exercise, is permissible. (Thus, the prohibition against draft-card mutilation was permissible because it was not aimed at inhibiting expression and served a legitimate purpose, the efficient management of the selective service system.)

In this spirit, the Supreme Court reasoned that Minnesota's public accommodation act does not aim at suppression of speech or distinguish between prohibited and permitted activity on the basis of viewpoint, or have as its purpose hampering the organization's ability to express its views. Even if the

result of enforcing the state's Human Rights Act is "some incidental abridg-
ment of the Jaycees' protected speech," Brennan argues, "that effect is no
greater than is necessary to accomplish the State's legitimate purpose."[9]

True, Minnesota's public accommodation law did not target Jaycees messages, but it did aim at the group's membership. If we accept the nexus between membership and expression, we should concede that a government-
mandated change in membership alters the association's voice. Whatever the
state's aim, the effect on expression is not circuitous or indirect. We also see
that the Court took upon itself the task of estimating the consequence of the
mandatory admission of women for the group's expression, concluding that it
would be trivial.

Membership and Message

The court of appeals ruling in *Roberts* had sensibly decided that if the association were forced to offer women full membership it was reasonable to expect
"some change in the Jaycees' philosophical cast." (Recall the resistance to
admitting women by male members; in 1981, Jaycees voted 67 percent to 33
percent in a national referendum not to change the membership status of
women.) The judges focused on the Jaycee creed—the avowed mission to
which members must subscribe:

> It is not hard to imagine . . . that if women become full-fledged members in any
> substantial numbers, it will not be long before efforts are made to change the Jaycee
> creed. . . . Young women may take a dim view of affirming the "brotherhood of man"
> or declaring how "free men" can win economic justice. . . . [S]uch phrases are not
> trivial.[10]

The Supreme Court rejected this claim in a graduated series of arguments
rising from the observation that the alleged nexus between Jaycees membership and message was speculative, to denial that any nexus exists, to the charge
that in asserting a nexus between male membership and political message the
Jaycees were engaging in precisely the sort of gender stereotyping the Minnesota antidiscrimination statute was designed to stop. By retracing these escalating steps, we can appreciate how crimped the Court's view of association
voice is. And how implausible in light of the genesis and practice not only of
messages but also of expressive associations themselves.

To qualify for First Amendment protection against compelled association,
Brennan began, there must be "a *logical nexus* between the discriminatory
membership policies and the group's purpose or message." In this case, the
nexus between membership and voice was "speculative." The Court could find
no factual basis in the record to support the prediction that admitting women
as full voting members would impede the group's ability to engage in its con-

stitutionally protected civic, charitable, lobbying, and fund-raising activities and to disseminate its preferred views. After all, Justice Brennan pointed out, the association is free to admit only women who espouse the Jaycee creed, and can screen out women applicants who do not support the group's purposes and messages.[11]

This proposed strategy for protecting expressive association fails for a simple reason that has a bearing on my subject as a whole. The Jaycees are not a political advocacy group organized to take public positions on defined issues. Like many groups that engage in substantial expressive activity, their "philosophy" and publicly stated purposes are broad and do not determine specific messages in advance. If Justice O'Connor is correct about the group's preoccupation with business and sales, perhaps ideological commitment to private enterprise and profit-making is a condition of membership, but that does not dictate positions on public policy. As a practical matter, a group that favors gun control might be able to exclude only those who oppose gun control; the Jaycees had no such test available.

Given the indeterminacy of the association's expression and the consequent difficulty of screening for compatible beliefs in practice, there is no "logical nexus" between membership and message that would predict the consequence of radically altered membership on public expression. So while it is unlikely that women would seek admission to the Jaycees under false pretenses— avowing beliefs they do not really hold in order to subvert the organization's public positions—it is also difficult to demonstrate that the association's public messages would be unchanged. The logical nexus Justice Brennan looks for is *necessarily* speculative.

Indeed, it is hard to see how on this reasoning *any* expressive association could defend a restrictive-membership policy. The standard hypothetical example of a strong nexus between membership and message is a white supremacist group whose exclusion of blacks is intrinsic to its ideological purpose. We need not engage in stereotyping to predict that African Americans would tend to have different views than Ku Klux Klan members, and that compelled association would subvert the group's message. "A suggestion that the admission of blacks . . . would not change the organization's philosophical cast would be laughable."[12] But it is not fanciful to think that the arguments applied to the Jaycees could apply here. The KKK could screen blacks for their views on white supremacy (presumably applicants would answer queries sincerely), and while those who choose to join would not reflect the views of most African Americans, it is conceivable that some—self-loathers or whatever—would be eligible for membership.[13] This would not change the group's voice, inasmuch as the Court identifies association voice with its racist public message. Conceivably, compelled integration might provoke white members to quit the KKK; the association's *viability* could be endangered, but not its message!

The Court does not stop to work out the implications of its notion of ideological "screening," because the ground of argument shifts. From asserting that the factual basis of a nexus between membership and message is too speculative to support a First Amendment claim, the Court moves on to insisting that as a matter of fact no nexus exists. The admission of women "would not curtail or intimidate any advocacy the association has pursued." Unlike the white racist group, say, the specific content of most Jaycees resolutions has nothing to do with sex. The association can point to no organizational goal to which women cannot and do not aspire, or to any public position regarding which sex mandates a point of view. In short, the Jaycees are accused of bootstrapping on their First Amendment activity.

A gender gap on public issues might conceivably bear on the relation between membership and message. Brennan accused the Jaycees of relying "solely on unsupported generalizations about the relative interests and perspectives of men and women." He forcefully condemned legal decision making that relies uncritically on assumptions of sexual difference. He did indicate vaguely that the Jaycees' generalizations about the relative interests and perspectives of men and women "may or may not have a statistical basis in fact with respect to particular positions adopted," but declined to say what a critical examination of empirical evidence would have to show. This left Justice O'Connor wondering what *would* satisfy the requirement of proof of a membership–message connection, and insulate a voluntary association from regulation.[14] Would Brennan's analysis have been different if the Jaycees "had a steady history of opposing public issues thought by the Court to be favored by women"?

The association took no position on the ERA, for example. If it had, the majority would likely have rejected the nexus claim even so, on grounds that views on the ERA have no logical or predictable relation to gender. We begin to see how crimped the Court's thinking is. After all, if an integrated membership decided what issues the Jaycees should take political positions on, they might have been more inclined to take a stance on the ERA. The group might justify its position for or against the ERA differently than if it were controlled exclusively by men. Certainly, the impact of its public expression would be altered by the fact that it no longer represented only men.

The Court moved easily from the observation that the interests and opinions expressed by the Jaycees are not peculiar to young men to the final escalation in its refusal to extend First Amendment protection to the group. It finds the Jaycees' nexus claim not just speculative or wrong, but vicious. The Jaycees "operate on the arbitrary sentiment that men have a natural monopoly on such advocacies; this only serves to perpetuate the chauvinistic myth that women are incapable of dealing with such matters." The Court would be complicitous if it gave credence to these invidious generalizations: "We decline to indulge in the sexual stereotyping that underlies appellee's contention that, by allowing women to vote, application of the Minnesota Act will change the content or impact of the organization's speech."[15]

This is the worst of the Court's three missteps. The fact that the group is expressive should insure that First Amendment protection is not seen as government endorsement of discriminatory beliefs and practices. More troubling, the Court appears to diminish the nexus claim in this case because it finds it noxious. It comes perilously close to treading directly on viewpoint. Indeed, we know that one reason for enforcing antidiscrimination law in this case was fear that people would be influenced by the implicit message sent by the group's restrictive membership practices.

The association voice created by compelling the Jaycees to admit women might or might not be significantly different from the original in the specific messages it communicates. But it could be accurately perceived as influenced by state policy, if not as an official artifact outright. The real fear is not an appearance of state endorsement of discrimination, but the reverse. Freedom from government influence is one classic purpose of the right of association as an ancillary First Amendment right. State interference with a group's control of its own membership "violates the most basic guarantee of the First Amendment—that citizens, not the government, control the content of public discussion."[16]

Membership and Voice

For freedom of association to do its work as ancillary to the First Amendment, a group's voice cannot be reduced to its current public messages. It is not hard to see why there must be protection for an association's unaltered voice, and not just for its actual, identifying messages. The religion cases discussed earlier provide a helpful analogy. Recall Justice Brennan's permissive concurrence in *Corporation of Presiding Bishop of the Church of Latter-Day Saints v. Amos*, decided three years after *Roberts*. In *Amos*, a Mormon Church-run gymnasium was exempted from Title VII of the Civil Rights Act on statutory grounds, and permitted to fire a janitor for failing to conform to their tenets of faith. The church's uncertainty as to whether a court would see its discriminatory policy as central to faith (hence permissible) or peripheral to faith (hence regulable) was key to the Court's decision that accommodation was constitutionally permissible. Uncertainty alone posed an onerous burden on the group: "Fear of potential liability might affect the way an organization carried out what it understood to be its religious mission."

I argued in chapter 3 that the *Amos* Court was too solicitous of the church, too loathe to engage in a case-by-case analysis of facts, and too willing to cede liberal democratic norms in the critical area of employment, where important aspects of moral education go on. The point for now is that Brennan's concurrence in *Amos* focused on insulating the church from conditions where "the community's process of self-definition would be shaped in part by the prospects of litigation." He does not reduce viability to survival, or to specific defining elements of the groups authority, discipline, doctrine, or management. Instead, he recognizes the ongoing, evolving character of associational life, and defines viability in terms of free "self-definition":

> Determining that certain activities are in furtherance of an organization's religious mission, and that only those committed to that mission should conduct them, is thus a means by which a religious community defines itself. Solicitude for a church's ability to do so reflects the idea that furtherance of the autonomy of religious organizations often furthers individual religious freedom as well.[17]

The same inhibition operates on expressive associations, but the majority in *Roberts* made no move to accept the group's ongoing self-definition as its voice. The Court examined the Jaycees' public messages for a logical nexus to its membership policy, and judged the connection speculative or nonexistent, and the claim itself invidious.

In contrast to Justice Brennan, O'Connor's concurrence in *Amos* paralleled her earlier reasoning in *Roberts*. She would relieve a religious organization of the burden of demonstrating that the particular activity is religious and would allow discrimination so long as an objective observer would perceive the government action as an accommodation of the exercise of religion rather than endorsement. Her opinion in *Roberts* follows the same lines. She sees freedom of association as instrumental to expression, and argues that once an association passes the threshold of engaging in predominantly expressive activity, both the content of its message and choice of members should be sheltered. "Protection of the association's right to define its membership derives from the recognition that the formation of an expressive association is the creation of a voice, and the selection of members is the definition of that voice."[18]

This understanding of the connection between membership and voice is consistent with the moral uses of pluralism. If we define the message of an association as the expression agreed to, following some recognized internal procedure, by willing and wanted members, then a nexus between membership and voice exists by definition. The two are inseparable. (The exception is a radically divided group, internally at war and on the way to schism.) The relation between membership and voice is not logical but expressive. What matters on this view is that the message is a communication of *these people*, voluntarily joined for some lawful purpose and moved to engage in expressive activity—whether public expression is regular and consistent or spontaneous and sporadic. The voice belongs to "this group." The association is not defined by its messages; the message is a creation of the association.

So the nexus between membership and voice rests on the group's self-understanding and unplanned dynamic. The message need not be a defining or characteristic one. Nothing dictates that the communication is decided on by a deliberative or democratic process, either, rather than by authoritative fiat, if the internal life of an association is undemocratic. Simply, as the Conference of Private Organizations observed in its brief, the communications of a membership association are "inherently linked to the essential character of the association, and that character is a product of its membership restrictions."[19] Being legally required to admit a class of unwelcome members changes the group's voice, even if its impact on the group's actual public communications cannot be predicted, or does not occur at all.

A principal part of any Jaycee communication is that the public positions the association takes, while they may not reflect views peculiar to young men, *are* views decided on by a class of young men between the ages of eigthteen and thirty-five. Brennan insisted that the group was "large and basically unselective," but that is incorrect.[20] They were a restricted-membership group, and the de facto selectivity of their admission procedures points up their social and professional homogeneity. Whatever its messages, it spoke as the voice of an identifiable segment of the male population.

The term "voice" reminds us, too, that the object of solicitude here is communication. The Court unaccountably leaves this out of consideration by ignoring the connection between an association's membership and the reception and effectiveness of its voice. The exercise of First Amendment rights of speech and association have as much to do with the speaker as with the ideational content or form of the message abstracted from the group. Despite the dominant view that the purpose of the First Amendment is maximizing the stock of ideas and information available for democratic deliberation, ideas are not free-floating, detached from their proponents. Expression has to do with who we are and are perceived to be, not just what we say. So associations with unwanted members, whether political parties required by state law to hold open primaries or integrated Jaycees, are vulnerable. The impact of messages can be affected even if the content is not.

All this would be too obvious to mention were it not for the Court's obliviousness. *Association* adds more to individual expression than the increased intensity of advocacy when speakers join together; and more than the measurable political impact that comes from aggregating voices (or money). It adds a new voice to the roster of communicators. Like the powers of charisma, reputation, or skill, an association's distinctive voice affects the probability of influence over others.[21]

Members' Messages

Justice Brennan is right to say that the connection between Jaycee membership and message is "speculative"; as I said before, it has to be. The Jaycees do not fit the mold of an advocacy group whose positions are settled and communications scripted in advance, which is why prospective members cannot be usefully screened for their opinions on public issues. The membership comprises a class of young men who come together for a variety of social, civic, and business-related activities, not to demonstrate a particular commitment to some cause. Together, voting members decide on whether to take public policy positions, and what these should be. The group's messages are unpredictable. They may be fickle or contradictory, sporadic, or pointed and consistent. In this, the Jaycees are typical. Association voice is often indeterminate and always shifting.

In a follow-on case, *New York State Club Association*, the Supreme Court conceded that "it is conceivable . . . that an association might be able to show that it is organized for specific expressive purposes and that it will not be able to advocate its desired viewpoints *nearly as effectively* if it cannot confine its membership to those who share the same sex, for example, or the same religion." But this consideration applies only to groups "organized for specific expressive purposes."[22] It excludes from First Amendment protection associations not dedicated to public expression, even though a substantial part of their activities fits this description.

If the permissibility of compelled association turns on a showing that it alters a group's communications or the advancement of beliefs and opinions in predictable ways, then the defense of expressive association is vulnerable. Not only for the Jaycees but even for political groups organized for public expression. Apart from single-issue advocacy groups, the broad original goal of political associations may be preserved, but groups will normally shift both their positions and the issues on which they pronounce, affected by the vicissitudes of events, by changes in leadership, and by the group's own membership policies. Nothing is more common than a change of message and strategy, alliances and forms and techniques of communication. Indeed, if we ranged expressive associations along a spectrum of more or less protected on the basis of a hierarchy of preferred freedoms, the quintessential political association—the political party—is potentially vulnerable to Brennan's stringent, strangling nexus test.

After all, it is said with some justice that the major political parties do not have identifiable or stable ideological positions, much less policy platforms. This fact has been used to justify permitting states to determine who can vote in party primaries. Recall the Democratic Party's First Amendment challenge to a state-mandated open primary in *Democratic Party v. Wisconsin*. The Supreme Court upheld the law allowing non-Democrats to vote in the primary without regard to party affiliation or requiring a public declaration of party preference.[23] The state interest in increasing political participation could justify requiring an open primary, but this public interest could not justify imposing the outcome of the primary on the party. So the Court also upheld the right of the national Democratic Party to follow its policy of seating only those delegates chosen by party members, voters who publicly record their party preferences.

The Democratic Party's rule was adopted after the 1968 elections. There, delegate selection had been largely the prerogative of party officials or caucuses. The idea motivating reform was to enhance the ability of rank-and-file party members to influence the choice of nominees and the formulation of the party platform through delegate selection. Allowing the votes by those who have endorsed other parties and by independents to bind delegates would undermine this effort to build a more effective and responsive party.[24] Freedom to associate for the "common advancement of political beliefs," the Court ruled, necessarily presupposes freedom to identify the people who constitute the association, and to limit the association to them. The party could screen out "those whose affiliation is . . . slight, tenuous or fleeting."[25]

Even here, where political expression is as salient as it can be for association membership, and where political efficacy is the association's whole purpose (the aim is "to control the levers of government") three dissenting Justices challenged the Democratic Party's claim of a nexus between membership and voice, and would have upheld Wisconsin's requirement that party delegates be bound by the results of the open primary. The dissenters were harsh: the National Party's "apparent concern that the outcome of the Wisconsin Presidential primary will be skewed cannot be taken seriously."

Their reasoning, like the Court's in *Roberts*, was that the association voice was insufficiently distinctive to sustain the claim that compelled association would change it. The Democratic Party had presented evidence that the voting patterns of crossover voters, who comprised as much as one-third of the participants in primary elections, differed significantly from the preferences of party members. Justices Blackmun and Rehnquist signed on to Justice Powell's objection that since the party has never made "a serious effort to establish . . . a monolithic ideological identity by excluding" differing views, it is unlikely that the influence of voters unwilling to publicly affiliate with the party will produce a delegation with preferences that differ from those represented by a substantial number of delegates from other parts of the country. To the dissent, the nexus requirement should be determinative:

> if appellant National Party were an organization with a particular ideological orientation or political mission, perhaps this regulation would present a different question. In such a case, the state law might well open the organization to participation by persons with incompatible beliefs and interfere with the associational rights of its founders. . . . [But the party] is not organized around the achievement of defined ideological goals.[26]

Like the Court in *Roberts*, they were willing to substitute the state's judgment for the association's on the relation between membership and message.[27]

The mistake here is fundamental. Political association does not presume prior agreement; it is rarely a simple tally of views. The reasons theorists give on behalf of deliberative democracy are reiterative; they reach down from official representative institutions to voluntary associations, both political and those that are nonpolitical but intermittently expressive. One of the chief points of a deliberative view of democracy is that fixed, pre-given preferences do not determine the bounds of discussion; there is the possibility of shaping new agenda issues and revising old ones. The electoral primary is one mechanism for determining the starting point of political preferences and to select the delegates that best express them on a range of issues. But parties must have the ability to seek compromises among the varied interests of their adherents. So they must be free to set standards for determining affiliation, and to decide whether they want to include only individuals with obviously shared purposes and views, or those with diverse views whom they wish to recruit.[28] (Which is why the same logic makes it unconstitutional for a state to condition voting in a party primary on a registration requirement that the party does not desire.)[29]

Anne Phillips admonishes, "As any reasonably diligent observer of the political process will confirm, policy decisions are not settled in advance by party programmes or election commitments."[30] The same holds for the articulation of partisan programs and election commitments in the first place. (It holds true for interest and advocacy groups as well; studies of internal debates and policy changes within the American Medical Association and member polling by Common Cause describe this in detail.)[31] To the extent that citizens acting as electors are structurally required to act as consumers choosing among existing "products," this should come as late in the process as possible. It is why association freedom to choose its membership is so important.

This does not mean that political parties have complete autonomy over who can associate, or should. The "White Primary" cases prohibited racial discrimination in party membership and primary voting. Major political parties structure electoral choices, and states give their candidates favored ballot access. Given rapidly changing government functions—something we saw in chapter 4 with regard to the similarity between homeowners' associations and local government—it is very hard to say whether a private association is performing an "essentially governmental" function. A better test of "state action," Laurence Tribe argues, is whether government can constitutionally leave certain decisions to private actors. In this case, the state had made the parties and primary outcomes integral to its electoral scheme, and would violate the rights of voters if it tolerated a system that gave racially segregated parties central place. This is one of the areas where the moral uses of pluralism require a strong background of liberal democratic public culture, and where restriction of voluntary association is justified. With this exception, independent control of membership is essential to association voice. Voice is defined by membership.

In contradiction to this, *Democratic Party*'s dissenters look for a "monolithic ideological identity." And the *Roberts* Court allowed the state to interfere with membership policy unless it could be shown that the group was formed for specific expressive purposes, and that "the ability of members to express only those views that brought them together" would be impaired.[32] This approach binds associations' hands, or mouths. It recalls the corporate law stricture that associations are licensed for specific purposes and must be held to them. (And brings to mind the reasons courts declined to hold religious associations to their original tenets, for fear of quashing spontaneous religious life and the evolution of doctrine.) Deciding on and attempting to insure orthodoxy, using impairment of orthodoxy as a test of the bounds of association freedom, is the trajectory of *Roberts*.

Extending the Logic of Nexus

Although the Court's typology of associations in *Roberts* does not refer to two-tier First Amendment doctrine, it reflects it. Association freedom to control its membership is most secure when members are contributing to public deliberation as citizens, not when they are acting as members, simply, "to achieve whatever it is that moved them to join the association." The typologies Justices Brennan and O'Connor create—commercial/expressive/intimate associations—fail to cover the vast majority of voluntary associations not formed for expressive purposes, but not commercial either: fraternal societies, cultural and ethnic associations, and so on.

If applying the nexus argument to political parties seems like a demand for congruence gone awry, applying it to ethnic or cultural groups seems absurd. But strong proponents of congruence between democratic citizenship and open, democratic membership groups have advocated just that. A Jewish leadership organization, for example, might be said to have nothing to do with perpetuating Jewish identity and heritage. It is only an organization designed to promote leadership skills that happens to be formed along religious lines. Similarly, "it strains the imagination to envision what could be 'Christian' or 'Jewish,' or 'black' about a country club whose principal activities are golf, tennis, and swimming." On this view, courts should allow exclusionary membership policies only if something central to the association's practices "affirmatively promotes identity and community." And even then, only if compelled association would evidently disrupt of the group's purposes. The nexus test is not intended to provide much latitude: "the inclusion of members of other cultural communities into a group that celebrates a particular ethnic or religious heritage should not normally be disruptive of the latter's associational purpose," because outsider status is so clear and membership patently nominal.[33]

This is a plausible extension of the stingy logic of *Roberts*. It can be explained as willful blindness, or as the lack of understanding of someone with no experience of ethnic or cultural self-organization. Fear that these groups would be compelled to open their membership is doubtless academic, absent a compelling state interest in regulating cultural group memberships: "The category of 'all non-Irish persons' is too large and diverse for them to be realistically stigmatized."[34] Nevertheless, this amplification of *Roberts* is significant for what it says about the pinched understanding of association voice, the depreciation of freedom of association, and the strange perception of association viability.

William Marshall, the constitutional scholar who would require the Jewish leadership group to admit non-Jews, allows for concessions at the limit if it could be shown that compelled integration would endanger the organization's viability: "Only if the existence of the group is severely threatened should the associational right prevail."[35] Whether the association is a cultural group or a gender-segregated group like the Jaycees, the test of "viability" has problems of the sort I discussed earlier in connection with religious associations. Beginning with the concept of "viability" itself.

Is viability a matter of stable internal structure and authority? If so, compulsory admission of unwanted members would seem to qualify as a sufficient threat. If viability is a matter of pursuing formal, avowed purposes, there are no agreed on empirical tests for when the group is effectively thwarted. Most important, as a limitation on government intervention, viability is an invitation to courts or legislatures to assess for themselves what is central and what is peripheral in group life, as the *Roberts* Court did. Government is permitted to substitute its judgment for the association's on the connection between membership and voice, and the consequences of compelled association.

We encountered a cautionary example earlier in Justice Goldberg's opinion in *Dade Christian Schools*. He argued that the church and school, which claimed racial exclusion as a matter of faith protected by the free exercise clause, would be unimpaired by the requirement to admit black students. Compelled association would not have any impact on the church's activities, Goldberg predicted, because racial segregation is only a "minor tenet" of faith. And because teachers, students, and parents could go on believing and effectively promulgating the message of racial segregation while being forced to practice integration, an argument that anticipated the Court's in *Roberts*. Involuntary enrollment of blacks in the church school would not be mistaken for a shift in the church's own message, Goldberg went on, employing an analogy to public accommodation law:

> much as merchants were freed by the Civil Rights Act of 1964 from any fear that white customers would react adversely to the acceptance of black business, parents and school leaders are freed by section 1981 from any fear that children will interpret acceptance of blacks as an indication of church approval of the practice.[36]

Sheer priority for the liberal principle of antidiscrimination over association freedom is preferable to the sort of bad faith claim we see here and again in *Roberts*. Balancing the right of association against the state interest is the best approach, but not when the group's stake is diminished to an elusive threshold "viability," or denied altogether. If compelled integration is not deemed a threat to the association's viability *as a distinctive voice*, then viability is reduced to a group's literal ability to attract and retain members, even if they are not the members the association wants.

The Emergence of Association Voice

My quarrel with the Court's account of expressive association is not that it singles out public expression as a distinct aspect of association life protected by the First Amendment. Rather, that this perfectly warranted solicitude is undercut by indifference to the dynamic by which voices are formed. For voluntary association typically *precedes* expression. Association voice emerges, when it does, as an indirect and often unpredictable result of group interests, activities, and membership practices. Out of obligation, interest, the ambition of leaders, civic-mindedness, or venom, associations of every kind find their voice and articulate some public message. It is a contingent matter whether members' purposes impel them to engage in expressive activity, then, and if so, whether the association's messages are logically related to its membership practices. But the possibility of rapid, unanticipated engagement in political expression is always there. The Boy Scouts of America brief put it baldly: many thousands of associations of all kinds are "actually or potentially pressure groups."[37]

The alternative assumption, that voice precedes association, supposes that independent individuals intend the same communication and that association simply aggregates and amplifies their voices. This describes a crowd of cheering sports fans, not a voluntary association. Advocacy groups are no exception; not even their messages are scripted. The American Civil Liberties Union is a model advocacy group, yet its positions are not predictable. There is internal disagreement over the Second Amendment right to bear arms, for example, and over limitations on speech posed by the disclosure requirements and other elements of campaign finance law. "Members of the National Rifle Association may be giving money to the organization because of a sporting purpose, but find the NRA is spending their money to attack a Democratic member on a Medicare or education issue"; in the event, they can (and have) disassociated and joined alternative groups.[38]

Compelled association alters this spontaneous dynamic. In Justice O'Connor's now familiar phrase, the creation of association and admission of members *is* the creation of a voice. That is why compelled association can operate as a sort of "prior restraint" on the emergence of a voice, even without aiming at content or viewpoint. Inattention to the dynamic of emergent voices is a common failing, evident in most attempts to categorize groups as private versus civic, say, or social versus political, with a view to which groups enhance democracy and foster democratic competencies and dispositions.

For the most part, the spontaneous emergence of association voice from the group's lived, daily activities is mundane, its expressions politics as usual. Homeowners' associations, for example, enter public arenas for hum-drum and usually multiple reasons, spurred by local events or internal complaints. This is the sound element in the optimistic liberal expectancy that civil society fuels political participation, and that "engaged men and women tend to be multiply engaged."[39]

> People engage in informal political discussions in these settings. . . . [T]he agenda at a meeting of even a non-political organization may include consideration of political issues. The weekly sermon at church may cover a political topic. Not only do these settings provide exposure to political messages, but . . . they are frequently the locus of political recruitment of citizen activists.[40]

Organizations also develop their own, often intermittent, political voices.

Of course, even if a group undertakes substantial expressive activity, it may not be the salient aspect of associational life for individual members. If it is, they acquire democratic competencies in religious groups or at work when they organize meetings or coordinate volunteers for a charity drive. (Or undemocratic skills in hierarchic or personality-driven associations.) Voluntary associations are indispensable for nudging issues into public consciousness or offering reasons that supplement, reinforce, or oppose the terms dominant in public discussion. Certainly, they have this use for their members personally.[41] In short, associations not formed for purposes of expression anticipate, foster, and mutate into political voices. First Amendment protection for a group's actual exports to the marketplace of ideas is not enough. Nor is concern for the viability of an already-formed political voice, and for its effective, uncensored political expression.

Women's groups draw attention to the transition from associations formed for apolitical purposes and unconcerned with communication on matters of public interest to advocacy groups. (Besides the fact that staunchly apolitical groups can facilitate this almost imperceptible shift for individual members.) The original purpose of association may have been as inward-oriented as "consciousness-raising," aimed mainly at overcoming members' passivity and self-abnegation, or as apolitical as charitable works and fellowship. Together, quasi-political and nonpolitical women's groups fueled a broad-based social reform movement. Local efforts spawned parallel groups in other places; alliances and federations formed. Against this background, formal lobbying organizations such as NOW and the National Black Feminist Organization recruit and advocate. Evans and Boyt report the twin processes at work. Women use organizational skills learned in nonpolitical associations to form groups geared to advocacy. At the same time, nonpolitical groups find a political voice:

> small "consciousness-raising" groups . . . repoliticized informal female networks—office friendships, neighborhood kaffeeklatsches—creating thousands of free social spaces. . . . Throughout the 1970s and early 1980s, massive numbers of women . . . simply shifted their activities in church and voluntary associations toward feminist concerns. Others began to organize specific constituencies of women: clerical workers, sociologists, day care providers, historians.[42]

Feminist groups also bring home the fact that what counts as a matter of public interest and as political expression is changing and contested. No delineation or interpretation of politically cognizable interests or needs is authoritative. It is not necessary to rehearse either the intellectual power or the actual effect on law and public policy of the phrase "the personal is political." Simply, it conveys the often subtle effect of patterns of power in structuring social and private life, and at the same time, the public significance of private experience—women's "vulnerability by marriage," child-rearing, and the structure of the labor market, to name the obvious. Women who used the phrase "the personal is political"

> meant by it that experiences that they had previously defined as private and applicable only to them individually they now saw as deriving from larger structures of human organization subject to human deliberation, decision and change. They meant that the most archtypically personal and private matters, the most minute and traditionally trivial matters, opened up under collective examination ways of understanding the world that challenged the foundations of public order.[43]

When neo-feminists today deemphasize gender solidarity and focus on fairness to individual women, they offer a corrective to the excesses of some (mostly academic) feminist theory. But in doing so they form associations of their own, like the Women's Freedom Network, evidence that they have not entirely lost sight of the fact that organizations and a sense of community are necessary for political movements, indeed for public expression.

Women's groups suffice to make us wary of a narrow, categorical approach to association freedom; expressive associations are not only those organized for specific expressive purposes. Though rarely as dramatic as feminism, the dynamic is general. Consider the regular process by which disorganized, ascriptive identity motivates voluntary association, and groups take on the color of expressive association. The elderly are a prime example. Or the physically handicapped. Associations of the speech-impaired metamorphose from self-help and support groups or small social groups into associations geared to public education and political lobbying. Goffman writes, "It is important to stress that, in America at least, no matter how small and how badly off a particular stigmatized category is, the viewpoint of its members is likely to be given public presentation of some kind."[44]

It may be superfluous to add that the prelude to the "politics of recognition," whether it aims at concrete distributive policies or mechanisms of political representation, is disorganized populations and a host of voluntary associations, some short-lived and barely tenable, others well-organized. That is where group-specific concerns originate, or should, as I discuss in chapter 9.

Association is the condition for collective action. Historically, it has been *the* resource of groups without the vote; before they achieved suffrage, women successfully fought for legislative protection for children and other social policies through their associations. It is the critical resource for those who lack influence based on economic resources, cultural hegemony, prestige, and so on. "This is the most fundamental claim about participation and democracy."[45] It is the bridge from parochial to national commitments.

But it is not a warrant for characterizing voluntary associations in ways reminiscent of democratic theorists' idealized open and independent "public sphere." Or for valuing them as civic. Caution is in order, because the tendency among theorists of grassroots organization especially is to portray what Harry Boyt calls "free public spaces" in exhilarating, moral terms. Inclusive and egalitarian, participatory, on this view, voluntary associations comprise "environments in which people are able to learn a new self-respect, a deeper and more assertive group identity, public skills, and values of cooperation and civic virtue." Feminist groups, black churches, the union movement before the NLRB were all "liberated zones."[46] No accident that both Boyt and Michael Sandel invoke the Knights of Labor as a model of democratic spirit; association is tied to populism with a sanguine civic face.[47]

It is a short step from here to the argument that the mobilization of "the right sort" of association merits government support. For Michael Walzer, that means labor unions, citizen groups, and cultural affinity groups that provide human services. It is a short step, too, to the view that certain associations merit special constitutional protection. Aviam Soifer urges legal recognition of the association rights of certain groups, distinct from the First Amendment rights of individual members. Soifer has in mind associations that constitute a sort of fifth estate. They parade, boycott, report, and engage in labor or nonprofit activities that check government. These associations serve "the 'checking value' we celebrate and expect of a robust free press" and merit "the gingerly concern we are accustomed to affording newspapers."[48]

This inventive constitutional interpretation aims at greater protection for certain expressive associations. But this concession, like Walzer's selective solicitude, is no substitute for insuring the most hospitable conditions possible for group formation and expression broadly. Protection for emergent association voices should not depend on a progressive, liberal democratic expectancy.

In the next chapters I discuss hate groups and secret societies. They demonstrate clearly that grassroots associations may be conservative and exclusive, racist and anti-Semitic. The "pockets of political activism that defy the trend toward civic disengagement and try to contend with economic forces that disempower communities and undermine civic life"[49] have sinister counterparts.

Religious groups reinforce my principal point: the unanticipated emergence of association voice. We know that neither separation of church and state nor fear of establishment prohibits political activity by religious associations, office-seeking by clerics, or advocacy on policy questions with or without a doctrinal nexus to articles of faith. But we also know that political expression can be divisive, a source of schism within religious groups. Deviation from a traditionally apolitical theology may be perceived as a necessity by some clergy and faithful: "When government abandons traditional morality or, worse yet, protects 'deviant' behavior, political action must be taken."[50] Believers may feel compelled to engage in public expression by the obligations of conscience, and aim at getting government to accommodate particular exercises of faith; the sort of advocacy responsible for the Religious Freedom Restoration Act.

The classic American example of the emergence of association voices is black churches, "which served as the organizational and visionary heart of the movement from slavery to civil rights."[51] (Though the thesis should not be overstated. The Dexter Avenue Baptist Church along with associations like the Southern Christian Leadership Conference assumed this tremendous advocacy role. But conservatism and accommodation to racism on the part of many black churches was an impetus to the rise of Elijah Muhammad and the Nation of Islam.)[52] The entry of new, religious voices into public discussion as a result of the fragmentation of denominational alliances and the rise of independent churches is continuous. And there has been a shift from political involvement under the leadership of clergy to initiatives by new activist institutions: "parachurch" groups, religion-based public affairs organizations, special agenda groups, and political lobbies that bear a closer resemblance to interest groups than churches.[53]

The same dynamic that marked women's groups holds for religion. From political expression in support of beliefs and interests—often in the form of protest and opposition. To political influence on specific issues through lobbying, advocacy, and coalition-building. To direct involvement in electoral processes to achieve political representation. The development of the Christian Right is a much-studied example: the Christian Coalition's evolution from a purist social protest movement to political activism oriented to agenda-setting and electoral victory.[54]

Given the indefinite purposes of religious-based groups and the mixed character of expression, we should not be surprised by efforts to exploit First

Amendment protections by arguing that religious proselytizing and political advocacy are constitutionally indistinguishable. Indeed, that religion is a distinctive viewpoint vis-à-vis secular voices. The idea is to qualify religious expression for government protection and support it would not receive on free exercise grounds and could not receive under the establishment clause.

Moves to categorize religious expression per se as an ideology in contemporary political debate received support from the Supreme Court in *Rosenberger v. University of Virginia*. The Court reviewed the university's decision, which Virginia justifed on standard establishment grounds, to prohibit using mandatory student activity fees to support a student religious publication, *Wide Awake*. Failure to support the religious paper would constitute viewpoint discrimination prohibited by the free speech clause, the majority ruled, in light of the fact that these funds were used to subsidize other student-run political publications.

Justice Souter dissented vigorously. If the university guidelines were written so as to limit only *Christian* evangelical efforts, the discrimination would be based on viewpoint. But Virginia's policy applies to Muslim, Jewish, and Buddhist advocacy, as well as to agnostics and atheists since they too promote particular beliefs about a deity. And the university's decision to fund a magazine about racism and not to fund publications aimed at urging repentance before God skews neither the debate about racism nor discussion of the desirability of religious conversion:

> The Court's decision equating a categorical exclusion of both sides of the religious debate with viewpoint discrimination suggests the Court has concluded that primarily religious and antireligious speech, grouped together, always provides an opposing (and not merely a related) viewpoint to any speech about a secular topic.[55]

The counterpart of efforts to assimilate religious speech to political viewpoint is the effort to draw a categorical *distinction* between religious and political expression. Liberal democratic society may not be secular, but politics must be, on the view of what Isaac Kramnick and R. Laurence Moore call "the party of godless politics."[56] Political activity by religious groups is divisive and uncompromising because it is grounded in reasons whose force depends on the existence of God, articles of faith, or the pronouncements of authority; a religiously informed politics is indistinguishable from a "politics of religious correctness." So only secular standards of public justification, "public reasons," or "mutually acceptable reasons" should be permissible in political discussion. At a minimum, citizens and officials should impose a religious gag rule on themselves.[57]

My objection to a logical nexus between membership and voice as a test of First Amendment protection for voluntary associations should be plain. Autonomy for the internal life of associations, certainly including control of membership, is a condition for the formation of an association voice. Since it is important to protect the array of associations that are neither predominantly expressive nor commercial, it undercuts O'Connor's commercial/expressive typology. My preferred approach is to respect associational rights to control membership. The exceptions are organizations judged public accommodations, and associations like major political parties with which government is powerfully implicated and which, left alone, might fatally undercut fundamental practices of democratic public life.

The usual course for those who would secure constitutional protection for a wider range of associations than *Roberts* allows is not faithful to the expressive uses of membership. Instead, the First Amendment link between association and expression is contorted or severed. The domain of "expressive" activity is enlarged beyond recognition; or the right of association is interpreted as a fundamental liberty; or the shield of "intrinsic" association is invoked for groups that do not fit that description.

Elastic Expression, Personal Liberty, and Intimate Association

When *Roberts* reserved First Amendment protection for associations specifically formed for the purposes of advocacy, or those whose message follows predictably from core purposes, it gave priority to speech intended and received as a contribution to public deliberation. Freedom of association is not only ancillary to expression; it tracks a two-tiered interpretation of freedom of expression. Identified with Alexander Meiklejohn, this position represents speech in the service of self-government, not expressive interests generally, as the constitutional value embodied in the First Amendment.[58] Even those who do not concede that political speech and association are the most important forms of expression are inclined to grant it primacy in the constitutional scheme. For government's incentive to regulate speech and association, and the likelihood of bias, are at their height when it comes to political disagreement, criticism, unpopularity, or fear of subversion.

The "pathological view" of the First Amendment has a lot to recommend it. The classic heart of freedom for association voice is mistrust of government to shape public debate, for reasons that begin but do not end with partisan motivations or the very real possibility of "political incest."[59] For Justice Scalia, regulations undercut "the absolutely central truth of the First Amendment: that government cannot be trusted to assure, through censorship, the 'fairness' of political debate."[60]

Whatever the merits of a two-tiered approach to constitutionally guaranteed speech, we have seen that when it comes to association it is constraining, even from the perspective of political expression. One response is to encompass a wider range of associations by expanding "expression" to include the messages communicated indirectly by a group's internal organization and affairs. This accepts the principal justification for group autonomy, and gives up any claim to the right of association independent of the First Amendment right of expression. The difference is that expression is not limited to intentional exports to the marketplace of ideas, or public discourse. Associations are expressive whether or not they engage in a substantial amount of public communication, as long as affiliation "advances" beliefs and ideas. The right of association entails the right to express one's attitudes or philosophies by membership in a group. "The act of association itself is a 'form of expression of opinion.'"[61]

The Conference on Private Organizations amicus brief in *Roberts* fleshed out this argument by pointing to the beliefs of the Knights of Columbus concerning the separate roles of men and women in society. Thus, the association's ceremonial 'rite of passage' was intended to imbue the initiate with a "manly" sense of pride in his Catholicism and a strong dedication to defend the faith. The insurance program was a medium for expressing the (male) breadwinner's economic responsibility for his family. The K of C Council was a place where Catholic men could find social sustenance for their struggle as a minority group in a hostile society, and for the militant promotion of Catholic interests. "This identification with masculinity was so strong that the resolution admitting women into the Order never reached the floor of the National Council, either in 1985 or at any subsequent meeting."[62]

The argument for expression by association holds for groups that by their very existence advance beliefs and opinions vis-à-vis a smaller community than society generally. An association of progressive Jewish women whose organization and practices "speaks to" the Jewish community, is expressive, its messages embodied in its activities.

Of course, Justice Brennan rejects this line of thinking. He dismisses the notion that admitting women into the Jaycees would impair the symbolic message conveyed by the very fact that they were prohibited from voting. For him, the voice of an association, and members' identification with it, is heard solely in its public pronouncements. Associations themselves are not counted as "public spaces" for expression; they may be public with respect to their members, but are nonpublic with respect to political society.[63]

On its own terms, this elastic notion of expression has intractable problems. All conduct is expressive of something. So is all joining. No voluntary relationship would fall outside First Amendment protection if the standard is whether it advances belief in the association's worth and implicates opinions. (Obviously, nothing is sharpened by the inverse claim that "expression of the right of freedom of association" is at issue.)[64] The argument for expression bleeds into a general case for personal liberty.

Which is why some advocates of expanded freedom of association abandon First Amendment protection and appeal directly to the broad umbrella of personal liberty. The Boy Scouts amicus brief in *Roberts* rejects the view of freedom of association as an appendage of enumerated First Amendment rights. Rather, it is "an independent constitutional value fundamental to our Nation's concept of liberty." The Scouts quote Tocqueville:

> The most natural privilege of man, next to the right of acting for himself, is that of combining his exertions with those of his fellow creatures and of acting in common with them. The right of association therefore appears to be as almost inalienable in its nature as the right of personal liberty. No legislator can attack it without impairing the foundations of society.[65]

In this spirit, George Kateb regrets that "only rarely does freedom of association receive a defense that honors it as integral to a free human life, to being a free person. Picking one's company is part of living as one likes; living as one likes (provided one does not injure the vital claims of others) is what being free means." He goes further: "a lot of the time, one is one's expression, one lives to express, one lives by expressing."[66]

It is hard to see how the argument from "personal liberty" could serve its purpose of strengthening association freedom, on any interpretation. If the identification of freedom of association with personal liberty means that whatever is lawful alone is lawful in a group, there is no constitutional anchor for the right at all. Simply, whatever legislatures judge lawful for individuals is lawful for associations, and any attempt to limit that conduct by a group is impermissible.[67]

Alternatively, this approach offers association the dubious protection of a "fundamental liberty" based on substantive due process. Given the constitutional history of fundamental personal liberties, this would firmly tether the right of association to judgments that a particular association is deeply rooted in national history and fosters traditional practices. The claims of small, unusual, or barely formed associations (to say nothing of noxious, counterculture groups) could be handily dismissed.[68]

A third course open to expansionists exploits Justice Brennan's protected category of "intimate" or "intrinsic" association. Brennan lists formal criteria for this type of group: "relative smallness . . . a high degree of selectivity in decisions to begin and maintain the affiliation, and seclusion from others in critical aspects of the relationship." (He adds "congeniality"—off-putting, if we have a cold eye on the dark side of intimate relationships!) The contours of intimate association are imprecise, but it was plain to every Justice that the 295,000-member Jaycees failed to meet the criteria. The category was intended for purely personal or "family-type" relations.

However, the decision provides an opening through which expansionists march when Brennan alludes to a spectrum of relations "that presuppose deep attachments and commitments to the necessarily few other individuals with whom one shares not only a special community of thoughts, experience, and beliefs but also distinctively personal aspects of one's life." Fraternal organizations have successfully claimed to qualify:

> The clubhouse is of course not on the same constitutional plane as is the bedroom or study with respect to the right of privacy, [still,] truly fraternal organizations attempt to replicate the bonds of literal fraternity; the relationship among members is close, intimate, and continuing. Its members having genuinely chosen each other as social intimates, the club functions as an extension of their homes.[69]

The most aggressive expansionist push exploits the fact that Brennan uses "intimate" and "intrinsic" association interchangeably. "The constitutional shelter afforded such relationships reflects the realization that individuals draw much of their emotional enrichment from close ties with others," Brennan explains. And, intrinsic association safeguards "the ability independently to define one's identity that is central to any concept of liberty." And, "certain kinds of personal bonds have played a critical role in the culture and traditions of the Nation by cultivating and transmitting shared ideals and beliefs."[70]

These elements of constitutionally protected "intrinsic association"—the ability to define one's identity, emotional enrichment, personal bonds through which ideals and beliefs are transmitted, and so on—confound a number of eminently confoundable associational goods. Intrinsic association seems to encompass groups that foster objective aspects of identity (traditions, say) as well as associations that elicit personal identification. They converge just where we would expect these often-confused elements to converge—on associations deemed significant for "personal identity-formation."

For Kateb, there is no reason to assume that intrinsic associations are also intimate ones. He resists the implication that the personal is superior to the impersonal when it comes to these personal uses of association: "It is an unattractive romanticism to believe that a self discloses or enhances itself only amidst loving immediacy." Certainly, "it is not up to courts (or any governmental entity) to rank associations for people, or to hold that close or intimate relationships are inherently more significant than other relationships and therefore more deserving of protection."[71]

Doubtless, Justice Brennan did not anticipate that intrinsic association would become its own elastic category and threaten to embrace pluralism *simpliciter*. Of course, all sorts of groups serve emotional and moral functions for particular members—we know from television comedies that the workplace can be experienced as a family. But not "intrinsically."

Coerced Expression

Although I have objected to the membership/message nexus as a standard for protecting the autonomy of expressive associations, I have respected the rubric of expression. It is one important approach to freedom of association. Affiliation with an association's public expression is one of the moral uses of pluralism, and merits consideration on its own. It is also independent of the substantive contribution associations make to public discourse.

If so, we must consider membership and voice from another angle. When membership in a group is compulsory, so is affiliation with the association's voice. Laws compel membership in union shops as a condition of employment, for example, and association with the union voice is involuntary. Dissenters can exit voluntary associations, but involuntary members of compelled associations authorized by the state cannot. Or not without losing their jobs. So compelled association is also compelled expression. The question is whether members who disagree with union messages should be able to exercise their First Amendment rights of speech and association to disassociate from them.

Compelled expression is a classic liberal taboo. Freedom from government censorship and constraint is a condition of liberty to speak and associate. Freedom from government-imposed obligations to profess beliefs or opinions is a condition of liberty *not* to speak or associate. "If there is any fixed star in our constitutional constellation, it is that no official, high or petty, can prescribe what shall be orthodox in politics, nationalism, religion, or other matters of opinion or force citizens to confess by word or act their faith therein."[72]

Government may not compel flag salutes or make citizens vote. It may not "require citizens to express support for or agreement with a cause with which he disagrees or concerning which he prefers to remain silent."[73] (Loyalty oaths are a testy exception; hardly exceptional if we consider that an estimated one-sixth of the total civilian labor force was subject to some type of loyalty qualification.)[74] When the Hatch Act prohibited federal employees from certain forms of political campaign activity, the rationale was partly to insure nonpartisan government operations and partly to see "that Government employees are free from pressure to vote in a certain way or perform political chores in order to curry favor with their superiors rather than to act out of their own beliefs."[75]

Of course, all taxpayers are coerced into expression when government "speaks." There is no establishment clause when it comes to official speech. And no *Abood* amount (explained below) that can be withheld from federal or state income taxes by citizens who object to government advocacy. Government speaks through the associations it subsidizes as well as directly. It conditions grants on their agreeing to convey publicly favored messages—or refrain from unfavored ones. *Rust v. Sullivan* upheld a prohibition on abortion-related advice imposed on recipients of federal funds for family planning. The most visible battle has been over public funding for the arts, on grounds that taxpayers should not be compelled to support expression they loathe.

There is no more dizzying area of law. For once regulation of expression can be attached as a condition for public support, and once the definition of support is open-ended and includes grants, loans, loan guarantees, tax exemptions, tax deductions, incorporated status, and so on, vulnerability to regulation is open-ended too.

Thus, the Supreme Court upheld a law prohibiting a nonprofit association from lobbying to influence legislation if it wished to retain its tax-exempt status on grounds that tax status was a form of largesse and there is no right to have speech subsidized by government. Eligibility for food stamps can be denied to households in which a worker is on strike. Legislators have proposed prohibiting nonprofit organizations that get federal grants from political advocacy vis-à-vis candidates or legislative proposals, even advocacy financed from privately raised funds, threatening to use what has been called Congress's "power to punish."[76] The public funding provisions of the Federal Election Campaign Act condition public support for election campaigns on accepting spending ceilings.[77] As we will see in the case of *Austin v. Michigan Chamber of Commerce*, limits on corporate political spending are upheld on grounds that corporate status is a valuable government-conferred benefit: "the corporate shield which the State granted to corporations [is] a form of *quid pro quo*" for various regulations, including limits on political activity.[78]

In these examples, laws change the costs of association, expression, and silence, and raise the question of compelled expression. More so when government transforms an association from a voluntary to a mandatory membership group and endows the group with authority to compel members to support its expressive activities. It would seem that if government cannot directly force people to contribute to organizations that work to elect party candidates or influence policy choices, then private groups exercising government-sanctioned authority cannot either.[79] Closed shop unions test this proposition.

Union Membership: Compelled Association and Coerced Expression

Recall that when Congress identifies unionization as part of a federal policy to stabilize labor–management relations and insure a countervailing power to industry, there is no protected conscientious objection to union membership as a condition of employment. Activities related to collective bargaining would be unstable if employees could withdraw support out of disagreement with negotiating policy. "Associations build on the need for mutual reliance," and in closed shops, government insures the viability of union "voice" by prohibiting free riders.[80] The belief that the right to strike is the road to serfdom for the working class is not grounds for disassociation. It does not violate First Amendment rights to compel workers to contribute financially to a union as a condition of employment.

The objectionable fiction is that compelled membership in a union is not coerced identification or expression. Involuntary members must pay periodic dues but no one is required to attend meetings or vote in elections, or to espouse the cause of unionism.

In practice, association is not always a simple arrangement of dues in return for contractual benefits. There was the once strong ideal of union brotherhood that called for loyalty and activism, and the civic ideal of workers as citizen-producers, revived in arguments like Carole Pateman's for workplace democracy as a school of citizenship. From these standpoints, disassociation from union advocacy may appear as a betrayal of solidarity, or democratic irresponsibility. Both demand support for union political advocacy and partisan activities. Many unions (perhaps all unions at times of crisis or declining prosperity) are more than coordinating structures that do not require commitment from members.

Less subjectively, the rise of union spending on political education, advocacy, and candidate support increases the occasions when members might resist being assessed for political expression they disavow. The amounts at stake are not trivial. Evidence in a case involving the Communications Workers of America showed that only 19 percent of the union's dues went toward defraying the costs of the union's activities as bargaining agent. The rest went toward other programs and causes, including contributions to the National Coalition against Domestic Violence, the National Coalition for Lower Tuition in Higher Education, financing a lobby for the Panama Canal Treaty, support for lifting sanctions against Zimbabwe, and "for the tormented people of Northern Ireland."[81]

There are limits to permissible expression; presumably the postal workers' association cannot transform itself into the postal workers' association for the advancement of the policies of the Democratic Party and still compel employee support.[82] But unions have come close. In 1996, the AFL-CIO raised a $35 million "war chest" from per capita assessments on member unions, to be spent on "political education" on salient issues like the minimum wage, Medicare, and workplace safety laws. These are not campaign contributions or direct political expenditures, and they narrowly avoid federal regulation. But they are plainly intended to direct union members to support Democratic candidates.[83]

Is compelled association limited to the union's core purposes—collective bargaining, administering labor contracts, and adjusting employment-related grievances? Or does it require support for all union activities? The terms of the debate inflamed discussion of business and nonprofit corporations in the United States for half a century. It continues to reappear in cases like *First National Bank v. Bellotti*.[84] It illuminates competing American ideologies of association broadly, and their consequences for membership and voice.

In 1947, Cecil B. DeMille went to court protesting his expulsion from the American Federation of Radio Artists for his refusal to contribute one dollar to the union's campaign against right-to-work laws. The union rules, he argued, infringed his constitutional right to free speech. DeMille could speak out against the legislation, a California court decided, but he was obligated to support the union financially. For its part, the union could devote its funds to any purpose calculated to promote its objects.[85]

This decision was set squarely in the context of the debate over "corporate personality" we encountered briefly in chapter 3. Like Gierke, Maitland, and the British pluralists, many American legal scholars insisted that corporations are "autonomous, self-sufficient, and self-renewing bodies."[86] The corporation has a spontaneous life and voice of its own, capable of changing to embrace matters beyond some original or core purpose, and they would assign corporations all the rights of natural persons. Labor unions are not corporations, but the closed shop is a state-conferred privilege, created by law, and in this respect thinking about union and corporate authority proceeded in tandem.

Operating on this theory in the DeMille case, the California court had no difficulty granting union leadership full discretion to spend members' dues. Union activities need not exhibit a nexus between political messages and bargaining over wages. The union is no more limited to this original purpose, narrowly construed, than a church is constrained to engage only in rituals explicitly prescribed by its tenets of faith, or than the directors of a business corporation are to lobby only against legislation that materially affects its assets. The corporate "personality" is expressive; association life and purposes evolve.

The contrasting view sees corporations as artificial entities. In Chief Justice Marshall's words: "a corporation is an artificial being, invisible, intangible, and existing only in contemplation of law. Being the mere creature of law, it possesses only those properties which the charter of creation confers upon it."[87] It follows that corporations are restricted to the specific purposes set out in their charters. The artificial entity position dictates a nexus between the legally stated purposes of membership/shareholding and corporate activity, including expression.

American Progressives ridiculed the natural entity idea and the fiction of a corporate will or personality. Corporations *are* legal artifacts formed to further certain economic goals. But as a practical matter, in order to insure the continuity of groups and economic development, the corporate form should not constrain their revolution.[88] Corporations have implied powers, and should not be held to *ultra vires* doctrine (limiting corporations to those transactions they were formed to do). The triumph of this realist conception was insured, and substantive state regulation undercut, because, in what Justice Brandeis referred to as "a race to the bottom," large companies could simply reincorporate in 'liberal' states. New Jersey and Delaware became favorite sites for incorporation, with their low taxes and permissive laws (Delaware's corporate purpose clause read "to engage in any lawful act or activity for which corporations may be organized under the General Corporation Law of Delaware").

This theoretical background was resurrected by the Supreme Court when it considered coerced union expression in 1961 in *International Association of Machinists v. Street.*[89] The case involved a union requirement that employees contribute to the campaigns of designated candidates for federal and state offices, and to propagating certain political and economic doctrines. The Justices agreed that compulsory unionism was designed to force employees to share in the cost of negotiation and settlement of disputes, not to advance political programs. And that political programs are not a necessary union expense. But they split on the question of whether the use of dues to advance these political programs infringes on members' constitutional rights.

Justice Frankfurter drew on writings by the British pluralist Harold Laski: "The law regards the union as a self-contained legal personality, exercising rights and subject to responsibilities wholly distinct from its individual members." The union could spend money collected from members under a closed shop for any purpose it chooses to endorse, and to allow political dissenters not to pay a contribution would invite them to free ride in as clear a way as if they were not to pay the rest of their dues.

On the other side, Justice Black opposed the use of dues for political causes of any kind as a violation of members' First Amendment free speech rights. He would have prohibited compulsory support even for political causes the union can show are crucial to its ends: "it makes no difference if, as is urged, political and legislative activities are helpful adjustments to collective bargaining."[90]

The middle ground, of course, is where a nexus exists between political activities and collective bargaining. In *Abood v. Detroit Board of Education* the Supreme Court seized it. It required the Detroit Federation of Teachers, an agency shop, to refund to dissenting teachers the portion of fees used to subsidize political and ideological activities "unrelated to its duties as exclusive bargaining representative"—a refund referred to as the "Abood amount." A union can constitutionally spend funds for the expression of political views, on behalf of political candidates, or toward the advancement of other ideological causes not germane to its duties. But employees cannot be compelled to finance these activities.

The burden is on individual employees to initiate proceedings to determine what part of the union's budget has been allocated to ideological activities unrelated to collective bargaining, and to show that withholding financial support is within his or her First Amendment protection.[91] There are exceptions; the International Association of Machinists collects its PAC war chest chiefly by means of one dollar per month payroll deductions and employees must specifically sign up for the withholding.[92] (The situation is potentially more coercive for management-level corporate employees, who are often directly solicited for contributions to PACs by their superiors.)[93]

O'Connor invokes the *Abood* ruling in support of her commercial/expressive typology in *Roberts*: "a State may compel association for the commercial purposes of engaging in collective bargaining, administering labor contracts, and adjusting employment-related grievances, but it may not infringe on association rights involving ideological or political associations."[94] Actually, *Abood* is more complicated than this. A union *can* compel members to subsidize political expression germane to its objectives as bargaining agent. But what is "germane"?

We recognize this question from earlier discussions. It parallels the need to determine whether a church's activity is "close to the heart" of religious faith and practice, and the need to demonstrate a "logical nexus" between membership and message in order to claim First Amendment protection for discriminatory membership practices. What nexus between membership and voice could override union members' protection against involuntary expression?

If we think that the purpose of federal labor law is to establish some sort of rough equivalence of economic power between labor and management, then "germaneness," or the nexus between politics and union policy, is open to enormous swings of interpretation. It turns on nothing less than "an understanding of the relationship between economic power and political action."[95]

If we begin with a more contracted view of union purposes, "germaneness" is still open-ended. Many aspects of economic and social life relate in some way to the interests of union members. A "woman's right to choose" affects all women but arguably has special relevance to women workers' ability to carry on with their normal employment. It could be a legitimate issue for any trade union, which could decide to affiliate with political organizations advocating freedom of choice.

"Germane" could be sharpened by restricting compulsory support to activities that help advance the interests of union members qua members in a particular sector of the economy, not qua workers generally or qua citizens.[96] Even here, review "takes the conscientious Justice deep into the history, purpose, and ideals of the union movement in general, and of the union involved in particular . . . the history of the industry with which the union negotiates, its attitudes, and its structure."[97]

It is easier to see the respects in which *Abood* permits coerced expression and curtails "the unfettered judgment of each citizen on matters of political concern." For one thing, "educational advertisements" of the sort I referred to earlier—really camouflaged electoral and issue advocacy—are legally funded from the AFL-CIO treasury. For another, *Abood* permits disassociation from only certain kinds of political advocacy. The Court's distinction was between *expressive activities* that are germane versus those that are unrelated to collective bargaining. Not between germane versus unrelated activities of all kinds. That leaves in place compulsory support for conventions, social activities, campaigns for recruiting members, charitable contributions, medical and legal services, publications, and so on.

Moral, religious, or political objections to core union activities are not grounds for disassociation—conflict between an employee's view of abortion and the union's policy in negotiating medical benefits, for example. An employee cannot disassociate from a union's activities on grounds that he or she objects to its wage policy as a violation of guidelines designed to limit inflation. Some issues such as a strike against a public agency may be "so controversial and of such general public concern" that it conflicts with employees' political beliefs.[98]

When the Court acknowledged that union membership was a condition of employment and allowed for disassociation from coerced political expression unrelated to union business, the idea was to spare workers from having to choose between funding political messages they find ideologically compromising and their jobs. Why not permit members to withhold support for any activity lacking a strict nexus to collective bargaining?

For the same reason we want to give religious and secular voluntary associations latitude, and reject a strict nexus between free exercise and religious doctrine, or between membership and voice. The inhibition of having to demonstrate that an activity is "germane" to a sharply delimited association purpose would be stifling. It would reduce the union to a coordinating mechanism. It would certainly inhibit its effectiveness. It would dampen rather than encourage the expressive aspect of associational life, particularly for groups that were not formed for specific expressive purposes.

Corporate Contributions, Germaneness, and Coerced Expression

Both coerced expression and a required nexus between corporate purpose and voice arise again in connection with corporate political expenditures. In *First National Bank of Boston v. Bellotti* the Supreme Court considered the constitutionality of a Massachusetts law that prohibited business corporations from political spending for or against referenda questions that did not materially affect their property or assets. Two Massachusetts banks and their fellow appellants (Gillette, Digital Equipment Corp., and Wyman-Gordon Co.) challenged the law by publicly advocating a "no" vote on a statewide referendum proposing a graduated personal income tax. The Court agreed that the corporations had a business interest in the referendum (the tax, the banks argued, would discourage executives from settling and working in Massachusetts, and would adversely affect their loans). More important, it overturned the state's requirement of a nexus between message and business purpose altogether, using now-familiar reasoning.[99]

Management could never be sure whether a court would disagree with its judgment about the effect of a particular referendum issue on business, and the uncertainty and expense of litigation in establishing a "complex and amorphous economic relationship" would be chilling. Put simply,

> If a legislature may direct business corporations to "stick to business," it also may limit other corporations—religious, charitable, or civic—to their respective "business" when addressing the public. Such power in government to channel the expression of views is unacceptable under the First Amendment.[100]

The *Bellotti* decision provoked opposition, again in familiar terms. Long after the demise of the view that corporate status is a special privilege, dissenters argued that incorporated associations have no constitutional protection when they act beyond their legal competence. Justice Rehnquist voted to uphold Massachusetts' restriction on corporate political spending on these grounds:

> a corporation is an artificial being. . . . Being the mere creature of law, it possesses only those properties which the charter of creation confers upon it. . . . A State grants to a business corporation the blessings of potentially perpetual life and limited liability to enhance its efficiency as an economic entity. It might reasonably be concluded that those properties, so beneficial in the economic sphere, pose special dangers in the political sphere.[101]

Though even Rehnquist would allow corporations to speak out on issues of direct concern to their shareholders.

The dissent also raised the question whether investment in a corporation constitutes consent to business's political expenditures, and whether the recourse of selling stock is adequate support for the First Amendment rights of shareholders who disagree with a company's political stances: "the State has a strong interest in assuring that its citizens are not forced to choose between supporting the propagation of views with which they disagree and passing up investment opportunities."[102]

"Expression by association" was addressed at length in 1990 in *Austin v. Michigan Chamber of Commerce*. Departing from *Bellotti*, the Court upheld a state law prohibiting expenditures from corporate treasury funds, this time in regard to candidates for state office. It argued in part that "the State surely has a compelling interest in preventing a corporation it has chartered from exploiting those who do not wish to contribute to the Chamber's political message."[103] "Ordinarily the expenditure of funds to promote political causes may be assumed to bear some relation to the fervency with which they are held." Spending from a corporation's general treasury, however, reflects "the economically motivated decisions of investors and customers," not popular support.[104] Corporate donations from voluntary segregated funds used solely for political purposes (PACs) on the other hand, are constitutionally protected. (Notice that *Austin* does not articulate an egalitarian standard. Nothing suggests that financial support must be related to the *actual number* of adherents an association can claim, only that expenditures from corporate treasury funds bear "no relation" to actual support, a point to which I return.)

We can see that a law requiring a voluntary segregated fund for corporate political expenditures relieves the economic burden on both association and individual expression when the two do not go in tandem. It protects the organization from the risk that it might have to gag itself in order to retain members or shareholders, and it protects individuals from having to sacrifice membership or investments to political beliefs.

This makes sense in the case of nonprofit, multipurpose groups that fall under this law, like the Michigan Chamber of Commerce, which brought suit in *Austin*. Even if they disagree with the association's political spending, members may be reluctant to withdraw because they do not want to lose the benefits of nonpolitical programs and business contacts.[105] The parallel to *Abood* does not depend on claiming that having to forego an investment or sell stock is on the order of having to seek jobs in nonunionized sectors of the economy.

But "exploiting" shareholders who may not wish to contribute to a business corporation's message is strong language. It is less clear that shareholders require a protection similar to union members who have the "out" of an *Abood* amount. There is not much question of mixed purposes in corporate shareholding. Stockholders' goals are pretty much limited to economic gain. Crises of conscience are more likely to arise with regard to unethical business practices or questionable products than campaign contributions or independent political expenditures. (The recourse in these cases is shareholder democracy, investor backlash, or challenges to management's exercise of its fiduciary responsibility.)

Besides, the assumption that stockholders feel personally implicated in corporate political expression and thus have an impetus to disavow it presumes a high and probably rare degree of political commitment to begin with. Where such commitment exists, disinvestment seems an appropriate response, and measures to protect the individual "ideological psyche" by allowing partial disassociation seem unnecessary. After all, selling corporate shares "does not ordinarily involve severe psychic trauma or economic disaster."

No wonder Justice Scalia disparaged constitutional protection for shareholders against coerced expression:

> The shareholder knows that management may take any action that is ultimately in accord with what the majority . . . of the shareholders wishes, so long as the action is designed to make a profit. That is the deal. The corporate actions to which the shareholder exposes himself, therefore, include many things that he may find politically or ideologically uncongenial: investment in South Africa, operation of an abor-

tion clinic, publication of a pornographic magazine, or even publication of a newspaper that adopts absurd political views and makes catastrophic political endorsements.[106]

We normally think of investment as eminently voluntary association, but that has changed significantly. Shareholders have little say over the investment of pension funds through an employer or mutual fund. Selling stock is not always possible. There is no reason to completely discount the compromise entailed by owning stock in a corporation that contributes money to the opposition party, or, what is more likely, that supports incumbents or hedges by contributing to both candidates in a race. Ultimately, this tension is the inevitable consequence of pluralism and our overlapping associations, with no obvious corrective. We can reconcile ourselves to it by noting that except for large institutional investors, disinvestment is probably a less effective form of disassociation than personal support for advocacy groups that oppose the corporate politics shareholders despise.

Still, we can appreciate the deeper thought that members' diverse uses of association can often be modestly facilitated. At least when it comes to expressive aspects of association, people should have reasonable flexibility. As few obstacles as possible should be set in the way of participation so that it can come as close as possible to Ronald Dworkin's notion that "agency consequences connect politics, for each individual, to his or her own moral experience; a decent political structure will allow people to participate not merely as voters but as moral agents who bring reason, passion, and conviction to the role."[107]

Curtailing Voices: Distortion, Corrosion, and Unfair Influence

Justice Scalia is skeptical that legislation requiring corporations to create separate voluntary political funds is motivated by concern for shareholders' First Amendment rights. After all, the Michigan law permits corporations to take political positions so long as they are unrelated to the election of a candidate for state office, and it curtails corporate political support even if shareholders unanimously authorize it.

Scalia is right, and not only because corporate PAC funds come from management in practice, rarely shareholders. *Austin*'s requirement that corporate political spending reflect popular support takes us far beyond the question of coerced expression. For advocates of curtailing certain association voices, in this case corporate voices, the point is the impact rather than the voluntarism of spending: "to restrict the influence of political war chests funneled through the corporate form"; "to curb the political influence of those who exercise control over large aggregations of capital."[108]

Austin and subsequent decisions sustain a vague and contested notion of undistorted democratic political process and an even more elusive notion of political equality. What is clear is that in discussions about limiting spending, the associational aspects of expression fall from view. The moral uses of expressive association for supporters personally and individually is eclipsed.

Constitutional law recognizes political contributions as a form of expression: "there is a communicative element inherent in the very act of funding itself." Less obviously, though apparent on reflection, contributions are a form of association. "Making a contribution, like joining a political party, serves to affiliate a person with a candidate. In addition, it enables like-minded persons to pool their resources in furtherance of common political goals." "Our past decisions have not drawn fine lines between contributors and members," the Supreme Court observed, "but have treated them interchangeably."[109] (In turn, the provisions of the Federal Election Campaign Act apply to partnerships, committees, associations, corporations—including nonprofits—or any other organization or group of persons.) Political theorists who chronically treat freedom of speech as if it were entirely separate from association, and vice versa, are forced to make an exception when it comes to political expenditures and campaign contributions.[110]

Justice White's dissent in *First National Bank of Boston v. Bellotti* set the stage for criticism of constitutional protection for political contributions as a form of expressive association: "vast amounts of money" may "dominate not only the economy but also the very heart of our democracy, the electoral process."[111] Judge Skelly Wright articulated the need "to prevent the mutilation of these communal thought processes" by "the unholy alliance of big spending, special interests, and election victory."[112]

The preponderance of legal and political commentary opposes the Court's decisions in *Bellotti*, where it overturned a prohibition on corporate spending to influence state referenda, as well as *Buckley v. Valeo*, where it overturned key provisions of the 1974 amendments to the Federal Election Campaign Act, and rejected the "highly paternalistic" view that public deliberation must be protected from the "undue influence" of money from individuals or associations that would "distort" or "pollute" the electoral process. In *Buckley*, the Court flatly declared that improving the quality of public debate was *not* a permissible justification for regulating association voices. The decision moved many to wonder, as Cass Sunstein did, "does the First Amendment undermine democracy"?[113]

The "quality of public debate" is, of course, the theoretical high ground and common starting point of arguments in support of regulating this form of political association. In democratic theory, the legitimacy of majority decision making derives from the fact that it comes at the end of public discussion. So justifications for curbing political voices by restricting contributions on the one hand and for enhancing voices by subsidizing them on the other rest on some conception of the requirements of adequate public deliberation. That said, even the most elementary aspects of democratic deliberation are contested.

To simplify, on some views, the point is to structure political expression to make it more likely that there will be a match between political decisions and the interests and opinions of a majority or plurality of voters. The chief concern is that salient positions be represented, and expressive associations, including campaign organizations, are conduits for channeling opinions and information into the deliberative mix.[114] It is easy to see why it is so difficult to delineate the range of existing voices, much less how the range of alternatives might be composed to improve the match.[115]

Alexander Meiklejohn remains a principal authority for a contrasting set of views, which deemphasizes the marketplace of ideas and associations and emphasizes the *quality* of the deliberative process. "What is essential is not that everyone shall speak, but that everything worth saying shall be said."[116] His heirs prescribe standards, conditions, and mechanisms for public discussion, sometimes based on rueful conclusions drawn from practical experience (the presumed effects of "negative" television advertising on campaigns, say), sometimes on sophisticated moral and epistemological notions of dialogic communication.

Neither standpoint dictates programmatic prescriptions. Both provide plausible theoretical bases for every policy alternative: supporting curbs on association expression, enhancing voices, and leaving the business of shaping participation and improving deliberation to political organizing and social reform, not legislatures and courts. Both perspectives on deliberation are consistent with acknowledging the chief reason to resist government management of the parties to deliberation and the process. That is, the assumption that we cannot regard ourselves as responsible political participants if we are protected by others (especially government officials) against the risk that we will be misinformed, manipulated, or overwhelmed.[117]

The limits on campaign contributions and public financing provisions upheld in *Buckley v. Valeo* have been described as Congress's effort "to use public money to facilitate and enlarge public discussion and participation in the electoral process, goals vital to a self-governing people." In fact, neither current nor proposed regulations are closely tied to improving the range of voices or the quality of deliberation.[118] (A possible exception is spending floors for campaign organizations, that is, inexpensive or free media time, reduced postal rates, franking privileges to challengers, and so on. They can plausibly enhance weak voices, at least "enough to make political effort something other than pointless."[119] But they cannot claim to reduce the impact of stronger association voices.)

Beyond this, however, if we ask why government should subsidize campaign organizations over and above the support they can garner from voluntary contributors, the answer has little to do with deliberation. Even if public funding laws do not amount to an "incumbent support act," they reinforce two-party contests (what Ralph Nader calls the "two-party duopoly") and do little to advance minor parties or independents. Public funding is *designed* to have this effect. Courts and Congress judge that government should not use public money to fund hopeless candidacies, create a system of splintered parties, or encourage unrestrained factionalism. More radical equalizing proposals are no better in this regard. Retired Senator Bill Bradley advocates a constitutional amendment that would ban PACs, soft money, and all large donations. On his plan, citizens would contribute to elections, not campaign organizations, with the money to be divided "between" the candidates.[120] The chief limitation of any such plan is apparent: it would displace spending from candidates and parties to independent spending on political advocacy by interest groups, similar to what goes on in contests over referenda issues.

The appeal of regulating political contributions cannot be explained by the existence of a clear, unified notion of fair democratic deliberation in the context of elections. Nor by compelling empirical demonstrations of how weak voices would be enhanced by restricting others; there is little evidence that constraining spending would level the electoral playing field, and some evidence to the contrary. Watery images of an "oversaturated" marketplace of ideas or some voices "drowning out" others are distressing, but they are metaphors.

Rather, the appeal is *curtailing* certain association voices. When the Court retreated from *Buckley* in *Austin v. Michigan Chamber of Commerce*, it echoed the predominant negative sentiment: political expenditures by corporations "will undermine the integrity of the political process."[121]

The Court had employed the formulation "undermining the integrity of the political process" earlier in *Buckley*, where it upheld government's compelling interest in preventing corruption or the appearance of corruption of elected officials—contributors getting favorable treatment from officials as a result of a quid pro quo, say.[122] Since the outcome of *Austin* was much less protective of association expression, "undermining the integrity of the political process" must have come to mean something more. The Court moves almost imperceptibly from the possibility that representatives will be corrupted to "a different type of corruption," a novel subset called "political corrosion." The decision points to "the corrosive and distorting effects that are accumulated with the help of the corporate form."[123]

Analyzing "distortion," "corrosion," or "unfair influence" turns out to be unenlightening. Michigan aimed at "aggregations of wealth" that "are accumulated with the help of the corporate form." These distort the process because they exploit a government-conferred advantage. State laws of incorporation "not only allow corporations to play a dominant role in the Nation's economy, but also permit them to use resources amassed in the economic marketplace to obtain an unfair advantage in the political marketplace."[124]

The problem is, we are not clear what state-conferred benefits constitute an "unfair advantage" to association voices in electoral politics. After all, the laws of incorporation are not selective; they are available to for-profit businesses large and small, and nonprofit organizations. Restrictions on contributions apply to them all. And the same rationale could apply to everything from enforcement of the laws of partnerships to tax-exempt status. Indeed, it could reasonably extend to economic inequalities overall insofar as they are seen to rest on public policy: "the use of existing distributions for political expenditures marks out government inaction. But . . . it should be clear that elections based on those distributions are actually a regulatory system, made possible and constituted through law."[125]

We cannot comprehend "distortion" or "corrosion" or understand why corporate status should be singled out as justifying restraint without articulating some baseline. Without that, we learn mainly that at least when it comes to corporate voices, the Supreme Court will defer to legislative judgments about "corrosion." Which is why Justice Scalia calls *Austin* "Orwellian."

We can say with confidence, however, that curtailing association expression is not an egalitarian ideal. The issue is some kind and degree of *inequality* among association voices. Neither the Court nor reform advocacy groups like Common Cause explain "unfair influence," but the attack on "aggregations of wealth" is plain enough. So is Skelly Wright's insistence that unchecked expenditures no less than crass censorship of ideas "may drown out opposing beliefs, vitiate the principle of political equality, and place some citizens under the damaging and arbitrary control of others."[126] Public discourse "cannot now plausibly be interpreted as an arena of free communicative exchange" if wealthy voices drown out others any more than contracts are voluntary if economic inequality makes one party vulnerable and dependent on the other.[127]

Like "big money," "unfair influence" is a political trigger. It invokes oligarchy or plutocracy, arousing recurrent American opposition to the perceived influence of (often unspecified) groups. Hence Walt Whitman's warning against "brawling office-holders . . . kept editors, bribers, compromisers, lobbiers, spongers . . . the lousy combines and born freedom-sellers of the earth."[128] In context, "unfair influence" may reflect concrete grievances, opposition to particular political outcomes supported by a particular "special interest." The target may be "interested money" per se, no matter what its source. Or classic populist targets, like "big business." But it always derives moral force, if not analytic strength, from democratic concerns whose roots go deeper than electoral influence: the perfectly accurate perception that concentrated economic power can undermine self-government.

Here, however, economic inequality is addressed at the level of political process, specifically, electoral campaigns rather than other forms of political participation or social structure. No proposed limitation on association voices corrects for the absence of a "poor-PAC" on Capitol Hill. Indeed, economic inequality is addressed at a single point in the political process, and not the one we might think is most salient: mechanisms of political representation, such as proportional schemes.[129]

Verba, Brady, and Schlozman draw mixed conclusions from their study of unequal political participation. On the other hand, they find that better educated and politically interested citizens are overrepresented in every electoral activity, including spending. On the other hand, representation is skewed because the politically active and inactive have different interests and priorities; elections create a picture of the public that is more informed, more tolerant of unpopular opinions, and more committed to activity for the community. "Thus, while the process exacerbates political inequality, it may enhance the quality of political discourse and democratic governance."[130]

In any case, economic inequality is more invoked than addressed. It could hardly be otherwise. American political thought harbors divergent ideas about both economic equality and political influence, and always has. Even those who have firm notions of the democratically acceptable parameters of either inequality of wealth or political influence are likely to be perplexed and divided about the just relation between them. We are not always sensitive to the *source* of political influence (money, or celebrity, or money garnered in specific ways). We disagree about whether we would curtail contributions to the political process if we thought that economic inequalities *were* morally justified.[131] We disagree about what constitutes illegitimate economic influence. Michael Sandel asks, "What, really, is the moral difference between a politician who buys votes and one who panders to economic self-interest? Both offer a financial reward in exchange for a vote." Another scholar proposes that for the purposes of participating in the electoral process, "all money is like . . . stolen money."[132]

Except for academic political philosophy, we have never thought that political influence should be strictly proportional to numbers, if that were conceivable. We lack norms for when political spending is wasteful, messages insubstantial, influence disproportionate, public discussion distorted, the system harmed.[133]

Money and Voice

Discussion of association by contribution is dominated by normative concerns about the electoral system as a whole, and by interpretation of the constitutional guarantees of freedom of association and expression. Its significance for individuals—the moral uses of association—falls from view. Except for the thought that curtailing political contributions is a solution to political apathy, the subjective side of contributions rarely comes up. The meaning of this form of participation for "members," that is, contributors, personally and individually, is unmentioned. Do the moral uses of association by contribution bear mention?

The most important aspect of the *Buckley* decision was the constitutional distinction drawn between independent expenditures and contributions. The distinction is unsupportable as a response to political corruption, its ostensible rationale. It may be that candidates are more likely to curry favor for contributions than for general pronouncements in favor of their positions.[134] But independent expenditures by supporters unconnected to candidates are hard to distinguish from those authorized or requested by a candidate or his or her agents.

The distinction is even less tenable as applied to political parties; attempts to judge whether they amount to contributions to campaigns or independent spending are scholastic, indeed, silly.[135] And the distinction invites evasion. "Uncoordinated" political spending by associations like the National Conservative Political Action Committee (NCPAC) directed against "liberal candidates" stretches credibility. Who can doubt that the NRA strategizes with conservative incumbents about its "independent" expenditures? Or the AFL-CIO with Democratic leadership in designing its "educational" campaign? The public is as likely to perceive candidates as beholden to PACs (permissible) as large individual donors (impermissible).

At the same time, and more significant for considering the personal uses of association, the Court reinforces this distinction by proposing that contributions are less "indispensable to democratic decisionmaking" than expenditures. *Buckley* effects something close to a scaling of the value of political association and expression.[136] By implication, contributions are a less consequential form of expression for contributors personally. Why?

Political contributions, the Court asserts, have two separate aspects. One is the association the gift effects and the 'moral' support it conveys. The other is that contributions translate into communication. Consider the relevant passage:

> A contribution serves as a general expression of support for the candidate and his views, but does not communicate the underlying basis for the support. The quality of communication by the contributor does not increase perceptibly with the size of his contribution, since the expression rests solely on the undifferentiated, symbolic act of contributing. . . . [T]he transformation of contributions into political debate involves speech by someone other than the contributor.

The first thought seems to be that since any contribution suffices to signal affiliation, a low ceiling does not alter the message, and additional money does not enhance attachment. This is doubtful. Like large donors to advocacy groups such as the ACLU, individuals who make significant contributions— either absolutely or relative to their own means and past experience—are likely to be more intensely committed to a candidate or issue. We know from experience the difference between writing a token check in response to persis-tent solicitation and being a strong supporter of candidates and causes, in which case our financial contributions may be larger and probably not the only way in which we indicate association. The dynamic works in reverse, too: what began as a "mere" contribution is more likely to turn into increasingly active involvement when the amount is significant, both because of the psy-chology of investment and because the large contributor is likely to be aggres-sively recruited to participate in other activities. In any case, the fact that affili-ation with a candidate or cause can be had for a small contribution does not make a larger one "symbolic."

A second element in the Court's depreciation of contributions, and the most important for freedom of association, is the suggestion that although as a mat-ter of law donations are designated speech and association, they are not the contributor's own expression. The actual expression donations generate is by another party—the campaign organization. It is speech by proxy.[137] This is a peculiar argument, since expression via membership in an association is *al-ways* communication by proxy. When a labor union or the Jaycees makes an independent political expenditure in the context of elections, or simply ex-presses its political views on some issue, members' express views via the association's voice. If contributions are vulnerable as second-hand speech, so are association voices generally. If the point is that an association voice is not really the voice of its members—not because it is somehow unrepresentative but because we must speak directly for ourselves—we should all resort to soapboxes or the internet.

PACs are the real proxy voices, of course. They are associations formed to meet the peculiar requirements of federal campaign law, substitutes for what would otherwise be direct contributions to associations whose voices people want to influence and support. *Austin* sustained Michigan's prohibition of the Chamber of Commerce's newspaper advertisement, which explained why the candidates it endorsed would improve economic conditions. Justice Scalia wonders why Michigan voters should be deprived of the information that own-ers and operators of a vast percentage of the industry of the state want to communicate. How else can voters evaluate corporate-supported policies and determine whether organizations "have earned credibility over a period of time"?

> It is important to the message that it represents the views of Michigan's leading corporations as corporations . . . not just the views of some *other* voluntary associa-tions to which some of the corporation's shareholders belong. [And,] the public is not interested in what a PAC says. . . . PAC's are interim, ad hoc organizations with little continuity or responsibility.[138]

Scalia's objection gains force if we consider unaffiliated PACs. Anyone trying to decipher the names and (often just the initials) of organizations sponsoring political advertisements, mailing literature, or soliciting donations comes up against their effective anonymity: the Society for Good Government, for example. Even their ideological identity is obscure. They are the associational equivalent of "stealth candidates."

Ultimately, the Court's depreciation of contributions by designating them expression by proxy makes sense only in contrast to direct expression, whether independent spending or other forms of political participation. The idea is that limiting contributions is merely an incidental constraint on expression as long as individuals and groups remain "free to . . . assist personally in the association's efforts on behalf of candidates." Contributions are "symbolic" in contrast to other, "real" forms of participation. Added to this is the belief that contributions inhibit those other modes of participation, and that limiting them would facilitate these forms of personal involvement in electoral politics.

Here is where the case for curtailing association and expression becomes particularly murky. Is the issue correcting for skewed political outcomes? Or promoting equal and universal political participation per se? For some advocates of managed spending and expression, the main objective is to prevent "distorted" political communication, undue influence, and hence unjustifiable policy outcomes. For others, however, the underlying concern is universal participation *simpliciter*. The political engagement of all citizens is valuable— for their personal moral development and for the well-being of democracy— without regard to whether or not enhanced participation has identifiable political consequences.

We would be more likely to concede that "nothing would do more to restore faith in democracy, as well as democracy's competence to address real problems, than radical campaign finance reform," if it were the case that "money talks louder than votes and voters increasingly stay home."[139] And if we were certain that voters stay home because "the access process makes them "cynical and discouraged."[140] Whether or not political disaffection is caused by uncurtailed (or inadequately curtailed) campaign spending, the notion that limiting contributions and substituting independent spending or public funding would be an antidote is sheer speculation. So is the thought that curtailing association voices would increase participation or shift citizens from participation by contribution to other forms. In particular, that individuals would shift from association by spending to direct personal involvement.

Verba and colleagues' study of political participation in America does not appear to support this speculation. They find that "for many people, political activity consists of giving money and nothing else." Of those who take part in campaigns, there are twice as many people (69 percent) who limit their involvement to check-writing as people who give only time or who give both time and money. There is no indication that contributing substitutes for other forms of participation, so that limiting it would impel people to contribute time instead of money. Or, inversely, that the inability to contribute financially diminishes other forms of participation.[141] Although economic resources increase the likelihood that people will participate in political campaigns, psychological engagement plays the same role as affluence. Once over the threshold of participation—having "mustered psychological engagement"—the poor are as politically active as their counterparts higher on the income ladder.

If there is a link between contributions and political disaffection on the part of activists themselves it is most likely that the activity that has gained in frequency and significance is comparatively unsatisfying. "Contributors garner relatively few gratifications, especially of a social sort, and are less likely to feel that what they did had an impact."[142]

We should be wary of judging contributions as a form of political association too harshly, however. Robert Lane advances the grim thesis that democratic *processes* (quite apart from outcomes) do not enhance individuals' sense of well-being: "democratic processes are generally painful, fail to contribute to good cheer in democratic publics and do very little to relieve what seems to be an epidemic of depression." For Lane, the pains of democracy are inherent and not simply a consequence of the fact that the predominant forms of participation lack gratification. Inherent in democratic processes are the frequency of frustration, the referral of distressing social problems and unpopular causes to government, the "hedonic toll" of democratic insistence on humane principles of justice.[143]

What can be said about contributions? Recall that contribution is association by individuals. And that "in many ways, the most striking fact in American campaign finance has been the persistence . . . of individual contributors as the dominant force."[144] So we should at least consider whether "check-writing," scorned in the democratic literature as passive at best and more often as subversive of "genuine" participation, might not actually be, as the Supreme Court said it is by law, a form of association that affords some experience of expressive association.

I pointed out earlier in connection with homeowners' associations that the romance of localism and revulsion at corporatism made it easy to disparage participation—the number of people who serve as directors, for example, in this pervasive form of proprietary community. Similarly, nothing is easier than to dismiss contributions as a personally insignificant form of participation. Indeed, for some critics, association by contribution is morally deficient, a form of anticivic substitution for doing one's duty: money buys "political mercenaries."[145] In practice, most experiences of political association and expression fall somewhere between ideal acts of participation to influence electoral outcomes on the one hand and voting on the other. Check writing in support of candidates or causes is a step up in involvement.

It is also an important locus of access to political affairs. Participation of any kind is not just a matter of personal individual disposition; it depends on access, which depends in turn on recruitment. Associations recruit members via requests for donations. Insofar as they do not perform mediating functions between members and political elites, and do not channel members into additional activities beyond check-writing, they have limited significance for their members as participatory associations. Even so, this kind and degree of association can be significant.

To understand that, check-writing must be disaggregated. Contributors have multiple goals. In the case of affiliated PACs, they may express professional or workplace solidarity. And contributors may see contributions as an entry to ongoing engagement; some corporations have active programs of political education, sending managers to Washington for seminars on the political process, or scheduling meetings with congressmen. In the case of unaffiliated PACs, contributions are a way for marginally active citizens to take on a political obligation beyond voting in support of some broad ideological loyalty or specific issue. The domain of contributions is not restricted to electoral campaigns.

Institutional innovations further blur the distinction between political activism and passive association by contribution. For example, lobbying was virtually defined in contrast to grassroots mobilization; it meant contact with legislators by professionals employed by government contractors or foreign governments. Or it signified powerful domestic alliances. (Less well known than the dairy association, say, is the Federal Judges Association, formed by federal judges to lobby Congress for better salaries and retirement benefits, it maintains a "federal coordinator" for national legislation relating to the courts.)[146]

Today, however, there is convergence between "influence peddling" and electoral campaigns.[147] Corporate "public affairs" committees engage employees and community leaders in local organizing, educational forums, and coalition-building.[148] Grassroots lobbying techniques invented by Ralph Nader's consumer-based groups have been adopted by all sorts of associations, which mobilize constituents to contact decision makers. Electronic networks allow them to send a personal mailgram to a legislator by a push of a phone button:

> the National Rifle Association generating three million telegrams in seventy-two hours and blanketing Capitol Hill with so many phone calls that members cannot make outgoing calls . . . the "grey lobby" dumping up to fifteen million postcards on [former Speaker] Jim Wright in one day to warn Congress not to tamper with Social Security cost-of-living adjustments.[149]

This form of political association and expression is disparaged too, as "astroturf" participation. Critics deny that it is a legitimate expression of popular sentiment because staff-led organizations orchestrate campaigns and motivate people to act manipulatively, by arousing fear on highly visible issues. Certainly, electronic mail fits no description of sober dialogue. But it is churlish to deny that this is democratic participation on a massive scale. Or that it is educative; it brings day-to-day politics that are otherwise distant and physically remote—especially decisions at the federal level—home. Whether this is "carpetbagging," a regrettable interference with the specific regional concerns of constituents, or the healthy nationalization of political consciousness ("PACs are the precincts of the 80s")[150] is another matter. It certainly engages the elderly more than mailing an AARP dues check in return for benefits.

Innovations in PACs prevent even this least favored form of political association from arid passivity, especially the variation called "bundling." PACs normally have an authoritarian structure. In affiliated PACs, decisions are typically made by the CEO; in unaffiliated PACs, they tend to be made by a single entrepreneurial founder. (There are exceptions; the International Machinists do not support campaigns unless the local union has endorsed a candidate.)[151] In new types of PACs, by contrast, a political group collects and "bundles" the checks of individual contributors and sends them to the candidates they specify. Emily's List is the best known example, an association that supports only "pro-choice," Democratic women candidates for the House and Senate (thus departing from the stereotypical PAC dedicated to buying access to incumbents). Contributors to Emily's List pledge a required sum to the List and a minimum of $100 each to a minimum of two candidates; the checks are written to specific campaign committees. So contributors are affiliated with both the organizing political group and the campaign organization to which they address their money. Emily's List blurs membership in an advocacy group and "mere" check-writing. "The PAC member enjoys new choices and new influence," and the association "suits the populist tenor of contemporary American political life."[152]

Voice and Vote

We can understand why contribution as a form of expressive association and its significance for individuals disappear from view if the operative assumption is that resources spent on elections translate directly into electoral outcomes. If expenditures are thought to have an unmediated political effect, democratic deliberation, which had been the starting point for regulating association voice, is also eclipsed. "Voting is what gives public political discussion its point,"[153] but discussion falls away if we assume that economic inequalities translate into unequal political expenditures, and expenditures translate directly into votes.

Criticism of the practical consequences of the Court's constitutional categorization of contributions as association and speech in *Buckley* and *Bellotti* has overshadowed the element of common sense at the heart of the decisions. By keeping association voice in view the Court indicated that campaign activities and political expenditures exercise their influence indirectly by influencing the beliefs and attitudes of voters.[154] Images and arguments persuade, manipulate, inform, excite, teach, cow, or inspire; they don't simply mobilize inert citizens to action. Spending is expressive and communicative. Jane Mansbridge makes the same point vis-à-vis interest groups; viewing them exclusively as the exercise of power, exertion of pressure, or adding a force to the equilibrium of interests ignores the way interest group politics can "change people's preferences and help them create new options."[155] I would even venture to apply this description to corporate political expenditures. In recent years, for example, "business mobilization" turned corporate attention from immediate favorable treatment for their own firms and sectors to formulating an overall interpretation of business (and employment) problems. The dominant narrative offered by business today centers on "government regulation," offering an interpretation of policy that is influential for reasons that go beyond the force of money. It provides a credible and politically attractive "growth model" of the American economy, and coincides with the preexisting antistatist inclinations of many groups.[156]

All this is denied when contributions are treated as raw exercises of political power that translate into votes. It is a short step to the view that democracy's commitment to political equality makes expenditures the moral and practical equivalent of votes, regulable by the same principles governing voting. Contributions should be withdrawn from the domain of First Amendment speech and association and political participation in general and set in the framework of ballot access and apportionment, the argument goes. The internal logic of this conception of political equality drives support for curtailing association expression. The counterpart of one person, one vote is the "equal-dollars-per-voter" rule, and the logical outcome of this line of thought is a voucher system.[157] Indeed, one constitutional scholar argues that spending vouchers are constitutionally required, entailed by the equal protection clause.[158]

Theories of political equality are not my subject; stingy views of association are. Here, proponents are less inclined to say that limiting some voices enhances others, since regulations on contributions are *intended* to suppress unequal voices. They set political equality squarely above freedom of association and expression. Even those normally protective of rights of expression and association reconcile themselves to government-imposed limits and regulations by segregating elections from the rest of political association, expression, and deliberation.[159] Association voices may be sacrificed in the context of election campaigns, so long as they are free in other spheres. Proponents of inhibiting contributions might concede that expression to affect "the longer-term and more general process of public political debate cannot be disposed of by considerations internal to the concept of election campaign deliberation."[160] But they agree with Justice Stevens' confident (but dubious) assertion, "there is a vast difference between lobbying and debating political issues on the one hand, and political campaigns for election to public office on the other."[161]

If we decline to segregate these aspects of association expression, and insist that there are other reasons for association within the electoral context than buying votes, and other mechanisms at work besides direct influence, then justifications for regulating association voices geared to voting overshoot the mark even when it comes to elections.

We know that campaigns are the principal setting for popular political discussion overall. Elections structure participation, create an audience, and provide foci for association on issues, policies, personalities, and ideals that may be only tangentially related to specific candidates and electoral results. Groups unaligned with candidates, minor political parties, and independent candidates and their supporters look for educational or ideological change, not electoral victory. My generation will recall that a handful of wealthy individuals made the presidential primary campaign of Senator Eugene McCarthy possible. McCarthy represented an antiwar agenda, and support for his candidacy reflected the donors' strategic judgment that ending America's involvement in the war in Vietnam would best be advanced by supporting this opposition primary campaign to "dump Johnson." Current campaign finance laws make this scenario impossible.

Association goals may be purely oppositional and defiant, combining spending with protest activities; the idea is not strategic advantage or compromise but radical discourse.[162] And there is noninstrumental expression— spending by associations whose members are inspired by a felt obligation to articulate "thoughts, attitudes, and feelings" quite apart from calculating the effect on electoral outcomes.[163] We can also understand association activity as a variation on the public standing argument I discussed earlier. Inside and outside the framework of elections, association expression aims at "recognition," a point to which I return in chapter 9.

Contributions are a distinctive form of political association, but there is every reason to think the full range of aims is at work. All this is lost when association via political expenditure is contemplated solely in terms of influencing votes, much less as the equivalent of a vote.

The strains on freedom of association posed by the Jaycees and unions, corporate spending, and political contributions could not be more interesting. They mirror the messy ideological mix that comprises our thinking about political association, democratic deliberation, and political equality. They challenge any notion we might have that there is general agreement about the value of political association, and whether when it comes to political expression via contributions, associations should be enhanced, curtailed, or left alone. They raise doubts about the usual descriptions of joining and membership by pointing up prominent cases of compelled association and coerced expression, and raising the question of whether contributions constitute expressive association or a sort of participation by proxy. Above all, they challenge us to look not only at systemic and constitutional concerns but also at the moral uses of association for members.

In terms of moral drama, however, the dilemmas these associations pose pale in comparison to overtly antiliberal, antidemocratic associations: secret societies, hate groups, private armies, conspiracists, and self-styled citizen militias. Some of these groups are rooted in nonliberal political ideologies. Anti-Semitic hate groups, for example, are by no means strange imports, alien to American society, but they are not outgrowths of liberal democracy (or of liberal democratic failings) either. Other associations, like some secret societies and citizen militias, have clear affinities to democratic ideology. They all exploit freedom of association for illiberal ends. Their ill effects seem apparent; their moral uses are not.

7

Secret Societies and Private Armies:
Conspiracism and Clear and Present Danger

Secrecy, Conspiracy, and Democracy

Avowedly exclusive, private clubs and restricted membership groups like the Jaycees are troublesome for democracy, but secret societies are anathema. Public tenets of equality and publicity are flouted when membership and rituals are concealed and association life is clandestine. The apparatus of signs, passwords, and especially oaths excites the belief that secret societies produce "selected, dedicated, indoctrinated, and rigidly disciplined members."[1] Presumably tightly organized and demanding blind obedience, they are believed to compromise national loyalty: "When a citizen of these United States kneels at the altar of masonry, when he swears allegiance to her laws, he snaps asunder the ties that bind him to this country; he cannot at the same time be the citizen of a free republic, and the subject of a despotic empire."[2]

It is not surprising that secret societies are often dubbed conspiracies. Even if they neither advocate nor engage in subversive action, they challenge the public ethos of democratic equality more than the usual interplay of social snobbery and deference, prejudice and self-affirmation. Though they rarely comprise an upper class, much less a pretended aristocracy, secret societies present an affront to elites of wealth and achievement, and they arouse "status anxiety" in those near the social bottom. "Combinations" challenge the ideals of free markets and open competition, and secret societies subvert "careers open to talent" by giving members hidden, unfair advantage. The antidemocratic ethos of secret societies is exacerbated when they espouse the inferiority of some group and are cemented by hate. The mother of a leader of the Southern White Knights of the Ku Klux Klan remarked, "It's a secret organization. So are the Masons. Secret. I don't see much good in it."[3]

Neither prohibition of titles of nobility nor extension of the franchise has eliminated secret societies or allayed recurrent fears that they are based on claims of superiority and translate into political supremacy. An early example is the Order of Cincinnati, a group of Revolutionary War officers with hereditary membership. Some worried that the Cincinnati order was a potential military threat, but the chief anxiety was that it would perpetuate a species of un-American nobility. The press attacked, Rhode Island considered disenfranchising members, and the Massachusetts legislature proclaimed it "dangerous to the peace, liberty, and safety of the Union."[4] In the same spirit, Jacksonians assaulted Freemasons, Catholics, and Mormons as intolerably antidemocratic. Lodges were burned, Masonic clergymen expelled from churches, legislative investigations launched, and secret society oaths prohibited in some states.

America remains rife with secret societies, and with voluntary associations formed to counter these presumably sinister elites and their antidemocratic schemes. Private groups range from respected associations like the Anti-Defamation League of B'nai Brith, which has monitored hate groups for over eighty years, to self-appointed inquisitors who make it their business to ferret out covert associations and expose members: the nativist, vigilante American Protective Association, for example, and the Jewish Defense League.

Secret societies inspire the formation of secretive counterparts to better resist them. When Robert Welch organized the John Birch Society to resist communism, he used the Party as a model, aiming to create a secret society of committed individuals who reject "debating-society" tactics in favor of "a monolithic body . . . under completely authoritative control."[5] The American Nazi Party explains its "iron chain of command" as a protective response to Jewish violence: it was "forced to organize along military lines to DEFEND itself from this constant illegal and immoral harassment."[6] Paramilitary groups especially provoke the creation of mirror images of themselves, rationalizing the militarization of ordinary life. Even the Klanwatch Project at the Southern Poverty Law Center has an extensive intelligence operation that includes "carefully conducted undercover operations."[7]

They also contribute to the militarization of domestic government institutions, at the extreme "federaliz[ing] the spirit of American vigilantism."[8] Counterconspiracy is institutionalized at every level of government, from the FBI and Bureau of Alcohol, Tobacco, and Firearms of the Treasury Department to intelligence units attached to each branch of the armed services and investigative units of the INS and IRS (including several hundred auditors in the recently formed Illegal Tax Protester Program). From state police and highway patrols to local police with their undercover units and "Red Squads," and the smallest sheriffs' department.[9] Counterconspiracy justifies "preventive intelligence": telephone tapping, mail tampering, seizing bank records, infiltration, entrapment, government-sponsored "disinformation," and the multiplication of informants, hired witnesses, and agents provocateurs.[10] The white supremacist National States Rights Party gave rise to the saying, "The only ones paying dues here are the FBI spies."[11] For some groups, nothing is as confirming as being under surveillance. Citizen militia leaders have been known to agree to regular meetings with the FBI; conspiracists all, they like to keep tabs on each other.

As Richard Hofstadter points out, some groups take the leap from the plausible view that secret societies have engaged in antidemocratic conspiracies to a conspiratorial view of history as a whole, so that the motive force in events is "plots long hatched and deeply premeditated."[12] Indeed, for Michael Rogin, "American political demonology" is at the center of American history. Certainly, at points in American history the culture of secrecy, conspiracy, and counterconspiracy has dominated political life. Colonial accounts of a conspiracy by the Church of England and the king's ministers fueled the Revolution. Jeffersonian charges that the Federalists wanted to reestablish monarchy spurred the countercharge that the Jeffersonians conspired to subvert Christianity. The belief that the annexation of Texas and war with Mexico was a machination of the southern Slave Power was another such period; the Ku Klux Klan during Reconstruction and revived in the civil rights era; the Red Scare of 1917–20 and the Palmer Raids, when the Justice Department summarily deported thousands of aliens. And of course McCarthyism. David Brion Davis proposes that fears of conspiracy were never as diverse or widespread as in the 1960s following President Kennedy's assassination.[13]

Today, conspiracy claims run the gamut from fluoridation of water to Neo-Luddite attacks on "large, bureaucratic, complex and secretive organizations of the industrial world."[14] They include claims of deliberate mongrelization of the white race by programs of forced integration, and the view of African Americans that crack cocaine and HIV are a government program of genocide, and that certain commercial products are contaminated, their producers linked to antiblack conspiracies. Or that as regards indigenous tribes, "an assimilationist ideal amounts to genocide."[15] Anti-Semitic charges of a world Jewish conspiracy are familiar: Jews are responsible for Marxism, the stock market, liberal religion, radicalism in universities, sensitivity training (a plot to make white Christians more receptive, that is, " 'sensitive' to the colored, the ne'er-do-wells"), and modern art.[16] Jews are responsible for importing slaves for the purpose of undermining American society.[17] As the author of *The Temple Bombing* points out, "Jews were the only people on earth ever accused by others of murdering God."[18]

There are some constants to conspiracism. Charges and countercharges inevitably tie subversion to moral laxity and sexual deviance. Catholic priests are libertines and convents licentious; polygamy and "the Mormon seraglio" reflect Joseph Smith's extraordinary animal magnetism; FBI Director J. Edgar Hoover was preoccupied with Martin Luther King's infidelities (and Hoover's enemies with his sexual preferences); and the Bureau reported to COIN-TELPRO field agents that "the two things foremost in the Black militant's mind are sex and money."[19] Communists are homosexuals and vice versa; leftists engage in "intellectual debauchery"; communes are scenes of perversion; the sexual misdeeds of leaders of paramilitary and survivalist groups are publicized to legitimize government intervention.

Always, government is the principal scene of betrayal, whether it is subverted by foreign enemies and their agents "inside," or traitorous officials. The Minutemen defined themselves as "a secret underground organization equipped to spy upon, harass, and destroy troops of any foreign power that might occupy the U.S.," that is, until the group switched to "counterrevolution" against tyrannical federal and state governments subverting the republic from within.[20]

The chief variable is what is read as the principal sign of conspiracy. Wearing the Revolutionary mantle of the independent militia that opposed the British army, citizen militias echo the conspiracist logic of that rebellion: the motive behind the Stamp Act was not simply to raise money from the colonies, John Adams had warned, but "to forge a fatal link between ecclesiastical and civil despotism by stripping colonies of the means of knowledge." The danger to America, it was believed, "was in fact only the small, immediately visible part of the greater whole whose ultimate manifestation would be the destruction of the English constitution with the rights and privileges embedded in it."[21] Today, public schools are a form of "conscription," and "a child in the age bracket for compulsory school attendance is like a combat soldier in the draft-age bracket." ("Comrade" John Dewey is a particular target; his stress on the need for children to get along in groups is viewed as preparation for socialism.)[22] Or, conspiracy to overthrow the United States and erect a New World Order is foreshadowed by the World Council of Churches and spearheaded, in the current version, by the United Nations. In July 1995, the *New York Times* reported that the Indiana transportation department changed its road signs after callers phoned in their fears that the maintenance codes on the back were secret messages for invading troops.[23] Above all, the federal income tax or gun control is the entering wedge of a conspiracy by a cabal of federal officials.

Conspiracy spirals become dense, convoluted, fantastic, and mutually reinforcing. Each side sees an emergency situation, a crisis. Each side in the strange dance of secret societies and official and unofficial counterconspirators claims to be the national redeemer. The prosecutor in the trial of Minutemen leaders for violating the National Firearms Act described "murderous arsenals secretly finding their way into the hands of . . . enemies of the public." The defense responded that the group's purpose was "to protect themselves and their homes against an uprising of an underground force which is—I don't want to go too far—advocating at least the overthrow of our present form of government. . . . We have been fighting around the world trying to protect other people from the same force."[24]

For in the United States, conspiratorial thinking typically revolves around who is genuinely faithful to American democracy. European subversives and the continental ideologies imported or adopted by groups here—communism, syndicalism, anarchism, Nazism—explicitly rejected democratic institutions. But many secret societies and private armies are American originals that represent themselves as defenders of "the democratic way of life" and the final bulwark against a conspiracy to betray democracy by government officials abetted by an unwitting public. We have indigenous associations on the right and the left. Ku Klux Klan members claim to be "patriots." Black militants may see themselves as colonized (and all blacks in jail as political prisoners). Still, the Black Panther program ended by quoting from the Declaration of Independence, and the group made at least a temporary alliance with the Student Nonviolent Coordinating Committee (SNCC), known for its Freedom Rides and voter registration drives.[25] This strange commitment of undemocratic groups to what they see as American democracy is clearest in the case of self-styled citizens' militias, the subject of the next chapter.

Nowhere is the reciprocal charge of subversion of democracy by secret societies and their inquisitors more striking or its baleful effects clearer than when groups are armed. My aim is to consider the battery of laws arrayed against these associations. And to consider the internal life of these groups in order to gain some insight into their abiding attraction for members, and to assess whether it is senseless to speak here of the moral uses of membership.

I also show why secret societies and private armies ought to arouse not only fear of "domestic terrorism" and fear for civil liberties, but also apprehension about the propensity for conspiracism that is a permanent element of American political life and a basis of voluntary association. "Clear and present danger" is both a constitutional doctrine and a state of mind.

The Internal Life of Paramilitary Groups

With the possible exception of religious cults, no association is more incongruent with liberal democracy than paramilitary groups. In addition to being secret, conspiracist, and separatist, their military organization sets them apart. After all, many radical political groups viewed as ideologically subversive are organizationally similar to the general run of political associations and parties; they may even be internally democratic. And the "grammar of violence" is pronounced by organized crime and by associations like urban street gangs and British football firms bent on injury and destruction.[26] They are neither secret (they mark out their territories and advertise their affiliation by dress and demeanor) nor militarist. Paramilitary groups cannot be characterized by a proclivity to violence or disorder, simply, then. They are both undemocratic and anticivilian, bent on preparation for combat. They have a command structure, hierarchy, and discipline according to the (sometimes eccentric) lights of leaders. The Black Panthers, for example, had an elaborate military structure, with the minister of defense at the top, a minister of information and chief of state, party field marshals, captains and assistant captains, and rank-and-file soldiers.[27]

In 1965, the NRA protested the "lies and insinuations" that led the American people "to believe that private armies are being formed by 'fanatics' and 'extremists.'"[28] That same year, the California attorney general wrote an eighty-one-page report on the American Nazi Party, the National States Rights Party, the California Rangers, the Black Muslims, and the Minutemen, a paramilitary group formed in 1960, which he described as "the fantastic situation of a private citizen raising a private military force to accomplish by violence whatever objective the citizen decides in his judgment is best for the country."[29]

The NRA was wrong. The number of paramilitary groups and private armies is not known for certain, much less the number of active members.[30] Like other associations, paramilitary groups have passive members, fellow-travelers, subscribers to their publications. Personal acquaintance is the principal way in, and members often join with friends. But recruitment also goes on openly at gun shows, groups use local newspaper ads, and application to some associations can be made by mail. The numbers are elusive. Directories and official tallies of paramilitary and hate groups appear to include not only small groups (fewer than six members) but a host of one-man organizations. The Anti-Defamation League's report on militia groups specifically estimated groups in forty states in 1995 (California has more than thirty), with about 15,000 members overall.

The demographics of membership is uncertain, too. Social science analysis focuses on electoral politics or on "right-wing" organizations generally, specifically excluding groups that advocate violence. Case studies of paramilitary groups cover a small sample. Altogether, accounts of members' socioeconomic status are inconclusive; one study concludes that members were "surprisingly diverse."[31]

Paramilitary groups come in many stripes, often benign. The Boy Scouts are modeled on military hierarchy, teach patriotism and discipline, and practice survival skills, riflery, and archery, but they are an open membership group and their activities are overt. (Statutes outlawing paramilitary organizations specifically exempt them.) In some groups, military organization is nominal. Ranks and uniforms, martial music, drilling, even preaching violence is a matter of attracting members and keeping up enthusiasm and contributions.

Paramilitary group activities run the gamut as well, many overt and lawful. Some groups have parallel political arms like the Minutemen's Patriotic Party, which endorsed George Wallace for president in 1968. The Black Panthers ran a slate of candidates for mayor, city council, and planning committee of Oakland. Radio broadcasts are a principal means of self-promotion, and groups use satellite linkups and shortwave outlets as well as regular stations. They have exploited public access cable television channels, and use the stations' recording facilities to produce master tapes that are aired in many states.[32]

Technological developments have extended these groups' reach and sharpened their self-presentation. Aryan Nations began to produce audiocassettes of sermons in 1979; Klan and Posse Comitatus leaders star in videos (Gordon Kahl, who would become a Posse martyr, urged sympathizers to play his tapes at home and in their pickup trucks and combine cabs). Telephone hotlines with recorded messages expound conspiracy theories from answering machines. Computer-literate sympathizers can hook up to electronic bulletin boards such as the Aryan Nations Net. Almost immediately after the Oklahoma City bombing in 1995, a computerized news service and bulletin board began issuing a flash suggesting that the CIA and FBI were behind the bombing, intent on discrediting militias.[33] (Norman Olson was forced to resign from the leadership of the Michigan Militia after members dissented from his public view that the Japanese had bombed the Murrah federal building in retaliation for nerve gas attacks in the Tokyo subway engineered by the United States.)

It would be a mistake to overestimate their technological sophistication, though: the usual rallies, marches, innumerable publications, and endless uninterrupted ideological speeches to passive listeners dominate their public activities. A "law school" called the Christian Liberty Academy was set up in one paramilitary compound in Wisconsin, and groups hold seminars on the use of legal weapons.[34]

But if recruitment and public activities are unexceptional, the internal life of paramilitary groups is distinctive because it revolves around preparation for combat, "self-defense," "public defense," "resistance," "counterrevolution," or "war." The answer to the question, "what do you do" is "maintain security, gather information, spread propaganda, recruit, stockpile and train."[35] Members are taught how to obtain, use, and conceal weapons, and how to manufacture munitions at home. Groups build arsenals of bazookas, mortars, hand grenades, machineguns, flame throwers, plastic explosives and ammonium nitrate, booby traps, rocket launchers, automatic weapons, and silencers. The leader of a New Hampshire militia boasts, "We're probably better armed than the Army."[36]

Training for fighting in every milieu is the defining purpose. Before it was eliminated in 1985 after an FBI raid, Covenant, Sword, and Arm of the Lord conducted training classes for outsiders for a fee at the "End Time Overcomer Survival Training School" that featured an urban gunfight training facility with pop-up targets similar to the FBI's camp at Quantico, Virginia.[37] Populist Party candidate Bo Gritz advertised training in "both street confrontation and deliberate shooting . . . along with instinctive 'Quick Kill' skills."[38] But mostly training and war game maneuvers are secreted in secluded compounds for members only.

There is training in psychological warfare, ambush, reconnaissance patrol, and "escape from controlled custody." (Radical groups in the 1960s, including the Black Panthers, encouraged [women] members to take courses in battlefield medicine.) Environmental groups sponsor workshops in blockades and tree-sitting in anticipation of confrontations; the difference is that paramilitarists look ahead to armed combat. (The misnamed environmental group, Wise Use, dedicated to opening federal lands, is an exception.)

There is survival training in every terrain. After all, apocalyptic groups anticipate the need to survive foreign invasion, nuclear war, race rioting, and economic chaos. Survivalism alone requires combat skills; we recall from the 1950s, owners of bomb shelters had to be able to defend themselves against the desperate attacks of those who find themselves unprepared for nuclear Armageddon. Minutemen leader DePugh, who was in the animal nutrient business, advised that a hundred-pound sack of dry dog food contains as many calories as a ton of potatoes.[39]

So a principal activity is "intelligence." One Militiaman reports that he travels about "keeping my eyes on the Commies."[40] Groups keep dossiers on local "subversives." They map the location of underground telephone cables, terminal boxes, power plants and transmission lines, supplies of arms, federal buildings, and ambush locations. Intrigue may have as much appeal as guns: members prepare for escape and evasion, hiding out, using mail drops, telephone tapping and bugging, and they communicate with one another on radios tuned to an agreed-on frequency so that "if there was an armed attack—an entry of armed people that come up here to do us dirt, like they did to Waco, well, we're not going to let that happen."[41]

In practice, maintaining secrecy may be the most consuming business. Members are warned to avoid using checks or postal money. *Privacy?* teaches how to become "invisible" to investigators: how to stop generating financial records and stay out of government files, conceal assets, obtain multiple addresses, "use hideouts, deep cover."[42] Members employ code names, aliases, and female impersonation. The Order, the most notorious and criminal of recent secret right-wing groups, urged public deception: "Until you can sit at a table or in a bar with a beautiful White woman and her nigger boyfriend or husband and convince them that you are overflowing with brotherly love and affection, you are not yet a completed agent of the White underground."[43] Defectors from an array of groups report that leaders are well practiced in using the media and that "public statements by spokesmen can be relied upon to contain calculated untruths."[44]

Actually, the chief preoccupation is with internal feuds and schisms, which should not be surprising given the dynamic of secrecy, conspiracism, and mistrust. Accommodating the ambitions of would-be "generals" is an additional reason for incessant splintering. "For leaders whose appeal is based on intransigence, outrage, and wrath, there is always the danger of being outflanked by those even more intransigent, more outrageous, more wrathful."[45] The national Klan is fragmented into an estimated thirty or forty organizations whose leaders are often overtly hostile to one another, reminiscent of religious schism and competition among corner churches, and mirrored in the fragmentation of black militant groups, Nazis and Neo-Nazis, and "citizen militias." At a "White Man's Weekend" in Georgia, a group of skinheads beat a leader of the White Aryan Resistance almost to death.[46] Indeed, "more effort is expended by leaders trying to draw members from competing brother groups than in trying to enroll the inexperienced."[47]

For the most part, it is easier to get people to join if they have already assumed the social risks of belonging to an unconventional association. The Klan is a recruiting ground for paramilitary groups that claim to have gotten beyond the "old" black–white issue and focus instead on Holocaust denial or antifederalism.[48] Hate groups may preach violence publicly, but rhetoric cannot hold everyone, and paramilitary groups recruit from less activist associations that seek to preserve respectability. The people "get in there [the John Birch Society] and they're told to write letters and they're told to study this, read that, and it's an endless repetition to a point where in time they become frustrated. . . . [T]hey tell them what's wrong but they offer no practical solution."[49] The Black Panthers' appeal was precisely that they scared "the white establishment": "These guys weren't like the Elijah Muhammad guys, who would sell you a two-week-old paper and laugh behind your back. They weren't like Don Warden, who was just on the radio and never did anything. Not like Martin Luther King or any of the others. These guys were *scary*."[50] The Order could boast that "instead of weak-chinned wimps in rented Nazi uniforms whining about getting a permit to parade in Skokie, the Survivalists offer Robert Jay Matthews, the Bruder Schweigen founder, who held off two hundred heavily armed FBI attackers for two days."[51] Jailed or dead martyrs give the groups standing to answer those who accuse them of just posturing. One writer observes that Posse martyr Gordon Kahl is to paramilitaries what John Brown was to antislavery forces after the attack on Harper's Ferry—a symbol that the time for talk had run out.[52]

The possibility of violence is "the bait that makes the organization visible and that draws members."[53] Very likely only a fraction of members have an active wish to harm others; physical confrontation is aggressive enough—the adrenaline rush of confrontations with hostile crowds when Klansmen gather, for example, where police provide protection from counterdemonstrators and only a show of courage is required. Members of most groups would bail out if there were armed combat. Still, occasional acts of violence or armed resistance are vital. Leaders may publicly disavow criminal acts by loose cannons or tiny cells, but some actual violence, even if it is anonymous and *not* the work of individuals closely associated with the groups, is indispensable to maintaining a vigilant membership.

This description sets the stage for a discussion of the laws governing paramilitary associations, and for clear and present danger as both doctrine and state of mind. First, however, I want to go a step farther in explaining the attraction these groups have and their significance for members by surveying the three powerful ideological threads interwoven in paramilitary groups in the United States.

Ideologies of hate are well known. The other threads are romantic militarism and separatist communitarianism. Their precise mix in any particular group is unique, and with it the group's hold on its members and the personal uses they make of association. Paramilitary groups are hybrids, amalgams of the dark underside of freedom of association.

Romantic Militarism

The chief emotional appeal of military organization and preparation for violence is its distance from the mundane, and there are as many romanticizations of soldiering and war as there are frustrations with ordinary civilian life.[54] The ethos of discipline and sacrifice is the reverse of dull utilitarianism and ordinary self-interest. Asceticism is the proud opposite of vulgar materialism. Spartan "survivalism" is an antidote to dependence and effeminacy. It resists the banality of civilianism. Especially unabidable are domesticity and the company of women.

Thus, paramilitary groups' obsession with military fatigues contrasts with both vain civilianism and with what members of the uniformed groups disdainfully describe as the mismatched, dirty robes of the Klan. There is express contempt for "average middle-class whites": "they're so worried about their color TV . . . that if it ever comes down to the war, when the electricity goes out and the power plants are blown up or whatever . . . they'll sit there in their living room . . . and wait for their TV to come back on."[55] There is members' exhilarating conviction that they are taking great risks in the company of comrades. Again, there is the exclusion of women.

None of this inspires a turn to the institutionalized military, which is, after all, the most bureaucratic state apparatus and the antithesis of romanticism. Some members of paramilitary groups are ex-soldiers, but most who did serve in the armed forces were enlisted men for a short time, often without combat experience, and several paramilitary leaders had been dishonorably discharged or left voluntarily in frustration and disgust.[56] Whether or not members are lapsed professional soldiers, they are attracted to what they have not had and can only imagine, not to what they have lost. Romanticism remakes the military world into one in which they are officers concocting strategies and imposing discipline, unhindered by regulations from above. This is not hard, given the size of these groups; almost everyone is a cadre leader or has a vital mission.

All of which helps make sense of the otherwise vacuous "romance of the gun." Paramilitarism is romantic insofar as the internal life of the group is more important than external activity, so long as uniforms serve less to intimidate outsiders than to reinforce members' fantasies about themselves.[57] Training and secrecy may be ends in themselves, or sources of comradery. Romantic militarism combined with race-hate may aim at self-transformation as much as action: "We believe that the only goal that can lift man out of unhappy selfishness into radiance of self-sacrificing idealism is the upward struggle of his race."[58] Where romanticism is a strong element of group life, paramilitarism is organized around expressive gestures and exhibitionistic defiance, in contrast to the symbolic or calculatedly subversive violence of political groups.[59]

Separatism

The second thread of paramilitarism is separatist communitarianism. Separatist "utopias" are an American commonplace. John Humphrey Noyes opened his *History of American Socialisms* by acknowledging that he was creating a record of failures—"all died young, and most of them before they were two years old"—but he accurately assessed the perennial attraction the United States has had for would-be community-builders: "a comparatively unperverted people, liberal institutions and cheap lands of the West."[60] Religiously inspired communities, often the work of indigenous religions like the Church of Latter-Day Saints, coexisted alongside socialist experiments like Brook Farm, social missions like Nashoba's—dedicated to educating slaves for freedom, secular communities based on ideals of friendship and love, environmentalist retreats, and military-style compounds.[61]

We tend to think of communitarianism in terms of a quest for harmony. Separatists like the Oneida Perfectionists saw their communities as "other-worldly" retreats and Noyes took pains to distinguish Oneida from the Mormons on this score: the Perfectionists do not defy civil authority, do not drill soldiers, do not try to increase their numbers by sending evangelists to proselytize abroad. But separatist compounds are also built for fearful self-defense or in anticipation of apocalyptic conflict. They are oases from which, after Armageddon, a new race or social order will emerge. The declared purpose of Richard Butler's Church of Jesus Christ Christian Survivalist compound in Coeur d'Alene, Idaho (disbanded in 1985), for example, was to build an ark for God's people during the coming tribulations. Some separatists are aggressively secessionist. Detachment indicates the illegitimacy of government and social authority, but also the determination to dismember the country, like the Aryan state projected for the Pacific Northwest. The aim is to make themselves indigestible, and ultimately independent. And every type of "utopia" has had its private army.

The Mormons are the best known historical case of a separatist group whose thought was never to try to exist as just another tolerated minority. America's destiny was to be the Mormon kingdom; Joseph Smith crowned himself its king and declared himself a candidate for the presidency in 1844, and an autonomous Mormon state of Deseret was established in 1849. The federal government extended its jurisdiction to Utah territory in 1850, but Brigham Young, the first governor, continued to rule the territory as a theocracy. "At least until the end of the Civil War," a Mormon historian observes, "many Mormons assumed that the federal government would dissolve in anarchy or become subordinate to the kingdom of God."[62]

The publication of Smith's revelations concerning the duty of plural marriage in 1852 is often said to have caused the invasion of Utah by federal troops five years later and enforcement of laws against the Mormon community, most notably antipolygamy law in *Reynolds v. United States.* These actions were driven by aversion to religious heterodoxy, but also by the determination to prohibit patriarchal polygamy as the core doctrine and practical support of a theocratic state within the state.

For plural marriage was just one aspect of Brigham Young's announcement of the Mormon political kingdom of God, which included a design for a scorched earth policy in the event of federal challenge. President Hayes explained what was at issue for the government: "Laws must be enacted which will take from the Mormon Church its temporal power. Mormonism as a sectarian idea is nothing, but as a system of government it is our duty to deal with it as an enemy of our institutions and its supporters and leaders as criminals." This was the thing "that grinds the feelings of American citizens," he continued, not the "social, immoral or polygamic features" of Mormonism "but the hostile, treasonable and the mutinous."[63]

It is not hard to comprehend paramilitary groups' proclivity toward separatism. Today, the "Freemen" anti-tax movement in Montana argues that the federal government deprives them of their rights and that they prefer to live by their own common law court system.[64] The Posse Comitatus makes plans for independent townships that will remain standing when banks fail, government collapses, and anarchy and outside invaders threaten.[65] At the very least it is good strategy to have a physical retreat, safe houses, a place for concealment and for practicing military and political purity. Of course, the ambition for separatist self-government may involve large-scale migration, to a Northwest Aryan homeland, for example. The only question is whether the territory would be voluntarily surrendered by the government to get rid of "a minority so indigestible that five states would be a small price to pay."[66]

The connection to ideologies of race-hate is also plain. A territory preserved for whites is necessary, if integration has become so pervasive that only withdrawal to an Aryan homeland (the "Northwest Imperative") can save the race. For black militants, one response to bondage and "100 years of forced citizenship" is control of all police forces in the "African colony," the right to tax

white merchants with business in the colony, control of all government funding to black people. Malcolm X promised a separatist homeland.[67]

Ideologies of Hate

The third ideological thread, then, is race-hate and anti-Semitism. Rogers
Smith has traced the tradition of ascriptive citizenship, which coexists alongside (and often successfully challenges) liberal democratic principles of
American political identity. It has been closely tied to notions of Anglo-Saxon
supremacy among civilizations and of Americans among Anglo-Saxons, on
the view that Americans are a new breed with a special cultural or racial capacity for liberty. So the definition of American has excluded "lower races," "sav-
ages," "unassimilables," "unnatural" criminals, and women. It is made manifest in actions to kill off Native American tribes, invent chattel slavery for
Africans, restrict immigration and naturalization, limit suffrage, and, as I show
in the next chapter, guide legislation on the ownership of guns.[68]

Ascriptive notions of political identity are not irrational impulses, Smith
contends, or residual prejudices, the unfinished business of liberal democracy.
They are supported by "elaborate, principled arguments for giving legal expression to people's ascribed place in various hereditary, inegalitarian cultural
and biological orders, valorized as natural, divinely approved, and just."[69]
They have been justified by scientific and medical writings, religion, and political ideologies of America as a distinct people, indeed, God's providentially
Chosen People.

Pedigreed associations of the Sons and Daughters of the American Revolution—those who "wished merely to live off the unearned increment of ancestral reputations"—are one thing.[70] "Southern-heritage" groups like Sons of
Confederate Veterans, which disavow the Klan but fly the rebel flag, come
closer to an organization based on ascriptive citizenship. But both fall short of
groups that impute disqualifying racial inferiority, as Americans have throughout U.S. history, to "lower classes of whites," blacks, and "non Anglo-Saxon
immigrants." (In 1835, Lyman Beecher denounced "the rapid influx of foreign
emigrants, the greater part unacquainted with our institutions, unaccustomed
to self-government, inaccessible to education, and easily accessible to prepos-
session, and inveterate credulity, and intrigue, and easily embodied and
wielded by sinister design.")[71] For these groups, "the world is made up of
racial groups" struggling for place and survival, a vision that obliterates cross-
cutting identifications, multiple affiliations, and inclusive images of democratic community or religious fellowship.[72]

It is not racism, nativism, or religious bigotry per se that distinguishes hate
groups from other secretive, restrictive associations, then. Or the fact that they

are based on a developed ideology rather than a disparate set of beliefs or thoughtless prejudices and impulses. But the specific claim that "we" are the "real citizens" and others are permanently alien and undeserving because their second-class citizenship is a matter of inherited or unalterable attributes.[73]

Gerald Smith brought these elements together after the Second World War in Christian Nationalist writings that are still influential, insisting that "America will rise or fall based upon its attitude toward Christ."[74] Distinctive churches, as well as theologies, eliminate the disjuncture members of hate groups experience between their daily immersion in racism and government conspiracism on the one side and ordinary Sunday services preaching unity on the other: "It was tearing them *apart*."[75] The redundancy in the name of the Aryan Nations church, Church of Jesus Christ, Christian, is there to assert that Christ was not a Jew. Right-wing paramilitary groups subscribe to the Christian Identity Movement, for example. Developed for America by Wesley Swift in 1946, and modeled after a nineteenth-century doctrine, British Israelism, it proves that Anglo-Saxons are the remnants of the Biblical nation of Israel. That the Jews are the sons of Cain (himself the product of a love affair between Satan and Eve). That Cain's children mated with animals to produce nonwhite "mud people." And that the legendary "lost tribe" of Israel crossed the ocean on the *Mayflower*, where God directly gave them sacred documents, the Declaration and Constitution, making America the promised land.[76] Pastor Pete Peters explains:

> Today's modern, state approved, tax exempt Christianity . . . is a refined, palatable, goody, goody religion that fits well with the plans of the one world Communist conspirators, [and] is tenderly embraced by an effeminate world, and is socially accepted by a Christless, Lawless, Humanistic society.[77]

White race-hate groups are not alone in forging this sort of amalgam. According to Elijah Muhammad's cosmology, "blacks were descended from the tribe of Shabazz, which 'came with the earth' . . . sixty-six trillion years ago. White people, by contrast, came into existence less than seven thousand years ago, the result of the genetic experiments of a wicked scientist named Yakub . . . drained not only of color but of humanity."[78] Nation of Islam leader Farrakhan praises Hitler, says Jews are wicked and practice a "dirty religion," and describes AIDS as a white plot. Farrakhan has been on good terms with white racial supremacists, as Elijah Muhammad was with George Lincoln Rockwell, whom he invited to address a 1962 Nation of Islam Convention in Chicago.[79]

We know that these ideologies are not the exclusive preserve of organized hate groups and secret societies. They are successful elements of popular culture, beginning with Griffith's spectacular hit film, *Birth of a Nation*, whose debut was the occasion for Klan rallies. A precursor to today's hate-mongering radio personalities was Father Charles Coughlin, a Catholic priest from Detroit, who explained the Depression as "an insidious conspiracy of international bankers and world communism."[80] Coughlin's Sunday afternoon radio program in the 1930s reached over 30 million people; baseball games were halted to broadcast his show. He lifted whole passages from Joseph Goebbels: "almost without exception the intellectual leaders . . . of Marxist atheism in Germany were Jews" who financed the Bolshevik Revolution as part of their design for world conquest. Jews are "blood-sucking parasites on the community of Christ."[81]

We also know that these ideologies permeate electoral politics, sometimes characterizing political parties, though never as successfully as the Know-Nothing Party in the 1850s, which sent seventy-five members to Congress and controlled several state legislatures. At the height of its influence in the 1920s, the Klan elected senators from Texas, Colorado, and Oregon, governors in Oregon and Maine, and dominated the state legislatures of Oregon and Indiana. The Liberty Lobby's Populist Party ran David Duke of the National Association for the Advancement of White People for president in 1988.[82] One careful study of Duke's successful run for the Louisiana state legislature concludes that the fact he was a Klansman was part of the message: "his Klan antecedents, as his finance manager later observed, tell white and black voters alike that 'he means business.' "[83]

I return to the convergence of popular ideology and secret societies shortly. For now, the point is that many paramilitary groups, like unarmed hate groups, make these ideologies the cement of association life. The Ku Klux Klan, the American Nazi Party and Neo-Nazi offshoots, and Aryan Nations are the best known groups forged by ideologies of hate. But there is an incredible array of hate groups and objects: rabid lesbian feminists, "men's liberation" groups, racist-environmental groups, even an organization of homosexual Nazis.[84]

It is not hard to see that romantic militarism, separatism, and ideologies of hate feed a proclivity to form private armies. Romantic militarism thrives on the discipline and homoeroticism of a military-style brotherhood; hate groups exhibit their superiority and loathing and are prepared at least for violence; separatist communities must defend themselves from hostile outsiders and millenarians must prepare for the final conflict and triumph.

These three sources came together in the now defunct Covenant, Sword, and Arm of the Lord. James Ellison ruled his compound in Arkansas (the membership of 150 included women and children), declared himself a descendant of King David and had himself anointed King of the Ozarks, and took an extra wife. The community had its own utilities, dormitories, and factories for making hand grenades and silencers, and means of support in a business in Neo-Nazi hate literature.[85]

What laws are arrayed against them?

Freedom of Association

There is nothing new about hate groups, subversive political associations, or revolutionary cells. These groups are often armed. Their internal organization often qualifies them as "paramilitary," with a command structure, hierarchy, and discipline. And they have engaged, at least peripherally, in unlawful activities, including in some cases for-profit criminal enterprises.

In the course of regulating these groups, federal and state laws prohibit the actions most feared from paramilitary associations: subversion, violence, civil disorder, terrorism, hate crimes, threatening government officials. Laws against conspiracies to deprive people of federal civil rights are designed to protect ordinary citizens from intimidation by private armed groups. Indeed, the rationale for public concern and legal action to regulate or outlaw paramilitary groups is their connection to hate crimes, weapons violations, bombings, assassinations, robbery, counterfeiting, bogus check-writing schemes, and other scams.

The best-known paramilitary groups, of course, are those that have come to trial: KKK members and Black Panther Huey Newton convicted for violating civil rights, conspiracy to further civil disorder, and murder; Minutemen leader Robert DePugh's prosecution on weapons charges in the 1960s and Randy Weaver's in the early 1990s; the Posse Comitatus made famous after Gordan Kahl's 1983 "self-defense"—prosecutors characterized it as a private declaration of war—against U.S. marshalls attempting to serve him with a warrant for probation violation in an income tax evasion case. (That shootout resulted in the death of two officers, and a third in a later attempt to arrest the fugitive.) Because so much of our knowledge of these groups comes from the reports of agent-informants and court records, illegal activity is one of the things we know best about them, at least after the fact.

There is little evidence that all or most paramilitary groups are engaged in serious criminal activity, though, or that all members know about or are involved in law-breaking committed by a few.[86] The citizen militias recently formed in forty states, mostly in rural communities and small towns, are organized, "armed and dangerous," but they typically are exhibitionistic and confrontational rather than violent. There are an unknown number of remnant left-wing groups with arsenals and plans, like the one accidentally uncovered by the New York police: "Whatever they are," one official observed, "they weren't doing a lot of it."[87]

I want to consider the justification for additional laws aimed not only at the criminal activities of paramilitary groups but also at their lawful core activities, and the justification for statutes that criminalize paramilitary associations themselves. Is this a matter of disabling disfavored groups, or a reasonable response to threats to national security or public safety? What protection can paramilitary groups expect to find in the constitutional right of association?

We have seen some of the ways in which government interferes with non-criminal groups, beginning with regulations that force groups to accept unwanted members. Government also interferes by proscribing activities integral to an association's purposes; anti-Klan statutes prohibiting wearing hoods and masks, for example. Public nuisance laws have been used to frustrate gang members from congregating in local parks (though injunctions against their propensity to "confront, intimidate, annoy, provoke, and challenge," have been challenged as unconstitutionally vague).[88]

Government has made membership painful and costly by ascribing guilt by association, a commonplace in federal loyalty programs affecting employment, restrictions on foreign travel, deportation rules, criminal sentencing, even eviction from public housing.[89] Guilt by association was facilitated by compulsory disclosure of membership lists. When a grand jury formed to indict Minutemen leader Robert DePugh issued a subpoena demanding Minutemen records, including a list of subscribers to its publication, *On Target*, DePugh successfully argued that the *NAACP* ruling protecting these lists applied to his group.

Investigation and prosecution may be the most effective constraint on freedom of association, weakening groups and encouraging self-censorship. After World War II, fear of communist conspiracy inspired infamous federal and state investigations, and during the "heyday" of indictments from 1970 to 1974, one-hundred grand juries in eighty-four cities subpoened more than one-thousand witnesses from groups of the New Left, Vietnam opposition, the Catholic left, and the women's movement.[90] Until recently charges of legalized oppression have been staples of the political left; today, paramilitary group leaders echo them. Like warrants, bail bonds, and legal fees, subpoenas and indictments divert resources and force groups to target fund-raising at financing legal battles. DePugh reports: "I was indicted on one charge after another—some of them totally without foundation, tentative hearsay evidence. But every time I was indicted I had to go to the bank, put up a bigger and bigger share of my company, money to make bond." DePugh was eventually convicted on weapons charges.[91]

Lawyers for Gordon Kahl insisted that it was not illegal activity that brought him to court in 1974—as records show, he hadn't paid income taxes since 1968—but a televised interview that established him as a tax protest leader, and IRS agents conceded that it was rare to take legal action against someone who made less than $10,000 annually.[92] The deadly shootout was precipitated by an attempt to serve him with a warrant for a misdemeanor probation violation. The cost is pervasive antilegalism on all sides: mistrust of the justice system, and its misuse by government.

Finally, of course, government can outlaw associations outright, punishing membership and attendance at meetings. The Smith Act aimed directly at association, making it a felony to hold membership in any organization advocating the overthrow of the government by force or violence. The Communist Party has been considered a special case because of its "long continued, systematic, disciplined activity directed by a foreign power," and the Supreme Court upheld the requirement to register membership lists in *Communist Party of the U.S. v. Subversive Activities Control Board.*[93]

In subsequent cases the Court became more discriminating. In *Scales v. United States* it reinterpreted the Smith Act so as to repudiate guilt by association. A "blanket prohibition of association with a group having both legal and illegal aims" would present "a real danger that legitimate political expression or association would be impaired."[94] Mere membership without specific intent to further the organization's illegal aims is protected. Only "active" members having guilty knowledge, with intent to further illegal aims and concrete involvement, are punishable. "Nominal, passive, inactive or purely technical" members, and "mere association"—despite its implications of assent, sympathy, and encouragement—are not.[95] In *NAACP v. Claiborne Hardware*, a case to which I return, the Court advised: "the right to associate does not lose protection merely because some members of the group may have participated in conduct or advocated doctrine that is not itself protected," including acts of violence.[96]

It is not hard to see that paramilitary groups pose special difficulties. There is the question of whether weapons instruction is speech or expressive activity, or constitutionally unprotected conduct. It is unclear that participation in paramilitary activities per se indicates membership. There is the attendant difficulty of distinguishing active from passive members: Can participation in paramilitary training and the activities I described above be "nominal"?

Beyond that, separating the legal from illegal activities of these groups is no easy task, which makes avoiding guilt by association and identifying active members with intent to commit a crime particularly difficult. (Leaving aside whether "intelligence-gathering" amounts to criminal conspiracy—the 1996 Anti-terrorism Act employs the INA definition of terrorism, which includes "gathering information on potential targets").

Clear and Present Danger

"Clear and present danger" (CPD) is not the universal test of the parameters of constitutionally protected speech and association (it is not used for commercial speech or "low-value" speech, for example), but it is the principal test for legislation aimed at the content or impact of expression.[97] Based on the law of criminal attempts, it proscribes speech and association under circumstances that create "clear and imminent danger that it will bring about forthwith certain substantive evils."[98] The test requires a factual estimate of the probable consequences of expressive activity. Who determines the degree of nexus between words and action? Legislatures? Juries? Justices reviewing each instance?

Mistrust of excitable juries, zealous prosecutors, and the "ineffabilities" of judges led Judge Learned Hand to contest Justice Holmes' formulation, and to shift First Amendment doctrine from assessing the likely consequences of advocacy to categories of speech. Advocacy of doctrine is protected, on this standard, but words that are a direct incitement—counsel, advice, advocacy, or command to violate the law—are not. The current rule from *Brandenburg v. Ohio* adds a restored CPD test to this formulation: statutes restricting speech and association must be limited to advocacy "directed to inciting or producing imminent lawless action" (Hand) and "likely to incite or produce such action" (Holmes). *Brandenburg* overturned the conviction of a KKK leader and the Ohio law that prohibited "assembly with others to advocate" crime, sabotage, violence, or unlawful methods of terrorism.[99]

Everything turns on how stringently the standard is applied, which is strikingly variable, as *NAACP v. Claiborne Hardware* (1982) indicates. At an NAACP-sponsored boycott of white merchants in Claiborne, Mississippi, Charles Evers told a crowd of several hundred that they would be watched, and that any uncle toms who broke the boycott would have their necks broken by their own people. White merchants charged that fear of reprisal had caused black citizens to withhold their patronage.

The case is notable because the context of Evers' speech was one of proven intimidation, threats, social ostracism, vilification, and violence. Boycott "Enforcers"—twenty-two "Black Hats" or Deacons, a paramilitary group formed during the boycott—were stationed in the vicinity and publicly displaying weapons. "Store watchers" stood outside to record the names of blacks who patronized merchants, and names were read aloud at the First Baptist Church and at NAACP meetings and published in a local black newspaper, branding them "traitors." There were records of destruction of goods purchased at boycotted stores, incidents of shots fired at a house and bricks thrown through windows.

The Supreme Court allowed that in the passionate atmosphere of the boycott, the speeches might have been understood as "intending to create a fear of violence whether or not improper discipline was specifically intended." Nonetheless the Court ruled that "mere advocacy of the use of force or violence does not remove speech from the protection of the First Amendment" or create the taint of force in otherwise peaceful picketing. "Social pressure" and the threat of ostracism are protected by the First Amendment. The fact that speech is intended to have a coercive impact does not remove protection, either. Comments like "necks would be broken" "implicitly conveyed a sterner message," the Court conceded, but do not indicate that improper discipline was specifically intended. It is necessary to establish that the group itself possessed unlawful goals and the individual had specific intent to further those illegal aims.

In short, the First Amendment does not forbid advocacy of the use of force or violation of the law except insofar as intent exists to incite imminent lawless action, and is likely to produce it, and there was no evidence that Evers' speech was followed immediately by acts of violence—these occurred weeks later. "When such appeals [for unity and action in a common cause] do not incite lawless action, they must be regarded as protected speech."[100]

Against this background we see that if paramilitary groups simply advocated weapons training, intelligence-gathering, or armed resistance to income tax auditors, they would be protected. On the other side, "violence has no sanctuary in the First Amendment, and the *use of* weapons, gunpowder, and gasoline may not constitutionally masquerade under the guise of advocacy."[101] That leaves paramilitary groups occupying a largely unmapped middle ground. Are forming and training private armies constitutionally protected by the First Amendment? And if not, are paramilitary associations lawful at all?

Anti-Paramilitary Training Statutes: Toward the Criminalization of Paramilitary Groups

As part of an effort to suppress labor unrest in Chicago, where workers armed for clashes with private company armies, police, and the National Guard, an early Illinois statute imposed a blanket prohibition on paramilitary groups. The statute at issue in *Presser v. Illinois* (1886) prohibited outright "any body of men whatever, other than the regular organized volunteer militia of this State, and the troops of the United States . . . to drill or parade with arms in any city, or town, of this State, without the license of the Governor." With exceptions for military academies and sword-carrying members of benevolent orders, citizens had no right to band together in paramilitary organizations.

Presser is not an apt guide to contemporary cases because the Court upheld the ban on paramilitary groups as part of the state's broad authority to forbid voluntary associations generally, a power judged necessary to prevent sedition.[102] The doctrine of freedom of association, as it has evolved since then, rejects this. Until recently, the statute has had few counterparts, but today, criminalization seems to have come full circle.

When the FBI went after the Minutemen in 1964, the legal mechanisms available to prohibit associations from collecting arms and training in military tactics were all geared to groups planning foreign attacks that threatened national security. Since the purported purpose of domestic paramilitary groups is self-protection against invasion, internal enemies, and abuse of government authority, the federal laws did not apply. The states were first to produce legislation specifically aimed at paramilitary groups.

In 1964, California Attorney General Lynch launched a campaign against the Minutemen (in the context of militancy on the left as well, with the Black Panthers active in the state): "This anarchism cannot be allowed. . . . Armed bands equipped with automatic weapons, grenades, tear gas devices, mortars and even cannons are a danger to the peace of our cities and a clear challenge to law enforcement." (The group retaliated by handing out calling cards reading "Lynch Lynch.")[103] The statute prohibits assembling as a paramilitary organization for the purpose of practicing with weapons intended for illegal use. Congress entered the arena in 1968 with an act that criminalizes teaching or demonstrating the use or production of firearms or explosives,

> knowing or having reason to know or intending that the same will be unlawfully employed for use in or in furtherance of a civil disorder which may in any way or degree obstruct, delay, or adversely affect commerce or the conduct or performance of any federally protected function.[104]

The U.S. Code applies only to paramilitary instructors. Instead of seeking to add criminal penalties for participants to the federal law, the Anti-Defamation League, a leader in drafting this legislation, advocated state restrictions. The advocacy group reasoned that state and local law enforcement have "traditionally dealt with weapons offenses and intrastate activities" and "have the resources and the inclination to engage in the type of investigatory activities needed to obtain conviction."[105] Twenty-four states have enacted anti-paramilitary training statutes on the ADL model, which subjects to fine or imprisonment

> whoever assembles with one or more persons for the purpose of training with, practicing with, or being instructed in the use of any firearm, explosive or incendiary device, or technique capable of causing injury or death to persons, intending to employ unlawfully the same for use in, or in furtherance of, a civil disorder.

Proponents insist that the statute is drafted narrowly to avoid violating First Amendment freedoms and "clearly does not prohibit legitimate lawful activities," meaning that rifle ranges and karate clubs are exempt.[106] As of 1996, the conformity of state statutes along this model to federal and state constitutions had not been challenged in court, but the federal law has.

United States v. Featherston (1972) involved leaders of the Black Afro Militant Movement (BAMM), who instructed members in assembling explosives in preparation "for the coming revolution."[107] The Court first ruled that the federal law on arms training was not unconstitutional on its face due to overbreadth or vagueness. It relied on an earlier case involving Black Panther Bobby Seale and five other plaintiffs charged with organizing to promote a riot in connection with the Democratic Convention in Chicago. The "knowing or having reason to know or intending" language "narrows the scope of the enactment by exempting innocent or inadvertent conduct from its proscription."[108]

Featherston goes on to address the charge that the statute is unconstitutional as applied because the prosecution failed to show a clear and present danger as mandated by the First Amendment. The Court started out by adopting the clear and present danger rule as the appropriate test. But intent to incite a *present* disorder cannot be readily inferred from defendants' statements; one appellant is quoted as saying, "We must get our heads and minds and bodies right for the revolution, no telling when the revolution might come."[109] On the *Brandenburg* standard, BAMM's preparation for "the coming revolution when the time is right" is like the rioter acquitted of incitement for urging "we'll take the streets later."[110] So, what explains the ruling that BAMM was constitutionally unprotected?

The majority opinion cites Justice Vinson's 1951 opinion in *Dennis v. United States*, which *rejected* Holmes' CPD test as inadequate security against subversion:

> If we must decide that this Act and its application are constitutional only if we are convinced that petitioner's conduct creates a "clear and present danger" of violent overthrow, we must appraise imponderables, including international and national phenomena which baffle the best informed foreign offices and our most experienced politicians. We would have to foresee and predict the effectiveness of Communist propaganda, opportunities for infiltration, whether, and when, a time will come that they consider propitious for action, and whether and how fast our existing government will deteriorate."[111]

Dennis had turned on the presumed nature of the Communist Party. When the constitutional provisions were written, Justice Jackson pointed out in his concurrence, the chief antagonists in the struggle between authority and liberty were the government and individual citizens. Problems are complicated with the intervention of "organized, well-financed, semi-secret and highly disciplined political organizations."[112]

Similar considerations produced the judgment that a clear and present danger existed in *Featherston*. The Court focused on the association's paramilitary organization:

> Here the evidence showed a cohesive organized group, led by Featherston and aided by Riley, engaged in preparation for "the coming revolution." This group included a force regularly trained in explosives and incendiary devices standing ready to strike transportation and communication facilities and law enforcement operations at a moment's notice.[113]

There is some ambiguity about whether the internal structure of the group—its cohesive, disciplined character is key? Or weapons training? Or the two in combination, with arms preparation as the overt act confirming that association members intended revolution? Or was the decisive factor testimony that Featherston had advised, "We must keep these ingredients around the house or one or two bombs made up so we could use them on a moment's notice"?[114]

The clear and present danger test was designed as a standard for laws directed at subversive advocacy, and was subsequently applied to dangerous ideas generally. Was the *Brandenburg* test, or any CPD standard, appropriate for paramilitary training?

On one view, anti-paramilitary training statutes violate the First Amendment and state constitutions insofar as they criminalize teaching and demonstrating the use of firearms or incendiary devices. These are forms of communication; indeed, they communicate knowledge. In order to prevent possible future disorder, the state does the impermissible: it aims at the content and communicative impact of expression, not just incidentally but directly.[115]

Alternatively, military exercises can be seen as "speech plus." The speech/conduct distinction is notoriously unhelpful, as is the degree of additional leeway for regulating the "plus." Like *any* form of conduct, military exercises express something. But are they predominantly expressive, like boycotts, picketing, and financial contributions? Does training communicate a particularized message, likely to be understood by others? (Citizen militias, for example, whose message is precisely that militia are the means of protecting rights against the government, are in a better position to make this claim than secret paramilitary groups.)[116] In fact, the question remains whether CPD applies only to the *communicative* activities of expressive groups or to any otherwise lawful activity integral to the communicative purposes of expressive associations protected by the First Amendment.

Finally, even if nothing prohibits training in the use of arms by law-abiding citizens alone or in association, it does not follow that these activities are constitutionally protected. (I leave aside security for paramilitary groups under the Second Amendment.) On this view, the typical activities of paramilitary associations are neither predominantly expressive nor integral to the group's communicative purposes, and can be restricted without interfering with its First Amendment rights. Restrictions neither aim at the "communicative impact of expressive conduct" nor interfere so substantially with the group's protected activity that they should be curtailed.

If forced to choose, I incline to the second position. We recognize it from *Roberts v. Jaycees*, where the Justices first categorized the association as predominantly expressive, and then tried to determine whether the group's membership practices were inseparable from its communicative purposes. Still, a categorical approach to the application of CPD (are paramilitary groups predominantly expressive/are their training activities predominantly expressive and integral to their message?) may be less helpful than one based directly on the reasoning that undergirds the CPD doctrine.

The basic premise is familiar. Advocacy is unlawful when no conceivable opportunity exists for crime to be averted by the intervention of more speech. "Only the emergency that makes it immediately dangerous to leave the correction of evil counsels to time warrants making any exception to the sweeping command, 'Congress shall make no law . . . abridging the freedom of speech.'"[117] The appropriateness of the CPD test depends, then, on the manner in which expression causes harm. It applies if harmful consequences depend on how the audience responds. It does not apply if speech causes harm directly, regardless of the audience's reaction, because the danger is not conceivably vulnerable to correction by more speech."[118]

We are now in a position to see how it is that *Featherston* both invokes the CPD rule and adopts Hand's categorical distinction between types of expression—between protected "keys of persuasion" and unprotected "triggers of action" literally applicable to the paramilitary group. In the context of a paramilitary association that is itself a trigger, words present a clear and present danger. The paramilitary structure of the group (leaders' tight control) and its purpose (to create a ready strike force) are evidence of intent and capacity to act "on a moment's notice." It is virtually impossible to predict the moment, but when it arrives, there will be no temporal lag between incitement and action. The assumption, in short, is that in paramilitary groups, advocacy amounts to command, and commands produce automatic, unreflective action.

(This reasoning applies to other types of association—fundamentalist religious groups, for example, insofar as clerics' preachings are assumed to be not just advocacy on even incitement but categorical imperatives. In the sedition trial of Sheik Omar Abdel Rahman, the charge of "conspiring to wage a war of urban terrorism" in the United States was based almost exclusively on his sermons about *jihad*, which were interpreted as commands to followers to wage a literal war.)[119]

Each element of this argument is spurious. The implicit suggestion is that CPD only applies in the context of dialogue and persuasion, whereas the test has teeth only if it extends to incitement in settings unamenable to free-flowing deliberation and dissent—to disciplined, hierarchical associations as well as liberal classrooms. Or to the facts of *Claiborne*, where the leaders' speech is in a context designed to have a coercive impact. Moreover, the assumption that the structure and purpose of a paramilitary group make the chance of any response to advocacy other than reflexive action impossible is unwarranted. The relation between leaders and members, internal cohesiveness, and so on is variable. So the empirical considerations demanded by *Brandenburg*'s CPD test are appropriate.

Using this test, ADL-model paramilitary statutes are not unconstitutional on their face: to obtain convictions it is necessary to prove that the goal of the individuals participating in paramilitary programs is to foster civil disorder.

But they are vulnerable to being unconstitutionally applied, because *Brandenburg* requires more: there must be incitement to violate laws; the incitement must call for an immediate lawless action; and the violation must be likely to occur. To satisfy these conditions, paramilitary training and "intelligence" are not enough. Planning for a specific criminal act would seem to be necessary. The Court in *Claiborne* made every effort to distinguish First Amendment clear and present danger considerations, applied in that case to people assembling in the boycott of white stores, from the circumstances that warrant prosecution for conspiracy against public order.[120] In practice, however, anti-paramilitary training statutes are an invitation to cast standard paramilitary activity as intent to engage in unlawful conduct, even in the absence of the things required to show conspiracy to commit a crime.

The ADL targets "hate groups . . . characterized by a *propensity* for lawlessness and violence," and its reports document the de facto effects of legislation, which can effectively shut down paramilitary activities. Thus, a leader of the North Carolina White Patriot Party was convicted under a state statute for conducting maneuvers for "an eventual attempt to overthrow the U.S. government and to create a racist state." A Florida statute was used to convict members of the United Klans of America for training with guns as part of a plan to incite blacks to riot so that whites would turn to the Klan for leadership: "the statute helped prevent a dangerous situation from escalating into the kind of violence which could easily have led to the loss of innocent life."

After Illinois passed its anti-paramilitary training statute, the Christian Patriots Defense League, a survivalist group that staged field maneuvers and weapons classes (in "Guns and Reloading" and "Knife Fighting"), moved its "freedom festivals" to Missouri. When Missouri passed its law, the CPDL director instructed people not to bring their firearms to the camp, and "many extremists apparently stayed away from the meeting for this reason."[121] The law "hangs over [people's] heads like a Sword of Damocles." That judges may ultimately exonerate those whose conduct is held lawful is not enough; famously, "the value of the sword of Damocles is that it hangs—not that it drops."[122]

Beyond Protection, Toward Criminalization

Conspiracy law does not require an actual crime for a conviction to be upheld, but the conspiracy must be specific. In *Vietnamese Fishermen's Association v. The Knights of the Ku Klux Klan*, for example, Louis Beam and the paramilitary arm of the Texas Knights of the KKK intimidated local Vietnamese with the purpose of stopping them from fishing in Galveston Bay during the shrimping season. Beam's rally, organized to support "American fishermen," featured a "security force" dressed in military garb, a promise to "fight fight fight," a warning that it may become necessary "to take the law into our own hands," and an offer to train American fishermen at one of his military camps, and the burning of a fishing boat and cross. This was followed a month later by a boat ride in sight of Vietnamese fishermen by persons wearing KKK robes and hoods, visibly armed, with a small cannon and a figure hung in effigy. All this occurred against the background of three unsolved cases of arson that destroyed boats owned and operated by Vietnamese.

Taken together, the court ruled, these actions constituted a violation of U.S. Code prohibiting conspiracy by private citizens to interfere with civil rights and the full and equal benefit of all laws, including making a living and freedom of contract. The Klan was also held in violation of the Sherman Anti-Trust Act; intimidation had the intent and effect of reducing competition.[123]

A conspiracy to commit specific crimes was reasonably clear here. In contrast, the Justice Department tried ten leaders of Aryan Nations, the Order, the Covenant, Sword, and Arm of the Lord, and the Klan for conspiring to overthrow the government at a gathering in Idaho in 1983.[124] (The group included a father and son, Choctaw Indians, who had been chosen Arkansas Farm Family of the Year.) Whatever else the defendants were guilty of (and several had been previously charged and convicted on weapons charges and in one case murder), openly conspiring to overthrow the government at a meeting of twenty or thirty people including strangers was an incredible charge, and they were acquitted by a federal jury.[125] Even conspiracists are rarely conspirators. Which is why Justice Stevens had cautioned in *Claiborne*:

> The term "concerted action" encompasses unlawful conspiracies and constitutionally protected assemblies [and advising:] in litigation of this kind the stakes are high.
> ... History teaches that special dangers are associated with conspiratorial activity.
> ... [T]he rights of political association are fragile enough without adding the additional threat of destruction by lawsuit.[126]

Given existing state and federal anticonspiracy laws, laws prohibiting violent acts, and laws regarding aiding and abetting the commission of a crime, it is not clear whether anti-paramilitary training statutes create a new substantive crime, or what purpose they serve. Existing laws cover the illegal activities of paramilitary groups without being directed at the association.

That may be the point behind anti-paramilitary training statutes. What they effectively do is shift the focus away from specific intent to engage in a specific crime and toward the paramilitary nature of the association. In practice, ADL model anti-paramilitary training statutes create a suspect class of association, and lower the First Amendment shield. If anti-paramilitary training laws do not actively invite prosecution aimed at disabling these groups, they enable it.

So it is not surprising that seventeen states have recently passed legislation that dispenses with conditions of intent to create civil disorder and, like the nineteenth-century Illinois law used against militant strikers in *Presser*, outlaws "unauthorized military organizations" outright. These statutes subject to punishment

> any two or more persons, whether with or without uniform, who associate, assemble or congregate together by or under any name in a military capacity for the purpose

of drilling, parading or marching at any time or place or otherwise take up or bear arms in any such capacity without authority of the governor.[127]

These state statutes also give law enforcement license to investigate groups to determine whether they fall under the law. Morris Dees proposes a blanket federal law regulating militia groups that are not authorized by state law.[128]

The laws vary at the margins. Some exempt the Boy Scouts and associations wholly composed of honorably discharged veterans. Some explicitly exempt the use of weapons for self-defense. One makes a point of including "women." North Carolina's 1994 supplement to the state code outlaws "oath-bound secret political or military" associations as well as designated activities, among them disguising voices; secret signs, grips, and passwords; mustering; and drilling.

I know of no test of these laws. The court in *Vietnamese Fishermen* applied a variety of criminal conspiracy laws to the KKK, but expressly declined to apply Texas's statute prohibiting the formation of private military organizations. The statute had not been interpreted by state courts, and the U.S. district court did not preempt them.[129] So the question remains: Is this categorical limitation on freedom of association justifiable?

The idea must be that paramilitary groups are not political associations. They are not characterized by predominantly expressive purposes and activities, which progress along a continuum culminating in paramilitary activity, lawful and unlawful. Rather, they are constitutionally unprotected associations that may or may not also engage in a certain amount of political expression. From this standpoint, there is no First Amendment claim, and no need to strike a balance between the right of association and public ends, or to demonstrate that any infringement on rights granted by the First Amendment is more than counterbalanced by a compelling government interest.[130]

Laws prohibiting "unauthorized military organizations" are just one example of the criminalization of associations. Typically this is done on grounds that the group's purpose is criminal, and that the only effective way to curtail its illegal activity is by disabling the organization directly, as in laws designed to fight organized crime. Does this justification hold for anti-paramilitary statutes?

Criminal Groups

The 1970 federal Racketeer-Influenced and Corrupt Organization Act (RICO) aims at "criminal enterprises" with a proven pattern of illegal activity. Traditional criminal laws were unsuccessful in reducing organized activity because prosecution of individuals could not touch the criminal organization. So the law aims at the association. Under the conspiracy provision, each defendant is held responsible for all the crimes committed by the organization. RICO also uses forfeiture provisions to attack the group's economic base, on the view that as long as the property of criminal enterprises remains intact, new leaders will step in to take over the group and its assets.

Laws designed to combat racketeering are recast and employed today against urban and suburban street gangs, described as criminal enterprises organized for drug trafficking, burglary, robbery, witness intimidation, car theft, loan-sharking, money-laundering, prostitution, and murder.[131] Sociologists define gangs without reference to crime or delinquency, but accounts of these groups as spontaneous and informal are mostly outdated. The purpose of membership can seldom be characterized as community loyalty (to the "hood") simply, nor can conflicts be seen as symbolic rivalry over turf and colors. (This has not stopped academics from describing gangs as surrogate families and proposing that they are protected by the First Amendment right of "intimate association"; for example, "street gangs more closely resemble family structures than any organization that the Court has thus far evaluated under the *Roberts* test.")[132]

Thirteen states have passed Street Terrorism Enforcement and Protection (STEP) Acts modeled after RICO, which create a substantive crime of participation in a street gang with knowledge that its members engage in a pattern of criminal gang activity, enhance sentences for gang-related felonies, and contain property forfeiture clauses.

Challenges to STEP laws on grounds that they are too broad and punish constitutionally protected association have been unsuccessful. The First Amendment *does* protect association with individuals who are involved in criminal conduct, but freedom of association for the purpose of planning crimes would mean that no RICO enterprise or conspiracy could be prosecuted. "Freedom of association is not a talisman that will ward off all government attempts to proscribe or regulate activity."[133] Street terrorism acts attempt to protect innocents by requiring "active" membership—a member must devote substantial time and effort to the gang to fall under its umbrella, and must be aware of the group's goals and intend to further its illegal activities.

The connection between racketeering laws and antigang STEP acts is reasonably clear, although prosecutors may have too much discretion to decide whether the statute applies to Neo-Nazi groups, skinheads, and other groups that are not gangs but may be involved in vandalism, graffiti, and intimidation, or to motorcycle gangs and prison gangs, and so on.[134]

RICO has also been applied to paramilitary groups. Does this parallel to organized crime hold up? In 1985, twenty-three members of the white supremacist group, the Order, were charged with violating racketeering law. Their crimes included the murder of Jewish radio talk show host Alan Berg and the execution of a member of the Order considered a traitor, all financed through counterfeiting and a string of armored-car robberies. Racketeering laws were also used against the Covenant, Sword, and Arm of the Lord for repeated episodes of arson and attempted bombing. The prosecution conceded that the crimes were conducted "for political reasons." If RICO and its analogues encompass not only enterprise crime but also social and political goals pursued wholly or in part through criminal violence, it is a reasonable legal weapon against paramilitary groups that engage in proven patterns of crime.

But paramilitary groups rarely exist to engage in criminal enterprises for profit (even to support political activities), and small-scale illegal gun manufacture and trading hardly fits the organized crime scenario of Scrips' drug-dealing. Recall, too, that subversive political groups do not become criminal enterprises because their ideological goals are illegal. Most important, the substantive justification for RICO is not combatting individual criminal acts but the character of the association, and in this respect the parallel between organized crime and paramilitary groups is seriously misleading.

Racketeering and street gangs endure across generations, though individual members leave, are killed, or are prosecuted and jailed. They are sophisticated organizations, able to sustain long-term patterns of activity; most gang activity in small cities and towns is an expansion of urban gang operations into lucrative new areas; more than thirty Los Angeles gangs have set up in twenty-one states outside California.[135]

Paramilitary groups, by contrast, are small, local, notoriously uncohesive, and short-lived. Unlike organized crime, they do not survive their leaders. Indeed, they have difficulty remaining intact at all. "People come in and stay awhile; they see nothing is happening; and they go away."[136] An enormous amount of energy is spent simply keeping a tiny group alive. Leaders feud. Everyone wants his own militia or klan. As often as groups confederate, they decompose again. Naturally enough, suspicion of conspiracy and infiltration are fatal to unity; conspiracist habits unravel groups from within. Tony Martinez reports on the internal dynamics of the paramilitary group, The Order: members criticized a proposal to cut off electricity to Los Angeles, arguing that it would cause urban riots and arouse animosity against their racist cause. But instead of seeing the proposed scheme as a well-intentioned error in strategy, it was taken as proof that leader Bob Matthews was a CIA field agent trying to trick the group into committing crimes that would discredit the Aryan movement.

Members are noticeably disloyal. Every account of paramilitary groups describes members who trade legal testimony for favors, as well as disaffected members and ex-leaders who voluntarily offer information to authorities or watch-dog groups like the Southern Poverty Law Center. To veterans of the radical left, who see these groups as political associations, not criminal enterprises, "turncoat witnesses" are an appalling betrayal.[137]

These groups are able to attract their nonjoiner members and are temporarily gripping precisely because they are intense and closed off. But they are not gripping enough to keep them. The evidence is that membership is fluid and that "recruits cycle in and out rapidly." "Some fraction of the members—a quarter? a third?—will drift away over the next four years."[138]

Paramilitarists cast their inability to create a movement or stabilize a local group in a favorable light, citing the tactical superiority of small cadres in eluding detection. A former Grand Dragon of the Texas Klan has advanced a strategy called "leaderless resistance," a virtual invitation to anarchic types and disorganized disorder. In fact, members appear to be politically and psychologically incapable of large-scale organization. Everyone wants his own organization. As often as groups confederate, they decompose again. Groups splinter, members lose interest, leaders are harassed or litigated out of existence by authorities, or some combination of these. At a standoff between federal agents and "Freemen" in Montana in 1996, paramilitary sympathizers turned against them: "The Freemen are using the Constitution as a facade to prevent their incarceration for illegal activity," Bo Gritz, a paramilitarist and Liberty Lobby spokesman, proposed, and he offered the FBI military advice: "A coordinated nonviolent strike against all four areas deep on a moonless night might well result in the capture of all 21 occupants without bodily injury to either side."[139]

Nonetheless, "criminal enterprise" and "domestic terrorist" paramilitary associations are officially grouped together as secret, disciplined associations plotting an ongoing pattern of unlawful acts. The same guidelines for federal investigation of organized crime apply to paramilitary groups. In both cases the declared objective is "to eliminate any perception that actual or imminent commission of a violent crime is a prerequisite to investigation."[140] The threshold for investigation—facts or circumstances that "reasonably indicate" the existence of a domestic security/terrorism enterprise—is substantially lower than the orthodox Fourth Amendment requirement of probable cause, and the grounds for opening a "preliminary inquiry" are even slimmer: any information or allegation "whose responsible handling requires some further scrutiny."

The distinguishing purpose of investigation is to obtain information about the nature and structure of the association (the relationship of the members, finances, past and future activities), warranting open-ended surveillance for long-range detection and prosecution. This differs from general crime investigations, which are limited to ninety days and terminate with the decision to prosecute or not. For when it comes to conspiracist groups "there may be no completed offense to provide a framework for the investigation"; indeed, "in some cases the enterprise may meet the threshold standard but be temporarily inactive . . . yet the composition, goals, and prior history of the group suggests the need for continuing federal interest."[141]

Short of investigation unambiguously motivated by desire to suppress a political movement, it is doubtful whether any investigation of any length—continuing for years—is unconstitutional.[142] The Arizona Viper Militia, characterized by prosecutors as "an urban terror cell," is the latest publicized case of long-term infiltration. Following the Oklahoma City bombing, the attorney general proposed tightening the 1983 guidelines, and it is no wonder even FBI Director Louis Freeh questioned the need for revision.[143]

Despite justified notoriety, the extent of criminal activity by paramilitary groups is difficult to assess. We know that acts reflexively attributed to them— and to organized hate groups generally—are frequently committed by outsiders—fellow-travelers, adolescent thugs (a New York City survey of hate crimes in 1990 noted that 70 percent of those arrested were younger than nineteen, for whom this is a social activity), or disaffected and paranoid lone wolves. "Most serious analysts figure that the bulk of racial violence and homophobic violence is carried out by unaffiliated individuals."[144] Genuinely disturbed men and women do not last long in any organization, including these. A 1981 report by the Connecticut Advisory Committee to the U.S. Commission on Civil Rights on Hate Groups and the State's Response concluded that activity from cross-burnings and anti-Semitic graffiti to fire-bombings could not be authoritatively traced to organized groups.

There is little evidence that paramilitary groups are criminal enterprises. What is certain is that the groups contribute to a "climate of hate, violence, and ingorance . . . that makes such acts acceptable."[145] How do we assess their danger to democracy?

Terrorism, Conspiracism, and Clear and Present Danger

Judgments of danger to government security and public order, compounded by elected officials' responsiveness to popular alarm, are always at work in enacting, interpreting, and applying restrictions on freedom of association. In particular, the perception of clear and present danger, understood not just as a test of the constitutionality of statutes but as a habit of mind, is a permanent element of American political thought.

Justice Holmes' opinion concerning the Russian immigrant anarchists in *Abrams v. United States* (1919) is the classic bold pronouncement of freedom for innocuous dissent by "poor and puny anonymities," license for "the surreptitious publishing of a silly leaflet by an unknown man."[146] In the same spirit, Justice Douglas's dissent in *Dennis* described the Communist Party in America as a "crippled political force" that has never made a respectable political showing and is incapable of presenting a clear and present danger.[147] The U.S. attorney who conducted the secret grand jury investigation of the Black Panthers commented, "I find it difficult to believe that a group of men who succeed in getting all their men exiled, in prison, or killed, are any real danger in overthrowing this country. It is too easy to convince middle Americans—the great silent majority—that it is good that they [government officials] are after people who are ignorant, black, crude, and violent."[148]

Lacking confidence that sober estimates will prevail, the current civil libertarian perspective on the First Amendment is "pathological": civil liberties must "do maximum service in those historical periods when intolerance of unorthodox ideas is most prevalent and when governments are most able and most likely to stifle dissent systematically." Justice Brandeis's opinion in *Whitney* promises the most latitude: "The fact that speech is likely to result in some violence or in the destruction of property is not enough to justify its suppression. There must be the probability of *serious injury to the State*."[149]

John Rawls interprets "serious injury to the state" stringently, to indicate constitutional crisis. Restrictions on liberty are warranted when conditions threaten the basic equal liberties of "the representative citizen."[150] As a hypothetical example, Rawls discusses legislation aimed at preventing the formation of paramilitary groups. In the context of sharp religious antagonisms, where members of rival sects collect weapons and form armed bands, he would endorse a legislative judgment that "the formation of paramilitary groups, which the passing of the statute [outlawing private ownership of guns] may forestall, is a much greater danger to the freedom of the average citizen than being held strictly liable for the possession of weapons." This restriction on association is not just; simply, all that can be done is to "aim for the least injustice that conditions allow."[151]

Contemporary paramilitary groups do not present the threat of "serious injury to the state" Rawls had in mind. There is nothing today to rival the hundreds of bombings of homes, schools, and churches throughout the South following the decision in *Brown v. Board of Education* in 1954, for example. Local disorder is the most likely danger: isolated confrontations, disturbances, melees, violence. Despicable and injurious, by themselves these activities should not inspire official or unofficial visions of a clear and present political danger. But circumstantial estimates of danger are vulnerable to the state of public feeling. What contributes to the high level of public anxiety in the United States?

The ease of launching groups exacerbates deep-seated fear of conspiracy, for one thing. Historically, for example, southern fear of the American Anti-Slavery Society was fed by cheap publication: "the sudden deluge of abolitionist publications lent credibility to the image of an enormous propaganda machine financed by British gold."[152] The technology of communication is more effective than ever today, and groups have easy access to arms and to online instruction in explosives.

It is also clear that the self-dramatizing conduct of paramilitarists arouses alarm. California passed the Mulford bill prohibiting the carrying of loaded firearms in public places in response to the audacity of the Panthers' guerrilla theater tactic of patrolling white neighborhoods. Members delight in uniformed and armed self-display, and in boasting—as one training pamphlet did in what must be an unconscious parody of the Communist Manifesto—that the

Minutemen "are the most experienced, most dedicated and best disciplined organization that is involved in this fight at the grass-roots level . . ."[153]

Paramilitary groups loom large, well-armed, and unstable when they confront, frustrate, and humiliate government agents, even if the group of forty "Christian patriots" holding Whatcom County, Washington police at bay for several days when they tried to serve an eviction notice on a seventy-year-old tax-evading veterinarian is more typical than Waco.

The outrage of local officials and the FBI does not make paramilitarists any more dangerous to the public generally, or a substantial political threat. Clearly, though, displays of weapons and persistent charges of treason do intimidate neighbors. When the Gainesville militia protested flying a United Nations flag at city hall in 1994, the city manager reported that at the city commission meeting "I felt more personal fear than any other public meeting I've attended."[154] Provocative behavior sets off spirals of organization and confrontation. Leaflets distributed by one group so upset a community in Queens that the citizens considered forming vigilante brigades to protect themselves.[155]

Finally, the attribution "domestic terrorism" invokes an additional, heightened set of fears. The now-familiar phrase is calculated to alarm. It shifts attention from revolution and political subversion, which are implausible in the United States today, to wanton harm to private citizens, which is always imaginable, and now terrifyingly real. It borrows impact from reports of international terrorism and fear of foreigners or those made alien by their suicidal fanaticism.[156] For "terrorist" implies a willingness to engage in unlimited mass destruction—a characteristic that does not appear to apply to domestic paramilitary groups. Attributing fearful hate crimes and political violence to "domestic terrorist" groups exploits this exaggerated sense of insecurity in order to solicit new government powers, which in turn can only create illusory security. The 1996 Anti-Terrorism and Effective Death Penalty and Public Safety Act was passed on the heels of the Oklahoma City bombing, though none of its provisions speak to crimes of that kind, and its success in diminishing civil liberties is plain.[157]

Perhaps the heaviest cost of this extravagance is skewed perceptions of public danger. "Domestic terrorism" minimizes the extent to which the violence that *does* make the day-to-day lives of ordinary people hellish is apolitical. A municipal judge in Montana described being threatened with kidnapping and murder by members of the paramilitary "Freemen" movement who were forced to appear in court in response to routine traffic tickets.[158] Unsettling and potentially dangerous, still, this is a rarity compared to the insecurity of urban judges and lawyers for whom metal detectors are a routine attempt to forestall commonplace violent disturbances inside and outside the courtroom. Or true domestic violence against women. Or neighborhood vulnerability to gangs that really do create war zones.

The Street Gang Terrorism and Protection Act is strangely named. Gangs frighten (and harm) law-abiding citizens—they can paralyze a neighborhood and keep people effectively hostage in their homes. But this has little to do with terrorism as a political strategy and type of crime. The atmosphere street gangs create is not a political crisis; it is a chronic condition. Unlike terrorist bombings, for example, it does not wake up those previously unaware, alerting them in frightening fashion that *this* is what it will look like, creating a potentially defining moment that could move a nation to condemn violence (and to condemn editors, political leaders, talk-show hosts, and others who encourage lawlessness and hate). For residents of inner-city war zones, the landscape of anarchy and violence is familiar, and the provisions of the street gang statute have little to do with the sort of measures that might actually allay their fear.

Nonetheless, the language of crisis, creating a compelling government interest that permits restriction of association, is significant. It is one element in the habit of mind that announces a clear and present danger and uses it to justify the creation of new substantive crimes of membership in certain groups, and methods of intervening.

Moreover, by identifying "domestic terrorism" with organized groups and arguing for anti-paramilitary statutes and enhanced enforcement as requirements of self-protection, the role of disconnected loners is eclipsed. In 1996, the rush to declare a national conspiracy of hate groups to burn black churches was unchecked by available evidence to the contrary, which shows that almost half the burnings involved churches whose congregations were all or mostly white. Evidence also indicates that while some burnings of black churches were hate crimes (apparently unconnected, except perhaps as copycat crimes), even these were not traced to organized groups. At least as many burnings were unplanned acts of vandalism by drunk teenagers, or attempts to conceal theft by black arsonists as well as white.[159] The two men accused in the 1995 bombing of the federal building in Oklahoma City attended several militia meetings but the tenuous connection falls well short of membership.

Paramilitary leaders are perfectly aware of the threat of unaffiliated loners: Minuteman Robert DePugh advised that it is better to have "kooks and nuts" inside the organization than out of it on their own:

> "Out," he told an interviewer, "they're liable to do most anything at any time without anybody knowing it except them. If they decide they want to go out and blow somebody up, okay, they go out and blow somebody up. But if they're part of a group . . . well, then there's a good chance someone in the organization will know about it and they're going to take steps to bring this person under control."[160]

Most important, "domestic terrorism" gives credence to conspiracist thinking rather than chastening it. Conspiracists are the avatars of clear and present danger. Paramilitary groups justify their organization and arms with conspiracist pronouncements of imminent crisis. The forces arrayed against them, official and unofficial, do the same. ADL announces the "alarming proliferation" of groups, describes all hate groups and paramilitary groups as "paranoid," and titles its 1995 report "A Response to Domestic Terrorism." The label "domestic terrorism" is inflammatory. So are the titles chosen by self-styled "posses" and "militias" to denote exactly the opposite: citizens authorized to maintain or restore public order. The conflict behind this war of names is the interesting heart of the matter. Legislation and judicial decisions are the concrete outgrowths of this dance of conspiracists.

The Life Cycle of Membership

What, if anything, can be said for freedom of association for paramilitary groups? David Brion Davis took the long historical view and found that certain conspiracist eras had unintended, progressive political consequences: anti-Masonry helped spread egalitarian ideals and democratize American politics, the image of a Slave Power conspiracy assisted in organizing Northern abolitionists, the crusade against communism led the United States to abandon isolationism.[161] Retrospective historical assessment is entirely different from thinking about the effect of paramilitary group life on members personally and individually, though, and from the moral uses of pluralism.

Undoubtedly, membership in paramilitary groups is serviceable for some people. If the activities of private armies are not criminal, they may provide relatively safe arenas for expressing antiliberal dispositions and gratifying militarist hungers. One commentator described a member of the Militia of Montana "alive with conspiracies. They whir in his mind and welter in his heart, and they fill him so full of outrage and nervousness that he cannot ever stay still."[162] He was securely ensconced in a northwestern compound, and probably benign. Asked in an interview whether he felt it was dangerous to provide "kooks and nuts" with a justification for their hostility, DePugh answered forthrightly, "Well, to a degree you're right there. . . . If our literature were not fairly provocative, we wouldn't find them in the first place."[163] Containment and the "safety valve" thesis are credible considerations.

A more ambitious, progressive argument is made for specific groups as politicizing, providing education in constitutionalism, say, or rights, beginning with the right to bear arms. I discuss the strategies of citizen militias in the next chapter—what I call their "legalistic antilegalism." Since the substantive politics of members is illiberal and undemocratic, the question is whether members move on from paramilitary and hate groups to channel their experiences into constructive associations. Published life histories of ex-members describe paths out of secret societies and paramilitary groups and away from arms.

The Black Panthers, for example, graduated political activists and community organizers, a law professor, and two members of Congress. In contrast to

the democratically inclined leaders of SNCC, however, Panthers Huey Newton, Eldridge Cleaver, and Bobby Seale spiraled down into drugs and criminal
violence, and, in 1995, H. Rap Brown was arraigned on weapons possessions
and assault charges. It appears that Panthers who went on to become democratic activists had been more involved in the group's social mission than its
military organization.[164] Tony Martinez, author of *Brotherhood of Hate*, became a lecturer for the Anti-Defamation League, though in his case the "way
out" was arrest for counterfeiting and service as an FBI informant. Similarly,
a leader of the Southern White Knights decided to start a new life by speaking
to the Southern Poverty Law Center about the Klan.[165] The groups themselves
did not seem to have a centrifugal political dynamic, then, and there is little to
suggest that the life histories of leaders, particularly those inclined to produce
autobiographies, are typical.

More helpful for thinking about the moral uses of association is Raphael
Ezekiel's study of white racist groups, which focuses on young joiners,
"scared, stranded white youths." Ezekiel shows that members are not driven by
hate to join a group that mirrors and acts on their already formed beliefs.
Instead, they were isolated and available. The group drew them in. And they
were taught anti-Semitism or conspiratorial views of federal agents set on dis-
possessing the people—beliefs that had little connection to their own experience. "Most were members in this extreme racist group because the membership served a function, not because they had to enact racism."[166]

The thrust of Ezekiel's study is that before they joined, members' lives were
markedly devoid of attachments. The Neo-Nazis in his study are young men in
their teens and twenties from families with at least one absent parent and few
extended family ties. "Church typically played no role in the family's life."
Nor did other social groups, or public agencies besides the police. They were
out of school (most had dropped out years before graduation) and had neither
work nor prospects of work. "Many people whom Miles' newsletter reaches
derive a degree of self-confidence and dignity from the suggestion that they are
engaged in a heroic struggle for the sake of a larger entity, the reborn family
of Whites." "The white supremacist movement—for a while, at least—is a
lifeline for these kids."[167]

This corresponds to descriptions of street gangs as sources of identity, support, and respect. This is not to say that "young people join gangs for the same
reasons as business people join ... the Rotary Club—to belong, to interact
with people who share their interest, to have support, to have instant friends,
and to socialize."[168] But it does provide association: relief from solitude and
the mutual regard of similar men. Greene describes a white supremacist from
the 1950s:

> He became an insider. When he met confederates, there were important words and
> counter-signs to exchange. ... [H]is telephone rang at odd hours. ... After work

there might be a key person to meet at a bar, or a lecture to attend. . . . [He] became a vital link in a chain of being.[169]

Sheer lack not only makes membership attractive but also goes some way toward explaining why joining this sort of group may be easy for them. In general, young men "have high energy, few restraining obligations, and little caution" but those inclined to paramilitarism stand out: "Most strikingly, recruits have little in their heads to *inhibit* their adopting these [Nazi] legends"; "nothing from family or environment got in the way."[170]

In practice, hate groups target prospective members from among the most disaffected and unaffiliated. The American Nazi Party's official stormtrooper's manual suggests rescuing "hordes of criminal teenagers by dealing with their need for aggression, action, danger, and excitement," cutting through the "nonsense of clubs and tea-parties."[171] The Black Panther organization included street hustlers, criminals, pimps, and gamblers along with sincere rural and urban blacks and young black intellectuals.[172]

During his term in jail DePugh wrote *Behind the Iron Mask*, in which he advocated rehabilitating prisoners: "a real and permanent change involves the formation of new social bonds . . . [so that] on his release, the prisoner need not return to the same old friends and neighborhood where all his social bonds involve a criminal's sense of personal identity."[173] Hate groups follow this recommendation and actively recruit in prisons. In the late 1970s, Aryan Nations initiated a "ministry" to white inmates, distributing literature and taped sermons, corresponding with prisoners, publishing a "prison outreach" newsletter, and operating a halfway house for released members of the Aryan Brotherhood, a white racist prison gang. Christian Identity, the religious organization tied to a number of paramilitary groups, was recognized by the federal courts as an official inmate religion.[174]

The fact that membership fulfills "needs" is no argument for the moral uses of association, certainly not if association fatally inhibits shifting involvements. Here as in other groups I have discussed, that is the critical point. William Pierce's novel, *The Turner Diaries*, a blueprint for paramilitarists, taught that "the Order" demands spiritual and social separatism and a "total moral environment."[175] These groups typically shut out the world by associating only with one another. Leaders assign members activities that isolate them and give them a feeling of accomplishment. To the extent that paramilitary groups form self-supporting compounds they are further withdrawn from moderating effects, in particular, regular employment. The destructiveness of these groups depends in large part on how successful they are in blocking out conflicting information and inhibiting "reality testing."

Although paramilitary groups are oddly literature-intense—the first introduction to them is often *The Turner Diaries* or hate propaganda—nothing is more isolating than conspiracist material. Since one of the first lessons of conspiracist groups is to mistrust outsiders, including the mainstream press and popular culture, countereducation may have little impact in any case. There is no way "into" conspiracy thinking, and no obvious corrective for its "deep lack of common sense."[176] Separation and exclusion have epistemological consequences: "A group may become ignorant at a level that would be appalling in an individual," and self-enforced ignorance is a function of the success of separation.[177]

As one assistant district attorney put it, "They're secretive, fanatical. You can't argue with them."[178] That does not mean paramilitarists decline to argue with others; only that the process is as far as possible from reciprocal: "he is not a receiver, he is a transmitter."[179] Their conduciveness to conspiracism, rather than arms, may be the gravest consequence of these associations, for members personally and for democracy generally.

Paramilitary groups have difficulty isolating most members for long, though. Other connections draw them outward despite the appeal of romantic militarism, separatist communitarianism, and ideologies of hate, and despite all the efforts of leaders. For individuals with even rudimentary personal and social attachments outside, the chief limiting factor is precisely the distracting pull of ordinary associations. Testimony shows that families are the most powerful counterforce against immersion in the group. "I've let alot of things slide," one Klan leader on his way out of the movement remarked, "you know, and you put the Klan first. And I'm tired of me suffering, my mother suffering . . . We don't *own* nothing. We don't *have* nothing. And as you know, most Klan leaders . . . are self-employed or don't work at all." One thirty-four-year old observed, "Girls that will put up with this are hard to come by. . . . I thought I had one, this girl here I dated for three years . . . but you know, when she'd want to do something on the weekend I'd say, 'Well, we got a rally.' . . . people expect the leaders to go to everything."[180] He left for love.

Leaders last longer; Richard Butler of Aryan Nations led groups for decades (despite the fact that his mother did not like his involvement and wanted him to stay in the family's aeronautical engineering business). But even for them, centrifugal forces operate, and many of the best-known paramilitarists do not persevere. The personal costs of secrecy and separatism are high. It is difficult to remain in a constant state of crisis, especially when there is little gratifying action. Theatrics become stale. There is no constructive program, and few measures of "success" beyond the pleasures of organizing itself.[181] Jail, legal troubles, the financial costs of organization, are wearing. Tom Metzger of White Aryan Resistance spoke grimly of the fact that underground organization means cutting ties with family, friends, everyone. As for terrorist or revolutionary tactics: "Personally, it's not wise," he advised; they don't live long.[182]

These forces for reintegration work uncalculatedly and unobserved, unrelated to organized democratic opposition to paramilitary groups. We know that hatemonger and paramilitarists *are* available for joining associations, after all; they may not be sturdy psychologically, Ezekiel reports, but they are not pathological or "kooks," incapable of adjusting to group norms or cooperative activity.

But these centrifugal forces are not operative for everyone. When individuals do not have competing connections and the experience of pluralism is unavailable to them, the life cycle of their membership is not extended but exit is more a matter of anomic drift than potentially constructive social pushes or pulls. Many ordinary members appear to have no more resources when they exit than when they joined, so that they rarely leave to find other involvements. They cycle in from and back out to chaos and personal disorganization—to drugs and alcohol, or arrest for unrelated crimes. The same absence of competing attachments that facilitated their entry haunts their exit. Just as no forces were at work in their lives to inhibit them from joining in the first place, none are inviting them once they leave.

Democratic Obligations

Ezekiel's portrait of joiners suggests that many others are similarly situated and available for membership in paramilitary or hate groups but do not happen to be recruited. Also that those who do join might have entered some other association if they were actively recruited. As he describes it, joining reflects not just the normal vicissitudes of personal experience, but thin social experience and an absence of alternatives. Ezekiel also emphasizes "the sense of belonging somewhere and having a continuing source of care" as the function these groups serve for their members.

So the life cycle of membership suggests that one corrective is the deliberate creation of compensatory attachments and mentoring, providing other places to go and to belong:

> Given an alternative group that offered comradeship, reassuring activities, glamour, and excitement, they could easily have switched their allegiances. They would have remained racist—like their neighbors who hadn't joined a group—but they would not have needed to carry out racist actions in a group setting.[183]

Not surprisingly, the alternatives envisioned correspond to specific interpretations of who joins, and why. Ezekiel links membership in white racist groups to an "economically devastated" white underclass, and his imagined alternative is membership in progressive political groups that directly address social needs. Alan Wolfe's macropolitical analysis of the "radical right" attributes their rise to mistaken political decisions by Democrats to forego political mobilization; he too sees political groups as alternatives.[184] Both approaches discount the unique attractions of paramilitary group life, which are not reducible to failures of political organizing. They minimize the extent to which certain forms of disaffection and depression are invulnerable to the usual proposals for participation because they are not gratifying. Members require unusually acute stimulation.

Not just any group could substitute, then. Paramilitary associations have the distinctive ideological and emotional attractions of romanticism, separatism, and ideologies of hate I have described, and the heightened intensity of militarism may be critical for breaking into the hard shell of anomie. Occasions for emotional expressions of contempt and confrontation, with their guns and exhilarating threat of violence, may be hard to duplicate.

Social theorists are generally less interested in alternative associations than in addressing the phenomenon "at its roots," the assumption being that the appeal of these antidemocratic groups is reducible to social factors. We know little about the economic background of paramilitary group members, however, except that it is mainly lower- and middle-class. Comprehensive studies of the American right wing are similarly inconclusive: "In spite of the massive amount of effort social scientists have invested in trying to find it, there is no single socioeconomic base for right-wing activism."[185]

Nor is there good evidence that economic insecurity is a condition of group activity. One version of the "frustration–aggression" thesis ties hate crimes to unemployment. A competing thesis advances the "power–threat hypothesis," positing group conflict in times of economic downturn. These links are tenuous, for one thing because vulnerable groups tend to become targets only when they are made the scapegoats of economic setbacks.[186]

Status explanations fare no better. With important exceptions, they see slippage in prestige as a result of disruption of a stable status hierarchy as the motivation for joining and hate crime. Today, these explanations focus on "life style" or "cultural values" as independent vehicles of status, and hence on the drive to sanctify one subculture and stigmatize others. Donald Green proposes an explanation based on specific configurations of demographic change. White hate crime coincides with the move of nonwhites into white strongholds; the motivation is defense of homogeneity and neighborhood identity, anticipated lack of control.[187]

Taking these contested social explanations together, correcting the conditions that presumably give rise to these groups would involve nothing less than eliminating economic insecurity, relieving status anxiety, and configuring policies to legitimize traditional values and communities (without depreciating contemporary liberal ones).

There is no "simple and overpowering psychological explanation" for who joins, either.[188] The classic frustration–aggression hypothesis has been applied indiscriminately to all manifestations of hostility and is dependent on explanations of frustration to begin with. Joining has been linked both to feelings of powerlessness and to people who seem to have a high sense of efficacy.[189]

Mass society theory sees membership as a case of fragmented egos coping with disorganization in the environment. A host of theses cast "deviant" groups as outlets for clinical maladjustment.

If secret societies, hate groups, and paramilitary associations serve unique functions and are ineliminable, the critical question is what obligations do democratic citizens have to counter their effects? Responsibility for speaking out should be general, of course, but in practice campaigns against them have remained the business of specialized associations. Like the ADL's lobbying efforts directed at denying license renewals to radio stations that broadcast "This Is Liberty Lobby." In 1995, for example, the shortwave radio station that had broadcast Michigan militia leader Mark Koernke's daily diatribes to 2.7 million listeners canceled his show. While not insignificant, these setbacks are unlikely to affect the calculations of prospective joiners.

Few associations have been more single-mindedly dedicated to organizing broader social forces and bringing them to bear against paramilitary and hate groups than the Center for Democratic Renewal. The association publishes *A Handbook of Effective Community Responses*, instructs on model state and local legislation and lobbying, and provides workshop training to labor unions, universities, religious institutions, human rights commissions, neighborhood groups, farm alliances, and so on. Nothing in this agenda is apt to persuade sympathizers to change their minds. Rather, the sound aim is to increase the costs of joining and supporting groups by forcing members and sympathizers to confront a hostile community. That means mobilizing people who are passively opposed to these groups, putting pressure on ordinary citizens to agitate, litigate, monitor, and confront—"to make as much noise as possible." The idea is to make public condemnation an obstacle potential members must overcome.[190]

In this mission, CDR is as interested in "intelligence-gathering" as the groups they oppose: they encourage subscribing to sinister publications to monitor what leaders tell their followers, dialing telephone hate-lines, sending representatives to rallies. CDR invites creative actions: "take photos of especially menacing skinheads, enlarge them, and poster them around town."[191] The association advises on how to refuse to let group members take over public meetings, how to turn publicly sponsored marches into private ones so that Klan floats can be legally excluded, how to eliminate community access cable channels to deny them platforms. CDR recommends that human rights advocates not appear on radio or television programs with white supremacists, because the confrontations these programs generate are attractive to some viewers and increase the number of joiners!

My view is that democratic obligations have less to do with eliminating these associations or inhibiting joiners than with aiding victims. Not only for humane reasons, but also because public support reduces fear of retaliation, one of the chief reasons for quiescence. The Connecticut report on hate groups contrasted the response to a fire-bombing in West Haven, where petitions were passed asking the victimized family to remain, demonstrations held, and neighbors volunteered to aid (and where police found the perpetrator) with East Haven, where there was no publicity and no community response.[192] A Billings, Montana community responded to a 1993 skinhead attack on a Jewish home by pasting drawings of a menorah printed by the *Billings Gazette* on their windows and staging a Martin Luther King Day march.

Vocal and above all visibly majoritarian opposition can overturn any perception of passive acquiescence and latent agreement—a sustaining thought for paramilitarists and their fellow-travelers. It was habitual nonvoters who came to the polls in a special election to vote *against* David Duke in his ultimately successful run for a seat in the Louisiana state legislature in 1989.[193] In 1990, Duke won 44 percent of the vote against an incumbent U.S. senator—a solid majority of white voters. The sensible hope is that by activating usually passive citizens, public sentiment will be so strongly opposed that groups become literal "extremists."

In fact, the importance of these groups is precisely their convergence with other elements of American political culture. Public exhibitions of opposition are critical—more critical than enhancing laws and law enforcement, precisely because liberal democratic dispositions are not always the ones most flagrantly displayed, and liberal democratic principles and practices are not always in the forefront of public consciousness.

Convergence

The designation "domestic terrorism" by "extremists," "fanatics," or "the paranoid fringe"—what one *New York Times* columnist described as "the danger posed by heavily armed hatemongers thrashing about in a fog of paranoia"—deflects attention from convergence. The erroneous implication is that in its beliefs and reasoning the group is peripheral. Categories like "extremist," applied to both the left and the right, suggest a great distance from a designable center. The assumption is that a stable "center" of legitimate political discourse and conduct exists. This is an empirical question. In fact, there are competing political traditions in America and a moving center.[194] It may not be broad and stable. That center may not be moderate, either. As one journalist wrote of a Militiaman: "He is a stranger *of* a strange land, warped not against his culture but by it, and the curve of his warp follows the curve of the culture; it is only steeper and continues farther, off the edge of the graph."[195] Those who speak hyperbolically of a paramilitary "movement" can point only to the fact that groups sometimes share propaganda literature and martyrs: Gordon Kahl, Randy Weaver, David Koresh.[196] The real clear and present danger is not a network of cells, but convergence with other, mainstream groups, at the level of public discourse and conduct, and moral disposition.

The Connecticut Advisory Committee on Civil Rights and Hate Groups reported that most crimes could not be traced to organized groups, but the committee insisted that extremist groups were responsible for the climate of hate that makes these actions conceivable. It is also important to acknowledge just the reverse, that paramilitary and hate groups are the *beneficiaries* of a climate of hate and antigovernmentalism they exploit but do not create. "What are the chances that people who first have been softened up by the awesome persuasive powers of a Jimmy Swaggart or a Pat Robertson will then be receptive to the similar preachings of a Thom Robb or some other Identity fanatic filled with venom?"[197]

The empirical question is how many citizens participate in the concerns, sympathize with the grievances, and tentatively incline to the habits of paramilitary and hate groups and their close cousins. In this connection, Henry Louis Gates Jr. struggled to assess the level of support Louis Farrakhan has among African Americans. Those who attend mosques affiliated with the Nation of Islam are not very numerous, he writes. "On the other hand, if you go by the number of people who consider him a legitimate voice of black protest, the ranks are much larger. (In a recent poll, more than half the blacks surveyed reported a favorable impression of him.)"[198] A recent survey of political views suggests that perpetrators of hate crimes are distinguished from the general public by their exclusionary impulses, their especially powerful political views on immigration, interracial marriage, and so on. White supremacists are more likely to see a need for activism. Sixteen percent of the whites under forty-five in the general population match the characteristics associated with these "extremists," a figure that does not begin to approach the estimated membership of these groups.[199] Leaders strategize with this in mind, seizing opportunities "to make an impression on a very receptive audience, if we move aggressively and use a reasonable degree of discretion."[200]

Paramilitary and hate groups keep the threads of romantic militarism, separatism, and hate alive and accessible. They enhance the apparent moderation and hence legitimacy of their less exhibitionistic counterparts. They make it easy for others to disavow conspiracist associations and violent activities, while conceding that "something must be done." The polemical objective behind the label "extremist" is to disavow this continuum.

Following the Oklahoma City bombing in the spring of 1995, President Clinton advised that radio show purveyors of hatred, division, and lies are intent on keeping people as paranoid as possible and the rest of us as torn up and upset with each other as possible. He was making the point that no group has a monopoly on antidemocratic affect or effectiveness.

The Christian Identity Church of the "survivalist right" delivers a more virulent message than what is commonly called the "religious right." But these evangelists, whose televised sermons and millenarian messages reach millions (one estimate is 40 percent of all households with a television), share the theme of a "Christian" America, declare hatred for homosexuals and atheists, and are obsessed with the Jews—whether that means destroying Israel or preserving it for the conversion that will presage the Second Coming.[201]

Popular hosts of mainstream radio call-in shows talk poisonously of ordinary politicians, attribute fantastic crimes to them, and speak jokingly of murdering political opponents.

> Any suggestion of conspiratorial evil against a prominent politician, no matter how extreme the charge or how scanty the evidence, glides from the margins of politics to the center, on a sort of media conveyor belt that carries it from the rantings of the fringe groups of the right and the left into the respectable zone of public discourse.[202]

Republican presidential contender Pat Buchanan writes of the "Manhattan Money Power" and the political influence of people with names like Rubin, Goldman, and Sachs. We have studies of how "conservatives exploited racial resentments to make 'liberal elites' and big government, rather than big business, the new target for right-leaning populist ire."[203] We know less about racism in the black media and popular culture, still less about racism harbored by quieter ethnic groups.

Rhetoric of warfare and violence is commonplace in everyday politics. In the course of a federal budget dispute Democrats accuse a Republican Congress of holding the whole country hostage, threatening to basically blow up the government, of using blackmail and bomb-throwing; Republicans accuse Democrats of terrorist tactics. There are always literalists who translate bad metaphors into prescriptions for action. Still, rhetoric reflects to some degree motivating effect; it certainly tries for impact. Politicians regularly try to earn trust by telling adherents they should mistrust their opponents. At a minimum, this sort of discourse exhibits a truly careless lack of self-restraint. On the other hand, if responsibility for every diminution of civility, regardless of context and content, is seen as a contribution to hate groups, we are liable to confuse decorum with democracy.

Finally, just as anticommunism provided a major unifying ideology in the 1950s and 1960s, antigovernmentalism is an emergent rallying point today. Antifederalism crosses the mainstream political spectrum. Severe mistrust and even loathing of officials at every level of government is widespread, as evidenced by the rush to home-schooling or the overlapping consensus that sees guns as justifiable for self-defense against assaults on homes, property, family, and livelihoods, and in some cases against zealous officials viewed as enemies. There has been a subtle but important shift in gun control from a crime issue to an issue of social control and sovereignty. When paramilitary groups style themselves citizen militias and represent their association as not just a constitutionally protected right but a democratic obligation, an expression of popular sovereignty, we enter the domain of "fusion republicanism," my next subject.

The trouble is, in daily life there may be no easy way to distinguish what we hear. When is hateful, militant talk just general incivility? When is it political rhetoric calculated to exploit popular feelings, or the exaggerated pose of partisans charging one another with disregard for some common good? When does it reflect the deep beliefs and herald the potentially violent action of extremists? When is it the considered judgment of presumptively virtuous democratic citizens, pushed to the limit by a sense of crisis?

As a practical matter, we must insist strongly on making these distinctions. But we must also explore the possibility of their profound relation to one another, and with it the question of political responsibility. Outraged objection to any suggestion of linkage is not enough. There is the empirical question of extremism: which associations and how many promulgate the disposition to militarism and hate, and which associations or leaders are carried away by extravagant rhetoric. There is also the question posed by the sociology of knowledge—how systematic elements of democratic and antidemocratic thought "move out" and become appropriated and transformed in popular discourse and the wild ravings of hateful fanatics.

President Clinton's effort to raise the matter of political responsibility received little sober consideration. The predominant response was lashing out: "the attempt to locate in society's political discourse the cause of a lunatic's action is . . . contemptible"; the connection between political speech and hateful crime is "grotesque and offensive."[204] Partisanship aside, this reflects the familiar (quasi-conspiracist) inclination to try to identify some fringe as solely responsible for fear and disorder. But the question in assessing paramilitary and hate groups, and association life generally, is the elusive one of general democratic accountability.

This suggests that the chief threat to liberal democracy may not be separatism, romantic militarism, ideologies of hate, or even arms, but pervasive, unwarranted mistrust, raised to the level of conspiracism. It is a widespread and entrenched habit of mind, brought to a pitch and embodied in these voluntary associations. Of course, secret societies do exist, conspiracies do occur, so does internal disloyalty, and often suspected acts can be confirmed. But for conspiracists themselves, verification is unimportant. Their own fragmentary experiences, personal testimony, and the confirmation of their fellows is enough. As a cognitive style, conspiracist thinking is a classic closed system, invulnerable to contradictory evidence. Conspiracists operate from the assumption that someone is 'in control': there are no accidents, coincidences, or unintended consequences. Jews do not make bad investments. Communists (or agents of the Trilateral Commission) are well funded and well armed. And paramilitary associations are terrorists ready and able to strike at a moment's notice. The strict internal logic of conspiracism finds a place for every piece of evidence in its narrative scheme.

The consequences are genuinely subversive of democratic politics and political thought, not only at the fringe. For the diffuse result is to undercut both the will and the capacity to analyze associations politically. A conspiracist habit of mind undercuts the ordinary political give and take of parties, ideologies, and interest groups. Substantive ideological divisions and contested social science findings appropriately guide our thinking and give meaning to our divergent assessments of political danger, but they are eclipsed as well. Thus, we have polar views of paramilitary groups: as terrorists on the one hand; as defenders of democracy on the other. The counterpart is polar views of gun control advocates: as the quintessential public interest lobby (guns are *the* national crisis) on the one hand; as agents of an official conspiracy to disarm citizens who have a right, necessity, and even moral obligation to arm on the other. Retreat from political analysis is apparent. Skepticism, argument backed by evidence, open-ended deliberation, even self-conscious ideology and articulated political preferences become exceptions rather than the rule.

Measured against virtually any norm of democratic discourse, conspiracy thinking is untenable. It is not the only form of irrationalism in American popular culture or democratic politics. "Expert authorities" on whom the public depends for guidance are likely to be self-appointed and self-publicizing ministers, gurus, celebrities, and self-styled patriots. What distinguishes conspiracism is that associations, not random individuals, are its carriers.

This challenge to democracy is more elusive and unregulable than any plot to create civil disorder. Which is why paramilitary and hate groups ought to arouse not only fear of "domestic terrorism" and fear for civil liberties, but also apprehension about the propensity for conspiracism that is a permanent element of American political life.

8

"Fusion Republicanism" and Paramilitary Paul Reveres

"Fusion Republicanism"

One classic formulation of the relation between civil society and liberal democracy emphasizes the political role of groups as countervailing forces to government. Like a wide dispersion of private property, a multiplicity of associations provides a check on authority and insures the possibility of political resistance. Voluntary associations threatened with loss of autonomy can be expected to appeal to this rationale for freedom of association; the Boy Scouts amicus brief in *Roberts v. Jaycees* invokes "Free Society v. Totalitarianism" as a knock-down argument for their right to decide who they will admit as members. The logic is available to any group; Tom Metzger, leader of the Aryan Nations, cautions: "As social power decreases faster and faster, state power increases faster and faster."[1]

The defensive political function of associations is a general thesis in favor of pluralism, and I have argued that it is difficult to predict which associations serve this purpose, and when. But some groups appoint themselves guardians of liberty, and arm to defend against oppression. "Citizen militias" are the fierce contemporary embodiment of private armies presenting themselves as public defenders.

Posse Comitatus, a paramilitary group founded in 1969, is one of the more histrionic and ideologically decentralist militias. The Posse Comitatus Act passed by Congress after the Civil War barred the federal government from using the army to enforce domestic laws, assigning this police power to county officials. Armed with this slim legal doctrine, Posse Comitatus claims that "in the formation of this constitutional republic, the county has always been and remains to this day, the TRUE seat of the government for the citizens," and that the sheriff is the only legal law enforcement officer. Moreover, in the Posse's skewed view, the sheriff's ordinary police functions are subordinate to the duty to protect citizens from government abuse. Local citizens must advise him (never her) when officials commit unlawful acts, and if the sheriff refuses to mobilize a posse, Posse Comitatus claims the right to act in his name. "In areas where the Posse numbers in the hundreds, they are being heard, with both respect and fear. . . . We are facing a lawless group in power who are in the process of destroying our freedoms and making us serfs of a ONE-WORLD GOVERNMENT." Posse members wear tiny gold hangman's nooses on their lapels: "This is no game for weak-knees or panty-waists. This calls for men with guts."[2]

By 1996, there were several hundred citizen militias, at least one in every state, with membership ranging from fewer than a dozen to over a thousand, all organized and armed to resist tyranny.[3] Donning the revolutionary mantle of the independent militia that opposed the British army, their conspiracist thinking echoes the logic of that rebellion. The motive behind the Stamp Act was not simply to raise money from the colonies, John Adams had warned, but "to forge a fatal link between ecclesiastical and civil despotism by stripping colonies of the means of knowledge." The danger to America "was in fact only the small, immediately visible part of the greater whole whose ultimate manifestation would be the destruction of the English constitution with the rights and privileges embedded in it."[4] Today, the federal income tax or gun control is the entering wedge of a conspiracy to confiscate property or deny citizens the means of self-protection.

Militias focus their opposition on law enforcement agencies and the justice system—not surprisingly, since that is where government coercion touches individual lives and errant authority hits home. Members engage in organized noncompliance. They refuse to appear in traffic court, for example, or to register automobiles. Individually and in small combinations, they have resisted arresting authorities. The Freemen standoff in Montana in 1996 captured headlines for weeks.

As important as their potential for violent resistance is their inventiveness at what I call "legalistic antilegalism." Posse Comitatus leaders advise members on techniques for invalidating loans and avoiding foreclosures. The publication "We the People" explains that citizens are not obliged to pay their debts because U.S. currency has been worthless since the country went off the gold standard. Groups conduct constitutional law seminars instructing that the income tax is unconstitutional. (The number of tax protesters has doubled every year since 1978 and is now many tens of thousands.) Groups file common law liens against the personal property of judges, district attorneys, and court commissioners to clog the system. When authorities are believed to operate outside the bounds of the Constitution, "citizens' juries" or "Christian grand juries" draw up "indictments" and hand down "arrest warrants" for local officials.[5] I discuss jury nullification shortly.

Negative, resistant, and self-appointed, still, militia groups cannot be usefully described as anarchist because they lack confidence that if political authority were erased, harmony would emerge from some natural or spontaneous social dynamic. They are antigovernment, and at the same time intensely political. They are attracted to the exercise of authority and contemptuous of the passive, apathetic, and powerless. Very likely leaders see themselves as "an intellectual elite fully capable of governing America."[6] There is little indication of what the proper allocation of authority should be, however; whether it should lie principally with states, counties, or localities, or with self-organized townships of "sovereign individuals." Like any purely reactive political group, citizen militias pronounce grievances, exaggerate danger, mobilize resentment, and name enemies but offer no positive programs or institutional designs. Unlike counterrevolutionaries, they cannot point to tangible political institutions they would conserve or restore, though faithfulness to the U.S. Constitution, properly understood, is their claim to legitimacy.

Citizen militias are neither anarchists nor reactionaries, then. Nor are they fatally negative. A member of a white supremacist group interviewed by Rafael Ezekiel recited all the things that had been denied him, called liberalism "E-V-I-L," and concluded, "I want everybody to get what I got: Nothing."[7] In contrast and like true radicals, militia members are optimistic, not nihilistic. They attest to feelings of political mistrust but not to desperate powerlessness. These groups imagine that patriotic action can usher in liberty and the good life.

They claim to be true republicans, unwavering defenders of the Constitution and the Bill of Rights, which makes every American one of them. And, like secret societies and paramilitary groups generally, their significance lies in convergence with other groups and affinity with the public temper.

In this chapter I discuss "fusion republicanism," the phrase I use to refer to the amalgam of democratic ideology, potential militancy, and invocation of civic virtue. "Fusion republicanism" incorporates a wide spectrum of positions, from respectable democratic theory to radical ideologies promulgated by extremists. It is the harsh face of democratic discontent.

Bernard Bailyn describes how Americans' alarm about a conspiracy of the king's ministers was confirmed by similar judgments coming from other political quarters for entirely different political reasons. If the constitutional crisis that led to the Revolution had not been evident to the colonists, Bailyn argues, they would have discovered it from the flood of newspapers, pamphlets, and letters pouring in from opposition sources in England.[8] Similarly, militias cannot be handily dismissed as "paranoid fringe" if their alarm about overweening federal government is reinforced by a flood of similar assertions by groups that would never describe themselves as extremist: libertarians, associations within the conservative mainstream, groups on the democratic left who see big government inexorably constricting state and local authority and individual liberty. As of 1995, fifteen states had reaffirmed the Tenth Amendment and passed resolutions asserting state sovereignty and rejecting all but a narrow role for the federal government.[9]

This is where the democratic virtue of mistrust—fear of concentrated power and official indifference or abuse that is essential to self-protective self-government—becomes generalized and unsupportable, detached from specific grievances. The finding that Americans have declining trust in "people in general" is significant. It fuels "fusion republicanism" indirectly, insofar as it encourages people to believe that they must rely on themselves; self-defense becomes a literal prescription. But it pales in comparison with wholesale, routine mistrust of government.

"Fusion republicanism" is not a matter of agreement about which policies are oppressive. The point of agreement is that mistrust in government is warranted and that one or another policy—"takings" of private property, gun control, school curricula, or the national debt—is a sign of uncontrolled centralized power. The date of the Great Betrayal varies. 1913, the year the federal income tax (characterized as a form of "involuntary servitude" and, opponents note, the second plank of the Communist Manifesto) was declared constitutional, or the New Deal. The public policies and judicial decisions of the 1960s ("forced" busing and changes in the legal status of women) or some more recent expansion of the federal role. At each point it can truthfully be said that never before has government so directly affected the day-to-day lives of so many. Whether officials act on their own or as tools of the forces of "one world government," multinational corporatism, or liberal elites and secular humanists, the federal government is seen as an uncontrolled force. Each policy is represented as a step in a considered move to deny citizens the means of self-government and the moral capacity to reclaim it.

With difficulty, we can try to sort out when these views are the expressions of principled antifederalists or of true believers in some fantastic conspiracy, and when they are opportunistically exploited by politicians—the exaggerated poses of partisans charging one another with disregard for the common good. The ideological threads of "fusion republicanism" are even more confused and confusing. They include capitalist and anticapitalist proponents, and those indifferent to the distinction. Groups seem to cycle back and forth between antifederalism and quasi-libertarianism, libertarianism and stern republicanism. (One militia defines republicanism as "sovereign individualism"!) This strange, shifting stew is theoretically incoherent, but that does not appear to inhibit a common sense of democratic disempowerment or to disturb adherents' confidence in their common sense.

In fact, catchall generalizations serve. They create a continuum between militias and Ronald Reagan's promise to end "fifty years of failed federal programs" and to curb "bureaucratic cadres."[10] Ubiquity leaves room for innumerable grievances over substance and process. The constant in "fusion republicanism" is that the line between hostility to government and hostility to arbitrary and unjust government is blurred. So is the distinction between unresponsive authority and systematic abuse of authority.

There is another point of convergence along the spectrum of "fusion republicanism." When government is perceived as the source of our difficulties and violator of rights, people are thrown back on themselves. So "fusion republicanism" inclines to direct popular action. Judging from polls, mistrust in political institutions is diffuse, and both political competence and political agency are eroded by "sadness, depression, dysphoria of all kinds."[11] Mostly, Robert Lane's "joyless polity" produces apathy and disassociation. The distinctive response of "fusion republicanism," by contrast, is a demand for *enhanced* self-government.

It is as if the less citizens have to do with conventional political activity, and the less satisfying it is for those who remain minimally active, the more groups across the spectrum of "fusion republicanism" insist on strenuous forms of participation. They find the give and take of political negotiation and compromise anathema. They distrust representation and have little interest in mundane voter registration and party participation. They insist on direct popular influence and immediate official accountability: term limits, rotation in office, popular recall, referenda, instructions in preference to deliberation, and plebiscites over party identification. In 1996, there were ninety initiatives on ballots in twenty states on issues ranging from hunting rights to a ban on affirmative-action programs. Groups agitate for record numbers of constitutional amendments to override judicial and legislative decisions on substantive policy matters like a balanced federal budget.

Political negativity and a depressed political mood seem to require some electric participatory jolt, and citizen militias provide the sharpest shot in the arm. For members and their sympathizers, "extremism in the cause of liberty" is excusable. David Brion Davis observes, that discovery of a national conspiracy could counteract the corrosive effects of lethargy "by allowing the people to re-enact the primal drama of patriotism."[12]

Militias promise vivid displays of empowerment, with their symbolism of the gun. Like other paramilitary groups, some harbor ideologies of hate, separatism, and romantic militarism. The difference is that militias represent themselves as republicans first of all, self-styled Paul Reveres. Their business is to alert and demonstrate preparedness, and to resist when officials threaten our liberties, beginning with freedom of association. Appropriating the title "Minutemen" in this way is a historical pattern:

> It is hardly accidental that, in 1799, Fisher Ames called for a new generation of Minute Men to rise against the Jacobins, or that the same image was invoked by the anti-Masons, anti-abolitionists, and anti-Catholics. In the 1880's a secret group of New York City Minute Men plotted aginst the Papists. And of course in our own time the heart-stirring name has been appropriated by militant right-wing extremists.[13]

Militias represent themselves not as ordinary voluntary associations, then, but as embodiments of popular sovereignty. The titles "posse" and "militia" invoke defense of liberty and order by an authorized group of virtuous citizens operating within the bounds of law, an implicit response to statutes that tie these groups to terrorism and criminal disorder. "Militias," the term suggests, are in the best tradition of American political history. The propensity for direct popular action is in part a question of what sort of engagement is a corrective to feelings of democratic powerlessness and demoralization. In part, it is foundational.

Popular Sovereignty and "Common Sense"

Intellectual historians and political theorists continue to debate whether the ideological origins of American government were principally republican or liberal, and activists join the dispute in their hunt for historical authorities to add credence to their political preferences. The basic tension between the two ideologies is familiar. Republicanism emphasizes popular sovereignty, active political engagement, and civic virtue. Liberal constitutional democracy is defined by its countermajoritarian emphasis on individual rights and by the predominance of institutional constraints over personal virtue as a guarantee of liberty.

Republicanism's first principle is that "there necessarily exists, in every government, a power from which there is no appeal, and which, for that reason, may be termed supreme, absolute, and uncontrollable," and which can only rest legitimately with the people.[14] It sees the chief threat to liberty in the sinister interests of an entrenched elite, a "natural aristocracy," or political representatives who are at such a distance from constituents that they are unaccountable. Which is why republicanism tends to invest authority in small political units. For republicans, the guarantee of free government "is not balance but responsibility."[15]

For its part, liberal constitutionalism restrains government even when it accurately reflects the popular will. It sees the chief threat to liberty in majority tyranny:

> wherever the real power in a Government lies, there is the danger of oppression. In our Governments the real power lies in the majority of the community, and the invasion of private rights is *chiefly* to be apprehended, not from acts of Government contrary to the sense of its constituents, but from acts in which the Government is the mere instrument of the major number of the Constituents.[16]

Enumerating, delegating, and balancing power, liberal democracy binds not only government but also citizens' hands.

No American thinker embodies the republican side of the tension and all its unsettling tendencies better than Thomas Paine. When he argued against hereditary government and enslavement to the past he had in view not only the ancien regime but any sacred, unalterable political order. Paine took consent of the governed to heart. It was not something to be granted once and for all in some original social contract; every political obligation must have the people's ongoing assent. He never doubted that the people are superior to constitutions and are justified in changing them whenever and however they please. Paine applauded the U.S. Constitution principally because it incorporated provisions for its own alteration. He would not restrict popular resistance and constitutional change to the Lockean terms set out in the Declaration of Independence, either—the right of the people to alter or abolish regimes when they systematically abuse power. Changing circumstances and opinions are sufficient reasons to revolt. "The earth belongs to the living" presumes a willingness to undo everything. It translates into "a revolution in every generation." Nothing could be more radical: "Every age and generation must be as free to act for itself, *in all cases*, as the ages and generations which preceded it."[17]

At least one militia group called its publication *Common Sense*, aptly, since militias follow Paine in rejecting every authority but the Bible, and rely solely on the evidence of their own experience. Paine's seldom noticed account of American political identity may also be part of his appeal. The Israelites, not the English, he argued, had the original republican constitution (before they betrayed it by crowning kings), and Americans have assumed their divine mission. Paine pointed to *Christian* Europe as the parent country. And he was prone to conspiracism and demonizing: Britain was a cruel monster, a "hellish power" that "stirred up the Indians and the Negroes to destroy us."[18]

Like Paine, militias do not rue instability or share Publius's fear of "disturbing the public tranquillity by interesting too strongly the public passions."[19] Above all, in rhetorical imitation of Paine's great familial metaphor, they insist that "while some say that the right to keep and bear arms is granted to Americans by the Constitution, just the opposite is true. The Federal government itself is the child of the armed citizen. We the people are the parent of the child we call government."[20]

There is an enormous difference, however. Like other Enlightenment thinkers, Paine had confidence in education and moral perfectability. He did not doubt that common sense would discern common principles, or that revolutionary turmoil would be progressive. Mistrust of fellow citizens (and of virtually every institution assigned to educate them) poses a problem for common sense today. Communism and Roosevelt's "selling" of the New Deal proved, for these groups, the manipulability of democratic citizens, and militia members are neither utopian republicans nor sanguine populists.[21] Leaders point out that the American Revolutionaries' indignation was extraordinary. They echo Patrick Henry's grim caution: "Virtue will slumber. The wicked will be continually watching: Consequently you will be undone."[22]

Their scorn is pronounced: those who are not part of the conspiracy to undo America are dupes, passive consumers, vegetables. The temper of their pronouncements is outraged virtue. "Patriots" are distinguished from nominal democratic citizens by their vigilance and readiness to resist authorities that betray the popular will. Citizen militias are not without a strong dose of authoritarian vangardism. *They* are civic fundamentalists.[23]

Of course, skepticism about the intentions and capacities of citizens and mistrust of the unchecked inclinations of political representatives is precisely the motive force behind liberal constitutionalism, which *is* countermajoritarian. Even the amending power is hemmed in by supermajoritarian requirements.[24] The whole idea is to devise a means to protect a democratic people from reducing themselves to subjection. But liberal constitutionalism is also designed to be constructive. Federalism and the separation of powers aim at an effective division of political functions: "it is one of the greatest advantages of a government of different branches, that each branch may be conveniently made conformable to the nature of the business assigned to it."[25] "Fusion republicanism," in contrast, inclines to "negative constitutionalism." The aim is to disable government rather than energize and empower it, at least when it comes to a strong, activist federal government.

The constitutional theme on which "fusion republicanism" converges is antifederalism. Curbing the power of federal courts and agencies and restoring the prerogatives of state legislatures is on every agenda. Beyond that, specific proposals for structural and constitutional change are all over the map: from striking the enabling phrase "provide for the general welfare" to eliminating every amendment added after the Bill of Rights. One group wants to return to the Articles of Confederation, where the states controlled naturalization, loyalty oaths, and treason.

"Fusion republicanism" cannot be identified with a "new federalism" or states' rights simply, however. Plenary state power is no better than federal. The idea is to reduce the national government in favor of the states; the states in favor of localities. And for citizen militias, local authority must be subject to the surveillance of self-organized citizens—always keeping in mind the reserved rights of the people. The Bill of Rights is invoked to reassert states' power but also in exhortatory defense of political liberty, with a particular focus on the Second Amendment's presumptive guarantee of the right to arm and form citizen militias.

Striking at the heart of personal and political liberty is government regulation of guns, and defense of "the right to keep and bear arms" is the respectable public face of militias. It is also an example of "fusion republicanism." It is where the personal right to self-protection in the face of government's inability to "insure domestic tranquillity," republican concern to preserve the possibility of popular self-defense against oppressive authority, and a sort of "civic fundamentalism" come together.

Self-Defense and the Failings of Public Order

A recent estimate of the number of guns in the United States is 200 million, but as the Senate Judiciary Committee Report pointed out, both sides have an interest in overstating it: gun control advocates to illustrate the extent of the gun problem, anti-gun control forces to illustrate the number of citizens whose rights are infringed by regulation.[26]

The first federal gun control laws were a response to the introduction of the Thompson submachine gun by organized crime. Today there are thousands of regulations on the use of firearms, from the National Firearms Acts of 1934 and 1938 to the Brady Bill and recent Gun Control and Omnibus Crime Control Acts. A labyrinth of state and local ordinances prohibit concealed weapons or open carry, ban assemblage, impose permit requirements, waiting periods, and age restrictions, require licenses to carry handguns in a public place (which may be denied for failure to demonstrate a personal safety hazard or for lack of "good character and reputation"), and so on.

Generally, the public is willing to consider the social costs and benefits of regulating private ownership. People are concerned about the extent to which guns contribute to violent crime, to accidents, and to the risk that dangerous weapons will fall into the hands of children. There is widespread acceptance of some regulation as prudent. "Law-abiding people who are not afraid of criminal attack do not generally insist on a right to carry a gun."[27]

Opponents of gun control reject cost–benefit analysis out of hand. They treat the right to private arms as a natural right or common law claim. Or as a fundamental constitutional right, like speech. Like free speech civil libertarians, some gun advocates are willing to concede that the right is not unqualified, but the NRA describes the right to keep and bear arms as "the right most valued by free men" and an absolute bar to government restriction.[28] Indeed, there are advocates who present gun ownership as a moral obligation: it is our responsibility to defend our families from attack, and to refuse to actively protect oneself demonstrates contempt for God's gift of life.

The popular justification for owning guns, handguns in particular, is self-protection. Public opinion has it that the Second Amendment guarantees private ownership for individual purposes; that "keep" means to keep in one's home and "bear" means to carry it about. Pro-gun historians reinforce this view, arguing erroneously that in the absence of police, self-protection was one impetus behind the constitutional right to keep arms. This is wrong; the military sense of "keep and bear arms" is well established.[29] But if personal use does not stand up as constitutional interpretation, the political implications are clear. Popular willingness to accept a pragmatic approach to regulation is vulnerable to fear. Gun ownership is justified if people lack confidence in government's capacity to get effectively tough on crime—whether the reasons have to do with rules that coddle criminals, incompetent law enforcement, or the sheer dimension of lawlessness.

The case for grim self-protection is strengthened by stories about good citizens able to fend off criminals (or not-so-good citizens, like Bernhard Goetz, who described his pleasure in shooting four black teenagers on a New York subway in 1984). Strangers invade our homes. Rogue law enforcement officers assault us on the street. No place is safe:

> Social workers . . . are increasingly at risk, threatened or attacked when they visit their clients' homes. . . . Utility workers fear being attacked when they shut off someone's service because of unpaid bills. In Texas, a man repossessing a car for a finance company was shot and killed, no questions asked, by the would-be owner who received considerable support from his community. The district attorney was reluctant to indict, in the apparent belief that a man has a right to open fire on someone who ventures onto his property.[30]

In fact, fear bears no logical relation to the statistical probability of being a victim. The most vehement defenders of armed self-defense tend to reside in nonurban areas where the violent crime rate is low and the likelihood that they will fall victim to attack (particularly by hated blacks or Jews) miniscule. Nonetheless, to the extent that prohibition of the illegal use of guns is ineffective, the feeling that it is sensible for individuals to have weapons will probably grow stronger. The NRA actively prescribes self-defense over reliance on law enforcement, and campaigns to convince women to arm.

For young men and boys (and increasingly girls) in inner-city neighborhoods, fearfulness and the disproportionate burden of violent crime they bear is well documented. Government's failure to keep the peace and offer protection is measurable. "Far less striking disparities in the scale of public expenditures has provoked extensive litigation in many states . . . [and] ambitious lawsuits," according to one commentator, who proposes a strategy of civil suits to hold state governments liable for damages to victims and their families.[31] The NRA has a more immediate plan. It champions the right of tenants in public housing projects to keep guns.[32]

For those who can afford it, the alternative to self-help is private security modeled after the police. Since the establishment of Pinkertons in 1850, well-equipped security forces have multiplied: campus police, special patrol agencies for neighborhoods, armored car units, plant protection units, industrial guards, and security guards.[33] "Private police" must obtain licenses in most states, but otherwise they are unregulated and possess the same powers as ordinary citizens. That means permission (but no obligation) to restrain and arrest suspects in misdemeanor and felony cases, with no obligation to observe the usual constitutional safeguards. Uniformed private police look like public officers and carry guns, but they are not required to issue Miranda warnings for statements obtained during interrogation, and physical evidence they obtain illegally is admissible in criminal prosecutions.

Voluntary self-defense associations like the neighborhood watches discussed in chapter 4 have multiplied too. We have dramatic reports of organized citizens coming to the aid of others. The Guardian Angels are unarmed, but groups with guns like the Hasidic Jewish patrols in New York City act as samaritans, or as vigilantes to avenge crimes. Militia leaders propose that their associations could be used in the war on drugs and to defend people "in their homes and in their stores and their livelihoods" against Los Angeles rioters.[34]

So self-protection is linked to government failure and justifies associations for self-defense. More so when people are regular targets of assault by hostile groups. It should be obvious that different experiences with organized violence, and differences in victims' ability to rely on government for protection, explain attitudes toward private armies and collective self-defense. Part of the background of militias is the fact that aggressors are abetted by law enforcement or go unchecked because of official indifference. Along with a history of efforts to make the targets of violence more vulnerable by disarming them. In the United States, nativism, racism, and gun control have gone hand in hand.

Militias, Self-Defense, and Second-Class Citizenship

State statutes outlawing open carry of weapons and prohibiting ownership appeared frequently in the North starting in the 1880s, coinciding with immigration from eastern and southern Europe and the rise of labor unions. The history of private armies is inseparable from industrial strife. Strikes brought threats of violence by unionists against strikebreakers and their armed protectors, by private company armies hired to attack union organizers and strikers, and by the National Guard, which was allied with employers. Sheriffs were often stationed on company property and had their salaries paid by owners. In some instances, police swore in civilians as deputies and formed posses to deal with labor threats. They were called citizen militias, contributing to unwillingness, until recently, to refer to any group as a militia.[35] "Industrial war" is no misnomer. The assault by National Guardsmen on striking Ludlow miners and their families in 1914 has been appropriately called a massacre.

In 1886, Herman Presser paraded in Chicago on horseback leading a company of four-hundred men armed with rifles. He headed one of a number of private armed clubs, this one formed by German socialists. According to Lehr und Wehr Verein's corporate charter, the group was organized to

> improve the mental and bodily condition of its members, so as to qualify them for the duties of citizens of a republic. Its members shall therefore obtain . . . a knowledge

of our laws and political economy, and shall also be instructed in military and gymnastic exercises.[36]

Presser was convicted under the Illinois statute banning paramilitary groups from organizing, drilling, or parading without a license from the governor. As we saw in the previous chapter, the *Presser* court allowed that "it is within the police powers of the Legislature to regulate the bearing of arms so as to forbid such unauthorized drills and parades."[37] The court also validated using the "select militia," that is, the National Guard, to suppress labor unrest.

Nothing in the opinion, which found this "armed socialistic organization" to be an unlawful conspiracy, tells us that Presser's army was formed to protect workers and their families from assaults by police and the National Guard, and to defend against physical intimidation at the polls. Or that the motivation was workers' resolve "never again to be shot and beaten without resistance."[38] In the trials following the Haymarket riot, Lehr und Wehr Verein was sympathetically described as "an armed proletarian corps" formed after "the shooting down of peaceably inclined wage-workers by the bloodhounds of 'law and order.' "[39]

The history of private armies for self-protection is also inseparable from race. African Americans have been repeatedly subject to public and private violence: slavery, forcible preservation of Jim Crow, lynching, attacks by police, violent backlashes after the Second World War and in connection with voter registration drives and court-mandated desegregation, to say nothing of wanton attacks by white supremacists. Frederick Douglass insisted that fugitive slaves should have weapons to resist kidnapping: "When government fails to protect the just rights of any individual man," he rests on "his original right of self-defense," and slaves without arms would never attain freedom.[40] Ida Wells-Barnett, the black antilynching activist, wrote:

> I had been warned repeatedly by my own people that something would happen if I did not cease harping on the lynching. . . . I had bought a pistol the first thing . . . because I expected some cowardly retaliation from the lynchers. I felt that one had better die fighting against injustice than to die like a dog or a rat in a trap. I had already determined to sell my life as dearly as possible if attacked. I felt if I could take one lyncher with me, this would even up the score a little bit.[41]

For much of this history, private armies of white citizen patrols or the Ku Klux Klan met no resistance from blacks or local law enforcement.

In northern cities, too, whites attacked black churches, homes, and businesses: the Providence Snowtown Riot of 1831, where for four days a mob destroyed black homes, Cincinnati mobs in 1841, the bloody riots in Boston aimed at abolitionists and blacks. A historian of Philadelphia reports that the bombardment of the city during the 1831–33 period "pinpointed the Negro ghetto as a target for socially acceptable violence."[42] A black newspaper at the time of the draft riots and lynchings in New York City in 1863 wrote, "Most of the colored men in Brooklyn who remained in the city were armed daily for self-defense."[43]

It is no accident that armed self-defense was rare. Regulations to insure white supremacy included prohibitions on gun ownership by blacks. Before the Civil War, slaves were presumed to be under their masters' control so state laws restricting arms were directed at free blacks. Florida was one of the first states to create white citizen patrols to "enter into all negro houses and suspected places, and search for arms and other offensive or improper weapons," enforce pass systems, and generally insure quiescence.[44] The Supreme Court advised in *Dred Scott* (1856) that keeping and carrying arms was among the "privileges and immunities" that would be extended to black Americans if they were recognized as citizens.

After the Civil War a burst of restrictive laws, nearly all in former states of the Confederacy, prohibited blacks only from carrying firearms without a license.[45] Mississippi's 1865 statute was typical:

> That no freedman, free negro or mulatto, not in the military service of the United States government, and not licensed so to do by the board of police of his or her county, shall keep or carry fire-arms of any kind, or any ammunition, dirk or bowie knife, and on conviction thereof . . . shall be punished by fine . . . and all such arms or ammunition forfeited to the informer."[46]

The law included fines and prison terms for any white selling, lending, or giving weapons to blacks.

For supporters of African American citizenship, deprivation of the right was a badge of servitude, and debates over the Fourteenth Amendment raised the question of equal protection for the right to arm. Former counsel for the slaveowner in *Dred Scott*, Senator Johnson, among others, opposed the Fourteenth Amendment on these grounds. *United States v. Cruickshank*, the 1876 case that serves as precedent for the ruling that the Second Amendment constrained Congress but not the states from regulating arms, was a race case. The Federal Enforcement Act of 1870 had been designed to prevent whites from conspiring to deprive blacks of their constitutional rights, and Cruickshank along with two others were charged by federal officers with violating the right of two black men to peaceably assemble with guns. The Supreme Court ruled that the Fourteenth Amendment did not protect citizens against private action, forcing African Americans to look to state and local governments for security and to preserve their right to arm. This, in the context of violence by white paramilitary groups in Colfax, Louisiana, committed to ridding the country of "Black Devils." *Cruickshank* cleared the way for disarming blacks in the Jim Crow era, leaving them defenseless against white state militias that patrolled and disarmed them, and against paramilitary groups.[47]

The connection between gun control and race has been officially acknowledged. In 1941, the Florida supreme court refused to prohibit carrying pistols in the glove compartment of a car, explaining that the intent behind the state law of 1893 and its amendment in 1901 was "for the purpose of disarming the negro laborers . . . and to give the white citizens in sparsely settled areas a better feeling of security. The statute was never intended to be applied to the white population and in practice has never been so applied."[48]

With individual self-protection futile, blacks formed private militia groups to deter white violence, like the African Greys formed by free blacks in Providence, Rhode Island, in 1821.[49] These militia guarded jailed blacks at risk from mobs, and forestalled lynchings. When the civil rights movement adopted nonviolence, its adherents were vulnerable to attack, and African Americans formed armed groups to protect targets like Daisy Bates, leader of the Little Rock NAACP. The Deacons for Defense and Justice stood vigil for months outside the house of a black doctor trying to get access to a swimming pool for children in North Carolina in 1957.[50] A second Deacons for Defense organized in Louisiana in 1964 would grow to fifty or sixty chapters across the state. The militia protected James Farmer, head of the Congress of Racial Equality, on his visits South. One self-declared "liberal skeptic" on restricting handguns recalls:

> As a civil rights worker in a Southern State during the early 1960's I found that the possession of firearms for self-defense was almost universally endorsed by the black community, for it could not depend on police for protection from the KKK. The leading civil rights lawyer in the state . . . went nowhere without a revolver. . . . The black lawyer for whom I worked . . . attributed the relative quiescence of the Klan to the fact that the black community was heavily armed. Everyone remembered an incident several years before, in which the state's Klansmen attempted to break up a civil rights meeting and were routed by return gunfire.[51]

After northern ghetto riots in the 1960s resulted in massive searches and seizures for arms by National Guardsmen and police, the Program of Afro-American Unity reaffirmed the right to bear arms for self-defense against unpunished violence. Malcolm X invoked the Second Amendment:

> Negroes don't realize this, that they are within their constitutional rights to own a rifle, to own a shotgun. When the bigoted white supremasists [sic] realize that they are dealing with Negroes who are ready to give their lives in defense of life and property, then these bigoted whites will change their whole strategy and their whole attitude.

A radicalized Stokely Carmichael and SNCC declared that every black man needs a gun: "Responsibility for the use of violence by black men, whether in self-defense or initiated by them, lies with the white community."[52] Huey Newton drew on Robert Williams' description of the Deacons of Defense in his book *Negros with Guns*, and exploited a California law allowing loaded rifles to be carried so long as they were publicly displayed and pointed at no one.[53]

Not all black paramilitary groups can plausibly appeal to a desperate need for collective self-protection. The full name of the Black Panther Party for Self-Defense implies that blacks in cities like Oakland, California, faced the same conspiracy of white violence and official complicity as those in areas of the South. In fact, the Panthers had a revolutionary and sometimes criminal agenda; their guns had other uses besides self-protection. They spun a con- spiracist line: the Mulford Act (passed to prohibit the group from carrying loaded firearms in public places) "aimed at keeping the black people disarmed and powerless . . . brings the hour of doom one step nearer," and they com- pared racist police agencies terrorizing, brutalizing, and murdering black peo- ple to "the war of genocide in Vietnam."[54] Among urban blacks today, arming for self-protection has to do with intraracial violence.

Individual and collective self-protection are justifed by the perceived inade- quacy, indifference, or partiality of government, then. Fear accounts for popu- lar sentiment, often reluctant, in support of private arms and private armies. But it does not produce a principled republican defense of freedom to arm and form armed groups. And courts have consistently rejected attempts to read a personal right to own guns for self-protection into the Second Amendment. Self-defense has a place in law, but not in constitutional interpretation.

That is why advocates of a broad personal right to gun ownership tried turning to the Fifth Amendment's "takings clause." Defendants in *Village of Morton Grove*, a case involving a local ban on all handguns, argued that the blanket prohibition amounted to destruction of the use and enjoyment of a legitimate private property right "without just compensation." The Court re- jected the argument, observing that owners could sell their handguns outside the city or store them at licensed gun clubs. Even if this circuitous route to protecting the right to private arms had been successful, it would not have addressed "fusion republican" preoccupation with the Second Amendment right as a matter not of gun ownership simply, but of freedom of association and republicanism.

The Structural Second Amendment

Alone among constitutional debates, this one cannot rely on Supreme Court decisions; there are too few. Lower federal courts, state courts, and the bulk of scholarship are seldom taken as authoritative on constitutional issues. Still, they coalesce around a republican reading of the Second Amendment. In fact, there are two republican interpretations. On the first, the right to keep and bear arms is a structural defense of the federal balance. On the second, it is a guarantee of republicanism generally, ultimately of the possibility of popular resistance. Both readings give considerable weight to the amendment's preamble, which seems to set out its purpose: "a well regulated Militia, being necessary to the security of a free State."[55]

For political theorists, republicanism evokes Machiavelli's insistence that a city must rely on its "own arms." Or James Harrington's advice that, "men accustomed unto their arms and their liberties will never endure the yoke." Or Algernon Sidney's: "Swords were given to men, that none might be Slaves, but such as know not how to use them."[56] Machiavelli blamed the foreign conquest of Italy on neglect of the militia, and insisted that, unlike hirelings, citizens would stand their ground in defense of the city. (Indeed, Machiavelli saw republics as successfully imperial; citizen armies are more aggressive in every instance.)

A citizen militia stands in moral as well as practical contrast to a "mercenary" army. Courage in defense of liberty is a civic virtue, so participation is a means of character development. A "well-regulated militia" mandates regular training and discipline, further insurance of virtue. In the American context, Akhil Amar adds, the *local* character of the militia was critical to avoiding the moral failings of a standing army:

> men serving alongside their families, friends, neighbors, classmates, and fellow parishioners—in short, their community—would be constantly reminded of civil(ian)/(ized) norms of conduct. They were less likely to become uncivilized marauders or servile brutes. Thus, the transcendent constitutional principle of civilian control over the military would be beautifully internalized in the everyday mindset of each militiaman.[57]

Except for aversion toward professional soldiers, however, the militia guaranteed by the Constitution bears little resemblance to classical republican notions. Even the aversion to a professional army can be overstated. The Constitution provided for a standing army, in part to overcome the military weaknesses displayed by the militia during the Revolution and Confederation. Service as officers in the Continental Army was influential in shaping nation-builders like Washington and Madison.

The key difference from classic republicanism is the militia's purpose in the American context. On a structural view of the Constitution, the militia is part of the federalist compromise, an element of the *internal* system of political checks, not just national defense. Article I, Section 8 gives the federal government "power to provide for organizing, arming, and disciplining the militia," and gives state governments the power of "appointment of the officers, and the authority of training the militia according to the discipline prescribed by congress." This division of labor was designed to preserve the states' hand in militias financed by the central government and imbued with a centralized code of discipline. The concern was states' capacity to resist potential centralized tyranny, military tyranny specifically.[58]

Understanding the Second Amendment is more difficult. It denies the federal government authority to disarm state militias, but it is not obvious that this amounts to much of a change, except symbolically. (Though *any* addition would have gone some way to allay antifederalist disaffection, which was the point.) Later the amendment began to have practical consequences. When the Fourteenth Amendment was effectively emasculated, and cases like *Cruickshank* unleashed private white armies and state militias to terrorize blacks, Congress debated whether it could disband southern state militias. The proposal was voted down as a violation of the Second Amendment.[59]

In 1903, federal legislation folded state militias into the National Guard, which on some views makes the Second Amendment moot and has inspired proposals to rescind it. Historians disagree about whether today's National Guard is the counterpart of the eighteenth-century militia or of the paid semi-professionals called the "select militia." In any case, the Guard has been integrated into the U.S. Army and Air Force.[60] So from a structural standpoint, its decentralizing function and role in preserving the federal–state balance would be further undermined by rescission.

The contours of a structural interpretation are fairly clear. The Second Amendment constrains the national government and leaves states free to regulate the ownership and use of arms with a view to insuring public peace, safety, and order. (Though the *Presser* Court cautioned that since the militia was a reserve military force of the United States, which Article II permits the president to call on to execute laws and suppress insurrection, the Second Amendment also prohibits the states from regulating arms in such a way as to deprive the federal government of this resource.)[61] *United States v. Miller* (1939) and a preponderance of modern cases confirm the Second Amendment as a restriction on Congress only.[62] This structural approach sees the Second Amendment as a guarantee of state militias, and state militias as key to the federal balance.

Regulation of guns has become the symbolic focus of the politics of that balance in practice. Given the amendment's core political content, it seems to follow that private gun ownership is regulable if it does not contribute to "the preservation or efficiency of a well-regulated militia." An early case upheld a law prohibiting concealed weapons on grounds that regulating the manner of bearing arms is not disarmament. *Miller* ruled that in the absence of evidence to the contrary, a double-barrel 12-gauge shotgun with a barrel less than eighteen inches long was irrelevant to militia effectiveness, and could be regulated. The problem is that legislatures and courts have little to guide them in assessing whether a particular weapon has a "reasonable relation" to militia effectiveness.

Opinions run the gamut. On the one hand, opponents of gun control worry that the "reasonable relation" test might permit a ban on handguns. On the other hand, the army expects all soldiers to be proficient in grenade launchers, anti-tank weapons, fragmentation grenades, and antipersonnel mines (none of which are legally available to civilians). The "reasonable relation" test might have the perverse result of leaving only antiques regulable and permitting private ownership of heavy weapons.[63] In reality, it has not operated as a constraint; in 1976, *United States v. Warin* upheld the Gun Control Act of 1968 outlawing private ownership of a 9-millimeter prototype submachine gun.

Not all measures tend in one direction, however. Since the early 1970s, a rash of state constitutional conventions have added provisions to *enhance* security for private ownership, like the provision of the Illinois constitution stating that "subject only to the police power, the right of the individual citizen to keep and bear arms shall not be infringed." The "right of the individual citizen" is a notable addition; by explicitly enunciating an individual right of ownership, Illinois attempted to broaden the scope of the right, to give it a libertarian and nonmilitary cast, and to conditionally protect all private arms, including handguns.[64]

In 1981, a middle-class Chicago suburb enacted the first general ban on handguns, and *Quilici v. Village of Morton Grove* tested whether the ordinance conflicted with the revised Illinois constitution. Because the ordinance did not prohibit the possession of *all* firearms, the court found that it did not violate the constitution. The right to any particular weapon had to be explicitly balanced against the police power: villages have "an obvious interest not only in reducing premeditated crime within their boundaries but also in minimizing the effects of domestic violence or spontaneous quarrels." The court judged the handgun ban reasonable. (Provoking intensified opposition to gun control nationwide; in Kennesaw, Georgia, the city council passed an ordinance requiring every household to have a gun.)[65]

The dissent in *Morton Grove* applied the same standard of review to reach the opposite conclusion. An absence of evidence of handgun-related crimes or injuries in the village meant that the ordinance failed to meet the minimal test of a rational means to accomplish a proper purpose. The dissenters were also skeptical that the handgun ordinance had been passed to protect public safety rather than "for the sole purpose of publicizing a political viewpoint."[66] Their skepticism was plausible. Policy experts disagree about whether widespread gun ownership increases crime, about whether it deters criminal violence, and about whether it lessens the likelihood that victims will be injured or puts private citizens at greater risk. Overall, "debates about gun ownership and gun control are driven more by values and ideology than by pragmatism."[67]

The heart of the ideological debate is the "fusion republican" concern for the federal balance. We see it operating in this case, too: handgun owners tried to bring their challenge to the Illinois state courts, but Morton Grove succeeded in getting it before a federal judge. Eleven states filed amicus briefs objecting to having a federal court decide the meaning of the Illinois constitution.

These themes came together in 1995 in *United States v. Lopez*, a case determining which level of government appropriately criminalizes certain uses of arms. It arose in the wake of moves by Congress to federalize a wide range of crimes already covered by state laws: carjacking, drive-by shootings, gang violence, crimes by juveniles involving handguns, stalking, and spouse abuse. In 1990, Congress used its authority under the commerce clause to pass an act forbidding "any individual knowingly to possess a firearm" in a school zone. A student carrying a 38-caliber handgun to high school in San Antonio was originally arrested for violating the Texas Penal Code, but federal agents preempted the state and charged the teenager under federal law.

The dissent in *Lopez* saw the Gun-Free Act as a legitimate exercise of the commerce power that ought to have survived standard rational basis review. The cumulative effect of weapons on the quality of education could be said to make citizens less productive, the argument goes, and this has an adverse impact on interstate commerce and competitiveness in foreign commerce. But in a move that abandoned deferential review, reined in the federal government, and set a potentially crucial precedent, Chief Justice Rehnquist struck the law down as an improper use of the commerce power. The criminal statute has nothing to do with economic enterprise, he argued; the effect of guns in school zones on interstate commerce is indirect and remote at best. "Under the theories that the Government presents . . . it is difficult to perceive any limitation on federal power, even in areas such as criminal law enforcement or education where States historically have been sovereign."[68]

Justice Kennedy's concurrence struck the antifederal note even more sharply. He defined the Supreme Court's role as defender of the structural elements of the Constitution. The Court has derived workable standards to preserve separation of powers and checks and balances, Kennedy argued, but has been "tenuous" in preserving the federal balance. Among other things, "devolving too much authority to the remote central power" and blurring boundaries between state and federal authority on matters of education and crime result in a dangerous inability to hold government responsible. "Federalism serves to assign political responsibility, not to obscure it."[69]

Not all groups assign the Supreme Court sole responsibility for defending the structural balance or for protecting constitutional rights generally. For militia groups, political responsibility lies ultimately with the people. This makes the federal balance just one aspect of the Second Amendment debate. Another aspect is freedom of association in defense of constitutional liberties. With this, advocates shift the focus from organized state militias to self-organized citizen militias, direct expressions of popular sovereignty.

Citizen Militias

Historically, the militia comprised all (white male) citizens of the community—"the people." A "select militia" was considered by some to be hardly less dangerous than a standing army:

> Should one fifth or one eighth part of the men capable of bearing arms, be made a select militia . . . and all the others put upon a plan that will render them of no importance, the former will answer all the purposes of an army, while the latter will be defenceless.[70]

Rotating service was key, and Tocqueville drew a parallel between militias and juries—"a certain number of citizens chosen by lot and invested with a temporary commission."[71] The 1903 statute that merged state militia with the National Guard also established an "unorganized militia" of all men between the ages of eighteen and forty-five, a reserve pool of citizens subject to being called up for service.[72] *United States v. Miller* confirmed for modern law that the militia comprises all citizens capable of bearing arms.

This does not resolve the question whether the Second Amendment protects a collective "right of the people" called up as a militia under the authority of states, or an individual right. Republican arguments seem to be consistent with an individual right, though. It is a right held by individuals, but qua citizens rather than as a personal civil liberty. It is a peculiarly political right, guaranteed for the purpose of having an armed citizenry capable of comprising a militia in defense of liberty.

Advocates of a personal and broadly libertarian right to arms are reluctant to concede this point:

> Naturally, the virtues of an armed populace or general militia were stressed in terms of its political value for a free society, since the ratification process involved political issues. Nonetheless the right to have weapons for nonpolitical purposes, such as self-protection or hunting . . . appeared so obviously to be the heritage of free people as never to be questioned.[73]

Perhaps this accurately describes historical assumptions, but it is not compelling constitutional interpretation. "To see the Amendment as primarily concerned with an individual right to hunt, or protect one's home, is like viewing the heart of the speech and assembly clauses as the right of persons to meet to play bridge, or to have sex."[74] In keeping with a "preferred freedoms" reading of the First Amendment, the Second Amendment right is political not personal.

Why is interpreting the Second Amendment as protection for individual rights important, then? Because on this reading, the Constitution not only secures officially authorized and disciplined companies of "the people" under the jurisdiction of governors. It also protects self-selected and self-trained companies of citizens. It reinforces the idea that the check provided by the Second Amendment goes beyond offsetting a concentration of military power in the national government and buffering state-controlled militias from evisceration. An additional element (for citizen militias, the predominant element) is a citizenry capable of resisting authority at any level.

The Second Amendment is not only protection for state-run militias, on this view. Nor protection for citizens at large to arm for purposes of their own. Rather, it protects individuals, as members or potential recruits, to form or join citizen militias. These are misdescribed as individuals banded together, and correctly described as citizens banded together under the mantle of the Constitution for specific purposes. Members of self-styled citizen militias argue that it guarantees them the right to keep and bear arms.[75]

This grants militias a constitutional basis for association outside the First Amendment. Yet we recognize this republican reading of the Second Amendment as parallelling the First Amendment freedom of association. Citizen militias are voluntary associations, not established by authority. And like the speech and assembly clauses, the right is geared to political self-defense against oppressive authority. Together, these rights look beyond regular democratic electoral processes to the possibility of direct popular action, constitutional conventions, ultimately the possibility of Locke's "appeal to heaven." Which requires not just the right to keep and bear arms but also freedom of association for citizen militias. From this perspective, "words and guns . . . had resulted in a successful revolution, and it is not surprising that the founding generation thought highly of both."[76]

Constitutional scholar Sanford Levinson advances this republican reading of the Second Amendment as a guarantee of the conditions of popular resistance:

> It seems foolhardy to assume that the armed state will necessarily be benevolent, the American political tradition is, for good or ill, based in large measure on a healthy mistrust of the state . . . [I]t is hard for me to see how one can argue that circumstances have so changed as to make mass disarmament constitutionally unproblematic.[77]

Levinson does not address where the right resides, however, or what groups can reasonably claim to exercise it in practice. It is unclear, finally, whether he finds an individual right to arm for resistance but not a right to associate as a militia. Or a collective right that remains unassigned. He has not proposed that the Second Amendment protects self-styled citizen militias.

L. A. Powe goes a step farther. He represents the individual right to keep arms and the First Amendment right to speech as complementary checks on government, and allows that the "no prior restraint" rule for speech applies to gun ownership. But he is unwilling to extend this liberty to citizen militias:

"Military groups not under state control are *per se* dangerous and are not constitutionally protected."[78] At least not by the Second Amendment.

There are good reasons for reticence and confusion. Neither the Second Amendment nor the Constitution as a whole offers support for a (legal) right of resistance or revolution. There is no guidance in the Constitution for determining whether or when self-organized militias can be judged to exercise the right. It is sheer speculation whether the Constitution contains a further implied right to form voluntary paramilitary associations to train and prepare in *anticipation* of the need for resistance. In sum, recent, thoughtful interpretations leave us with a novel picture of constitutional checks and balances: a Second Amendment right to arm for resistance (but not necessarily to form citizen militias in advance) set against constitutional provisions empowering Congress to call out state militias to put down insurrections.

Of course, it is possible to argue that armed resistance against tyranny is justifiable and rooted in the American political tradition, and at the same time that the Second Amendment is designed exclusively to establish organized state militias to *prevent* insurrection. The right of revolution exists, Garry Wills concedes, "yet the right to *overthrow* government is not given by government. It arises when government no longer has any authority. One cannot say one rebels by right of that nonexistent authority."[79]

Testifying before the Senate Subcommittee on Militias, Normon Olson of the Michigan militia agrees:

> It makes no sense whatsoever to look to the Constitution of the United States or that of any state for *permission* to form a citizen militia since logically, the power to permit is also the power to deny. . . . [T]he Second Amendment is not the source of the right to form a militia nor to keep and bear arms. . . . The enumeration of those rights in the Constitution only underscores their natural occurrence and importance.[80]

If there is a natural right of revolution, which people can and do exercise, it is irrelevant whether that right is "constitutional." (Though some forms of resistance, like civil disobedience, have a special status in constitutional democracies, and not all acts of resistance are a Lockean state of war or return to a state of nature. This involves an extensive argument outside my present purpose.)

In any case, from a republican perspective arms and organization have purposes other than violent resistance. "A state facing a totally disarmed population is in a far better position, for good or for ill, to suppress popular demonstrations and uprisings than one that must calculate the possibilities of its soldiers and officials being injured or killed," Levinson insists.[81] Put extravagantly, as it was by a member of the U.S. House of Representatives: militia groups in a position to *threaten* government are a defining characteristic of democracy because "we have democracy when the government is afraid of the people."[82] Armed and organized citizens may be a deterrent to overweening government action in the first place. The threat of disorder can force government to compromise.[83] It can provoke political reassessment and shifts in policy.

The aims and rationales parallel civil disobedience perhaps more than revolution, particularly when civil disobedience aims at making the costs of enforcing hated or unjust public policy morally insurmountable.

Citizen Militias, Civic Virtue, and Political Identity

With this emphasis on political rights and popular sovereignty, it is not surprising that the strongest legal precedents for gun ownership as a personal, civil liberty rather than a guarantee of authorized militias comes from state court opinions granting the right to unnaturalized foreign-born residents. Or that the republican account of militias will be concerned with political identity and eligibility for citizenship.

From the early colonial period, Americans modified the English common law right to be armed by changing the way it was qualified. In England, it was restricted to Protestants "suitable to their condition": game laws regulated the kind and use of arms by the poor, the rights of religious dissenters were restricted, Irish and Scots were disarmed, American Indians were disarmed, and the British adopted increasingly stringent policies for the colonists, including home searches.

The need for posses and the irrelevance of game laws favored a broad prerogative of keeping arms in America. We have already seen that qualifications on the right to keep guns were based on race rather than class or religion. The same was true of militia service:

> An armed and universally deputized white population was necessary not only to ward off dangers from the armies of other European powers, but also to ward off attacks from the indigenous population. . . . [It] was also essential to maintain social control over blacks and Indians who toiled unwillingly as slaves and servants in English settlements.[84]

As Cottrol and Diamond review the history, a 1639 Virginia statute requiring that white men be armed at public expense neither specified nor prohibited black men from arming themselves. But by 1680, Virginia had prohibited black freemen and slaves from carrying arms, and other colonial militias exempted blacks or required them to perform substitute service on public works projects. The Uniform Militia Act, passed by Congress one year after the Second Amendment, was one of the earliest federal statutes to make a racial distinction. It called for enrollment in the militia of every free, able-bodied white male citizen between the ages of eighteen and forty-five.

To the extent that contemporary self-styled citizen militias are imbued with race-hate and anti-Semitism, subscribe to ascriptive notions of political identity and second-class citizenship, and impose these as criteria of admission, their claims to be republican defenders cannot be entertained—quite apart from their constitutional standing and the merits of their grievances.[85] Their "civic fundamentalism" is tainted as well as extravagant if it is a matter of "taking back our country" from *them*.

On the other hand, by itself the fact that citizen militias are self-appointed and draw "heavily from groups who feel unjustly disempowered by recent events—angry white males, conservative christians, rural residents"—or that militias recruit from "like-minded persons" does not automatically undermine their claim to arm and associate in defense of constitutional liberty, as some have argued.[86] Citizens are not equally vulnerable or vigilant.

A number of legal scholars propose that Second Amendment protection for citizen militias is conditional on people exhibiting "a high degree of civic virtue and homogeneity." Moral circumstances distinguish bona fide citizen militias from actual paramilitary groups, and "arming the populace is not the same as recreating a universal militia." A militia must have a "consensual epistemology" and "a consensual body of rules." The point is, "if we do not have a universal militia, then we do not have a right of revolution. And if we do not have a right to revolution, then we do not have a right to arms to make a revolution."[87] And, "defending our individual right to bear arms, will hardly transform us into such citizens."[88]

Naturally, militia groups reject the challenge from political morality. *They*, at least, are vigilant patriots, ready to sacrifice for the common good. They would agree with Garry Wills in assigning a purely military meaning to "keep and bear arms."[89] They are "well regulated." They train and demonstrate discipline.

Besides, conditions like homogeneity and civic virtue are singularly unhelpful in assessing the standing and claims of self-styled democratic defenders. "The people" is always a part, defined in contrast to the Crown or nobility, sinister or special interests. Disputes about designating some part as representative of a people rather than a faction, much less designating them virtuous, is a *cause* of resistance, after all. Only an ahistoric sensibility could imagine that contemporaries agree "as a body" on characterizing political action as legitimate revolution, violence by a group for its own selfish ends, or civil war. The American Revolution had its loyalists, holdouts, and pacifists. "Common sense" is a hope (and a brief against tutelary authority), not a test of political insight.

Whether resistance or preparation for it is justifiable or not cannot be settled by the group's composition or numbers.[90] Neither Lockean liberalism nor civic republicanism insists that a majority be victims of tyranny or prepared to fight for resistance to be legitimate, only that it be in the general interest. A self-styled militia becomes the voice of the people on the basis of its judgment, not membership simply.

We can imagine a set of propositions and steps for thinking about how a subset of people should act on a bona fide claim of tyranny with a view to winning over significant popular support. Studies of the American Revolution have traced the course for that rebellion.[91] Analyzing these steps is a project for political philosophy, too, particularly for discussions of civil disobedience, which requires novel and typically unlawful actions by self-appointed agents of justice.

Militias see themselves as alternately a vangard and a "saving remnant." They would have the adherence of a majority (who agree with them "at a gut level") if they were not forced by authorities to arm and train covertly. The current doctrine of "leaderless resistance" (the title of a manual written by Louis Beam) takes diffuse pockets of self-organized militia to the limit. It assigns responsibility to citizens to "know exactly what they are doing, and exactly how to do it," though it assures patriots that "newspapers, leaflets, computers, on-line services, and word of mouth will keep the true citizen soldier informed of events, allowing a planned response."[92] Leaderless resistance can be understood as a tactical response to the effective infiltration of militia groups by the FBI and other law enforcement agencies and their "top-down" assault on these associations. It responds directly to pragmatic dismissals of citizen militias as impotent.

Practical objections to reading the Second Amendment as protection for citizen militias are frequently said to be so strong as to quash the relevance of the constitutional right altogether. Roscoe Pound advised that "nothing in the Bill of Rights can or ought to be ignored, though some provisions, such as the right to bear arms have a much altered significance under the conditions of popular uprisings against oppression under the conditions of military operations today."[93] Militias do not concede the prudential argument any more than they do the moral one. Their response to the notion that resistance in an age of technologically sophisticated weapons is a wild fantasy is to train for urban guerrilla warfare and survivalism.

Whether or not citizen militias have a Second Amendment claim (I discussed the First Amendment argument in the previous chapter), they pretend to arm and organize in the common interest. What public good do they defend? The Montana Human Rights Network had an answer: "In Montana, apparently mainstream people are arguing that formation of a domestic army to fight the government is an appropriate response to the passage of federal legislation regarding gun control."[94] Gun control is the chief evidence of a larger anti-democratic scheme whose success depends on a disarmed populace. The idea is to "break our will to resist. . . . This is what gun control is all about."[95] Hence the widespread tendency to make martyrs and folk heroes (endorsed by jury nullification) out of those who resist a foreclosure sale, or stand up to an agent of the Agriculture Department, or vigilante Bernhard Goetz.

Citizen Militias and the Conspiracy to Disarm

For militias and other groups along the spectrum of "fusion republicanism," gun control is not just questionable anticrime policy or a violation of a constitutionally guaranteed right. Rather, legislative moves from imposing penalties for illegal weapons transactions and for the illegal use of guns to restricting their sale was the entering wedge. Subsequent regulations and bans on some weapons all tend in one direction, toward outlawing and confiscating arms. The conspiracist tenor of statements by NRA leaders and other mainstream groups is pronounced:

> A document secretly delivered to me reveals frightening evidence that the full-scale war to crush your gun rights has not only begun, but is well underway . . . not just to ban all handguns or all semi-automatics, but to eliminate private firearms ownership completely and forever.[96]

As we have seen, day-to-day political rhetoric is infused with conspiracism, and this particular conspiracy is no exception: "What were those British soldiers coming for my friends?" Patrick Buchanan asked during his 1996 presidential primary campaign. "They were coming for the arsenal at Concord. . . . [T]hey could impose their rule upon them, they could crush them. . . . That right ain't about shooting ducks. That right is about a man's right to defend his wife, his family, his freedom and his country."[97]

Fueling opposition and widening the spectrum of "fusion republicans" alert to oppression is the fact that gun control is accompanied by expanded police authority, and by measures that are arguably independent violations of civil liberty: random and unannounced searches, even warrantless searches without probable cause, home invasions, metal detectors in public places. The NRA and paramilitary leaders refer to Bureau of Tobacco and Firearms agents as stormtroopers kicking down doors. It was a computer programmer in Indiana, not a Michigan patriot, who said, "I feel it is more likely that I will be killed by an agent of the government than by a crook. It's gotten that bad."[98] Gun control and its enforcement brings in its wake "law enforcement excesses, discriminatory enforcement and police corruption, criminal profits, bureaucratic abuse, overloading courts and corrections . . . diversion of resources, and loss of respect for the law."[99]

Detached from conspiracism and allowing that law enforcement is predominantly fair and honest, these concerns cannot be dismissed. The Fourth

Amendment, not the Second, may be the most important protection for gun owners, including militia, today.

In 1988, the Chicago Housing Authority's "Operation Clean Sweep" was the first attempt by city government to run surprise warrantless searches of public housing projects. Sixty police and dozens of CHA employees cordoned off buildings and searched door to door for illegal drugs, guns, and residents. There is no more straightforward form of government intrusion. Political scientist and criminologist James Q. Wilson supported these raids as a defense of victims held hostage in their apartments. It is a fundamental duty of government to "insure domestic tranquillity," he explained, and the sweeps were part of an effort to provide the basic right of security to civilians living in a veritable "war zone." "We are not infringing on rights," the CHA director claimed. "We are restoring our residents' rights to a safe and decent environment."[100] Given this mission, we can understand why "civil libertarians who opposed the searches were likely to be labeled 'elitist' and accused of sacrificing the everyday safety of residents for more abstract concepts of Fourth Amendment law."[101]

Although many residents supported the searches as a necessary measure, not everyone acquiesced: "We aren't all hardened criminals. The law is not supposed to be just for the rich."[102] The ACLU filed a class action suit on behalf of the 150,000 or so residents of the projects, and according to the terms of the consent decree, police may only accompany CHA staff who must conduct the inspections and contents of homes not in plain view cannot be searched.

Do legal grounds exist for warrantless searches for guns? The "emergency" exception to the Fourth Amendment does not seem to apply here because there are no specific, exigent circumstances. The searches are explicitly discretionary. The "emergency" situation is, in fact, a chronic condition of unsafety. Problems with gangs, drugs, and crime are acute in Chicago housing projects, but the same rationale would permit warrantless searches for weapons in private homes in crime-ridden neighborhoods where residents are hostages to street violence.

Evolving law in this area seems to favor surprise warrantless searches. The Supreme Court has embraced an exception to the warrant requirement called "special government needs" in connection with the operation of schools, offices, prisons, and regulated industries. It allows government supervisors to conduct warrantless, work-related searches of employees' desks and offices without probable cause; school officials to conduct searches of some student property, also without probable cause; and sobriety tests at automobile check points.[103] Presumably the doctrine of "special governmental needs" could apply to the Chicago Housing Authority, which is "statutorily charged with maintaining and supervising a decent, safe, and sanitary public housing environment."[104]

Small wonder some paramilitary groups oppose capital punishment and lengthy prison terms; they see themselves as more likely to be victims of government's criminal laws than of crime. Victimization is not equivalent to innocence. But as Wendy Kaminer points out, it does imbue people with a sense of righteousness and garners sympathy from far-flung segments of the community.

> The recent 51 day siege and massacre of nearly one hundred men, women and children in Waco, Texas, was a crime of the greatest magnitude . . . a cruel, sadistic, brutal crime. It was a crime which violated nearly every article of the Bill of Rights. . . . It resembled the burning and obliteration of Christian cities and the annihilation of their inhabitants by Mogul hordes.[105]

Combined with deep antigovernment sentiment, it explains the transformation of noncompliants and vigilantes into heroes. Who is martyred and why depends on who you think presents the real clear and present danger. Which fear is greatest: ordinary crime? "domestic terrorism"? or seemingly unaccountable law enforcement agents of the state?

This divides African Americans who see government's "punitive" war on drugs and guns as "genocide" from those who see underenforcement of the criminal law in black communities as willful reluctance to protect black victims.[106] Not surprisingly, some blacks are ambivalent about the criminal justice system, and polls show them more inclined than whites both to fear crime and to oppose stiff mandatory sentencing and capital punishment.[107]

Who judges? Is there an appeal to "the people" besides the threat of armed resistance?

Legalistic Antilegalism

Preparation for armed resistance conforms to paramilitarists' limited taste and tolerance for regular political institutions and democratic processes. It is not the only course; a great deal of the life of militias involves "legalistic antilegalism." One form of direct action available close to home is the jury, with its irreversible power to acquit in disregard of the law.

Jury trial in criminal cases is mandated by Article III of the Constitution and juries are at the heart of the Bill of Rights: the Fifth Amendment safeguards the role of the grand jury; the Sixth, the criminal petit jury; and the Seventh, the civil jury. Before the "search and seizure clause" and the "probable cause" clause of the Fourth Amendment were collapsed, it was read to permit warrantless searches on the understanding that juries (rather than issuing magistrates) would assess their reasonableness.[108] The jury is the final judge of who is victim and victimizer, patriot and subversive. The double jeopardy rule prohibits appellate reversal of a jury's decision to acquit, regardless of its reasons. Nullification is a shield against overzealous prosecutors, corrupt judges, and oppressive laws.

Historical examples of nullification cut in all directions: Boston juries' refusal to convict under the Fugitive Slave Law as well as all-white juries that routinely refused to convict whites charged with violating the civil rights of blacks, effectively undoing Reconstruction statutes. Jury nullification was successfully used by opponents of the Vietnam War prosecuted in the 1960s, and was unsuccessfully urged by Operation Rescue defendants more recently. Leaders of Aryan Nation and other white supremacist groups were tried for sedition in 1988 and acquitted by a sympathetic jury, though here as in most cases it is uncertain whether the government case was simply improbable or nullification was at work, or both.[109]

Political theorists typically stress the jury's educative function:

> it teaches men to practice equity; every man learns to judge his neighbor as he would himself be judged. . . . *It may be regarded as a gratuitous public school*, ever open, in which every juror learns his rights, enters into daily communication with the most learned and enlightened members of the upper classes, and becomes practically acquainted with the laws.[110]

But jury duty has always been more than a tutorial. It is a direct exercise of democratic will. *A Maryland Farmer* argued that the jury trial is more important than representation in the legislature because "those usurpations, which silently undermine the spirit of liberty, under the sanction of law, are more dangerous than direct and open legislative attacks."[111] For Tocqueville, "the jury system as it is understood in America appears to me to be as direct and extreme a consequence of the sovereignty of the people as universal suffrage."[112] Trial by jury is a constitutionally explicit, structural aspect of republicanism as well as an individual right and guarantee of a fair trial to the accused.

So once again, debates about qualifications for jury service and the composition of juries revolve around questions of political identity first-class citizenship, and civic virtue. "The conscience of the community," the jury is a popular body. Like the militia, panelists are ordinary citizens, and the composition of juries has been continuously disputed, chiefly for their exclusion of women and minorities. Four of the ten points of the Black Panther program concerned police and prison. No. 9 demanded that

> all black people when brought to court . . . be tried by a jury of their peer group from the black communities, as defined by the Constitution of the United States . . . a person from a similar economic, social, religious, geographical, environmental, his-

torical, and racial background. . . . We have been and are being tried by all-white juries that have no understanding of the "average reasoning man" of the black community.[113]

The issue is not just the right of the accused to a fair trial. The jury has always performed a legitimizing function as well: assurance that the justice system prevents arbitrariness and abuse.

The complex relation between a representative jury and an impartial jury is at a pitch when juries engage in nullification. The issue in jury nullification is not whether the crime alleged was committed. Normally defendants admit to evading taxes, shooting at law enforcement officers, or trespassing on the grounds of abortion clinics. Rather, the issue is whether in a particular case the penalty attached is extreme and warrants merciful acquittal. Or whether the law itself is unconstitutional, or unjust in light of some "higher law" so that the jury refuses to enforce it by refusing to punish violators. In 1895, the Supreme Court rejected the right of criminal juries to judge the law (though it conceded that in practice the results of jury nullification could not be set aside). Today, judges in forty-eight states tell juries that their duty is to determine the facts and to apply the law as it is explained to them, whether they think it legitimate or not.[114] But this restraint on the democratic function of juries is not always effective, and some constitutional scholars have advocated instructions to juries from the bench on nullification and the right of lawyers to argue unconstitutionality as a defense. In 1990, the "Fully Informed Jury Association" was founded to lobby for laws bolstering nullification. Its members mirror the messy mix of "fusion republican" and democratic discontent: "NRA members, antilogging environmentalists, advocates for the legalization of marijuana, tax protesters, and bikers opposed to mandatory helmet laws."[115]

Clearly, when juries act as minilegislatures, authority is returned to local arenas, giving effect to bias and parochialism and handing power to local associations. Intimidation, not only a sense of justice, accounts for jury nullification. (Tocqueville gives an account of the state militia's refusal to protect an unpopular newspaper editor, and the jury's subsequent decision to acquit his murderers.)[116] Nullification invites violation of due process, undermining the legalistic virtues of predictability and uniformity. Plainly, no judicial system could function if it made "every jury, impanelled in every court in the United States . . . the rightful and final judge of the existence, construction, and effect of every law."[117]

For militia groups, that is the point. Jury nullification should not be restricted to rare instances when conscience and law conflict because acquittal seems like an act of mercy or a specific law is deemed unjust. It is a program of resistance. After all, it is in the courts that hateful tax and bankruptcy laws and "unconstitutional" weapons laws are enforced. Patriots should be eager to serve, and insist not only on legally mandated trial by jury but also on trial by jury in any case where "principles" are involved, including IRS audits.[118]

Moreover, since not all citizens are patriots, militias do not look to the jury for democratic deliberation. They would prefer a rule requiring jurors to cast secret ballots rather than retiring to consult. They advise sympathizers to hang the jury by themselves, if necessary. And it follows from their conspiratorial view of authority that virtuous citizens should dissemble about their knowledge of jury nullification:

> You must not let the judge or prosecutor know that you are an informed American who now has clout. You will need a blank face and go along with the whole process because these judges and prosecutors are government employees and they don't want anyone on the jury who can't be manipulated.[119]

The grounds proposed for jury nullification by African Americans are similarly radical. Jurors should consider the evidence in light of a criminal justice system that is discriminatory against blacks, the argument goes. Not only enforcement of criminal laws but the laws themselves are unjust, and not just isolated laws like mandatory punishment for drug crimes that have a disparate impact on blacks, or gun laws, but criminal laws generally: and even laws of property that "protect the status quo." Where estimates are that between one-third and two-thirds of black men aged eighteen to thirty-five are under some form of state supervision—jail, probation, parole, or awaiting trial—the description police state has seemed apt.

Today, racially based jury nullification by African Americans is documented in some jurisdictions, and one legal scholar has offered "a principled framework" for these acts in practice. Paul Butler proposes the principle that "the black community is better off when some nonviolent lawbreakers remain in the community rather than go to prison" and that "the decision as to what kind of conduct by African-Americans ought to be punished is better made by African-Americans themselves, based on the costs and benefits to their community, than by the traditional criminal justice process, which is controlled by white lawmakers and white law enforcers."[120]

The parallel to militias' insistence on the communal rationale for nullification continues if we consider the proposition that black jurors who engage in nullification "might be morally obligated to participate in black self-help programs," including community enforcement of norms against antisocial conduct, like the Nation of Islam guards that patrol public housing projects.[121] An advocate of jury nullification urges that information about it should be publicly disseminated in church, through rap music, newspapers and magazines, and so on.[122] (He also argues that it is morally justifiable for prospective black jurors to commit perjury about their racial sympathies and likelihood of nullification during voir dire, to avoid being challenged: "as an African-American . . . it is difficult for me to encourage my people to relinquish the greatest power they have against the tyranny of the majority.")[123]

Clear and Present Danger: Reprise

We can see, then, the reasons for disagreement about the right to arm and to associate in self-styled militias. The constitutional standing of militia groups, the legitimacy of their grievances, and their freedom to prepare for resistance in defense of rights and interests are part of a more profound problem. That is, assessing whether a group can be reasonably interpreted as political at all, much less whether its actions are justified. The categorical First Amendment issue I discussed in the previous chapter—whether paramilitary groups are predominantly political associations, their activities predominantly expressive? or constitutionally unprotected but justifiable and presumptively lawful? or criminals bent on their own selfish or wantonly destructive ends? is a variant of this larger problem. To speak of "Timothy McVeigh's rebellion" or the Unabomber's "Luddite dissent" is to declare at the outset that their acts were intended and are appropriately interpreted as political "terrorism" rather then mass or serial murder on the order of the "Mad Bomber" in New York City in the 1950s. It preempts sober attempts to understand the character and significance of these acts, and to explore the ideological orientations that guide our interpretations of them.

Obstacles to understanding are created in part by conspiracist habits of mind and constant, exaggerated mutual accusations of tyranny and terrorism. Militias justify their organization and arms with conspiracist pronouncements of crisis; the forces arrayed against them, official and unofficial, do the same. Conspiracism sees clear and present danger everywhere. This habit of mind is sufficiently widespread to color public discussion generally. Disregard for evidence, failure to discriminate among cases, and inability to bear ambiguity are marks of conspiracist thinking, whose chief cognitive feature is the conviction that someone is 'in control.'

Again, retreat from political analysis is endemic. Despite laudable motives, advocacy groups like the Anti-Defamation League fuel it by characterizing all paramilitary associations as "paranoid" and "domestic terrorists." In the same spirit, absent a criminal conspiracy of hate groups to burn black churches, Jesse Jackson conjures up a "cultural conspiracy" linking arsonists in "white sheets" with Supreme Court Justices "in black robes" and politicians "in blue suits."[124]

When conspiracism does not hold sway, it is hard enough to think soberly about whether resistance or disorder can be traced to political frustration or economic hardship, or whether a grievance is merely cosmetic or rhetorical.[125]

Are urban riots errant undirected chaos, sheer "unreason"? Or opportunistic occasions for looting? Or spontaneous political uprisings? No champion of racial justice, the NRA embraced rioters in Los Angeles in 1992 as comrades in arms, who "kept police out of their neighborhoods for several days."[126] (This is as fanciful as the gang of football thugs, who, after overturning cars and breaking store windows during an international match in Turin, declared: "We did it. We took the city.")[127] Only if urban rioting is interpreted as politically inspired and/or politically corrigible do questions of justification and efficacy (and whether there are appropriate official responses besides punishment) arise.

The same holds for jury nullification as an exercise of "black power." If crime by blacks is "a symptom of internalized white supremacy" or "a reasonable response to the racial and economic subordination every African-American faces every day"; if stealing cars for joyrides is social protest; or if antisocial conduct generally (or nonviolent crime specifically) is "resistance to one particularly destructive instrument of white supremacy—American criminal justice," then conflicting interpretations of punishment and nullification will proliferate. Admirers of African American lawbreakers will associate them with "race-war guerrillas": "There is . . . no other overtly political alternative that constitutes as provocative, creative, crass, hard-nosed, and daring an assault on the status quo as does the culture of young black male criminals."[128] Crime will generate pride and admiration in some quarters: "We can't help but feel some satisfaction seeing a brother, a black man, get over on these people, on these people, on their system. . . . We know they represent rebellion—what little is left in us." At least, black jurors will get the message that they "should not send another black man to prison."[129]

If it is easier to absorb the Catholic priest Richard John Neuhaus's claim that "it is not hyperbole to say that we are at a point at which millions of conscientious American citizens are reflecting upon whether this is a legitimate regime," that is because "reflecting" is not a call to arms.[130]

Are militias paramilitary Paul Reveres, terrorists, self-serving tax evaders, or entrepreneurs engaged in illegal gun trading for profit? Are actions calculated to provoke authorities into reacting with force the behavior of a few paranoid nuts? Or is this civil disobedience gone awry?

President Clinton was adamant that militias are not just criminals but crazy domestic terrorists: "There is nothing patriotic about hating your government, or pretending you can hate government and love your country. How dare you suggest that we in the freest nation on earth live in tyranny."[131] This is powerful rhetoric, but both parts of the proposition would meet disagreement from "fusion republican" groups, with some justice. It *is* possible to love your country and hate its government. And even the freest nation on earth may not be free enough, and may be in the grip of officials duping an unwitting people.

Discussion and understanding come to a dead stop unless we consider specific associations, with specific grievances, engaged in specific activities, and the ideologies that cause us to cast them in divergent ways.

Covert militia are few people's image of a republican uprising. It is hard to accept armed members of remote religious enclaves as Minutemen, or isolated standoffs against Treasury agents and farmers defending their property from foreclosure as contemporary equivalents of Shays Rebellion. The broad spectrum of "fusion republicanism" helps sustain militia members' sense of their rightness and provides some credence for their grievances against federal power, on Second Amendment issues and the right of association in particular. But despite constitutional arguments and "legalistic" strategies, their political theory consists mainly of "conspiracy."[132] Sadly, since fantastic accounts of abuse of power are not alien to American political thought, conspiracism may be the most credible aspect of militias, and make their claims more rather than less accessible.

The point I raised in the previous chapter about linkage and political responsibility applies here as well. "Fusion republicanism" denotes a spectrum of positions, potentially mutually reinforcing. The comforting assumption is that fringe groups are responsible for the climate of hostility that makes a general tenor of antigovernment hate conceivable. But precisely the opposite relation holds as well: extremists and "civic fundamentalists" are the beneficiaries of a diffuse climate of hostility and mistrust and of widespread agitation for direct action to correct the sense of disempowerment. They exploit democratic discontent, but do not create it.

Besides willful blindness, thinking through the relation between political rhetoric and the actions of self-styled citizen militia groups is hampered by a deficit of understanding. We have little insight into the relation among wild ideas, ideology, and republican political philosophy, because neither a detailed history of ideas nor a sociology of knowledge, crucial here, has been applied to "fusion republicanism."

Ultimately, it is impossible to identify self-styled citizen militias with republicanism, less because they are private armies with no good claim to be representative than because of the barrier erected by militias' own chronic mistrust of their fellow citizens and all officials. Above all, there is militiamen's abject denial that government officials are also "private citizens." "Revealed in the broad light of an Oklahoma day, the companionable virtues gave the lie to the caricature of demonic government. . . . At the time of the explosion the 'pagan tyrants' supposedly feeding on the substance of an enslaved citizenry had been paying farm subsidies, arranging student loans, looking after children."[133]

9

Identity Groups and Voluntary Association: Filling in the Empty Politics of Recognition

Latent Voices

Celebrations of diversity are a recurrent part of American life and thought, as familiar as aversion toward alien differences. Delight in diversity is not a constant; ethnic and cultural pluralism as an ideal has ebbed and flowed along with competing ideals: the melting pot, "Americanism" as identification with a set of beliefs and values, and of course Anglo-Saxon racism.[1] But during identifiable periods, "Roycean provinces, Bourne's ethnic groups, DuBois's races, and Odum's regions" were endowed with the ability to redeem America, or, less spectacularly, to provide cultural resources that add pleasure and value to people's lives.[2] No rhetoric is more common than moral and aesthetic affirmation of the American "mosaic." It generates sympathy for resistance to cultural hegemony and counters to cultural vacuity: the "insipidity," "flabbiness," and "tasteless, colorless fluid of uniformity" Randolph Bourne abhorred.[3]

In *Roberts v. Jaycees* we caught the whisper of an argument for constitutional protection for ethnic and cultural groups that affirm and transmit differences. Recall the point in the majority opinion where Justice Brennan created the category "intrinsic association." It comes linked to "intimate association," that is, to "deep attachments and commitments to the necessarily few other individuals with whom one shares not only a special community of thoughts, experience, and beliefs but also distinctively personal aspects of one's life":

> without precisely identifying every consideration that may underlie this type of constitutional protection, we have noted that certain kinds of personal bonds have played a critical role in the culture and traditions of the Nation by cultivating and transmitting shared ideals and beliefs; they thereby foster diversity and act as critical buffers between the individual and the power of the State.[4]

Brennan brings together the classic liberal view of pluralist centers of power as bulwarks against government with the intimate ties of families, and both of these with associations fostering cultural diversity. The amalgam casts a sort of spell, which we will see reiterated. The personal bonds and emotional connection of "intimate association" spill over onto "intrinsic associations" based on ancestry, tradition, and the company of others who share a "way of life."

"Intrinsic association" has not caught on as a legal category, but it is clear enough why the Jaycees unequivocally fell outside the proposed parameters: "The Jaycees is not the type of association central to the communitarian ethic, and the admission of women to that organization will not significantly diminish cultural richness and pluralism."[5]

A particular conception of cultural identity and of the associations that transmit it is at work here. Early on, I referred half facetiously to "our multiculturalism" in order to draw attention to associations based on a coherent system of secular values, practices, and organization—corporate culture, for example, or the distinctive cultural forms developed by some gay men and lesbians, the evolving mores of the aging that comprise a way of life in retirement communities, or "support" and "recovery" groups.

These deserve at least the designation "subcultures." The intensity with which people identify themselves as ex-addicts or survivors of sexual abuse, for example, rivals ethnic identity, and the ideology of self-help provides a standpoint from which people judge everything from their own relationships to candidates for public office. Voters' identification with Marion Barry, when he ran for reelection as mayor of Washington, D.C., after a stint in jail for cocaine possession, is a prominent case of casting personal weakness and recovery as representative. Barry, one commentator remarked, "seems to see 'people in recovery' as a constituency," and he connected effectively to all those who have "been there and back, just like so many folks."[6]

My point is that Justice Brennan is solicitous of "custom" when it is combined with "tradition," not cultural pluralism. He also categorizes associations that transmit "shared ideals and beliefs" as nonpolitical. Cultural groups aim at fostering and maintaining their members' heritage at home and in designated social and charitable arenas, on the model of religion. The category "intrinsic association" is allied with intimate relations in the family and juxtaposed to "expressive association."

We know, however, that associations organized around ethnicity, race, or culture may take up a political cause or spin off an advocacy group: promoting the provision of public services in their language or public funding for museums or social agencies, seeking exemptions from dress codes in schools or the military, or public celebrations of their holidays, agitating for immigration reform or for the presence of their leaders on local committees and boards. I have emphasized the unanticipated emergence of political voices from the day-to-day activities of groups formed for other purposes and motivated to public expression by reasons peculiar to their ongoing activities, by the impetus of particular members, or in response to external contingencies. This dynamic is as true for "intrinsic" type associations as other groups. Cultural affirmation straddles the divide between apolitical celebration of distinctiveness and participation in the normal political give and take of interest group pluralism.

We may be tempted to think of freedom of association for ethnic, racial, cultural groups—particularly if they are expressive—as a precursor to the contemporary "politics of recognition." The politics of recognition sets itself apart from voluntary association and political pluralism, however, in its declared purposes, in the measures prescribed, and in the justifications it offers. Contrastive strategies are also employed to distinguish the goals of "recognition" from the standard aims of antidiscrimination law and policy.

The "politics of recognition" is the name political theorists have given to "an emancipatory politics that affirms group difference," and to the demand by minority groups for "recognition of their identity, and accommodation of their cultural differences."[7] Its current outlines were anticipated in Isaiah Berlin's famous discussion of the search for status in "Two Concepts of Liberty." Lack of "proper recognition" inclines people to seek to avoid being "ignored, or patronized, or despised, or being taken too much for granted—in short, not being treated as an individual, having my uniqueness insufficiently recognized . . . and what is true of the individual is true of groups." It can lead, Berlin observed, to Mill's "pagan self-assertion" in a collectivized form.[8]

The notable thing for my purposes is that the politics of recognition reverses the dynamic by which voices emerge from the normal activities of voluntary associations. The identity group is synonymous with "culture" or "community," and "culture" or "community" exists on the basis of objective characteristics such as ancestry, language, or history; some notion of "primordial affinities"; or an inventory of specific beliefs and practices thought to comprise a distinctive "way of life."[9] These have nothing to do with concrete voluntary associations with regular membership practices. Moreover, the relevant "culture" may not be adequately represented by advocacy groups or other voluntary associations that register members' interests and opinions. Whether because they are silenced or disorganized for reasons having to do with lack of resources or leadership, these groups often lack associations. The racial, cultural, or ethnic group's members are unaffiliated and may even be isolated, except vicariously or ascriptively.

Nonetheless, unity and coherence are attributed to groups—more aptly, populations. The assumption is that a latent voice is "there." If groups *did have* a presence in social and political forums, the argument goes, their representatives would express characteristic opinions or "perspectives" on matters of public concern. Where Justice O'Connor saw the formation of an association as the creation of a voice, here, the formation of an association makes an antecedent, inchoate voice manifest.

Proponents of "recognition" are not content to wait for the spontaneous creation of voluntary associations and attempts to gain a presence in social and political arenas by the usual means. Self-appointed spokespersons invoke the group—"virtual" representatives, in the absence of associations that make representation conceivable much less democratically accountable. Or, peculiarly empathic public officials pick up and interpret latent voices. Judges "perhaps enjoy a situational advantage over the people at large in listening for voices from the margins," Frank Michelman has suggested; they can bring "to legal-doctrinal presence the hitherto absent voices of emergently self-conscious social groups."[10] But this falls short of authentic expressivism. So official "recognition" in the form of public subsidy and support, and institutional reforms guaranteeing presence, are often deemed necessary to stimulate and structure authoritative group voices.

Although the politics of recognition is typically discussed detached from any consideration of voluntary associations, it is a vital part of my subject. My interest in whether we legally enforce congruence with the public norms of liberal democracy, or should, or whether we should secure freedom for the internal life of associations stems from their power to affect the moral disposition of members. The politics of recognition speaks directly to the theme of the moral uses of pluralism. In fact, it ratchets up the claim that "membership" shapes character. Groups are said to be constitutive in the deepest sense. They mold nothing less than members' identity tout court. Charles Taylor has explored "the supposed links between recognition and identity, where this latter term designates something like a person's understanding of who they are, of their fundamental defining characteristics as a human being."[11] Recognition and the programs of reform it entails are justified by assertions about the dependence of personal identity on membership.

Only here, the moral uses of membership have nothing to do with the fact that individuals cooperate in associational life. Unlike homeowners' associations, churches, or militias, no actual association imposes its authority and terms of participation on willing members. Cultures and communities claim people as their own, positing a nexus between ascriptive membership and message. It is not only that there is no joining. Or that the significance of belonging is taken for granted, regardless of whether or not an individual avows affiliation or is subjectively identified with the group. Beyond that, "members" need not be involved in ethnic, cultural, or race-based associations at all. I refer in what follows to the "politics of recognition" in general, knowing that there are variations in both theory and practical prescriptions. Still, they share this fundamental feature: they refer to groups, cultures, and communities as undifferentiated entities, quite apart from the concrete voluntary associations in which their members act together and from which voices emerge.

The politics of recognition is part of my subject, too, because it advances a new understanding of the obligations of liberal democracy vis-à-vis ethnic, cultural, or racial groups. The idea is that public institutions have failed "to recognize or respect the particular cultural identities of citizens." It is a long way from orthodox rationales for supporting and including social groups with definable interests or disadvantages as a matter of procedural fairness or social justice, to the thought that liberal democracy is responsible not only for insuring opportunities for representation in public institutions but also for the group's collective survival and flourishing. "Liberal democratic states are obligated to help disadvantaged groups preserve their culture against intrusions by majoritarian or 'mass' culture," the argument goes.[12] It is farther still to the idea that recognition is a condition for members' stable personal identity and self-respect.

The politics of recognition departs from standard celebratory rationales for fostering ethnic, racial, and cultural pluralism in another respect. "The heart of the great cry for recognition on the part of both individuals and groups is a bitter longing for status," Berlin explains.[13] Not surprisingly, groups may look on their status as just one piece in the American mosaic as anathema. They may settle for "recognition" only because they cannot enjoy predominance. Demands for recognition can be desperate, and exclusively on behalf of one's own group, especially if the motivation is protracted experience of fear and violence. But desperation is no prerequisite for casting a group as not only "different" but exemplary. Or for disregarding other groups and the pluralist "mosaic," and casting the wider society as homogeneous and uniformly imperialist. In short, nothing in the politics of recognition promises that a group sees itself as one among a plurality, acknowledging that the conditions for other groups to flourish are special to *them*. Much less assumes the more onerous task of affording recognition to other groups on *their* terms. In short, recognition, which may amount to deference to a group's vision of itself, is not necessarily reciprocal. The politics of recognition looks for public acknowledgment of the group's singularity and its unique public standing.

The Politics of Recognition and Personal Identity

The politics of recognition, with its claims for public assistance and exemptions, rights and representation, draws its force from the distinctive moral use cultural groups are said to have for members.

Nothing less than "the self" is at stake, and the term "identity group" is useful shorthand for the heightened pitch at which the argument proceeds. The phrase also captures a movement of thought that often goes unremarked. That is, the shift back and forth between some objectively determinable element of *identity* ascribed to individuals as a way of characterizing them for certain purposes to *identification*, a specific psychological state of emotional attachment, personal commitment, and motivation. The relation between the two needs explaining, since nothing in the objective markers of identity dictates whether we have a conception of ourselves as dedicated to *our* history, *our* culture, *our* identity.[14] Or warrants us in thinking that members of a group are actually so inclined.

K. Anthony Appiah makes the point:

> There is . . . a set of theoretically committed criteria for ascription, not all of which are held by everybody, and which may not be consistent with one another even in the ascriptions of a single person; and there is then a process of identification in which the label shapes the intentional acts of (some of) those who fall under it.[15]

"If we did not have identifications, that is, commitments, it would not matter so much that we have the quasi objective identities we have," Russell Hardin advises.[16] Michael Walzer alludes to the distinction, albeit cryptically. "It is entirely possible to inherit a life and still possess it as one's own," he writes. The words are elusive but the tightrope Walzer gingerly walks is plain. Cultural groups transmit not only a "way of life" but a life.[17] Identity and identification are fused in the notion that one can "inherit a life." At the same time, "possess it as one's own" disentangles them. It invokes individual autonomy. There is the hint of self-distancing: possessions, including inheritances, are alienable.

The concept of a constitutive group or culture or community, which brings together identity and identification, has made huge inroads in contemporary political theory, including liberal democratic thought. The idea is not simply that "we all come from somewhere" and that to *some* extent we make decisions within the range of options provided by specific cultural contexts. This is true by definition. Everyone has access to *culture*, after all, even in transitional societies and in the extremis of war. We speak without irony of a "culture of alienation." The question is, why should ethnic or cultural identity be predominant in individual lives and prescriptive in liberal democratic politics? (Particularly if we separate out race, which is typically physically inescapable and, in the United States, socially and legally salient and a trigger for differential treatment.)

The politics of recognition advances the additional claim that there is a profound human need to belong to *a* culture that can only be served by a culture of *one's own*: "it is in the interest of every person to be fully integrated into a cultural group."[18] Why? Because it gives meaning to life:

> Only through being socialized in a culture can one tap the options that give life a meaning. By and large, one's cultural membership determines the horizon of one's opportunities, of what one may become, or (if one is older) what one might have been. . . . [F]or most people, membership is a major determinant of their sense of who they are; it contributes to what we have come to call their sense of identity.[19]

However culture is conveyed—and surprisingly little attention is paid to family practices or specific mediating associations—it provides the materials closest to hand for conceiving the world and courses of action. Language in particular, and the people with whom we regularly speak, is a large part of how we come to know anything at all. Our culture supplies the initial tools of cognitive judgment and confers "the primary pigment of individual identity on the persons it comprehends."[20]

The politics of recognition goes on to say that "the horizon of one's opportunities" created by one's own culture are uniquely meaningful. Sometimes unwittingly but more often with intent, proponents shift from group membership as an initial source of meaning in the epistemological sense to ongoing meaningfulness. Cultures instill in members their ideas of goodness and value, evil and worthlessness. It follows that self-distancing, transition from one context to another, appropriating and piecing together disparate elements of cultural pluralism are all epistemologically difficult, perhaps impossible. Indeed, this difficulty seems to *define* cultural identity:

> The core options that give meaning to our lives . . . are open only to those who master them, but their complexity and the density of their details defy explicit learning or comprehensive articulation. They are available only to those who have or can acquire practical knowledge of them . . . embodied in social practices and transmitted by habituation.[21]

The moral stakes are ratcheted up yet another notch by a final psychological claim: personal dignity and self-respect are bound up with the esteem in which the group is held by others, particularly members of the presumptively unified, dominant culture. Identity is mediated by recognition.[22] The spread of the idea that a person's understanding of who he or she is is formed by recognition means, as Charles Taylor has explained, that "misrecognition has now graduated to the rank of a harm that can be hardheadedly enumerated along with" (not reducible to) inequality, exploitation, and injustice.[23]

Demands for legal and political "recognition" flow from this moral psychology. Liberal democracy should assist in stabilizing minority cultures or communities that confer identity on their members; protect them from the forces that tempt members away; exercise self-restraint in mandating internal changes in accord with public norms; impose checks on external economic and political forces pressuring groups to integrate in the wider society. The operative measures go beyond antidiscrimination policy such as equal protection, affirmative action, and the mandatory social changes aimed at putting an end to stigma. They also go beyond normal assurance of opportunities for political participation.[24] In particular, political recognition often entails guaranteed presence—whether proportional, equal, or threshold—in the public arenas where decisions are made.

Of course, even if the constitutive claims of the politics of recognition were valid, and if reforms could secure cultures and satisfy the longing for recognition, there are reasons to resist the conclusion that liberal democracy should take the recommended steps. Critics are rightly disturbed by proposals of public affirmation and support for incongruent groups whose beliefs and practices restrict members' civil and political liberties, curtail internal division and dissent, and inhibit voluntary association even among their own.

Radical incongruence has driven advocates to concede the need to condition public recognition of groups, above all when they are effectively antiliberal because they enjoy a measure of self-government. But where the goal is maximum possible accommodation, concessions are minimal. Charles Taylor points to habeus corpus as his example of "fundamental liberties that should never be infringed." Writing from within a liberal theory of the self and committed to a framework of liberal democracy, Will Kymlicka harbors a "liberal expectancy" with regard to minority national communities. Meanwhile, though, he explicitly supports intervention in the "societal cultures" of indigenous North American tribes only when they are guilty of "gross and systematic violation of human rights, such as slavery or genocide or mass torture and expulsions."[25] This ground has been well covered. My concern here is the solicitude for identity underlying accommodation.

"Collective identities have a tendency . . . to 'go imperial,'" Appiah observes, and the important point is that proponents of recognition appear to have no regrets.[26] Few positively applaud efforts to hinder individuals from electing to disassociate from groups, to marginalize and shame them, make them invisible, or publicly brand them as traitors. On the other hand, nothing in the psychology of the politics of recognition acknowledges reasons for wanting to escape ascriptive connections that are presumptively, "irrepressibly me." They do not acknowledge the innumerable reasons, including the simplest requirements of personal happiness, to make ethnic or cultural or racial identity less central to our lives. Or the reasons to fight against our habitual inclinations to demonstrate solidarity and rise to symbolic tests of loyalty, when exhibitions of identification go against our better judgment. There is not a glimmer of the thought that alienation may have morally constructive functions.

Rather, proponents of the politics of recognition seem to wish identification with the group on others, and to encourage the thought that that is all members can have. Because of external labeling, but also because subjective membership is inalienable. The plain thrust is to give priority to moral affirmation and material assistance to the cultural group over members' freedom to shift involvements. "Political society is not neutral between those who value remaining true to the culture of our ancestors and those who might want to cut loose in the name of some individual goal of self-development," Taylor clarifies. In sharp contrast to antidiscrimination policy, the aim is to "maintain and cherish distinctness, not just now but forever. After all, if we're concerned with identity, then what is more legitimate than one's aspiration that it never be lost?"[27] Groups are not to be viewed or treated as voluntary associations.

Throughout, I have highlighted the positive moral uses of incongruent associations that do not conform (and do not wish to conform) to liberal democratic norms. They may cultivate virtues, even if not peculiarly liberal or democratic ones, still, moral dispositions that are appreciated in liberal democracy. They may contain vices, allowing them relatively safe expression. Where the conditions for shifting involvements exist, membership may compensate for a deficit of social experience in other areas. But I have defended this freedom for *voluntary associations*, where membership is willing, not ascriptive. I have argued for freedom of association, not mandatory legal recognition or strategic use of public resources. And I have tried to suggest that the alternative to association may be anomie, which inhibits forming and exercising moral dispositions of every kind.

A similar suggestion undergirds the politics of recognition. Generally, its thrust is less affirmative (that *this* particular group's way of life is valuable and warrants public preservation) than negative. Without recognition and support for "their" culture, individuals are liable to spiral down into disorganization and personal chaos. Which is why people are said not only to have a (group) identity but also to require "the safety of effortless secure belonging," that is, a stable environment and unchallenged, undisturbed identification.[28]

Cultural Identity and Personal Chaos

This assumption about the moral uses of cultural group membership is grandiose. In the context of accommodation of religious groups I pointed out that "viability" was not used as a sociological term of art but as a sort of moral challenge, to justify accommodation. Here too, some minimal attempt at differentiation is in order: the survival of a community from weakened institutions; transitions in structures and values from the adoption and exploitation of resources made available by other groups (some of which, in a pluralist society, are likely also be one's own); declining numbers of willing members— these are independent conditions.

Moreover, the relation between changes in a cultural group's institutions and beliefs and the moral grounding of individuals is complex. We cannot assume they move in tandem. It is a sleight of hand to shift from descriptions of large-scale historic processes—weakening, transition, gradual or forcible assimilation—to assertions about their significance at any moment for men and women personally and individually. Both "stable and secure culture" and "assimilation" are abstractions with regard to cultural groups. They do not always capture social processes. They correspond even less to personal experience.

Assumptions about the fragility of personal identity are therefore overblown as well. For individuals, too, there is a difference between repudiation of membership on the one hand and self-distancing from a specific mark or test of solidarity, which is variable in degree and across dimensions on the other.

Neither one is synonymous with "assimilation"—which draws an unsupportably sharp divide between particular group identity and allegiance and a presumptively homogeneous, undifferentiated social self. And none of these alternatives is equivalent to anomie.

Nevertheless, the suggestion is that cultural or communal dictates are either experienced as categorical imperatives or religious commands or they are not genuinely experienced at all. And that the alternative is to be without resources, haplessly cognitively and morally adrift. The weakening of what are taken to be traditional group norms and structures (even if they are actually recent creations) so that they are less "rich and secure" is not the same as living in a moral vacuum, however, and pluralism with all its tensions is not the same as social dislocation, moral chaos, or personal, psychological disorder. Certainly, when talking about the development of moral dispositions within a stable liberal society like the United States, it is important to preserve the distinction between the range of options provided by a fragmented pluralist environment and the conditions that give rise to fearful anomie.

Consider some of the points where generalizations about identity and identification go wrong. At the most mundane psychological level, pointing to cultural group membership as the source of whatever meaning members' lives have is extravagant. The objects with which we identify may have little to do with giving life meaning in a moral sense. And those who step back from the brink of suicide tell us that their reasons for wanting to live range from pets to visitations by a personal angel. The minutiae of personal experience and temperament, the wildly varied resources individuals have immediately at hand all suggest the aridity of representing a "culture" as the source of value in anyone's life. Unless we resort to the reductive logic that since every object and belief that makes a person want to get up in the morning is a cultural construction, and that adherence to it is an expression of cultural identity.

More important, identification with a cultural group is perfectly compatible with an acute sense of meaninglessness. If well-being is (or is believed to be) conditioned by ascriptive membership, and if members regularly endure hunger, disease, violence, personal insecurity, unemployment, family breakdown, sleep deprivation brought on by a genuinely anarchic environment, and so on, they may be emotionally spent. If self-styled "communities" cannot help provide minimally hopeful futures for their members, the probable result is apathy, depression, and self-loathing. Walzer paraphrases Edmund Burke: "If people are to love their country, their country must be lovely." The thought applies to identity groups as well as nations, and points in opposite directions: to postmodernist perspectivism and the rejection of aesthetic canons, but also, as Walzer intends, to the need for minimal standards of loveliness.[29]

Kymlicka rightly insists that "societal cultures" should have freedom to change their characters. Individuals are not irrevocably identified with a particular way of life either, certainly not in the United States. This is not to say that they should be held collectively or individually responsible for failing to alter practices that re-create desperation and despair. But it does invite us to recharacterize the failure. How should we think about groups which, lacking organizations that provide for or effectively advocate minimal well-being, nevertheless want to segregate themselves, rail against "assimilation" by their children, and continue the cycle of impoverishment and hopelessness? Are they irrationally devoid of normal self-protection and concern for their descendants? Or hobbled by an incapacity to revise their ideas and exploit other paths? Constrained by externally imposed obstacles to change? Or caught up in an ideology of resistance? In any case, it is a distortion to describe this as self-affirmation and cultural self-preservation.

From inside, from the standpoint of members, comparisons are inevitable. "Misrecognition" is not the only or principal impediment to self-respect. The individual ashamed of his or her ascriptive affiliation, justifiably or not, is a staple of novels and confessional memoirs. I have argued that membership in voluntary associations fosters self-respect, as a result of cooperation and experiencing appreciation for one's contributions to the association's goals. *Voluntary associations*, perhaps especially when they are based on race or culture and are intentionally geared to self-affirmation, help buffer members against the harms of exclusion, misrecognition, and deprivation. They are sources of comfort and solidarity. But undifferentiated "culture" or "community" is simply unintelligible as self-protection.

And "recognition" is a doubtful corrective for people identified with a group that has difficulty sustaining rudimentary institutions, including a fluid array of voluntary associations. Or with a group whose collective self-definition is largely in terms of discrimination and disadvantage. For them, public "recognition" of the group and avowals of worth can seem like hypocritical patronizing. Insuring the essentials of economic well-being will make members materially better off. But why should we imagine that support is perceived as "recognition," or that it enhances individual self-respect? Or that resources necessarily sustain a particular culture or community, especially if it is unclear that members share a distinctive common culture of beliefs, values, and practices that they do not share with others?

The principal difficulty with both the fact of a presumptively weakened culture and its presumed significance for members' identification with it is abstractness. Insofar as personal identity is mediated through ethnic or cultural belonging, belonging is mediated through concrete associations. Inattention to voluntary associations is a significant cause of the vacuity of the politics of recognition. Despite boasted solicitude for "difference" and "identity," the politics of recognition violates the elementary lessons of the moral uses of pluralism. It fails to orient us toward the variability of actual associations and the vicissitudes of personal development. Consider briefly the two steps that move the politics of recognition *away from* the considerations that make sense of the moral uses of pluralism.

The first step is to transfer individuality from persons to the group. "If we value autonomy," Walzer writes, "we will want individual men and women to have their own lives," and the same argument holds for "the people/nation."[30] This step is facilitated by a disembodied view of groups. Concrete associations reveal a group's internal diversity. Through their activities and alliances, associations indicate greater and lesser degrees of affinity and integration with "outside" groups, giving the lie to the grand contrastive strategy of posing a unique cultural or racial identity against a homogeneous wider society.

Then, in a second step away from the moral uses of pluralism, individualism is further subverted by categorical claims about the constitutive effects of membership on personal identity and self-respect. (Thus replicating the error of racism or sexism, though the motives are benign.) Cultures do not imprint their objective characteristics uniformly; even if they did we would still expect variability in members' *identification*.

How we come to have group identity makes all the difference. Borrowing terms favored by some theorists of recognition, the "dialogical" character by which we define our identity must refer to dialogue with "significant others" in specific contexts to be instructive. For example, parental anxieties and interpretations of culture have as much to do with the substantive content of identity and the quality of identification in particular instances as the group's objective well-being or its status.

Erik Erikson illustrates the power of family narratives and feelings with the story of a young Jewish boy whose parents moved to a perfectly congenial Gentile neighborhood: "he was a Jew, a matter by no means solely or even primarily brought to his attention by the neighbors; for his own parents had persistently indicated that a little Jew had to be especially good in order not to be especially bad."[31] Contrast this with the Jewish baseball player who "felt generally smiled upon in life, a feeling not uncommon in a natural athlete." Contrast both with the self-defensive disposition of "black Jews" in the South, despised even by co-religionists, who firmly believed it was possible to be altogether "too Jewish."[32]

Depending on our objectives, disregard for the dynamics of identity and identification need not be a failing; political theory can plausibly carry on without it. The power of philosophical arguments about the self is unaffected by an absence of psychological or sociological realism, for example. And it may be sober political pragmatism under certain circumstances to follow the dictate that "recent history suggests that *to some extent* national identities must be taken as givens."[33] Generalizations are the basis of arguments for group rights based on rectifying historical injustice, other strong distributive claims, changing the composition of political elites, or realistic calculations of what sort of power-sharing is required for political stability. In multinational societies, people from minority national groups "will only share an allegiance to the larger polity if they see it as the context within which their national identity is nurtured, rather than subordinated," Kymlicka observes.[34]

Although the United States has national minority groups (Native Americans, Puerto Ricans, and native Hawaiians), they are exceptions. In Kymlicka's useful terms, the United States is a polyethnic multicultural society. Ethnic, racial, and cultural groups here do not have homelands. They are neither separatists nor advocates of consociational or group-based federal arrangements, and only rarely do they agitate for self-government in areas such as property rights or family law.

As a generalization about political strategy it may make sense to say that the politics of recognition is anti-assimilationist. But when it comes to accounts of *personal* identity and the moral uses of membership, disregard for the dynamics of membership produces misleading conclusions. "Identification," "assimilation," and "anomie" do not exhaust the possibilities. Walzer concedes that there is an alternative to "inheriting a life." As he puts it, it is "to find a life, literally light upon it, with no forethought at all."[35] He appears to view the inheritor as the more fortunate. This leaves the vast field between these thoughtless extremes unexplored.

Micro and Macro "Ethnic Options"

The range becomes clearer if we consider that the politics of recognition flies in the face of a number of important observations about ethnic and cultural identity in the United States.

For one thing, there is the phenomenon Mary Waters has called "ethnic options." For white ethnics, the predominant experience is neither assimilation nor the preservation of traditional communities or practices. Rather, there is a generational pattern:

> To make it in this country required transitions of such difficulty that people often sacrificed their entire lives so that their children would feel at home. Only when the work was done—the language mastered, the parochialism put aside, the passage assured—could they, or their children, then afford the token gestures toward their origins that passes for ethnic consciousness in America.[36]

"Token gestures" is disparaging and often inaccurate. "Vestigial" is misleading, too, if we think that "the ethnic group in American society became not a survival from the age of mass immigration but a new social form."[37] The point is, white ethnic identity is frequently symbolic and elective.

Elective, because identification with one's ethnic or cultural ancestry—or with one idiosyncratically selected thread of mixed ancestry, which is commonplace—is voluntary. It is an option, despite the rhetoric of group belonging and the fact that individuals may *believe* their identity is ascriptive, or an inheritance. Intermarriage is well documented. So are the reasons, often serendipitous, why individuals identify themselves with one or another of their parents' or grandparents' background. (We also know that ethnic identification waxes and wanes over the life cycle.)

When over half of those from "European-origin" groups marry outside the group, the ethnic identification of descendants—the ancestry and elements of culture they feel they possess—is bound to be elective in some sense. Intermarriage by Asians runs 30 percent or more, and similar figures hold for Hispanics. People with a tiny fraction of Native American ancestry call themselves American Indian.[38] The revival of white ethnicity in the 1970s led to the addition of the ancestry question to the U.S. census. Now, people of mixed races, ancestry, and ethnicity insist that the census form provide them with a separate box to check, too. The multiplication of official options in response to popular demands has done nothing to stem the confusion. Nathan Glazer reports Americans' understandable incomprehension when asked to differentiate race from ancestry from religion (Jewish does not count as ancestry) from national origin.

Group identity is symbolic as well as elective because typically the ethnic option does not affect individuals' choice of partner, friends, residence, or chances of success. Belonging corresponds to the personal desire for status and feeling special, interesting, or elite rather than just "plain vanilla American."[39] What is the *moral* significance, if any, of designating oneself "1/32 Cherokee"?

In this crucial respect, white ethnicity and culture in the United States diverges from race, or what Appiah carefully calls "racial identity." "It is because ascription of racial identities . . . is based on more than intentional identification that there can be a gap between what a person ascriptively is and the racial identity he performs," which allows people to "pass."[40] Because ascriptive identity is normally inescapable for African Americans, identification remains strong as well, perpetuated by discrimination, residential segregation, and obstacles to intermarriage. "Race in America means blacks"; and black is more a matter of the social meaning attributed to biological variations in skin color than ancestry.[41]

Alex Haley is the African American writer who traced his family history back to the African slave trade in the highly publicized novel and television show *Roots*. It has been pointed out that if Haley had carried out the genealogical inquiry on his father's side, he would have experienced his great moment of self-knowledge in Ireland, not Gambia.[42] Of course, Haley's dark skin determines that he will be automatically identified as African American by both whites and blacks. He is inhibited from electing to accentuate his Irish ancestry.

The "ethnic option" affords Americans an imagined community. The process of identification frequently occurs in actual isolation from a wider ethnic group or community, much less membership in specific associations. That is why Americans are prone to erroneously characterize their own family's idiosyncratic rituals and behavior as "Jewish" or "Irish." "One can have a strong sense of identity without a specific idea of that identity meaning anything."[43]

The macro challenge to the politics of recognition, and to the dichotomy between identification and assimilation that is part of its moral apparatus, is the fact that in America ethnic and cultural identity is preserved, adopted, and altered within a *system* of cultural pluralism. Groups insist on their uniqueness while exhibiting similar, recognizable patterns of cultural affirmation. Symbols of defiance are transferred from group to group. Even the content of ethnic and cultural "difference" overlaps. Leaders may insist that their culture is "real, historical, orthodox, organic, faithful, uncorrupted, pure, and enduring." But "the same ethnic qualities seemed to exist divorced from whatever ethnic label one happened to attach to them."[44] Sociologists find that "a variety of different ethnic groups all claimed to be special because they placed particular importance on patriotism, the family, and education."[45] In short, Americans often assume what amounts to general ethnic identities.

(A similar observation has been made about the signature marks of black youth culture:

> Black American culture is always already in the public domain where it is ripe to be ripped off by anyone paying attention. Adherence to black cultural modes and mores cannot be used as a sign of solidarity or as a mark of economic authenticity or group origin [like a Kosher designation]. . . . It is impossible to exclude whites from black cultural production.)[46]

Werner Sollors describes the assertion of difference itself as peculiarly American. The tendency to represent groups as marginalized is part of a characteristic process of ethnic and cultural group affirmation. Self-exoticization as "different" and juxtaposing one's group to an allegedly homogeneous culture are common strategies available to everyone. There is a common political vocabulary of debased public standing, marginality and exclusion, and distrust of governing elites. Logically, of course, minority status applies to everyone. So members of self-styled identity groups are "insulted, wounded, hurt, offended, bypassed, not invited, ignored, left out, and shunted aside." Each group "evaluates their treatment through the lens of pride, dignity, honour, propriety, legitimacy, and recognition."[47]

In this connection, historians propose that heightened, politicized race-consciousness in the 1960s gave renewed legitimacy to ethnicity, in particular to the notion of "unmeltable ethnics." The wave of ethnic revival was "directly influenced by the black civil rights movement and strengthened by its radicalization."[48] There is disagreement whether this was a "racist response" to black power or part of an effort to reduce racial tension by pointing up the diversity of groups in order to dilute the harsh division between white and black. The American Jewish Committee's National Project on Ethnic America was designated a "depolarization project."[49]

"Casting oneself as an outsider may in fact be considered a dominant cultural trait," Sollors concludes.[50] Small wonder getting the "multiracial" designation on official documents became a political cause; thousands gathered on the Mall in Washington in a display of pride, power, and unity under the banner of the "Multiracial Solidarity March."[51] It is no surprise that when "privileged groups" cease to "ignore their own specificity" and recognize that they had been "parad[ing] their norms as universal or neutral," they are more apt to see themselves as a beleaguered minority than oppressors. Iris Young optimistically anticipated that relativizing the "dominant culture" and "contextualizing it" leads to rueful recognition of past domination. In fact, the common reaction is solidarity and vigorous self-protection.[52] Male Jaycees reflexively presented themselves as a minority embattled by a hostile public, and compared their organization to the NAACP and NOW.

The prominence of ethnic options and overlapping cultural content of groups does not mean that navigating the disparate elements of a multicultural environment is always easy, or that it is universal. Legal categorization is sometimes critical for the distribution of rights and benefits. Who counts as a Cherokee or Mashpee Indian has produced endless court cases and a cottage industry of articles. Tribes themselves are divided over who belongs, their positions dictated by political strategy as well as anthropology; nothing is as elusive as cultural authenticity.

Deflating the psychological claims made by advocates of the politics of recognition is not to deny the strong account of identity and identification that holds for some members of self-removed groups like the Amish or Lubavitchers, tribal members residing on reservations, and minorities condemned to a ghetto "culture of segregation." Simply, when they fail to hold their members, as they often do, it is a mistake to automatically portray disassociation as assimilation or anomie.

This was Figgis's point when he wrote that "the notion of isolated individuality is the shadow of a dream":

> You are not merely John Doe ... but as John may probably be a member of the Christian church by baptism, a Doe by family, and Englishman by [nationality]. . . .
> In addition to this you are a member of a school, an alumnus of a college, a sharer in this club . . . and so forth. All these groups and unions have their effect, and limit and develop your life, make you do, or refrain from doing, what otherwise you would not,

and in so far prevent you being a free and untrammelled citizen of the state. More than that, they penetrate your imagination and your thought, and alter not only what you do but what you want to do. Between all these groups there will be relations.[53]

Multiple involvements also "prevent you being a free and untrammelled" member of an identity group. Figgis's portrait of personal pluralism is more common than one of untrammeled identification with an identity group, but it does not always obtain, either. I have not deflated the psychological claims of the politics of recognition in order to suggest that everyone is identified with more than one formative association, or with any. The moral uses of pluralism are not always exploited.

The principal point is that an overblown and undynamic account of identity constituted by membership is an insecure basis for the politics of recognition.

The Politics of Presence versus the Politics of Interest

The politics of recognition is often motivated by compassion for sufferers of discrimination and exclusion. It is tender toward the self-understanding of victims, and obeys the admonition that "the voices of the victims must always be heard first . . . to attend to their interpretations of the situation."[54]

A lot can be said for providing public occasions for victims to tell what happened to them, and to acknowledge suffering and injustice. (We could be more inventive in creating forums less banal than confessional television talk shows.) International "Truth Commissions" serve this function. But the "recognition" they afford has little to do with affirming sufferers of injury, individually or as a group, or with appreciation for "differences." It is simply to say that they really have been wronged. And it undercuts the power of oppressors, which comes in part from their ability to convince their victims that they are invisible, and that no one will ever know.

The politics of recognition is not principally about witnessing and documenting, acknowledging fury and resentment, or giving charges of "misrecognition" a hearing, in any case. Perhaps the most important item in the catalogue of measures that count as recognition is the idea of institutionalizing group voices. The idea is that designated identity groups should have public standing in "all arenas of potentially transformative dialogue," in "all the institutions of collective life."[55] That means reforming both public venues and an ambitious range of semipublic/semiprivate "spaces." Notoriously indefinite, "public spaces" can refer to any forum in which matters of public interest are discussed, including virtually any voluntary association, or to guaranteed political representation in elected assemblies and other policy-making bodies.

Since the justification for "recognition" is the psychology of identification I have described, representation is synonymous with "presence." The personal characteristics of representatives and their avowed membership insures that they speak in an authentic voice:

> no amount of thought or sympathy, no matter how careful or honest, could jump the barriers of experience. And conversely, it seems, experience is enough of a guarantee of representativeness: the adequacy of the representation depended on the degree to which that experience was shared.[56]

Underlying the need for presence is the insistent claim that cultural group voices articulate more than objectively identifiable interests and opinions. Unique "perspectives," normally inaccessible to outsiders, are the real expression. As Charles Taylor explains, owing to the intellectual history of romanticism, expression emerges in response to an inner intuition about what is "right for us." (We are reminded of the romantic law of the heart.)

Plainly, "some of the disadvantages that oppressed groups suffer can be remedied in policy only by an affirmative acknowledgment of the group's specificity."[57] But as Anne Phillips has pointed out, we generally allow that opinions and interests can be represented by those who are not like us and are not "one of our own," so long as they share our views on salient issues and are skilled advocates. We do not imagine that only industrial workers can represent the interests of labor, or those who have grown up in poverty can represent the poor. Opportunity to choose representatives and protection of interests need not go hand in hand with presence. Where responsiveness to citizen interests is at stake, the participatory/representative/constituency links are complex. From the standpoint of the politics of recognition, however, representatives must be "physically, culturally, and psychologically connected to their constituency base."[58]

Beyond that, the group's self-conception, its view of what is required for secure and stable identity, must be acknowledged as authoritative. "Recognition" of disadvantage, moral harms and status injuries, and interpretations of need are, almost by definition, on the group's own terms. Anything else is deficient, perhaps a harmful "misrecognition." At the extreme, "recognition" means that "what is just for the group ought to be defined by it alone. What is due to people—what in hot politics, their 'rights' are—is for them to say."[59] Thus Iris Young proposes veto power over specific policies that affect a group directly, such as reproductive rights policy for women.[60]

So it is striking that theorists of the politics of recognition go to considerable length to sever the goals of "presence" from the standard goals of political representation. The reason presence is required is not strategic. It is not a matter of better advocacy and more effective advancement of interests and opinions, or only secondarily, and properly understood. Presence *is* representation, *simpliciter.* "Shared experience" takes precedence over shared ideas, interests, and political programs. And presence matters, regardless of consequences for public policy.

One reason for attenuating the connection between presence and a politics of interest is readily comprehensible. It immunizes guaranteed representation from the failure to protect group interests in practice. Political presence is perfectly compatible with political impotence, after all, for reasons ranging from skill in negotiating and forming alliances to limited resources. The constraints on local decision making I discussed in chapter 4, for example, apply regardless of the identity of political elites. In periods of fiscal crisis, black mayors and city councils may be unable to substantially improve or alter services. Weak government is a particular problem for weak groups.

The vehemence and heat behind severance of the politics of recognition from interests clearly run deeper than this, however. It is thoroughgoing, beginning with members' express identification with the group. Recognition proceeds from the claim that "we value our group and therefore we have an interest in its success." Interests arise from identity. The perfectly plausible counterpart is that "for historical personal reasons of the particularity of our experience, our interests are causally associated with our group's interest." Identity arises from interests. Naturally, it is not lost on leaders that *identification* facilitates coordination, and coordination creates power.[61] So it is striking when political theorists side-step self-interested identification as if it were unseemly. Joseph Raz, to take one example, argues that "individual freedom and prosperity depend on full and unimpeded membership in a respected and flourishing cultural group," but respect eclipses flourishing in his account of liberal multiculturalism, and prosperity drops away.[62]

Of course, associations representing "cultures" or "communities" frequently pursue material and political advantages. They lobby for public money, subsidized schools and curriculum control, employment and contract quotas, and so on. Kenneth Karst has cautioned against concluding that "values," abstracted from mundane struggles for economic goods and opportunities, social services, and political influence lie behind every conflict. "In American history . . . the expressed concern for values has often provided the excuse—as well as the emotional fuel—for hostile action aimed at preserving interests that are mainly economic."[63]

In contrast, the politics of recognition persistently portrays benefits to the group as public acknowledgment of what is vital to viability and members' self-respect. Benign "empowerment" is substituted for power. What explains these efforts to oppose the politics of presence to interest group pluralism?

We are familiar with moral criticisms of political pluralism based on the (erroneous) idea that interests simply *are* selfish interests, the pursuit of "naked preferences." Even if interests are based on opinions about the common good (cf. the proliferation of public interest lobbies and representatives on corporate boards), there are moral objections to a process in which political decisions are the result of aggregation, deal-making, or "raw power."[64] Critics have no sympathy with Karst's unapologetic observation that "horse-trading is an honored calling in this country."[65]

We are also familiar with political attacks on interest group pluralism: as the capture of government by factions, the effective disenfranchisement of "discrete and insular minorities" (or diffuse majorities), or in particular cases the enfranchisement of a specific bigoted or unjust set of interests. Political scientists have long studied these failings, observing that "not all groups and interests are represented by politically effective associations," that some are not represented at all, and that like everyone else, voiceless citizens have interests to protect and opinions to advance. They observe that objectively salient interests are absent, perhaps willfully excluded, from the political agenda. "The interests that come up short in the end are those that are so deprived of resources that they never even establish a foothold in the process."[66] These criticisms are generally a stimulus to reform rather than a rejection of political pluralism.

The politics of recognition, in contrast, tends to reject strategic conceptions of representation altogether. The "distributive paradigm" is inattentive to the independent good of political presence, the argument goes. The "Neo-Nietzschean" emphasis on power and counterpower is said to miss the driving force of this kind of politics—the search for recognition and respect. "The reduction of all intellectual disagreements to conflicts of group interest" is indefensible.[67] To which the correct response is yes, and no. Any kind of reductionism is flawed. Power is certainly not the sole motive for political conflict (or injustice), any more than greed is. The politics of recognition as an agonistic contest for respect is a partial concept of democracy, too.

In the end, the deficiencies of interest group politics are simply insufficient to account for heated and strenuous efforts to distance recognition and presence from political pluralism. What does explain it?

Does it reflect a tendency to represent minority groups as victims, and victims as innocents, morally superior? The politics of recognition is not only presumably self-defensive but also untainted by political claims stemming from boiling anger and revenge. Advantages are not selfish if they are for oneself qua member of a culture or community, and if the ultimate aim is public standing and self-respect.

Or is the move subtly pragmatic? Given profound political resistance to egalitarian redistribution in America, recasting demands in terms of respect for cultural values may be divisive, but it circumvents explicit arguments for equalization.

Abstraction from interests also helps keep in view a group's unique status and needs. It obscures the unhappy fact that minorities are likely to conflict even when they are united by basic objective interests. There is no "rainbow coalition" in the United States.[68]

The main reason for separating the politics of presence from interest group pluralism, however, is the psychological logic of recognition itself. Political compromises are intolerable if they are seen as compromises of who we are rather than as efforts to secure for members their share, fair or not, of jobs and positions, opportunities and influence. Another damper is the fact that interests are normally integrative. "Religious and ethnic activists begin by defending the interests of their own community," Walzer points out, "and end up in political coalitions, fighting for a place on balanced tickets, and talking (at least) about the common good."[69] Indeed, from the point of view of the politics of presence, a politics of interest may look like assimilation:

> Cultural politics is a historically validated avenue to recognition and acceptance for members of minority cultures and especially for their leaders. . . . Each success for the group in the politics of the wider community, each material advance, integrates more and more members of the group into the institutions and processes of the dominant culture with the inevitable result that the group declines as a separate political force.[70]

"Perspectives" and "shared experience," on the other hand, preserve the aura of incommensurability, giving representation a permanent foothold as a key element of "recognition."

"All that remained," one critic observed, "was to find a method by which the routines of authentication could be decently bureaucratized."[71] That "remainder" comprises the domain of political representation. It puts in relief a blindspot in political theories of group recognition: inattention to voluntary associations.

Voluntary Association and Accountability: Message and Voice

It is fair to say that political theorists focus on normative justifications for the specific types of representation, public subsidy, and support that count as recognition of differences. The difficult matter of determining the parameters of cultural groups or communities, and of deciding which groups qualify as claimants follows as a secondary concern.

Proponents may restrict recognition to minority cultural communities whose viability is threatened, or more narrowly to previously self-governing, territorially concentrated national minorities.[72] Another proposed category is groups whose distinctive histories and cultural forms have their origin in oppression, which includes but is not limited to cultural domination.[73] Alternatively, candidates for recognition are groups that suffer persistent, systemic subordination and disadvantage, regardless of the history and cause of disadvantage, and whether or not members are stigmatized and despised.[74]

Every version of the politics of recognition takes a particular group as its model, if only implicitly. So the prospect of endless balkanization and unbearable strains on public resources looms large only if we imagine accepting every incommensurate basis for recognition. Fear of a slippery slope into the "hyperpluralism trap" is exaggerated.[75] The real slippery slope is from cultural to social groups, which is a problem if we accept that what underlies the idea of guaranteed "presence" is the incommensurability and quasi-incommunicability of distinct perspectives. Conflicts among social groups seldom spring from mutual unintelligibility.

If we concede a fit between the moral grounds for recognition and a designated group, the critical problem is who speaks in the group's authentic political voice. How do we assess representativeness? As long as discussion focuses on undifferentiated culture or community, the consideration at the heart of constitutional freedom of association for political groups—the relation between membership and message—is *necessarily* obscure. As a result, representatives' accountability *to* members *for* identifiable outcomes is obscure as well.

Interest groups and ideological groups have a relatively high degree of political cohesion; "when a political movement sees itself as based on shared ideals and goals .., then commitment to these goals seems the only legitimate qualification for membership."[76] Historically, the technique used to enhance accountability has been to authorize representatives to advocate a more or less specific political agenda. Labor groups and parties in systems of proportionate representation have traditionally favored a delegate view of representation. By severing the politics of presence from the politics of interest, and concentrating on "perspectives," the politics of recognition deprives itself of the standard touchstones of responsiveness and accountability.

What is the alternative? Essentialism, or some presumed identity of interest among all members, promises a spontaneous and inerrant fit between representatives and their culture or community, but in *politics* certainly, essentialism is spectacularly implausible. Few inferences about interests and opinions, except at a very high level of generality, and even fewer inferences about policy preferences, can be drawn from self-identified membership in an ethnic, cultural, or racial group. Hence the propensity for symbolic gestures designed to elicit shows of solidarity.

The absence of a single or universal interest of all members is consistent with some concerns being especially salient if not exclusive to a particular group:

> That some women do not bear children does not make pregnancy a gender-neutral event; that women disagree so profoundly on abortion does not make its legal availability a matter of equal concern to both women and men; that women occupy such different positions in the occupational hierarchy does not mean they have the same interests as men in their class.[77]

As this example makes perfectly clear, interpretations of salient interests diverge, and so will views of who is representative. It is an orthodoxy of feminist thought that the candidacy of a woman does not mean she can claim a mandate derived from her sex or that she advances women's shared interests. Mirroring, the heart of "presence," may be necessary but it is not sufficient.

We know this for a certainty as soon as members of an identity group form voluntary associations. The proliferation of women's advocacy groups, including antifeminist women's associations, may be the best known example. (The current configuration prompted Wendy Kaminer's question, "Will class trump gender?")[78] Although a separatist sense of identification is particularly acute for African Americans, we cannot infer a sense of what justice (or any less demanding standard) requires from racial identity. Kimberle Crenshaw has described the division of race and gender on the issue of domestic violence.[79] Michael Dawson points to young poor blacks as pro-nationalist, ideologically hostile to anything but a black political party.[80] Adolph Reed has suggested that the only political initiatives that have benefited all blacks are those that reduce police brutality. Studies show a discrepancy between the political preferences of politically active and inactive African Americans.[81]

Political accountability is always difficult, conceptually and operationally. But never more so than when "presence" rather than objective interests and common agendas is the standard of representativeness.[82] Shared experience may be a starting point for representation, but it is not politically directive. In the absence of goals generated and communicated through associations, shared experience is liable to be politically incoherent or vacuous. *Associations* serve representative purposes, not cultures or communities.

This problem undermines the effectiveness of voices that emerge from electoral arrangements like race-conscious districting, which are designed to secure the group's presence in elected assemblies. Race and geography are uncertain proxies for interests, and "safe seats" may act as disincentives to political organizing. That is one of Lani Guinier's critiques of "the theory of black electoral success."[83] Evidence of the unintended consequences accumulates: safe seats reduce the need for incumbents to mobilize local support; dampen debate; discourage cross-racial coalitions; and attenuate accountability.

Precisely because demand for presence predominates, cynical self-interest and political ambition can make opportunistic use of a politics of recognition. Self-styled representatives are likely to be better at gestures and media moments—like those favored by the American Indian Movement—than either advocacy or deliberation in decision-making arenas.[84] Leaders may be more adept at channeling frustration (often in conspiratorial terms) than advancing interests; and more inclined to do so since interests are divisive. And a politics of presence encourages people to look on this as what representation is all about, rather than as demagoguery. (Political theorists do not acknowledge "In your face!" for the powerful element of voice it clearly is.)

A politics of presence does not dictate that members' various objective ends are ignored or sacrificed, but it is enabling. As Adolph Reed put the problem, the differential class impact of laws is disguised or defused "through the legerdemain of symbolic racial collectivism."[85] Which is obviously helped along by demonization of blacks by some whites, and by the division of African Americans into "two nations," middle-class and pathological.[86]

No wonder it is safer to focus on the unfairness and indignity of exclusion than on what is expected from presence. Put mildly, "there is an asymmetry . . . between what alerts us to a problem and what counts as a satisfactory solution."[87]

What can narrow the disjuncture between diffuse and ascriptive membership and voice? The chief security for responsiveness is a background of voluntary associations. Members of identity groups develop and articulate their specific concerns in political advocacy groups and in the caucuses and conferences of wider voluntary associations committed to issues at work, ideology, or aspects of social life. The mechanisms of democratic accountability operate via associations, too. This is a political science commonplace. Voluntary associations are resources for promoting leaders. They create conditions for consultation. Representativeness depends on the basis on which elites can learn and respond to their constituents. For the most part, elected representatives "build coalitions of minorities, each one of which is especially concerned with a particular subset of issues"; withdrawing support is a way to "veto" the representative's policy choices.[88] So there must be means for ascertaining what various members of a diffuse group want; what shared experiences count; which internal divisions are negotiable and which are not; and how these might translate into policy—and to give these voice. Whatever the goal, representation depends on the field of associations from which leaders emerge, to which representatives recur, and which holds them accountable.

The self-organization of groups into voluntary associations capable of giving representatives a voice and message cannot be assured. Grant McConnell points out that the phrase "potential interest groups" is unreasonably optimistic because it suggests that for every group interest an association will be formed.[89] There are public inducements, however. Benefits such as government grants, contracts, employment, and so on are not only parceled out among organized groups; they generate claimants. We know that the increase in the number of private nonprofit associations is correlated to increased government spending. The NEA not only funds but also gives rise to arts organizations claiming to express identity groups' aesthetics.

Recently, democratic theorists have begun to propose public assistance geared directly at organizing associations to enable political engagement. Michael Walzer argues that a crisis of civil society exists such that "it makes sense to call the state to the rescue." He advocates government sponsorship and subsidy of select groups ("the right sort of groups"): unions, "cultural associations," tenants' housing cooperatives, and so on.[90] But whether and how associations become politically active is up to them. Associations may not be entirely spontaneous and independent, but Walzer is not looking to make associations mere artifacts of public policy.

Solicitous of the self-understanding of identity groups and focused on "presence," the politics of recognition is hesitant, fatally ambiguous really, about the genesis of representative voices. Latent voices are "there," but how are they institutionalized? The relevant identity groups are disorganized or silenced, and advocates do not expect authentic voices to emerge from spontaneous mobilization. Again, they do not explore the ground between undifferentiated "culture" and "community" on the one side and "presence" on the other, the ground where voluntary associations secure a connection between membership and message. Instead, advocates propose institutional reforms and targeted public resources aimed at stimulating the "self-organization" of groups "so that they achieve collective empowerment and a reflective understanding of their collective experience."[91] Briefly, guaranteed political presence *precedes* political association and is an impetus to it. Again, the dynamic of membership and voice is reversed.

With this, we observe the instability of the politics of recognition, its vacillation between artifactual and romantic. It emerges clearly in proposals to reform "public spaces" to elicit voices in a fashion that serves specific conceptions of democratic processes and fair outcomes. As it does when the politics of recognition is joined in a strange and brittle amalgam with deliberative democracy.

Deliberation and Artifactual Groups

The moment discussion turns from the moral psychology of membership and from justifications of group recognition in hypothetical "public spaces" to *political* representation, we encounter the ideal of democratic deliberation.[92] The affinity between these two developments in contemporary democratic theory—recognition and deliberation—is plain: mutual disdain for interest group politics and for anything approaching a delegate theory of accountability to particular constituents. Moreover, each has something to offer the other. Deliberation promises to unsettle majorities, dislodge fixed alliances, and challenge cultural preconceptions. From the perspective of recognition, a group's lack of power stands to be less significant if decision making is governed by deliberative norms rather than bargaining.[93] From the perspective of democratic deliberation, the voices joined in public discussion must be inclusive, and a politics of "presence" offers additional assurance of representativeness beyond the usual electoral and party mechanisms.

Moreover, deliberative democracy seems to resolve one of the problems of representation that beset the politics of recognition. Deliberation is premised on a reiterative process of elucidating and altering initial preferences and opinions. A feature of deliberation is that participants "regard themselves as bound only by the results of their deliberation. . . . [T]heir consideration of proposals is not constrained by the authority of prior norms or requirements."[94] Which means that "perspectives" rather than objective interests or programs *are* appropriate bases of representation. Anne Phillips explains: "Against this background, the deliberative retreat from stricter notions of accountability should not be viewed as a failure of democratic integrity. On the contrary, it gives extra theoretical legitimacy to the implications of a politics of presence."[95]

Deliberation speaks to the dark side of interest groups and identity groups—the possibility that the opinions, values, preferences, and "perspectives" the politics of recognition would make authoritative are products of illegitimate constraints, blind and unself-reflexive, arrived at without all relevant information and under conditions that obstruct awareness of alternatives and opportunities. Properly contrived, deliberation can ward off the sour observation that "the authority of existing preferences, as criteria of salience, is tainted by their causal history."[96]

Of course, preferences and commitments are altered in the give and take of ordinary interest group pluralism, too. Programs are seldom fixed in advance of discussion. Understanding, if not agreement, is enhanced, and the grounds of persistent disagreement clarified. Legislators change their minds when presented with new points of view. In practice, institutional features—the structure of legislative committees and agenda-setting, for example—affect the alternative programs actually available for discussion, so that outcomes may not represent even a "majority" choice, as social choice theory explains. Political pluralism obviously entails public argument and persuasion, negotiation, bargaining, strategic voting, and accommodation. "Interest aggregation" is both naive and misleading if it suggests simple vectors, or balancing, or that there is only one way of amalgamating preferences. In short, the distinction between strategic and deliberative democracy does not turn on predetermined unchanging preferences versus reasonable flexibility. Deliberative theorists exaggerate the power of interests in their disregard for the institutional constraints on decision making.

Instead, the mark of deliberative democracy is the normative conditions imposed on decision making. In deliberative arenas, representatives are assigned public roles, conform to regulations regarding the arguments brought to discussion, and take on publicly designated purposes, chief among them discussion designed to culminate in votes. From this standpoint, group presence must not only be justified; it must be made compatible with deliberation. As Amy Gutmann and Dennis Thompson argue, group representation is not itself a moral end.[97] Specifically, deliberation requires public reasonableness. It demands that preferences be backed up with reasons and arguments that can be shared by all reasonable citizens. In this way, Joshua Cohen and Joel Rogers argue, deliberation contributes to shaping the preferences and convictions that are brought to public affairs, with the result that "deliberation . . . focuses debate on the common good."[98]

Deliberative theorists sometimes emphasize the legitimacy of outcomes, other times their justice. In some cases, the idea is that decisions should conform to an independent standard for evaluating political practices, and presence is simply a precondition for knowing this standard and reaching correct outcomes.[99] In every case, public forums, when they are deliberative, do more than stimulate voices; they configure them.

The notion that a deliberative framework provides not only a standard of justification for democratic decisions but also a source of motivation is at the core of every deliberative account:

> Under current or perhaps even ideal conditions, a deliberative politics is an imperfect guarantee of public-regarding outcomes. But by disciplining the kinds of reasons that may be offered in support of legislation, it increases the likelihood that they will come about.[100]

A formative ambition is at work that extends beyond deliberative arenas. Thus, Joshua Cohen and Joel Rogers propose using taxes, public subsidies, and sanctions to support associations that represent major social interests in ways that contribute to qualitative democratic decision making. They would make it a condition of sponsorship and access to decision-making institutions that groups satisfy democratic norms in their internal organization and be other-regarding in their participation in policy-making. The purpose of subsidized association is not to amplify the voices of independent groups with self-selected purposes and uncensored expression, which do not owe their existence or purposes to the direction of government. It is to recruit citizens and to alter the "terms, conditions, and public status of groups" so that they engage in what Cohen and Rogers call "an artful democratic politics of secondary associations."[101]

Cohen and Rogers are principally concerned with social interests, described as lineal descendants of unions and employers, rather than identity groups. But similar arguments are made for incorporating ethnic, cultural, or racial presences in public arenas charged with deliberation. Deliberation does not require leaving "particularities" behind, exactly. Only that "public reason" frames political discussion. And that the process of deliberation shapes and refines views and generates reasons congruent with the public norms of liberal democracy.[102] Which *does* require representatives to distance themselves from the unique, intuitive commitment to what is right "for us" that gave the politics of recognition its psychological force.

From the point of view of ideal democratic theory, there is nothing to regret in the subordination of group voices to the requirements of deliberation. The business of political philosophy is to articulate norms of democratic procedure and substance. Thus, for Charles Taylor, "the struggle for recognition can find only one satisfactory solution, and that is a regime of reciprocal recognition among equals."[103] This regime appears to require a unity of purpose. There is little reason to think commitment to reciprocity has much of a foothold in the shared experience that justifies the politics of recognition, though. The starting point for presence is the conviction that the group's standing is unique, after all. From "inside" the politics of recognition, reciprocity, the magnanimity of "acknowledging the moral status of a position that one opposes," the imperative that public deliberation rely "only on forms of reasoning and evidence that are publicly accessible and available to citizens generally" is not only morally stringent, but likely to be viewed as compromising and counterproductive.[104]

And in a regime of "reciprocal recognition among equals" representatives would be *less* rather than more responsive to their own groups. The whole thrust of deliberation is away from partiality and incommensurable perspectives. No "invisible hand" can bring the system into moral equilibrium when representatives are chiefly concerned with the well-being of their jurisdiction. Deliberators must address their reasons to everyone and are accountable to everyone directly affected by their decisions: citizens generally, and "potential moral constituents"—nonresidents and future generations.[105]

Once the democratic goal is "to preserve the integrity of public debate . . . to safeguard the conditions for true and free collective self-determination," cracks appear in the brittle amalgam of the politics of recognition and democratic deliberation.[106] We see them in the tenor of discussion, in the gap between the intense emotions and rhetoric accompanying claims to recognition on the one hand, and hyperrational concern with the way group-specific needs and interests must be justified on the other. (That what goes on in "public spaces" is the "dialogic, interactive generation of universality.")[107] The disjuncture is apparent in the gap between the justification for recognition insofar as it rests on moral psychology on the one hand and for deliberation on the other. In Gutmann and Thompson's terms, "deliberative democracy does not specify a single form of representation. It searches for modes of representation that support the give-and-take of serious and sustained moral argument within legislative bodies, between legislators and citizens, and among citizens themselves."[108] This may explain why democratic theorists argue, as John Dryzek has, that it may make good sense for groups to resist political inclusion and maintain an "oppositional" presence, mainly in the semipublic arenas of civil society where:

> discourse need not be suppressed in the interests of strategic advantage; goals and interests need not be compromised or subordinated to the pursuit of office or access; embarrassing troublemakers need not be repressed; the indeterminacy of outcome inherent in democracy need not be subordinated to state policy.[109]

Public Forums

The managed tenor of "public spaces," epecially when discourse is guided by "public reason," is sharpened if we recall the spirit of public forums. Given life in First Amendment jurisprudence twenty-five years ago, public forum doctrine originated with a categorical division of government property. Government's ability to regulate expressive activities on property designated a public forum is strictly limited, while in nonpublic forums, government has considerable latitude to admit or exclude speakers and regulate modes of expression. The prerogatives of government's proprietary rights outside the traditional forums of streets and parks and the degree of discretion government has in prohibiting uses incompatible with official business in schools, airports, or post offices continue to be debated. So do extensions of what amounts, in effect, to a public subsidy for expression.

Thus, drawing an analogy between the university's subsidy for student publications and a public forum, the Supreme Court ruled in *Rosenberger v. University of Virginia* that the state must provide equal access to the school's activities fund for all student groups, including the religious paper, *Wide Awake*.[110] The dissent saw paying students' groups' printing bills as a new economic benefit that had nothing to do with public forums. It also saw this as direct aid to religion in violation of the establishment clause, correctly in my view.

The vagaries of public forum doctrine are not germane here, but the underlying purpose of the public forum *is*: to protect "uninhibited, robust and wide-open" speech on public issues.[111] The liberal democratic promise is tolerance and the civic respect of a public hearing. Public forums give a hearing to the KKK in Muncie, the Hare Krishna at O'Hare Airport, and the Million Man March on the Washington Mall.

Public forums "functionally defined" and expanded to include privately owned shopping malls or streets of a homeowners' association are obviously not arenas for decision making, much less ideal "public spaces" for deliberation. The difference was plain to Alexander Meiklejohn, who opposed the "responsible and regulated discussion" of the town meeting to the "unregulated talkativeness" of Hyde Park. The public forum is aptly described as a scene of insistent communication. Speakers impose on listeners and the message is, however briefly, inescapable. The possibility of being heard in a context dense with people, where the involuntary audience cannot close their doors or ears, gives it importance for groups with unwelcome messages and styles of expression. It provides an opportunity to tangibly demonstrate strength of numbers and intensity of feelings.

Public forums set in motion unregulated and indeterminate political interactions, in short. Time, place, and manner rules are not suspended there, but they are generous.[112] Forums invite unmanaged self-affirmation and exhibitions of difference. Public expression is exhibitionistic, in fact, and often unseemly, aggressive, unreasonable. There is potential affinity to the politics of recognition, which often takes the form of aggressive self-assertion and symbolic gestures. Expression in public forums has a (safely contained) coercive edge. Insistent communication can compel a hearing.

Public forums can compel a hearing but not "recognition," which is what members of identity groups say they need. The politics of recognition is principally about the obligations public officials in liberal democracy have to provide assistance, including guaranteed presence in social and political institutions. But the same moral psychology places demands on private citizens, personally and individually, as well. Most insistently, it is said to require that outside official arenas, in day-to-day interactions, everyone exhibit behavior and demeanor that group members take as a sign of understanding and respect. The politics of recognition imposes an obligation of active response. It demands a kind of deference. It provokes the question, What do we owe one another in democracy in everyday life?

Conclusion _____

Navigating Pluralism:
The Democracy of Everyday Life

Beyond Associations: Shifting Involvements
   and the Democracy of Everyday Life

American democracy generates every imaginable formal organization and informal enclave, from admirable religious and civic associations to groups that are patent obstacles to cultivating specifically liberal and democratic dispositions.

I have attempted to describe and advocate the moral uses of this pluralism. I have supported an expansive notion of the moral dispositions wanted in a liberal democracy, and of the groups that may cultivate these virtues. I have drawn attention to the ideological underpinnings that give incongruent groups a permanent foothold in this country. But also, by focusing on the dynamics of membership rather than the formal purpose, structure, or legal categorization of groups, I have attended to the often unintended and unanticipated moral benefits of membership in unpromising groups like proprietary homeowners' associations, even loathsome hate groups. I have emphasized the ineradicability of vices, and the need to contain them. Voluntary associations act as "safety valves," relatively confined spheres of expression. Simply by the fact that individuals have an occasion not only to belong but also to exclude others, some place where their contributions are affirmed and where the likelihood of failure is reduced, associations normally instill a sense of self-respect. Perhaps, too, the proliferation of groups operates as a brake on hostile outbreaks of social envy, and worse.

The moral uses of pluralism militate for expansive freedom of association, and against a strategy of deliberately legislating schools of virtue, by government inducements or legally mandated congruence. By now, my cautions are familiar. We cannot assume that a group's formative effects on members can be predicted on the basis of its express purpose or organization. The sources of illiberalism (and worse) vary among individuals, so it really should not be surprising that what works as an effective school of virtue will vary too, depending on whether the obstacle in each instance is arrant self-interest, some gripping group identification, or anomie. Individuals bring predispositions, temperaments and constitutions, prior histories, and ideological expectations to membership. They attribute meaning to association and respond morally and emotionally to belonging in ways that are far from generalizable.

The moral uses of pluralism are guided by the thought that the variable experiences groups offer members and the vicissitudes of development can be exploited. One experience of associational life can offset others. Associations can compensate for deficits and deprivations suffered outside. When they are not indirect schools of virtue, they may provide a sort of reparation. The unifying theme of this book is that the moral uses of pluralism depend on effective freedom of association and on the *experience of pluralism* by men and women, personally and individually. That is, on shifting involvements.

At numerous points, I have observed that government should insure background conditions that make forming, joining, and leaving groups practicable. Shifting involvements also entails the personal capacity and inclination to adjust to changing social contexts. In the course of navigating pluralism, however, we are called on to exhibit certain moral dispositions all the time. That is, to display a certain moral constancy.

We do not always find ourselves in voluntary associations where as willing members we conform to the particular internal norms of the group, or in official public arenas where we are expected to conform to liberal democratic practices. Much of life "in public" is carried on in the interstices of groups and attachments. A foundational moral temperament allows us to get along. The democracy of everyday life is a habitual way of going about our ordinary business as we move about among groups and institutions, public and private. For many moments we are all on our own in society. So the democracy of everyday life has to do with mundane face-to-face interactions and involves encounters with strangers, since involuntary association is a fact of social life.

The democracy of everyday life is a fitting conclusion to this book in another respect. I have been consistently skeptical about an official public obligation for moral education, particularly of the responsibility to instill or protect self-respect. My opposition stems from resistance to tutorial government and from recognition of the countervailing power of formative voluntary associations, not complacency. Still, it provides me with added impetus to conclude with an affirmation of what we *do* owe one another in everyday life.

By definition, the requisites of democracy in everyday life are simple, involving competencies anyone and everyone is capable of developing without enormous conscious effort. And they are a matter of habitual disposition rather than principle, severe obligation, or some virtue that is called for only intermittently. The virtues I have in mind are simple and in constant use. They are *treating people identically and with easy spontaneity*, a phrase I borrow from Judith Shklar, and *speaking out against ordinary injustice*.[1]

These dispositions, which permit democracy in everyday life to flourish, are nothing very grand. They certainly do not exhaust the elements of liberal democratic character, much less moral character tout court. Yet they are as important as other moral and political competencies for maintaining the social climate in which liberal democratic institutions can flourish. We have as much to fear from their eclipse as we do from the absence of more orthodox virtues, from political ignorance and irrationality, or from anomie. For apart from the fear violent crime strikes in ordinary citizens, it is the absence of democracy in everyday life that makes daily interactions unbearable. It can heighten the propensity to stick with "our own" and what we know, and contributes to anomie. Those incapable of exhibiting these dispositions in mundane affairs put themselves outside the pale of liberal democratic society. Those who as a normal matter cannot expect to be treated with easy spontaneity are truly excluded.

Easy Spontaneity

The easy spontaneity of individuals toward one another has often struck foreign visitors to the United States. Michael Walzer observed that Americans have only one form of address, "Mr." (the feminine form, "Ms.," has not caught on everywhere). Today people are likely to refer to one another more familiarly by first names, even in chance encounters.

Easy spontaneity is a rejection of deference, a habitual disregard for social and economic standing, ethnic and cultural differences. It also means disregarding meritorious hierarchies and claims to public recognition.

Treating everyone regardless of status similarly betrays the origin of this democratic competence; along with anxiety about the survival of a "regal fungus" and attacks on monopoly, it was a core element of political ideology in the Jacksonian era. The demand to give and receive recognition for one's particular attributes, earned or inherited or ascribed, has rightly been associated with an antidemocratic ethos. Carefully calculating social status, making fine cultural or racial distinctions, and taking exquisite pains to avoid slights are wholly out of keeping with democracy in everyday life. The demand to treat people identically is simple because it does not require us to assess the social origin and place or the sensibilities of everyone we meet and adjust our conduct accordingly. The disposition to disregard inequalities and differences is specifically and unmistakably political.

I am reluctant to identify the democracy of everyday life with civility rules. Across time and cultures, most forms of civility have been patently undemocratic in their attention to rank, class, office, affiliation, or social standing. The French term *precedences* captures the tie to hierarchy. Also, these norms have typically judged democratic spontaneity uncivil. Easy spontaneity is particularly anathema to those who value distinct marks of social standing and see civility as the discipline that preserves them. From this standpoint spontaneity appears as errant self-indulgence. In fact, it is a good faith extension of resistance to deference and hypocrisy. Treating people similarly and with easy spontaneity exhibits a sort of democratic self-respect, being true to oneself in a way that falls far short of sheer romantic expressivism. It also exhibits a sort of democratic respect for others. For it invites reciprocity. Plain speaking, transparency of interests and needs, and an open countenance that reveals intensity of feeling can be reasonably understood as an exhibition of social trust.

Still, like basic norms of civility, easy spontaneity is an exhibition of self-control that signals the intention to deal with others peacefully.

> Good demeanor is what is required of an actor if he is to be transformed into someone who can be relied upon to maintain himself as an interactant, poised for communication, and to act so that others do not endanger themselves by presenting themselves as interactants to him.[2]

Indeed, Americans tend to use the term 'incivility' euphemistically to refer to flagrant lack of self-control, explosive expressions of prejudice and hate, rhetorical excess, cruelty, even physical threats. From the standpoint of popular discourse, we can see why civility is not an adequate shorthand for democracy in everyday life, which goes beyond barebones self-restraint.

On the other hand, treating people similarly and with easy spontaneity falls short of stern democratic requirements of public shows of respect. Democracy is defined by political philosophers as a regime of "reciprocal recognition among equals." Mutual respect is its essence, and public exhibition of respectful treatment is a categorical imperative.

This shift from easy spontaneity to moral obligation is grounded in discussions of *self-respect* as a "primary good," vital to well-being. The moral stakes are ratcheted up further with the claim that personal dignity and a sense of self-worth are bound up with the esteem in which we are held by others, that identity is mediated by public recognition. Self-respect requires positive recognition.

This shift has practical significance as applied to the dispositions exhibited by men and women in everyday life. The disposition to treat people similarly began as oppositional. It was a proud exhibition of one's own standing in democratic society. Easy spontaneity was, and remains, a way of demonstrating rejection of deference and hypocrisy; even if one is objectively vulnerable to those wielding greater wealth and power or some ideology of hate, one is not a dupe, taken in by their claims to superiority. In the moral philosophy of respect, by contrast, the valence shifts away from the democratic disposition as personal pride and a fighting creed.

Instead, exhibitions of democratic dispositions in everyday life are important for what they signify about the moral status of others. We are obliged to conduct ourselves civilly in order to avoid inflicting dignity harms and to in-sure others' sense of self-worth. Democratic civility is not just the tenor of a regime of social equals but tender solicitude for historic, perceived, or self-declared unequals. One result is that democratic demeanor, which originated as a bottom-up force—as resistance to deferential practices—has taken on the character of a top-down inculcation of rigorous moral education.

With these shifts come psychological strains. The democracy of everyday life always required self-discipline, but the discipline involved in treating peo-ple similarly was modest. For one thing, men and women could see its utility; uniform and simple forms of civility greased the wheels of democratic society, facilitating social mobility. More important, it was not morally onerous be-cause it was not supposed to reflect our *real* sentiments about whether individ-uals or groups warrant our respect, or whether we think they have grounds for respecting themselves. Precisely the opposite is the case today. Civility is im-perative because it is supposed to signal "recognition," that is, to afford others actual respect. It entails not only personal and public responsibility *to* others for our outward demeanor, but also responsibility *for* others—active solicitude for their sense of self-worth.

So the corollary of easy spontaneity toward others is the inclination to make allowances for them, and to resist the impulse to magnify slights. In short, a thick skin. It means not standing on one's rights or "true merits" in ordinary interactions or demanding recognition for one's unique individuality and au-thenticity. Exquisite romantic sensibilities who yearn to have their "true selves" acknowledged will always be frustrated.

This is a sort of tolerance liberal democratic theory overlooks: the self-discipline to tolerate being misunderstood. To "exercise extraordinary self-restraint toward injurious behavior as a means of symbolically demonstrating a capacity for self-control toward feelings that necessarily must play a role throughout social interaction but which also have a tendency to get out of hand."[3] Part of Lee Bollinger's defense of freedom of speech, this suggests the psychology behind making allowances.

Not everyone can abide democratic treatment. Thin-skinned types are per-petually offended. They regularly express outrage at the perfectly unremark-able conduct of others, which generally falls short of standards of refinement and sensitivity. We all know those pained by ordinary vices: "what I'd call average hypocrisy, just the incidental little whiffs of the social machine, was terribly hard on her."[4] Democratic dispositions find "good enough" behavior abidable, and are disposed to make allowances. This is not expecting too little of others; it is antiperfectionism. Liberal democracy does not demand an Emersonian faith in individuals.

Personal experience points up the importance of this competence for every-day life, and helps define it. We can all come up with examples of mundane dealings that were uncomfortably undemocratic—when we were treated deferentially or ceremoniously, patronized or demeaned. We can offer instances where, in retrospect, we recognize that interpreting some action as a slight and reacting defensively (or aggressively) was unwarranted and caused needless offense in turn.

Because democracy in everyday life is sometimes actively rejected, we also know it from its opposite. Elijah Anderson describes the "codes of the streets" that govern day-to-day interactions among some young African American men (as well as their conduct toward outsiders).[5] Far from disregarding status, the heart of the code is creating and preserving one's place in a precarious hierarchy of deference and respect. There is nothing here of treating people identically, much less spontaneously. Every nuance of dress and comportment—from sneakers to swagger—is orchestrated to signal the treatment expected from others. Protecting one's place depends on being keenly attuned to advances and slights, so demeanor also deters transgressions by signaling the predisposition to aggressively defend one's standing. The response to a failure to receive the proper show of respect (being "dissed") is physical confrontation; dishonor demands violent revenge.[6]

In contrast, Mitchell Duneier describes an exemplary scene of identical treatment and easy spontaneity. *Slim's Table* is an account of an integrated Chicago cafeteria serving working-class and "working-poor" black men and white men of somewhat broader social strata. Duneier describes an encounter between a police officer and a man who had been imprisoned for armed robbery. Green asked the officer if he minded if he sat down at his table.

> The patrolman's answer, "It's a public restaurant," unenthusiastic as it was, made it plain that the man's presence at his table would not be viewed as an encroachment. Valois [cafeteria] provided occasions for interaction between people who would not normally have an opportunity to talk, much less take a meal together. . . . [The man convicted of a crime] could transcend his stigma, putting it behind him if only for those moments, and the cop could transcend his role. In telling me some of the things he had said to Green, the officer emphasized that they were both "only human."[7]

It is not hard to see what is democratic here—a disregard for differences in dealing with one another outside formal public arenas and organized groups. It is a way of acting in the world that does not overtly proclaim "equal citizenship" or "reciprocity" but is indifferent to inequalities and a host of cultural differences. Better, it is dependably acting *as if* these differences were a matter of indifference in our views of one another. Easy spontaneity and making allowances are not necessarily signs of civic virtue or mutual respect. As Shklar reminded us, we are not all convinced that all men and women are entitled to respect, but most of us are able to act as if we did believe it. And that is what counts.[8]

The Politics of Recognition

At the same time it is not hard to see why this requirement of the democracy of everyday life might come under attack. It is anathema to the "politics of recognition," which encourages us to see ourselves as members of particular groups, often insists that affiliations are the most important thing about us, and demands displays of consideration in ordinary social dealings, even from strangers. The recognition claimed is not for social class or status, to be sure, but for defining elements of personal identity, for past or present suffering, or for group merits and accomplishments—the worth of one's culture.

The comfort some people find in group loyalty and pride is undeniable. And the politics of recognition is an understandable response to exclusion and inequality. Against that background, everyday offenses will be assigned public significance. Regular slights and grievances will assume a pattern of oppression. It is also undeniable, though, that the politics of recognition amplifies the inevitable vices of pluralism. It heightens sensitivity to presumably defining differences and does nothing to moderate mutual mistrust. It breeds reverse snobbery. It encourages a hypocritical pretense that variations of experience among "us," members of the group, do not matter, and accusations of betrayal when they do.

Precisely because it is a way to personally navigate the contradictions of pluralist society and not a demand on others, the democracy of everyday life cannot suffice for those who look for recognition. By definition, the politics of recognition seeks to alter the behavior of others. It looks for specific attestations of appreciation, or deference.[9] Not content with "easy spontaneity," it forces people's hands and demands substantive acknowledgment of one's own sense of standing.

Carried over into everyday interactions, recognition is liable to be impracticable in any case. For one thing, because it is so demanding. It requires considerable self-discipline to avoid specific actions or gestures that group members regard as a slight or say will diminish their self-respect, and to adjust our demeanor and conduct to what counts for them as an adequate demonstration of regard. Especially since what counts as respect become increasingly differentiated and refined. The inscrutability and insatiability of the needs of those vulnerable to dignity harms tax emotional and moral resources. If "the heart of the great cry for recognition on the part of individuals and groups is a bitter longing for status," as Isaiah Berlin thought, it follows that what counts as recognition is by definition on the groups's own terms. Who else can interpret members' needs? Anything else is deficient, perhaps a harmful "misrecognition."

That this is an invitation to hypocrisy—to currying favor or patronizing compliance rather than political decency is clear. It is also an invitation to demand displays of respect by engaging in unmistakable forms of self-assertion. We begin to see why the claims of recognition impose strains on all parties. Claimants to recognition feel obliged to demonstrate that they are self-respecting. And others feel that they are being asked to be deferential. It is not surprising that people resist changing their habitual demeanor on command, especially when they take their disposition to be spontaneous and unbiased. The demand for recognition in everyday life will be experienced as coercive.

The politics of recognition is not simple in any objective sense, either. It requires considerable sociological and cultural discernment to differentiate members of particular social and cultural groups in a wildly pluralist society, and to assess the treatment appropriate to particular individuals (as members) in ordinary situations. Figuring out who is who and how to behave can become paralyzingly difficult if we happen to recall the facts of mixed and elective identity. Few affiliations are patent, in part because few people are just one thing. Many people willfully throw off their ascriptive connections, choosing not to identify themselves as Jewish or Catholic or Polish, or not to present themselves as such in everyday life. Others who are identified with groups, nonetheless find unsolicited "recognition" unwelcome. So the politics of recognition requires us to know not just *what* but *when* differential conduct is appropriate.

It goes without saying that treating people identically in everyday life does not dictate a position on the merits of group representation in public and quasi-public forums, and it is unrelated to questions of public policy toward racial or cultural groups; it has nothing to contribute to debates about whether school curricula should be revamped. It speaks only to the need for steady, habitual interactions and the disposition to make allowances in mundane dealings. The alternative to the politics of recognition in everyday life is not license to express one's opinions or prejudices but treating everyone identically and with easy spontaneity.

Speaking Up

The second disposition required for democracy in everyday life is a willingness to respond at least minimally to ordinary injustice, an iota of recognition when someone is taken advantage of. I am not speaking here about sensational cases of citizens passively witnessing a crime or failing to report some awful abuse. Nor do I have in mind invoking legal rights or taking political action, initiating grievance procedures, or lodging formal complaints. What daily interactions call for is speaking up on the spot, saying, "No!"

We encounter arbitrariness and unfairness all the time: a senior colleague who sloughs committee work off onto a new assistant professor; a store clerk who speaks abusively to a teenager or ignores a non-English-speaking customer. Women are still liable to be underserved and overcharged when it comes to certain goods and services. "There can hardly be a black person in urban America who has not been denied entry to a store, closely watched, snubbed, questioned about her or his ability to pay for an item, or stopped and detained for shoplifting."[10] As clients of government agencies, consumers at an airline ticket counter, or hospital patients we have all been dealt with peremptorily, arbitrarily, or worse, with inconvenient or injurious consequences. We typically understand that the agent is not responsible for policy, but often enough an official's or employee's own manifest passivity, indifference, runaround, or caprice is at issue. The democracy of everyday life requires us to speak up for ourselves (insisting "I was next" to a bakery clerk who cannot be bothered with the nicety of lines, for example) or on behalf of others (insisting "it's her turn").

Overcoming passivity and speaking out against mistreatment is not a matter of having warm and deep sympathy for others. No one is required to display what George Bernard Shaw called the "nauseous sham goodfellowship" put on by politicians. And unlike good samaritanism and resistance to political injustice, it is not a duty. Speaking out is best understood as a virtually automatic response to the indignation we feel in the face of flagrant, if small and ordinary, injustices.

The response need not be an effective corrective, either. In most situations we do not expect anything more than cathartic relief from speaking out, if that. We don't imagine that the woman at the counter selling rolls is suddenly infused with a deep sense of fairness. Moreover, the disposition to object to ordinary injustice is not necessarily a sign that the speaker himself or herself is "empowered," sees arbitrariness as part of a pattern of systematic injustice, or wants to "empower" the victim. In fact, day-to-day mistreatment, even when it involves prejudice, may *not* be corrigible by political reform. Ordinary unfairness may well be the incidental result of personal moral flaws rather than political and legal wrongs.

In any case, the disposition to object indicates nothing about whether our political understanding is sophisticated. Nor does it translate into an active political concern for social justice, or a contribution to righting wrongs. Although speaking up is allied to "rights-consciousness," one is no guarantee of the other and the two diverge in practice. Rights invoke institutional supports and public enforcement. We are the sole agents of democracy in everyday life, personally and individually.

And the provocation to speaking up is small dominations, hauteur and arbitrariness, bullying and humiliation. Speaking up against injustice is not principled but rather a simple, unexceptional impulse. Saying "no!" is as definite a feeling as hunger, almost a physiological imperative.

Nonetheless, speaking up *is* an exhibition of a peculiarly democratic virtue. It is a public reminder to everyone involved in the incident that democracy invites everyone to express indignation at mistreatment and that no one should have to restrain his or her reflexive impulse to say "No!"[11] Vaclav Havel reminds us in "The Power of the Powerless" of the cost of confrontation in undemocratic regimes. People cannot be expected to speak out as a matter of course under conditions of political oppression, or in divided societies where political ideology dictates that some people's sense of injustice simply does not deserve a hearing. The disposition to speak up is peculiarly democratic.

For the person speaking up, it is a matter of democratic pride. The shame and regret we may feel thinking back to occasions when we could have objected but kept silent is for a civic, not merely private moral failing. And passivity in the face of everyday injustice is debilitating.

Even citizens with fully developed civic virtues may not have the dispositions I have described. They may be secure in their own, laudable associations, and admirably attuned to issues of social justice. And at the same time meekly passive in mundane situations. We are as likely to be insecure, bullied, or cowed as we are to be adventurous democratic individualists boldy navigating pluralism. So it is worth attending to the inhibitions on speaking up against ordinary injustice.

Fear and Democratic Responsibility

Among the obstacles is the vestigial ideology of deference and its counterparts, snobbery and condescension, as well as new ideologies of status and deference like the "code of the streets." Fear of violent retaliation operates too. Not confident that everyone around us has even a miniscule amount of self-restraint, we may be loathe to speak out because we are afraid of provoking a physical confrontation.

Most often the inhibition at work is a sense of propriety; we are reluctant to object because we don't want to cause a scene. Why? At bottom, I think, because we lack faith that others share our indignation. We imagine that in admonishing a bank teller who treats a customer unfairly we will be met with indifference or hostility from those who have been kept waiting in line. We do not expect encouragement and agreement. This is a specific instance of the generalized mistrust surveys document. It is an area in which latent mistrust *is* reiterative. That is why we are delighted by stories of people who do speak out; their example encourages us to think that we are not alone, and may inspire the iota of trust, the leap of faith, we need to overcome passivity ourselves. Like "copycat" crimes, the dynamic of democracy in everyday life operates in part by imitation.

Of course, the grim expectation that speaking out will be met with hostility or indifference simply repeats the question of why men and women are frequently passive in the face of everyday injustice. Almost certainly the disposition to speak up in the face of arbitrariness and unfairness in daily affairs is based on a modicum of identification with others. Our indignation at *any* mistreatment may be visceral, but we are more likely to actively object when the stranger is like us, less inclined to imagine that speaking out is somebody else's business. I am more apt to rise to the defense of an older woman treated roughly or dismissively.

Despite very real inhibitions on speaking out, most of us have objected to injustice or been defended ourselves by perfect strangers. When these instances occur, they are an exhilarating and indisputably political experience. It is a limited sort of political experience, of course. The habit of easy spontaneity and not rising to every slight may or may not produce sensitivity to inequality. The habit of objecting to ordinary unfairness may or may not translate into political participation on behalf of social justice. But they are the vital stuff of democracy in everyday life. They are part of the repair work necessary to build up a reservoir of social trust. These virtues are part of the background that indirectly enables shifting involvements.

Everyday Virtue and Where It Is Learned

Like any other competence, the habits of democracy in everyday life are learned. Almost certainly they are learned in the associations of civil society, but where do we find practices like treating people identically and speaking up among strangers? With this question I reenter the terrain on which I began in the introduction. It is an apt conclusion, because it allows me a final opportunity to point up the unanticipated moral consequences of membership in voluntary associations. To demonstrate once more the moral uses of pluralism, and its dependence on shifting involvements.

Of course, like most moral dispositions, treating people identically and with easy spontaneity and speaking up about injustice are first learned at home. If we have been dealt with erratically or abusively by parents or undisciplined siblings, and if the familiar complaint "that's not fair" has never worked for us, we are likely to become inured to arbitrariness. If we are accustomed to fearful dependence or physical aggression at home, we are unlikely to develop the habit of speaking out. If we are not trained to have minimal self-control, and are unused to seeing others restrain themselves, then even the relatively simple demand to treat people identically in ordinary encounters will be experienced as unbearably onerous. Throughout this book, I have focused on adult experiences. So where, apart from the family, can the dispositions that make democracy in everyday life possible be cultivated today?

A significant development and social countertrend to "bowling alone" is the phenomenal growth of a new type of small group that goes by the general name "support group." There are an estimated 3 million small groups in the

United States today. These include small religious groups—Bible study groups, prayer groups, and "home churches" numbering about 900,000—which have changed the face of religious organization in the United States by shifting the focus of religion from doctrine to "fellowship." There are roughly 500,000 self-help and recovery groups nationwide, forums for testifying to personal addictions, vices, and problems, and aiming at moral and spiritual self-improvement. And an estimated 250,000 specialized secular support groups—for single parents, for example, or reading groups. Robert Wuthnow reports in his authoritative study that "at present, four out of every ten Americans belong to a small group that meets regularly and provides caring and support for its members." (That is, 75,000,000 adults.)[12] These are voluntary associations. But they are a novel development, differing most obviously by their informality and size, and by their avowed purpose of providing "small portable sources of interpersonal support."

How should we assess their significance for moral development? Members of small groups often testify that "community" is what they are searching for, but it is clear that these groups do not meet democratic theorists' hopes for associations capable of compensating for the failures of political community. Wuthnow points out that far from countering tendencies to social and political disengagement, support groups are an adaptive response to community decline. Because an array of groups is available almost everywhere to help people deal with personal crises, they reinforce rather than replace individualist norms. These groups facilitate mobility, loosening of familial and community attachments, even increased pressure at work. "If small groups are the glue holding together American society (as some argue), they are then a social solvent as well."[13]

The failure to provide community is not surprising if we consider that small groups are particularly fluid voluntary associations, easily joined and costlessly exited. In many places a crowded marketplace of groups compete with one another for members, who shop around and regularly shift membership, in the process electing the elements of identity they will bring to the fore. In my diffuse desire for "support" I can choose to identify myself as a Jew, a woman, and a professor and join a synogogue group for orthodox women academics; or I can see myself as an adult child of an alcoholic and enter recovery; and I can reshuffle these attributes and change memberships at will.

These groups do not create sustained responsibilities, either; the chief obligation is to attend meetings regularly. The support they provide is emotional rather than practical, and almost never financial. (They bear no resemblance to that model democratic association, the mutual aid society.) The small group movement is not a revival of civic associations; it does little to encourage members to look outward toward participation. In fact, most steer clear of talk of politics much less political agendas. Few engage in projects in or for the larger community. Even when group life revolves around shared problems that have social roots (the difficulties of working mothers, say, or addictions), they typically avert attention from public policy.

Instead they offer opportunities for emotional support—"caring," defined as hearing one another out uncritically, and encouragement in facing up to the difficulties of everyday life. The proposed solution to most problems is self-transformation, not collective action or social change, and the goal is happiness, feeling good about ourselves. Critics are concerned that "an apolitical movement that helps shape the identities of a few million people will have political consequences," all negative.[14]

But if small groups do not meet the tests of community or civic association, it does not follow that they contribute nothing to cultivating democratic dispositions. Small groups are an example of the fact that the democratic valence of association life is often indeterminate and sometimes surprising. The substantive "stuff" of group life may be an apolitical preoccupation with personal problems, at its worst a narcissistic testifying about oneself, and at the same time call up capacities high on any democratic list. In short, if we focus on creating and joining groups rather than on the ideology of "fellowship" or "recovery," they clearly serve as incubators of organizational skills. This is not large-scale institution-building, but even the most informal groups must be formed and "run," with meeting times, planning, rules, and some material resources. This is "grassroots" organizing and, taking into account the ceaseless proliferation of new groups, leadership is astonishingly widespread.

More important, the structural attributes that discourage the hope of democratic theorists that small groups would function as communities or civic associations may be positive forces for cultivating certain moral dispositions. Precisely because they are *not* minicommunities and involve only weak ties, small groups may be a training ground for ordinary interactions. They are all about face-to-face relations and dealing freely with people who are initially strangers. Of course, most small groups are not mirrors of social diversity, though an urban meeting of AA may come close. Like any voluntary association some area of common interest (if only longing for "support") is their reason for being in the first place. But we should not exaggerate their homogeneity, overlook the fact that they are among the most permeable of associations (with few if any membership requirements or lists), or fail to appreciate that small groups are "horizontal" associations where members have equal standing.

Finally, the internal dynamic of small group life may be suited to developing the dispositions required for democracy in everyday life. The norms of these groups vary, and may be arbitrary, even idiosyncratic. But the announced norm of all support groups is treating people identically and with easy spontaneity. And small groups provide the experience of reciprocity: even if members mainly take turns speaking about themselves, they do take turns, and they are expected to take a turn at encouraging others. This is important if we consider that group members are explicit about their lack of alternative social connections and supports. Although the bulk of members may not suffer dire privatization and anomie, small groups do reach the isolated and excluded. "Probably the most important way in which small groups influence the wider community," Wuthnow concludes, "is by freeing individuals from their own insecurities so that they can reach out more charitably toward other people."[15]

Small groups also impel people to speak out about day-to-day injustice. That is their main business, after all. At their worst, they do nothing to distinguish injustice from bad habits and purely personal complaints. They may encourage the senseless equation of incest victims with "victims" of overeating: "in recovery, whether or not you were housed, schooled, clothed, and fed in childhood, you can still claim to be metaphorically homeless."[16] And members typically attend for the gratification of testifying to the injuries they have suffered, not to speak out on behalf of others. Even so, this is the reverse of humility and passivity. These groups accustom people to express their indignation, and to expect support when they do. With this, they may cultivate the iota of trust necessary for speaking out about ordinary injustice. They may encourage, if only in a miniscule way, the expectation that indignation at arbitrariness and unfairness will not be met with indifference or hostility.

Navigating Pluralism

These are tentative and in any case modest suggestions. Support groups are doubtless not the only context, and it may not be possible to locate with precision the contexts in which dispositions to treat people identically and to speak up about against ordinary injustice are developed.

That said, the disposition to perform the small daily acts that make up democracy in everyday life are critical for navigating the pluralism that *is* everyday life. They shape its character. Democracy in everyday life does not compensate for the educative limitations of public institutions, erase the effects of illiberal and antidemocratic associations, or repair the inequalities and exclusions they impose on both members and outsiders. Still, occasions for easy spontaneity and speaking out are all around us. We are called on to exhibit these dispositions all the time. And they are *political* virtues. When we demonstrate them in the course of our day-to-day interactions we don't have the common ground of democratic citizenship in mind, but we reinforce it despite ourselves.

This book explains why this is so important. The variety of association life is unalterable, unregrettably so. Under conditions of constitutionally protected liberties, pluralism has an exuberant life, which eludes the grasp of systematic political theory.

Where new affiliations are formed all the time for every conceivable purpose, and where individuals shift involvements and cycle through social spheres, the valence of associational life overall is bound to be indeterminate. And given the vicissitudes of individual development, the formative effects of membership in a particular association cannot be predicted dependably on the basis of the association's ideology or governance structure. Which is why I have looked in some detail at specific associations, the laws and ideologies with which we try to understand and govern them, and the way they target specific moral deficits, assist in repairing them, and in some cases contain irreparable vices.

The moral uses of pluralism are inconsistent with systematic programs for cultivating civic competence, with "congruence." I have tried to step back from sweeping generalities about the relation between civil society and liberal democracy. It seems fair to say that pluralism is difficult to *colonize* short of utopian institutional redesign, that *congruence* is difficult to enforce without a vast illiberal increase in legal intervention into private and social life, and that the Tocquevillian notion of indirect political education through *mediating* groups is an optimistic "liberal expectancy."

Experience confirms the variable, often unpredictable personal moral significance of membership. An ounce of psychological realism confirms the hybrid character of associations and the vicissitudes of individual development. The messy constitutional law of freedom of association and American political ideology insure the moral uses of pluralism will continue to fall short of both exalted possibilities of schools of virtue and jeremiahs of viciousness and anomie. I have tried to make this vivid.

Notes

Introduction

1. George Kateb, "The Value of Association," in Amy Gutmann, ed., *Freedom of Association* (Princeton, N.J.: Princeton University Press, forthcoming), pp. 3, 13.

2. William Galston, *Liberal Purposes* (Cambridge: Cambridge University Press, 1991), p. 6.

3. Ibid., p. 233.

4. Werner Sollors, *Beyond Ethnicity* (Oxford: Oxford University Press, 1986), pp. 175–86.

5. J. S. Mill, *On Liberty* (New York: Norton, 1975), p. 13.

6. "Civil Disobedience," in Nancy L. Rosenblum, ed., *Thoreau: Political Writings* (Cambridge: Cambridge University Press, 1996), p. 18.

7. Robert Wuthnow, *Sharing the Journey* (Princeton, N.J.: Princeton University Press, 1994).

8. Wendy Kaminer, *I'm Dysfunctional, You're Dysfunctional* (Reading, Mass.: Addison-Wesley, 1993).

9. Michael Kelly, "The Road to Paranoia," *New Yorker*, June 19, 1995, pp. 60–75, at p. 60.

10. Raphael Ezekiel, *The Racist Mind* (Cambridge, Mass.: Harvard University Press, 1995), pp. 24, 288.

11. Lewis White Beck, ed., *Immanual Kant on History* (Indianapolis: Bobbs-Merrill, 1963), pp. 112–13.

12. Montesquieu, *The Spirit of the Laws* (New York: Hafner, 1949), pp. 296–97

13. J. S. Mill, "M. De Tocqueville on Democracy in America," in Marshall Cohen, ed., *The Philosophy of John Stuart Mill: Ethical, Political, and Religious* (New York: Modern Library, 1961), pp. 145, 143.

14. Immanuel Kant, "Perpetual Peace," in Beck, ed., *Kant on History*, pp. 111–12.

15. Judith Shklar, *Ordinary Vices* (Cambridge, Mass.: Harvard University Press, 1984), p. 197.

16. Galston, *Liberal Purposes*, pp. 96, 298.

17. John Rawls, *A Theory of Justice* (Cambridge, Mass.: Harvard University Press, 1971), p. 506.

18. J. David Greenstone, "Group Theories," Fred Greenstein and Nelson Polsby, eds., *Handbook of Political Science* vol. 2, *Micropolitical Theory* (Reading, Mass.: Addison-Wesley, 1975), pp. 243–318.

19. Galston, *Liberal Purposes*, p. 254.

20. George Kateb, "The Moral Distinctiveness of Representative Democracy," *Ethics* 91 (1981): 357–74.

21. Galston, *Liberal Purposes*, p. 225. James Q. Wilson, "The Rediscovery of Character: Private Virtue and Public Policy," *Public Interest* 81 (1985): 13–16, at pp. 15–16.

22. Justice Jackson in *West Virginia State Board of Education v. Barnette*, 319 U.S. 624 (1943).

23. Peter Berkowitz, *Virtue and the Making of Modern Liberalism*, unpublished ms., p. 14. Stephen Holmes, *The Anatomy of Antiliberalism* (Cambridge, Mass.: Harvard University Press, 1993).

24. Nancy L. Rosenblum, ed., *Liberalism and the Moral Life* (Cambridge, Mass.: Harvard University Press, 1989).

25. James Q. Wilson, *The Moral Sense* (New York: Free Press, 1993), p. 54.

26. Albert Camus, *The Rebel* (New York: Vintage, 1956), p. ix.

27. Michael Sandel, *Democracy's Discontent* (Cambridge, Mass.: Harvard University Press, 1996), p. 326.

28. Alan Ryan, "The Liberal Community," in John Chapman and Ian Shapiro, eds., *Democratic Community: Nomos XXV*. (New York: New York University Press, 1993).

29. Saul V. Levine, *Radical Departures* (New York: Harcourt Brace Jovanovich, 1984), p. 179.

30. Cited in Guy Dodge, *Benjamin Constant's Philosophy of Liberalism* (Chapel Hill: University of North Carolina Press, 1980), p. 29.

31. Shklar, *Ordinary Vices*, pp. 234, 5.

32. L. T. Hobhouse, *Liberalism* (Oxford: Oxford University Press, 1964), p. 24.

33. Samuel Huntington, "The Democratic Distemper," *Public Interest* 41 (1975): 9–38.

34. Ezekiel, *Racist Mind*, pp. 153, xxiv, 158, 150, 109–10.

35. Joseph Raz, *The Morality of Freedom* (Oxford: Clarendon, 1983), p. 203.

36. Nancy Sherman, *The Fabric of Character* (Oxford: Clarendon, 1989), p. 2. Martha Nussbaum, "Non-Relative Virtues: An Aristotelian Approach," *Midwest Studies in Philosophy* 13 (1988): 32–53.

37. Ernest Gellner, *Conditions of Liberty: Civil Society and Its Rivals* (New York: Allen Lane, 1994), p. 103.

Chapter 1

1. Wilhelm von Humboldt, *The Sphere and Duties of Government* (London: John Chapman, 1854), pp. 11, 53, 114, 116–17.

2. Clifford Geertz, "The Uses of Diversity," *Michigan Quarterly Review* 75 (Winter 1986): 105–23, at p. 114.

3. *Philosophy of Right* (Oxford: Oxford University Press, 1952), p. 266 (Addition to ¶182).

4. Krishan Kumar, "Civil Society: An Inquiry into the Usefulness of an Historical Term," *British Journal of Sociology* 44, no. 3 (1993): 375–95. Andrew Arato and Jean Cohen, *Civil Society and Democratic Theory* (Cambridge, Mass.: MIT, 1991).

5. *Philosophy of Right*, p. 148 (¶238); p. 276 (Addition to ¶238); p. 154 (¶255); p. 124.

6. Ibid., p. 123 (¶185); p. 126 (¶189); p. 130 (¶200); p. 123 (¶183); p. 128 (¶193).

7. *The Philosophy of History*, trans. J. Sibree (New York: Dover, 1956), p. 448; p. 129 (¶197); p. 124 (¶187).

8. *Philosophy of Right*, p. 84 (¶124); p. 147 (¶235); p. 267 (Addition to ¶182).

9. Ibid., p. 291 (Addition to ¶297); p. 276 (Addition to ¶234).

10. *Philosophy of History*, p. 452.

11. *Philosophy of Right*, p. 133 (¶207); p. 278 (Addition to ¶255).

12. Ibid., p. 153 (¶253); p. 193 (¶296).

13. T. M. Knox, ed. note, ibid., pp. 353–54, 365.

14. Ibid., pp. 123–24; p. 150 (¶244–45).

15. Shlomo Avineri, *Hegel's Theory of the Modern State* (Cambridge: Cambridge University Press, 1972), pp. 240–41, and Z. A. Pelczynski, "Nation, Civil Society, State: Hegelian Sources of the Marxian Non-theory of Nationality," in *The State and Civil Society: Studies in Hegel's Political Philosophy* (Cambridge: Cambridge University Press, 1984), pp. 262–78. *Philosophy of Right*, p. 278 (Addition to ¶255).

16. Charles Taylor, *Hegel and Modern Society* (Cambridge: Cambridge University Press, 1979), p. 129.

17. Samuel L. Popkin, *The Reasoning Voter* (Chicago: University of Chicago Press, 1991).

18. Robert Lane, "The Joyless Polity," forthcoming in Stephen Elkin, ed. *Citizen Competence* (University Park: Pennsylvania State University Press).

19. Michael Walzer, "The Idea of Civil Society," *Dissent* (Spring 1991): 293–304, at p. 302.

20. Robert Putnam, "Bowling Alone: America's Declining Social Capital," *Journal of Democracy* 6, no. 1 (1995): p. 65–78, at pp. 69, 73; and idem, "Tuning In, Tuning Out: The Strange Disappearance of Social Capital in America," *American Political Science Review* (October 1995): 4–5. For a skeptical view, see Seymour Martin Lipset, "Malaise and Resiliency in America," *Journal of Democracy* 16, no. 1 (1995): 4–18.

21. Ralph M. Kramer, "The Future of the Voluntary Agency in a Mixed Economy," *Journal of Applied Behavioral Science* 21, no. 4 (1985): 377–91, at p. 377.

22. Walzer, "Civil Society," pp. 293, 298; John Gray, "Totalitarianism, Reform and Civil Society," in *Post Liberalism: Studies in Political Thought* (New York: Routledge, 1993), p. 157.

23. Reinhard Bendix, "State, Legitimation, and 'Civil Society,'" *Telos* 86 (1990–91): 143–52.

24. Jean Cohen, *Class and Civil Society: The Limits of Marxian Critical Theory* (Amherst: University of Massachusetts Press, 1982), pp. 50, 214. Jürgen Habermas, "Further Reflections on the Public Sphere," in Craig Calhoun, ed., *Habermas and the Public Sphere* (Cambridge, Mass.: MIT Press, 1992), pp. 421–61, at pp. 438, 453–54. David H. Watt, "United States: Cultural Challenges to the Voluntary Sector," in Robert Wuthnow, ed., *Between States and Markets: The Voluntary Sector in Comparative Perspective* (Princeton, N.J.: Princeton University Press, 1991), p. 270.

25. Walzer, "Civil Society," p. 293.

26. Peter L. Berger and Richard John Neuhaus, *To Empower People: The Role of Mediating Structures in Public Policy* (Washington, D.C.: The American Enterprise Institute, 1977), pp. 6, 3, 41.

27. William Galston, *Liberal Purposes* (Cambridge: Cambridge University Press, 1991), p. 255.

28. Joan Didion, "Slouching towards Bethlehem," in *Slouching towards Bethlehem* (New York: Washington Square Press, 1961), p. 94.

29. Berger and Neuhaus, *To Empower People*, p. 42.

30. See Lester M. Salamon, "The Rise of the Nonprofit Sector," *Foreign Affairs* 73, no. 4 (1994): 109–22.

31. Peter Berger, *The Capitalist Revolution*, cited in David H. Watt, "United States: Cultural Challenges to the Voluntary Sector," in Robert Wuthnow, ed., *Between States and Markets: The Voluntary Sector in Comparative Perspective* (Princeton, N.J.: Princeton University Press, 1991), p. 255.

32. Joseph Raz, "Multiculturalism: A Liberal Perpsective," *Dissent* (Winter 1994): 67–79, at p. 72.

33. Michael Walzer, "Constitutional Rights and the Shape of Civil Society," in Robert E. Calvert, ed., *The Constitution of the People* (Lawrence: University Press of Kansas, 1991), pp. 123, 125.

34. Frances Fitzgerald, *Cities on a Hill* (New York: Simon & Schuster, 1981), p. 22.

35. Joan Didion, *Miami* (New York: Simon & Schuster, 1987), p. 13.

36. Cited in John Keane, ed., *Civil Society and the State: New European Perspectives* (London: Verso, 1988), p. 5.

37. Vaclav Benda in H. Gordon Skilling, "Parallel Polis, or an Independent Society in Central and Eastern Europe: An Inquiry," *Social Research* 55, nos. 1–2 (1988): 211–46, at p. 218.

38. Jan Simsa, in Skilling, ed., ibid., p. 245.

39. For an overview, see David N. Nelson, "Civil Society Endangered: The Perils of Post-Communism," *East European Studies Occasional Paper*, 42, Woodrow Wilson Center.

40. For analyses, see Andrew Arato, "Civil Society against the State," *Telos* 47 (1981): 23–47.

41. Grant McConnell, "The Public Values of the Private Association," in J. Roland Pennock and John W. Chapman, eds., *Nomos XI: Voluntary Associations* (New York: Atherton, 1969), p. 155.

42. "Gingrich's Welfare Vision: Charities Find It in the Clouds," *New York Times*, June 4, 1995, p. 30.

43. Lester M. Salamon, *Partners in Public Service: Government–Nonprofit Relations in the Modern Welfare State* (Baltimore: Johns Hopkins University Press, 1995).

44. See Stephen Holmes, *Passions and Constraint* (Chicago: University of Chicago Press, 1995); Ellen Wood, "The Uses and Abuses of Civil Society," cited in Kumar, "Civil Society," p. 390.

45. Salamon, "Nonprofit Sector," p. 118.

46. Salamon, *Partners in Public Service*, pp. 44–45.

47. The exception in the United States is "semisovereign" nations, indigenous tribes on reservations.

48. See Nancy L. Rosenblum, "Democratic Character and Community: The Logic of Congruence?" *Journal of Political Philosophy* 2 (1994): 67–97.

49. Walzer, "Civil Society," pp. 293–304, at pp. 302–3.

50. Habermas, "Public Sphere," pp. 453–56; Claus Offe, "New Social Movements: Challenging the Boundaries of Institutional Politics," *Social Research* 52 (1985): 817–68. Philippe Schmitter argues that, "secondary citizenship cannot find expression there," in "Democratic Theory and Neocorporatist Practice," *Social Research* 50, no.4 (1983): 885–928, at pp. 925, 914.

51. Michael Sandel, *Democracy's Discontent* (Cambridge, Mass.: Harvard University Press, 1996), p. 305.

52. Cited in Robert B. Westbrook, *John Dewey and American Democracy* (Ithaca, N.Y.: Cornell University Press, 1991), pp. 534, 192.

53. Carole Pateman, *Participation and Democratic Theory* (Cambridge: Cambridge University Press, 1970). See too Joshua Cohen, "Contractualism and Property Systems," in John Chapman and J. Roland Pennock, eds., *Markets and Justice, Nomos XXXI* (New York: New York University Press, 1989), pp. 72–85, at p. 74; Robert Dahl, *Democracy and Its Critics* (New Haven, Conn.: Yale University Press, 1989), p. 331.

54. Adina Schwartz, "Meaningful Work," *Ethics* 92 (1982): 634–46. Carmi Schooler and Milvin Kohn, "Occupational Experience and Psychological Functioning," American Sociological Review 38, no. 1 (1973): 97–118.

55. Jon Elster, "Self-Realization in Work and Politics: The Marxist Conception of the Good Life," *Social Philosophy and Policy* 32 (1986): 97–126.

56. Sandel, *Democracy's Discontent*, p. 233.

57. Gabriel A. Almond and Sidney Verba, *The Civic Culture* (Princeton, N.J.: Princeton University Press, 1963).

58. Pateman, *Participation and Democratic Theory*, pp. 12–13, 48, 46, 52–53, 55, 74.

59. For Robert Dahl's argument, see *A Preface to Economic Democracy* (Berkeley: University of California Press, 1985), pp. 57–58, 94, 115, 118.

60. J. David Greenstone, "Group Theories," in Fred Greenstein and Nelson Polsby, eds., *Handbook of Political Science,* vol. 2, *Micropolitical Theory* (Reading, Mass.: Addison-Wesley, 1975), pp. 243–318. Dietrich Rueschemeyer, "The Self-Organization of Society and Democratic Rule: Specifying the Relationship," unpublished ms.

61. Harry Eckstein, "Civic Inclusion and Its Discontents," in Regarding Politics: Essays on Political Theory, Stability, and Change (Berkeley: University of California Press, 1992), pp. 343–77.

62. T. Richard Witmer, "Civil Liberties and the Trade Union," *Yale Law Journal* 621 (1941) at 627.

63. Stephen Macedo, "Community, Diversity and Civic Education: Toward a Liberal Political Science of Group Life," *Social Philosophy and Policy Foundation* 13, no. 1 (1996): 240–268, at pp. 264, 250.

64. Susan Okin, *Justice, Gender, and the Family* (New York: Basic, 1989).

65. Frank Michelman, "Law's Republic," 97 *Yale Law Journal* 1493 (1988); Cass Sunstein, "Beyond the Republican Revival," 97 *Yale Law Journal* 1593 (1988).

66. Robert Audi, "The Separation of Church and State and the Obligations of Citizenship," *Philosophy and Public Affairs* 18 (1989): 269–96, at p. 265. Kent Greenawalt, *Private Consciences and Public Reasons* (New York: Oxford University Press, 1995).

67. John Keane, ed., "Introduction," *Civil Society and the State: New European Perspectives* (London: Verso, 1988), p. 15.

68. Walzer, "Constitutional Rights," p. 125.

69. Joshua Cohen and Joel Rogers, "Secondary Associations and Democratic Governance," *Politics and Society,* 20, no. 4 (1992): 393–472, at p. 395.

70. John S. Dryzek, "Political Inclusion and the Dynamics of Democratization," *American Political Science Review* 90, no. 1 (1996): 475–87.

71. John Rawls, *A Theory of Justice* (Cambridge, Mass.: Harvard University Press, 1971), pp. 298–300, 441.

72. Putnam, "Bowling Alone," p. 67. Francis Fukuyama, *Trust: The Social Virtues and the Creation of Prosperity* (New York: Free Press, 1995), pp. 6–7.

73. Alan Silver, "The Curious Importance of Small Groups in American Sociology," in Herbert J. Gans, ed., *Sociology in America* (Newbury Park: Sage, 1990), pp. 61–72, at p. 70.

74. Ibid. pp. 63, 65; Kramer, "Voluntary Agency," p. 387.

75. "Tuning In, Tuning Out," p. 2.

76. Fukuyama, *Trust*, pp. 351, 43, 159, 325.

77. Nathan Glazer, "The Street Gangs and Ethnic Enterprise," *Public Interest* 28 (1972): 83–89.

78. See Paul Q. Hirst, ed., *The Pluralist Theory of the State: Selected Writings of G. D. H. Cole, J. N. Figgis, and H. J. Laski* (London: Routledge, 1989).

79. Figgis, "Great Leviathan," in ibid., p. 113.

80. Ibid. p. 125.

81. Robert Putnam, *Making Democracy Work: Civic Traditions in Modern Italy* (Princeton, N.J.: Princeton University Press, 1993), p. 90.

82. Alexis de Tocqueville, *Democracy in America*, ed. J. P. Mayer (New York: Harper & Row, 1966), p. 515. James T. Schliefer, *The Making of Tocqueville's Democracy in America* (Chapel Hill: University of North Carolina Press, 1980).

83. Tocqueville, *Democracy in America* p. 514.

84. Ibid., pp. 514, 516.

85. Ibid. p. 527.

86. Samuel Bowls and Herbert Gintis, "From the I.R.S. to the P.T.A," *New York Times*, April 19, 1995.

87. The phrase is Peter Berkowitz's, unpublished ms., p. 46. Michael McConnell, "Accommodation of Religion: An Update and a Response to the Critics," 60 *George Washington Law Review* 685 (1992).

88. Raz, "Multiculturalism," pp. 78–79.

89. Yael Tamir, "Seedbed of Democracy?" unpublished paper, American Political Science Association, August 1995, p. 32. For another formula, see John Keane, "The Limits of State Action," in John Keane, ed., *Democracy and Civil Society* (London: Verso, 1988).

90. Gray, "Hobbes and the Modern State," pp. 4, 17; "The Politics of Cultural Diversity," p. 266; "What Is Living and What Is Dead in Liberalism?" p. 288 in *Post-Liberalism: Studies in Political Thought*. See, too, Ernest Gellner, *Conditions of Liberty: Civic Society and Its Rivals* (New York: Allen Lane, 1994).

91. Chandran Kukathas, "Freedom of Association and Liberty of Conscience," unpublished paper, American Political Science Association, August 1995, p. 15.

Chapter 2

1. Robert Putnam, *Making Democracy Work: Civic Traditions in Modern Italy* (Princeton, N.J.: Princeton University Press, 1993), pp. 157–58.

2. Alan Zuckerman, Nicholas Valentino, and Ezra Zuckerman, "A Structural Theory of Vote Choice," *Journal of Politics* 56 (1994): 1008–33.

3. Mark Granovetter, "Economic Action and Social Structure: The Problem of Embeddedness," *American Journal of Sociology* 91, no. 3 (1985): 481–510, at p. 489.

4. See Nancy L. Rosenblum, "Studying Authority: Keeping Pluralism in Mind," in J. Roland Pennock and John W. Chapman, eds., *Authority Revisited: Nomos XXIX* (New York: New York University Press, 1987), pp. 102–30.

5. Erik H. Erikson, *Identity and the Life Cycle* (New York: Norton, 1980), p. 58.

6. John Rawls, *A Theory of Justice* (Cambridge, Mass.: Harvard University Press, 1971), p. 515.

7. Ibid., pp. 469–70, 494–95.

8. Ibid., p. 474.

9. Ibid.

10. Ibid., pp. 468–69, 496.

11. Ibid., pp. 496, 506. Rawls, "The Idea of an Overlapping Consensus,"*Oxford Journal of Legal Studies* 7, no. 1 (1987): 1–15, at p. 7.

12. Rawls, *Theory of Justice*, p. 516. The morality of principle may be necessary only for "a substantial majority of politically active" members, "Overlapping Consensus," pp. 19, 17, 22, 4n.

13. Rawls, *Theory of Justice*, pp. 473, 475, 472. See, too, *Political Liberalism* (New York: Columbia University Press, 1993), pp. 40–42 and n. 44.

14. William Galston, *Liberal Purposes* (Cambridge: Cambridge University Press, 1991), pp. 243–44.

15. Yael Tamir, *Liberal Nationalism* (Princeton, N.J.: Princeton University Press, 1993), pp. 135–38.

16. Rawls, *Political Liberalism*, p. 301.

17. Rawls, *Theory of Justice*, p. 527.

18. Ibid., p. 242.

19. Ibid., p. 7.

20. Ibid., pp. 463–65.

21. Ibid., p. 463. For creative efforts to secure conditions for effective parenting, see Carole Stack, *All Our Kin: Strategies for Survival in a Black Community* (New York: Harper & Row, 1974); On "recombinant family life" in the working class, see Judith Stacy, *Brave New Families* (New York: Basic, 1990). Susan Okin, *Justice, Gender, and the Family* (New York: Basic, 1989), p. 17, 22.

22. Rawls, *Theory of Justice*, pp. 225–26.

23. Ibid., p. 8.

24. Michael Sandel, *Liberalism and the Limits of Justice* (Cambridge: Cambridge University Press, 1982), p. 151. Rawls, *Theory of Justice* p. 523.

25. For the technical sense of "the strains of commitment," see Allen E. Buchanan, *Marx and Justice* (Totowa, N.J.: Rowman & Littlefield, 1982), p. 119.

26. *Political Liberalism*, p. 12.

27. Ibid., p. 146, n. 13. Rawls, "The Priority of Right and Ideas of the Good," *Philosophy and Public Affairs* 17, no. 4 (1988): 251–76, at p. 252.

28. "Justice as Fairness: Political Not Metaphysical," *Philosophy and Public Affairs* 14, no. 3 (1985): 223–51, at p. 241; *Political Liberalism*, p. 13.

29. Andrew Sharp, "Representing Justice and the Maori: On Why It Ought Not to Be Construed as a Postmodernist Text," *Political Theory Newsletter* 4 (1992): 27–38, at p. 33.

30. "Justice as Fairness," p. 241.

31. Rawls, "Kantian Constructivism in Moral Theory," *Journal of Philosophy* 77, no. 9 (1980): 515–72, at p. 545.

32. Buchanan, *Marx and Justice*, p. 149.

33. *Political Liberalism*, p. 85n.

34. "Priority of Right," p. 265.

35. Galston, *Liberal Purposes*, p. 292.

36. Steven Macedo, *Liberal Virtues* (New York: Clarendon, 1990), p. 53.

37. Galston, *Liberal Purposes*, p. 255, 296–97, 295.

38. George Kateb, "Notes on Pluralism," *Social Research* 61, no. 3 (1994): 511–37, at p. 521.

39. Will Kymlicka, "The Rights of Minority Cultures: Reply to Kukathas," *Political Theory* 20 (1992): 140–46, at p. 144.

40. Joseph Raz, "Multiculturalism: A Liberal Perpsective," *Dissent*, vol. 41 (Winter) 1994: 67–79, at pp. 77, 76.

41. Galston, *Liberal Purposes*, p. 295.

42. Raz, "Multiculturalism," p. 73.

43. Granovetter, "Economic Action," p. 492. Altruism toward strangers is an exception; James Q. Wilson, *The Moral Sense* (New York: Free Press, 1993), p. 36.

44. Macedo, *Liberal Virtues*, pp. 254–85.

45. Lewis Coser, *Greedy Institutions* (New York: Free Press, 1974), p. 17.

46. Rawls, *Theory of Justice*, p. 441.

47. Tamir, "Seedbed of Democracy?" unpublished paper, American Political Science Association, August 1995, p. 85.

48. Kateb, "Notes on Pluralism," pp. 524, 525, 527.

49. K. Anthony Appiah and Amy Gutmann, *Color Conscious* (Princeton, N.J.: Princeton University Press, 1990), "Race, Culture, Identity: Misunderstood Connections," p. 90. Appiah also laments the negative consequences of racial ascription.

50. I am grateful to John Tomasi for this observation. For a full discussion, see ibid., pp. 80ff.

51. *Political Liberalism*, pp. 277–78.

52. "Overlapping Consensus," p. 19; *Theory of Justice*, p. 234.

53. Judith Shklar, *American Citizenship: The Quest for Inclusion* (Cambridge, Mass.: Harvard University Press, 1991), p. 63.

54. Alexis de Tocqueville, *Democracy in America*, ed. J. P. Mayer (New York: Harper & Row, 1966), p. 604.

55. Rawls, *Theory of Justice*, pp. 537, 545, 536–37.

56. Ibid., p. 472.

57. James Madison, cited in Kateb, "Notes of Pluralism," p. 518.

58. Rawls, *Theory of Justice* p. 544.

59. Ibid., p. 212.

60. Hazel Markus and Paula Nurius, "Possible Selves," *American Psychologist* 41 (September 1986): 954–67.

61. Daniel Levinson et al., *Seasons of a Man's Life* (New York: Ballantine, 1978). Heinz Kohut, *Self Psychology and the Humanities* (New York: Norton, 1985), p. 11. For an exposition of developmental theory from the standpoint of political theory, see Jack Crittenden, *Beyond Individualism: Reconstituting the Liberal Self* (Oxford: Oxford University Press, 1992).

62. Erikson, *Identity*, pp. 122, 125. For the romanticism of life-cycle theory, see Nancy L. Rosenblum, *Another Liberalism* (Cambridge, Mass.: Harvard University Press, 1987), pp. 147–50.

63. Morris Eagle, *Recent Developments in Psychoanalysis: A Critical Evaluation* (Cambridge, Mass.: Harvard University Press, 1987), p. 155.

64. Anne Colby and William Damon, *Some Do Care: Contemporary Lives of Moral Commitment* (New York: Free Press, 1992).

65. Cited in Frances Fitzgerald, *Cities on the Hill* (New York: Simon & Schuster, 1981), p. 211.

66. Richard Flathman, "Liberal versus Civic, Republican, Democratic, and Other Vocational Educations," *Political Theory* 24, no. 1 (1996): 4–32, at p. 17.

67. Raymond Williams, *The Politics of Modernism* (New York: Verso, 1989), p. 116.

68. See Judy Dunn and Robert Plomin, *Separate Lives: Why Siblings Are So Different* (New York: Basic, 1990).

69. This is contingent on adult circumstances and experiences, of course, but trust and trustworthiness are learned first as a child at home.

70. William Damon, *The Moral Child* (New York: Free Press, 1988), pp. 35, 42–49.

71. Mary C. Waters, *Ethnic Options* (Berkeley: University of California Press, 1990), p. 59.

72. For disconfirmation of "the impressionable years hypothesis" as it applies to political attitudes, see Duane Alwin and Jon Krosnick, "Aging, Cohorts, and the Stability of Sociopolitical Orientations over the Life Span," *American Journal of Sociology* 97, no. 1 (1991): 169–95.

73. Useful studies include: Amy Gutmann, *Democratic Education* (Princeton, N.J.: Princeton University Press, 1987), pp. 105–7; Timothy E. Cook, "The Bear Market in Political Socialization and the Costs of Misunderstood Psychological Theories," *American Political Science Review* 79 (1985): 1080; Judith Torney-Purta, "Youth in Relation to Social Institutions," in S. Shirley Feldman and Glen R. Elliott, eds., *At the Threshold: The Developing Adolescent* (Cambridge, Mass.: Harvard University Press, 1990), pp. 463–64; Paul Allen Beck and M. Kent Jennings, "Pathways to Participation," *American Political Science Review* 76 (1982): 94–107; Herbert J. Gans, "The Balanced Community: Homogeneity or Heterogeneity in Residential Areas," in Jon Pynoos, Robert Schafer, and Chester W. Hartman, eds., *Housing in Urban America* (New York: Aldine 1980), pp. 141–52.

74. Alan Wolfe, *Marginalized in the Middle* (Chicago: University of Chicago Press, 1996), p. 132.

75. Erikson, *Identity* pp. 106–7.

76. Kohut, *Self Psychology and The Restoration of the Self* (Madison: International Universities Press, 1977); Eagle, *Psychoanalysis*, pp. 39, 48, 190–91.

77. Rawls, *Theory of Justice*, pp. 514–15.

78. "Big Government, Big Brothers," *New Republic*, December 25, 1995, p. 7.

79. Robert Kegan, *The Evolving Self* (Cambridge, Mass.: Harvard University Press, 1982), pp. 181, 255–57, 262.

80. Saul V. Levine, *Radical Departures* (New York: Harcourt Brace Jovanovich, 1984), p. 2.

81. Jagger and Richards, "You Can't Always Get What You Want," *Let It Bleed*, 1969.

82. Dunn and Plomin, *Separate Lives*, p. 149.

Chapter 3

1. Laurence Tribe, *American Constitutional Law* (Mineola, N.Y.: Foundation, 1978), p. 701.

2. Thomas Pickrell and Mitchell Horwich, "Religion as an Engine of Civil Policy: A Comment on the First Amendment Limitations on the Church–State Partnership in the Social Welfare Field," *Law and Contemporary Problems* 44, no. 2 (1981): 111–42, at pp. 139–40.

3. Peter L. Berger, *The Sacred Canopy* (New York: Doubleday, 1967), pp. 130ff., at p. 146.

4. Virginia Statute of Religious Freedom, passed in 1786; *Torcaso v. Watkins*, 367 U.S. 488 (1961); *McDaniel v. Paty*, 435 U.S. 618 (1978). See Isaac Kramnick and R. Laurence Moore, *The Godless Constitution* (New York: Norton, 1996), pp. 32ff. Also, Mary Ann Glendon and Raul Yanes, "Structural Free Exercise," 90 *Michigan Law Review* 477 (1991) at p. 479. *Everson v. Board of Education*, 330 U.S. 1 (1947) "elevated the separation of church and state to the status of a constitutional end in itself," p. 481.

5. William Galston, *Liberal Purposes* (Cambridge: Cambridge University Press, 1991), wants a "principled middle ground," p. 257.

6. Richard Posner and Michael McConnell, "An Economic Approach to Issues of Religious Freedom," 56 *University of Chicago Law Review* 1 (Winter) 1989 at p. 49.

7. Wilhelm von Humboldt, *The Sphere and Duties of Government* (London: John Chapman, 1854), p. 75.

8. Sacvan Bercovitch, *The American Jeremiad* (Madison: University of Wisconsin Press, 1978), p. 180. Barnaby Feder, "Ministers Who Work around the Flock," *New York Times*, October 3, 1996, p. D1.

9. Michael McConnell, "Accommodation of Religion: An Update and a Response to the Critics," 60 *George Washington Law Review* 685 (1992) at p. 739.

10. Tocqueville, *Democracy in America*, ed. J. P. Mayer (New York: Harper & Row, 1969), p. 448.

11. *Bowen v. Kendrick*, 487 U.S. 589, 605; "Gingrich's Welfare Vision: Charities Find It in the Clouds," *New York Times*, June 4, 1995, p. A30.

12. Nathan Hatch, *The Democratization of American Christianity* (New Haven, Conn.: Yale University Press, 1989). On American liberalism and Calvinism, see John P. Diggins, *The Lost Soul of American Politics* (New York: Basic, 1984). Harold Bloom, *The American Religion: The Emergence of the Post-Christian Nation* (New York: Simon & Schuster, 1992).

13. Conor Cruise O'Brien, *Godland* (Cambridge, Mass.: Harvard University Press, 1988). Carl Esbeck, "Establishment Clause Limits on Governmental Interference with Religious Organizations," 41 *Washington and Lee Law Review* 347 (1984) at 366n. Andrew Greeley and Michael Hout, "Musical Chairs: Patterns of Denominational Change," *Sociology and Social Research* 72, no. 2 (1988): 75–86.

14. *Zorach v. Clauson*, 343 U.S. 306, at 312; 313 (1952).

15. Kramnick and Moore, *Godless Constitution*, p. 56. The exception is some universities, where public expressions of religiosity are marginalized; I am grateful to Ann Wald for this observation.

16. Cited in Wendy Kaminer, "The Last Taboo," *New Republic*, vol. 215, October 14, 1996; pp. 24–32, at p. 26.

17. Joseph Grinstein, "Jihad and the Constitution: The First Amendment Implications of Combating Religiously Motivated Terrorism," 105 *Yale Law Journal* 1347 (1996).

18. George Kateb, "On Political Evil," in *The Inner Ocean* (Ithaca, N.Y.: Cornell University Press, 1992), pp. 199–221.

19. Kramnick and Moore, *Godless Constitution*, p. 61.

20. *Lynch v. Donnelly*, 465 U.S. 668 (1984), at 636.

21. Thomas James, "Rights of Conscience and State School Systems in Nineteenth-Century America," in Paul Finkelman and Stephen Gottlieb, eds. *Toward a Usable Past* (Athens: University of Georgia Press, 1991), pp. 117–47.

22. *Allegheny v. ACLU*, 109 S. Ct. 3086 (1989), at 3090, 3104.

23. *Lynch*, at 693.

24. A. Heschel, cited by the dissent in *Marsh v. Chambers*, 463 U.S. 783, at 810; "prayer is fundamentally and necessarily religious," at 783.

25. *Lynch*, 465 U.S. at 688.

26. Glendon and Yanes, "Structural Free Exercise," pp. 494–95. McConnell, "Accommodation," p. 740, and "Religious Freedom at a Crossroads," in Geoffrey Stone, Richard Epstein, and Cass Sunstein, eds., *The Bill of Rights in the Modern State* (Chicago: University of Chicago Press, 1992), pp. 117, 129, 188, 190–91.

27. Joseph Raz, "Multiculturalism: A Liberal Perspective," *Dissent*, vol. 41 (Winter 1994): 67–79, at p. 69.

28. McConnell characterizes Kathleen Sullivan's position this way; "Accommodation," p. 124n.; Sullivan, "Religion and Liberal Democracy," in *The Bill of Rights in the Modern State*.

29. Lawrence Foster, "Cults in Conflict: New Religious Movements and the Mainstream Religious Tradition in America," in Robert Bellah and Frederick Greenspahn, eds., *Uncivil Religion* (New York: Crossroad, 1987), p. 186. John Davison Hunter, *Culture Wars* (New York: Basic, 1991), p. 73.

30. Don DeLillo, *Mao II* (New York: Viking, 1991), p. 1.

31. For a response, see Judge Lively's opinion in *Mozert v. Hawkins County Bd. of Education*, 827 F. 2d 1058 (1987), at 1069.

32. Douglas Laycock, "Towards a General Theory of the Religion Clauses: The Case of Church Labor Relations and the Right to Church Autonomy," *Columbia Law Review* 81, no. 7 (1981): 1373–1417, at p. 1413.

33. Frederick M. Gedicks, "Toward a Constitutional Jursiprudence of Religious Group Rights," *Wisconsin Law Review* (1989): 99–169, at pp. 158, 162.

34. Claude Morgan, "The Significance of Church Organizational Structure in Litigation and Government Action," *Valparaiso University Law Review* 16 (1981): 145–62.

35. *Kedroff v. Saint Nicholas Cathedral*, 344 U.S. 94 (1952). *Watson v. Jones*, 13 U.S. 679 (1871) was decided without appealing to the First Amendment. *Presbyterian Church in the U.S. v Mary Elizabeth Blue Hull Memorial Church*, 393 U.S. 440.

36. *Granfield v. Catholic Univ. of America. National Labor Relations Board v. Catholic Bishop of Chicago*, 440 U.S. 490 (1979). In *Sister Reardon v. Brother Lemoyne*, 122 N.H. 1042 (1982).

37. Judge Reed in *Jones v. Wolf*, 443 U.S. 595, 613 (1979).

38. Despite variations in organization, courts recognize just two forms of religious polity: hierarchical and congregational. *Jones v. Wolf*, 443 U.S. 595 (1979). Arlin Adams and William Hanlon, "Jones v. Wolf: Church Autonomy and The Religion Clauses of the First Amendment," 128 *University of Pennsylvania Law Review* 1291 (1986).

39. *Kedroff*, at 195.

40. *Serbian*, at 164–65, 167, 168. In *Watson v. Jones*, 13 Wall 679 (1872). *Kedroff v. St. Nicholas Cathedral*, 344 U.S. 94. *Presbyterian Church v. Blue Hull Memorial Church*, 393 U.S. 440 (1969). *Melish v. Rector, Church Wardens and Vestrymen of the Church of the Holy Trinity*, 301 N.Y. 679 (1949).

41. *Serbian*, at 168.

42. *Serbian*, at 175, 176. For precedents where courts held that church societies had contravened their own rules, see 177, 180.

43. Cited by Glendon and Yanes, "Structural Free Exercise," p. 537.

44. Tribe, *American Constitutional Law*, p. 853.

45. 374 U.S. 398 (1963). *Lyng v. Northwest Indian Cemetery Protective Association*, 485 U.S. 439 (1988). See David Williams and Susan Williams, "Volitionalism and Religious Liberty," 76 *Cornell Law Review* 769 (1991). See too *Employment Division, Department of Human Resources v. Smith*, 110 S. Ct. 1595 (1990). On the criminalization of Mormon polygamy in *Reynolds v. United States*, see Nancy L. Rosenblum, "Democratic Sex," in David Estlund and Martha Nussbaum, eds., *Sex, Preference, and Family* (Oxford: Oxford University Press, 1997), pp. 63–85.

46. *Serbian*, at 167.

47. McConnell, "Bill of Rights," p. 173.

48. Michael Sandel, "Religious Liberty—Freedom of Conscience or Freedom of Choice?" 3 *Utah Law Review* 597 (1989).

49. See Robert Cover, "The Supreme Court 1982 Term: Foreword: Nomos and Narrative," 97 *Harvard Law Review* 1 (1983) at 33. Gustav Niebuhr, "Getting Below the Surface of U.S. Catholics' Beliefs," *New York Times*, April 13, 1996, p. B11.

50. Brennan, in 426 U.S. 696, at 709, citing *Watson v. Jones* at 728–29.

51. *Zorach v. Clauson*, 343 U.S. 306, 313 (1952).

52. Robert Post, *Constitutional Domains* (Cambridge, Mass.: Harvard University Press, 1995), p. 104.

53. Foster, "Cults in Conflict," pp. 188–89. Anson Shupe, "Constructing Evil as a Social Process: The Unification Church and the Media," in Robert Bellah and Frederick Greenspahn, eds., *Uncivil Religion* (New York: Crossroad, 1987), pp. 206ff.

54. Mark DeWolfe Howe, *The Garden and the Wilderness: Religion and Government in American Constitutional History* (Chicago: University of Chicago Press, 1965), and Adams and Hanon, "Jones v. Wolf," at 1300n. and 1303.

55. Cited in Hatch, *Democratization of American Christianity*, p. 300 n. 24.

56. Robert Wuthnow, *The Restructuring of American Religion: Society and Faith since World War II* (Princeton, N.J.: Princeton University Press, 1988), p. 98.

57. Posner and McConnell, "Issues of Religious Freedom," p. 58.

58. Raz, "Multiculturalism," p. 7.

59. Kren Arenson, "Donations to a Jewish Philanthropy Ebb," *New York Times*, December 27, 1995, p. A10.

60. Ernest Barker and F. W. Maitland, cited in Sheldon Leader, *Freedom of Association: A Study in Labor Law and Political Theory* (New Haven, Conn.: Yale University Press, 1992), p. 56; Paul Q. Hirst, ed., *The Pluralist Theory of the State* (London: Routledge, 1989).

61. Morris Cohen, "Communal Ghosts and Other Perils in Social Philosophy," *Journal of Philosophy, Psychology, and Scientific Methods* 16, no. 25 (1919): 673–690, at pp. 680–81.

62. Figgis, "Churches in the Modern State," in *Pluralist Theory of the State*, p. 121. For a contemporary discussion of church autonomy and state sovereignty, see Laycock, "Religion Clauses," pp. 1400–1401.

63. David Bromwich, "Culturalism, the Euthanasia of Liberalism," *Dissent*, vol. 42 (Winter 1995): 89–102.

64. *Employment Division v. Smith*, 110 S. Ct. 1595 (1990), at 1605.

65. Richard J. Neuhaus, *A New Order of Religious Freedom*, cited in Glendon and Yanes, "Structural Free Exercise," p. 486. Ira Lupu, "Where Rights Begin: The Problem of Burdens on the Free Exercise of Religion," 102 *Harvard Law Review* 933 (1989) at 947. Richard Epstein, "The Supreme Court, 1987 Term—Foreword: Unconstitutional Conditions, State Power, and the Limits of Consent," 102 *Harvard Law Review* 4 (1988). William P. Marshall, "In Defense of Smith and Free Exercise Revisionism," 59 *University of Chicago Law Review* 308 (1991) at 322.

66. Richard Epstein, "The Bill of Rights at 200 Years: Bicentennial Perspective: Religious Liberty in the Welfare State," 31 *William and Mary Law Review* 375 (1990).

67. *U.S. v. Seeger*, 380 U.S. 163 (1965). John Davison Hunter, "Religious Freedom and the Challenge of Modern Pluralism," in John Davison Hunter and O. Guinness, eds., *Articles of Faith, Articles of Peace* (Washington, D.C.: Brookings Institution, 1990), pp. 54–74.

68. Bruce N. Bagni, "Discrimination in the Name of the Lord: A Critical Evaluation of Discrimination by Religious Organizations," 79 *Columbia Law Review* 1514 (1979) at 1526–27.

69. Cited in Laycock, "Religion Clauses," p. 1375.

70. Ibid. p. 1377.

71. Bagni, "Discrimination," p. 1535.

72. *Amos*, 483 U.S. 327 (1987), at 801. The case involved a challenge to a statutory exemption of religious employees to Title VII of the Civil Rights Act, on establishment grounds, where employment bore no nexus to religious administration or trends of faith. *Amos*, at 335–36.

73. *Amos*, at 332. Gedicks, "Religious Group Rights," pp. 113–14.

74. *Amos*, at 343.

75. 397 U.S. 664. Lod Justice Balcombe, "The Attitude of the Law to Religion in Secular Society" (Oxford Centre for Postgraduate Hebrew Studies and the Institute for Advanced Legal Studies, 1989), pp. 13–15. Esbeck, "Establishment Clause Limits," pp. 399–400 and notes.

76. *National Labor Relations Board v. Catholic Bishop of Chicago*, 440 U.S. 490, at 501, 503, 496.

77. *Lemon v. Kurzman*, 403 U.S. 607 (1971). Religious associations may have to choose between independence and aid—described as "Caesar's revenge."

78. *NLRB*, at 104.

79. Scalia in *Employment Division v. Smith*, 110 S. Ct. (1990), at 1505, 1605–6. Walter Berns, *The First Amendment and the Future of American Democracy* (New York: Basic, 1970), p. 42.

80. Laycock, "Religion Clauses," pp. 1406–9, at p. 1409.

81. Gedicks, "Religious Groups Rights," pp. 154–55.

82. Bromwich, "Culturalism."

83. *Amos*, 483 U.S., at 342.

84. Wuthnow, *Restructuring of American Religion*, p. 5.

85. Esbeck, "Establishment Clause Limits," p. 381.

86. Will Kymlicka, *Multicultural Citizenship: A Liberal Theory of Minority Rights* (New York: Oxford University Press, 1995), pp. 84–85. John Tomasi, "Liberalism and Cultural Identity: Freedom Within or Freedom From?" unpublished paper, American Political Science Association, August 1995. Raz, "Multiculturalism," p. 69.

87. These problems recur vis-à-vis tribal membership, property, and the preservation of community in *Santa Clara Pueblo v. Martinez*, 436 U.S. 49 (1978).

88. 566 F. 2d 310 (1977), at 314.

89. *Dade*, at 321.

90. 556 F. 2d 310 (1977), Goldberg at 322.

91. Figgis, cited in Hirst, *Pluralist Theory*, p. 111.

92. O'Connor, *Roberts*, 83–724.

93. 556 F. 2d 310, at 321.

94. 406 U.S. 205, at 211.

95. See Justice Coleman's dissent in *Dade* at 326. Kent Greenawalt, "Freedom of Association and Religious Association," unpublished paper, pp. 15–16.

96. Frances Fitzgerald, *Cities on a Hill* (New York: Simon & Schuster, 1981), p. 138.

97. DeLillo, *Mao II*, p. 9.

98. L. T. Hobhouse, *Liberalism* (Oxford: Oxford University Press, 1964), p. 24.

99. Stephen Holmes, *Passions and Constraint* (Chicago: University of Chicago Press, 1995), p. 11.

100. Cited in David H. Watt, "United States: Cultural Challenges to the Voluntary Sector," in Robert Wuthnow, ed., *Between States and Markets: The Voluntary Sector in Comparative Perspective* (Princeton, N.J.: Princeton University Press, 1991), pp. 243–87, at p. 277

101. Gustav Niebuhr, "The Minister as Marketer: Learning from Business," *New York Times*, April 18, 1995, p. A20.

102. 471 U.S. 290, at 300.

103. Laycock, "Religion Clauses," p. 1403. At the opposite pole is Ira Lupu, "Free Exercise Exemptions and Religious Institutions: The Case of Employment Discrimination" 67 *Boston University Law Review*. 391 (1987).

104. *Wisconsin v. Yoder*, 406 U.S. 205 (1972).

105. Amy Gutmann, "Children, Paternalism, and Education: A Liberal Argument," *Philosophy and Public Affairs* 9, no. 4 (1980): 338–58, at pp. 342, 351.

106. *U.S. v. Lee*, 455. U.S. 252 (1982).

107. Raz, "Multiculturalism," p. 76.

108. See Abner S. Greene, "The Political Balance of the Religion Clauses" 102 *Yale Law Journal* 1611: (1993).

109. Fitzgerald, *Cities on a Hill*, p. 141.

110. Saul Levine, *Radical Departures* (New York: Harcourt Brace, 1984), p. 113.

111. Werner Sollors, *Beyond Ethnicity: Consent and Descent in American Culture* (Oxford: Oxford University Press, 1986), p. 32. Stephen J. Dubner, "Choosing My Religion," *New York Times Magazine*, March 31, 1996, pp. 36–41.

112. Greeley and Haut, "Musical Chairs," pp. 75–86. R. Stephen Warner, "Work in Progress toward a New Paradigm for the Sociological Study of Religion in the United States," *American Journal of Sociology* 98, no. 5 (March 1993): 1044–93, at p. 1075.

113. Gustav Niebuhr, "Protestantism Shifts toward a New Model of How 'Church' Is Done," *New York Times*, April 29, 1995, p. A12.

114. Gustav Niebuhr, "Where Religion Gets a Big Dose of Shopping-Mall Culture," *New York Times*, April 16, 1995, p. A14, and "The Minister as Marketer: Learning from Business," *New York Times*, April 18, 1995, p. A20.

115. Wuthnow, *Restructuring of American Religion*, pp. 121ff.

116. Horace McMullen, "The Institutional Church as House Church: A Vision and a Reality," in Arthur L. Foster, ed., *The House Church Evolving* (Chicago: Exploration, 1976), pp. 98–115.

117. Robert Bellah, Richard Madsen, William Sullivan, Ann Swidler, and Steven Tipton, *Habits of the Heart* (Berkeley: University of California Press, 1985), pp. 236, 414. Catherine E. Ross, "Religion and Psychological Distress," *Journal for the Scientific Study of Religion* 29, no. 2 (1990): 236–45.

118. *Everson v. Board of Education* 330 U.S. 1 (1946).

119. Stephen Carter, *Culture of Disbelief: How American Law and Politics Trivialize Religious Devotion* (New York: Basic, 1993).

120. Barbara Grizzuti Harrison, *Visions of Glory: A History and a Memory of Jehovah's Witnesses* (New York: Simon & Schuster, 1978), pp. 191–92.

121. Ibid., pp. 19, 185, 199–201, 196.

122. 465 U.S. (1984), at 668; 473 U.S. at 429.

123. McConnell, "Crossroads," p. 139. Watt, "United States," p. 266. Laycock, "Summary and Synthesis: The Crisis in Religious Liberty," 60 *George Washington Law Review* 841 (1990) at 849.

124. Harry Hirsch, *A Theory of Liberty* (New York: Routledge, 1992), p. 267.

125. Raz, "Multicultural," p. 77. On "Americanization" via religious membership, see Warner, "New Paradigm," pp. 1062–63.

126. Hunter, "Religious Freedom," p. 95.

127. Ibid., pp. 263–65.

128. Fitzgerald, *Cities on a Hill*, p. 160.

129. Derrick Z. Jackson, "Desegregating Sundays," *Boston Globe*, October 26, 1994, p. 28.

130. Jaroslaw Anders, "Dogma and Democracy," *New Republic*, vol. 208, May 17, 1993, pp. 42–48, at p. 45.

131. Leon Wieseltier, "The True Fire," *New Republic*, May 17, 1993, pp. 25–27, at pp. 25, 26.

132. Jacob Heilbrunn, "Neocon v. Theocon," *New Republic*, vol. 215, December 30, 1996, pp. 20–24, at p. 24. Jean Bethke Elshtain, "The Hard Questions: Cardinal Virtue," *New Republic*, vol. 215, December 9, 1996, p. 25.

133. Raz, "Multiculturalism," p. 75; Anders, "Dogma and Democracy," p. 46.

Chapter 4

1. For estimates, see Evan McKenzie, *Privatopia: Homeowner Associations and the Rise of Residential Private Government* (New Haven, Conn.: Yale University Press, 1994), p. 11.

2. *Nahrstedt v. Lakeside Village Condo*, 33 Cal. Rptr. 2d 63 (Cal. 1994), at 70. The estimate is from *Residential Community Associations: Private Governments in the Intergovernmental System?* (Washington, D.C.: Advisory Commission on Intergovernmental Relations, May 1989), A-112, p. 1. Current figures are cited in *Nahrstedt*, at 70. The 50 percent figure is from Fred Foldvary, *Public Goods and Private Communities: The Market Provision of Social Services* (Brookfield, Vt.: E. Elgar, 1994), p. 103. The New York figure is from *New York Times*, October 30, 1995, p. B2.

3. *Residential Community Associations*, p. 3.

4. Robert Jay Dilger, *Neighborhood Politics: Residential Community Associations in American Governance* (New York: New York University Press, 1992), p. 2.

5. McKenzie, *Privatopia*, pp. 18–19.

6. Constance Perin, *Belonging in America* (Madison: University of Wisconsin Press, 1988), p. 63.

7. *Residential Community Associations*, p. 18.

8. Carol Weisbrod, The Boundaries of Utopia (New York: Pantheon, 1980), pp. 77–79, 119, 54.

9. Ibid., citing a 1826 Maine case, p. 130.

10. Clayton P. Gillette, "Courts, Covenants, and Communities," 61 *University of Chicago Law Review* 1375 (1994) at 1381.

11. James L. Winokur, "The Mixed Blessings of Promissory Servitudes: Toward Optimizing Economic Utility, Individual Liberty, and Personal Identity," *Wisconsin Law Review* 1 (1989): 5.

12. Uriel Reichman, "Residential Private Governments: An Introductory Survey," 43 *University of Chicago Law Review* 253 (1976) at 258.

13. Winokur, *"Promissory Servitudes,"* p. 4.

14. McKenzie, *Privatopia*, p. 135, 138, 143, 126.

15. Reichman, "Residential Private Governments," p. 256.

16. *Hidden Harbour Estates v. Norman*, 309 So. 2d 180 (Fla. Dist. Ct. 1975).

17. McKenzie, *Privatopia*, pp. 14, 17.

18. See Daniel J. Monti, "People in Control: A Comparison of Residents in Two U.S. Housing Developments," in R. Allen Hays, ed., *Ownership, Control, and the Future of Housing Policy* (Westport, Conn.: Greenwood, 1993), p. 188.

19. For data on litigation, see Winokur, "Rejoinder: Reforming Servitude Regimes: Toward Associational Federalism and Community," 2 *Wisconsin Law Review* 537 (1990) at 546.

20. Bruce Ackerman, *Private Property and the Constitution* (New Haven, Conn.: Yale University Press, 1977), pp. 97–100.

21. Perin, *Belonging in America*, p. 30.

22. Gregory S. Alexander, "Dilemmas of Group Autonomy: Residential Associations and Community," 75 *Cornell Law Review* 1 (1989), at 9.

23. Ronald J. Oakerson, "Private Street Associations in St. Louis County: Subdivisions as Service Providers," in *Residential Community Associations*, p. 107.

24. Cited in Perin, *Belonging in America*, p. 31.

25. Ibid. pp. 64, 65, 64, 26, 44, 45.

26. Winokur, "Rejoinder," p. 539.

27. Perin, *Belonging in America*, pp. 68, 80.

28. James Buchanan, "The Domain of Constitutional Economics," 1 *Constitutional Political Economy* 1 (1990), at 3.

29. Gillette, "Courts, Convenants, and Communities," p. 1395.

30. Dilger, *Neighborhood Politics*, pp. 89–90.

31. Richard Epstein, "Covenants and Constitutions," 73 *Cornell Law Review* 906 (1988), at 917.

32. A. Dan Tarlock, "Residential Community Associations and Land Use Control," in *Residential Community Associations*, p. 75.

33. "Judicial Review of Condominium Rulemaking," 94 *Harvard Law Review* 647 (1981) at 648–50.

34. Winokur, "Promissory Servitudes," p. 59.

35. Cited in Marc H. Choko, "Homeownership: From Dream to Materiality," in Hays, ed., *Housing Policy*, p. 25. Hazel Morrow-Jones, "Black–White Differences in the Demographic Structure of the Move to Homeownership in the United States," in Hays, ed., *Housing Policy*, pp. 39–73, at pp. 52, 47.

36. Perin, *Belonging in America*, p. 30; Mark Baldassare, *Trouble in Paradise: The Suburban Transformation of America* (New York: Columbia University Press, 1986), p. 68.

37. Baldassare, *Trouble in Paradise*, p. 53.

38. Douglas S. Massey and Nancy A. Denton, *American Apartheid: Segregation and the Making of the Underclass* (Cambridge, Mass.: Harvard University Press, 1993), pp. 69–70.

39. Jim Kemeny, *The Myth of Home Ownership: Private versus Public Choices in Housing Tenure* (London: Routledge, 1981), pp. 56, 4, 60. Morrow-Jones, in Hays, ed., *Housing Policy*, pp. 39–73.

40. Gregory Alexander, "Freedom, Coercion, and the Law of Servitudes," 73 *Cornell Law Review* 883 (1988) at 893–94, 895.

41. Joe Klein, "The True Disadvantage," *New Republic* October 28, 1996, pp. 32–36, at p. 32.

42. Citations are from Winokur, "Promissory Servitudes," pp. 51, 74.

43. Jeremy Bentham, *The Theory of Legislation* (New York: Harcourt Brace, 1931), p. 115; Nancy L. Rosenblum, *Bentham's Theory of the Modern State* (Cambridge, Mass.: Harvard University Press, 1978).

44. Margaret Jane Radin, "Time, Possession, and Alienation," 64 *Washington University Law Quarterly* 739 (1986) at 757.

45. Foldvary, *Public Goods and Private Communities*, p. 106.

46. Gillette, "Courts, Convenants, and Communities," p. 1379.

47. *Holleman v. Mission Trace Homeowners Asssociation*, 1977, cited in "Judicial Review of Condominium Rulemaking," 94 *Harvard Law Review* 647 (1981) at 182.

48. *Neck Association v. New York City/Long Island County Services Group*, 472 N.Y. S. 2d 901 (1984), at 907. George Liebmann, *The Little Platoons: Sub-Local Governments in Modern History* (Westport, Conn.: Praeger, 1995), p. 60. On judicial resolution of conflict between covenants and social policies, see Gillette, "Courts, Convenants, and Communities," pp. 1433–34.

49. *Oakbrook Civic Associations*, 481 So. 2d 1008 (La. 1986).

50. Ibid.

51. See, too, Gerald Korngold, "Reply: Resolving the Flaws of Residential Servitudes and Owners Associations: For Reformation Not Termination," *Wisconsin Law Review* (1990): 513–35, at pp. 524–25. Reichman, "Residential Private Governments," pp. 293–94.

52. The debate focuses on the perpetuity of servitude regimes and whether courts or owners ought to interpret "changed conditions": Winokur, "Promissory Servitudes," p. 38; Epstein, "Covenants and Constitutions," pp. 919, 923; Posner cited in Winokur, "Promissory Servitudes," p. 27 nn. 109–10.

53. Alexander, "Dilemmas of Group Autonomy," p. 12, n. 44.

54. "Judicial Review of Condominium Rulemaking," 94 *Harvard Law Review* 647 (1981) at 659.

55. Robert Ellickson, *Cities and Homeowners Associations* (Philadelphia: University of Pennsylvania Law School, 1982) pp. 1519–80, at pp. 1526, 1528.

56. *Holleman v. Mission Trace Homeowners Association*, 1977, cited in "Judicial Review of Condominium Rulemaking," 94 *Harvard Law Review* 647 (1981) at 182, n. 69.

57. *Basso*, cited in Ellickson, *Cities* p. 1529.

58. Ibid., p. 1528.

59. Alexander, "Dilemmas of Group Autonomy," pp. 58–59, 60. Gillette, "Courts, Convenants, and Communities," pp. 1414ff., 1423.

60. *Nahrstedt*, at 65.

61. Ibid., at 80. Italics added.

62. Ibid., at 80, 81, 85. Though the association makes exceptions for domestic fish and (squawking) birds at 83.

63. Ibid., at 76.

64. *Serbian Eastern Orthodox Diocese of America and Canada v. Milivojevich* (1976), at 167.

65. Gillette, "Courts, Convenants, and Communities," p. 1401.

66. Wayne S. Hyatt and James B. Rhoads, "Concepts of Liability in the Development and Administration of Condominium and Home Owners Associations" 12 *Wake Forest Law Review* 915 (1976) at 919.

67. Ibid., p. 916.

68. Robert A. G. Monks and Nell Minow, *Power and Accountability* (New York: HarperBusiness, 1981), p. 76.

69. Cited in *Village Green*, 42 Cal. 3d. 490, at 527. See the Model Business Corporation Act, sec. 8.30(a), cited in Monks and Minow, *Power and Accountability*, p. 87.

70. "Judicial Review of Condominium Rulemaking," 94 *Harvard Law Review* 647 (1981) at 655, 648.

71. Hyatt and Rhoads, "Concepts of Liability," p. 936. For an overview of fiduciary/personal responsibility, see *Frances T. v. Village Green Owners Assn.*, 42 Cal. 3d 490 (1986).

72. Judge Benjamin Cardozo, cited in Monks and Minow, *Power and Accountability*, p. 85.

73. Ibid. p. 164.

74. Tarlock, "Residential Community Associations," p. 77; Korngold, "Reply," p. 530. Elliott J. Weiss, "Social Regulation of Business," 28 *UCLA Law Review* 343 (1981), at 365.

75. Tarlock, "Residential Community Associations," p. 78.

76. "Judicial Review of Condominium Rulemaking," 94 *Harvard Law Review* 647 (1981) at 654.

77. McKenzie, *Privatopia*, pp. 25, 132, 135, 138.

78. Stephen E. Barton and Carol J. Silverman, "The Political Life of Mandatory Homeowners' Associations," in *Residential Community Associations*, p. 32.

79. Monk and Minow, *Power and Accountability*, p. 32.

80. Cited in ibid., pp. 204–5.

81. Ibid., pp. 194, 184.

82. Jesse Choper, John Coffee Jr., and C. Robert Morris Jr., *Cases and Materials on Corporations* (Boston: Little, Brown, 1989), p. 30. David L. Engel, "An Approach to Corporate Social Responsibility," 32 *Stanford Law Review* 1 (1979).

83. Epstein, "Covenants and Constitutions"; Ellickson, *Cities* n. 61; Reichman, "Residential Private Governments," p. 282, n. 97.

84. Frank Michelman, "Universal Resident Suffrage: A Liberal Defense," 130 *University of Pennsylvania Law Review* 1581 (1982) at 1585. Ellickson, *Cities*, pp. 1554, 1563.

85. Ellickson, *Cities* pp. 1538, 1535–39. For the economic model of competition among communities in the provision of collective goods, see Charles Tiebout, "A Pure Theory of Local Expenditures," *Journal of Political Economy* 64, no. 5 (1956): 416–24. For discussion, see Richard Briffault, "Our Localism: Part II: Localism and Legal Theory," 90 *Columbia Law Review* 346 (1990), at 406; on the failure to consider interlocal inequality, pp. 407ff., 422.

86. Ellickson, *Cities* pp. 1559, 1538, 1535–39.

87. 451 U.S. 355, at 373, 375–76. *Ball v. James*, 451 U.S. 355 (1981), at 370, 366, 371, 373. "Judicial Review of Condominium Rulemaking," 94 *Harvard Law Review* 647 (1981) distinguishes exclusion cases from inclusion cases at 1494–96.

88. See "Comment: Democracy in the New Towns," 36 *University of Chicago Law Review* 379 (1969); Winokur, "Promissory Servitudes," p. 65.

89. Laurence Tribe, *American Constitutional Law* (Mineola, N.Y.: Foundation, 1978), pp. 1163–67.

90. Gerald E. Frug, "The City as a Legal Concept," 93 *Harvard Law Review* 1056 (1980) at 1071.

91. Dilger, *Neighborhood Politics*, p. 34.

92. Jane Mansbridge, "Does Participation Make Better Citizens?" forthcoming, in Stephen L. Elkin and Karol E. Soltin, eds. (Philadelphia: Pennsylvania State University Press).

93. Albert A. Foer, "Democracy in the New Towns," 36 *University of Chicago Law Review*, 379 (1969) at 381.

94. Michael J. Sandel, *Democracy's Discontent* (Cambridge, Mass.: Harvard University Press, 1996), p. 314.

95. Frug, "The City," pp. 1069, 1068, 1083ff., 1126.

96. Jane Mansbridge, *Beyond Adversary Democracy* (Chicago: University of Chicago Press, 1980), and Robert Dahl and Edward R. Tufte, *Size and Democracy* (Stanford, Calif.: Stanford University Press, 1973).

97. Reichman, "Residential Private Governments," p. 263.

98. Korngold, "Reply," p. 522; Mansbridge cited in Briffault II, "Our Localism" p. 398.

99. Typical attendance at RCA general membership meetings in 1986 ranged from 25 to 50 percent according to Dilger, *Neighborhood Politics*, p. 140. Other data cited in Winokur, "Promissory Servitudes," p. 62, n. 259. The Florida study is cited in ibid., n. 259 and p. 88, and Winokur, "Rejoinder," p. 547, n. 50.

100. Barton and Silverman, "Public Life in Private Governments: The Transformation of Urban Social Space," in *Gentrification and Urban Change: Research in Urban Sociology*, vol. 2 (Greensich, Conn. JAI, 1992), pp. 95–111, at 108. Alexander, "Dilemmas of Group Autonomy," p. 902.

101. Barton and Silverman, "Public Life," pp. 104, 105.

102. Dilger, *Neighborhood Politics*, p. 129.

103. Winokur, "Promissory Servitudes," pp. 6, 79, 81, and "Rejoinder," pp. 550, 537, 549, 552.

104. Barton and Silverman, "Public Life," pp. 34, 96.

105. Frances Fitzgerald, *Cities on the Hill* (New York: Simon & Schuster, 1981), p. 222.

106. For a libertarian program, see Foldvary, *Public Goods and Private Communities*, p. 206.

107. Liebmann, *Little Platoons*, p. 59.

108. Robert H. Nelson, "The Privatization of Local Government: From Zoning to RCAs," in *Residential Community Associations*, pp. 46–47. Ronald J. Oakerson, "Private Street Associations in St. Louis County: Subdivisions as Service Providers," in *Residential Community Associations*.

109. Dilger, *Neighborhood Politics*, p. 92.

110. Nelson, "Privatization," p. 49. Idem, "Private Neighborhoods: A New Direction for the Neighborhood Movement," in Charles C. Geisler and Frank J. Popper, eds., *Land Reform, American Style* (Totowa, N.J.: Rowman & Allenheld, 1984), p. 328. Mark Frazier, "Seeding Grass Roots Recovery: New Catalysts for Community Associations," in *Residential Community Associations*, p. 65.

111. Nelson, "Private Neighborhoods," pp. 328, 320. Frazier, "Grass Roots Recovery," p. 64.

112. Justice Black, cited in *Eastlake v. Forest City Enterprises*, 426 U.S. 668 (1975), at 679. *Euclid v. Ambler Realty Co.*, 272 U.S. 365 (1926), cited in *Eastlake*, at 677.

113. Edwin M. Epstein, "Societal, Managerial, and Legal Perspectives on Corporate Social Responsibility—Produce and Process," *Hastings Law Journal*, vol. 30 (May 1979): 1287–1320, at 1291.

114. Rosabeth Moss Kanter, "Cities Need New Sources of Leadership," *Boston Globe*, December 5, 1995, p. A15.

115. Engel, "Corporate Social Responsibility," p. 62.

116. Chopper, Coffee, and Morris, *Corporations*, p. 34, 32ff.

117. Epstein, "Establishment Clause Limits," p. 1313. Cited in ibid., p. 1316.

118. Elliott J. Weiss, "Social Regulation of Business," 28 *UCLA Law Review*, 343 (1981), at 345. Victor Brudney, "Business Corporations and Stockholders' Rights under the First Amendment," 91 *Yale Law Journal* 235 (1981) at 238–39. Engel, "Corporate Social Responsibility," pp. 71–75.

119. Robert Dahl, *A Preface to Economic Democracy* (Berkeley: University of California Press, 1985).

120. Robert Kuttner, "Corporate 'Good Behavior,'" *Boston Globe*, March 4, 1996, p. 11.

121. Monk and Minow, *Power and Accountability*, pp. 141, 143.

122. The title is from Richard Briffault, "Our Localism: Part I—The Structure of Local Government Law," 90 *Columbia Law Review* at p. 2 n.1.

123. "The Wrong Way to Lure Business," *New York Times*, editorial, September 8, 1996, sec. 4, p. 16. Richard Epstein, *Bargaining with the State* (Princeton, N.J.: Princeton University Press, 1993), pp. 188–89.

124. Briffault, "Our Localism II," p. 364.

125. Cited in Briffault, "Our Localism I," p. 5.

126. Briffault, "Our Localism II," pp. 346ff.; for figures, see p. 348. William Schneider, "The Suburban Century Begins," *Atlantic Monthly*, vol. 270, July 1992, p. 33.

127. Briffault, "Our Localism I," p. 112.

128. See the dissent in *Ball v. James* (1981), at 387–88.

129. Briffault, "Our Localism I," p. 84.

130. Ibid., p. 77. On RCAs electing to become municipal governments; Ellickson, *Cities*, p. 1575; Foldvary, *Public Goods and Private Communities*, p. 209. *Residential Community Associations*, p. 19.

131. Standard State Zoning Enabling Act 1926, cited in David Keating, "Exclusionary Zoning: In Whose Interests Should the Police Power Be Exercised?" 23 *Real Estate Law Journal* 4 (1995) at 304–31, esp. p. 305, n. 10.

132. *Eastlake v. Forest City Enterprises*, 426 U.S. 668 (1975), at 682.

133. Keating, "Exclusionary Zoning," p. 304.

134. 402 U.S. 143, cited in Briffault, "Our Localism I," p. 105. Mobile homes have captured a high proportion of the housing market; exclusionary zoning has been effectively prejudicial; Margaret J. Drury, *Mobile Homes: The Unrecognized Revolution in American Housing* (New York: Praeger, 1972), p. 134.

135. 424 U.S. 1 (1976), at 560.

136. Briffault, "Our Localism I," p. 21.

137. Briffault, "Our Localism II," p. 441.

138. *Belle Terre*, 416 U.S. 1 (1974), at 9. Though *Moore v. City of E. Cleveland* settled that muncipalities could not circumscribe the *composition* of a family. 431 U.S. 494 (1977).

139. Nelson, "Privatization," p. 46.

140. Sandel, *Democracy's Discontent*, p. 202, 205.

141. For these considerations played out in federal arrangements, see *Garcia v. San Antonio Metropolitan Transit Authority*, 469 U.S. 528 (1985).

142. Paul E. Peterson, *The Price of Federalism* (Washington, D.C.: Brookings Institution, 1995), p. 187.

143. Melissa Fay Greene, *The Temple Bombing* (Reading, Mass.: Addison-Wesley, 1996), pp. 28–29.

144. Peterson, *Price of Federalism* pp. 27–29.

145. Herbert J. Gans, "The Balanced Community: Homogeneity or Heterogeneity in Residential Areas," in Jon Pynoos, Robert Schafer, and Chester W. Hartman, eds., *Housing in Urban America* (New York: Aldine, 1980), pp. 141–52, at p. 141.

146. *Southern Burlington County N.A.A.C.P. v. Township of Mount Laurel*, 336 A. 2d 713 (N.J. 1975).

147. Subsequent cases using a regional measure of community include *Berenson v. Town of New Castle*, 341 N.W. 2d 236 (N.Y. 1975), *Township of Willistown v. Chesterdale Farms, Inc.*, 341 A. 2d 466 (Pa. 1975), and *Britton v. Town of Chester*, 595 A. 2d 492 (N. H. 1991).

148. John M. Payne, "Rethinking Fair Share: The Judicial Enforcement of Affordable Housing Policies," 16 *Real Estate Law Journal* 20 (1987), at 33, 20–21, 38.

149. Ibid., p. 30.

150. Cited in Briffault, "Our Localism I," p. 44, n. 175; cited in ibid., p. 56.

151. Briffault, "Our Localism II," pp. 387, 382, 384–85.

152. David Popenoe, "The Roots of Declining Social Virtue: Family, Community, and the Need for a Natural Communities Policy," in Mary Ann Glendon and Blankenhorn, eds., *Seedbeds of Virtue* (Md.: Institute for American Values, 1995), pp. 97, 94.

153. Tribe, *Constitutional Law*, p. 989.

154. See Morton J. Horwitz, "Santa Clara Revisited: The Development of Corporate Theory," 88 *West Virginia Law Review* 173 (1985).

155. Gans, "Balanced Community," p. 149.

156. Nelson, "Privatization," p. 50.

157. Dilger, *Neighborhood Politics*, p. 119–20, 129.

158. Gillette, "Courts, Covenants, and Communities," p. 1393.

159. Baldassare, *Trouble in Paradise*, pp. 46, 6–7, 169ff., 1–2.

160. Amy Gutmann and Dennis Thompson, *Democracy and Disagreement* (Cambridge, Mass.: Harvard University Press, 1996), p. 146.

161. Ibid. p. 228.

162. Peterson, *Price of Federalism*, pp. 174, 30–33.

163. Robert Reich, "Secession of the Successful," *New York Times Magazine*, January 20, 1991, p. 16.

164. Douglas S. Massey and Nancy A. Denton, *American Apartheid: Segregation and the Making of the Underclass* (Cambridge, Mass.: Harvard University Press, 1993), pp. 145, 150.

165. John Yinger, *Closed Doors, Opportunities Lost: The Continuing Costs of Housing Discrimination* (New York: Russell Sage, 1995), p. 106.

166. Massey and Denton, *American Apartheid*, pp. 150–51; 67, 85, 87. The pattern is unique compared to Hispanics or Asians; p. 153.

167. Ibid., p. 2.

168. Ibid., p. 77; on an autonomous cultural system, see pp. 169, 172.

169. Ibid., pp. 92, 213; Yinger, *Closed Doors*, pp. 13, 118–19.

170. Ibid. pp. 105, 116ff. On legal obstacles to integrating public housing projects and maintaining integration, see pp. 131ff., 200ff.

171. Ibid., p. 96.

172. Massey and Denton, *American Apartheid*, pp. 69–70, 9.

173. Greene, *Temple Bombing*, p. 90.

174. *O'Connor v. Village Green Owners Assn.*, 33 Cal. 3d 790 (1983), at 790, 795, 796. Justice Mosk dissented at 803.

175. On the ineffectiveness of these measures, see Massey and Denton, *American Apartheid*, pp. 198–200, 207.

176. *White Egret Condominium, Inc. v. Franklin*, Fla. 379 So. 2d 346, at 350, 351.

177. Cited in Fitzgerald, *Cities on the Hill*, p. 211.

178. McKenzie, *Privatopia*, pp. 23, 141.

179. Fitzgerald, *Cities on the Hill*, pp. 11, 13.

180. *Toronto Globe and Mail*, July 25, 1995, p. A1.

181. Eve Darian-Smith, "Neighborhood Watch—Who Watches Whom? Reinterpreting the Concept of Neighborhood," *Human Organization* 1, no. 52 (1993): 83–88, at p. 83.

182. *Marsh v. Alabama*, 326 U.S. 501 (1946), at 510–11.

183. *Laguna Publishing Co. v. Golden Rain Foundation of Laguna Hills*, 131 Cal. App. 3d 816 (1982), at 845.

184. Ibid. When discrimination is added to the picture, "the balance tips to the side of the scale which imports the presence of state action per *Mulkey* and the lunch counter cases" (ibid., at 843).

185. Ibid., at 839.

186. *Marsh*, at 506, 513. For an alternative approach to constitutionalizing RCAs, see Katharine Rosenberry, "The Application of the Federal and State Constitutions to Condominiums, Cooperatives and Planned Developments," *Real Property, Probate and Trust Journal* 19 (1984): 1–31, at pp. 8, 13–14. Tribe, on the "chaos" of state action doctrine, *Constitutional Law*, p. 1149.

187. Dilger, *Neighborhood Politics* pp. 26–27.

188. McKenzie, *Privatopia*, p. 27.

189. Reichman, "Residential Private Developments," pp. 263–64.

190. Barton and Silverman, "Public Life in Private Governments," p. 107. These studies lag behind the greatest growth in RCAs; I know of no more recent ones.

191. Dilger, *Neighborhood Politics*, p. 87.

192. Lester M. Salamon, *Partners in Public Service: Government–Nonprofit Relations in the Modern Welfare State* (Baltimore: Johns Hopkins University Press, 1995), p. 7.

193. Dilger, *Neighborhood Politics*, pp. 30–31.

194. McKenzie, *Privatopia*, p. 195.

195. Advisory Committee on Intergovernmental Relations, cited in ibid., p. 22. Dilger, *Neighborhood Politics*, p. 63.

196. Doug Lasdon and Sue Halpern, "When Neighborhoods Are Privatized," *New York Times*, November 30, 1995, p. A23.

197. McKenzie, *Privatopia*, p. 196.

198. Baldassare, *Trouble in Paradise*, p. 123.

199. Schneider, "Suburban Century," p. 39.

200. McKenzie, *Privatopia*, p. 143 (italics added); Louv, cited in ibid., p. 144.

201. Fitzgerald, *Cities on the Hill*, pp. 230ff.

202. Dilger, *Neighborhood Politics*, p. 57.

203. Case cited in ibid., p. 62.

204 Christopher Beam, "Civil Society in America: A Public Debate about Political Theory," Working Paper, National Commission on Civic Renewal, 1996, p. 29.

205. Zechariah Chafee Jr., "The Internal Affairs of Associations Not for Profit," cited in Richard Ellickson, "Cities and Homeowners Associations," 130 *University of Pennsylvania Law Review* 1519 (1982) at n. 31.

Chapter 5

1. For criticism of this view, see Seymour Martin Lipset, "Malaise and Resiliency in America," *Journal of Democracy* 6, no. 1 (1995): 4–18, at p. 14.

2. *International Association of Machinists v. Street*, 367 U.S. 740 (1961), at 775.

3. Brief amicus curiae of the Conference of Private Organizations to the Court of Appeals, 83–724.

4. Herbert Wechsler, "Toward Neutral Principles of Constitutional Law," 73 *Harvard Law Review* 1 (1959).

5. *Roberts v. Jaycees*, 468 U.S. 609 (1984), at 633.

6. *Democratic Party of the U.S. et al. v. Wisconsin Ex Rel. La Follette*, 450 U.S. 107 (1980), at 130.

7. I discuss *Abood v. Detroit Board of Education*, 431 U.S. 209 (1976) in chapter 6.

8. Harry H. Wellington, "The Constitution, the Labor Union, and 'Governmental Action,'" 74 *Yale Law Journal* 344 (1961) at 345.

9. Thomas I. Emerson, "Freedom of Association and Freedom of Expression," 74 *Yale Law Journal* 1 (1964): 32. *Shelton v. Tucker*, 364 U.S. 479 (1960).

10. Three times since 1958 the Supreme Court has upheld the NAACP's claims: *NAACP v. Alabama ex rel. Patterson*, 1959; *NAACP v. Gallion*, 1961; *NAACP v. Alabama ex rel. Flowers*, 1964.

11. 104 S. Ct. 3574, cited in Sheila D'Ambrosio, "Wrongful Expulsion from Voluntary Social Organization," 44 *Proof of Fact* 2d 455, at 465.

12. Cited in Douglas O. Linder, "Freedom of Association after *Roberts v. United States Jaycees*," 82 *Michigan Law Review* 1878 (1984) at 1881n.

13. Brief amicus curiae for the American Civil Liberties Union in *Roberts v. Jaycees*, cited in ibid., p. 1880.

14. Kathleen Sullivan, "Rainbow Republicanism," 93 *Yale Law Journal* 1713 (1988) at 1714–15.

15. *Cornelius v. Benevolent Protective Order of the Elks*, 382 Fed. Suppl. 1182 (1974), at 1199.

16. Kenneth Karst, *Belonging to America: Equal Citizenship and the Constitution* (New Haven, Conn.: Yale University Press, 1989), p. 4.

17. 109 U.S. 26, at 59.

18. John Theuman, "Annotation: Exclusion of One Sex from Admission to or Enjoyment of Equal Privileges in Places of Accommodation or Entertainment as Actionable Sex Discrimination under State Law" 38 *American Law Review* 4th 628 (1991).

19. *Moose Lodge No. 107 v. Irvis*, 407 U.S. 163 (1972), at 180.

20. For a critical discussion, see Aviam Soifer, "Toward a Generalized Notion of the Right to Form or Join an Association: An Essay for Tom Emerson," 38 *Case Western Reserve Law Review* 640 (1988).

21. *Board of Directors of Rotary Int'l v. Rotary Club*, 481 U.S. 537 (1987), and *New York State Club Ass'n v. City of New York*, 487 U.S. 1 (1988).

22. The district court ruled in favor of the state. The eighth circuit court of appeals overturned the decision, finding in favor of the Jaycees, though it split sharply. The Supreme Court decision was unanimous, though Chief Justice Burger and Justice Blackmun, past members of the St. Paul and Minneapolis Jaycees respectively, took no part in the decision.

23. Appellant's brief on appeal from the U.S. court of appeals for the eighth circuit, 83–724.

24. *Roberts* at 636, 638, 633.

25. Ibid., at 635.

26. *Boston Globe*, April 1, 1995, p. A24.

27. Brief of amicus curiae, 83–724.

28. *U.S. Jaycees v. McClure* 709 F. 2d 1560 (1983), at 1569.

29. *Roberts*, at 638.

30. Wendy Kaminer, *Women Volunteering* (New York: Anchor, 1984), p. 5.

31. Arthur M. Schlesinger, "Biography of a Nation of Joiners," *American Historical Review* 50, no. 1 (1944): 1–25, at pp. 11–13, 12. Morton Horwitz, "Santa Clara Revisited: The Development of Corporate Theory," 88 *West Virginia Law Review* 173 (1985), at 206–7.

32. *Roberts*, at 608.

33. Robert C. Post, *Constitutional Domains* (Cambridge, Mass.: Harvard University Press, 1995), p. 56.

34. Charles L. Black Jr., "The Lawfulness of the Desegregation Decision" 69 *Yale Law Journal* 421 (1960) at 427.

35. Judith Shklar, *American Citizenship: The Quest for Inclusion* (Cambridge, Mass.: Harvard University Press, 1991), p. 52; Douglass cited at p. 56.

36. Ibid., p. 18.

37. Charles Beitz, *Political Equality* (Princeton, N.J.: Princeton University Press, 1989), p. 110.

38. *Wyman v. James*, 400 U.S. 309 (1970), at 331, 332; Marshall cited at 347, 332.

39. *Goldberg v. Kelley*, 397 U.S. 254 (1970), at 265. Sylvia Law, "Some Reflections on *Goldberg v. Kelley* at Twenty Years," 56 *Brooklyn Law Review* 805 (1990).

40. Appellee brief, *Roberts v. Jaycees*, 83–724. On the demographics of membership, see *U.S. Jaycees v. McClure*, at 1571.

41. Deborah L. Rhode, "Association and Assimilation," 81 *Northwestern University Law Review* 106 (1986) at 106.

42. Karst, *Belonging to America*, p. 213.

43. *Rotary*, at 542.

44. Cited in *New York Club*, 487 U.S. 1, at 5–6, 16–17, 20, 21. *Elks*, at 1203.

45. *U.S. Jaycees v. McClure*, at 1572.

46. Christopher Jencks, *Rethinking Social Policy: Race, Poverty, and the Under-class* (Cambridge, Mass.: Harvard University Press, 1992), p. 48, and idem *Inequality* (New York: Basic, 1972), p. 261.

47. Linder, "Freedom of Association," p. 1890.

48. *U.S. Jaycees v. McClure*, at 1572.

49. Rhode, "Association and Assimilation," pp. 105, 113, 128, 121, 127.

50. Grant McConnell, "The Public Values of Private Associations," in J. Roland Pennock and John W. Chapman, eds., *Voluntary Associations, Nomos XI* (New York: Atherton, 1969), p. 158.

51. Schlesinger, "Biography," p. 23.

52. Rotary International brief of amicus curiae, 83–724.

53. Arthur Kinoy, cited in Karst, *Belonging to America*, p. 60.

54. *Roberts*, at 624.

55. Rhode, "Association and Assimilation," p. 109.

56. Andrew Koppelman, *Antidiscrimination Law and Social Equality* (New Haven, Conn.: Yale University Press (1996) p. 9.

57. Ibid., pp. 93, 218–19.

58. Rhode, "Association and Assimilation," p. 123.

59. *Rotary*, at 538.

60. Jencks, *Rethinking Social Policy*, p. 40; Richard Epstein, *Forbidden Grounds: The Case against Employment Discrimination Laws* (Cambridge, Mass.: Harvard University Press, 1992), pp. 61, 65, 68.

61. Reported in Jeffrey Rosen, "Like Race, Like Gender?" *New Republic*, February 19, 1996, pp. 21–27, at p. 24.

62. William P. Marshall, "Discrimination and the Right of Association," 81 *Northwestern University Law Review* 1 (1986), at 70.

63. Koppelman, *Antidiscrimination Law*, pp. 71, 4, 7.

64. The issue was recently joined in challenges to the exclusion of gay men and women from St. Patrick's Day parades in *Hurley and South Boston Allied War Veterans Council v. Irish-American Gay, Lesbian and Bisexual Group of Boston*, 115 S. Ct. 2388 (1995).

65. "Note: State Power and Discrimination by Private Clubs: First Amendment Protection for Nonexpressive Associations," 104 *Harvard Law Review* 1835 (1991) at 1849.

66. Ibid., pp. 1854, 1849, 1853.

67. Daniel Schwartz, "Discrimination on Campus: A Critical Examination of Single-Sex College Social Organizations," 75 *California Law Review* 2117 (1987) at 2123.

68. William Galston, *Liberal Purposes* (Cambridge: Cambridge University Press, 1991), p. 3.

69. Karst, *Belonging to America*, p. 79.

70. Erving Goffman, *Stigma: Notes on the Management of Spoiled Identity* (Englewood Cliffs, N.J. Prentice-Hall, 1963), pp. 105–6.

71. 347 U.S. 483 (1954), at 484.

72. Jencks, *Rethinking Social Policy*, p. 48.

73. John Rawls, *Political Liberalism* (New York: Columbia University Press, 1993), p. 316.

74. Iris Marion Young, *Justice and the Politics of Difference* (Princeton, N.J.: Princeton University Press, 1990), p. 174.

75. Hannah Arendt, "Reflections on Little Rock," *Dissent* 6 (Winter 1959): 45–56. See, too, Martha Minow, *Making All the Difference* (Ithaca, N.Y.: Cornell University Press, 1990), pp. 39–40.

76. Kristin Bumiller, *The Civil Rights Society: The Social Construction of Victims* (Baltimore: Johns Hopkins University Press, 1988), pp. 94, 109. This section is indebted to her argument.

77. Jencks, *Rethinking Social Policy*, pp. 48–49.

78. Bumiller, *Civil Rights Society*, p. 70.

79. Ibid., p. 93.

80. Shklar, *American Citizenship*, p. 98.

81. Michael Sandel, *Democracy's Discontent: America in Search of a Public Philosophy* (Cambridge, Mass.: Harvard University Press, 1996). See Claus Offe, "Full Employment: Asking the Wrong Question," *Dissent*, vol. 42 (Winter 1995): 77–81.

82. Jencks, *Rethinking Social Policy*, pp. 127, 158.

83. Carol B. Stack, *All Our Kin: Strategies for Survival in a Black Community* (New York: Harper & Row, 1974).

84. Cited in Sandel, *Democracy's Discontent*, p. 303.

85. Judith Shklar, *Ordinary Vices* (Cambridge, Mass.: Harvard University Press, 1984), p. 88.

86. Judith Shklar, *The Faces of Injustice* (New Haven, Conn.: Yale University Press, 1990), p. 94.

87. Arendt, "Reply to Critics," p. 179.

88. Mary C. Waters, *Ethnic Options* (Berkeley: University of California Press, 1990), pp. 140–42.

89. Melissa Fay Greene, *The Temple Bombing* (Boston: Addison-Wesley, 1996), p. 67.

90. Larry Alexander, "Banning Hate Speech and the Sticks and Stones Defense," 13 *Constitutional Commentary* 71 (1995) at 98.

91. Erving Goffman, "The Nature of Deference and Demeanor," *American Anthropologist* 58, no. 3 (1956): 473–502, at p. 479.

92. Cited in Lyman Tower Sargent, ed., *Extremism in America* (New York: New York University Press, 1995), pp. 271–72.

93. John Rawls, *A Theory of Justice* (Cambridge, Mass.: Harvard University Press, 1971), pp. 441, 544, 545.

94. Cited in Schlesinger, "Biography," p. 24.

95. Werner Sollors, *Beyond Ethnicity* (Oxford: Oxford University Press, 1986), pp. 29, 175–76; the Malcolm X reference is from his work.

96. Schlesinger, "Biography," p. 15.

97. David Brion Davis, "Some Themes of Countersubversion: An Annal of Anti-Masonic, Anti-Catholic, and Anti-Mormon Literature," in Richard Curry and Thomas Brown, eds., *Conspiracy: The Fear of Subversion in American History* (New York: Holt, Rinehart, Winston, 1972), p. 64.

98. Schlesinger, "Biography," p. 7.

99. Steven Simpson, "Political Economy and the Workers," in Joseph Blau, ed., *Social Theories of Jacksonian Democracy* (New York: Bobbs-Merrill, 1954), pp. 145, 156.

100. William Leggett, "Rich and Poor," in Blau, ed., *Special Theories*, p. 67.

101. Henry James, "Hawthorne," in Edmund Wilson, *The Shock of Recognition* (New York: Doubleday, 1943), pp. 460, 436. George Santayana, *The Genteel Tradition* (Cambridge, Mass.: Harvard University Press, 1967), p. 44. See Nancy L. Rosenblum, "Romantic Communitarianism," in Cornelius F. Delaney, ed., *The Liberalism-Communitarianism Debate* (Lanham, Md.: Rowman & Littlefield, 1994), pp. 57–90.

102. *Democracy in America*, ed. J. P. Mayer (New York: Harper & Row, 1969), p. 604.

103. Sam Bass Warner, *The Private City* (Philadelphia: University of Pennsylvania Press, 1968), p. 72.

104. Schlesinger, "Biography," p. 8.

105. Cited in Leo Stoller, *After Walden* (Stanford, Calif.: Stanford University Press, 1967), p. 17; Nancy L. Rosenblum, ed., *Thoreau: Political Writings* (Cambridge: Cambridge University Press, 1996); "Economy" from Walden, p. 34.

106. Schlesinger, "Biography," p. 20.

107. Russell Hardin, *One for All* (Princeton, N.J.: Princeton University Press, 1995), p. 217.

108. Karst, *Belonging To America*, p. 89.

109. Sidney Verba, Kay L. Schlozman, and Henry E. Brady, *Voice and Equality: Civic Voluntarism in American Politics* (Cambridge, Mass.: Harvard University Press, 1995), pp. 16, 527, 312.

110. Robert Kennedy, cited in Sandel, *Democracy's Discontent*, p. 302.

111. Jencks, *Rethinking Social Politics*, pp. 143–45, 170.

112. *Boston Globe*, May 31, 1993, p. 1.

113. Daniel J. Monti, "People in Control: A Comparison of Residents in Two U.S. Housing Developments," in R. Allen Hays, ed., *Ownership, Control, and the Future of Housing Policy* (Westport, Conn.: Greenwood, 1993), p. 188.

114. Nathan Glazer, "The Street Gangs and Ethnic Enterprise," *Public Interest* 28 (1972): 82–89, at p. 89.

Chapter 6

1. Thomas Emerson, "Freedom of Association and Freedom of Expression," 74 *Yale Law Journal* 1 (1964) at 15.

2. 372 U.S. 568.

3. 357 U.S. 449, 460 (1958).

4. *U.S. Jaycees v. McClure*, 709 F. 2d 1560 (8th Cir. 1983), at 1567. Laurence Tribe, *American Constitutional Law* (Mineola N.Y.: Foundation, 1978), pp. 701–2. For the broader view, see *U.S. Jaycees v. McClure*, 534 F. Suppl. 766 (1982); the district court cited circuit court opinions, including "The First Amendment protects the right of one citizen to associate with other citizens for any lawful purpose free from government interference," at 770. See Raggi, "An Independent Right to Freedom of Association," 12 *Harvard Civil Rights-Civil Liberties Law Review* 1 (1977). See

Aviam Soifer, *Law and the Company We Keep* (Cambridge, Mass.: Harvard University Press, 1995).

5. *Roberts*, 468 U.S. 609 (1984), at 617.

6. Kalven, cited in John Rawls, *Political Liberalism* (New York: Columbia University Press, 1993), p. 342. On democratic reasons, see Kent Greenawalt, *Fighting Words* (Princeton, N.J.: Princeton University Press, 1995), pp. 3–5.

7. *Roberts*, at 621.

8. Douglas O. Linder, "Freedom of Association after *Roberts v. United States Jaycees*," 82 *Michican Law Review* 1878 (1984) at 1889–90.

9. *Roberts*, at 623.

10. *U.S. Jaycees v. McClure*, 709 F. 2d 1560 (8th Cir. 1983), at 1569.

11. *Roberts*, at 608, 626, 609.

12. Linder, "Freedom of Association," p. 1892.

13. William P. Marshall, "Discrimination and the Right of Association," 81 *Northwestern University Law Review* 68 (1986), at 104.

14. *Roberts*, at 626, 632.

15. The quote is from the dissent in *U.S. Jaycees v. McClure*, at 1579. *Roberts*, at 626.

16. Cass R. Sunstein, *Democracy and the Problem of Free Speech* (New York: Free Press, 1993), p. 155.

17. *Amos*, 483 U.S. 327 (1986), at 342.

18. *Roberts*, at 633.

19. Brief amicus curiae to the eighth circuit, 83–724.

20. *Roberts*, at 619.

21. Ronald Dworkin, "What Is Equality? Part 4: Political Equality," 22 *University of San Francisco Law Review* 1 (1987), at 10.

22. *New York State Club Association v. City of New York*, 487 U.S. 1 (1987), at 14, 13.

23. 450 U.S. 107 (1980), at 110–11.

24. See Julia E. Guttman, "Primary Elections and the Collective Right of Freedom of Association," 94 *Yale Law Journal* 1 (1984): 117–36, at pp. 131–32, 122.

25. Rehnquist makes this observation in *Cousins v. Wigoda*, 419 U.S. 477 (1975), at 495. *Democratic Party of the U.S. et al. v. Wisconsin ex rel. La Follette*, 450 U.S. 107, at 122, 123.

26. *Democratic Party*, at 131.

27. Ibid., at 133, 132, 130.

28. Guttman, "Primary Elections," pp. 125, 128–29.

29. *Tashijian v. Republican Party of Connecticut*, 107 S. Ct. 544 (1986).

30. Anne Phillips, *The Politics of Presence* (Oxford: Oxford University Press, 1995), p. 44.

31. Cited in H. R. Mahood, *Interest Group Politics in America* (Englewood Cliffs, N.J.: Prentice-Hall, 1990), p. 42.

32. *Roberts*, at 623.

33. Marshall, "Discrimination," pp. 90–91.

34. Ibid., pp. 80, 97n, 90–91, 104n, 98–99.

35. Ibid., p. 104n.

36. 556 F. 2d 310, 321.

37. Brief amicus curiae to the eighth circuit, 83–724.

38. Robert Dreyfus, "Political Snipers," *American Prospect* 23 (Fall 1995): 28–36, at p. 32.

39. Michael Walzer, *What It Means to Be an American* (New York: Marsilio, 1992), p. 11.

40. Sidney Verba, Kay Lehman Schlozman, and Henry E. Brady, *Voice and Equality: Civic Voluntarism in American Politics* (Cambridge, Mass.: Harvard University Press, 1995), pp. 310, 309.

41. See Rawls, *Political Liberalism*, p. 335.

42. Sara M. Evans and Harry C. Boyt, *Free Spaces* (New York: Harper & Row, 1992), pp. 105, 107.

43. Jane Mansbridge, "Feminism and Democratic Community," unpublished paper, 1990, p. 44.

44. Erving Goffman, *Stigma: Notes on the Management of Spoiled Identity* (Englewood Cliffs, N.J.: Prentice-Hall, 1963), pp. 25, 24.

45. Dietrich Rueschemeyer, "The Self-Organization of Society and Democratic Rule: Specifying the Relationship," forthcoming in D. Rueschemeyer, Marilyn Rueschemeyer, and Bjorn Wittrock, eds., *Participation and Democracy: East and West*, unpublished ms.

46. Evans and Boyt, *Free Spaces*, pp. 17, 189, vii. See, too, Franklin Gamwell, *Beyond Preference* (Chicago: University of Chicago Press, 1984).

47. Michael J. Sandel, *Democracy's Discontent* (Cambridge, Mass.: Harvard University Press, 1996).

48. Soifer, *Law*, pp. 49–50, 100.

49. Sandel, *Democracy's Discontent*, p. 333.

50. Lyman Kellstedt and Corwin Smidt, "Onward Christian Soldiers: Religious Activist Groups in American Politics," in Allan Cigler and Burdett Loomis, eds., *Interest Group Politics* (Washington, D.C.: Congressional Quarterly Press 1983), pp. 55–75, at p. 67.

51. Evans and Boyt, *Free Spaces*, pp. 17, 189.

52. Henry Louis Gates Jr., "The Charmer," *New Yorker*, vol. 72, April 29 and May 6, 1996, pp. 116–31, at p. 119. Michael C. Dawson, "Black Power in 1995 and the Demonization of African Americans," *P.S.: Political Science and Politics*, September 1996, pp. 456–60.

53. John Davis Hunter, *Culture Wars: The Struggle to Define America* (New York: Basic, 1991), pp. 97, 163.

54. Matthew C. Moen, "The Evolving Politics of the Christian Right," *P.S.: Political Science and Politics*, September 1996, pp. 461–66.

55. 115 S. Ct. 2510. *Rosenberger*, at 38–39.

56. Isaac Kramnick and R. Laurence Moore, *The Godless Constitution* (New York: Norton, 1996), p. 12.

57. Robert Audi, "The Separation of Church and State and the Obligations of Citizenship," *Philosophy and Public Affairs* 18, no. 3 (1989): 278–88. In contrast, Rawls, *Political Liberalism*, pp. 213, 247ff.

58. Alexander Meiklejohn, *Political Freedom* (New York: Harper, 1960).

59. The phrase is Justice Burger's in *Buckley*, at 248. See Sunstein, *Free Speech*, p. 134.

60. *Austin v. Michigan Chamber of Commerce*, 494 U.S. 652 (1990), at 1408.

61. *Griswold v. Connecticut*, 381 U.S. 479 (1965).

62. Brief amicus curiae to the eighth circuit, 83–724.

63. *Political Liberalism*, pp. 220–21.

64. Raggi, "Freedom of Association," p. 8.

65. Brief amicus curiae to the eighth circuit, 83–724.

66. George Kateb, "The Value of Association," in Amy Gutmann, ed., *Freedom of Association* (forthcoming, Princeton University Press), pp. 3, 30.

67. Raggi, "Freedom of Association," pp. 15–16.

68. Soifer, *Law*, p. 97.

69. *Cornelius v. Benevolent Protective Order of Elks*, 382 F. Suppl. 1182 (1974), at 1195–96, 1202.

70. *Roberts*, at 609, 617.

71. Kateb, "Association," pp. 24, 19, 7.

72. *West Virginia State Bd. of Education v. Barnette*, 319 U.S. 624 (1943), at 642. *Abood v. Detroit Board of Education*, 431 U.S. 209 (1976), at 210.

73. White dissent in *Bellotti*, at 813.

74. Cited in Geoffrey Stone, Louis Seidman, Cass Sunstein, and Mark Tushnet *Constitutional Law* (Boston: Little, Brown, 1991), p. 1384.

75. *U.S. Civil Service Commission v. National Association of Letter Carriers*, 413 U.S. 548 (1973). See, too, *Elrod v. Burns*, 427 U.S. 347 (1976); *Branti v. Finkel*, 445 U.S. 507 (1980); *Rutan v. Republican Party of Illinois*, 497 U.S. 62 (1990).

76. Anthony Lewis, "Power to Punish," *New York Times*, September 22, 1995, p. A31.

77. *Regan v. Taxation with Representation of Washington, Inc.*, 461 U.S. 540 (1983). *Lyng v. International Union*, 485 U.S. 360 (1986).

78. Cited in *FEC v. Massachusetts Citizens for Life*, 479 U.S. 238 (1986), at 270.

79. Justice Douglas, *International Association of Machinists v. Street*, 367 U.S. 740, at 777.

80. Sheldon Leader, *Freedom of Association: A Study in Labor Law and Political Theory* (New Haven, Conn.: Yale University Press, 1992), pp. 93, 105.

81. Ibid., p. 94.

82. Ibid., p. 110.

83. *New York Times*, August 6, 1996, p. A1.

84. Morton Horwitz, "Santa Clara Revisited: The Development of Corporate Theory," 88 *West Virginia Law Review* 173 (1985). See Harold Laski, "The Personality of Associations," 29 *Harvard Law Review* 404 (1916) and on the other side, Morris Cohen, "Communal Ghosts," *Journal of Philosophy, Psychology and Scientific Methods* 16, no. 25 (1919): 673–90.

85. 31 Cal. 2d 139. I am indebted to the careful arguments of Leader, *Freedom of Association*, pp. 242–43.

86. Cited in Horwitz, p. 218.

87. Cited in Rehnquist's dissent, *Bellotti*, at 823.

88. Of course, the law of corporations imposes constraints. Jesse Choper, John

Coffee Jr., and C. Robert Morris, Jr. *Cases and Materials on Corporations* (Boston: Little, Brown, 1989), pp. 140–41.

89. 367 U.S. 740 (1961).

90. *International Association of Machinists v. Street*, at 788.

91. 431 U.S. 209 (1976), at 235–36.

92. Philip Stern, *Still the Best Congress Money Can Buy* (Washington, D.C.: Regnery Gateway, 1992), p. 152.

93. See Dan Clawson, Alan Neustadtl, and Denise Scott, *Money Talks* (New York: Basic, 1992), pp. 34–43.

94. *Roberts*, at 636. O'Connor is wrong more generally; cf. the majority opinion in *Bellotti* protecting corporate speech in the electoral context and protections accorded commercial speech. Frank Easterbrook, "Implicit and Explicit Rights of Association," 10 *Harvard Journal of Law and Public Policy* 91 (1987), at 98.

95. Harry H. Wellington, "The Constitution, the Labor Union, and 'Governmental Action,'" 70 *Yale Law Journal* 345 (1961), at 363.

96. Leader, *Freedom of Association*, pp. 102, 253.

97. Wellington, "Constitution," p. 364.

98. *Abood*, Rehnquist concurrence at 243.

99. *First National Bank of Boston v. Bellotti*, 435 U.S. 765.

100. *Bellotti*, at 785.

101. Ibid., at 826.

102. White dissent at 818.

103. *Austin v. Michigan Chamber of Commerce*, 494 U.S. 652 (1990), at 1403, 660. Marshall's concurrence, 494 U.S. 675 (1990), cited in 110 Supreme Court Reporter 1391, at 1406.

104. *First National Bank of Boston v. Bellotti*, 435 U.S. 765, at 810.

105. *Austin*, at 1399.

106. Ibid., at 1412.

107. Ronald Dworkin, "What Is Equality? Part 4: Political Equality," 22 *University of San Francisco Law Review* 1 (1987): at 5.

108. *FEC v. Massachusetts Citizens for Life*, at 257.

109. *Buckley v. Valeo*, 424 U.S. 1, at 22; 66, 23.

110. See, for example, Sunstein, *Democracy*.

111. 435 U.S. 765 (1978), at 803–4.

112. J. Skelly Wright, "Money and the Pollution of Politics: Is the First Amendment an Obstacle to Political Equality?" 82 *Columbia Law Review* 609 (1982) at p. 622, 639, 633, 636, 637.

113. Sunstein, *Democracy*, p. 93.

114. *Bellotti*, at 776, 777, 805, 783.

115. Charles Beitz, *Political Equality* (Princeton, N.J.: Princeton University Press, 1989), p. 179.

116. Cited in Robert C. Post, *Constitutional Domains* (Cambridge, Mass.: Harvard University Press, 1995), p. 270.

117. Sunstein, *Democracy*, 140. Beitz, *Political Equality*, p. 192.

118. *Buckley*, at 92–23. Frank J. Sorauf, "Adaptation and Innovation in Political Action Committees," in Allan J. Cigler and Burdett A. Loomis, eds. *Interest Group Politics* (Washington, D.C.: Congressional Quarterly Press, 1983), pp. 175–92, at p.

187. Vincent Blasi, "Free Speech and the Widening Gyre of Fund-Raising," 94 *Columbia Law Review* 1281 (1991) at 1284–85, 1287.

119. Dworkin, "What Is Equality?" p. 22. For a participant's view of campaign finance reform, see Greg D. Kubiak, *The Gilded Dome* (Norman: University of Oklahoma Press, 1994).

120. Robert Kuttner, "Campaign Reform Depends on Grass-Roots Action," *Boston Globe*, March 25, 1996, p. A23. Bill Bradley, "Congress Won't Act. Will You?" *New York Times* November 11, 1996, p. A15. One scheme was considered in *Buckley*, at 92, n. 125.

121. *Austin*, at 1402, 1398. For Rawls on *Buckley*, see *Political Liberalism*, p. 363.

122. *Buckley*, at 55–57.

123. *Austin*, at 1397.

124. Ibid., at 1397.

125. Sunstein, *Democracy*, p. 98.

126. Wright, "Money," pp. 636, 637.

127. Post, *Constitutional Domains*, p. 282.

128. Cited in Fred Cook, *Lobbying in American Politics* (New York: Franklin Watts, 1976), p. 25.

129. Beitz, *Political Equality*, p. 193.

130. Verba et al., *Voice and Equality*, p. 506.

131. See Edward B. Foley, "Equal-Dollars-Per-Voter: A Constitutional Principle of Campaign Finance," 94 *Columbia Law Review* 1204 (1994) at 1209, n. 15, 1238.

132. Michael Sandel, "Votes for Sale," *New Republic*, vol. 215, November 18, 1996, p. 25. Foley "Equal-Dollars-Per-Voter," p. 1242.

133. Political equality is not "a distinct dimension of equality, with its own distinct metric." Dworkin, "What Is Equality?" p. 6.

134. Tribe, *Constitutional Law*, p. 805.

135. *Colorado Republican Federal Campaign Committee v. FEC*, 110 S. Ct. 2309 (1996).

136. Blasi, "Free Speech," p. 1290.

137. *Buckley*, at 241, 243.

138. *Austin*, at 1416.

139. Kuttner, "Campaign Reform,"p. A23.

140. Clawson et al., *Money Talks*, p. 126.

141. Verba et al., *Voice and Equality*, pp. 506, 507. Money does tend to create a general distortion in a conservative direction, pp. 364, 366, 477–80.

142. Ibid., p. 531.

143. Robert Lane, "The Joyless Polity," in Stephen Elkin, ed., *Citizen Competence* (forthcoming, Pennsylvania State University Press), pp. 2, 23.

144. Report of the Twentieth Century Fund Task Force on Political Action Committees, *What Price PACs?* (New York: The Twentieth Century Fund, 1984), p. 85.

145. Ibid., p. 83.

146. Mahood, *Interest Group Politics*, p. 158.

147. Allan Cigler and Burdett Loomis, "Contemporary Interest Group Politics: More Than 'More of the Same,'" in *Interest Group Politics*, pp. 393–406.

148. Edward Grefe and Marty Linsky, *The New Corporate Activism* (New York: McGraw-Hill, 1995).

149. Hedrick Smith, cited in Cigler and Loomis, "Interest Group Politics," p. 395.

150. David Adamany, cited in John R. Wright, *Interest Groups and Congress* (Boston: Allyn & Bacon, 1996), p. 157.

151. Stern, *Best Congress*, p. 152.

152. Sorauf, "Political Action Committee," pp. 177, 181, 185.

153. David Estlund, "Democratic Discussion: Part I," unpublished paper, 1991, p. 24. Bernard Manin, "On Legitimacy and Political Deliberation," *Political Theory* 15, no. 3 (1987): 338–68.

154. Beitz, *Political Equality*, p. 202.

155. Jane J. Mansbridge, "A Deliberative Theory of Interest Representation," in Mark P. Petracca, ed., *The Politics of Interests* (Boulder, Colo.: Westview, 1992), pp. 32–58, at p. 32; on "collaborative deliberation," p. 39.

156. David Plotke, "The Political Mobilization of Business," in Petracca, ed., *Politics of Interests*, pp. 175–91.

157. Sunstein, *Democracy*, p. 20; Beitz, *Political Equality*, p. 195.

158. Foley, "Equal-Dollars-Per-Voter," p. 1205.

159. *Buckley*, at 48

160. Beitz, *Political Equality*, p. 212.

161. *Austin*, at 1407.

162. John S. Dryzek, "Political Inclusion and the Dynamics of Democratization," *American Political Science Review* 90, no. 1 (1996): 475–87.

163. Joshua Cohen, "Freedom of Expression," *Philosophy and Public Affairs* 22 (1993): 207–63, at p. 224.

Chapter 7

1. Justice Robert Jackson, cited in David Brion Davis, ed., *The Fear of Conspiracy* (Ithaca, N.Y.: Cornell University Press, 1971), p. 294.

2. Speech at the Anti-Masonic Convention, 1830, in ibid., p. 80.

3. Raphael S. Ezekiel, *The Racist Mind* (New York: Viking, 1995), p. 93.

4. Arthur Schlesinger, "Biography of a Nation of Joiners," *American Historical Review*, 50, no. 1 (1944): 1–25, at pp. 8–9.

5. Cited in Davis, *Fear of Conspiracy*, p. 327.

6. Lyman T. Sargent, *Extremism in America* (New York: New York University Press, 1995), p. 122. This is a collection of documents taken from the Wilcox Collection of Contemporary Movements at the University of Kansas, from the 1920s to the present.

7. Morris Dees and James Corcoran, *The Gathering Storm* (New York: Harper-Collins, 1996).

8. Joel Kovel, *Red Hunting in the Promised Land: Anticommunism and the Making of America* (New York: Basic, 1994), p. 95.

9. James Coates, *Armed and Dangerous: The Rise of the Survivalist Right* (New York: Hill & Wang, 1987), pp. 111–12.

10. Bud Schultz and Ruth Schultz, eds., *It Did Happen Here: Recollections of Political Repression in America* (Berkeley: University of California Press, 1989), p. 287. John George and Laird Wilcox, *Nazis, Communists, Klansmen, and Others on the Fringe* (Buffalo: Prometheus, 1992), p. 285.

11. Melissa Fay Greene, *The Temple Bombing* (Reading, Mass.: Addison-Wesley, 1996), p. 226.

12. Cited in Richard Hofstadter, *The Paranoid Style in American Politics and Other Essays* (New York: Vintage, 1964), p. 12. Writing in 1964, Hofstadter was confident that "the paranoid style" was the preferred style only of minority movements, p. 7. Rogin, cited in William B. Hixson Jr., *Search for the American Right Wing: An Analysis of the Social Science Record, 1955–1987* (Princeton, N.J.: Princeton University Press, 1992), p. 110.

13. Davis, *Fear of Conspiracy*, pp. 268–69.

14. Kirkpatrick Sale, "Setting Limits on Technology," *The Nation*, vol. 260, June 5, 1995, pp. 785–88, at p. 788.

15. Iris Marion Young, *Justice and the Politics of Difference* (Princeton, N.J.: Princeton University Press, 1990), p. 182.

16. Cited in Sargent, *Extremism*, p. 199.

17. "The Freemen Network," Anti-Defamation League, 1996, p. 2.

18. Greene, *Temple Bombing*, p. 202.

19. Cited in Hugh Pearson, *The Shadow of the Panther: Huey Newton and the Price of Black Power in America* (Reading, Mass.: Addison-Wesley, 1994), p. 179.

20. Sargent, *Extremism*, pp. 144–45.

21. Bernard Dailyn, "The Logic of Rebellion: Conspiracy Fears and the American Revolution," in Richard Curry and Thomas Brown, eds., *Conspiracy: The Fear of Subversion in American History* (New York: Holt, Rinehart, Winston, 1972), p. 22.

22. Cited in Sargent, *Extremism*, pp. 92, 216.

23. *New York Times*, July 6, 1995, p. B9.

24. J. Harry Jones Jr. *The Minutemen* (Garden City, N.Y.: Doubleday, 1968), pp. 260–62.

25. Junta of Militant Organizations, cited in Sargent, *Extremism*, p. 193.

26. The phrase is from Lewis H. Lapham, "Seen But Not Heard: The Message of the Oklahoma Bombing," *Harper's Magazine*, vol. 291, July 1995, pp. 29–36, at p. 29.

27. Pearson, *Shadow of the Panther*, p. 176.

28. George and Wilcox, *Nazis*, p. 279.

29. Jones, *Minutemen*, pp. 133–34.

30. The estimates for white racist groups put out by the Center for Democratic Renewal and the Southern Poverty Law Center includes 23,000 or more members; 150,000 sympathizers who buy literature or attend rallies; Ezekiel, *Racist Mind*, p. xxi. The latest figures on militia groups, taken from Klanwatch by Senator Arlen Specter, Chairman of the Senate Subcommittee on Terrorism hearings, is 224 groups active in 39 states and rumored to be present in all 50 states, p. 2.

31. See Hixson, *Right Wing*, pp. xvi, 297. Ezekiel reports, and cites James Aho, that the extremists he has studied come from a representative slice of American society, *Racist Mind*, p. xxviii. See, too, James Corcoran, *Bitter Harvest: Gordon Kahl and the Posse Comitatus: Murder in the Heartland* (New York: Penguin, 1991).

32. Coates, *Armed and Dangerous*, p. 216.

33. Alex Heard, "The Road to Oklahoma City," *New Republic*, vol. 212, May 15, 1995, p. 20.

34. Coates, *Armed and Dangerous* pp. 124, 154.

35. Jones, *Minutemen*, p. 364.

36. ADL, "Fact Finding Report: Beyond the Bombing: The Militia Menace Grows," 1995, p. 25.

37. Coates, *Armed and Dangerous*, p. 137.

38. Senate Subcommittee on Terrorism Hearing on the Militia Movement in the U.S., June 15, 1995. Montana Human Rights Network report, p. 7.

39. Coates, *Armed and Dangerous*, p. 236.

40. Cited in Jones, *Minutemen*, p. 126.

41. Cited in Michael Kelly, "The Road to Paranoia," *New Yorker*, vol. 71, June 19, 1995, pp. 60–75, p. at 75.

42. Coates, *Armed and Dangerous*, p. 54.

43. Thomas Martinez and John Guinther, *Brotherhood of Murder* (New York: McGraw-Hill, 1988), p. 55.

44. Richard P. Albares, *Nativist Paramilitarism in the United States: The Minutemen Organization* (Chicago: Center for Social Organization Studies, University of Chicago, 1968), p. 2; also reported by Jones, *Minutemen*, p. 370.

45. Henry Louis Gates Jr., "The Charmer," *New Yorker*, April 29, 1996, pp. 116–31, at p. 131.

46. Dees and Corcoran, *Gathering Storm*, p. 92.

47. Ezekiel, *Racist Mind*, p. 62.

48. Ibid., p. 112.

49. De Pugh, cited in Jones, *Minutemen*, p. 114.

50. Cited in Pearson, *Shadow of the Panther*, p. 116.

51. Coates, *Armed and Dangerous*, pp. 15–16.

52. Corcoran, *Bitter Harvest*, p. 148.

53. Ezekiel, *Racist Mind*, p. xxx.

54. Nancy L. Rosenblum, *Another Liberalism* (Cambridge, Mass.: Harvard University Press, 1987), p. 9.

55. Tom Metzger, cited in Ezekiel, *Racist Mind*, p. 85; skinhead, cited in ibid., p. 246.

56. George and Wilcox on the Minutemen leaders, *Nazis*, p. 288.

57. Martinez and Guinther, *Brotherhood*, p. 55.

58. Gerald Smith, in Sargent, *Extremism*, p. 121.

59. On the romanticization of urban gangs by social critics, see Alan Wolfe, *Marginalized in the Middle* (Chicago: University of Chicago Press, 1996), pp. 42–44.

60. John Humphrey Noyes, *History of American Socialisms* (New York: Hilary House, 1961), p. 61.

61. See Nancy L. Rosenblum, "Democratic Sex," in David Estlund and Martha Nussbaum, eds., *Sex, Preference, and Family* (Oxford: Oxford University Press, 1997), pp. 63–85.

62. Cited in Rex Eugene Cooper, *Promises Made to the Fathers: Mormon Covenant Organization* (Salt Lake City: University of Utah Press, 1990), p. 185.

63. Cited in Klaus J. Hansen, *Mormonism and the American Experience* (Chicago: University of Chicago Press, 1981), p. 144. J. H. Beadle, a Catholic critic, writing in 1870, cited in Carol Weisbrod, *The Boundaries of Utopia* (New York: Pantheon, 1980), p. 26.

64. Cited in ADL, Anti-Paramilitary Training, p. 2.

65. Corcoran, *Bitter Harvest*, p. 77.

66. Michael Barkun, *Religion and the Racist Right* (Chapel Hill: University of North Carolina Press, 1994), p. 237.

67. Junta of Militant Organizations, cited in Sargent, *Extremism*, p. 193.

68. Rogers Smith, *Civic Ideals: Conflicting Visions of Citizenship in American Public Law*, ch. 1, p. 7 of manuscript. David H. Bennett, *The Party of Fear* (Chapel Hill: University of North Carolina Press, 1988).

69. Smith, *Civic Ideals*, ch. 1, p. 7.

70. Schlesinger, "Biography," p. 19.

71. "A Plea for the West," in Davis, ed., *Fear of Conspiracy*, p. 89.

72. Ezekiel, *Racist Mind*, p. 66.

73. See Joel Kovel, *White Racism: A Psychohistory* (New York: Columbia University Press, 1984).

74. Cited in Sargent, *Extremism*, p. 31. From the earliest studies of the American right, Protestant fundamentalism has figured in some explanatory guise; Hixson, *Right Wing*, p. 78.

75. Cited in Ezekiel, *Racist Mind*, p. 131.

76. Cited in Martinez and Guinther, *Brotherhood*, p. 100. Corcoran, *Bitter Harvest*, p. 38. Coates, *Armed and Dangerous*, p. 80. Barkun, *Religion and the Racist Right*.

77. Cited in Dees and Corcoran, *Gathering Storm*, p. 2.

78. Gates, "Charmer," p. 119.

79. George and Wilcox, *Nazis*, p. 349.

80. Cited in James Shenton, "Fascism and Father Coughlin," in Curry and Brown, *Conspiracy*, p. 181.

81. Cited in Kovel, *Red Hunting*, p. 27.

82. Lorenzo Crowell Jr., "U.S. Domestic Terrorism: An Historical Perspective," *Quarterly Journal of Ideology* 11, no. 3 (1987): 45–56, at p. 51. Ingo Hasselbach, "Extremism: A Global Network," *New York Times*, April 1995, p. A25.

83. Lawrence N. Powell, "Slouching toward Baton Rouge: The 1989 Legislative Election of David Duke," in Douglas D. Rose, ed., *The Emergence of David Duke and the Politics of Race* (Chapel Hill: University of North Carolina Press, 1991), pp. 11–40, at pp. 16, 18.

84. Sargent, *Extremism*, p. 117.

85. Coates, *Armed and Dangerous*, p. 136; Ezekiel, *Racist Mind*, p. 34.

86. Despite notoriety, the extent of criminal activity is difficult to assess. *When Hate Groups Come to Town: A Handbook of Effective Community Response* (Atlanta: Center for Democratic Renewal, 1992), p. 113. For figures, see *Klanwatch*, October 1995, p. 11.

87. "Child's Cries Lead to Cult Arsenal, Officials Say," *New York Times*, November 13, 1996, p. 1.

88. *People ex. rel. Gallo v. Acuna*, 43 Cal. App. 4th 1341 (1995).

89. On prison gang membership in sentencing hearings, see *Dawson v. Delaware*, 112 S. Ct. 1093 (1992).

90. Schultz and Schultz, *Recollections*, pp. 71, 290.

91. DePugh, cited in George and Wilcox, *Nazis*, p. 281.

92. Corcoran, *Armed and Dangerous*, pp. 54, 71.

93. 367 U.S. 1 (1961).

94. *Scales*, 367 U.S. 203 (1961), at 209. See, too, *Elfbrandt v. Russell*, 384 U.S. 11 (1966).

95. 367 U.S. 203 (1961).

96. *Claiborne*, 458 U.S. 898 (1982), at 909.

97. Tom Hentoff, "Speech, Harm, and Self-Government: Understanding the Ambit of the Clear and Present Danger Test," 91 *Columbia Law Review* 1453 (1991) at 1463. See, too, Bernard Schwartz, "Holmes and Hand: Clear and Present Danger or Advocacy of Unlawful Actions," 5 *Supreme Court Review* 209 (1994).

98. Holmes, in *Abrams*, 250 U.S. 616 (1919), at 627.

99. 395 U.S. 444 (1969), at 447–48.

100. 458 U.S. 898 (1982), at 902, 3431, 3433, 928.

101. Cited in *Claiborne*, at 917.

102. *Presser v. Illinois*, 116 U.S. 252 (1885).

103. Jones, *Minutemen*, pp. 129ff.

104. 18 U.S. Code 231(a)(1)(1968).

105. ADL, "The Anti-Paramilitary Training Statute: A Response to Domestic Terrorism," 1995, p. 4.

106. Anti-Defamation League, Special Report, "Paranoia as Patriotism: Far-Right Influences on the Militia Movement," 1995, p. 4.

107. 461 F. 2d 1119 (5th Cir. 1972), at 1122. State statutes delete "having reason to know," further obviating that problem.

108. *National Mobilization Committee to End the War in Vietnam v. Foran*, 411 F. 2d 934 (7th Cir. 1969), at 937, 938.

109. John R. Moore argues that the *Featherston* decision was invalid under *Brandenburg*, "Oregon's Paramilitary Statute: A Sneak Attack on the First Amendment," 30 *Willamette Law Review* 335 (1984) at 340–41.

110. *Hess v. Indiana*, 414 U.S. 105 (1973).

111. 341 U.S. 494 (1951), at 509.

112. 341 U.S. 494 (1951), cited in *Featherston*, at 1122.

113. 461 F. 2d., at 1122.

114. Ibid.

115. Testimony of Stevie Remington, Executive Director of the ACLU, on HB3001 (Oregon), June 13, 1983. Moore, "Oregon's Paramilitary Statute," pp. 343–44.

116. Joelle E. Polesky, "The Rise of Private Militia: A First and Second Amendment Analysis of the Right to Organize and the Right to Train," 144 *University of Pennsylvania Law Review* 1593 (1996) at 1612.

117. *Abrams v. U.S.*, 250 U.S. 616 (1919), at 630.

118. Hentoff, "Speech," p. 1470.

119. Joseph Grinstein, "Jihad and the Constitution: The First Amendment Implications of Combating Religiously Motivated Terrorism," 105 *Yale Law Journal* 1347 (1996), at 1375.

120. 458 U.S. 886, at 908–9.

121. ADL, "Anti-Paramilitary Training Statute," pp. 3, 1. For a case involving a consent decree to cease paramilitary organizing brought against Glen Miller and the White Patriot Party, see *Person v. Miller*, 854 F. 2d 656 (1988).

122. Marshall dissenting in *Arnett v. Kennedy*, 415 U.S. 134 (1974), at 231.

123. 518 F. Suppl. 993 (1981).

124. For articles on the "Fort Smith" trial in 1988, see the *New York Times*, February 18, p. A17; February 19, p. A13; February 28, p. A25; April 6, p. A14;

125. Morris Dees attributes the acquittal to "an all-white Arkansas jury"; *Gathering Storm*, pp. 2, 44.

126. 458 U.S., at 932.

127. Title 31. Code of Alabama ¶31–2–125 (1995).

128. Dees and Corcoran, *Gathering Storm*, p. 183.

129. The state laws have "almost never been enforced" or, I assume, challenged. Ibid., pp. 220–21.

130. Anti-Defamation League, "Anti-Paramilitary Training Statute" (New York: Anti-Defamation League, 1995).

131. David R. Truman, "The Jets and the Sharks Are Dead: State Statutory Responses to Criminal Street Gangs," 73 *Washington University Law Quarterly* 683 (1991) at 685.

132. "Notes: Jail, Jail, the Gang's All Here: Senate Crime Bill Section 521, The Criminal Street Gang Provision," 36 *Boston College Law Review* 527 (1995), at 546.

133. Cited in Truman, "State Statutory Responses," p. 717, n. 189. I disagree with Alexander Molina's First Amendment analysis in "California's Anti-Gang Street Terrorism Enforcement and Prevention Act: One Step Forward, Two Steps Back?" 22 *Southwestern Law Review* 457 (1993) at 466, 468.

134. Molina, "California's . . . Act," p. 476.

135. Truman, "State Statutory Responses," pp. 728, 683.

136. Ezekiel, *Racist Mind*, p. xxii.

137. Ibid., p. 28.

138. Ibid., p. xxii.

139. "Freemen Earn Enmity of Once-Sympathetic Mediators," *New York Times*, May 25, 1996, p. 8.

140. William French Smith, 1983, cited in *National Law Journal*, May 8, 1995, p. A28. New guidelines were established in 1976 and further revised in 1983 following FBI abuses, including politically motivated investigations in the 1960s and 1970s. For a survey, see *Alliance to End Repression v. City of Chicago*, 742 F. 2d 1007 (1984). The justification for these expansive powers is provided by Judge Posner in *Alliance to End Repression* at 1016, 1010.

141. *National Law Journal*, May 8, 1995, p. A28.

142. Judge Cudahy dissent in *Alliance to End Repression* at 1020.

143. Freeh cited in *National Law Journal*, p. A28. "Law Enforcement Agencies Differ on Need for More Power to Spy on Terror Suspects," *New York Times*, April 26, 1995, p. A23.

144. CDR, p. 113. "Hate Groups and Acts of Bigotry: Connecticut's Response," A report based on a fact-finding meeting sponsored by the Connecticut Advisory Committee to the U.S. Commission on Civil Rights, September 24, 1981, p. 24. For more recent figures, see *Klanwatch*, October 1995, p. 11. Missouri State Highway Patrol Testimony, "The Militia Movement in the United States," Senate Committee on the Judiciary, Subcommittee on Terrorism, Technology, and Government Information, June 15, 1995. Ezekiel, *Racist Mind*, pp. 24, 288, xxiii.

145. "Hate Groups and Acts of Bigotry: Connecticut's Response," September 24, 1981, p. 24.

146. *Abrams*, 250 U.S., at 628, 629.

147. 341 U.S., at 588.

148. Cited in Pearson, *Shadow of the Panther*, p. 211.

149. Vincent Blasi, "The Pathological Perspective and the First Amendment," cited in Geoffrey Stone, Louis Seidman, Cass Sunstein, and Mark Tushnet, eds., *Constitutional Law* (New York: McGraw-Hill, 1991), p. 1075. *Whitney*, 274 U.S. 357, at 378.

150. John Rawls, *Political Liberalism* (New York: Columbia University Press, 1993), p. 355.

151. John Rawls, *A Theory of Justice* (Cambridge, Mass.: Harvard University Press, 1971), pp. 242–43.

152. Davis, *Fear of Conspiracy*, pp. xxii, 107.

153. Jones, *Minutemen*, p. 7.

154. Anti-Defamation League, Fact Finding Report, "Beyond the Bombing: The Militia Menace Grows," 1995, p. 11.

155. Jones, *Minutemen*, p. 304. On public officials' involvement in these groups, see ibid., pp. 292–93; Montana Human Rights Network report, Senate Subcommittee on Terrorism, Technology and Government Information Hearing on the Militia Movement in the U.S., June 15, 1995, p. 12; Coates, *Armed and Dangerous*, p. 135; ADL Fact-Finding 1994, p. 6; Center for Democratic Renewal, p. 164.

156. For a discussion of the 1987 Anti-Terrorism Act directed at the PLO and domestic supporters, see *Mendelsohn v. Meese*, 695 F. Suppl. 1474 (1988). Center for National Security Studies, "Recent Trends in Domestic and International Terrorism," April 26, 1995.

157. The 1996 bill authorizes the secretary of state to designate any foreign group a "terrorist" organization based on an effectively nonreviewable judgment that that group's activities threaten national security.

158. Martha Bethel, "Terror in Montana," *New York Times*, July 20, 1995, p. A23.

159. Michael Kelly, "Playing with Fire," *New Yorker*, vol. 72, July 15, 1996, pp. 28–35, at p. 31.

160. Cited in Ezekiel, *Racist Mind*, pp. 24, 288.

161. Davis, *Fear of Conspiracy*, p. 361.

162. Michael Kelly, "The Road to Paranoia," *New Yorker*, June 19, 1995, pp. 60–75, at p. 60.

163. Jones, *Minutemen*, pp. 90–91.

164. Pearson, *Shadow of the Panther*, p. 338.

165. Ezekiel, *Racist Mind*, p. 25.

166. Ibid., p. 159.

167. Ibid., pp. 154, 32, 150.

168. Cited in Molina, "California's . . . Act," p. 463.

169. Greene, *Temple Bombing*, p. 50.

170. Ezekiel, *Racist Mind*, pp. 153, xxiv, 158.

171. Cited in Sargent, *Extremism*, pp. 135–36.

172. Pearson, *Shadow of the Panther*, p. 94.

173. George and Wilcox, *Nazis*, p. 283.

174. Corcoran, *Bitter Harvest*, p. 39; on racist prison gangs, pp. 218, 224.

175. Cited in Sargent, *Extremism*, pp. 180–81.

176. Ezekiel, *Racist Mind*, p. 66.

177. Russell Hardin, *One for All* (Princeton, N.J.: Princeton University Press, 1995), p. 102.

178. Jones, *Minutemen*, p. 311.

179. Hofstadter, *Paranoid Style*, p. 38.

180. Ezekiel, *Racist Mind*, pp. 109–10.

181. Ibid., pp. 127, 79.

182. Jones, *Minutemen*, p. 211.

183. Ezekiel, *Racist Mind*, p. 159.

184. Alan Wolfe, "Sociology, Liberalism, and the Radical Right," *New Left Review* 28 (1981): 3–27, at p. 18.

185. Hixson, *Right Wing*, p. xxv.

186. This is the assumption of nonacademics in the field; see Dees and Corcoran, *Gathering Storm*, p. 116. For corrections, see Donald Green, Jack Glaser, and Andrew Rich, "From Lynching to Gay-Bashing: The Elusive Connection between Economic Conditions and Hate Crime," unpublished paper. Green with Margaret Garnett and Robert Abelson, "The Distinctive Political Views of Hate Crime Perpetrators and White Supremacists: A Report to the Harry Frank Guggenheim Foundation," unpublished paper. Green, with Janelle Wong and Dara Strolovitch, "The Effects of Demographic Change on Hate Crime," unpublished paper.

187. Green et al., "Demographic Change," pp. 20, 21.

188. Hixson, *Right Wing*, pp. 83, 90.

189. George and Wilcox, *Nazis*, pp. 258–59, 263.

190. *When Hate Groups Come to Town*, p. 81. CDR, p. 125.

191. CDR, p. 115.

192. Connecticut report, p. 5.

193. Powell, "David Duke," p. 27.

194. Wolfe, "Sociology, Liberalism, and the Radical Right."

195. Kelly, "Read to Paranoia," p. 62.

196. Coates, *Armed and Dangerous*, p. 4. Dees and Corcoran argue that the "infiltration" of militia by hate group leaders is creating "a single movement" in *Gathering Storm*, p. 42. Dees believes that the alleged McVeigh/Nichols bombing in Oklahoma was part of a larger plot, p. 164.

197. Coates, *Armed and Dangerous*, p. 167.

198. Gates, "Charmer," p. 128.

199. Green et al., "Distinctive Political Views," pp. 13, 17.

200. William Pierce, cited in Dees and Corcoran, *Gathering Storm*, p. 77.

201 Coates, *Armed and Dangerous*, pp. 259, 258.

202. Kelly, "Road to Paranoia," p. 66.

203. Powell, "David Duke," pp. 16, 18.

204. Columnist George Will, cited in Lapham, "Oklahoma Bombing," p. 32; Newt Gingrich, Speaker of the House of Representatives, cited in ibid., p. 34.

Chapter 8

1. Tom Metzger, cited in Raphael S. Ezekiel, *The Racist Mind: Portraits of American Neo-Nazis and Klansmen* (New York: Viking, 1995), p. 72.

2. Cited in Lyman T. Sargent, *Extremism in America* (New York: New York University Press, 1995), p. 346.

3. Morris Dees and James Corcoran, *The Gathering Storm* (New York: Harper-Collins, 1996), p. 199. The figures proposed by Senator Arlen Specter in Senate Subcommittee on Terrorism, Technology and Government Information Hearing on Militia Organizations, June 15, 1995, is that "at least 224 militias operate in this country."

4. Bernard Bailyn, "The Logic of Rebellion: Conspiracy Fears and the American Revolution," in Richard Curry and Thomas Brown, eds., *Conspiracy: The Fear of Subversion in American History* (New York: Holt, Rinehart, Winston, 1972), p. 22.

5. Tom Reiss, "Home on the Range," *New York Times*, May 26, 1995, p. A27. James Coates, *Armed and Dangerous: The Rise of the Survivalist Right* (New York: Hill & Wang, 1987), p. 118; James Corcoran, *Bitter Harvest: Gordon Kahl and the Posse Comitatus: Murder in the Heartland* (New York: Penguin, 1991), p. 32. Coates, *Armed and Dangerous*, pp. 111, 119. Anti-Defamation League, Special Report, "Paranoia as Patriotism: Far-Right Influences on the Militia Movement," 1995, p. 7. Anti-Defamation League, "The Freemen Network," 1996. Montana Human Rights Network, May 1994, p. 11.

6. This is Melissa Fay Greene's description of leaders of the National States Rights Party in the 1950s in *The Temple Bombing* (Reading, Mass.: Addison-Wesley, 1996), p. 213.

7. Ezekiel, *Racist Mind*, p. 326.

8. Bailyn, "Logic of Rebellion."

9. *New York Times*, July 6, 1996, p. A1.

10. Cited in David H. Bennett, *The Party of Fear* (Chapel Hill: University of North Carolina Press, 1988), p. 344.

11. Robert E. Lane, "The Joyless Polity: Contributions of Democratic Processes to Ill-Being," unpublished paper.

12. David Brion Davis, ed., *The Fear of Conspiracy* (Ithaca, N.Y.:Cornell University Press, 1971), p. xxii.

13. Ibid..

14. James Wilson, cited in Akhil Amar, "Popular Sovereignty and Constitutional Amendment," in Sanford Levinson, ed., *Responding to Imperfection: The Theory and Practice of Constitutional Amendment* (Princeton, N.J.: Princeton University Press, 1995), p. 98.

15. Herbert J. Storing, *What the Anti-Federalists Were For* (Chicago: University of Chicago Press, 1981), p. 56.

16. James Madison, cited in ibid., p. 39.

17. *The Rights of Man*, in *Thomas Paine: Collected Writings* (New York: Library of America, 1995), pp. 438, 594.

18. Thomas Paine, *Common Sense* (New York: Library of America: 1995), p. 35.

19. Publius, cited by Storing, *Anti-Federalists*, p. 74.

20. Norman Olson, testimony before Senate Subcommittee on Militias, June 1995.

21. The strongest affinity between citizen militias and populists is defense of local communities against outside interference. The key to militias is not the classic populist resentment at classes above and below. William B. Hixson Jr. *Search for the American Right Wing: An Analysis of the Social Science Record, 1955–87* (Princeton, N.J.: Princeton University Press, 1992), p. 224.

22. Cited in Storing, *Anti-Federalists*, p. 52.

23. J. Harry Jones Jr., *The Minutemen* (Garden City, N.Y.: Doubleday, 1968), p. 57.

24. John Vile, "The Case against Implicit Limits on the Amending Process," in Sanford Levinson, ed., *Responding to Imperfection* (Princeton, N.J.: Princeton University Press, 1995), p. 194.

25. Cited in Storing, *Anti-Federalists*, p. 60. Stephen Holmes, *Passions and Constraint* (Chicago: University of Chicago Press, 1995), pp. 164–65.

26. Report of the Subcommittee on the Constitution of the Committee of the Judiciary, U.S. Senate, 1982, in Earl Kruschke, *The Right to Keep and Bear Arms* (Springfield, Ill.: Thomas, 1985), p. 144.

27. Clayton E. Craymer, *For the Defense of Themselves and the State* (Westport, Conn.: Praeger, 1994), pp. 165, 194.

28. Cited in Sanford Levinson, "The Embarrassing Second Amendment." 99 *Yale Law Journal* 637 (1989) at 641.

29. Garry Wills, "To Keep and Bear Arms," *New York Review of Books*, vol. 42, September 21, 1995, pp. 62–73, at p. 66.

30. Wendy Kaminer, *It's All the Rage: Crime and Culture* (Reading, Mass.: Addison-Wesley, 1995), p. 58.

31. Jeremy Rabkin, "Sue the Government," *New Republic*, vol. 212, May 8, 1995, pp. 16–19, at p. 18.

32. Cited in Kaminer, *All the Rage*, pp. 236, 232.

33. See Theodore M. Becker, "The Place of Private Police in Society: An Area of Research for the Social Sciences," *Social Problems* 21, no. 3 (1974): 438–53, at p. 441. The only constraints on most private police are criminal prosecution and tort liability, p. 447. See, too, Susan Guarino Ghezzi, "A Private Network of Social Control: Insurance Investigation Units," *Social Problems* 30, no. 5 (1983): 521–31.

34. Cited in Dees and Corcoran, *Gathering Storm*, p. 54.

35. Craymer, *Defense*, pp. 194, 168, 133.

36. *Presser v. Illinois*, 116 U.S. 252 (1885), at 259.

37. Cited in Craymer, *Defense*, p. 131.

38. Cited in Levinson, "Second Amendment," p. 653, n. 78.

39. Cited in Stephen P. Halbrook, *That Every Man Be Armed* (Albuquerque: University of New Mexico Press, 1984), p. 250, n. 33.

40. Cited in ibid., p. 104.

41. Cited in Robert Cottrol and Ray Diamond, "The Second Amendment: Towards an Afro-American Reconsideration," 80 *Georgetown Law Journal* 309 (1991) at 353.

42. Ibid., p. 340. Sam Bass Warner, *The Private City* (Philadephia: University of Pennsylvania Press, 1968), p. 128.

43. Cited in Halbrook, *Every Man*, p. 105.

44. Cottrol and Diamond, "Second Amendment," p. 337.

45. Craymer, *Defense*, p. 138.

46. Cited in Halbrook, *Every Man*, p. 108.

47. For a review of the intent to incorporate the Second Amendment into the Fourteenth to allow blacks to arm, see L. A. Powe Jr., "Guns, Words, and Interpretation," *American Political Science Association*, unpublished paper, 1996, p. 62; forthcoming in *William and Mary Law Review*.

48. Craymer, *Defense*, p. 200. On the connection drawn between gun control and race today, see Halbrook, *Every Man*, pp. 185, 196, 264, n. 31.

49. Cottrol and Diamond, ''Second Amendment,'' pp. 340–42.

50. Hugh Pearson, *The Shadow of the Panther: Huey Newton and the Price of Black Power in America* (Reading, Mass.: Addison-Wesley, 1994), pp. 25–26.

51. Donald B. Kates Jr., cited in Cottrol and Diamond, "Second Amendment," p. 357, n. 267.

52. Cited in Craymer, *Defense*, pp. 199, 200.

53. Pearson, *Shadow of the Panther*, p. 109.

54. Bobby Seale, cited in ibid., pp. 131–32, 134.

55. For a discussion of originalist interpretation of the Second Amendment, see Powe, "Guns," pp. 26ff.

56. Cited in Halbrook, *Every Man*, pp. 28, 31.

57. Akhil Amar, "The Bill of Rights as a Constitution," *Yale Law Journal* 100 (1991): 1131–1210, at pp. 1170–71.

58. Garry Wills does not allow that the militias were part of the federal balance, and identifies the militia entirely with state governments suppressing insurrections, "Arms," pp. 69–70.

59. Halbrook, *Every Man*, pp. 135–38.

60. On the position of parties to the historical debate, see Powe, "Guns," pp. 18ff. "Guardsmen Fight Cuts by Pentagon," *New York Times*, December 26, 1995, p. 1.

61. *Presser*, at 265.

62. 307 U.S. 174 (1939); see, too, *Lewis v. U.S.*, 445 U.S. 55 (1980).

63. Cottrol and Diamond, "Second Amendment," p. 315, n. 20.

64. Cited in Halbrook, *Every Man*, p. 121.

65. Craymer, *Defense*, p. 264.

66. *Morton Grove*, cited in Kurschke, *Arms*, pp. 85, 83, 116–17, 121–22.

67. Wendy Kaminer, "Second Thoughts on the Second Amendment," *Atlantic Monthly*, March 1996, pp. 32–45. For current debates about the efficacy of gun control and self-defense, see Powe, "Guns," pp. 81ff.

68. *U.S. v. Lopez*, 63 U.S. 4343 (1995), at 4363–64, 4347.

69. Ibid., at 4351.

70. Richard Henry Lee, *Letters from a Federal Farmer*, cited in Halbrook, *Every Man*, p. 70.

71. Cited in Amar, "Bill of Rights," p. 1189.

72. Thomas Halpern and Brian Levin, *The Limits of Dissent: The Constitutional Status of Armed Civilian Militias* (Amherst: Altheia, 1996), p. 36.

73. Halbrook, *Every Man*, p. 69. Halbrook admits that the amendment does not foreclose gun control. "Handgun Prohibition and the Original Meaning of the Second Amendment," 82 *Michigan Law Review* 204 (1983).

74. Amar, "Bill of Rights," p. 1164.

75. *U.S. v. Oakes*, 564 F. 2d 384 (1977).

76. Powe, "Guns," p. 56.

77. Levinson, "Second Amendment," pp. 656, 657.

78. Powe, "Guns," p. 94.

79. Wills, "Arms," p. 69.

80. Norman Olson, testimony, Senate Subcommittee.

81. Levinson, "Second Amendment," pp. 656, 657.

82. Helen Chenoweth of Idaho, reported in Sidney Blumenthal, "Her Own Private Idaho," *New Yorker*, vo. 71, July 10, 1995, p. 28.

83. John Levin, "Bearing Arms," in Kruschke, *Arms*, p. 30.

84. Cottrol and Diamond, "Second Amendment," p. 324.

85. Dees and Corcoran see government overregulation and overtaxation as simply a "repackaging" of the essential racist message, *Gathering Storm*, pp. 4–5.

86. For quotation and a contrary view, see David C. Williams, "The Militia Movement and Second Amendment Revolution: Conjuring with the People," American Political Science Association, unpublished paper, August 22, 1995, pp. 55, 29, 89.

87. Williams, "Militia Movement," pp. 58, 76, 4, 79. Williams, "The Constitutional Right to Conservative Revolution," American Political Science Association, 1996, San Francisco, pp. 19, 12, n. 33.

88. Wendy Brown, "Guns, Cowboys, Philadelphia Mayors, and Civic Republicanism: On Sanford Levinson's 'The Embarrassing Second Amendment,' " 99 *Yale Law Journal* 661 (1989) at 663.

89. Wills, "Arms," pp. 64–66.

90. Williams, "Militia Movement," p. 4.

91. Pauline Maier, *From Resistance to Revolution* (New York: Knopf, 1974).

92. Cited in Kenneth S. Stern, *A Force upon the Plain: The American Militia Movement and the Politics of Hate* (New York: Simon & Shuster, 1996), p. 35; cited in Dees and Corcoran, *Gathering Storm*, p. 206.

93. Cited in Halbrook, *Every Man*, p. 193.

94. Statement to the Senate Subcommittee, p. 20.

95. Cited in Williams, "Militia Movement," p. 31.

96. From the NRA magazine *American Rifleman*, cited in "Bearing Arms and Harsh Words," *New York Times*, May 8, 1995, p. A17.

97. "Gun Owners No Easy Audience for Candidates," *New York Times*, January 15, 1996, p. A12.

98. Cited in Stern, *A Force upon the Plain*, p. 107.

99. Halbrook, *Every Man* p. 196, and citation on p. 196.

100. Cited in Steven Yarosh, "A Place for Safe Housing in the Fourth Amendment," *Responsive Community*, Summer 1994, pp. 29–41, at p. 39.

101. Kaminer, *Crime and Culture*, p. 231, on whom I rely for this paragraph.

102. Cited in Ira Glasser, "First, Protect the Tenants," *New York Times*, May 7, 1994, p. 23.

103. In 1987, *Griffin v. Wisconsin* extended this category to warrantless entry and search of a probationer's home without probable cause, 107 S. Ct. 3164 (1987).

104. Yarosh, "Safe Housing," p. 37.

105. Cited in Williams, "Militia Movement," p. 16, n. 32.

106. Paul Butler, "Racially Based Jury Nullification: Black Power in the Criminal Justice System," 105 *Yale Law Journal* 677 (1995), citing Randall Kennedy at 697–98.

107. Ibid., p. 699.

108. Amar, ''Bill of Rights," pp. 1178–80.

109. Tom Reiss, "Home on the Range," *New York Times*, May 26, 1995, p. A27; Ezekiel, *Racist Mind*, p. 26.

110. Tocqueville, cited in Amar, "Bill of Rights," p. 1186.

111. Cited in Storing, *Anti-Federalists*, pp. 19, 64.

112. Cited in Amar, "Bill of Rights," pp. 1185, 1196.

113. Cited in Pearson, *Shadow of the Panther*, p. 111.

114. 156 U.S. 51, in Jeffrey Abramson, *We, the Jury: The Jury System and the Ideal of Democracy* (New York: Basic, 1994), pp. 85, 62–63.

115. Ibid., p. 59.

116. Cited in Lorenzo Crowell Jr., "U.S. Domestic Terrorism: An Historical Perspective," *Quarterly Journal of Ideology* 11, no. 3 (1987): 45–56, at p. 48.

117. Benjamin Curtis vis-à-vis the Fugitive Slave Law, cited in Abramson, *We, the Jury*, 81.

118. Sargent, *Extremism*, p. 66.

119. Cited in ibid., pp. 68, 301.

120. Butler, "Jury Nullification," at 679.

121. Butler, "Jury Nullification," p. 717, n. 214. For statistics on the number of black males arrested, imprisoned, and under some form of criminal supervision, see ibid., pp. 690, 691. David Remnick, "The Situationist," *New Yorker*, vol. 70, September 5, 1994, pp. 87–101, at p. 93.

122. Butler, "Jury Nullification," p. 723.

123. Ibid., 724, n. 236.

124. Michael Kelly, "The Road to Paranoia," *New Yorker*, June 19, 1995, pp. 60–75, at p. 31.

125. Bill Buford, *Among the Thugs* (New York: Vintage, 1990), p. 218.

126. Wendy Kaminer, "Second Thoughts on the Second Amendment," *Atlantic Monthly*, vol. 277, March 1996, p. 34.

127. Buford, *Among the Thugs*, p. 93.

128. Regina Austin, "The Black Community, Its Lawbreakers, and a Politics of Identification," 65 *Southern California Law Review* 1769 (1992) at 1780.

129. Butler, "Jury Nullification," pp. 680, 690. John Edgar Wideman, cited in Austin, "Black Community," pp. 1778–79.

130. Cited in Jacob Heilbrunn, "Neocon v. Theocon," *New Republic*, vol. 215, December 30, 1996, pp. 20–24, at p. 20.

131. Cited in Dees and Corcoran, *Gathering Storm*, p. 180.

132. In contrast to the theory-laden crafting of handouts by left-wing groups, Ezekiel, *Racist Mind*, p. 315.

133. Lewis H. Lapham, "Seen But Not Heard: The Message of the Oklahoma Bombing," *Harper's Magazine*, vol. 291, July 1995, p. 35.

Chapter 9

1. Philip Gleason, "American Identity and Americanization," in William Peterson, Michael Novak, and Philip Gleason, *Concepts of Ethnicity* (Cambridge, Mass.: Belknap, 1982), p. 105.

2. Werner Sollors, *Beyond Ethnicity* (Oxford: Oxford University Press, 1986), p. 193.

3. Randolph Bourne, "Trans-National America" (1916), cited in ibid., p. 183. The classic early statement is Horace Kallen, "Democracy versus the Melting Pot: A Study of American Nationality," *Nation*, February 1915.

4. *Roberts v. Jaycees*, 468 U.S. 609, at 617.

5. Douglas O. Linder, "Freedom of Association after *Roberts v. United States Jaycees*," 82 *Michigan Law Review* 1878 (1984) at 1903.

6. David Remnick, "The Situationist," *New Yorker*, vol. 70, September 5, 1994, pp. 87–101, at p. 88.

7. Iris Marion Young, *Justice and the Politics of Difference* (Princeton, N.J.: Princeton University Press, 1990), p. 157; Will Kymlicka, *Multicultural Citizenship* (Oxford: Oxford University Press, 1995), p. 10.

8. Isaiah Berlin, "Two Concepts of Liberty," in *Four Essays on Liberty* (Oxford: Oxford University Press, 1969), pp. 155–59.

9. Kenneth Karst, *Belonging to America: Equal Citizenship and the Constitution* (New Haven, Conn.: Yale University Press, 1989), p. 308.

10. Frank Michelman, "Law's Republic," 97 *Yale Law Journal*, 1493 (1988), at 1529–30, 1537; Cass Sunstein, "Beyond the Republican Revival," 97 *Yale Law Journal* 1539 (1988) at 1574–75.

11. Charles Taylor, "The Politics of Recognition," in Amy Gutmann, ed., *Multiculturalism and "the Politics of Recognition"* (Princeton, N.J.:. Princeton University Press, 1992), p. 25.

12. Amy Gutmann, "Introduction," *Multiculturalism and the Politics of Recognition* (Princeton, N.J.: Princeton University Press, 1992), pp. 3, 5.

13. Berlin, "Two Concepts of Liberty," p. 157.

14. Michael Walzer, "Nation and Universe," *The Tanner Lectures on Human Values, XI* (Salt Lake City: University of Utah Press, 1990).

15. K. Anthony Appiah, "Race, Culture, Identity: Misunderstood Connections," in Amy Gutmann, ed., *Color Conscious* (Princeton, N.J.: Princeton University Press, 1996), p. 80.

16. For an extended discussion, see Russell Hardin, *One for All* (Princeton, N.J.: Princeton University Press, 1995), p. 7.

17. Walzer, "Nation and Universe," p. 520.

18. Joseph Raz, "Multiculturalism: A Liberal Perpsective," *Dissent* (Winter 1994): 67–79, at p. 71. For a critical discussion, see John Tomasi, "Kymlicka, Liberalism, and Respect for Cultural Minorities," *Ethnics* 105 (1995): 580–603.

19. Raz, "Multiculturalism," p. 71. David Bromwich, "Culturalism, the Euthanasia of Liberalism," *Dissent* (Winter 1995): 89–102.

20. Bromwich, "Culturalism," p. 89.

21. Raz, "Multiculturalism," p. 71.

22. Margalit and Raz, cited in Kymlicka, *Multicultural Citizenship*, p. 89.

23. Taylor, "Politics of Recognition," pp. 35–36.

24. For a discussion, see Jacob T. Levy, "Classifying Cultural Rights," in Ian Shapiro and Will Kymlicka, eds., *Ethnicity and Group Rights* (New York: New York University Press, 1997).

25. Taylor, "Politics of Recognition," pp. 59, 62, 61; Kymlicka, *Multicultural Citizenship*, p. 169.

26. Appiah, "Race," p. 103.

27. Taylor, "Politics of Recognition," pp. 58, 40. The obligation of "recognition" is sometimes directed at preserving the group's distinctiveness "through indefinite future generations"; p. 41n.; p. 58.

28. Raz, "Multiculturalism," p. 71.

29. Walzer, "Nation and Universe," p. 521.

30. Ibid., p. 519.

31. Erik Erikson, *Childhood and Society* (New York: Norton, 1963), p. 36.

32. Melissa Fay Greene, *The Temple Bombing* (Reading, Mass.: Addison-Wesley, 1996), pp. 20, 57, 127.

33. Kymlicka, *Multicultural Citizenship*, p. 184.

34. Will Kymlicka, "Social Unity in a Liberal State," paper prepared for the Social Philosophy and Policy Conference on "Community, Individual, and the State," Palo Alto, October 1994, p. 33.

35. Walzer, "Nation and Universe," p. 520.

36. Alan Wolfe, *Marginalized in the Middle* (Chicago: University of Chicago Press, 1996), p. 105.

37. Milton Gordon, cited in Gleason, "American Identity," p. 131.

38. Nathan Glazer, "Race for the Cure," *New Republic*, vol. 15, October 7, 1996, p. 29.

39. Mary Waters, *Ethnic Options* (Berkeley: University of California Press, 1990), p. 151.

40. Appiah, "Race," p. 79.

41. Glazer, "Race," p. 29; Appiah, "Race," p. 70.

42. David A. Hollinger, "Postethnic America," *Contention* 2, no. 1 (1992): 79–96, at p. 79.

43. Mary Waters, cited in Wolfe, *Marginalized*, p. 103.

44. Walzer, "Nation and Universe," p. 545.

45. Waters, *Ethnic Options*, p. 145.

46. Regina Austin, "A Nation of Thieves: Securing Black People's Right to Shop and to Sell in White America," 1 *Utah Law Review* 147 (1994) at 165.

47. Cited in Anne Phillips, *The Politics of Presence* (Oxford: Oxford University Press, 1995), p. 131.

48. Studies cited in Waters, *Ethnic Options*, pp. 156–57.

49. On the political background of race-consciousness and ethnic revivals, see Gleason, "American Identity," pp. 129, 135.

50. Sollors, *Beyond Ethnicity*, pp. 31, 36.

51. *New York Times*, July 20, 1996, p. A1.

52. Young, *Justice*, pp. 165, 171.

53. J. N. Figgis, "The Great Leviathan," in Paul Q. Hirst, ed., *The Pluralist Theory of the State* (London: Routledge, 1989), p. 125.

54. Judith Shklar, *The Faces of Injustice* (New Haven, Conn.: Yale University Press, 1990), p. 81.

55. Sunstein, "Republican Revival," pp. 1574–55. Michelman, "Laws Republic," p. 1531.

56. The terms are Anne Phillips' (*The Politics of Presence* [New York: Oxford University Press, 1995], p. 52).

57. Young, "Justice," p. 174.

58. Lani Guinier, "The Representation of Minority Interests: The Question of Single Member Districts," 14 *Cardozo Law Review* 1135 (1993) at 1152.

59. Andrew Sharp, "Representing Justice and the Maori: On Why It Ought Not to Be Construed as a Postmodernist Text," *Political Theory Newsletter* 4 (1992), pp. 27–38, at p. 33.

60. Young, "Justice," p. 184.

61. Hardin, *One for All*, pp. 217, 64, 48, 30.

62. Raz, "Multiculturalism," p. 69.

63. Karst, *Belonging to America*, p. 227.

64. Cass R. Sunstein, "Naked Preferences and the Constitution," 84 *Columbia Law Review* 1689 (1984).

65. Karst, *Belonging to America*, p. 89.

66. Sidney Verba, Kay Lehman Schlozman, and Henry E. Brady, *Voice and Equality: Civic Voluntarism in American Politics* (Cambridge, Mass.: Harvard University Press, 1995), p. 158.

67. Gutmann, "Introduction," p. 19; Taylor, "Politics of Recognition," p. 70.

68. Wolfe, *Marginalized*, p. 53.

69. Michael Walzer, "Multiculturalism and Individualism," *Dissent* (Spring 1994): 185–91, at pp. 190–91.

70. Karst, *Belonging to America*, p. 93.

71. Bromwich, "Culturalism," p. 76.

72. Will Kymlicka's model of a cultural group is aboriginal tribes in Canada in *Multicultural Citizenship* and *Liberalism, Community, and Culture* (Oxford: Clarendon, 1989), p. 10.

73. For Iris Young, feminist and black liberation movements are exemplary candidates for group representation in *Justice and the Politics of Difference*.

74. Owen Fiss, "Groups and the Equal Protection Clause," *Philosophy and Public Affairs* 5, no. 2 (1976): 107–77, at p. 155.

75. The phrase is Jonathan Rauch's, "The Hyperpluralism Trap," *New Republic*, June 6, 1994, pp. 22–25, at 22.

76. Phillips, *Politics of Presence*, p. 9.

77. Ibid., p. 68.

78. Wendy Kaminer, "Will Class Trump Gender?" *American Prospect* 29 (1996): 44–52.

79. Kimberle Crenshaw, "Whose Story Is It, Anyway? Feminist and Antiracist Appropriations of Anita Hill," in Toni Morrison, ed., *Racing Justice, En-Gendering Power* (New York: Pantheon, 1992).

80. Michael C. Dawson, "Black Power in 1996 and the Demonization of African Americans," *PS: Political Science and Politics* 29 (1996): 456–61, at p. 460. Reed cited in Phillips, *Presence of Politics*, p. 101.

81. Cited in Jennifer Hochschild, "Practical Politics and *Voice and Equality*," *American Political Science Review* 91, no. 2 1997): 425–27, at p. 425.

82. Hardin, *One for All*, p. 73.

83. Guinier, "Minority Interests," 1148, n. 52; her prescription is "proportionate interest representation," p. 1140.

84. Russell Means with Marvin Wolf, *Where White Men Fear to Tread: The Autobiography of Russell Means* (New York: St. Martin's, 1995).

85. Cited in Phillips, *Politics of Presence*, p. 101.

86. Dawson, "Black Power."

87. Phillips, *Politics of Presence*, p. 54.

88. For a representative statement, see William H. Riker and Barry R. Weingast, "Constitutional Regulation of Legislative Choice: The Political Consequences of Judicial Deference to Legislatures," 74 *Virginia Law Review* 373 (1988) at 396.

89. Grant McConnell, "The Public Values of the Private Association," in *Nomos XI: Voluntary Associations* (New York: Atherton, 1969), pp. 147–160, at p. 159.

90. Michael Walzer, "Constitutional Rights and the Shape of Civil Society," in Robert Calvert, ed., *The Constitution of the People* (Lawrence: University of Kansas Press, 1991), p. 125.

91. Young, *Justice*, p. 184.

92. On this point Rawls takes issue with Jürgen Habermas; the conditions of deliberation and public justification must obtain only in official public arenas, in "Reply to Habermas," *Journal of Philosophy* 42, no. 3 (1995): 132–80, at p. 140.

93. Amy Gutmann and Dennis Thompson, *Democracy and Disagreement* (Cambridge, Mass.: Harvard University Press, 1996), p. 133.

94. Joshua Cohen, "Deliberation and Democratic Legitimacy," in A. Hamlin and P. Petit, eds., *The Good Polity* (Oxford: Oxford University Press, 1989), p. 22.

95. Phillips, *Politics of Presence*, p. 156, 159.

96. Charles Beitz, *Political Equality* (Princeton, N.J.: Princeton University Press, 1989), pp. 179, 171–73.

97. Gutmann and Thompson, *Multiculturalism*, p. 154.

98. "Secondary Associations and Democratic Governance," *Politics and Society* 20 (1992): 393–472.

99. David Estlund, "Who's Afraid of Deliberative Democracy?" 71 *Texas Law Review* 1437 (1993) at 1467–68.

100. Cass Sunstein, "Interest Groups in American Public Law," 38 *Stanford Law Review* 29 (1985) at 84. On "reasonable pluralism" applied, see Stephen Macedo, "Liberal Civic Education and Religious Fundamentalism: The Case of God v. John Rawls," *Ethics* 105 (1995): 468–96.

101. Cohen and Rogers, "Secondary Associations," p. 395.

102. For Rawls, "this basic case of public justification is one in which the shared political conception is the common ground," in "Reply to Habermas," p. 144.

103. Taylor, "Politics of Recognition," p. 50.

104. Macedo, "Liberal Civic Education," p. 493.

105. Gutmann and Thompson, *Multiculturalism*, pp. 82, 145, 146.

106. Cass Sunstein, *Democracy and the Problem of Free Speech* (New York: Free Press, 1993), p. 18.

107. Seyla Benhabib, "The Generalized and the Concrete Other," in S. Benhabib and D. Cornell, eds., *Feminism as Critique* (Minneapolis: University of Minnesota Press, 1987), p. 92.

108. Gutmann and Thompson, *Multiculturalism*, p. 131.

109. John S. Dryzek, "Political Inclusion and the Dynamics of Democratization," *American Political Science Review* 90, no. 1 (1996): 475–87, at p. 482.

110. *Rosenberger v. University of Virginia*, 115 S. Ct. 2510 (1995), at 19.

111. Kalven, cited in Robert C. Post, *Constitutional Domains* (Cambridge, Mass.: Harvard University Press, 1995), p. 201.

112. Ibid., p. 430.

Conclusion

1. Judith Shklar, *Ordinary Vices* (Cambridge, Mass.: Harvard University Press, 1984), p. 136.

2. Erving Goffman, "The Nature of Deference and Demeanor," *American Anthropologist* 58, no. 3 (1956): 473–502, at p. 489. On "self-control," see James Q. Wilson, *The Moral Sense* (New York: Free Press, 1993), ch. 4.

3. Lee C. Bollinger, *The Tolerant Society* (Oxford: Clarendon, 1986), pp. 142–43, 157.

4. Saul Bellow, *The Adventures of Augie March* (New York: Penguin, 1949), p. 379.

5. "The Code of the Streets," *Atlantic Monthly*, vol. 273, May 1994, pp. 81–94. Bill Buford, *Among the Thugs* (New York: Vintage, 1990).

6. Undercutting Peter Berger's thesis in "On the Obsolescence of the Concept of Honour," in Michael Sandel, ed., *Liberalism and Its Critics* (New York: New York University Press, 1984), pp. 149–58, at p. 149.

7. Mitchell Duneier, *Slim's Table: Race, Respectability, and Masculinity* (Chicago: University of Chicago Press, 1992), p. 92.

8. Shklar, *Ordinary Vices*, p. 77.

9. Goffman, "Deference and Demeanor," p. 485.

10. Regina Austin, "A Nation of Thieves": Securing Black People's Right to Shop and to Sell in White America," 1 *Utah Law Review* 147 (1994), at 148.

11. Judith Shklar, *Faces of Injustice* (New Haven, Conn.: Yale University Press, 1990).

12. Robert Wuthnow, *Sharing the Journey* (Princeton, N.J.: Princeton University Press, 1994), pp. 45, 71, 73, 4. See, too, Allan Silver, "The Curious Importance of Small Groups in American Sociology," in Herbert Gans, ed., *Sociology in America* (Newbury Park: Sage, 1990).

13. Wuthnow, *Sharing the Journal* p. 25.

14. Wendy Kaminer, *I'm Dysfunctional, You're Dysfunctional: The Recovery Movement and Other Self-Help Fashions* (Reading, Mass.: Addison-Wesley, 1992), p. 162.

15. Wuthnow, *Sharing the Journey*, p. 323.

16. Kaminer, *Recovery Movement*, p. 155.

Index

About the Author

Nancy L. Rosenblum is Henry Merritt Wriston Professor and Professor of Political Science at Brown University. She is the author of *Another Liberalism: Romanticism and the Reconstruction of Liberal Thought* and *Bentham's Theory of the Modern State*. She is the editor of *Liberalism and the Moral Life* and *Thoreau's Political Writings*.